To Arthur

Acquisitions Editor
Scott Rogers

Technical Editor
Phil Schmaeder

Project Editor
Judy Ziajka

Copy Editor
Paul Medoff

Proofreader
Linda Medoff

Indexer
Valerie Robbins

Computer Designer
Mickey Galicia

Cover Design
Mason Fong
Bay Graphics, Inc.

Contents at a Glance

Contents

Acknowledgments

When I first discussed the design, contents, and layout for *DOS Inside & Out* with the editors at Osborne, our goal was to produce a book that helped you easily master DOS, was easy to read, contained the answers to your questions, and was fun to use. With the help of Osborne's talented editors, artists, and production team, our goal has been met. After an author submits the manuscript to a publisher, a team of copy editors, proofreaders, and designers spends countless weeks ensuring the book's correctness, ease of use, and quality. The pride the Osborne team places in its work shows on the pages of this book. Please take time to note the names of the individuals who worked to ensure this book's quality.

Introduction

Since its release in 1981, over 90 million people have learned how to use DOS. Over the years, the capabilities DOS provides have grown considerably. DOS version 6 continues this trend, providing you with many new ways to make your computer easier to use and more efficient. Regardless of whether you use your computer for word processing, spreadsheets, or another application, the more you know about DOS, the more productive your time at the computer will become.

Bookstore shelves are filled with books on DOS. Most of these books contain technical jargon that gets in your way and keeps you from learning about DOS. As a result, most users get frustrated, give up, and never really learn how to use DOS effectively.

DOS Inside & Out, Second Edition, assumes you don't have much time to learn to use DOS. Thus, it breaks apart everything you need to know to use DOS and organizes this information into a series of 15- to 20-minute lessons. Each chapter begins by presenting a topic, such as creating DOS subdirectories, and tells how the topic affects the way you work. Next, you will get some practice trying out the steps you need to use the topic. By following the book's steps, you cannot hurt your computer or the information it contains. Then, unlike other DOS books, each chapter teaches you how to perform similar steps within the user-friendly shell of DOS 5 and later versions. Chapters contain a list of key terms employed in that chapter, and each chapter ends with a review of the essential points you should take with you from that topic.

With *DOS Inside & Out, Second Edition*, you can read and learn at your own pace. Each time you finish a lesson, your confidence and DOS capabilities will grow.

Special Offer

One of the greatest frustrations users experience when working with DOS is forgetting a command. **DOS HELP** is a software program you can copy to your hard disk; it contains all of the answers to your DOS questions.

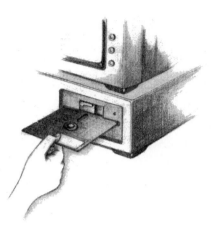

DOS HELP displays a friendly menu that summarizes all the DOS commands. By highlighting a command with your arrow keys and pressing ENTER, you can discover command specifics, view common examples of the command in use, and read tips that make you even more effective.

Every computer user should have a copy of **DOS HELP**!

Ordering Information

Domestic Orders:
Please send $24.95 (includes shipping and handling) to the address below. For fastest service, please send a money order or cashier's check. Please allow 2 to 3 weeks for delivery.

Foreign Orders:
Please send $29.95 (USD; includes shipping and handling) to the address below. For fastest service, please send an international money order. Please allow 4 to 6 weeks for delivery.

(Credit card orders not accepted)

Order Today!

Please send _____ copies of **DOS HELP**. Enclosed is my check/money order for $ _____

Name: _____

Address: _____

City: _____ State: _____ ZIP: _____

Country: _____ Phone: _____

Please send your order with payment to:

Concept Software
P.O. Box 26981
Las Vegas, NV 89126

CHAPTER

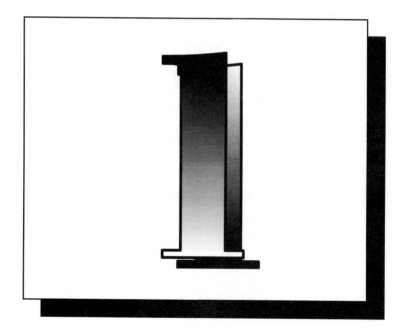

Understanding Your System

*E*very day, each of us is exposed to countless examples of the tremendous capabilities computers possess. In grocery stores, banks, airports, hospitals, and offices, computers are used on a routine basis to make our lives easier. We are only at the early stages of the computer's influence on our society. Each day someone new is using a computer to solve another difficult task. With these continual reminders of the computer's seemingly unlimited potential, it is no wonder we are awed by such a machine.

Before you start working with DOS, you should have a good under-standing of each piece that makes up your computer system, as well as how these pieces function. Your computer is composed of several distinct devices. Once you are familiar with the function of each device, your computer will appear much less complex and the processing that it performs will seem much more straightforward.

In addition to discussing the devices that are common to most personal computers, this chapter presents several steps you can follow to ensure that your computer is in working order each time your system starts. When you complete this chapter, you will be ready to start DOS.

Common System Components

Most systems have, at a minimum, a screen display, a chassis (some-times called the *system unit*), a keyboard, and a printer (see Figure 1-1). Actually, the specific types of these devices (color screen, monochrome screen, laser printer, tractor-feed printer, and so on) are of little conse-quence to DOS. Later in this book you will learn how to customize DOS for your specific devices.

The *keyboard* allows you to enter information into your computer. This information can be as simple as a yes or no response or as complex as a letter, report, or even a chapter of a book. As you work with your computer, your *screen display* (also called a *monitor*) serves as the message center. In most cases, the information you type in at the keyboard will be shown on the screen display. Your printer allows you to get a printed version of your information. This is called *hard copy.*

The most complex component of your system is the computer's *chassis.* It houses your computer's disk drives, memory, and processor.

FIGURE 1-1   Common system components

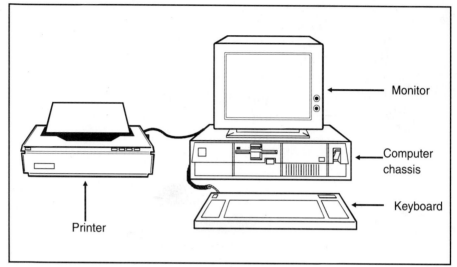

All the computations your computer performs occur in the hardware components that reside within the chassis.

Later in this chapter you will learn about additional devices that you can connect to your computer. For now, however, Table 1-1 summarizes the functions of your computer's primary devices.

Three Simple Steps

In spite of its seeming complexity, the computer actually performs only three basic operations: input, processing, and output. Regardless of the application the computer is performing, it does so in these three simple steps. Let's take a look at each.

What Is Input?

Input is the process of getting information into the computer. For example, most of us get a consolidated bank statement each month that

TABLE
1-1 Primary Devices and Their Functions

Component	Function
Monitor	Allows programs to display meaningful information and also allows you to view information you type at the keyboard.
Keyboard	Allows you to respond to prompts for information from your programs or to type in information for storage or manipulation.
Disk	Allows you to store information from one computer session to the next.
Printer	Allows you to obtain a printed copy of your information, called hard copy.
Chassis	Houses your computer's *central processing unit* (CPU), memory, and other hardware boards. Your disk drives are in your computer's chassis.

FIGURE
1-2 A bank statement

Statement

DATE OF THIS STATEMENT 10/22/93
PAGE 1 OF 1

CHECKING	04356-02374	CUSTOM FLAT FEE CHECKING PLAN	**CUSTOMER SINCE 1983**

SUMMARY
PREVIOUS STATEMENT BALANCE ON 09-23-93 _____ 2,412.69
TOTAL OF 2 DEPOSITS FOR _____ 1,823.83
TOTAL OF 5 CHECKS FOR _____ 1,624.72
STATEMENT BALANCE ON 10-22-93 _____ 2,611.80

CHECKS/
OTHER
DEBITS

CHECK NUMBER	DATE POSTED	AMOUNT	CHECK NUMBER	DATE POSTED	AMOUNT
102	09-27	1,063.54	105	10-13	151.28
103	10-04	39.24	106	10-18	121.79
104	10-08	248.87			

DEPOSITS   DEPOSITS

DATE POSTED	AMOUNT		DATE POSTED	AMOUNT
09-27	1,246.82		10-12	577.01

lists our current bank balance along with the amount for each check we wrote that month. Figure 1-2 shows such a statement.

Before the computer could generate this account summary, someone had to type in, or input, information specific to each check. Once this information has been input into the computer, the second step, processing, can occur.

The keyboard is the most obvious input device. However, several other devices are quite commonly used for input, as shown in Figure 1-3.

What Is Processing?

Processing is the execution of a computer program (called software) that takes the input information and converts it into a desired output. Processing can be as simple as adding two numbers and displaying the sum or as complex as coordinating takeoffs and landings in a busy air-traffic control tower. In the bank statement example, processing

Common input devices

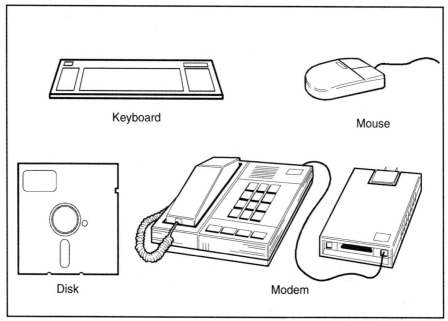

Keyboard

Mouse

Disk

Modem

would be the selecting and sorting of checks specific to your account and also the corresponding maintenance of your account's balance.

Pictorially, processing is most often associated with your computer's chassis, shown here, which houses your computer's memory and central processing unit (CPU):

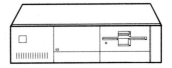

Once processing is complete, your computer is ready to display or print a meaningful result.

What Is Output?

Output is the printing or screen display of meaningful information to the end user. In the bank statement example, the output is your printed bank statement. Although output is normally associated with your computer's screen or printer, several other devices can be used for output, as shown in Figure 1-4.

All three steps in order—input, processing, and output—are illustrated here:

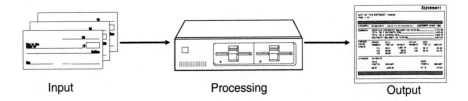

Input   Processing   Output

As you will find, no matter how complex a computer application at first appears, it consists of these three steps. With this fact in mind, you can easily identify the devices on your system that exist for input or output, or for both.

Common output devices

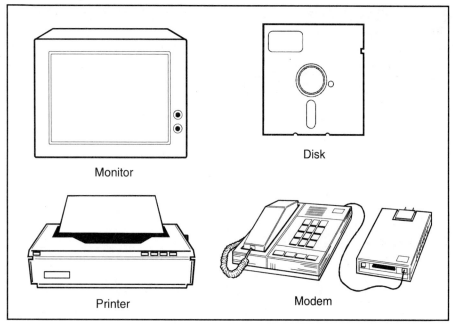

What's in a Name?

Throughout this book, the terms *personal computer* and *PC* refer to any personal computer capable of running DOS. Such computers include the IBM PS/2 line of computers, the IBM PC, and PC-compatible clones. Today, countless vendors sell computers that are IBM PC compatible. In general, two computers are *compatible* if they can run the same programs. An IBM PC, for example, can run the same programs as a PC made by Compaq. However, because the PC and Macintosh are not compatible, they cannot run the same programs. In many cases, you can even exchange hardware components (such as a screen display or keyboard) between compatible computers.

Getting Familiar with Your System

As you have seen, your computer's chassis contains the central processing unit and your computer's memory. In addition, it houses the disk drives for hard or floppy disks, as shown here:

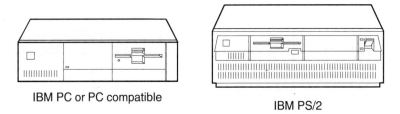

IBM PC or PC compatible

IBM PS/2

Disks store programs and information. When you purchase a software program, such as a word processor, the program that your computer will eventually run resides on disk. Also, if you need to store information from one working session to another, you store the information in a file on a disk. Later in this book you will see how DOS actually stores this information; for now, keep in mind that disks are used to store programs and information. Floppy disks can be removed from your computer, but

Comparison of Floppy and Hard Disks

Disk Type	Speed	Storage	Cost	Can Be Removed	Can Be Damaged
Floppy	Much slower than hard disk	380,000 to 2,900,000 characters	25 cents to several dollars	Yes	Yes
Hard	Fast	10,000,000 to several hundred million characters	$200 to $1000+	No	Yes

hard disks are attached to your computer's chassis. Hard disks are much faster and can store many times more information than can floppy disks. This book will examine hard and floppy disks in detail; the differences between hard and floppy disks are described in Table 1-2. (You can convert the information about disk memory in the table to pages of text by applying the formula 4,000 characters = one page of text.)

Depending on your system's configuration, your computer will have one or more floppy disk drives and possibly a hard disk (also called a *fixed disk*). Each disk drive on your system has a single-letter name, starting with A, B, C, and so on. If your system has a single floppy disk drive, the drive name is A. If your system has two floppy disk drives, the drive names will be A and B, as shown here:

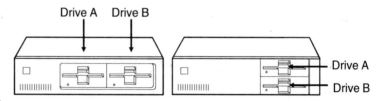

Systems with dual floppy disk drives

Finally, a hard disk drive (the first if there are more than one) is always named drive C, as shown here:

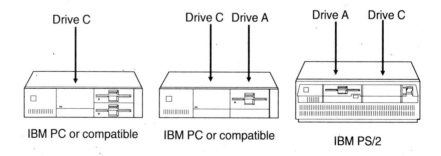

In the past, most systems had dual floppy disk drives and no hard disk. Today, however, almost all systems are shipped with a hard disk.

Optional Hardware Devices

Earlier in this chapter you reviewed a "standard" personal computer configuration, which contained a monitor, a chassis, a keyboard, and a printer, as shown in Figure 1-1. Many users, however, add additional hardware devices to their systems, as shown in Figure 1-5.

A *mouse* is an input device that can simplify the manner in which you use software by allowing you to move a pointer on the screen wherever you like and click a button on the mouse to trigger certain actions. DOS, for example, provides a very convenient menu-driven *user interface* (which means the way the screen is displayed) called the DOS shell.

A mouse allows you to select menu options quickly. Figure 1-6 shows an example menu and the choices you can click with the mouse. If you are going to use the DOS shell on a regular basis, a mouse is a very sound investment.

Many computers exchange information with other computers, which may reside at different geographic locations. A *modem* is a hardware device that allows two computers to communicate over standard telephone lines (see Figure 1-7) by *MOdulating* the computer's digital signal into a telephone's analog signal and sending it over the phone lines to the receiving computer, whose modem *DEModulates* the signal back into a digital signal for the receiving computer. There are two common types

**FIGURE
1-5**

System with modem and mouse

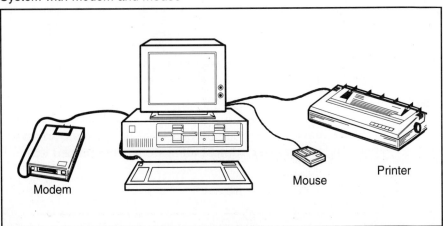

Modem

Mouse

Printer

FIGURE 1-6 Menu-driven DOS shell user interface

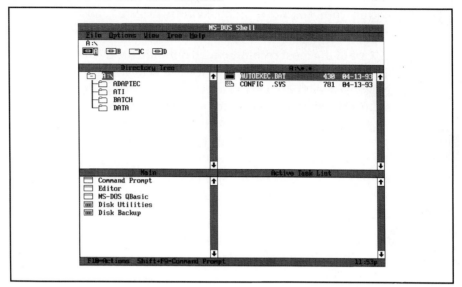

FIGURE 1-7 Sending information over telephone lines with a modem

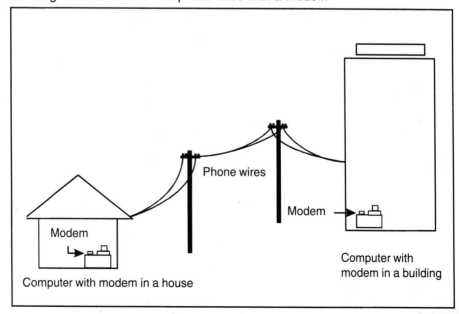

of modems: internal and external modems. An *internal modem* resides within your computer's chassis. An *external modem* resides outside of the chassis. In either case, both modem types perform the same task.

One of the most recommended optional hardware accessories available is a *surge suppressor.* This device protects your computer from abnormal power surges that may come across your power line. A surge suppressor sits between your wall outlet and your computer. Should a large surge of power come down your power line, the suppressor captures the excess power before it can damage your computer's internal circuitry. Many computers have been damaged by lightning that strikes several miles away. A surge suppressor can prevent such damage.

There are several types of surge suppressors. Some look like simple multiple-plug adapters, as shown here:

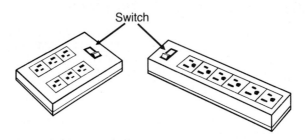

If you purchase this type of adapter, make sure that it is indeed an approved surge suppressor and not just a multiple-plug adapter.

The most convenient type of suppressor is shown here:

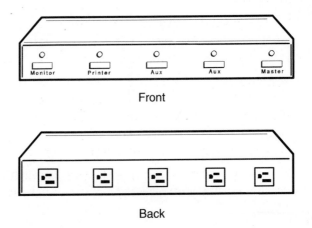

As you can see, this suppressor allows you to turn many devices on and off from one location. Whether you have been using your system for some time or have just purchased it, a surge suppressor is a sound investment.

 Note Surge suppressors only eliminate high spikes of power traveling down power lines. A surge suppressor will not protect your data from power loss. For that, you need an uninterruptible power supply or UPS. A UPS will typically provide you with 10 to 15 minutes of power, which is normally more than enough time to save your current data to disk. UPS prices range anywhere from several hundred to several thousand dollars. Most users do not have a UPS.

Turning On Your System

If your computer is already up and running, you might simply want to skim this section, referring to the steps you can take when your system fails to start. If, instead, you have just purchased your computer, this section will ensure that your system is correctly installed.

Installing a computer system is quite simple nowadays. Ignoring your printer for the time being, begin by attaching your keyboard and video monitor to your computer's chassis, as shown in Figure 1-8. On most systems, the keyboard cable is plugged into the lower-center portion of the back of the chassis. The cable for your video monitor will have either a 9-pin (for a CGA or EGA monitor) or a 15-pin (for a VGA monitor) plug, which should be plugged into the corresponding connector on the back of the computer.

Now you should plug all your computer components into the surge suppressor and plug your surge suppressor into the wall. Once you complete this step, your system is ready to be turned on.

With no floppy disks in your computer's disk drives, turn on your screen display and computer chassis. Your computer will begin its power-on sequence. Each time your system starts, your computer examines its own internal components to ensure they are working correctly. Many people refer to this process as the computer's *power-on self-test.*

If your computer encounters an error during its self-test, it will in most cases display an error message on your screen. Write down any error

FIGURE
1-8

Connecting your keyboard and video monitor

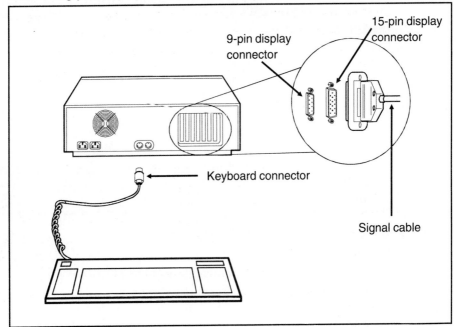

messages your system displays so you can later read them to your computer retailer. If such an error occurs, turn off your system, wait about ten seconds, and then turn it back on. This process is known as *cycling* the computer's power. In some cases, cycling the power will clear the error.

When some computers complete the self-test successfully, they will then display the amount of memory they find in your system like this:

```
00640 KB OK
```

Next, assuming that your system has a floppy disk in drive A or a hard disk that already contains DOS, your system may prompt you to enter the current date, as shown here:

```
Current date is Tue 04-06-1993
Enter new date (mm-dd-yy):
```

If your system prompts you for a date, simply press ENTER for now, leaving the current date unchanged. Your system may then prompt you for the current time. Again press ENTER. In Chapter 3, "Issuing DOS Commands," you will learn how to set the system date and time. Your system may display characters similar to the following; this is called the *DOS prompt.*

```
C:\>
```

DOS displays this prompt whenever it is waiting for you to type in a command. Instead of the DOS prompt, your system may display a graphical user interface such as the DOS shell shown earlier in Figure 1-6, the DOS 4 shell shown in Figure 1-9, or the Microsoft Windows shell shown in Figure 1-10. (The DOS shells come with your DOS package and can be loaded by typing **DOSSHELL** on the command line; you will learn more about giving commands in the next two chapters.)

Has your computer started properly? Here are some things to look for:

❏ Can you hear your computer's fan running? If not, make sure your computer is properly plugged in and turned on. If it is plugged in but makes no noise, test the wall outlet with a working appliance. If your system still does not work, it may have a power supply problem.

❏ Does your screen display work? If not, make sure that it is properly plugged in and turned on. Again, you may want to check the wall outlet and also be sure that the display is connected to the back of your computer's chassis.

FIGURE 1-9

The DOS 4 shell interface

```
 08-13-91                    Start Programs              10:04 pm
 Program  Group  Exit                                    F1=Help
                            Main Group
            To select an item, use the up and down arrows.
         To start a program or display a new group, press Enter.

 Command Prompt
 File System
 Change Colors
 DOS Utilities...
 Business Programs...
 WordPerfect Version 5.1
 Backup Operations...
 View File
```

❑   Does your computer display its operational memory? If your system begins displaying a count of the memory it contains but does not complete this count, the problem is your computer's memory. Cycle the power on your system to see if this error goes away. If it does not, notify your retailer.

Record any other error messages that your system displays so that you can read them to your retailer.

Practice

Throughout this chapter you have seen examples of several computer configurations. Using the illustrations in this chapter as your guide (refer to Figure 1-11 if you have a PS/2 model), locate and identify the disk drives that reside on your system. You will need to know the location of each drive before you start DOS.

Next, examine your computer's power cables. If you have several plugs attached to the same wall outlet, you should strongly consider a surge suppressor. The surge suppressor not only protects your hardware, but it also offers a convenient way to turn individual devices on and off.

The Microsoft Windows shell

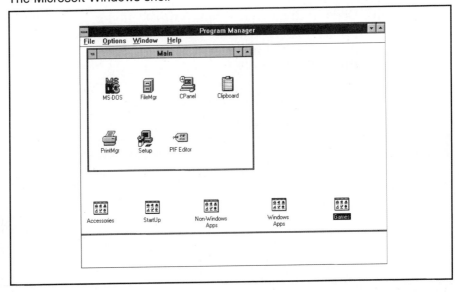

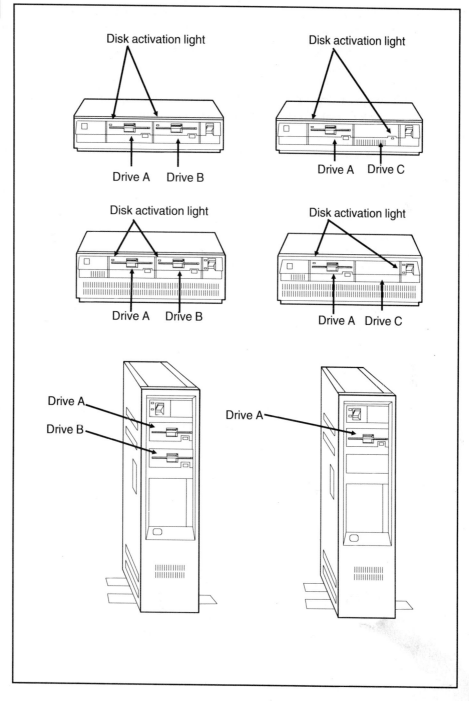

Disk drives on PS/2 models

FIGURE 1-11

If your screen display and chassis are plugged in, check your keyboard and monitor to ensure that each is properly connected to your computer chassis. If so, you are ready to turn on your system. Remove any floppy disks from your system. Next, turn on your screen display and chassis. You will hear your computer's fan as your computer begins its power-on sequence. If your system fails to start, use the guidelines presented earlier in this chapter to isolate your error. Record any error messages your system displays so that you can read it to your retailer.

If your system instead displays

```
Current date is Tue 04-06-1993
Enter new date (mm-dd-yy):
```

or

```
C:\>
```

or a shell interface, DOS is already installed on your system. You are ready to proceed to the next chapter.

Review

Answers to review questions are in Appendix A.

1. Any computer application can be broken down into three distinct steps. What are they?
2. What is input?
3. What is processing?
4. What is output?
5. Label the devices in Figure 1-12 as input, output, or both.
6. Fill in the blank: _____ exist to store programs and information.
7. Label the disk drives in the systems shown in Figure 1-13.

FIGURE 1-12

Computer devices

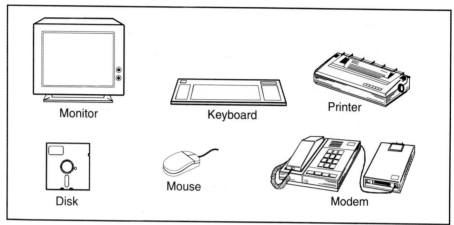

Monitor   Keyboard   Printer

Disk   Mouse   Modem

FIGURE 1-13

Disk drives

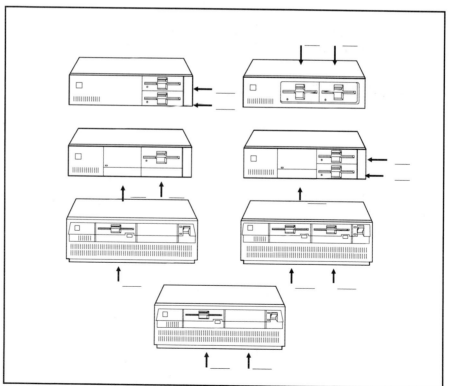

8. Define "PC compatible."

9. How does a hard disk differ from a floppy disk?

10. Discuss three optional hardware devices.

11. How do you cycle your computer's power?

12. What is the computer's self-test?

Key Points

Input

Input is the process of getting information into the computer. The term "input" also is used as a name for that information.

Processing

Processing is the execution of a computer program (software) that converts input to output.

Output

Output is the displaying or printing of meaningful information for the end user.

Disks

Disks, either hard or floppy, exist for one purpose: to store information.

CHAPTER

Getting Started
with DOS

Chapter 1, "Understanding Your System," examined many of the hardware components that make up your system. However, hardware is only half of the picture. Without software, your hardware is basically useless. This chapter examines the first software program your computer must be running before you can run other programs: DOS.

In this chapter you will learn how to start DOS from floppy disks as well as from your hard disk. You will also learn how to run your first DOS commands.

Software

Software is any computer program—a word processor, a spreadsheet, or even DOS. Hardware and software work together to help you perform various tasks with your computer. Although hardware performs the actual processing, software tells the hardware what to do.

Before your computer can execute a program, the program must reside in the computer's electronic memory. Therefore, the program must be read from disk and loaded into your computer's memory for execution.

Once you start your computer, DOS takes over the process of loading your programs into memory for execution. Thus, DOS gives you the ability to run other programs, as shown here:

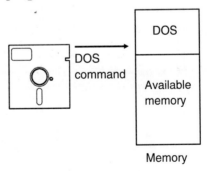

Memory

The software programs that you will execute are classified as either application or system software. *Application software* includes such programs as word processors, database management packages, and even, in some cases, computer games. Application software consists of the programs that you run in order to accomplish a specific task, or *applica-*

tion. System software, on the other hand, helps your computer to function and allows you to execute other programs.

The most common example of system software is an *operating system.* An operating system is a software program that serves as the overseer of your computer and all of its resources. The operating system allows you to run other programs, save information to disk, and use devices such as your printer.

DOS: An Operating System

DOS is a special software program. DOS stands for *disk operating system.* Because, as an operating system, DOS oversees your computer's resources, such as your printer and disk drives, it provides an interface to your hardware devices, as illustrated here:

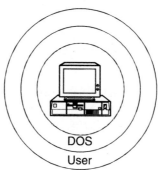

Before you can use other software programs, your system must be running DOS. This in turn makes DOS the interface to your application software, as illustrated here:

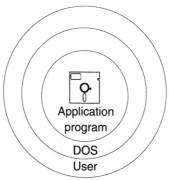

How PC-DOS and MS-DOS Differ

Many users become confused when they try to distinguish between PC-DOS and MS-DOS. Quite simply, both names refer to DOS, the disk operating system for personal computers. The two differ in their developers; Microsoft licenses MS-DOS, and IBM licenses PC-DOS. MS-DOS is used most often on PC-compatible clones. PC-DOS, on the other hand, is the most common operating system for the IBM PC, PC AT, and PS/2 line of computers.

For the end user, MS-DOS and PC-DOS are functionally identical. Each serves as your interface to your computer's hardware as well as to your application programs. MS-DOS and PC-DOS support the same set of commands.

Why DOS Version 6 Is Special

DOS was first announced in 1981 in conjunction with the IBM PC. Since then, several versions of DOS have been released. When a new version of DOS becomes available, the DOS developers change the DOS version number, dependent upon the degree of the changes that have occurred since the last release. Each DOS version number is composed of two parts, a major version number and minor version number. For DOS version 6.0, for example, 6 is the major version number and 0 is the minor version number.

When DOS developers release a new version of DOS, the following guidelines determine whether to increment the major or minor version number:

❏ If the previous version has been upgraded only to fix bugs (errors) or to make enhancements in the operating system, the developers increment the minor version number. An example is upgrading DOS 3.2 to DOS 3.3.

❏ If the previous version has been upgraded with major enhancements to the operating system (for example, a new user interface based on pull-down menus), the developers increment the major version number. An example is upgrading DOS 4.01 to DOS 5.0.

Version numbers help a user determine whether or not to purchase a new version. Unless you have specific needs that are met by minor-version upgrades, you usually need to purchase only major upgrades.

DOS 6 is a major DOS upgrade. Like DOS versions 4 and 5, DOS 6 provides a user-friendly, menu-driven interface, as shown in Figure 2-1, as well as improved memory management and a collection of file and disk recovery commands. In addition, DOS 6 provides utility programs that help laptop computer users exchange files with their desktop PC, utilities that check for and remove viruses, and network programs for users connected to local area networks using Windows for Workgroups.

How DOS Differs from Windows

One of the most popular programs of the 1990s is Microsoft Windows, a graphical (picture-oriented) user interface from which you can quickly

FIGURE 2-1

DOS 6 user-friendly shell interface

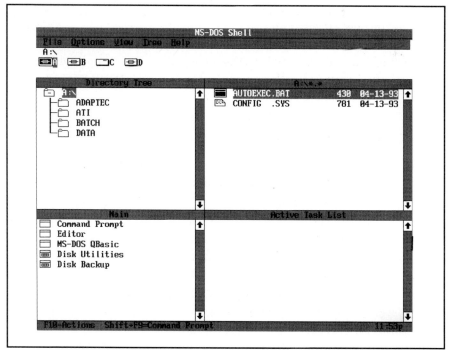

run your programs. Windows is so popular, in fact, that many retailers include Windows when you purchase your computer.

When Windows is running, users can execute programs by aiming a mouse pointer at the program on the screen and clicking the mouse select button. This "point-and-click" program execution makes Windows very easy to use.

Many users ask why, if they are using Windows, they need DOS. As discussed earlier, your computer must run DOS before it can run any other program. Windows is no exception. When your computer starts, it will first load DOS; once DOS is active, you can then run Windows.

Disks and Disk Drives

All personal computers have at least one floppy disk drive. Depending on the type of computer you are using (an IBM PC-compatible or a PS/2), the types of floppy disk drives found on your system may vary. The two most common types of disk drives are 5 1/4-inch and 3 1/2-inch, as shown here:

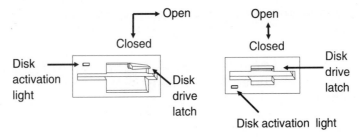

If you are using 5 1/4-inch disks, your disk drives have a drive latch (which you must close after you insert a disk), as shown in the preceding illustration.

If you are using 3 1/2-inch micro floppy disks, no disk drive latch is present. Instead, when you have finished using the floppy disk that the drive contains, you simply push the disk-eject button located at the side of the disk drive, as shown here:

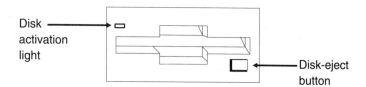

Disk activation light

Disk-eject button

Regardless of the type, your disk drive contains a small light called the *disk activation light.* Each time your computer reads or writes information to your disk drive, it illuminates this light. Never remove a disk from the disk drive or turn off the computer while this light is illuminated. Doing so could destroy your disk, causing you to lose the information that it contains.

Floppy Disk Storage Capacity

Although two floppy disks may be the same physical size, such as two 5 1/4- or two 3 1/2-inch disks, the individual disks may vary in storage capacity. When the IBM PC was first released in 1981, 5 1/4-inch disks stored 160Kb (1Kb is 1,024 bytes, each of which stores about one character or letter). Since that time, improvements in technology have increased the amount of information a disk can store. Depending on the age of your computer, however, your floppy disk drive may only be able to read disks up to a certain size. In general, 5 1/4-inch disks store either 360Kb or 1.2Mb (1Mb is slightly more than a million bytes). Because the 1.2Mb disks store four times as much information as the 360Kb disks, they are called *quad-density* (or *high-density*) disks.

If you have a 1.2Mb floppy disk drive, your drive can read and write information on both 360Kb and 1.2Mb disks. If your computer is older, and has a 360Kb disk drive, your drive can only read and write 360Kb disks and cannot use 1.2Mb disks formatted to use their full capacity. As you will learn in Chapter 3, you can format and use a 1.2Mb disk as a 360Kb disk.

In a similar manner, 3 1/2-inch disks store 720Kb, 1.44Mb, or 2.88Mb. Depending on the age of your computer, your 3 1/2-inch drive will support 720Kb, 1.44Mb, or 2.88Mb disks.

Inserting a Floppy Disk

When you insert a floppy disk into a disk drive, always insert it so that the end containing the disk label is the last end of the disk inserted into your computer. Also make sure that the disk label is facing upward, as shown here:

If your disk is unlabeled, locate the small write-protect notch that is on your disk:

Write-protect notch

Insert the disk so that this notch is on the left and the end of the disk containing the notch is inserted last.

If you are using 3 1/2-inch floppy disks, insert the disk so that the label is facing up and is inserted last. If your disk is unlabeled, locate the disk spindle and shutter:

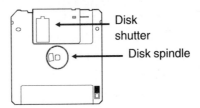

Disk
shutter

Disk spindle

Insert the disk so that the spindle is facing down and the end of the disk containing the shutter is inserted first.

Write-Protecting Your Disks

If you examine a 5 1/4-inch floppy disk, you will notice a small notch in the upper-right corner of the disk. This is called the *write-protect notch*.

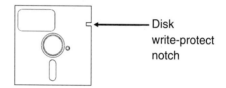

When this notch is visible, DOS is free to write information to the disk. You probably do not want DOS to write information to your original software disks, so you must protect each disk by placing a *write-protect tab*, a small rectangular piece of opaque adhesive tape, over the disk notch, as shown here:

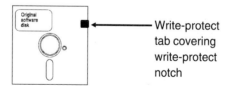

When you purchase a box of disks, the manufacturer usually includes a sheet of these tabs. Simply peel off a tab from the sheet and place it over the write-protect notch.

Later in this book you will create disks that contain information that is specific to an application, such as letters or documents for a word processor or data for a database management package. You will want

DOS to be able to write information to these disks, so you should not place write-protect tabs on them.

If you are using 3 1/2-inch disks, they do not have a write-protect notch. Instead, they have a *write-protect switch*. When this switch is up so that the hole is covered, DOS is free to write to your disk. When the switch is down, exposing the hole, as shown here, the disk is write protected and DOS cannot modify its contents:

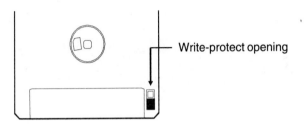

Write-protect opening

Rules for Handling Your Disks

Although floppy disks are very convenient, they are also very easily damaged. You need to treat your disks with great care. Figure 2-2 gives you a list of guidelines that you should follow when working with either 5 1/4-inch or 3 1/2-inch disks. If you follow these guidelines, your disks will last you quite some time.

Restarting DOS

There may be times when one of your programs contains an error that causes it to malfunction. In such cases, the only way to continue may be to restart DOS. To restart DOS you have two choices. First, you can turn your computer's power off and then back on. Second, you can hold down the CTRL-ALT-DEL keys by first holding down the CTRL key, followed by ALT, followed by DEL. All three keys must be held down at the same time.

FIGURE 2-2

Rules for working with disks

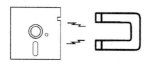

Never place the disk near magnetic devices.

Always place disks back in disk envelopes when you are not using the disks.

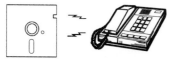

Keep your disk away from your telephone.

Store your floppy disks in a safe location.

Never touch your floppy disk media.

Always make a backup copy of your floppy disk.

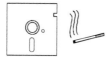

Never smoke near floppy disks.

Keep room temperature in the range 50° F and 110° F.

Never bend floppy disks.

Practice

To begin, start your computer. If your computer displays one of the shell interface programs shown in Figures 1-6, 1-9, or 1-10 in Chapter 1, exit the program by choosing the Exit option (or, if "Exit" doesn't appear on screen, first choose File and the Exit option that will then appear). Your screen should eventually display characters similar to the following:

```
C:\>
```

These characters are the DOS prompt. DOS displays its prompt whenever it is ready for you to issue a command. Press the ENTER key several times, as shown here:

```
C:\>  <ENTER>
C:\>  <ENTER>
C:\>  <ENTER>
```

DOS provides a group of commands, each of which performs a separate function. To execute a DOS command, you simply type the command's name at the DOS prompt and press ENTER. For example, the CLS command (CLS is an abbreviation for "clear screen") erases your current screen contents and places the cursor at your screen's upper-left corner. To execute CLS, simply type **CLS** at the DOS prompt (the line you've typed on is the *command line*) and press ENTER.

```
C:\>  CLS  <ENTER>
```

When you press the ENTER key, DOS will execute the CLS command, which directs DOS to clear the screen display and redisplay its prompt in the upper-left corner of the screen. Congratulations—CLS is your first DOS command!

In the next chapter you will examine several additional DOS commands as you prepare several disks for use by DOS. You will issue each of these commands by typing its command name at the DOS prompt.

You are now ready to continue with the commands presented in Chapter 3, "Issuing DOS Commands."

Review

1. Software can be categorized into one of two classes, depending on its function. What are these two classes?
2. What does "DOS" stand for?
3. What is an operating system?
4. Explain DOS version numbers.
5. How do MS-DOS and PC-DOS differ?
6. What is the disk activation light?
7. What is the DOS prompt?
8. Discuss two ways of restarting DOS.
9. What is the function of the DOS CLS command?

Key Points

Your Computer System

Your computer is composed of many hardware devices, each having a unique function. Hardware, however, is only half the picture. Before your computer hardware can function, software (computer programs) must tell the hardware what to do. Hardware and software, together, form your computer system.

Software: Computer Programs

A computer program is nothing more than a list of instructions for your computer to perform. Thus, software tells the hardware what to do.

continues . . .

Disk Activation Light

Remember never to remove a disk from the disk drive or turn off your computer while the disk activation light is illuminated. You risk losing the information contained on the disk.

Write-Protecting a 5 1/4-inch Disk

Most disks have a write-protect notch in the upper-right corner. When this notch is exposed, DOS is free to overwrite the contents of the disk. When you cover this notch with a write-protect tab, DOS can no longer write information to the disk. This prevents an errant DOS command from destroying information on your disk.

Always write-protect your original disks before using them. DOS can still execute programs or read information that resides on a write-protected disk. It simply cannot change the disk's contents.

Write-Protecting a 3 1/2-inch Disk

Unlike 5 1/4-inch disks, which have a write-protect notch on one side, 3 1/2-inch disks have a write-protect switch. When the switch is in the up position, covering the hole, DOS can fully access your disk. When the switch is in the down position, exposing the hole, the disk is write-protected.

CHAPTER

Issuing DOS Commands

*I*n Chapter 2, "Getting Started with DOS," you learned about the DOS prompt and issued your first DOS command. In this chapter you will learn how to issue several other DOS commands, and you should begin to feel more comfortable working with DOS. In addition, you will make backup copies of your original DOS disks so that you can put the originals in a safe location. Finally, you will examine the DOS FORMAT command, which prepares disks for use by DOS.

Before you get started, make sure that you have three or four unused floppy disks available you can use with the DISKCOPY and FORMAT commands.

Throughout this book, example commands will be shown in uppercase letters, like this:

```
C:\> CLS <ENTER>
```

DOS also allows you to enter commands in lowercase, as in

```
C:\> cls <ENTER>
```

or in both upper- and lowercase, as in

```
C:\> Cls <ENTER>
```

This book uses uppercase commands for consistency and to make the commands easy to see; however, you can use either case, or both, as you enter commands yourself.

Displaying the Current DOS Version Number

In Chapter 2 you learned that the CLS command clears the contents of your screen display and places the cursor in the screen's upper-left corner. To execute CLS, you simply typed in the command name and pressed ENTER. In a similar manner, to invoke the VER command, type **VER** at the DOS prompt and press ENTER. This causes the VER command (short for "version") to display the current DOS version number on your screen:

```
C:\> VER <ENTER>
MS-DOS Version 6.00

C:\>
```

The DOS version number has two parts, a major and a minor version number. In this case, 6 is the major and 0 is the minor version number. When DOS was initially released in 1981, it was version 1.0. Over the past years, DOS has undergone many changes resulting in several different versions of DOS being used throughout the world. Unless specifically stated, the commands in this book apply to all versions of DOS.

It is not uncommon for new versions of a software package to be released shortly after a major upgrade in order to fix errors in the major upgrade. Since these newer releases have only minor changes, you might see 6.0 become 6.01, and so on.

Setting or Displaying the System Date

A critical step in your computer work is making sure that the system date and time are correct. In the future, it will be important to you to know when your files were created; this is recorded by the DATE command. The DATE command allows you to set your system's date. To invoke it, simply type **DATE** at the DOS prompt and press ENTER. DOS will then invoke the DATE command, which displays the following:

```
C:\> DATE <ENTER>
Current date is Tue 04-06-1993
Enter new date (mm-dd-yy):
```

In this case, DATE is displaying the current system date and is prompting you to enter a new date. If you just want to display the current date and leave the system date unchanged, press the ENTER key. DOS will leave the current date unchanged, and it will redisplay its prompt, as shown here:

```
C:\> DATE <ENTER>
Current date is Tue 04-06-1993
Enter new date (mm-dd-yy): <ENTER>

C:\>
```

If, however, you want to change the system date, you must type in the date that you desire in the form *mm-dd-yy,* where *mm* specifies the current month, from 1 to 12, *dd* is the current day, from 1 to 31, and *yy* is the last two digits of the current year, as in 91.

In this example, you will set the current date to December 25, 1993 (12-25-93). Invoke the DATE command, and when you are prompted for the date, type **12-25-93**, as shown here:

```
C:\> DATE <ENTER>
Current date is Tue 04-06-1993
Enter new date (mm-dd-yy): 12-25-93 <ENTER>
```

If you enter an invalid date, possibly typing the month and day in the wrong order, DATE will display an error message and prompt you to enter a new date:

```
C:\> DATE <ENTER>
Current date is Sat 12-25-1993
Enter new date (mm-dd-yy): 25-12-93 <ENTER>

Invalid date
Enter new date (mm-dd-yy):
```

Make sure you have specified the date in the form *mm-dd-yy*, and reenter the correct date. To verify that the date has indeed been changed, simply invoke DATE once again:

```
C:\> DATE <ENTER>
Current date is Sat 12-25-1993
Enter new date (mm-dd-yy):
```

Leave the date unchanged by pressing ENTER.

In addition to allowing you to specify a date when prompted, the DATE command also allows you to specify a date when you invoke the command, as shown here:

```
C:\> DATE 12-25-93 <ENTER>
```

Since this command includes the desired date, DATE has no need to prompt you for one. DATE will simply update the system date as specified and display the DOS prompt. Again, if you specify an invalid date in your command line, DOS will display an error message and prompt you to enter the correct date:

```
C:\> DATE 25-12-93 <ENTER>
Invalid date
Enter new date (mm-dd-yy):
```

If you have changed your system date to any other than the current date, remember to set your system date back to the current date before continuing.

Setting or Displaying the System Time

Just as the DATE command allows you to set or display the current system date, the TIME command allows you to set or display the system's current time. When you enter this command at the DOS prompt, TIME will display the current system time and prompt you to enter a new time:

```
C:\> TIME <ENTER>
Current time is  4:50:56.52p
Enter new time:
```

Use the format *hh:mm:ss.nn,* where *hh* specifies the current hours from 0 to 23, *mm* specifies the current minutes from 0 to 59, *ss* specifies the current seconds from 0 to 59, and *nn* specifies hundredths of a second from 0 to 99. Although TIME allows you to specify the time accurately to hundredths of a second, it only requires you to specify hours and minutes. If you are using DOS 3.3 or earlier, TIME uses a 24-hour military clock. Table 3-1 lists the military times. If you are using DOS 4 or later, DOS lets you include the letter "A" or "P" to the right of your time to signify A.M. or P.M.

In this example, you will set the time to 12:30 P.M.:

```
C:\> TIME <ENTER>
Current time is  4:50:56.52p
Enter new time: 12:30 <ENTER>

C:\>
```

You can also specify the hundredths of a second:

```
C:\> TIME <ENTER>
Current time is  4:50:56.52p
Enter new time: 12:30:00.11 <ENTER>

C:\>
```

If you just want to display the current system time without changing it, simply press ENTER when prompted for a new time.

TABLE 3-1   Military and Standard Time Equivalents

Military Time	Standard Time	Military Time	Standard Time
0	12:00 Midnight	12	12:00 Noon
1	1:00 A.M.	13	1:00 P.M.
2	2:00 A.M.	14	2:00 P.M.
3	3:00 A.M.	15	3:00 P.M.
4	4:00 A.M.	16	4:00 P.M.
5	5:00 A.M.	17	5:00 P.M.
6	6:00 A.M.	18	6:00 P.M.
7	7:00 A.M.	19	7:00 P.M.
8	8:00 A.M.	20	8:00 P.M.
9	9:00 A.M.	21	9:00 P.M.
10	10:00 A.M.	22	10:00 P.M.
11	11:00 A.M.	23	11:00 P.M.

If the time that you specify is invalid, TIME will display an error message and prompt you to enter a correct time, as shown here:

```
C:\> TIME <ENTER>
Current time is 12:31:47.50p
Enter new time: 12:62 <ENTER>

Invalid time
Enter new time:
```

Again, reset the system time to the current time before proceeding.

Internal and External Commands

So far, you have issued the CLS, VER, DATE, and TIME commands. As briefly discussed in Chapter 2, "Getting Started with DOS," before a program can execute, the program must reside in your computer's memory. DOS commands are themselves programs. Each time DOS starts, it loads several of the smaller and most commonly used commands into memory, where they reside permanently throughout your working session with your computer. Since these commands are present in memory as soon as your system starts, there is no need for DOS to load them from a disk into memory each time you invoke them. These preloaded commands are called *internal commands.*

Because there are so many DOS commands, the DOS developers could not possibly make all of them internal commands. There isn't enough memory available in the system to hold them all. Instead, the developers put many DOS commands on disk. Each time you invoke one of these commands, DOS must load the program from disk into memory so the program can execute, as shown here:

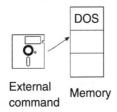

External   Memory
command

Since these commands reside on disk instead of in memory, they are called *external commands.* The distinction between internal and external commands is important because when you issue an external command, you must make sure that the command resides on the disk or in the directory that you are using. Later in this chapter you will execute the FORMAT and DISKCOPY commands. Both are external commands that reside in a directory named DOS on your hard disk.

If You Mistype a Command

As you enter more and more commands at the DOS prompt, you will eventually mistype a command. For example, you might misspell "TIME" as "TIMM." If you do, DOS will display this error message:

```
C:\> TIMM <ENTER>
Bad command or file name
```

When this error message occurs, one of two things has happened. Either you have misspelled the command or, if the command is an external command, it is not on the disk or in the directory of files you are currently using. If you are sure your spelling is correct, use the DIR command to locate the command on disk, as described next.

Listing the Contents of Your Disk

Chapter 4, "Getting Started with DOS Files," covers DOS files in detail. There you will learn more about several concepts you will use briefly here. DOS stores information on your disk in a *file*, much like you would organize information in an office by using a paper file. A *directory* is a collection of files. The best way to visualize a directory is as a drawer of a filing cabinet. Just as the filing cabinet can contain several drawers of related files, your disk can hold many directories of related files. The DIR command displays information about files stored in the current directory. For example, enter the following:

```
C:\> DIR <ENTER>
```

You will see the disk activation light illuminate briefly as DOS reads the contents of the disk. Next, DOS will display the list of files that resides in the directory.

Later in this chapter you will use the DISKCOPY and FORMAT commands—two external commands that reside on your disk. Typically, these external commands reside in a directory named DOS. Issue the following DIR command to display the external DOS commands:

```
C:\> DIR \DOS <ENTER>
```

Including a directory name in the DIR command line is similar to opening a specific drawer of the filing cabinet. If the file names scroll past you faster than you can read them, don't worry. In Chapter 4 you will learn how to display the directory list one screen at a time.

In addition to letting you list information about the files in a directory, DIR lets you display information about a specific file. The following command displays directory information concerning the DISKCOPY command:

```
C:\> DIR \DOS\DISKCOPY  <ENTER>
```

In DOS 6, your screen will appear similar to the following:

```
C:\> DIR   \DOS\DISKCOPY   <ENTER>

 Volume in drive C is DOS
 Volume Serial Number is 1A54-45E0
 Directory of C:\DOS

DISKCOPY COM     11879 02-12-93    6:00a
       1 file(s)      11879 bytes
                   16605184 bytes free
```

Note the last two lines of the DIR command's output. They tell you the number of files DIR listed, the amount of disk space those files consume, and the amount of disk space still available.

In a similar manner, this command displays directory information about the FORMAT command:

```
C:\> DIR   \DOS\FORMAT   <ENTER>

 Volume in drive C is DOS
 Volume Serial Number is 1A54-45E0
 Directory of C:\DOS
```

```
FORMAT    COM     22717 02-12-93    6:00a
        1 file(s)        22717 bytes
                       16605184 bytes free
```

If DIR cannot find a file matching the name you specify, DIR will display a message saying no such file was found:

```
File not found
```

If this error message appears, make sure you are spelling the file name correctly and that you are specifying the name of the directory within which the file resides.

Remember, only external commands reside on your disk. Internal commands like CLS, VER, DATE, and TIME always reside in your computer's memory and do not have a file on disk.

Making Duplicate Copies of Your Disks

One of the first steps you should perform with any software package is to make duplicate copies of your original disks with the DISKCOPY command. Once you create a duplicate set of *working copies* for your disks, you can place the originals in a safe location and use the working copies as needed.

If your system has two floppy disk drives of the same size and capacity, such as 5 1/4-inch high-density drives, place the disk you want to copy in drive A and an unused disk in drive B. Issue the command

```
C:\> DISKCOPY A: B: <ENTER>
```

to copy the contents of the disk in drive A to the disk in drive B. DISKCOPY will prompt you to insert the source disk in drive A and the target disk in drive B. The *source disk* is the one you want to copy, and the *target disk* is the unused disk you are copying to, as shown here:

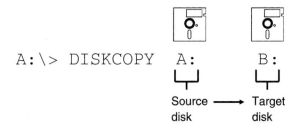

```
A:\> DISKCOPY   A:        B:
```

Source ──────▶ Target
disk   disk

To copy one of the original floppy disks containing DOS, you would first write-protect the disk and place it in drive A. Next, you would place an unused floppy disk in drive B. This concept is shown in Figure 3-1.

Warning   DISKCOPY will overwrite the contents of the target disk. If your target disk already contains programs or information, DISKCOPY will overwrite these contents and they will be lost. Always be sure you

FIGURE 3-1   Copying the source disk in drive A to the target disk in drive B

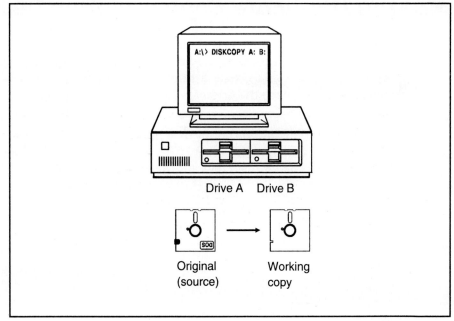

have placed the correct disk in the drive specified and have write-protected the original.

Once you have inserted the disks in the correct drives, press ENTER. DOS will begin copying the disk, displaying

```
A:\> DISKCOPY A: B: <ENTER>
Insert SOURCE diskette in drive A:
Insert TARGET diskette in drive B:
Press any key to continue...
```

As DISKCOPY copies your disk, you will first see the activation light for drive A illuminate as DISKCOPY reads information from that disk. Next, you will see the disk activation light for drive B turn on as DISKCOPY writes information to that disk. This cycle will continue until the copy is complete.

If your system only has a single floppy disk drive or your floppy drives are different sizes or capacities, you can still duplicate your disks with DISKCOPY. In this case, however, your command becomes

```
C:\> DISKCOPY  A: A: <ENTER>
```

To perform a single-drive copy in this manner, you must repeatedly exchange disks (see Figure 3-2). DISKCOPY will first prompt you to insert the *source disk* (the disk you want to copy) in drive A. As before, you would place the disk to copy in drive A and press ENTER. DISKCOPY will begin reading information from it. Next, DISKCOPY will prompt you to place the *target disk* (the unused disk you are copying to) in drive A. Insert the unused disk into the drive and press ENTER. DISKCOPY will begin writing information to the new disk. Depending on your disk type, you may have to exchange the source and target disks in the drive several times.

Regardless of whether you are performing a single disk drive copy or a dual disk drive copy, when it completes its processing DISKCOPY will prompt

```
Copy another diskette (Y/N)?
```

FIGURE
3-2

Disk copying on a system with a single floppy disk drive

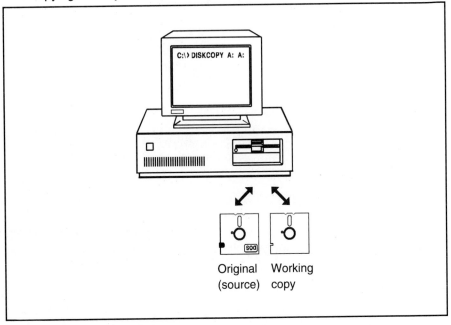

If you want to make additional disk copies, type **Y** (for yes) and press
ENTER. DISKCOPY will again prompt you to insert the source disk you
want to copy into the drive. If you have finished making copies, type **N**
and press ENTER. DISKCOPY will end, and DOS will display its prompt
and wait for your next command.

To label the newly created disk, use one of the labels that accompanied
your box of disks. Label it as shown here:

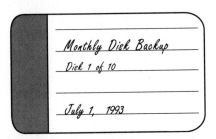

Never write on a label that has already been placed on a disk; you might
damage the disk and lose the information that the disk contains.

If you need to change a disk label, use a new label and place it over the existing label on the disk.

Repeat the DISKCOPY process for all your original disks.

Preparing a Disk for Use by DOS

In Chapter 29, "A Closer Look at Disks," you will take a close look at how DOS actually stores information on your disk. For now, you will simply learn how to prepare a disk for use by DOS by means of the FORMAT command.

The manufacturer of a disk has no idea if you intend to use it on an IBM PC, a Commodore, or an Apple computer, so the manufacturer does not prepare the disk for use on a specific system. Instead, you must prepare your disk for DOS by using the FORMAT command.

 Warning   FORMAT overwrites the contents of the target disk. You may not be able to recover the original information on a disk that FORMAT has overwritten. If you accidentally format the wrong disk and you are using DOS 5 or later, refer to the UNFORMAT command in this book's Command Reference.

Place an unused disk in drive A and issue the FORMAT command. FORMAT will prompt you to insert a new disk into the specified disk drive:

```
C:\> FORMAT A:  <ENTER>
Insert new diskette for drive A:
and press ENTER when ready...
```

Make sure the disk you are formatting is an unused disk. FORMAT completely overwrites the contents of a disk, destroying any information that it previously contained.

Since you have already inserted a new disk into the specified drive, press ENTER. FORMAT will begin preparing the disk for use. Depending on your DOS version, the information FORMAT displays on your screen will differ. In DOS 6, FORMAT displays the following:

```
C:\> FORMAT A: <ENTER>
Insert new diskette for drive A:
and press ENTER when ready...

Checking existing disk format.
Formatting 1.44M

1 percent completed
```

When FORMAT completes, it will inform you and prompt you to enter a volume label:

```
Format complete.
Volume label (11 characters, ENTER for none)?
```

A *volume label* is nothing more than a name you can assign to your disk. If, for example, you are creating a disk to keep your school notes on, you might call your disk SCHOOL. Volume labels can contain up to 11 characters. In this example, type **DOS** at the label prompt and press ENTER:

```
Volume label (11 characters, ENTER for none)? DOS <ENTER>
```

FORMAT will continue by displaying disk usage information:

```
1457664 bytes total disk space
1457664 bytes available on disk

   512 bytes in each allocation unit.
  2847 allocation units available on disk.

Volume Serial Number is 2B15-14EB

Format another (Y/N)?
```

The first line tells you the total amount of disk space present on the disk. Depending on your disk type, this value may vary, as shown in Table 3-2.

Notice that the amount of disk space is specified in *bytes*. A byte is equivalent to a character of information. A typed single-spaced page consumes about 4,000 bytes; a 1.44Mb disk, which contains 1,457,664 bytes, can store over 360 such pages.

The next line that FORMAT displays tells you how much disk space is actually available for your use. In some cases, disks contain damaged locations that DOS cannot use to store information. These damaged locations reduce the amount of available disk space. In fact, one of the primary functions of FORMAT is to identify these damaged areas on the disk and to mark them as unusable by DOS. This keeps DOS from placing information in areas where, because of damage, a disk may not be able to record the information.

TABLE 3-2

Storage Capacities of Disks

Disk Size	Disk Description	Storage	DOS Versions
5 1/4	360Kb	368,640 bytes	DOS 2.0 and later
5 1/4	1.2Mb	1,228,800 bytes	DOS 3.0 and later
3 1/2	720Kb	737,280 bytes	DOS 3.2 and later
3 1/2	1.44Mb	1,474,560 bytes	DOS 3.3 and later
3 1/2	2.88Mb	2,949,120 bytes	DOS 5.0 and later

If FORMAT locates damaged areas on your disk, it will display the number of bytes it found: for example,

```
4096 bytes in bad sectors
```

Note that FORMAT has subtracted the amount of damaged disk space from the total disk space to produce the amount of available disk space:

```
1457664  bytes total disk space
   4096 bytes in bad sectors
1453568  bytes available on disk
```

Floppy disk technology has increased greatly over the past few years, so most floppy disks do not contain damaged locations. If your disks often have damaged locations, however, you should consider buying a different brand of disk.

Finally, FORMAT prompts you to determine whether you want to prepare another disk for use by DOS:

```
Format another (Y/N)?
```

To prepare another disk, type **Y** and press ENTER. FORMAT will then prompt you to insert a new disk in the drive, and this cycle will continue. If you do not want to format additional disks, simply type **N** and press ENTER. In this case, the FORMAT command will terminate and DOS will redisplay its prompt.

Safe Formatting with DOS 5 or Later

Beginning with version 5, DOS provides the UNFORMAT command, which helps you recover from an inadvertent disk format operation on a needed disk. To assist UNFORMAT, the FORMAT command performs a safe format operation (unless you tell it to do otherwise by using the /U switch, as described in the FORMAT section of the Command Reference in this book). If the disk you are formatting contains information, a safe format does not actually overwrite the existing information. Instead, the safe format makes the disk appear to DOS as newly formatted, just as you would normally want. If you then place new information on the disk, the old information will be overwritten. However, if you immediately use UNFORMAT on a safe formatted disk, you can probably recover the disk's previous contents.

To assist UNFORMAT, the safe format also stores information UNFORMAT can use to recover the disk. As it saves this information, FORMAT will display the following message on your screen:

```
Saving UNFORMAT information
```

For more information on FORMAT, turn to the Command Reference at the end of this book.

High-Density Disk Users

If your computer has a 1.2Mb disk drive, you need to know how to exchange disks with users who have 360Kb disk drives. 1.2Mb disk drives are designed to use a disk called a quad-density disk. 360Kb disk drives, however, use a double-sided, double-density disk.

To get the best use out of your 1.2Mb disk drive, you should purchase the 1.2Mb quad-density disks. However, if you have 360Kb disks available or you have to exchange disks with a user who has 360Kb disk drives, the FORMAT command allows you to prepare a 360Kb disk in your 1.2Mb drive. For FORMAT to do so, however, you must include the /4 switch in the FORMAT command, as shown here:

```
C:\> FORMAT A: /4 <ENTER>
```

When FORMAT prompts you for the new disk to format, place your 360Kb disk in the drive and press ENTER. The actual formatting process will be the same as discussed previously. Remember, the only time you need to use the /4 switch is when you are preparing a 360Kb disk in a 1.2Mb disk drive. If you are using a 1.44Mb 3 1/2-inch disk drive and need to format a disk for a user with a 720Kb drive, see the /F switch of the FORMAT command in the Command Reference section of this book.

Write Protection with FORMAT and DISKCOPY

Earlier you learned that write-protecting your disks could prevent them from being overwritten by the DOS DISKCOPY or FORMAT command. Here's a quick example of why.

Assume that you have write-protected the disk in drive A and you issue the command

```
C:\> FORMAT A: <ENTER>
```

Because your DOS disk is write protected, FORMAT will not overwrite the disk's contents. Instead, it will display

```
Write protect error
Format terminated.
Format another (Y/N)?
```

Type **N** to end the format operation.

As you can see, write-protecting your floppy disks when their content is not going to change is a very smart step. Had FORMAT overwritten one of your disks, the disk's contents would have been lost unless you immediately used the UNFORMAT command.

Practice

If your system is displaying the DOS prompt, issue the VER command:

```
C:\> VER <ENTER>
MS-DOS Version 6.00

C:\>
```

As you may recall, VER is an internal DOS command that always resides in your computer's memory once DOS starts.

Invoke the DATE command to display the current system date:

```
C:\> DATE <ENTER>
Current date is Tue 04-06-1993
Enter new date (mm-dd-yy):
```

In this case, leave the date unchanged by pressing ENTER.

Next, repeat the DATE command, this time setting the system date to July 4, 1993:

```
C:\> DATE <ENTER>
Current date is Tue 04-06-1993
Enter new date (mm-dd-yy): 7-4-93 <ENTER>

C:\>
```

Verify that the date has indeed been changed by again invoking DATE:

```
C:\> DATE <ENTER>
Current date is Sun 07-04-1993
Enter new date (mm-dd-yy):
```

This time, use today's date to reset your system date. Don't forget that DATE allows you to specify a date in the command line when you invoke DATE.

Next, rather than entering the DATE command, misspell "DATE" as "DART." When you invoke this command, DOS will display the message

```
C:\> DART <ENTER>
Bad command or file name

C:\>
```

Next, from the DOS prompt, issue the TIME command. TIME will display the current system time and prompt you to enter the desired time:

```
C:\> TIME <ENTER>
Current time is  2:04:55.02p
Enter new time:
```

Leave the time unchanged by pressing ENTER.

Since the TIME command allows you to specify a time in the command line, let's set the current system time to 1:30 P.M. using military time:

```
C:\> TIME 13:30 <ENTER>
```

If you are using DOS 4 or later, repeat the command as shown here:

```
C:\> TIME 1:30p <ENTER>
```

If you invoke TIME once again, you can verify that the system time has indeed changed:

```
C:\> TIME <ENTER>
Current time is  1:30:02.03p
Enter new time:
```

Set the system time to the correct time before proceeding.

In order to have several disks for the later chapters of this book, you need to use the FORMAT command to prepare new disks:

```
C:\> FORMAT A: <ENTER>
```

When FORMAT prompts

```
Insert new diskette for drive A:
and press ENTER when ready...
```

place an unused disk in the specified drive and press ENTER to continue. FORMAT will prepare your disk for use, displaying

```
C:\> FORMAT A: <ENTER>
Insert new diskette for drive A:
and press ENTER when ready...
Checking existing disk format.
Formatting 360K

1 percent completed
```

Use FORMAT to prepare several floppy disks. Remember, if you are using double-sided, double-density disks (360Kb disks) in a 1.2Mb drive, you will have to add the /4 switch to the FORMAT command.

By now you should be feeling a little more comfortable with issuing DOS commands. This means you are now ready to learn the specifics of DOS files.

Review

Answers to review questions are in Appendix A.

1. What command displays the DOS version number?

2. What is the function of the following command?

   ```
   C:\> DATE 12-25-93  <ENTER>
   ```

3. What DOS TIME command should you use to set the system time to 6:30 P.M.?

4. When does the following error message occur?

   ```
   Bad command or file name
   ```

5. How does an internal DOS command differ from an external DOS command?

6. How can you display your current system date or time without modifying it?

7. How do you locate an external command on disk?

8. How do you write protect a disk? When would you want to do so?

9. How can you make duplicate copies of your original disks?

10. What are working copies?

11. Define source and target disks.

12. What does the DOS FORMAT command do?

13. What is a disk volume label?

14. What happens if your new disk contains damaged locations?

Key Points

VER

The VER command displays the major and minor version numbers of the DOS version you are using. To execute VER, simply type **VER** at the DOS prompt and press ENTER:

```
C:\> VER <ENTER>
```

DATE

The DATE command allows you to set or display the computer's current system date. To invoke DATE, type **DATE** at the DOS prompt. When DATE prompts you to enter a date, type in a date in the format *mm-dd-yy*, or press ENTER to leave the date unchanged.

DATE also allows you to include a date in the command line, as shown here:

```
C:\> DATE 2-23-93 <ENTER>
```

TIME

The TIME command allows you to set or display the current system time. To invoke TIME, simply type **TIME** at the DOS prompt. When TIME prompts you to enter a time, enter it in the format *hh:mm:ss.nn*, or simply press ENTER to leave the time unchanged.

Although TIME allows you to specify a time that is accurate to hundredths of a second, it only requires you to specify hours and minutes. Remember, prior to DOS 4, TIME uses a 24-hour clock.

continues . . .

Like DATE, TIME allows you to include a time in the command line, as shown here:

```
C:\> TIME 12:30 <ENTER>
```

Internal and External Commands

DOS commands are categorized as internal or external. Each time DOS starts, it loads several smaller, commonly used commands into memory. Commands such as CLS, DATE, TIME, and VER are examples. Since these commands are always in memory, DOS does not have to load them from disk when you execute them. They are internal DOS commands.

External commands, however, reside on disk. These include commands such as FORMAT and DISKCOPY. When you execute an external DOS command, DOS must load the command from disk into memory.

Bad Command or File Name

If you misspell a DOS command or if the command is an external command, it does not reside on the disk or in the directory of files you are using. DOS will display an error message:

```
Bad command or file name
```

If you are sure of your typing, use the DIR command to locate the external command on disk.

continues . . .

DIR

A directory is a list of file names. The DIR command displays information about each file in the list. To invoke DIR, type **DIR** at the DOS prompt and press ENTER. To display the files contained in a specific directory, include the directory name:

```
C:\> DIR \DOS <ENTER>
```

To display a directory for a specific file, include the file name.

```
C:\> DIR \DOS\FORMAT <ENTER>
```

DISKCOPY

The DISKCOPY command allows you to make duplicate copies of your disks. DISKCOPY is an external DOS command. If your system has two floppy disk drives, you can invoke DISKCOPY as

```
C:\> DISKCOPY A: B: <ENTER>
```

If you have a single floppy disk drive system, use

```
C:\> DISKCOPY A: A: <ENTER>
```

CHAPTER

Getting Started with DOS Files

A s you know, both floppy and hard disks are used to store programs and information. You have seen that DOS keeps all of its external commands (such as DISKCOPY and FORMAT) on disk by name. In the case of your hard disk, the DOS commands reside in a directory that is named DOS.

DOS stores information on your disk by placing your programs and information into individual storage facilities called *files.* A file on disk can be compared to a paper file in a filing cabinet; both are used to store information.

Later in this book you will learn that DOS allows you to create, modify, rename, and later discard files, just as you would a file in your office. Before you learn about such operations, however, you should learn more about DOS files in general.

Understanding DOS File Names

Every file on your disk has a unique *file name.* DOS uses the file name to distinguish one file from another. DOS file names are composed of two parts: a *base name* that can contain from one to eight characters, and an optional *extension* containing from one to three characters. DOS uses a period to separate the file name from the extension, as shown here:

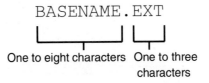

For example, the DISKCOPY command, which is an external command, is kept on disk in a file named DISKCOPY.COM:

DISKCOPY is the eight-character base name, and COM is the three-character extension.

So far, using the DIR command, you have simply specified the base name in the DIR command, as shown here:

```
C:\> DIR \DOS\DISKCOPY <ENTER>
```

However, if you know a file's extension, you can include it as well:

```
C:\> DIR \DOS \DISKCOPY.COM <ENTER>

 Volume in drive C is DOS
 Volume Serial Number is 1A54-45E0
 Directory of C:\DOS

DISKCOPY COM      11879 02-12-93   6:00a
        1 file(s)       11879 bytes
                     16607232 bytes free
```

As you can see, if you include an extension, you must separate it from the base name with a period, even though DIR does not show the period on the screen. DIR separates the base name from the extension by one or more blank characters instead.

If you use DIR to list all the files in your DOS directory, DIR will show the following display:

```
C:\> DIR   \DOS <ENTER>

 Volume in drive C is DOS
 Volume Serial Number is 1A54-45E0
 Directory of C:\DOS


 .            <DIR>      11-23-92   9:26p
 ..           <DIR>      11-23-92   9:26p
DBLSPACE BIN     50284 02-12-93   6:00a
FORMAT   COM     22717 02-12-93   6:00a
```

```
NLSFUNC  EXE      7036 02-12-93    6:00a
UNTRY  SYS       17066 02-12-93    6:00a
KEYB     COM     14983 02-12-93    6:00a
KEYBOARD SYS     34694 02-12-93    6:00a
ANSI     SYS      9065 02-12-93    6:00a
ATTRIB   EXE     11165 02-12-93    6:00a
CHKDSK   EXE     12908 02-12-93    6:00a
EDIT     COM       413 02-12-93    6:00a
  :        :        :        :          :
MWAVMGR  DLL     21712 02-12-93    6:00a
MWAVTSR  EXE     17328 02-12-93    6:00a
COMMAND  COM     52925 02-12-93    6:00a
QBASIC   INI       132 02-20-93   12:10p
MOUSE    INI        28 02-03-93   11:54a
DEFAULT  CAT        66 02-08-93    7:51p
       130 file(s)    5826340 bytes
                     16601088 bytes free
```

Note that the file extensions vary in this listing. The file's extension will often help you determine what information the file contains.

Understanding File Extensions

DOS file names can have an optional three-character extension. This extension can tell you about the contents of the file. For example, if your file contains a letter, the file's extension might be LTR; for a report, the extension might be RPT. The following list of file extensions is standard for DOS files:

Extension	File Contents
LTR	File containing a letter
RPT	File containing a report
DAT	File containing data for a program
BAK	Backup copy of a file
BAS	File containing a BASIC program

Extension	File Contents
TXT	Text or word processing file

If you examine your DOS disks, you will find files with the following extensions:

Extension	File Contents
COM	File containing a DOS command
EXE	File containing a DOS command
SYS	Operating system file used by DOS
BAT	DOS batch file that contains a list of DOS commands
CPI	Code-page information file used for international character sets
HLP	File containing DOS help information
OVL	Overlay files used by executable programs
DLL	Dynamic link library files used by executable programs
INI	Initialization files used by specific programs

By examining a file's extension, you usually can determine the file's contents. Here are some examples:

File Name	File Contents
DISKCOPY.COM	File containing a DOS command
GRANDMA.LTR	File containing a letter
CONFIG.SYS	Operating system file used by DOS
AUTOEXEC.BAT	DOS batch file that contains a list of commands
CHAPTER4.TXT	Text or word processing file

Naming Your Own Files

Later in this book you will create files to store your own information. As you do so, one of the most important things you should do is to use meaningful file names. DOS file names should tell you about the contents of a file. Although the extension is very useful in telling you about the type of a file, the eight-character base name is equally important.

For example, if you examine the file names X.LTR, Y.LTR, and Z.LTR, the extension LTR tells you that each file contains a letter. However, X, Y, and Z do not give you much information. Contrast these file names to the following names:

GRANDMA.LTR
LAWYER.LTR
BANKLOAN.LTR

Here, the eight-character base name gives you the specifics.

When you name your files, make your file names meaningful. As the number of files on your disk increases, meaningful file names will greatly increase your file organization.

DOS allows you to use the characters in the alphabet ("A" through "Z") and the digits 0 through 9 within your file names, as well as the following characters:

! @ # $ ^ & ( ) – { } ' % ~ _

With this additional set of characters, your file names can become quite meaningful, as shown here:

PROFIT93.$$$	1993.TAX	PHONE.#S
MY–COST.NOV	CLASS(A).GRD	PHOTO.A&W

If you use lowercase letters in your file names, DOS will convert them to uppercase for standardization.

Directories

To organize your files, DOS keeps track of each file by maintaining a list of files on the disk. This list is called a directory. A directory listing refers to displaying the names of the files in a specific directory. The DIR command (short for "directory"), which we looked at in Chapter 3, "Issuing DOS Commands," displays a directory listing of your disk. This listing contains file names and other important information.

The Directory Listing

Issue the following DIR command:

```
C:\> DIR <ENTER>
```

Unless you specify a file or directory name in the DIR command line, DIR lists all of the files in the current directory. The directory listing contains more than just the name of each file on the disk. If you examine the first two lines of the directory listing, you will find that DIR displays the letter of the disk drive that you are examining, as well as the optional disk name, which DOS calls the volume label:

```
Volume in drive C is DOS 6 DISK
```

If the disk does not contain a volume label, DIR will display

```
Volume in drive A has no label
```

Beginning with DOS 4, DIR also displays the disk's serial number.

```
Volume Serial Number is 16F6-3B73
```

Next, DIR displays the directory name followed by file names and extensions:

```
Directory of C:\

CONFIG   SYS        128 03-09-93  10:31a
AUTOEXEC BAT        119 03-09-93  11:42a
DOS           <DIR>     01-22-93   7:19a
MASM          <DIR>     02-22-93   7:31a
```

In addition to the file name and extension, DIR displays the size of the file in bytes. Remember, as previously discussed, a byte is equivalent to a character of information; if a file is 512 bytes in length, it contains 512 characters of information.

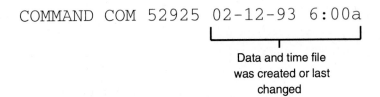

DIR then displays the date and time at which the file was created or last modified:

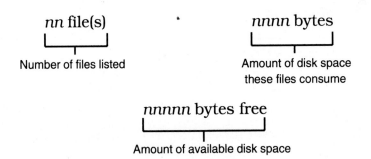

Chapter 3, "Issuing DOS Commands," discussed setting your system date and time. Each time you modify or create a file on disk, DOS assigns the current system date and time to the directory entry for the file. You can then use this date and time to determine when a specific file was created or changed.

Finally, DIR displays the total number of files on the disk, the amount of disk space the files occupy, and the amount still available on the disk:

nn file(s)   *nnnn* bytes

Number of files listed   Amount of disk space
                                                  these files consume

nnnnn bytes free

Amount of available disk space

Additional Features of DIR

Depending on the number of files on your disk, the file names may have scrolled past you quite rapidly when you issued the DIR command. When this occurs you can use the /P switch (a *switch* is a modifier to a DOS command), which directs DIR to *pause* with each screenful of information displayed:

```
C:\> DIR /P <ENTER>
```

In this case, when DIR displays the first screenful of files, it pauses and displays the following message:

```
Press any key to continue . . .
```

If you press any key, DIR will display the next screenful of files, repeating this prompt if additional files exist. If you don't want to display additional files, you can end the directory listing by pressing CTRL-C.

There may be times when you do not need to see the size, date, and time fields for each file. The /W switch directs DIR to display (*wide* across the screen) only the file names and extensions for each of the files on your disk, with five file names and extensions per line, as shown here:

```
C:\> DIR  \DOS  /W <ENTER>

 Volume in drive C is DOS
 Volume Serial Number is 1A54-45E0
 Directory of C:\DOS


[.]           [..]          DBLSPACE.BIN  FORMAT.COM    NLSFUNC.EXE
COUNTRY.SYS   KEYB.COM      KEYBOARD.SYS  ANSI.SYS      ATTRIB.EXE
CHKDSK.EXE    EDIT.COM      EXPAND.EXE    MORE.COM      MSD.EXE
QBASIC.EXE    RESTORE.EXE   SYS.COM       UNFORMAT.COM  UNDELETE.INI
README.TXT    DEBUG.EXE     FDISK.EXE     DOSSHELL.VID  DOSSHELL.INI
   :             :             :             :             :
SIZER.EXE     MONOUMB.386   MSTOOLS.DLL   MSAV.EXE      MSAV.HLP
```

```
 MSAVHELP.OVL  MSAVIRUS.LST  VSAFE.COM    MWAVDOSL.DLL  MWAVDRVL.DLL
MWAVDLG.DLL   MWAVSCAN.DLL  MWAV.EXE     MWAVABSI.DLL  MWAV.HLP
DEFAULT.SET   DEFAULT.SLT   MWAVSOS.DLL  MWAVMGR.DLL   MWAVTSR.EXE
COMMAND.COM   QBASIC.INI    MOUSE.INI    DEFAULT.CAT
        129 file(s)    5826340 bytes
                      16607232 bytes free
```

If you are using DOS 5 or later, DIR also provides the /O, /S, /A, /B, and /L switches.

By default, DIR displays file names in the order the files appear in your directory listing. Using the /O switch, you can direct DIR to display files sorted by name, extension, size, or date. For example, the following DIR command uses /O:N to sort the files by names.

```
C:\> DIR  \DOS  /O:N  <ENTER>

 Volume in drive C is DOS
 Volume Serial Number is 1A54-45E0
 Directory of C:\DOS

 .            <DIR>         11-23-92    9:26p
 ..           <DIR>         11-23-92    9:26p
ANSI     SYS      9065 02-12-93    6:00a
APPEND   EXE     10774 02-12-93    6:00a
ATTRIB   EXE     11165 02-12-93    6:00a
CHKDSK   EXE     12908 02-12-93    6:00a
CHKSTATE SYS     41600 02-12-93    6:00a
CHOICE   COM      1754 02-12-93    6:00a
COMMAND  COM     52925 02-12-93    6:00a
COUNTRY  SYS     17066 02-12-93    6:00a
DBLSPACE BIN     50284 02-12-93    6:00a
DBLSPACE EXE    273068 02-12-93    6:00a
DBLSPACE HLP     72173 02-12-93    6:00a
DBLSPACE INF      2166 02-12-93    6:00a
   :        :        :       :         :
UNDELETE INI       235 02-23-93    1:04a
UNDELETE EXE     26420 02-12-93    6:00a
UNFORMAT COM     12738 02-12-93    6:00a
VFINTD   386      5295 02-12-93    6:00a
```

```
VSAFE     COM      62576 02-12-93    6:00a
WNTOOLS   GRP       2205 02-22-93    3:17p
XCOPY     EXE      15820 02-12-93    6:00a
        129 file(s)    5826340 bytes
                      16607232 bytes free
```

In this case, DIR listed the files alphabetically from "A" to "Z." If you want to display the files sorted from "Z" to "A," use the /O:–N switch, as shown here:

```
C:\> DIR  \DOS  /O:-N <ENTER>

 Volume in drive C is DOS
 Volume Serial Number is 1A54-45E0
 Directory of C:\DOS

XCOPY     EXE      15820 02-12-93    6:00a
WNTOOLS   GRP       2205 02-22-93    3:17p
VSAFE     COM      62576 02-12-93    6:00a
VFINTD    386       5295 02-12-93    6:00a
UNFORMAT  COM      12738 02-12-93    6:00a
UNDELETE  INI        235 02-23-93    1:04a
UNDELETE  EXE      26420 02-12-93    6:00a
   :        :        :        :         :
DBLSPACE  EXE     273068 02-12-93    6:00a
DBLSPACE  HLP      72173 02-12-93    6:00a
DBLSPACE  INF       2166 02-12-93    6:00a
DBLSPACE  SYS        339 02-12-93    6:00a
COUNTRY   SYS      17066 02-12-93    6:00a
COMMAND   COM      52925 02-12-93    6:00a
CHOICE    COM       1754 02-12-93    6:00a
CHKSTATE  SYS      41600 02-12-93    6:00a
CHKDSK    EXE      12908 02-12-93    6:00a
ATTRIB    EXE      11165 02-12-93    6:00a
APPEND    EXE      10774 02-12-93    6:00a
ANSI      SYS       9065 02-12-93    6:00a
  ..             <DIR>      11-23-92    9:26p
  .              <DIR>      11-23-92    9:26p
        129 file(s)    5826340 bytes
                      16607232 bytes free
```

Table 4-1 briefly describes the options you can specify with /O.

In Chapter 11, "Getting Started with File Organization," you will learn how DOS helps you organize your disk by creating subdirectories. The /S switch directs DIR to not only display the files in the current directory, but also files that reside in subdirectories.

Using DIR /S, the following command lists every file on your disk:

```
C:\> DIR \*.* /S <ENTER>
```

In Chapter 25, "Advanced File Manipulation," you will learn that each file has a unique set of characteristics that DOS calls attributes and that the DIR /A switch lets you list files by their attributes.

**TABLE
4-1**

DIR /O Sort Options Provided with DOS 5 or Later

Option	Sort Order
D	By date, oldest to newest
–D	By date, newest to oldest
E	By extension, A to Z
–E	By extension, Z to A
G	Directory names before files
–G	Directory names after files
N	By base name, A to Z
–N	By base name, Z to A
S	By size, smallest to largest
–S	By size, largest to smallest
C	By compression ratio, smallest to largest
–C	By compression ratio, largest to smallest

The /B switch directs DIR to display file names, one name per line, suppressing the file size, date, and time stamp information, as shown here:

```
C:\> DIR \DOS /B <ENTER>
DBLSPACE.BIN
FORMAT.COM
NLSFUNC.EXE
COUNTRY.SYS
KEYB.COM
KEYBOARD.SYS
ANSI.SYS
ATTRIB.EXE
CHKDSK.EXE
   :
   :
COMMAND.COM
QBASIC.INI
MOUSE.INI
DEFAULT.CAT
```

Finally, the /L switch directs DIR to display the directory listing in lowercase letters:

```
C:\> DIR \DOS /L <ENTER>

 Volume in drive C is DOS
 Volume Serial Number is 1A54-45E0
 Directory of C:\DOS


 .            <DIR>       11-23-92    9:26p
 ..           <DIR>       11-23-92    9:26p
 dblspace bin     50284 02-12-93    6:00a
 format   com     22717 02-12-93    6:00a
 nlsfunc  exe      7036 02-12-93    6:00a
 country  sys     17066 02-12-93    6:00a
 keyb     com     14983 02-12-93    6:00a
 keyboard sys     34694 02-12-93    6:00a
 ansi     sys      9065 02-12-93    6:00a
```

```
attrib    exe      11165 02-12-93    6:00a
chkdsk    exe      12908 02-12-93    6:00a
  :        :         :     :          :
  :        :         :     :          :
qbasic    ini        132 02-20-93   12:10p
mouse     ini         28 02-03-93   11:54a
default   cat         66 02-08-93    7:51p
        129 file(s)      5826340 bytes
                       16607232 bytes free
```

File Not Found

In Chapter 3, "Issuing DOS Commands," you used the DOS DIR command to locate specific files on your disk:

```
C:\> DIR \DOS\DISKCOPY <ENTER>

 Volume in drive C is DOS
 Volume Serial Number is 1A54-45E0
 Directory of C:\DOS

DISKCOPY COM      11879 02-12-93    6:00a
        1 file(s)        11879 bytes
                      16607232 bytes free
```

At that time, you found that if the file you were searching for did not exist in the directory, DOS displayed the message

```
File not found
```

DOS is telling you that you have either misspelled the file name in the DIR command line or that the file simply does not exist in the directory that you are using.

 Note   It is important to distinguish between the error message "File not found" and the message "Bad command or file name." With the first message, DOS is telling you that the command that you ran (such as

DIR) is valid, but DOS could not find the file that was specified in the command line. With the second message, DOS is telling you that the command you typed does not exist as specified or is not in the directory that you are using.

Abort, Retry, Fail?

As your floppy disk usage increases, so too will the likelihood of seeing the error message

```
Not ready reading drive A
Abort, Retry, Fail?
```

This error message is most common when you have either failed to insert a floppy disk in the specified disk drive or when you have not closed the disk drive latch after you inserted the disk. DOS is telling you that it cannot access the specified disk drive and that it wants you to tell it how to continue. Your options are to type **A**, **R**, or **F** for Abort, Retry, or Fail.

❑ **Abort** The Abort option directs DOS to terminate the command that attempted to access the unprepared disk drive. When you type **A**, DOS terminates the current program and redisplays the DOS prompt.

❑ **Retry** The Retry option directs DOS to retry the operation that accessed the disk drive. You normally select this operation after you have inserted a disk in the drive or closed the disk drive latch. When you type **R**, the command may continue as if the error never occurred.

❑ **Fail** The Fail option directs DOS to ignore the error and try to access the disk. DOS will sometimes display the "Abort, Retry, Fail?" message when you have a disk in the drive and the drive latch is closed. This is your first warning that the disk in the disk drive is starting to go bad. In some cases—if you are lucky—the Fail option can convince DOS to ignore the error, allowing you to access the disk. If this is the case, you will need to copy files from the disk, as discussed in Chapter 8, "Basic File Operations."

Listing a Group of Files

So far, you have used the DIR command either to list all the files in your directory with

```
C:\> DIR <ENTER>
```

or to list a specific file with

```
C:\> DIR \DOS\DISKCOPY <ENTER>
```

DIR provides another capability: it can list a group of files that have similar file names or extensions. To display a directory listing of specific files, you will use two characters, the asterisk (*) and the question mark (?). These are called the DOS *wildcard characters*. Let's take a look at some uses of the asterisk wildcard character.

Most users use the asterisk wildcard character when they do not care about either the base name or the extension. For example, the command

```
C:\> DIR   \DOS\*.COM <ENTER>
```

requests that DIR display all of the files in the DOS directory that have the COM extension.

The output becomes the following:

```
C:\> DIR   \DOS\*.COM <ENTER>

 Volume in drive C is DOS
 Volume Serial Number is 1A54-45E0
 Directory of C:\DOS

FORMAT    COM     22717 02-12-93    6:00a
KEYB      COM     14983 02-12-93    6:00a
EDIT      COM       413 02-12-93    6:00a
```

```
MORE       COM      2546 02-12-93    6:00a
SYS        COM      9379 02-12-93    6:00a
UNFORMAT   COM     12738 02-12-93    6:00a
CHOICE     COM      1754 02-12-93    6:00a
DOSSHELL   COM      4620 02-12-93    6:00a
HELP       COM       413 02-12-93    6:00a
MODE       COM     23521 02-12-93    6:00a
DISKCOMP   COM     10620 02-12-93    6:00a
DISKCOPY   COM     11879 02-12-93    6:00a
GRAPHICS   COM     19694 02-12-93    6:00a
LOADFIX    COM      1131 02-12-93    6:00a
TREE       COM      6898 02-12-93    6:00a
DOSKEY     COM      5883 02-12-93    6:00a
MOUSE      COM     56408 02-12-93    6:00a
VSAFE      COM     62576 02-12-93    6:00a
COMMAND    COM     52925 02-12-93    6:00a
         19 file(s)      321098 bytes
                       16607232 bytes free
```

The asterisk wildcard character told DIR to ignore the base name portion of the name and simply list all of the files that have the extension COM. In a similar manner, the command

```
C:\> DIR \DOS\*.EXE <ENTER>
```

makes DIR display all of the files that have the extension EXE.

To display all of the files in the DOS directory that begin with the letter "A," you would use the following command:

```
C:\> DIR  \DOS\A*.* <ENTER>
```

In the case of DOS 6, DIR displays the following:

```
C:\> DIR  \DOS\A*.* <ENTER>

 Volume in drive C is DOS
```

```
Volume Serial Number is 1A54-45E0
Directory of C:\DOS

ANSI     SYS      9065 02-12-93    6:00a
ATTRIB   EXE     11165 02-12-93    6:00a
APPEND   EXE     10774 02-12-93    6:00a
        3 file(s)        31004 bytes
                      16607232 bytes free
```

When you do not specify a file name or an extension, DIR defaults to the asterisk wildcard character. That's why the command

```
C:\> DIR \DOS\FORMAT <ENTER>
```

produces the same result as

```
C:\> DIR \DOS\FORMAT.COM <ENTER>
```

Since no extension was given in the first command, DOS defaulted to *.
If you issue the command

```
C:\> DIR \DOS\FORMAT.* <ENTER>
```

DOS will display the following:

```
C:\> DIR \DOS\FORMAT.* <ENTER>

Volume in drive C is DOS
Volume Serial Number is 1A54-45E0
Directory of C:\DOS
```

```
FORMAT    COM      22717 02-12-93   6:00a
         1 file(s)        22717 bytes
                      16607232 bytes free
```

The second DOS wildcard character, the question mark, allows you to be a little more precise with your directory listings. Assume, for example, that you have created several data files on a disk, as shown here:

```
Volume in drive C is DOS 6 DISK
Volume Serial Number is 16F6-3B73
Directory of C:\

BILLS-01 93          128 01-09-93   10:31a
BILLS-02 93          128 02-09-93   10:31a
BILLS-03 93          128 03-09-93   10:31a
BILLS-04 93          128 04-09-93   10:31a
BILLS-05 93          128 05-09-93   10:31a
BILLS-06 93          128 06-09-93   10:31a
BILLS-07 93          128 07-09-93   10:31a
BILLS-08 93          128 08-09-93   10:31a
BILLS-09 93          128 09-09-93   10:31a
BILLS-10 93          128 10-09-93   10:31a
BILLS-11 93          128 11-09-93   10:31a
BILLS-12 93          128 12-09-93   10:31a
         12 file(s)         1536 bytes
                      151904256 bytes free
```

The files in this case contain your monthly bills (months 1 to 12) for the year 1993. The command

```
C:\> DIR *.93 <ENTER>
```

displays all of the files with the extension 93, as you might expect. If you wanted to list a specific file, such as BILLS-01.93, you would specify its file name in this command:

```
C:\> DIR BILLS-01.93 <ENTER>

 Volume in drive C is DOS 6 DISK
 Volume Serial Number is 16F6-3B73
 Directory of C:\

BILLS-01 93         128 01-09-93  10:31a
        1 file(s)         128 bytes
                    151904256 bytes free
```

Using the question mark wildcard character, you can perform selective group listings. For example, in the command

```
C:\> DIR BILLS-1?.93 <ENTER>
```

the question mark wildcard character directs DIR to ignore the character in the eighth character position of the file name. DIR will display

```
C:\> DIR BILLS-1?.93 <ENTER>

 Volume in drive C is DOS 6 DISK
 Volume Serial Number is 16F6-3B73
 Directory of C:\

BILLS-10 93         128 10-09-93  10:31a
BILLS-11 93         128 11-09-93  10:31a
BILLS-12 93         128 12-09-93  10:31a
        3 file(s)         384 bytes
                    151904256 bytes free
```

This command told DOS to display any file with a name that started with BILLS-1 and had the extension 93. To display files for the first three quarters of 1993 (files that have 0 in position 7 of the file name), your command becomes

```
C:\> DIR BILLS-0?.93 <ENTER>

Volume in drive C is DOS 6 DISK
Volume Serial Number is 16F6-3B73
Directory of C:\

BILLS-01 93          128 01-09-93  10:31a
BILLS-02 93          128 02-09-93  10:31a
BILLS-03 93          128 03-09-93  10:31a
BILLS-04 93          128 04-09-93  10:31a
BILLS-05 93          128 05-09-93  10:31a
BILLS-06 93          128 06-09-93  10:31a
BILLS-07 93          128 07-09-93  10:31a
BILLS-08 93          128 08-09-93  10:31a
BILLS-09 93          128 09-09-93  10:31a
         9 file(s)        1152 bytes
                    151871488 bytes free
```

If you instead issue the command

```
C:\> DIR BILLS-?2.93 <ENTER>
```

you are telling DIR to list any file whose name starts with "BILLS-", has 2 in position 8 of the file name, and has an extension of 93. Since two files meet this criteria, DIR will display

```
C:\> DIR BILLS-?2.93 <ENTER>
Volume in drive C is DOS 6 DISK
Volume Serial Number is 16F6-3B73
Directory of C:\

BILLS-02 93          128 02-09-93  10:31a
BILLS-12 93          128 12-09-93  10:31a
         2 file(s)         256 bytes
                    151871488 bytes free
```

Because all of the files on this example disk contain the extension 93, you could have omitted the file extension in each of the preceding DIR commands. The extension was included in the examples simply to reduce confusion.

The asterisk and question mark wildcard characters are actually quite similar. The question mark directs DOS to ignore the character in a specific location in a file name or extension. The asterisk wildcard character directs DOS not only to ignore the character at a specific location, but also to ignore any characters that follow the asterisk throughout the file name or extension. For example, if the asterisk appears in the first position of a file name, as in

```
C:\> DIR *  <ENTER>
```

or the command

```
C:\> DIR *ILENAME.EXT <ENTER>
```

DOS will ignore all eight characters in the file name. Remember, the asterisk wildcard character directs DOS not only to ignore the characters in the position containing the asterisk, but also all of the character positions that follow the command.

The command

```
C:\> DIR F*LENAME.EXT <ENTER>
```

directs DIR to ignore the characters in positions 2 through 8 of the file name, even though the letters are present in the command line. That's why, given the previous directory of files, the command

```
C:\> DIR BILLS-*1.93 <ENTER>
```

and the command

```
C:\> DIR BILLS-*.93 <ENTER>
```

produce the same results.

Practice

If your system is not turned on, start DOS. When DOS displays its prompt, issue the command

```
C:\> DIR \DOS <ENTER>
```

Depending on your system, the file names that reside on your disk may scroll past you quite rapidly, which makes locating a specific file on your disk difficult at best. Therefore, repeat the DIR command, this time including the /P switch:

```
C:\> DIR \DOS /P <ENTER>
```

By including this switch, you direct DIR to pause with each screenful of files, displaying the message

```
Press any key to continue . . .
```

To continue your directory listing, press any key.

Next, suppress the display of the size, date, and time stamps for each file by using the /W switch, as shown here:

```
C:\> DIR \DOS /W <ENTER>
```

/W directs DIR to display your directory listing in a wide format, with five names and extensions per line. Once DOS displays the directory listing, note the different file extensions. Finally, note the amount of available space that resides on the disk.

Open the disk drive latch for drive A if you are using 5 1/4-inch disks, or if you are using 3 1/2-inch disks, eject the floppy disk from drive A. Issue the command

```
C:\> DIR A: <ENTER>
```

When DOS displays the message

```
Not ready reading drive A:
Abort, Retry, Fail?
```

type **A**. As you will recall, the Abort option directs DOS to terminate the application that is accessing the unprepared disk drive. When you type **A** to abort the DIR command, DOS will redisplay its prompt:

```
C:\> DIR   A: <ENTER>
Not ready reading drive A
Abort, Retry, Fail? A

C:\>
```

Again invoke the DIR command, and when DOS displays the message

```
C:\> DIR A: <ENTER>
Not ready reading drive A
Abort, Retry, Fail?
```

close the disk drive latch or insert a disk into the drive, and type **R**. This tells DOS to retry the operation responsible for the error message. Since you have corrected the cause of the problem (by readying a disk in the drive), the DIR command can continue as if the error had never occurred.

Next, issue the command

```
C:\> DIR XXX <ENTER>
```

When DIR displays the message

```
File not found
```

it is telling you that a file named XXX does not exist in your current directory. However, DOS did successfully execute the DIR command. This time, misspell DIR as shown here:

```
C:\> DRI <ENTER>
```

When DOS displays the message

```
Bad command or file name
```

it is telling you that it did not execute the specified command; the command was not an internal DOS command in memory or an external command on the current disk.

Now let's try the DOS wildcard characters. Issue the command

```
C:\> DIR \DOS\*.COM <ENTER>
```

In this case, DOS will display all of the files in the DOS directory that have the extension COM. Repeat this technique using the following command:

```
C:\> DIR \DOS\*.EXE <ENTER>
```

Throughout the remainder of the book you will examine many commands that support DOS wildcard characters. Take time now to ensure that you understand how they work.

Review

1. How does DOS keep track of information on your disk?
2. What is a directory?

3. What DOS command displays a directory listing of your disk?

4. DOS file names are composed of two parts. What are they?

5. What characters can you use in DOS file names?

6. Using file extensions as your guide, determine the contents of the following files.

   ```
   DISKCOMP.COM
   ANSI.SYS
   AUTOEXEC.BAT
   JONES.LTR
   ```

7. What is the function of the /P switch command shown here?

   ```
   C:\> DIR /P <ENTER>
   ```

8. How can you suppress the display of each file's size, date, and time stamp when you perform your directory listings?

9. List five things displayed by the DIR command.

10. What are DOS wildcard characters?

11. What is the result of the following commands?

    ```
    C:\> DIR \DOS\*.COM <ENTER>
    C:\> DIR \DOS\A*.* <ENTER>
    C:\> DIR \DOS\DISKCO??.COM <ENTER>
    ```

Key Points

DIR Switches

The DIR /P switch directs DIR to pause after each screen and to display the message "Press any key to continue. . ." To continue the directory list, simply press a key.

The DIR /W switch directs DIR to suppress the display of the file's size, date, and time fields. With /W, DIR displays five files across the screen.

continues....

Key Points
(continued)

Abort, Retry, Fail?

If DOS displays the "Abort, Retry, Fail?" message on your screen display, you have either not placed a disk in the specified drive or not closed the disk drive latch. DOS expects you to enter **A** for Abort, which terminates the application causing the error, **R** for Retry, which directs DOS to retry the operation that caused the error (normally after inserting a disk in the specified drive or closing the disk drive latch), or **F** for Fail.

If you have a disk in the drive with the latch closed and DOS still displays this error message, the disk is probably bad.

*The * Wildcard Character*

The DOS asterisk (*) wildcard character directs DOS not only to ignore the character contained in the file name position that contains the asterisk, but also all of the characters that follow it.

The ? Wildcard Character

The DOS question mark (?) wildcard character directs DOS to ignore the character in the file name position that contains the question mark during file search operations.

CHAPTER

Upgrading to DOS 6

When you purchase DOS 6 with a new computer, the company from which you purchased the computer should install DOS 6 on your hard disk for you. If you are currently using a different version of DOS, you can purchase and install the DOS 6 upgrade as discussed here.

Unlike other chapters in this book, this chapter does not have a "Practice" or "Review" section. Instead, the entire chapter is meant to be hands-on.

Performing the Upgrade

The DOS 6 upgrade ships on several 3 1/2- or 5 1/4-inch disks, as shown in Figure 5-1.

During the upgrade, the Setup program will ask you to insert one or two floppy disks that you have labeled Uninstall #1 and Uninstall #2, as shown in Figure 5-2. Thus, you will have two unused floppy disks available before you begin the upgrade.

FIGURE 5-1

The DOS 6 upgrade requires multiple disks

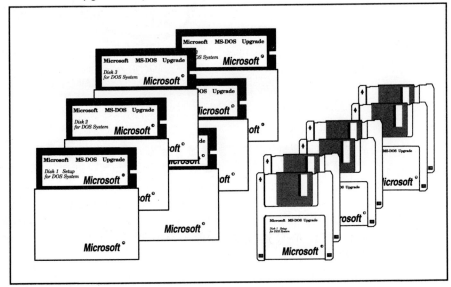

FIGURE 5-2 The DOS 6 upgrade requires two blank floppy disks

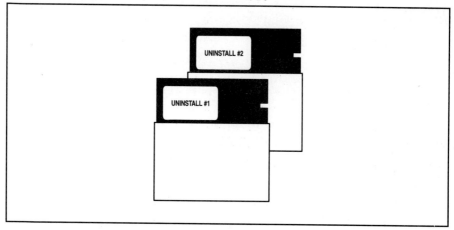

To begin the installation, place Disk 1 of the upgrade disks in drive A, select drive A as the current drive, and issue the SETUP command as shown here:

```
A:\> SETUP <ENTER>
```

Setup will display the screen shown in Figure 5-3, which welcomes you to DOS 6 Setup.

To continue the upgrade, press ENTER. Setup will display the screen shown in Figure 5-4, which informs you that it requires the two Uninstall disks.

Press ENTER to continue the upgrade. Setup will then display a screen containing specifics about your system, as shown in Figure 5-5.

If the information displayed is correct, press ENTER to continue the upgrade. If one or more of the items displayed is not correct, use the arrow keys to highlight the entry and press ENTER. Type the correct setting. When the entries are correct, press ENTER to continue the upgrade. Setup will display the screen shown in Figure 5-6, which lets you direct it to install its backup, undelete, and anti-virus utilities for DOS or Windows, or for both.

FIGURE
5-3

The Welcome to Setup screen for DOS 6

```
Microsoft MS-DOS 6 Setup
════════════════════════

          Welcome to Setup.

          The Setup program prepares MS-DOS 6 to run on your
          computer.

          • To set up MS-DOS now, press ENTER.

          • To learn more about Setup before continuing, press F1.

          • To quit Setup without installing MS-DOS, press F3.




ENTER=Continue  F1=Help  F3=Exit  F5=Remove Color
```

FIGURE
5-4

The Setup Uninstall overview screen

```
Microsoft MS-DOS 6 Setup
════════════════════════

          During Setup, you will need to provide and label one
          or two floppy disks. Each disk can be unformatted
          or newly formatted and must work in drive A. (If you
          use 360K disks, you may need two disks; otherwise,
          you need only one disk.)

          Label the disk(s) as follows:

              UNINSTALL #1
              UNINSTALL #2 (if needed)

          Setup saves some of your original DOS files on the
          UNINSTALL disk(s), and others on your hard disk in a
          directory named OLD_DOS.x. With these files, you can
          restore your original DOS if necessary.

            • When you finish labeling your UNINSTALL disk(s),
              press ENTER to continue Setup.

ENTER=Continue  F1=Help  F3=Exit
```

FIGURE 5-5

The Setup system information screen

```
Microsoft MS-DOS 6 Setup
═══════════════════════════

        Setup will use the following system settings:

        ┌─────────────────────────────────────────────────┐
        │  DOS Type:       MS-DOS                          │
        │  MS-DOS Path:    C:\DOS                           │
        │  Display Type:   VGA                             │
        │                                                  │
        │  The settings are correct.                       │
        └─────────────────────────────────────────────────┘

        If all the settings are correct, press ENTER.

        To change a setting, press the UP ARROW or DOWN ARROW key until
        the setting is selected. Then press ENTER to see alternatives.




ENTER=Continue  F1=Help  F3=Exit
```

FIGURE 5-6

The Setup utility screen

```
Microsoft MS-DOS 6 Setup
═══════════════════════════

        The following programs can be installed on your computer.

                        Program for             Bytes used
        ┌─────────────────────────────────────────────────┐
        │  Backup:       Windows only            884,736   │
        │  Undelete:     Windows only            278,528   │
        │  Anti-Virus:   Windows only            786,432   │
        │                                                  │
        │  Install the listed programs.                    │
        └─────────────────────────────────────────────────┘

        Space required for MS-DOS and programs:    6,149,696
        Space available on drive C:               11,583,488

        The free disk space reported here may differ from that of DIR
        or CHKDSK. See 'Diagnosing and Solving Problems' for details.

        To install the listed programs, press ENTER.  To see a list
        of available options, press the UP or DOWN ARROW key to
        highlight a program, and then press ENTER.

ENTER=Continue  F1=Help  F3=Exit
```

If you use Windows, you will want Setup to install the Windows utilities. If you have sufficient disk space, you will want Setup to install the utilities for Windows and DOS. To control which utilities Setup installs, use the arrow keys to highlight an entry and press ENTER. Setup will display a screen similar to that shown in Figure 5-7, which lets you select the desired utilities.

Highlight the utility option you desire and press ENTER. After you select the desired options, press ENTER to continue the upgrade. If you directed Setup to install the Windows-based utilities, Setup will display a screen asking you to verify the directory containing your Windows files. If the directory specified is correct, press ENTER to continue the upgrade. Setup will then display the screen shown in Figure 5-8, which states that it is ready to perform the DOS 6 upgrade.

Type **Y** to continue the upgrade. Setup will begin copying files to your hard disk, periodically prompting you to insert the Uninstall disk or a DOS 6 disk. Insert the disk specified and press ENTER to continue the upgrade. Eventually, Setup will display a screen directing you to remove all floppy disks and to press ENTER. Setup will then display a screen stating that the upgrade is complete, and that on the Uninstall disk it has saved your AUTOEXEC.BAT and CONFIG.SYS files in files with the DAT extension. To restart your computer under DOS 6, press ENTER.

After your system starts and you verify that it is running correctly, you can remove the DOS files that corresponded to your previous DOS version by issuing the DELOLDOS command as shown here:

```
C:\> DELOLDOS  <ENTER>
```

Respond to the screens DELOLDOS displays.

Using the Uninstall Disks

The Uninstall disk let you restore your system to its state immediately before you began the DOS 6 installation. Should you experience a fatal error during the DOS 6 upgrade, place the disk labeled Uninstall #1 in drive A and restart your system. Follow the messages that appear on your screen to restore your previous DOS version.

FIGURE
5-7

The Setup utility selection screen

```
Microsoft MS-DOS 6 Setup
─────────────────────────────

        Backup for:

        ┌──────────────────────────────────────────────────┐
        │ Windows and MS-DOS                               │
        │ Windows only                                      │
        │ MS-DOS only                                       │
        │ None                                              │
        └──────────────────────────────────────────────────┘

        If you want to install the highlighted program, press ENTER.
        To select a different option, press the UP or DOWN ARROW
        key to highlight the program you want. Then press ENTER to
        choose it.




ENTER=Continue  F1=Help  F3=Exit  ESC=Previous Screen
```

FIGURE
5-8

The Setup ready-to-upgrade screen

```
Microsoft MS-DOS 6 Setup
─────────────────────────────




        ┌──────────────────────────────────────────────────┐
        │ Setup is ready to upgrade your system to MS-DOS 6.│
        │ Do not interrupt Setup during the upgrade process.│
        │                                                   │
        │   • To install MS-DOS 6 files now, press Y.       │
        │                                                   │
        │   • To exit Setup without installing MS-DOS, press F3. │
        └──────────────────────────────────────────────────┘




F3=Exit  Y=Install MS-DOS
```

CHAPTER

Getting Started with the DOS Shell

*B*eginning with DOS 4, DOS provides a menu-driven user interface called the *DOS shell,* from which you can run your programs or perform your file operations such as viewing, printing, and copying files. The advantage of using the shell as opposed to typing commands at the DOS prompt is ease of use. As you will learn in this chapter, the shell displays your file and directory names on the screen, allowing you to quickly select them. In addition, rather than forcing you to memorize several different DOS commands, the shell lets you select commands from a series of menus.

This chapter introduces you to the DOS 5 and 6 shell. As you learn different DOS commands and concepts throughout the remaining chapters, you will learn to perform the commands not only from the DOS prompt, but, when applicable, also from within the shell.

Becoming Familiar with the DOS Shell

To start the DOS shell, invoke the DOSSHELL command from the DOS prompt, as shown here:

```
C:\> DOSSHELL  <ENTER>
```

DOS will display a screen similar to that shown in Figure 6-1.

As you can see, the shell contains several different parts; this section briefly examines each. To move from one section of the shell to the next, press the TAB key.

The *title bar* appears at the top of the shell display and contains the title "MS-DOS Shell." Immediately below the title bar is the shell's *menu bar,* which contains a list of available menus. To select a specific menu, hold down the ALT key and press the key corresponding to the first letter of the menu name. For example, to select the File menu you would press ALT-F. Likewise, to select the Options menu you would press ALT-O. When you select a menu, the shell will display a pull-down menu of options. In the case of the File menu, the shell displays the menu of options shown in Figure 6-2.

FIGURE
6-1

The DOS 5 and 6 shell

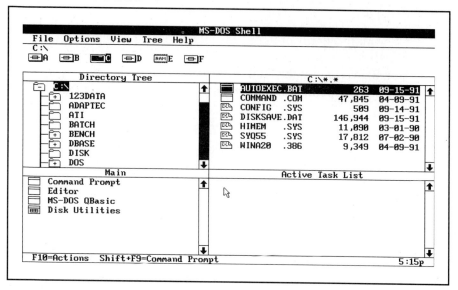

Using your keyboard's UP ARROW and DOWN ARROW keys, you can highlight a menu option and press ENTER to select it. In some cases, one or more menu items may appear in dim letters, which indicates the option is not currently available. Many of the File menu options, for example, require you to first select a file. After you have selected a file, the shell

FIGURE
6-2

The File menu

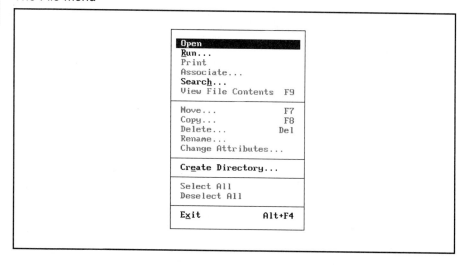

will make the menu options available, displaying their names in dark letters.

Many menu options are followed by three dots (...), called ellipses. When you select such an option, the shell will display a *dialog box* that asks you for additional information. For example, if you select the Copy option, the shell will display the following dialog box:

```
┌──────────────────────────────────────────────────────┐
│                    ▐ Copy File ▌                      │
│                                                        │
│                                                        │
│     From:    ┌FILENAME.EXT─────────────────┐          │
│              └─────────────────────────────┘          │
│     To:      ┌C:\──────────────────────────┐          │
│              └─────────────────────────────┘          │
│                                                        │
│                                                        │
│       (   OK   )      ( Cancel )      ( Help )         │
│                                                        │
└──────────────────────────────────────────────────────┘
```

A dialog box is simply a way for the shell to get additional information it needs to perform a command. If you invoke a menu and decide not to select an option, you can cancel the menu by pressing the ESC key.

If you examine the File menu, you will see that several menu options have keys such as F7, F8, or F9 to their right. These keys are called *hot keys.* You select the corresponding menu option any time the shell is active by pressing the hot key. Using hot keys eliminates the need to invoke a menu before selecting the option with your keyboard.

Immediately below the menu bar, the shell displays the name of the current directory and disk drive icons for the available disk drives. An *icon* is simply a graphic, or pictorial representation. Depending on your system, the number and types of disk drive icons will differ. Table 6-1 lists the different icon types you may see.

The shell highlights your current disk drive by displaying the drive icon in black. As you will learn in Chapter 9, "Getting Around on Your Disk Drives," you can change the current drive by holding down the CTRL key and pressing the letter of the drive you desire. To select the hard drive C, for example, you would press CTRL-C.

As briefly discussed earlier, a directory is a list of files, similar to a drawer of a filing cabinet. As you increase the number of files you store on your disk, you should use directories to help organize your files.

TABLE 6-1

The Disk Drive Icons

Icon	Disk Drive Type
A	Floppy disk drive
C	Hard disk drive
[RAM] D	RAM drive
[NET] F	Network drive
[CD] E	CD-ROM

Immediately beneath the disk drive icons, the shell displays the *directory tree* (the list of directories) for the current disk. Using your keyboard arrow keys, you can highlight a directory, and the shell will display the names of files the directory contains in the file list that appears to the right of the directory tree. Changing directories in this way is similar to closing one drawer of a filing cabinet and opening another.

The *file list* contains the directory information for each file in the current directory, which includes the file name, extension, size, and date stamp. Using your keyboard's arrow keys, you can scroll through the list of files. If you highlight a file with the COM, EXE, or BAT extension, you can execute the file by pressing ENTER. To select a specific file for printing, copying, or some other file operation, simply highlight the file by using your keyboard arrow keys.

As you view the files in the file list, you will notice that each file is preceded by an icon. The shell uses one of two icon types, as shown in Table 6-2.

As already mentioned, after you highlight an executable file, you can run the command by pressing ENTER.

Beneath the directory tree, in a window labeled "Main," the shell displays a list of program names, called the *program list*. Table 6-3 briefly describes the program list entries DOS provides. As you will learn in

TABLE 6-2

The File Icons

Icon	File Type
	Executable EXE, COM, or BAT file
	Nonexecutable file

TABLE
6-3

Program List Entries Provided by DOS

Entry Name	Function
Command Prompt	Temporarily exits the shell to the DOS prompt
Editor	Invokes EDIT (see Chapter 16, "Using Edit"), letting you edit a new or existing file
MS-DOS QBasic	Invokes the QBasic interpreter (see the Command Reference)
Disk Utilities	Displays a menu of commonly used disk utilities

Chapter 31, "Advanced Shell Concepts," the shell lets you add or change entries in this list.

Once again, the shell precedes each program list entry with one of two icons, depending on whether the entry immediately involves a command or displays a menu of additional entries. Table 6-4 describes each icon.

To select a program list entry, highlight the entry by using your keyboard arrow keys and press ENTER. If you select the Disk Utilities entry, for example, the shell will display the following options:

You will use several of these options throughout the later chapters of this book.

TABLE
6-4

The Program Icons

Icon	Entry Type
	Program entry
	Program group

Using a Mouse Within the Shell

The DOS shell exists to make running programs and performing file operations easier. If your computer has a mouse, you can use the mouse within the shell to select files, directories, disk drives, menu options, and so on. Before you can use the mouse, however, you must tell DOS about the mouse. Generally you tell DOS about your mouse by running a command named MOUSE.COM or by placing a DEVICE= entry in your CONFIG.SYS file (see Chapter 27, "Customizing Your System Using CONFIG.SYS"). Refer to the documentation that accompanied your mouse for specifics.

The shell displays your mouse pointer as a small arrow if your screen is in graphics mode and as a small rectangular box in text mode. As you move the mouse on your desk, the shell will move the mouse pointer across your screen. To select a menu, disk drive, or file by using your mouse, simply move the mouse pointer on top of the item you desire and click the left mouse button. The process of selecting an object by moving the mouse pointer to the object and clicking the mouse button is called "point and shoot."

Exiting the Shell

The shell lets you exit temporarily or permanently. If you press the F3 function key, the shell program will end, and DOS will redisplay its prompt. If you later want to use the shell again, you must invoke the shell by using the DOSSHELL command. As a rule, you should always exit the shell to DOS by pressing F3 before you turn off your computer.

As you will learn in Chapter 31, "Advanced Shell Concepts," the shell lets you load several different programs into memory at one time. By using the shell, you can switch between programs. If you turn off your computer while one of these programs (such as a word processor) has a file opened or unsaved information, you might damage the file or lose the information that it contains. By exiting the shell to DOS before turning off your computer, you will eliminate the chance of losing information in this way.

There may be times when you want to temporarily exit the shell to the DOS prompt. If you press the SHIFT-F9 key combination or select the Command Prompt entry from the program list, the shell will let you temporarily exit to the DOS prompt. If you have loaded several programs as previously discussed, the programs are temporarily suspended. When you have finished issuing commands from the DOS prompt, you can return to the shell by issuing the EXIT command:

```
C:\> EXIT <ENTER>
```

DOS will redisplay the shell, allowing you to continue as if you had never exited. If you turn your computer off when you have only temporarily exited the shell, you risk losing the information unsaved by programs you previously suspended.

Working with Multiple Files

Before you can use many of the File menu options, you must select a file. As you have learned, there may be times when you want to perform an operation on two or more files. For example, you might want to print the contents of two files or copy the files to a different disk.

If the files you want to select appear in the file list in consecutive order, you can select the files by using your keyboard, as follows:

1. Use the arrow keys to highlight the first file.

2. Hold down the SHIFT key and use the arrow keys to highlight the additional files. The shell will highlight each selected file name in reverse video.

Select consecutive files by using your mouse as follows:

1. Aim the mouse pointer at the first file you want to select in the list and click the left mouse button to select the file.

2. Hold down the SHIFT key and aim the mouse pointer at the last file you want to select in the list. When you press the left mouse button, the shell will highlight the selected files in reverse video.

If the files you desire are dispersed throughout the file list, you can select the files by using your keyboard, as follows:

1. Use your arrow keys to highlight the first file you desire. Next, press the SHIFT-F8 keyboard combination. The shell will display the word "ADD" at the bottom of your screen to the left of the current time. Press the SPACEBAR to select the file.

2. Use your arrow keys to highlight the next file, pressing the SPACEBAR to select the file. Repeat this process for each file you desire.

3. Press SHIFT-F8 to tell the shell you have selected the last file.

To select dispersed files by using your mouse, simply hold down the CTRL key when you click the file name.

Using the Shell's Built-in Help

The shell provides built-in help that you can use to learn about different dialog boxes, menu options, or shell procedures. To use the shell's built-in help, press the F1 function key or press ALT-H to display the Help menu, shown here:

Table 6-5 briefly describes the Help menu options.

If you select the Keyboard option, for example, the shell will display a large Help window similar to the one in Figure 6-3.

FIGURE 6-3   The Help window within the shell

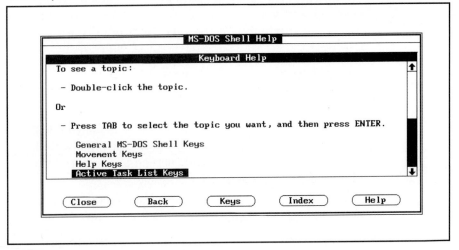

Using your keyboard arrow keys, you can scroll through the Help window's text. As you do so, you will see text highlighted in reverse video or a different color. Help uses these highlights to indicate it has additional help text available on the topic. If you highlight such text and press ENTER,

TABLE 6-5   Help's Menu Options

Menu Option	Display
Index	Index of topics available within Help
Keyboard	Index of keyboard topics
Shell Basics	Index of fundamental operations you should know as you work with the shell
Commands	Index of shell menu options
Procedures	Index of steps you must follow to perform various tasks
Using Help	Index of topics on how to use Help
About Shell	The shell's copyright notice

Help will display text about the topic. If you examine the Help window shown in Figure 6-3, you will find Help displays several options at the bottom of the window. To select one of these options, press the TAB key to highlight the option and press ENTER or click on the option using your mouse. Table 6-6 briefly describes each option.

To end a Help session you can either select the Close option or press the ESC key.

Understanding and Using Scroll Bars

If you look to the right of the directory tree, file list, or program list section, you will find a rectangular strip called a *scroll bar*. As you move up and down through one of these lists, the shell moves a small slide along the bar; this slide indicates your relative position in the list. If the slide appears near the top of the bar, you are currently near the top of the list. Likewise, if the slide appears near the bottom of the bar, you are near the bottom of the list.

If you are using a mouse, you can quickly traverse the list by aiming the mouse pointer at the slide, holding down the mouse button, and moving the slide in either direction.

TABLE 6-6

Help Window Options

Help Window Option	Function
Close	Ends the Help session
Back	Displays the help text for the previous topic
Keys	Displays an index of keyboard-related topics
Index	Displays the index of available topics
Help	Displays Help text on using Help

Practice

Invoke the DOS shell if you have not already done so:

```
C:\> DOSSHELL <ENTER>
```

When the shell appears on your screen, press the TAB key several times to select different sections of the shell. Next, select the directory tree. Use your keyboard arrow keys to scroll through the directory names. As you do so, watch the names that appear in the file list change.

Next, press the ALT-F keyboard combination to invoke the File menu. If you press the RIGHT ARROW or LEFT ARROW key, you can display the different menus. Press the ESC key to remove the menu.

Press the F1 key to invoke the shell's built-in Help. Use your arrow keys to scroll through the Help text. Select text that appears in a second color. Help will display text related to the topic. Press ESC to end the Help session.

Many of the chapters that follow will have you perform specific operations within the shell. For now, press the F3 function key to exit from the shell.

Review

1. How do you invoke the DOS shell?
2. How do you move from one section in the shell to another?
3. How do you invoke a shell menu?
4. What is a dialog box?
5. How do you exit the shell?
6. What is an icon?

CHAPTER

Using Your Keyboard and Mouse

Most new DOS users feel uncomfortable when they first sit down at a computer simply because they aren't used to working with the keyboard. Because they spend so much time typing at the keyboard, new users often feel they could perform the same functions faster by hand. This lesson will introduce you to several techniques you can use as you enter DOS commands at the keyboard. These keyboard techniques will save you time and reduce your typing. One of the techniques you will learn about in this chapter is the use of DOS *keyboard combinations*. A keyboard combination is simply two or more keys that you hold down in the specified order. For example, to enter the CTRL-C key combination, you first hold down the CTRL key, and while that key is down, you press the C key.

By using the keyboard secrets this chapter presents, you will soon find working with DOS to be much easier, and in many cases, your keyboard mastery will make you much more productive. Finally, this lesson examines using a mouse to travel through the DOS shell.

PC and PC AT Keyboards

Figure 7-1 illustrates the keyboards commonly found on the IBM PC and the PC AT, as well as the newer extended keyboard. Although the extended keyboard is larger and provides additional keys, all three of these keyboards are functionally equivalent when working with DOS. Each of the capabilities discussed in this chapter can be performed easily on any of these keyboards.

Using BACKSPACE to Delete Characters

You may have already made several typing mistakes as you've entered DOS commands (if you haven't, you will eventually). The BACKSPACE key, shown in Figure 7-2, allows you to erase characters that precede the cursor on the current line.

FIGURE 7-1

The PC, PC AT, and the newer extended keyboard

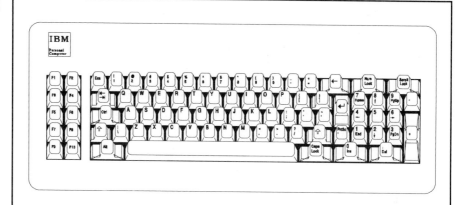

Original PC keyboard

PC AT keyboard

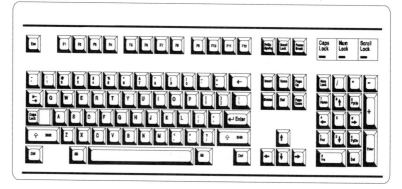

Extended keyboard

FIGURE 7-2

Location of the BACKSPACE key

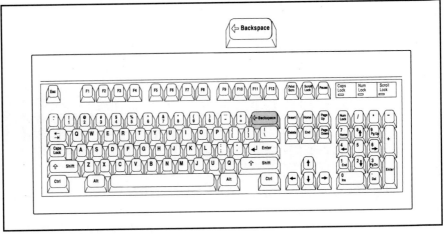

For example, assume that you have typed in the TIME command as

```
C:\> TINE_
```

but you have not yet pressed the ENTER key to execute the command. Since the letter "E" immediately precedes the cursor, pressing the BACKSPACE key deletes it, as shown here:

```
C:\> TIN_
```

If you press the BACKSPACE key again, DOS will erase the "N," thus yielding

```
C:\> TI_
```

You can now correct your mistake by typing **ME**, as shown here:

```
C:\> TIME_
```

Using CTRL-ALT-DEL to Restart DOS

As you work with DOS, you may have to restart DOS by using the CTRL-ALT-DEL key combination, shown in Figure 7-3. In some cases, a program that you are running may contain an error that causes it to fail, locking up your system. If this occurs, your computer will appear to ignore all of your entries from the keyboard. In many cases, the only way to resume work with your system is to press the CTRL-ALT-DEL key combination. If DOS does not respond to this by restarting, you will have to cycle your computer's power off and on.

Use the CTRL-ALT-DEL key combination only as needed. If you have a program running that is accessing one or more of your files, restarting DOS with CTRL-ALT-DEL might damage the files, causing DOS to lose the information that the files contain. CTRL-ALT-DEL should be used only as a last resort. The process of restarting DOS by pressing the CTRL-ALT-DEL keyboard combination is called a *warm boot.* When you boot DOS by turning your computer's power off and on, you perform a *cold boot.*

FIGURE
7-3

Location of CTRL, ALT, and DEL keys

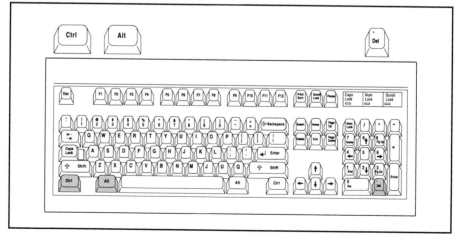

Using *CTRL-BREAK* to Terminate a Command

It's not uncommon to invoke a command and then later decide to terminate the command before it completes. The CTRL-BREAK key combination, shown in Figure 7-4, allows you to terminate a DOS command.

For example, assume you have invoked the FORMAT command with

```
C:\> FORMAT A: <ENTER>
```

only to find that you don't have any blank disks available for formatting. When FORMAT prompts

```
C:\> FORMAT A:
Insert new diskette for drive A:
and press ENTER when ready...
```

you can simply press the CTRL-BREAK key combination to terminate the command. In this case, DOS will redisplay its prompt as shown here:

FIGURE 7-4

Location of CTRL and BREAK keys

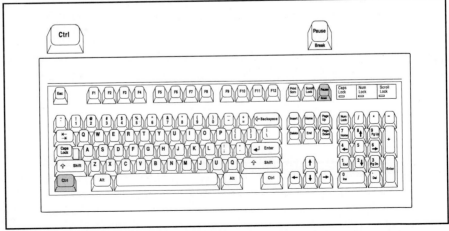

```
C:\> FORMAT A:
Insert new diskette for drive A:
and press ENTER when ready...^C


C:\>
```

Note the ^C on the screen display. The caret (^) is often called the *Control character*, so the ^C is read as "Control C." DOS allows you to use either CTRL-C or CTRL-BREAK to terminate a DOS command. Do not use CTRL-BREAK to end your application programs, such as your word processor. If the program has files open and you end the program by using CTRL-BREAK, you might lose the information the files contained.

Using CTRL-S to Suspend Output

Earlier in this book when you executed the DIR command, many of the files scrolled quite rapidly across the screen. As a solution, you used the DIR command with the /P (*pause*) switch:

```
C:\> DIR   /P <ENTER>
```

This causes DIR to suspend scrolling with each screenful of files and wait for you to press a key before displaying the next screen.

Unfortunately, most DOS commands do not include a /P qualifier to suspend output in this fashion. Instead, to prevent the output from scrolling rapidly past you, you can use the CTRL-S (*suspend*) key combination. For example, if you enter the command

```
C:\> DIR \DOS <ENTER>
```

files will begin scrolling past you quite quickly. Press the CTRL-S key combination, and output will stop as shown here:

```
Volume in drive C is DOS
Volume Serial Number is 1A54-45E0
Directory of C:\DOS

.                <DIR>        11-23-92    9:26p
..               <DIR>        11-23-92    9:26p
DBLSPACE BIN       50284 02-12-93    6:00a
FORMAT   COM       22717 02-12-93    6:00a
NLSFUNC  EXE        7036 02-12-93    6:00a
COUNTRY  SYS       17066 02-12-93    6:00a
KEYB     COM       14983 02-12-93    6:00a
KEYBOARD SYS       34694 02-12-93    6:00a
ANSI     SYS        9065 02-12-93    6:00a
ATTRIB   EXE       11165 02-12-93    6:00a
CHKDSK   EXE       12908 02-12-93    6:00a
EDIT     COM         413 02-12-93    6:00a
EXPAND   EXE       16129 02-12-93    6:00a
MORE     COM        2546 02-12-93    6:00a
MSD      EXE      158470 02-12-93    6:00a
QBASIC   EXE      194309 02-12-93    6:00a
RESTORE  EXE       38294 02-12-93    6:00a
SYS      COM        9379
```

DOS does not display any messages on your screen telling you why the output was suspended.

To resume output, press any key, and you will see the rest of the files.

Using ESC to Cancel a Command

It is not uncommon to make typing errors as you enter your DOS commands. Consider this misspelling of the DISKCOPY command:

```
C:\> DISSCOPY  A:  B:_
```

As you have seen, you can correct this error by using the BACKSPACE key on your keyboard to erase characters that precede the cursor. However, in some cases you may find it simpler to retype the command from the DOS prompt. If you type the command

```
C:\> DISSCOPY   A:   B:  <ENTER>
```

DOS will search your disk for a command called DISSCOPY and then display the message

```
Bad command or file name
```

Although DOS will redisplay its prompt and you can retype the command, you had to wait until DOS searched your disk for the command. Depending on the number of files on your disk, this command search could be quite time consuming.

As an alternative, DOS allows you to press the ESC key at the end of your command line. When you do so, DOS displays a backslash (\) to represent the ESC keypress and ignores the command line. For example, with the command line

```
C:\> DISSCOPY   A:   B:_
```

if you press ESC, DOS will display a slash at the end of your command line and will advance the cursor to the next line, immediately below the command, as shown here:

```
C:\> DISSCOPY   A:   B:\
     _
```

You can now type in the correct command and press ENTER to execute it. If you simply press ENTER, DOS will display a new prompt.

Using the Function Keys with DOS

In working with the DOS shell, you have had to use some of the function keys. The function keys are F1 through F10 on most keyboards and F1 through F12 on others, as shown in Figure 7-5.

As you will see in the section "Using Predefined Keys with the Shell," later in this chapter, several of the DOS function keys have predefined meanings within the DOS shell. As you will see here, you can also use the DOS function keys when you issue commands at the DOS prompt:

Issue the command

```
C:\> DIR <ENTER>
```

When DOS executes this command, it does two things. First, it displays a listing of your files. Second, it stores the command in a keyboard buffer, which allows it to remember the command that you just executed so that you can quickly repeat it. Here's where the DOS function keys come into use. Press the F1 function key. DOS will display the letter "D" on your screen:

```
C:\> D_
```

Location of function keys

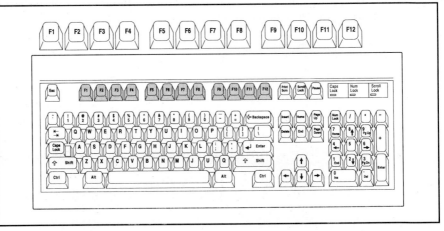

F1 directs DOS to use the letter from the same character position in the previous command. Since "D" was the first letter of the previous DIR command, it is displayed. If you press F1 again, DOS will display

```
C:\> DI_
```

Pressing F1 a third time results in

```
C:\> DIR_
```

Press F1 again:

```
C:\> DIR_
```

Nothing happens. This makes sense, because you have used up all of the characters from the previous command.

At this point, you can simply execute the command by pressing ENTER or you can add to the command, specifying additional information, such as a file name. In this case, simply execute the command by pressing the ENTER key:

```
C:\> DIR <ENTER>
```

Once the command completes, press the F3 key. DOS will display the entire previous command:

```
C:\> DIR_
```

The F3 key will repeat the characters from the previous command line, starting at the location that matches the cursor's position in your new command line. Users often use F1 and F3 in conjunction to make quick changes to the previously entered commands, thereby editing their command lines.

Assume, for example, that your previous command was

```
C:\> DISSCOPY  A:  B: <ENTER>
Bad command or file name
```

Rather than having to retype the entire line, you can use F1 and F3. First press the F1 key three times, and DOS will display

```
C:\> DIS_
```

Next, type **K**, yielding

```
C:\> DISK_
```

You can now copy the remaining characters from the previous command by pressing the F3 key. DOS will display

```
C:\> DISKCOPY  A:  B:
```

Your command is ready to execute.

In a similar manner, if your command line contains

```
C:\> TINE  12:30:05_
```

and you have not yet pressed ENTER, DOS allows you to edit the current command line with the function keys. First press the F5 key. DOS will display

```
C:\> TINE  12:30:05@
        _
```

Notice that the cursor is located on the line immediately below the command line. Press the F1 key twice. DOS will display

```
C:\> TINE  12:30:05@
     TI_
```

Next, type **M** to correct the error:

```
C:\> TINE  12:30:05@
     TIM_
```

Pressing the F3 key completes the command:

```
C:\> TINE  12:30:05@
     TIME 12:30:05
```

You can now execute your command by pressing the ENTER key.

Finally, the F2 and F4 function keys allow you to edit your command line based upon specific letters. First, the F2 key directs DOS to copy all of the letters that precede the letter that you type immediately after pressing F2. For example, assume that your previous command was

```
C:\> DIR  FORMAT <ENTER>
```

When the command completes, you can reissue the DIR command by pressing the F2 key followed immediately by the letter "F." DOS will display

```
C:\> DIR _
```

Since "F" was the letter that you typed immediately after pressing the F2 key, DOS copied all of the characters in the previous command line up to that letter.

In a similar manner, the F4 key directs DOS to skip all of the letters up to, but not including, the character that you type immediately after pressing F4. Again assume that your previous command was

```
C:\> DIR   FORMAT
```

If the current directory contains the FORMAT command, you can execute FORMAT by pressing the F4 key and typing **F**. Then press F3. In this case, DOS will display the following.

```
C:\> FORMAT_
```

To execute the command, simply press ENTER. As you can see, the DOS function keys can save you considerable time and keystrokes.

Using INS to Insert Characters

So far, all of the command-line editing you have performed has dealt with a mistyped character, such as the command

```
C:\> FORMMT   A:
```

In some cases, however, you may simply omit a letter, as shown here:

```
C:\> FOMAT   A:   <ENTER>
Bad command or file name
```

If this occurs, use the F1 key to locate the character position that is missing the character:

```
C:\> FO_
```

Next, press the INS key, shown in Figure 7-6. DOS now allows you to insert characters in the previous command line. In this case, type **R**. When you press the F3 key, DOS will complete the command line as shown here:

```
C:\> FORMAT  A:_
```

As you can see, DOS has inserted the letter "R" as desired. The INS key
is a toggle key. If you had not pressed the INS key, DOS would have been
in overstrike mode; it would have overwritten the "M" when you typed
"R," as shown here:

```
C:\> FORAT  A:_
```

Using DEL to Delete Characters

Just as the INS key allows you to insert characters into the previous
command line, the DEL key allows you to delete characters from the
command. Assuming that your previous command line was

```
C:\> FORRMAT  A: <ENTER>
Bad command or file name
```

| FIGURE 7-6 | Location of INS key |

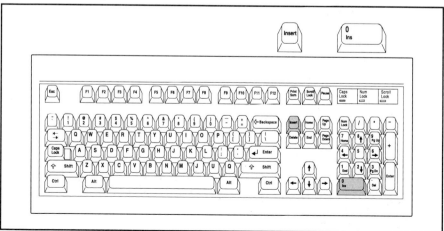

press the F1 key three times. DOS will display

```
C:\> FOR_
```

Next, press the DEL key followed by the F3 key. DOS will display the corrected line, as follows:

```
C:\> FORMAT  A:_
```

Using Predefined Keys with the Shell

The DOS shell predefines several keys, as shown in Table 7-1. Using these keys helps you to work effectively in the shell. You will use these keys within the shell throughout the remainder of this book.

TABLE 7-1

Predefined Keys for the DOS Shell

Key	Action
F1	Invokes interactive online help
F3	Terminates the shell or file system menu
SHIFT-F9	Temporarily exits the DOS shell, providing command-line access
F10	Selects the action bar
ESC	Cancels a menu option
TAB	Selects different sections of the file system menu

Using a Mouse

The DOS shell fully supports a mouse interface:

If you don't have one yet, you will find a mouse to be an excellent investment.

If you are using a mouse with the DOS 4 shell, you must tell DOS your mouse type when you invoke the shell. To do so, you will need to edit the DOSSHELL.BAT file. DOSSHELL.BAT is a DOS batch file. (Chapter 18, "Using Batch Files," discusses DOS batch files in detail.) If you have a word processor, you can use it to edit the DOSSHELL.BAT file. If you do not have a word processor, you can use the DOS EDLIN editor, EDIT, or a different editor.

If you examine the DOSSHELL.BAT file by using the TYPE command, you will find in it a line that contains the following:

```
C:\> TYPE  DOSSHELL.BAT <ENTER>
@SHELLC /MOS:PCIBMDRV.MOS/TRAN/COLOR/DOS/MENU/MUL/SND
/MEU:SHELL.MEU/CLR:SHELL.CLR/PROMPT/MAINT/EXIT/SWAP/DATE
```

Find the /MOS switch in this line. The /MOS switch allows you to specify the device driver software DOS requires to use your mouse. By default, DOS provides device driver support for three mouse types:

PCIBMDRV.MOS	(IBM PC PS/2 mouse)
PCMSDRV.MOS	(Microsoft serial mouse)
PCMSPDRV.MOS	(Microsoft parallel mouse)

If you are using a different brand of mouse, simply remove the /MOS switch from the line and install your mouse driver as specified in the documentation that accompanied your mouse.

FIGURE 7-7

Mouse pointer in the DOS 5 or later shell (in Active Task list box)

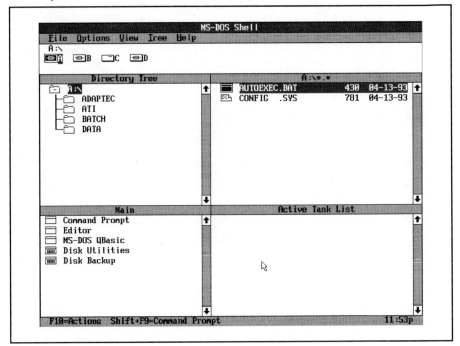

If you are using the DOS 5 or later shell, you must first install the mouse device driver. Depending on your mouse type, you may need to place a DEVICE= entry in your CONFIG.SYS file (see Chapter 27, "Customizing Your System Using CONFIG.SYS") or place a mouse command in your AUTOEXEC.BAT file (see Chapter 18).

Once your mouse is installed, DOS allows you to use it to select shell menu options. In this case, DOS will display a mouse pointer on your screen that you can move by sliding your mouse along your desk top. Figure 7-7 illustrates the mouse pointer within the DOS shell. To select an option, double-click the left button on your mouse while pointing at it. To double-click the mouse, you must press the mouse button two times in quick succession.

Practice

In this lesson you will use several of the key combinations discussed in this chapter. First issue the DATE command:

```
C:\> DATE <ENTER>
Current date is Tue 04-06-1993
Enter new date (mm-dd-yy):
```

Now cancel the command by pressing the CTRL-BREAK key combination. DOS will display

```
C:\> DATE
Current date is Tue 04-06-1993
Enter new date (mm-dd-yy): ^C

C:\>
```

Next, invoke the TIME command:

```
C:\> TIME <ENTER>
Current time is  9:47:36.94a
Enter new time:
```

Use CTRL-C to verify that it functions in the same manner as CTRL-BREAK. When you press CTRL-C, DOS will terminate the command, displaying

```
C:\> TIME
Current time is  9:47:36.94a
Enter new time: ^C

C:\>
```

Now, press the F1 key four times:

```
C:\> TIME_
```

As you can see, DOS displays the previously issued command. In this case, rather than pressing ENTER to invoke the TIME command, press the ESC key, and DOS will display

```
C:\> TIME\
      _
```

You can now type in your next command. In this case, simply press ENTER to redisplay the DOS prompt.

Execute the DIR command:

```
C:\> DIR <ENTER>
```

When the command completes, press the F3 function key:

```
C:\> DIR_
```

Before you press ENTER to repeat the command, locate the CTRL and S keys on your keyboard. Be ready to press this key combination to suspend scrolling after you press ENTER. Once you have suspended scrolling, simply press any key to resume scrolling.

Next, type in the following command, including the misspelling, as shown here:

```
C:\> DISKCCPY  A:  B: <ENTER>
Bad command or file name
```

As should happen, DOS displayed an error message. Press the F1 key five times, displaying

```
C:\> DISKC_
```

Type **O** and press the F3 function key. DOS will correct the command line
as shown:

```
C:\> DISKCOPY A: B:_
```

Cancel this command by pressing the ESC key and then ENTER.

Next, type the command

```
C:\> DISCOPY A: B:_
```

omitting the "K," but do not press ENTER. Instead, press the F5 key to edit
the command line:

```
C:\> DISCOPY A: B:@
     _
```

DOS will allow you to edit the current command line. Press the F2 key
and type **C**. DOS will display

```
C:\> DISCOPY A: B:@
     DIS_
```

Press the INS key and type **K**:

```
C:\> DISCOPY A: B:@
     DISK
```

Now press the F3 key, and DOS will display the correct command line,
after which you can press ENTER to invoke the command:

```
C:\> DISCOPY A: B:@
      DISKCOPY A: B: <ENTER>

Insert SOURCE diskette in drive A:

Insert TARGET diskette in drive B:

Press any key to continue . . .
```

Now use the CTRL-BREAK key combination to terminate the command.

Enter the following command:

```
C:\> FORRMAT A: <ENTER>
Bad command or file name
```

To edit the misspelled command, press the F1 key three times:

```
C:\> FOR_
```

Next, press the DEL key followed by F3:

```
C:\> FORMAT A:_
```

Use ESC to cancel the command.

Finally, use the command

```
C:\> DIR \DOS\FORMAT <ENTER>
```

Press the F4 key, type **F**, and press F3. DOS will display

```
C:\> FORMAT_
```

You could easily execute this command by pressing ENTER. Instead, however, use the BACKSPACE key to erase the command, leaving the DOS prompt.

Review

1. When you execute a DOS command, DOS does two things. What are they?

2. Briefly describe the functions provided by the following keys: F1, F2, F3, F4, BACKSPACE, INS, DEL, and ESC.

3. If your previous command line contains the following:

```
C:\> FOMAT A:  <ENTER>
Bad command or file name
```

what is the fastest way to correct it?

4. If you own a mouse, what steps must you perform to use the mouse in the DOS shell?

Key Points

The BACKSPACE key allows you to delete the character that immediately precedes the cursor.

The CTRL-ALT-DEL key combination restarts DOS. Use this key combination as a last resort. If you are running a program that has open files, resetting DOS with CTRL-ALT-DEL can damage the files, destroying their contents.

continues . . .

*Key Points
(continued)*

The CTRL-BREAK key combination directs DOS to terminate the current command. DOS allows you to use either the CTRL-BREAK or the CTRL-C key combination to terminate a command. To reduce the chance of losing data, do not use CTRL-BREAK to end your application programs.

The CTRL-S key combination directs DOS to temporarily suspend the output of a command. To resume program output, press any key.

The ESC key directs DOS to ignore a command if you press it at the end of the command line. When you press ESC, DOS will display the backslash character at the end of your command line, and when you press ENTER, DOS will ignore the command and redisplay its prompt.

The F1 key directs DOS to repeat in your current command the character in the same character position in the previous command.

The F3 key directs DOS to repeat the characters in the previous command line from the current cursor position forward.

The F5 key allows you to edit the current command line. When you press F5, DOS displays the @ character and moves the cursor down one position:

```
C:\> DISSCOPY A: B: @
```

You can now use F1 and F3 to edit the command line.

continues . . .

The F2 key directs DOS to copy characters from the previous command line, up to but not including the character you type immediately after pressing F2.

The F4 key directs DOS to skip all of the characters up to but not including the character you type immediately after pressing F4. After you press F4, you must press either F1 or F3 to recall the remainder of the command line.

The INS key allows you to insert characters when you are editing a command line. The INS key works as a toggle. The first time you press it, DOS supports inserting. The second time you press it, DOS begins overstrike mode.

The DEL key allows you to delete characters as you perform command-line editing. DEL deletes the character in the cursor position.

The DOS shell fully supports a mouse-driven interface. However, before you can use the mouse, you must install it. If you are using the DOS 4 shell, you must edit the DOSSHELL.BAT batch file. If you are using DOS 5 (or later), you must install the mouse device driver as explained in the documentation that accompanied your mouse.

CHAPTER

Basic File Operations

You learned earlier that files exist for one reason: to store programs and information. You have learned that DOS assigns unique names to each of your files on disk, placing each file name into a list of names called a directory. Each file name has the format

FILENAME.EXT

and contains from one to eight characters with an optional one- to three-character extension.

In this chapter you will learn the fundamental DOS file-manipulation commands that you will need in your daily use of DOS. By the end of this chapter you will know how to copy, rename, and delete files not only from the DOS prompt, but also from within the DOS shell. This chapter lays the foundation you will build on throughout the remainder of the book as you manipulate files with DOS.

Making a Copy of Your Files

So that you will have a disk to work with without affecting your DOS disks, place a blank disk in drive A and issue the following FORMAT command:

```
C:\> FORMAT  A: /S <ENTER>
```

When you examine the structure of a DOS disk in Chapter 29, "A Closer Look at Disks," you will learn more about the /S switch. For now, all you need to know is that /S directs FORMAT to create a floppy disk that you can use to boot DOS. It directs FORMAT to place the COM-MAND.COM file on the disk. This file contains the DOS internal commands (such as CLS, DIR, and DATE) and is responsible for processing the commands you enter at the DOS prompt. When the FORMAT command completes, use the DIR command to display the files that reside on the disk:

```
C:\> DIR  A:  <ENTER>

 Volume in drive A has no label
 Volume Serial Number is 203B-1E03
 Directory of A:\

COMMAND  COM     52925 02-12-93   6:00a
        1 file(s)       52925 bytes
                      1160704 bytes free
```

The characters "A:" direct DIR to display the contents of the disk in drive A. In Chapter 9, "Getting Around on Your Disk Drives," you will learn more about working with disk drives. In this chapter, each of the commands uses A: to create the files on drive A. By using drive A, you reduce the file clutter on your hard disk and the possibility of deleting or overwriting needed files. As you can see, COMMAND.COM is currently the only file on the disk in drive A.

Earlier in this book you used the DISKCOPY command to duplicate your disks. In a similar manner, you can use the COPY command to make duplicate copies of a file. DOS can create a duplicate on the same disk or on a different disk. The basic format of the COPY command is as follows:

```
C:\>  COPY SOURCE.EXT TARGET.EXT
```

The *SOURCE.EXT* file is the file that you want to copy, and *TARGET.EXT* is the name of the duplicate copy you will create:

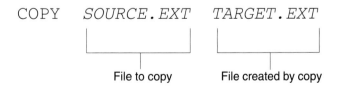

If you issue the command

```
C:\> COPY  A:COMMAND.COM  A:TEST.COM  <ENTER>
```

COPY will make a copy of the file COMMAND.COM that resides on drive
A, naming the file copy TEST.COM. In this case, the A: before the file
name TEST.COM directs COPY to place the file on drive A.

A directory listing of the disk in drive A reveals the following:

```
C:\> DIR  A:  <ENTER>

 Volume in drive A has no label
 Volume Serial Number is 203B-1E03
 Directory of A:\

COMMAND   COM     52925 02-12-93    6:00a
TEST      COM     52925 02-12-93    6:00a
        2 file(s)      105850 bytes
                      1107456 bytes free
```

The COPY command fully supports the wildcard characters discussed
in Chapter 4, "Getting Started with DOS Files." The following COPY
command uses wildcards to copy all the files on drive A with the extension
COM to files with the extension DOS:

```
C:\> COPY  A:*.COM  A:*.DOS  <ENTER>
```

A directory listing of the disk reveals the following:

```
C:\> DIR  A:  <ENTER>

 Volume in drive A has no label
 Volume Serial Number is 203B-1E03
 Directory of A:\

COMMAND   COM     52925 02-12-93    6:00a
COMMAND   DOS     52925 02-12-93    6:00a
```

```
TEST       COM      52925 02-12-93    6:00a
TEST       DOS      52925 02-12-93    6:00a
        4 file(s)       211700 bytes
                       1000960 bytes free
```

If you don't specify an extension on your target file, as in this command:

```
C:\> COPY  A:COMMAND.COM  A:*  <ENTER>
```

COPY will create the file without an extension. In this case, COPY will create the file COMMAND on drive A, as shown here:

```
C:\> DIR   A:  <ENTER>

  Volume in drive A has no label
 Volume Serial Number is 203B-1E03
 Directory of A:\

COMMAND   COM      52925 02-12-93    6:00a
COMMAND   DOS      52925 02-12-93    6:00a
TEST      COM      52925 02-12-93    6:00a
TEST      DOS      52925 02-12-93    6:00a
COMMAND            52925 02-12-93    6:00a
        5 file(s)       264625 bytes
                        947712 bytes free
```

In the next chapter you will learn how to copy files from one disk to another.

 Warning!   If a file already exists in your directory with the same name as the target file in a COPY command, COPY will overwrite the existing file's contents. In Chapter 25, "Advanced File Manipulation," you will learn how to protect files from being overwritten in this way by using the ATTRIB command.

Renaming Files on Disk

Just as there are times when you need to assign a new name to a file in your office, there are times when you will have to rename a DOS file on disk. The RENAME command allows you to rename a file. The basic format of this command is

```
C:\>RENAME OLDNAME.EXT   NEWNAME.EXT
```

First, list the current contents of the disk in drive A:

```
C:\> DIR  A: <ENTER>

 Volume in drive A has no label
 Volume Serial Number is 203B-1E03
 Directory of A:\

COMMAND   COM     52925 02-12-93    6:00a
COMMAND   DOS     52925 02-12-93    6:00a
TEST      COM     52925 02-12-93    6:00a
TEST      DOS     52925 02-12-93    6:00a
COMMAND           52925 02-12-93    6:00a
          5 file(s)     264625 bytes
                        947712 bytes free
```

You can use the RENAME command shown here to rename the file TEST.COM to NEWTEST.COM:

```
C:\> RENAME  A:TEST.COM  NEWTEST.COM <ENTER>
```

Note that the target file name NEWTEST.COM does not have a disk drive specifier (such as A:) in front of it. RENAME knows the file TEST.COM resides on drive A, and RENAME may only create target files on the same drive as the source drive. Thus the file NEWTEST.COM must also reside on drive A. In fact, if you include a drive specifier before the target file name, the command will fail. A directory listing of the disk reveals that the file name has been changed as desired:

```
C:\> DIR   A:  <ENTER>

 Volume in drive A has no label
 Volume Serial Number is 203B-1E03
 Directory of A:\

COMMAND   COM       52925 02-12-93     6:00a
COMMAND   DOS       52925 02-12-93     6:00a
NEWTEST   COM       52925 02-12-93     6:00a
TEST      DOS       52925 02-12-93     6:00a
COMMAND             52925 02-12-93     6:00a
          5 file(s)       264625 bytes
                          947712 bytes free
```

Because the RENAME command is frequently used, DOS lets you abbreviate the command as simply REN. Using REN, the following command renames the file COMMAND.DOS to COMMAND.EXT:

```
C:\> REN   A:COMMAND.DOS   COMMAND.EXT <ENTER>
```

A directory listing of the disk now reveals the new file name:

```
C:\> DIR   A:  <ENTER>

 Volume in drive A has no label
 Volume Serial Number is 203B-1E03
 Directory of A:\

COMMAND   COM       52925 02-12-93     6:00a
COMMAND   EXT       52925 02-12-93     6:00a
NEWTEST   COM       52925 02-12-93     6:00a
TEST      DOS       52925 02-12-93     6:00a
COMMAND             52925 02-12-93     6:00a
          5 file(s)       264625 bytes
                          947712 bytes free
```

Unlike COPY, which overwrites files with the same name as the target file, RENAME will not change the name of a file on disk to the name of a file that already exists on the disk. Thus, the following command fails because the COMMAND.EXT file already exists on disk:

```
C:\> REN  A:TEST.DOS  COMMAND.EXT <ENTER>
Duplicate file name or file not found
```

Like COPY, RENAME also fully supports the wildcard characters. The following RENAME command renames all the files on drive A with the COM extension to files with the NEW extension:

```
C:\> REN  A:*.COM  *.NEW <ENTER>
```

A directory listing of drive A reveals the following:

```
C:\> DIR  A: <ENTER>

 Volume in drive A has no label
 Volume Serial Number is 203B-1E03
 Directory of A:\

COMMAND   NEW      52925 02-12-93    6:00a
COMMAND   EXT      52925 02-12-93    6:00a
NEWTEST   NEW      52925 02-12-93    6:00a
TEST      DOS      52925 02-12-93    6:00a
COMMAND            52925 02-12-93    6:00a
        5 file(s)       264625 bytes
                        947712 bytes free
```

Deleting Files from Disk

Just as you throw away files in your office when they are no longer needed, the DEL command allows you to delete from your disk files you no longer need. The format of the DEL command is as follows:

```
C:\>DEL FILENAME.EXT
```

Given the following files on drive A,

```
C:\> DIR   A:  <ENTER>

 Volume in drive A has no label
 Volume Serial Number is 203B-1E03
 Directory of A:\

COMMAND   NEW       52925 02-12-93    6:00a
COMMAND   EXT       52925 02-12-93    6:00a
NEWTEST   NEW       52925 02-12-93    6:00a
TEST      DOS       52925 02-12-93    6:00a
COMMAND             52925 02-12-93    6:00a
        5 file(s)      264625 bytes
                       947712 bytes free
```

the command

```
C:\> DEL   A:COMMAND.EXT  <ENTER>
```

deletes the COMMAND.EXT file from your disk.

A directory listing of drive A reveals the file has been deleted, as shown here:

```
C:\> DIR   A:  <ENTER>

 Volume in drive A has no label
 Volume Serial Number is 203B-1E03
 Directory of A:\

COMMAND   NEW     52925 02-12-93    6:00a
NEWTEST   NEW     52925 02-12-93    6:00a
TEST      DOS     52925 02-12-93    6:00a
COMMAND           52925 02-12-93    6:00a
        4 file(s)     211700 bytes
                     1000960 bytes free
```

DEL also fully supports DOS wildcard characters, but you should be very careful when you use DEL in conjunction with them. An errant

```
C:\> DEL   A:*.*  <ENTER>
```

you are directing DOS to delete all of the files that reside in the current directory of the disk in drive A. If you invoke this command in error, the command could have devastating results. To protect your files from such disaster, DEL issues the following prompt before deleting the files:

```
All files in directory will be deleted!
Are you sure (Y/N)?
```

If you really want to delete all of the files, type **Y** and press ENTER. Otherwise, type **N** and press ENTER to terminate the command.

To help reduce your chances of deleting a file inadvertently, DOS 4 and later provide the /P qualifier, which directs DEL to display the following prompt before deleting a file:

```
FILENAME.EXT, Delete (Y/N)?
```

If you are sure that you want to delete the file, type **Y** and press ENTER. If you instead type **N** and press ENTER, DOS will leave the file on disk. If you use /P in conjunction with the wildcard characters, as in

```
C:\> DEL   A:*.* /P <ENTER>
```

DEL will prompt you before deleting each file.

Undeleting Inadvertently Deleted Files

If you accidentally delete the wrong files, you may be able to recover the files using either a third-party disk utility program or the DOS 5 or later UNDELETE command. If you are using DOS 5 or later, turn to Chapter 30, "DOS 5 or Later File and Disk Recovery," for information on UNDELETE. If you accidentally delete files, do not copy any new files to your disk until you undelete the files. If you copy new files to the disk, you may overwrite the information that DOS needs to undelete the information.

Manipulating Files Within the Shell

You can perform file copy, rename, and delete operations from within the DOS shell. As discussed in Chapter 6, "Getting Started with the DOS Shell," when you invoke the shell, your screen will display your files and directories as shown in Figure 8-1.

Note   The shell shown here is the DOS 5 and 6 shell; the DOS 4 shell has a different appearance, but performs essentially the same functions.

Using the TAB key, you can highlight the first file in the list. Next, use your keyboard's arrow keys to highlight the desired file. Once you have done so, press ALT-F to invoke the File menu shown in Figure 8-2.

The DOS shell user interface (DOS 5 and later)

FIGURE
8-1

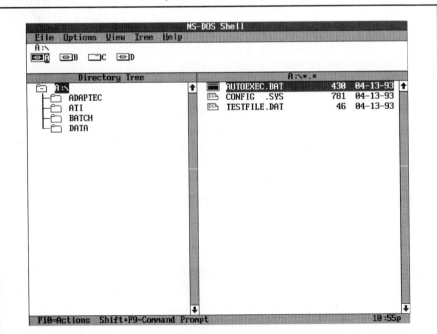

FIGURE 8-2

The File menu

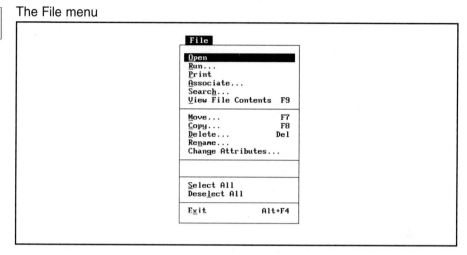

As you can see, the menu in Figure 8-2 displays the Copy, Rename, and Delete options. If you select the Copy option, the shell will display the following dialog box, asking you the name of the target file. Type in the name you desire and press ENTER. The shell will copy the file.

Renaming a file within the shell is very similar. As before, use the TAB key to highlight the file list and the arrow keys to highlight the file you want to rename. Next, select the File menu Rename option. The shell will display the following dialog box:

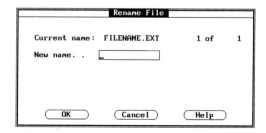

Type in the file name that you desire and press ENTER.

The File menu Rename option, like the RENAME command, does not allow you to rename a file from one disk drive to another or from one directory to another. Thus, the shell does not allow you to include a disk drive specifier (A:) in the target file name. If you do so, the command will fail and the shell will display the following dialog box:

To delete a file, highlight the file as previously discussed and invoke the File menu Delete option. The shell will then display the following dialog box:

Select the Yes option and press ENTER. The shell will remove the file as desired.

Practice

This section will examine each of the file-manipulation routines discussed in this chapter. To get started, issue the following FORMAT command to create a floppy disk containing only the file COM-MAND.COM:

```
C:\> FORMAT  A: /S <ENTER>
```

When the FORMAT command completes, you will have a disk containing the COMMAND.COM file. Using the COPY command, copy the COMMAND.COM file to a file called CMD.COM. When you then use the DIR command, the files on the disk will be displayed:

```
C:\> COPY  A:COMMAND.COM  A:CMD.COM  <ENTER>
C:\> DIR  A:<ENTER>
```

Repeat the command, creating a file called TEST.COM on drive A. You should repeat the DIR command as well so you can view the results of the COPY operation:

```
C:\> COPY  A:COMMAND.COM  A:TEST.COM  <ENTER>
C:\> DIR  A:  <ENTER>
```

Using the wildcard characters, copy the files with a COM extension to files with the extension DOS. Then you can use the DIR command to display the new files:

```
C:\> COPY  A:*.COM  A:*.DOS  <ENTER>
C:\> DIR  A:  <ENTER>
```

Next, using the RENAME command, rename the CMD.COM file to CMD.NEW, then use the DIR command to display the files on drive A:

```
C:\> RENAME  A:CMD.COM  CMD.NEW  <ENTER>
C:\> DIR  A:  <ENTER>
```

Using the DEL command, delete the CMD.NEW file, and then use the DIR command again:

```
C:\> DEL  A:CMD.NEW  <ENTER>
C:\> DIR  A:<ENTER>
```

Next, using the wildcard character, delete all files on drive A with the COM extension:

```
C:\> DEL  A:*.COM <ENTER>
C:\> DIR  A: <ENTER>
```

Finally, issue the following command to delete all the files on drive A:

```
C:\> DEL  A:*.* <ENTER>
```

Because you are using the wildcard character for both the file name and extension, DEL prompts you with the following:

```
All files in directory will be deleted!
Are you sure (Y/N)?
```

In this case, press **N** to terminate the DEL command. Use the DIR command to verify that the files are still on drive A:

```
C:\> DIR  A: <ENTER>
```

Next, invoke the DOS shell. Press the ALT-A keyboard combination to select drive A as the current drive. Using the TAB key, highlight the first file in the list of files. Next, using the UP ARROW and DOWN ARROW keys, select the file TEST.DOS. Press the ALT-F keyboard combination to invoke the File menu. Select the Copy option. The shell will display the following dialog box:

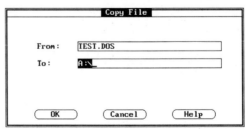

Type in the file name **TESTCOPY.EXT** and press ENTER. The shell will copy your file, updating your directory listing to display the newly created file as shown:

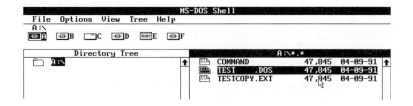

Now select the TESTCOPY.EXT file and invoke the File menu again.
Select the Rename option. The shell will display the following dialog box:

Type **FILENAME.EXT** and press ENTER to rename the file. When the
Rename operation completes, select the file TEST.DOS. Using the File
menu Delete option, delete the file. In this case, the shell will display the
following dialog box:

Select the Yes option and press ENTER. The shell will delete the file as
desired.

This discussion has been an introduction to DOS file-manipulation
basics from both the DOS prompt and the shell. You will expand your
knowledge of DOS file manipulation throughout the remaining chapters
of this book.

Review

1. What are the source file and target file in the following COPY command?

   ```
   C:\> COPY  BUDGET.RPT  BUDGET.SAV <ENTER>
   ```

2. What is the function of the following command?

   ```
   C:\> COPY  A:*.EXE  A:*.SAV <ENTER>
   ```

3. What happens if you copy a file using the name of a file that already exists on disk?

4. What is the function of the following command?

   ```
   C:\> REN  BUDGET.RPT  *.SAV <ENTER>
   ```

5. How can you restore an inadvertently deleted file?

6. What is the function of DEL's /P switch?

Key Points

COPY Command

The COPY command allows you to copy one or more files from one disk or directory to another. The following COPY command, for example, copies the file BUDGET.RPT as BUDGET.OLD:

```
C:\> COPY  BUDGET.RPT  BUDGET.OLD <ENTER>
```

continues...

Key Points
(continued)

RENAME Command

The RENAME command lets you change the name of a file on your disk. Because of its frequency of use, DOS lets you abbreviate the RENAME command as REN. The following RENAME command renames the file BUDGET.DAT as BUDGET.OLD:

```
C:\> RENAME  BUDGET.DAT  BUDGET.OLD  <ENTER>
```

You cannot rename a file to a file name that is already in use. If you try to do so, the RENAME command will fail.

DEL Command

The DEL command allows you to delete one or more files from your disk. The following DEL command, for example, deletes the file BUDGET.OLD:

```
C:\> DEL  BUDGET.OLD  <ENTER>
```

The DEL *.* Command

If you attempt to delete all of the files in your directory by using the wildcard characters *.*, DEL will first display the following warning:

```
All files in directory will be deleted!
Are you sure (Y/N)?
```

continues . . .

Key Points
(continued)

If you press **Y** and press ENTER, DEL will delete the files from disk. If you instead press **N**, the DEL command will end and the files will remain.

UNDELETE Command

The UNDELETE command (DOS 5 or later) allows you to recover, in certain circumstances, files that you have accidentally erased. For more information on this command, turn to Chapter 30 or the Command Reference.

CHAPTER

Getting Around on Your Disk Drives

With the exception of the FORMAT and DISKCOPY commands, the commands presented in the previous chapters have used only drive C. In this chapter you will learn how to manipulate DOS files and external commands on disk drives other than drive C.

The Default Drive

Each of your disk drives has a unique name, such as the floppy drives A and B and your hard disk drive C. When you work with DOS, you must select one of these drives for use. DOS defines the *default disk drive* (also called the *current drive*) as the drive that it searches, by default, for your files and external commands. For example, if you issue the command

```
C:\> DIR <ENTER>
```

DOS will display the files that reside in the current directory of drive C because drive C is your current drive.

Normally, the DOS prompt contains the drive letter of the default drive:

```
C:\>
```
↑
Current drive is drive C

DOS lets you change the current drive by typing the desired drive letter followed by a colon (such as A:) and pressing ENTER. Place a formatted floppy disk in drive A. To select drive A as the current drive, issue the following command:

```
C:\> A: <ENTER>
```

When you press ENTER to change the current drive, DOS will change the appearance of your DOS prompt, as shown here:

```
C:\> A: <ENTER>
A:\>
```

As you can see, the new prompt contains the new default drive. If you now issue the following DIR command:

```
A:\> DIR <ENTER>
```

you will see the disk activation light for drive A illuminate as DIR reads and displays the names of files contained on the disk in drive A. As you can see by the directory listing, DOS has changed your current disk drive as desired.

Changing the Default Drive from the Shell

The DOS shell also allows you to quickly change disk drives. As shown in Figure 9-1, the shell displays disk drive icons for the available disk drives, which in this case include drives A, B, and C.

Using the TAB key, highlight a drive in the row of disk drives. Next, use the right and left arrow keys to toggle between the disk drives. To select a specific disk drive, simply highlight the disk drive and press ENTER.

DOS will display a brief message on the screen stating that it is reading information from the disk. You will see the disk activation light illuminate for the selected drive as DOS reads the files that it contains. DOS will then display the new list of files for the new drive.

You can also select a disk drive by holding down the CTRL key and pressing the key of the drive desired. Later in this chapter you will learn how to use the shell to display simultaneously the files that reside on two different disk drives.

Disk drive icons within the DOS 5 and 6 shell (A, B, and C in upper-left corner); drive A is current

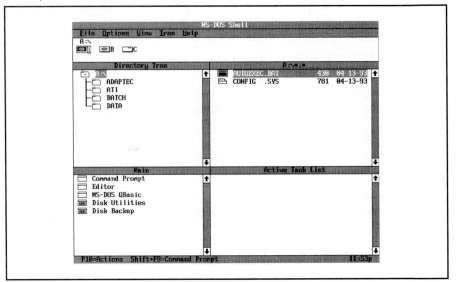

Listing Files on Another Disk Drive

By default, the DIR command displays the files that reside on the default disk drive. The following DIR command, for example, lists the files that reside on drive C:

```
C:\> DIR <ENTER>
```

To display the files that reside on another disk drive, you can first change the default drive as you learned in the previous section and then issue the DIR command:

```
C:\> A: <ENTER>
A:\> DIR <ENTER>
```

However, the DIR command provides an easier alternative. DIR allows you to specify a disk drive letter in your command line, as shown here:

```
C:\> DIR  A:  <ENTER>
```

In a similar manner, to display a directory listing for a specific file that resides on a disk drive other than the default, simply precede the file name with the disk drive specifier, as shown here:

```
C:\> DIR  A:FILENAME.EXT <ENTER>
```

You can also use wildcard characters after a disk drive specifier, as shown in these two commands:

```
C:\> DIR  A:*.COM <ENTER>
C:\> DIR  A:*.* <ENTER>
```

Viewing Multiple Disk Drives

One of the most powerful features of the DOS shell is that it allows you to display the files that reside on two different disks (or subdirectories) at the same time. Invoke the View menu option. The shell will display the following menu:

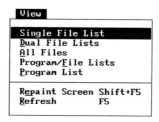

Select the Dual File Lists option. DOS will split your screen display and show you two directory listings, as shown in Figure 9-2.

In this case, DOS is displaying the directory listing for drive A twice, displaying the BATCH subdirectory in the lower window. To view files that reside on two different disks simultaneously, press the TAB key until

FIGURE 9-2   Displaying dual file lists within the shell

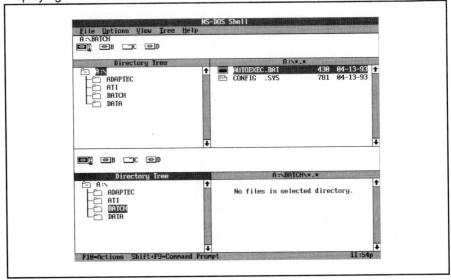

DOS highlights the second set of disk drives. Next, using the right and left arrow keys, highlight one of the other disks shown. When you press ENTER, DOS will display the files that reside on both disks simultaneously.

As you examine the DOS file-manipulation commands later in this book, the ability to view and work with files that reside in different directories will be very convenient.

Executing a Command Stored on Another Disk

You have learned in this chapter that you can change your default drive easily. Assume, for example, that the disk containing a program named BUDGET resides in drive A.

One way to execute the command is to select drive A as your default drive, as shown here:

```
C:\> A:  <ENTER>
A:\> BUDGET  <ENTER>
```

As an alternative, DOS allows you to precede the command name with the corresponding disk drive letter, as shown here:

```
C:\> A:BUDGET  <ENTER>
```

When DOS encounters "A:" before the command name, DOS will search the disk in drive A for the BUDGET program. All DOS external commands can be executed in this manner.

Moving Files to Other Disk Drives

Chapter 8, "Basic File Operations," discussed several DOS file-manipulation commands. At that time, you found that the COPY command allows you to copy the contents of a file to a new file that resides on either the same or a different disk. Given the command

```
C:\> COPY  COMMAND.COM  TARGET.COM  <ENTER>
```

COPY will copy the contents of the COMMAND.COM file to a file named TARGET.COM that resides on the same disk. By simply preceding the source or target file name with a disk drive letter, however, you can direct COPY to copy files across disk drives. For example, the command

```
C:\> COPY  COMMAND.COM  A:TARGET.COM  <ENTER>
```

causes COPY to create a duplicate copy of COMMAND.COM on drive A, naming it TARGET.COM. Figure 9-3 illustrates this file copy process.

FIGURE 9-3 Copying the file COMMAND.COM from drive C to drive A

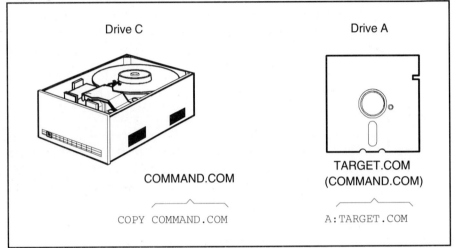

In a similar way, the following command copies COMMAND.COM from drive C to drive A, naming the file copy on drive A COMMAND.COM:

```
C:\> COPY  COMMAND.COM  A:COMMAND.COM  <ENTER>
```

Assuming the disk in drive A contains a file named BUDGET93.DAT, which you want to copy to your hard disk, you can issue the following COPY command:

```
C:\> COPY  A:BUDGET93.DAT  BUDGET93.DAT  <ENTER>
```

In this case, the drive specifier (A:) before the source file name tells DOS to copy the file from drive A.

You can place a disk drive specifier in front of your file names for each of the commands that you examined in Chapter 8. For example, the following DEL command directs DEL to erase the file TARGET.COM from the disk in drive A:

```
C:\> DEL  A:TARGET.COM  <ENTER>
```

command can have devastating results. If you are not sure which files might be deleted, always perform a DIR command with the same wildcard characters you plan to delete. For example, if you want to delete files with the extension NEW, you should issue this DIR command first to be sure you are aware of all NEW files:

```
C:\> DIR   A:*.NEW  <ENTER>

 Volume in drive A has no label
 Volume Serial Number is 203B-1E03
 Directory of A:\

COMMAND   NEW      52925 02-12-93    6:00a
NEWTEST   NEW      52925 02-12-93    6:00a
        2 file(s)      105850 bytes
                      1000960 bytes free
```

With these files in mind, issue the following DEL command:

```
C:\> DEL   A:*.NEW  <ENTER>
```

A directory listing of drive A reveals the following:

```
C:\> DIR   A:  <ENTER>

 Volume in drive A has no label
 Volume Serial Number is 203B-1E03
 Directory of A:\

TEST      DOS      52925 02-12-93    6:00a
COMMAND            52925 02-12-93    6:00a
        2 file(s)      105850 bytes
                      1107456 bytes free
```

The DEL command is one of the most important commands you will use on a daily basis. However, it can also be one of the most destructive. If, for example, you issue the command

Although the RENAME command is similar, you must remember one rule when you invoke RENAME: Because RENAME does not allow you to move a file from one disk to another, you cannot specify a disk drive letter before the target file name. RENAME assumes the target file disk drive is identical to the source file disk drive. For example, the command

```
C:\> RENAME  A:FILENAME.EXT FILENAME.NEW <ENTER>
```

renames the *FILENAME.EXT* file that resides on drive A as *FILENAME.NEW*, and the *FILENAME.NEW* file remains on drive A. If you do precede the target file name with a disk drive, the command will fail and DOS will display the following:

```
C:\> REN  A:FILENAME.EXT  A:FILENAME.NEW <ENTER>
Invalid parameter
```

Using Wildcards to Copy Files to Other Drives

When you are copying files from one disk to another, the wildcard characters can be very convenient. For example, the command

```
C:\> COPY  COMMAND.COM  A:COMMAND.COM <ENTER>
```

directs COPY to copy the contents of the COMMAND.COM file to drive A, creating a file on drive A called COMMAND.COM. Had you instead used wildcards for the target file name, as shown here:

```
C:\> COPY  COMMAND.COM  A:*.* <ENTER>
```

COPY would have performed the same processing. In this case, A: tells COPY the target disk is drive A, and *.* directs COPY to use the same file name as the source file for the target. In a similar manner, the command

```
C:\> COPY  *.COM  A:*.* <ENTER>
```

directs DOS to copy all of the files with the extension COM to the disk in drive A. DOS will assign the original file names to each of the copies.

If you specify only a disk drive letter for the target file name, as in the following command:

```
C:\> COPY  *.COM  A:  <ENTER>
```

DOS defaults the target file name to the same name it had on the source drive. Thus, the following commands are identical in function:

```
C:\> COPY DISKCOPY.COM  A:DISKCOPY.COM <ENTER>
C:\> COPY DISKCOPY.COM  A:*.* <ENTER>

C:\> COPY  FORMAT.COM  A:*.* <ENTER>
C:\> COPY  FORMAT.COM  A:  <ENTER>

C:\> COPY  A:FORMAT.COM  *.* <ENTER>
C:\> COPY  A:FORMAT.COM <ENTER>
```

By knowing these few simple rules, you can greatly reduce the amount of typing you must perform as you use DOS commands.

Copying Files to Other Drives with the Shell

In Chapter 8 you found that when you copy files with the shell, the shell displays the dialog box shown here:

```
┌─────────────────────────────────────────────┐
│                  Copy File                   │
├─────────────────────────────────────────────┤
│                                              │
│   From:  │AUTOEXEC.BAT            │          │
│                                              │
│   To:    │C:\                    │           │
│                                              │
│                                              │
│    ( OK )      ( Cancel )      ( Help )       │
└─────────────────────────────────────────────┘
```

If you include a disk drive specifier before the file name in the dialog box's To: option, you direct the shell to copy the file to another disk.

Practice

Issue the following invalid command name:

```
C:\> BAD_NAME <ENTER>
```

The disk drive activation light for drive C illuminates briefly as DOS searches for the command on disk. In this case, DOS will not be able to find a command called BAD_NAME, and it will display the following message:

```
C:\> BAD_NAME <ENTER>
Bad command or file name

C:\>
```

DOS looked on drive C because drive C is the current drive.

Place a floppy disk in drive A and issue the following command to select drive A as the default:

```
C:\> A: <ENTER>
A:\>
```

This time, when you invoke the BAD_NAME command,

```
A:\> BAD_NAME <ENTER>
```

DOS will look on drive A for the command because drive A is now the default disk drive, as the DOS prompt shows.

Next, with either drive A or drive C as your default drive, issue the DIR command:

```
A:\> DIR <ENTER>
```

DIR will display the files contained on the current disk. Select drive C as the current drive if you have not already done so:

```
A:\> C: <ENTER>
```

To display the files on the disk in drive A, issue the command

```
C:\> DIR  A: <ENTER>
```

Next, by using the following COPY command, copy the contents of the DISKCOPY.COM file from the DOS directory to a file called DCOPY.COM, which resides on drive A:

```
C:\> COPY  \DOS\DISKCOPY.COM  A:DCOPY.COM <ENTER>
```

Perform a directory listing of drive A to reveal the file:

```
C:\> DIR  A: <ENTER>
```

Using the RENAME command, rename this file to DC.COM. First, issue this RENAME command:

```
C:\> REN  A:DCOPY.COM  A:DC.COM <ENTER>
```

Because the command precedes the target file name with a disk drive specifier, the command will fail, and DOS will display the following:

```
C:\> REN  A:DCOPY.COM  A:DC.COM <ENTER>
Invalid parameter

C:\>
```

Remember, RENAME does not allow you to put a disk drive letter in front of the target file name. Instead, use the command

```
C:\> REN   A:DCOPY.COM   DC.COM  <ENTER>
```

Finally, using the DEL command, delete the file from disk:

```
C:\> DEL   A:DC.COM  <ENTER>
```

Invoke the shell and select either drive A or drive C as the current disk drive. As you will see, DOS displays the files that reside on that disk. Next, using the View menu, select the Dual File Lists option. Display the contents of either drives A and B or drives A and C, depending on your configuration.

Next, select a file from drive C and then choose the Copy option from the File menu. When DOS then displays the Copy File dialog box, type **A:NEWFILE.EXT** to copy the file to drive A with the name NEWFILE.EXT.

Next, locate the file NEWFILE.EXT on drive A and select it. Using the Delete option on the File menu, delete the file as discussed in Chapter 8. You have now performed DOS file-manipulation commands across disk drives from within the shell and at the DOS prompt.

Review

1. What is the default drive?
2. How do you change the default drive?
3. How do you list the files that reside on drive A?
4. How do you execute external commands that reside on drive A if drive C is the default drive?
5. What is the function of the following command?

```
C:\> COPY COMMAND.COM   A:TEST.COM  <ENTER>
```

6. How do the following commands differ in their effects?

```
C:\> COPY  COMMAND.COM  A:COMMAND.COM <ENTER>
C:\> COPY  COMMAND.COM  A:*.* <ENTER>
C:\> COPY  COMMAND.COM  A: <ENTER>
```

7. What is the major limitation of the RENAME command?

8. What command would delete the TEST.COM file from drive A if drive C were the current default?

9. How do you change the current disk drive from the DOS shell?

Key Points

Default Drive

DOS defines the current or default disk drive as the drive that, unless you tell it to look elsewhere, DOS will search for your external commands and files. In most cases, the DOS prompt will contain the drive letter of the default drive.

Selecting a New Default Drive

To change your current disk drive, simply type in the new drive letter followed by a colon and press ENTER. For example, the following command changes the current drive from drive A to drive C.

```
A:\> C: <ENTER>
```

When you press ENTER, DOS will select the new drive and change its prompt to indicate the new current drive:

continues . . .

Key Points
(continued)

```
C:\>
```

Changing Disk Drives from the Shell

To change the current drive within the shell, press the TAB key until DOS highlights one of the disk drives in the list of drives that appear on your screen. Next, use the RIGHT ARROW and LEFT ARROW keys to highlight the desired drive. Once you have done so, press ENTER. DOS will display the files that reside on the disk you have selected. In addition, pressing the CTRL key and the letter of the drive you desire also causes DOS to select the disk; for example, you can press CTRL-A for drive A.

Displaying Files on a Drive Other Than the Default Drive

To list the files that reside on a disk other than the default, place the drive letter desired, followed immediately by a colon, in the DIR command line, as shown here:

```
C:\> DIR A:  <ENTER>
```

Accessing Specific Files on a Disk Drive Other Than the Default

Most DOS commands allow you to access files on disk drives other than the default. To do so, precede the file name with a disk drive letter, as shown here:

continues . . .

```
C:\> DIR  A:FILENAME.EXT <ENTER>
```

Displaying Files on Two Disks Simultaneously

The shell allows you to display the contents of two disks (or subdirectories) at the same time. To do so, select the Dual File Lists option from the View menu. DOS will split your screen in half, displaying the files that reside on one or more disks.

Executing a Command Stored on a Disk Other Than the Default

To execute an external DOS command that resides on a disk other than the one in the default drive, precede the command name with the drive letter and a colon, as shown here:

```
C:\> A:PAYROLL <ENTER>
```

Using COPY to Copy Files to Other Drives

To copy a file to or from a disk other than the one in the default drive, precede the file name with the desired drive letter and a colon, as shown here:

```
C:\> COPY  AUTOEXEC.BAT  A:AUTOEXEC.BAT <ENTER>
```

CHAPTER

Creating and Displaying Files

So far, you have learned to copy, rename, and delete files from the DOS prompt and also from the DOS shell. However, you still don't know how to create files. In this lesson, you will learn how to create simple files from the DOS prompt and how to display those files by using the TYPE command and the shell.

Many of your DOS files contain characters that prevent their display. For example, if you attempt to display a DOS command, such as DISKCOPY, your screen will fill with meaningless characters. The files examined in this lesson are called *text files* because they contain only standard characters (such as "A" to "Z" and 0 to 9) and common punctuation marks. These characters are what you normally see in a letter, a book, and other forms of text.

Creating Files at Your Keyboard

In Chapter 8, "Basic File Operations," you learned that the COPY command allows you to copy the contents of a file to another file that resides on either the default drive or another disk drive. COPY also allows you to create a file by typing in text at the keyboard. To do this, you must use the device name CON (*console*) as the source of your file copy, as shown here:

```
C:\>COPY CON FILENAME.EXT
```

Source file   Target file

Just as DOS assigns unique names to the files on your disk, it also assigns names to your hardware devices. In this case, the device name CON refers to your keyboard device.

At the DOS prompt, type in the following:

```
C:\> COPY  CON  TESTFILE.DAT <ENTER>
This is a test file. <ENTER>
It contains two lines. <ENTER>
```

When you have typed in these lines, you must tell DOS you have finished entering text in the file. In this case, press the F6 function key, and DOS will display the Control Z character (^Z), as shown here:

```
C:\> COPY  CON  TESTFILE.DAT
This is a test file.
It contains two lines.
^Z
```

DOS uses the ^Z character to signify the end of a file. When you press the ENTER key, DOS will create the file, displaying the following:

```
C:\> COPY  CON  TESTFILE.DAT
This is a test file.
It contains two lines.
^Z <ENTER>
    1 File(s) copied

C:\>
```

A directory listing of the file reveals

```
C:\> DIR  TESTFILE.DAT <ENTER>

 Volume in drive C is DOS 6 DISK
 Volume Serial Number is 16F6-3B73
 Directory of C:\

TESTFILE DAT         46 03-08-93   8:10a
        1 file(s)         46 bytes
                   151986176 bytes free

C:\>
```

Repeat this process to create the ONE.DAT file as shown here:

```
C:\> COPY  CON  ONE.DAT <ENTER>
1 <ENTER>

ONE <ENTER>
^Z <ENTER>
    1 File(s) copied

C:\>
```

A directory listing of your disk displays the following:

```
C:\> DIR  ONE.DAT <ENTER>

 Volume in drive C is DOS 6 DISK
 Volume Serial Number is 16F6-3B73
 Directory of C:\

ONE       DAT          5 03-08-93   8:10a
         1 file(s)             5 bytes
                  151982080 bytes free

C:\>
```

Displaying Your Files with TYPE

Once you create a text file by copying it from your keyboard, the TYPE command allows you to display the file's contents. TYPE is an internal DOS command. To display the contents of the TESTFILE.DAT file, for example, using the TYPE command results in the following:

```
C:\> TYPE  TESTFILE.DAT <ENTER>
This is a test file.
It contains two lines.

C:\>
```

If the file whose contents you want to display using TYPE resides on a different disk, simply precede the file name with a disk drive specifier, as discussed in Chapter 9, "Getting Around on Your Disk Drives. The following TYPE command, for example, displays the contents of a file that resides on drive A:

```
C:\> TYPE   A:FILENAME.EXT <ENTER>
```

If your file is longer than one screen and scrolls past you faster than you can read it, you can use the MORE command, which is discussed in Chapter 20, "I/O Redirection with the DOS Pipe," or the Command Reference, to display the file's contents one screen at a time.

Also, remember that not all files are text files. If you use the command

```
C:\> TYPE   COMMAND.COM
```

to display the contents of the COMMAND.COM file, for example, your screen will fill with meaningless characters, and your computer's bell will probably beep.

Displaying Your Files from the Shell

One of the problems you will experience when using the TYPE command is that in order to redisplay a portion of the file that has already scrolled off the screen, you must issue a second TYPE command. The DOS shell, however, provides the File menu View File Contents option, which allows you to view parts of the file a screenful at a time by using the PGUP and PGDN keys on your keyboard, as shown in Figure 10-1.

Invoke the DOS shell and select the TESTFILE.DAT file:

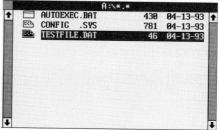

FIGURE 10-1

Location of PGUP and PGDN keys

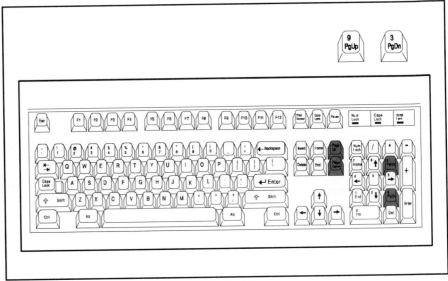

Next, select the File menu. Select the View File Contents option. The shell will display the file, as shown here:

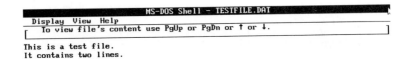

In this case, the file is only two lines long. If the file instead contained several pages of text, you could traverse each page a screenful at a time by using the PGUP and PGDN keys. When you have finished viewing the file, press the ESC key to return to the shell.

If the file you wish to see resides on a different disk, you simply select the disk drive, as discussed in Chapter 9, "Getting Around on Your Disk Drives." Then you select the file and invoke the View File Contents option, as in the previous example.

Don't forget to delete the TESTFILE.DAT and ONE.DAT files before continuing.

Practice

From the DOS prompt, issue the following command:

```
C:\> COPY  CON  MEETINGS.DAT <ENTER>
```

Next, type in the following:

```
MONDAY   12:00 MEET WITH LAWYER <ENTER>
MONDAY   14:00 BANK WITH LOAN OFFICER <ENTER>
TUESDAY 11:30 CHIROPRACTOR <ENTER>
TUESDAY 13:00 HAIRCUT <ENTER>
```

When you finish typing in this text, use F6 to inform DOS that you have reached the end of your file. After you then press ENTER, your screen should appear as follows:

```
C:\> COPY  CON  MEETINGS.DAT
MONDAY   12:00 MEET WITH LAWYER
MONDAY   14:00 BANK WITH LOAN OFFICER
TUESDAY 11:30 CHIROPRACTOR
TUESDAY 13:00 HAIRCUT
^Z
     1 File(s) copied

C:\>
```

Once you have created this file, use the TYPE command to display its contents:

```
C:\> TYPE  MEETINGS.DAT <ENTER>
```

Finally, to practice traversing a large file from within the shell, create a file called NUMBERS.DAT, and enter in it the numbers 1 to 100, as shown here:

```
C:\> COPY  CON  NUMBERS.DAT <ENTER>
01 <ENTER>
02 <ENTER>
03 <ENTER>
04 <ENTER>
05 <ENTER>
.. <ENTER>
.. <ENTER>
.. <ENTER>
96 <ENTER>
97 <ENTER>
98 <ENTER>
99 <ENTER>
100 <ENTER>
^Z <ENTER>
     1 File(s) copied
```

Invoke the shell and select the NUMBERS.DAT file. Next, invoke the File menu View File Contents option. The shell will display the file's contents, as shown in Figure 10-2.

Using the PGUP and PGDN keys, traverse the file. When you have finished, press the ESC key to return to the shell. Don't forget to delete the MEETINGS.DAT and NUMBERS.DAT files before proceeding.

Review

1. What is a text file?
2. How do you create a text file with DOS from your keyboard?
3. What is the function of the TYPE command?
4. How do you display the contents of a file that resides on a disk other than the current default?
5. How do you display a file from within the shell?

FIGURE 10-2 Displaying the file NUMBERS.DAT

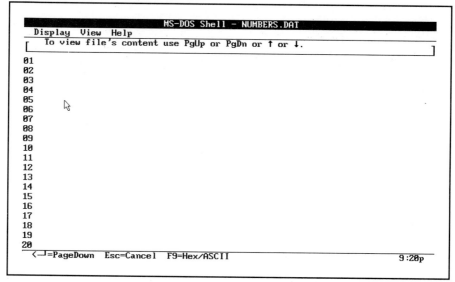

Key Points

The F6 Function Key

The F6 function key directs DOS to place an end-of-file marker in your file when you create a file by copying it from the keyboard.

```
C:\> COPY CON FILENAME.EXT
Last line in file
^Z  ←——————————————————————  F6 pressed here
```

When you press F6, DOS will display the characters ^Z, which are pronounced "Control Z." When you press ENTER following ^Z, DOS will create your file.

continues . . .

***Key Points
(continued)***

Using CON

To create DOS files from your keyboard, use the device name CON as the source in your COPY command, as shown here:

```
C:\> COPY  CON FILENAME.EXT <ENTER>
```

DOS will copy the information you type into the specified file until you enter a ^Z by pressing the F6 function key.

The TYPE Command

The TYPE command allows you to display the contents of a file on your screen. To do so, specify the file in the TYPE command line, as shown here:

```
C:\> TYPE FILENAME.EXT <ENTER>
```

If the file resides on a different disk, simply precede the file name with a disk drive specifier, as shown here:

```
C:\> TYPE  A:FILENAME.EXT <ENTER>
```

Viewing a File from the Shell

To display the contents of file from within the DOS shell, select the desired file. Next, using the File menu, select the View File Contents option. The shell will display your file. You can page through information a screenful at a time by using the PGUP and PGDN keys. When you have finished viewing the file, press ESC to return to the shell.

CHAPTER

Getting Started with File Organization

*E*arlier in this book, when you first issued the DIR command, you learned that DOS keeps track of the files on your disk by placing them into a list of files called a directory. The DIR command displays the files that reside in the directory. In this chapter you will learn that DOS allows you to divide a directory into organized groups of files called *subdirectories.* By creating directories on your disk, you can group related files in the same location. For example, you can place all of your business files in one directory, your DOS commands in another, and your memos in a third. The actual number of subdirectories you will create depends on the number of different types of files you have. Before you learn about DOS subdirectories in detail, however, let's review the basics of file organization.

Basic File Organization for Floppy Disks

If you use a floppy disk based system, you still need to organize your disks and files in order to prevent misplacing critical programs or files. Most people use a word processor to create letters and reports. Assuming that your word processing software resides on one floppy disk, you will probably want to create individual disks for letters, memos, and reports, as shown here:

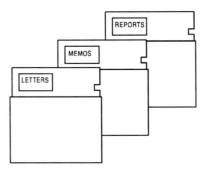

You will then find that you spend much less time looking for your files and that you also reduce the number of duplicate files that you have spread out across several disks.

Assume, for example, that you want to keep track of your class notes on disk for your math, Spanish, and history classes. For each class, you type your notes into files named

LESSON1.SPA
LESSON1.MAT
LESSON1.HIS

Before long, your disk can contain a large number of files, as shown in the following:

```
C:\> DIR  A:  <ENTER>

Volume in drive A has no label
Volume Serial Number is 19DA-2F7C
Directory of A:\

LESSON1   SPA     37637 04-09-93    6:55a
LESSON1   HIS        38 04-09-93    6:55a
LESSON1   MAT        96 04-09-93    6:55a
LESSON2   SPA     12838 04-09-93    6:55a
LESSON2   HIS     10428 04-11-93    7:55a
LESSON2   MAT     15741 04-11-93    7:55a
LESSON3   SPA     70151 04-11-93    7:55a
LESSON3   HIS     22923 04-11-93    7:55a
LESSON3   MAT     14759 04-11-93    7:55a
LESSON4   SPA     23360 04-11-93    7:55a
LESSON4   MAT     17199 04-11-93    7:55a
LESSON4   HIS      3674 04-11-93    7:55a
       12 file(s)      228844 bytes
                        59392 bytes free
```

Because you have used meaningful file extensions, you can determine which files belong to which class. For example, the following command lists your Spanish files:

```
C:\> DIR  *.SPA <ENTER>
```

However, in many cases you would much rather separate your class files into three distinct disks, as shown here:

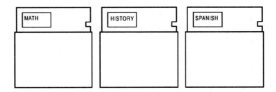

If you have organized all of your files by disk, finding files specific to one class will no longer be dependent on the file extension. You can change your file name from the less meaningful LESSON1.HIS to something more specific, like CIVILWAR.LS1. Doing so will let you know at a glance which lesson the notes relate to (LS1) and also the topic discussed (CIVILWAR).

How Many Files Can My Directory Hold?

Each time you format a disk, DOS sets aside a fixed amount of space on the disk specifically for one primary directory. As you create files, DOS adds the file name, size, date, and time information to the directory. DOS records directory information on your disk.

Because the amount of space that DOS reserves for your disk's primary directory is fixed, DOS is restricted to a specific number of files in the directory. In the case of a 360Kb floppy disk, the maximum number of files that the disk can store is 112, regardless of the files' sizes.

If you attempt to create a 113th file on the disk, DOS will display the error message

```
Cannot make directory entry - FILENAME.EXT
```

and the file will not be created. Whether you are using 360K, 1.2Mb, or even a hard disk, DOS still restricts the number of files that you can place in the primary directory on your disk. The only difference between disk types in this case is that the larger disks support more files. Table 11-1 lists the number of files (directory entries) that each disk type supports.

Unlike the primary directory on your disk, which is fixed in size, the number of files in DOS subdirectories is not restricted.

TABLE 11-1 Number of Files Supported by Hard and Floppy Disks

Disk Type	Files
Single-sided	64
Double-sided	112
Quad-density	224
Hard disk	512

Subdirectories

Think of a DOS directory as a list of files. Likewise, think of a DOS subdirectory as simply a sublist of files. If, for example, you want to track your class notes for Spanish, math, and history as previously discussed, but you want all of your files to reside on one disk (a hard disk, for example), DOS allows you to create three subdirectories on the disk to group your files logically. In this case, the subdirectory names might be SPANISH, MATH, and HISTORY. The concept is similar to placing your notes into one large filing cabinet, but with each class in a separate drawer. The disk is your filing cabinet, and subdirectories are drawers.

The organization of subdirectories on your disk can be represented in this way:

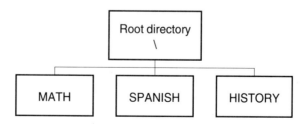

Each time you create a file for one of your classes, you will place the file into the corresponding directory. This in turn ensures that your files remain organized.

Creating DOS Subdirectories

Just as DOS allows you to create files on your disk, it also allows you to create subdirectories. The MKDIR (make directory) command creates a directory on your disk. To begin, place a newly formatted disk in disk drive A. Issue the DIR command:

```
C:\> DIR   A:  <ENTER>

Volume in drive A has no label
Volume Serial Number is 4428-16F4
Directory of  A:\


File not found
```

As you can see, the disk does not yet contain any files. Since in this example you will track class notes by subject, you will create directories named MATH, SPANISH, and HISTORY. To start, issue the following MKDIR command to create the directory MATH on drive A:

```
C:\> MKDIR   A:\MATH  <ENTER>
```

Later in this chapter you will learn about the backslash character (\), which is the DOS character that means "directory," you have placed before the subdirectory name. For now, simply include this character as shown in the example.

If you perform a directory listing of the disk in drive A, DOS will now display

```
C:\> DIR   A:  <ENTER>

 Volume in drive A has no label
 Volume Serial Number is 4428-16F4
 Directory of A:\

MATH           <DIR>        04-09-93   7:00a
        1 file(s)            0 bytes
                      320512 bytes free
```

Note that DOS has replaced the file-size field with <DIR> in the directory listing. This tells you that MATH is a DOS subdirectory.

Repeat this process to create the SPANISH subdirectory:

```
C:\> MKDIR  A:\SPANISH <ENTER>
```

Because of its frequency of use, DOS allows you to abbreviate the MKDIR command as MD. Using MD, create the HISTORY subdirectory:

```
C:\> MD  A:\HISTORY <ENTER>
```

A directory listing of your disk now reveals

```
C:\> DIR  A: <ENTER>

 Volume in drive A has no label
 Volume Serial Number is 4428-16F4
 Directory of A:\

MATH           <DIR>       04-09-93    7:00a
SPANISH        <DIR>       04-09-93    7:01a
HISTORY        <DIR>       04-09-93    7:01a
        3 file(s)              0 bytes
                         318464 bytes free
```

DOS has created all three directories for your use in organizing your files. Now that you know how to create DOS subdirectories, let's find out how to use them.

Selecting the Current Directory

As you know, DOS defines the default disk as the disk drive that, by default, it searches for your external commands or files. DOS also defines the current directory. So far, each time you have issued the DIR command, DOS has displayed the files contained in the primary DOS directory. DOS assigns the backslash (\), with no other name after it, as the name of this subdirectory:

```
C:\> DIR  A: <ENTER>


Volume in drive A has no label
Volume Serial Number is 4428-16F4
Directory of  A:\
```

Root directory

Many people refer to this main directory as the *root directory* because all the subdirectories you create appear to grow from it.

Until now, the root directory has always been the current directory. To select a directory other than the root as your current directory, you must use the CHDIR (change directory) command. CHDIR directs DOS to select or display the current directory. If you simply type **CHDIR** at the DOS prompt (or CHDIR with a different drive specifier) DOS will display the current directory for the current drive or the drive specified:

```
C:\> CHDIR  A: <ENTER>
A:\

C:\>
```

In this case, DOS is telling you that the root directory (\) is the current directory on drive A. To select the MATH subdirectory as your current directory, use the command

```
C:\> CHDIR  A:\MATH <ENTER>
```

A directory listing of your disk reveals that DOS has selected MATH as your current directory:

```
C:\> DIR  A: <ENTER>

Volume in drive A has no label
Volume Serial Number is 4428-16F4
Directory of A:\MATH

.              <DIR>      04-09-93   7:07a
..             <DIR>      04-09-93   7:07a
        2 file(s)            0 bytes
                        319488 bytes free
```

Note the two directories that appear in the directory listing. DOS predefines two abbreviations in each subdirectory that you create. You will learn about them later in this chapter. For now simply note that DOS places them in each directory that you create.

To select the SPANISH subdirectory as your current directory, enter

```
C:\> CHDIR  A:\SPANISH <ENTER>
```

A directory listing of your disk reveals

```
C:\> DIR  A: <ENTER>

Volume in drive A has no label
Volume Serial Number is 4428-16F4
Directory of A:\SPANISH

.              <DIR>      04-09-93   7:01a
..             <DIR>      04-09-93   7:01a
        2 file(s)            0 bytes
                        318464 bytes free
```

Remember, if you simply type **CHDIR** at the DOS prompt without specifying a directory name, CHDIR will display the current directory:

```
C:\> CHDIR  A: <ENTER>
A:\SPANISH

C:\>
```

Again, because of its frequency of use, DOS allows you to abbreviate the CHDIR command as CD. Use CD to select the HISTORY directory as your current directory:

```
C:\> CD  A:\HISTORY <ENTER>
```

With HISTORY as your current directory, create a file named CIVILWAR.LS1, as shown here:

```
C:\> COPY  CON  A:CIVILWAR.LS1 <ENTER>
The civil war lasted from <ENTER>
1861 to 1865. <ENTER>
^Z <ENTER>
     1 File(s) copied

C:\>
```

A directory listing of your disk reveals

```
C:\> DIR  A: <ENTER>

 Volume in drive A has no label
 Volume Serial Number is 4428-16F4
 Directory of A:\HISTORY

 .            <DIR>      04-09-93   7:01a
 ..           <DIR>      04-09-93   7:01a
 CIVILWAR LS1       42 04-09-93   7:02a
       3 file(s)          42 bytes
                      317440 bytes free
```

Next, select the root directory as drive A's current default directory:

```
C:\> CHDIR  A:\  <ENTER>
```

Issue the DIR command. Note that the CIVILWAR.LS1 file does not appear in the directory listing. DOS is displaying the list of files that reside in the root directory; CIVILWAR.LS1 resides in the HISTORY subdirectory.

Removing a DOS Subdirectory

Just as there are times when you no longer need a specific file that resides on disk, there will also be times when you want to remove a subdirectory. The DEL command does not allow you to delete a DOS subdirectory. Given the directory listing

```
C:\> DIR  A:  <ENTER>

 Volume in drive A has no label
 Volume Serial Number is 4428-16F4
 Directory of A:\

MATH         <DIR>      04-09-93    7:00a
SPANISH      <DIR>      04-09-93    7:01a
HISTORY      <DIR>      04-09-93    7:01a
       3 file(s)            0 bytes
                      317440 bytes free
```

if you issue the following DEL command:

```
C:\> DEL  MATH.DIR  <ENTER>
```

the command will fail and DOS will display the following:

```
File not found
```

The DEL command works for DOS files. DOS treats files and subdirectories differently. To remove a DOS subdirectory from your disk, you must use the RMDIR (remove directory) command. For example, to remove the MATH subdirectory, use the command

```
C:\> RMDIR  A:\MATH <ENTER>
```

A directory listing of your disk reveals the following:

```
C:\> DIR  A: <ENTER>

 Volume in drive A has no label
 Volume Serial Number is 4428-16F4
 Directory of A:\

SPANISH        <DIR>      04-09-93   7:01a
HISTORY        <DIR>      04-09-93   7:01a
         2 file(s)             0 bytes
                         318464 bytes free
```

RMDIR does not allow you to delete a subdirectory that contains files. If you attempt to remove the subdirectory HISTORY, which contains the CIVILWAR.LS1 file, DOS will display

```
C:\> RMDIR  A:\HISTORY <ENTER>
Invalid path, not directory,
or directory not empty
```

Before you can remove the subdirectory, you must delete the files that the subdirectory contains.

DOS allows you to abbreviate the RMDIR command as RD. Using RD, remove the SPANISH subdirectory, as shown here:

```
C:\> RD  A:\SPANISH <ENTER>
```

Your directory listing should now contain the following:

```
C:\> DIR  A: <ENTER>

 Volume in drive A has no label
 Volume Serial Number is 4428-16F4
 Directory of A:\

HISTORY      <DIR>      04-09-93    7:01a
       1 file(s)            0 bytes
                      319488 bytes free
```

Creating Multiple Levels of Subdirectories

Just as creating the MATH, SPANISH, and HISTORY subdirectories improved your disk organization, there may be many times when further dividing your DOS subdirectories into additional subdirectories will improve your disk organization to an even greater extent. Given the directory structure

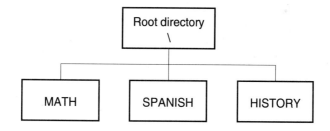

you might want to further divide your files into the NOTES, HOMEWORK, and TESTS subdirectories, as shown in Figure 11-1.

To create the NOTES subdirectory within the HISTORY subdirectory, your MKDIR command becomes

```
C:\> MKDIR  A:\HISTORY\NOTES <ENTER>
```

Subdirectories added to directory structure

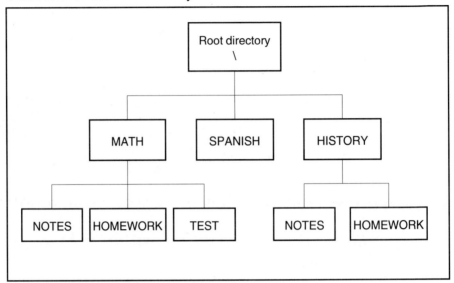

In this case, a directory listing of HISTORY reveals

```
C:\> DIR  A:\HISTORY  <ENTER>

 Volume in drive A has no label
 Volume Serial Number is 4428-16F4
 Directory of A:\HISTORY

 .            <DIR>      04-09-93   7:01a
 ..           <DIR>      04-09-93   7:01a
 CIVILWAR LS1        42 04-09-93   7:02a
 NOTES        <DIR>      04-09-93   7:04a
        4 file(s)           42 bytes
                       318464 bytes free
```

Likewise, to create the HOMEWORK subdirectory, use the command

```
C:\> MKDIR  A:\HISTORY\HOMEWORK  <ENTER>
```

Pictorially, the directory structure would now look like this:

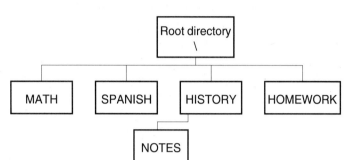

In both cases, the \HISTORY part of the command preceding the directory name tells DOS to create the subdirectory specified within the HISTORY directory. If you omit \HISTORY and use

```
C:\> MKDIR   A:\HOMEWORK  <ENTER>
```

DOS will create the directory below the root directory.

When you create a DOS subdirectory, DOS examines the name that you are specifying in the MKDIR command line and performs the following processing:

❑   If the subdirectory name begins with a backslash, as in

```
C:\> MD   A:\HISTORY  <ENTER>
```

DOS begins at the root directory and traverses any directories that may precede the subdirectory to create a new one. In this case, DOS would start at the root and create the HISTORY subdirectory. Given the command

```
C:\> MD   A:\HISTORY\TESTS  <ENTER>
```

DOS will start at the root, traverse the HISTORY directory, and then create the TESTS subdirectory within HISTORY.

❏ If your subdirectory name does not begin with a backslash, as in the following,

```
C:\> MD  A:TESTS <ENTER>
```

DOS will create the subdirectory (TESTS) within the current directory on drive A. As long as you know what the current directory is, you can omit the backslash and preceding directory names, and DOS will create the subdirectory in the current directory.

Naming Your Directories

DOS directories and subdirectories follow the same naming conventions as DOS files. The following characters are valid in both DOS directory and subdirectory names:

! @ $ % ^ & ( ) – { } ' ~ _

The following rules will guide you as you create your DOS directories and subdirectories:

❏ Unless you start the name at the root directory by placing a backslash (\) before the name, DOS will create the directory or subdirectory within the current directory.
❏ Including a disk drive specifier allows you to create a directory on a disk other than the current default disk, as shown here:

```
C:\> MKDIR  A:\HISTORY <ENTER>
```

❏ Do not create a DOS directory or subdirectory with the same name as a file that will reside in that directory.
❏ The longest directory or subdirectory path name that DOS will support is 63 characters.
❏ The maximum number of files that you can place on your disk when you do not use subdirectories is restricted (see Table 11-1).

The . and .. Directories

Earlier, you found that DOS creates two subdirectories within each subdirectory that you create:

```
Volume in drive A has no label
 Volume Serial Number is 4428-16F4
 Directory of A:\MATH

.            <DIR>      04-09-93   7:04a
..           <DIR>      04-09-93   7:04a
       2 file(s)           0 bytes
                      317440 bytes free
```

These two subdirectories are simply abbreviations:

. is an abbreviation for the current directory.

.. is an abbreviation for the directory immediately above the current directory. For example, if the current directory is \SPANISH, the abbreviation .. refers to the root directory. If the current directory is \SPANISH\NOTES, the abbreviation .. refers to \SPANISH, the directory immediately above the current directory.

Given the directory structure

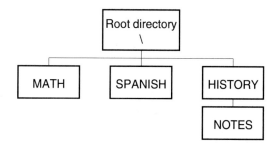

and the current directory \HISTORY\NOTES, the command

```
C:\> DIR A:.  <ENTER>
```

```
C:\> CHDIR  A:\HISTORY <ENTER>
```

You can verify this by invoking CHDIR as follows:

```
C:\> CHDIR <ENTER>
C:\

C:\> CHDIR  A: <ENTER>
A:\HISTORY

C:\>
```

As you can see, DOS keeps track of the current directory for each of your disk drives.

Manipulating Directories from Within the Shell

Just as you can create, select, and later remove subdirectories from the DOS prompt, the DOS shell also allows you to quickly perform directory manipulation. Insert a blank disk in drive A, and invoke the shell. Next, press CTRL-A to select drive A as the current drive and invoke the File menu, shown in Figure 11-2.

Note the Create Directory menu option. When you select this option, the shell will display the following dialog box prompting you for the directory name to create:

```
┌──────────────────Create Directory──────────────────┐
│                                                     │
│   Parent name: A:\                                  │
│                                                     │
│   New directory name. .    [_            ]          │
│                                                     │
│                                                     │
│                                                     │
│      ( OK )        ( Cancel )        ( Help )        │
└─────────────────────────────────────────────────────┘
```

FIGURE
11-2

The File menu

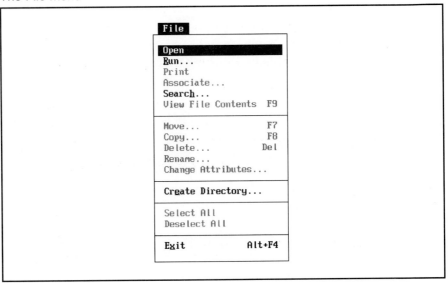

If you have not already created the HISTORY subdirectory, type **HISTORY** and press ENTER. The shell will create the subdirectory and add it to the directory tree. The shell will display the new directory in drive A's directory tree, as shown in Figure 11-3.

FIGURE
11-3

The new subdirectory shown in drive A's directory tree

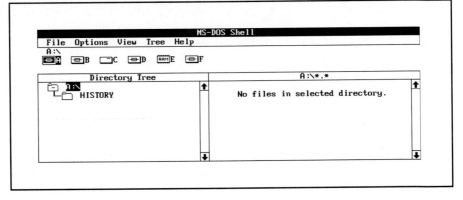

Selecting a directory as your current directory is very similar to selecting a file. In this case, press the TAB key until DOS highlights the first subdirectory name in the directory tree area. Next, use the UP ARROW and DOWN ARROW keys to highlight the desired directory. Once the directory is highlighted, press ENTER to select it.

To remove a DOS subdirectory by using the shell, select the directory to delete as the current directory, as just discussed. Next, invoke the File menu again and select the Delete option. The shell will display the following dialog box:

To remove the directory, select the Yes option and press ENTER.

Working with Directory Trees

By default, the shell only displays the first level of your directory tree, in other words, the directories whose names appear within the root directory. If you examine the icons that appear next to the directory names, you will find some icons contain a plus sign, some a minus sign, and some are blank. The directories whose icons are blank do not contain additional directories. The directories whose icons contain a plus sign have additional levels of directories that are not currently displayed. A directory whose icon contains a minus sign has all of its next level directories visible.

Using your mouse or keyboard, you can select a directory and *expand* (make visible) or *collapse* (remove from view) one or more levels of directories beneath the directory.

Expanding the Next Level of Directories

The shell provides you with several ways to expand a directory to its next level of directories. First, you can click on the plus sign that appears in the directory's icon with your mouse. If you are using your keyboard, use your arrow keys to highlight the directory and press the plus sign or invoke the Tree menu and select the Expand One Level option. Note the plus sign to the right of the option indicating the option's hot key.

Expanding a Directory's Tree

To expand all the directories beneath a directory, click on the directory name with your mouse or use your arrow keys to select the directory. Next, type an asterisk (*). To expand your entire directory tree, you can select the root directory and type * or you can press the CTRL-* key combination, regardless of the current directory.

Collapsing a Directory's Branches

To collapse the branches beneath a directory, click on the minus sign that appears in the directory's icon or highlight the entry with your arrow keys and press the minus sign. The minus sign is the hot key corresponding to the Tree menu's Collapse Branch option.

Practice

In this lesson you will experiment with the MKDIR, CHDIR, and RMDIR commands, as well as perform directory manipulation from within the DOS shell.

DOS subdirectories improve your file organization. You will use them on a daily basis. Take time to ensure that you fully understand each example presented in this section.

Place a newly formatted disk in drive A and issue the command

```
C:\> DIR  A: <ENTER>

Volume in drive A has no label
Volume Serial Number is 4428-16F4
Directory of  A:\

File not found
```

Although the directory listing tells you that there are no files on the disk, it also tells you that you are examining the root directory on drive A (A:\).

Create the EXPENSES, INCOME, and TAXES subdirectories on your disk. To start, issue the command

```
C:\> MKDIR  A:\EXPENSES <ENTER>
```

A directory listing of your disk reveals the newly created file:

```
C:\> DIR  A: <ENTER>

 Volume in drive A has no label
 Volume Serial Number is 4428-16F4
 Directory of A:\

EXPENSES     <DIR>      04-09-93   7:07a
       1 file(s)            0 bytes
                      320512 bytes free
```

Using the MD abbreviation of the MKDIR command, create the IN-COME and TAXES subdirectories:

```
C:\> MD  A:\TAXES <ENTER>

C:\> MD  A:\INCOME <ENTER>
```

Using the CHDIR command, select TAXES as your current directory:

```
C:\> CHDIR   A:\TAXES <ENTER>
```

A directory listing of your disk now displays the following:

```
C:\> DIR   A: <ENTER>

 Volume in drive A has no label
 Volume Serial Number is 4428-16F4
 Directory of A:\TAXES

.               <DIR>      04-09-93    7:07a
..              <DIR>      04-09-93    7:07a
       2 file(s)              0 bytes
                         319488 bytes free
```

Remember that . and .. are simply abbreviations.

Issue the DIR command

```
C:\> DIR   A:. <ENTER>
```

to display the contents of the current directory, followed by

```
C:\> DIR   A:.. <ENTER>
```

to display the directory that resides immediately above TAXES, which in this case is the root directory. Next, issue the command

```
C:\> CHDIR   A:INCOME <ENTER>
```

In this case, the command fails and DOS displays

```
Invalid directory
```

If you don't precede a directory name with a backslash (\), DOS will search for the directory specified within the current directory. In this case, INCOME resides not below the TAXES subdirectory but below the root directory. The easiest way to select INCOME as the current directory would be

```
C:\> CHDIR   A:\INCOME  <ENTER>
```

You could also select the root directory as the current directory with

```
C:\> CHDIR   A:\  <ENTER>
```

and then issue the command

```
C:\> CHDIR   A:INCOME  <ENTER>
```

In this case, since INCOME resides within the current directory, DOS allows you to omit the backslash before the name.

Using the RMDIR command, delete the EXPENSES subdirectory:

```
C:\> RMDIR   A:\EXPENSES  <ENTER>
```

Invoke the shell, and place the disk containing your newly created subdirectories in drive A. Select drive A, and the shell will present the display shown in Figure 11-4.

Notice the entries in the directory tree area. To start, use the File menu and select the Create Directory option. When DOS prompts you for a subdirectory, type **EXPENSES** to place that subdirectory back on your disk. When the command completes, DOS will update your directory tree with the new subdirectory, as shown in Figure 11-5.

Press the TAB key until the first subdirectory in the directory tree is highlighted. Next, using the UP ARROW and DOWN ARROW keys, highlight the INCOME subdirectory. When you press ENTER, the shell will select INCOME as your current directory.

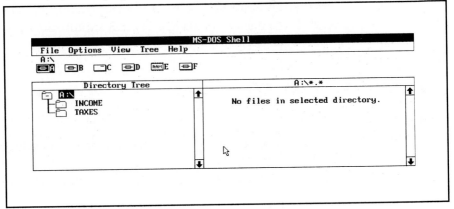

FIGURE 11-4

Subdirectories displayed in drive A's directory tree

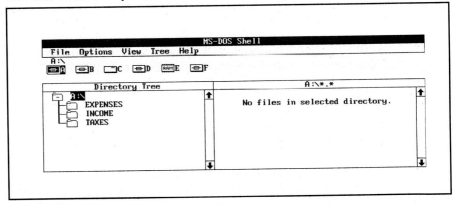

FIGURE 11-5

The new subdirectory shown in drive A's directory tree

Next, since the INCOME subdirectory does not contain any files, you can remove it. Select the Delete option from the File menu, and the shell will display the following dialog box:

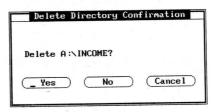

Delete the subdirectory. When DOS redisplays your directory tree, note that INCOME no longer appears.

The ability to manipulate DOS subdirectories is critical to your success. The next two chapters explore more DOS subdirectory concepts that will help you manage your files effectively.

Review

1. What is a subdirectory?

2. What DOS command creates a DOS subdirectory? What is its abbreviation?

3. What is the current directory?

4. What command selects the current directory? What is its abbreviation?

5. Why doesn't the DEL command remove a subdirectory?

6. What are the . and .. directories?

7. If you do not use DOS subdirectories, your disks are restricted to a specific number of files. Why?

8. How do you select the current directory from within the shell?

9. How do you remove a directory from within the shell?

10. Draw the directory structure created by these commands:

```
C:\> MKDIR ONE <ENTER>

C:\> MD TWO <ENTER>

C:\> MKDIR  \THREE <ENTER>

C:\> CD ONE <ENTER>

C:\> MKDIR A <ENTER>

C:\> RMDIR \TWO <ENTER>

C:\> MD \THREE\B <ENTER>
```

Disk Organization

If you are using a floppy disk based system, you will eventually use several different disks for each of your applications. Make sure that each disk is properly labeled and that each of your files is named meaningfully. This will make locating specific files in the future much simpler.

The MKDIR (or MD) Command

The MKDIR command allows you to create a subdirectory on the default disk or a specified disk:

```
A:\> MKDIR \HISTORY <ENTER>

C:\> MKDIR A:\HISTORY <ENTER>
```

DOS allows you to abbreviate the MKDIR command as MD. The following commands are functionally equivalent:

```
C:\> MKDIR A:\MATH <ENTER>

C:\> MD  A:\MATH <ENTER>
```

Root Directory (\ )

Every DOS disk has a main directory called the root directory. DOS uses the backslash (\), with no name after it, to represent the root. All of the other subdirectories that you create on your disk appear to grow out of the root like branches on a tree.

continues . . .

Key Points
(continued)

The CHDIR (or CD) Command

The CHDIR command allows you to select or display the current directory on the default disk or a specified disk:

```
A:\> CHDIR  \MATH <ENTER>

C:\> CHDIR  A:\MATH <ENTER>
```

DOS allows you to abbreviate the CHDIR command as CD. The following commands are functionally equivalent:

```
C:\> CHDIR  A:\MATH <ENTER>

C:\> CD  A:\MATH <ENTER>
```

The RMDIR (or RD) Command

The RMDIR command allows you to remove a subdirectory from your disk. The subdirectory must not contain files, or the command will not execute; therefore, you must delete all of the files in the subdirectory first.

DOS allows you to abbreviate the RMDIR command as RD. The following commands are functionally equivalent:

```
C:\> RMDIR  A:\SPANISH <ENTER>

C:\> RD  A:\SPANISH <ENTER>
```

CHAPTER

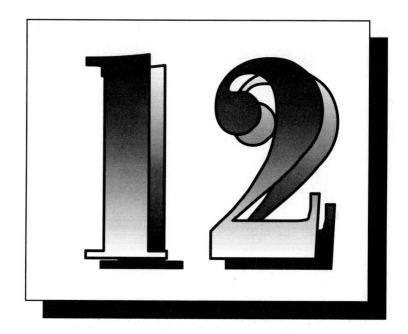

Using DOS Directories

*I*n Chapter 11, "Getting Started with File Information," you learned what directories are; how to create, select, and later remove them; and the rationale for using them. However, Chapter 11 did not teach you how to manipulate files that reside in DOS directories. In this chapter you will learn how to list the contents of a specific directory, copy files from one directory to another, rename files in a directory, and display and delete files that reside in directories. As you will see, you'll still be using DIR, COPY, REN, TYPE, and DEL; the only difference now is that you must precede each file name with the directory name that contains the file.

Listing Files in a Directory

So you don't clutter up your hard disk with the directories we will create in this lesson, you will create the directories on a floppy disk in drive A. To begin, place a blank, formatted disk in drive A. Select drive A as the current drive, as discussed in Chapter 9, "Getting Around on Your Disk Drives," and shown here:

```
C:\> A:  <ENTER>
A:\>
```

Next, create the DOS, LOTUS, and DBASE directories, as shown here:

```
A:\> MKDIR  \DOS  <ENTER>
A:\> MKDIR  \LOTUS  <ENTER>
A:\> MKDIR  \DBASE  <ENTER>
```

A directory listing of your disk will show the results of your commands:

```
A\> DIR  <ENTER>

 Volume in drive A has no label
 Volume Serial Number is 1837-14F3
 Directory of A:\
```

```
DOS            <DIR>        04-11-93   12:05p
LOTUS          <DIR>        04-11-93   12:05p
DBASE          <DIR>        04-11-93   12:05p
        3 file(s)                0 bytes
                         258048 bytes free
```

Using the CHDIR command, select DOS as your current directory and issue the COPY command to create the file DOS.NTS:

```
A:\> CHDIR  \DOS <ENTER>
A:\DOS> COPY  CON  DOS.NTS <ENTER>
DOS Version 6 provides a shell interface <ENTER>
and several disk utilities. <ENTER>
^Z <ENTER>
     1 File(s) copied

A:\DOS>
```

Use DIR to display the file's directory listing:

```
A:\DOS> DIR <ENTER>

 Volume in drive A has no label
 Volume Serial Number is 1837-14F3
 Directory of A:\DOS

.              <DIR>        04-11-93   12:05p
..             <DIR>        04-11-93   12:05p
DOS      NTS        71 04-11-93   12:05p
        3 file(s)              71 bytes
                         257024 bytes free
```

Remember that unless you specify otherwise, DIR displays the files in the current directory. Using the following commands, select the root directory as your current directory, and then issue the DIR command:

```
A:\DOS> CD  \ <ENTER>
A:\> DIR <ENTER>
```

DIR will display the contents of the current directory, which is now the root. Note that the DOS.NTS file does not appear in the directory listing. It shouldn't—the DOS.NTS file resides in the DOS directory.

To list the files in the DOS subdirectory, use the command

```
A:\> DIR   \DOS <ENTER>

 Volume in drive A has no label
 Volume Serial Number is 1837-14F3
 Directory of A:\DOS

 .              <DIR>      04-11-93   12:05p
 ..             <DIR>      04-11-93   12:05p
 DOS    NTS          71   04-11-93   12:05p
        3 file(s)             71 bytes
                         257024 bytes free
```

Likewise, to display the files in the LOTUS subdirectory, your command becomes the following:

```
A:\> DIR   \LOTUS <ENTER>

 Volume in drive A has no label
 Volume Serial Number is 1837-14F3
 Directory of A:\LOTUS

 .              <DIR>      04-11-93   12:05p
 ..             <DIR>      04-11-93   12:05p
        2 file(s)              0 bytes
                         257024 bytes free
```

Because your command line contains a specific directory name, DIR displays the files in that directory instead of the current directory. As before, you can list a specific file, as shown here:

```
A:\> DIR   \DOS\DOS.NTS <ENTER>

 Volume in drive A has no label
```

```
Volume Serial Number is 1837-14F3
Directory of A:\DOS

DOS        NTS        71 04-11-93  12:05p
           1 file(s)            71 bytes
                          257024 bytes free
```

Displaying the Contents of a File in a Subdirectory

Select the DOS subdirectory as your current directory, and then issue the TYPE command shown here:

```
A:\> CD  \DOS <ENTER>
A:\DOS> TYPE  DOS.NTS <ENTER>
DOS Version 6 provides a shell interface
and several disk utilities.

A:\DOS>
```

In this case, the TYPE command succeeds because the DOS.NTS file resides in the current directory. If, however, you select the root directory as your current directory with the command

```
A:\> CHDIR  \ <ENTER>
```

you must change your TYPE command to include the name of the subdirectory that contains the DOS.NTS file:

```
A:\> TYPE  \DOS\DOS.NTS <ENTER>
DOS Version 6 provides a shell interface
and several disk utilities.

A:\>
```

If the file had resided on drive B, you would simply include a disk drive specifier for drive B, as shown here:

```
A:\> TYPE  B:\DOS\DOS.NTS <ENTER>
```

Deleting a File from a Subdirectory

As you will see, deleting a file that resides in a subdirectory is quite straightforward. Issue the DEL command to delete the file DOS.NTS from the DOS directory:

```
A:\> DEL  \DOS\DOS.NTS <ENTER>
```

As you learned earlier, any time you specify the wildcard characters *.* with the DEL command, DEL will display the following:

```
All files in directory will be deleted!
Are you sure (Y/N)?
```

As you can see, the command does not delete all the files from your disk, but rather the files in the directory that you specify. For example, if you issue the command:

```
A:\> DEL  \LOTUS\*.* <ENTER>
```

DEL will delete all of the files from the LOTUS directory, leaving files in other directories untouched.

Select the LOTUS directory as the current directory and create the file LOTUS.NTS:

```
A:\DOS> CD  \LOTUS <ENTER>
A:\LOTUS> COPY  CON  LOTUS.NTS <ENTER>
Lotus 1-2-3 is a spreadsheet program. <ENTER>
```

```
^Z <ENTER>
      1 File(s) copied

A:\>
```

Next, select the root directory as your current directory and issue the following TYPE command:

```
A:\LOTUS> CD   \ <ENTER>
A:\> TYPE   LOTUS.NTS <ENTER>
File not found - LOTUS.NTS
```

In this case, DOS could not find the file because the file does not reside in the current directory, but rather in the LOTUS directory. The correct command in this case becomes the following:

```
A:\> TYPE   \LOTUS\LOTUS.NTS <ENTER>
```

Next, issue the following DEL command:

```
A:\> DEL   LOTUS.NTS <ENTER>
File not found
```

Once again, you must specify a complete directory name for the file, as shown here:

```
A:\> DEL   \LOTUS\LOTUS.NTS <ENTER>
```

Renaming a File in a Directory

In order to have a file that you can manipulate, create the following file:

```
A:\> COPY  CON  \DBASE\NOTES.DAT <ENTER>
DBASE is a database program. <ENTER>
^Z <ENTER>
     1 File(s) copied

A:\>
```

A directory of the DBASE directory reveals the following:

```
A\> DIR   \DBASE <ENTER>

 Volume in drive A has no label
 Volume Serial Number is 1837-14F3
 Directory of A:\DBASE

.               <DIR>      04-11-93   12:05p
..              <DIR>      04-11-93   12:05p
NOTES    DAT          30 04-11-93   12:07p
        3 file(s)          30 bytes
                       256000 bytes free
```

Next, using the RENAME command, try to rename the file as shown here:

```
A:\> REN  \DBASE\NOTES.DAT  \DBASE\DBASE.DAT <ENTER>
```

In this case, your command will fail, and RENAME will display the following:

```
Invalid filename or file not found
```

As discussed in Chapter 8, "Basic File Operations," RENAME doesn't let you rename a file from one disk or directory to another. Therefore, you cannot specify a directory name as the target of a RENAME command. In the previous example, the correct RENAME command is the following:

```
A:\> REN   \DBASE\NOTES.DAT   DBASE.DAT <ENTER>
```

Use the DIR command to verify the file has been renamed as desired:

```
A:\> DIR   \DBASE <ENTER>
```

Copying Files from One Directory to Another

Earlier in this chapter, you used the command

```
A:\> COPY   CON   \LOTUS\LOTUS.NTS <ENTER>
```

to create a file in the LOTUS subdirectory. To copy files from one DOS subdirectory to another, you simply need to specify subdirectory names before the source and target file names, as shown here:

```
A:\> COPY NAME.EXT   \TARGET\FILENAME.EXT
```

Use the following command to create the file NOTES.DAT:

```
A:\> COPY   CON   \LOTUS\NOTES.DAT <ENTER>
This is a sample file. <ENTER>
^Z <ENTER>

A:\>
```

To copy the file NOTES.DAT to a file named NOTES.123 that also resides in the LOTUS subdirectory, you would issue the following command:

```
A:\> COPY   \LOTUS\NOTES.DAT   \LOTUS\NOTES.123 <ENTER>
```

A directory listing of the LOTUS subdirectory reveals the following:

```
A:\> DIR   \LOTUS <ENTER>

 Volume in drive A has no label
 Volume Serial Number is 1837-14F3
 Directory of A:\LOTUS

 .               <DIR>      04-11-93   12:05p
 ..              <DIR>      04-11-93   12:05p
 LOTUS    123          24 04-11-93   12:09p
 NOTES    DAT          24 04-11-93   12:09p
         4 file(s)           63 bytes
                         253952 bytes free
```

Likewise, to copy the same file into the DBASE subdirectory, use the following COPY command:

```
A:\> COPY   \LOTUS\NOTES.DAT   \DBASE\DBASE.DAT <ENTER>
```

Listing the DBASE subdirectory files reveals the following:

```
A:\> DIR   \DBASE <ENTER>

 Volume in drive A has no label
 Volume Serial Number is 1837-14F3
 Directory of A:\DBASE

 .               <DIR>      04-11-93   12:05p
 ..              <DIR>      04-11-93   12:05p
 DBASE    DAT          24 04-11-93   12:09p
         3 file(s)           24 bytes
                         252928 bytes free
```

Don't forget about the wildcard characters. For example, to copy all of the files in the LOTUS subdirectory to DBASE, use the following:

```
A:\> COPY   \LOTUS\*.*   \DBASE\*.* <ENTER>
```

In a similar manner, if you don't specify a target directory name in the COPY command, as in the following:

```
A:\> COPY  \LOTUS\*.*   *.* <ENTER>
```

DOS will copy all the files in the LOTUS directory into the current directory. Had you wanted to copy the files to the disk in drive B, your command would have been

```
A:\> COPY  \LOTUS\*.*   B:*.* <ENTER>
```

Just as you don't have to specify a target file name when you copy files between disks, the same holds true when you copy files between directories. For example, the following command will copy the file NOTES.DAT to the DBASE directory, using the same file name:

```
A:\> COPY  \LOTUS\NOTES.DAT  \DBASE <ENTER>
```

Thus, the following shows two different ways of entering four different COPY commands:

```
COPY   \LOTUS\123.DAT   \DBASE\123.DAT   COPY   \LOTUS\123.DAT   \DBASE\*.*

COPY   \LOTUS\123.DAT   \DBASE\123.DAT   COPY   \LOTUS\123.DAT   \DBASE

COPY   \LOTUS\*.*   \DBASE\*.*                COPY   \LOTUS\123.DAT   \DBASE

COPY   \LOTUS\*.*   \DBASE                    COPY   \LOTUS\DBASE
```

Moving Files from One Disk or Directory to Another

In the past, the only way to move a file from one disk or directory to another was to use the COPY command to first copy the file and then to use DEL to erase the file. DOS 6, however, provides the MOVE command that lets you quickly perform such operations. The format of the MOVE command is as follows:

```
MOVE [drive:][path]SourceFile [drive:][path]TargetFile
```

The *SourceFile* specifies the file you want to move. The *TargetFile* specifies the desired file location. The following command, for example, moves the file REPORT93.DAT from the current directory into the DATA directory:

```
C:\SUBDIR> MOVE REPORT93.DAT \DATA\*.* <ENTER>
c:\subdir\report93.dat => c:\data\report93.dat [ok]
```

The MOVE command fully supports DOS wildcards. The following command, for example, moves all of the current directory data files into the DATA directory:

```
C:\SUBDIR> MOVE *.DAT \DATA\*.* <ENTER>
```

You can also use MOVE to move a file from one disk to another. The following command, for example, moves the file FILENAME.EXT from the current directory to the disk in drive A:

```
C:\SUBDIR> MOVE FILENAME.EXT A:*.* <ENTER>
```

Last, you can use the MOVE command to rename a directory. The following command, for example, renames the directory OLD_DATA to NEW_DATA:

```
C:\> MOVE \OLD_DATA \NEW_DATA <ENTER>
```

Executing a Command That Resides in a DOS Subdirectory

In Chapter 9, "Getting Around on Your Disk Drives," you learned that to execute an external command that resides on a disk other than the current default, you have to precede the command name with a disk drive letter and colon, as shown here:

```
C:\> A:BUDGET  <ENTER>
```

In this case, DOS would execute a program named BUDGET that resides on the floppy disk in drive A.

Select drive C as your current drive, if it isn't. As you have read, your DOS commands reside in a directory named DOS. To display the contents of this directory, use the following DIR command:

```
C:\> DIR  \DOS  <ENTER>
```

DOS will display your external DOS commands and system files, as shown here:

```
C:\> DIR  \DOS  <ENTER>

 Volume in drive C is DOS
 Volume Serial Number is 1A54-45E0
 Directory of C:\DOS

 .               <DIR>        11-23-92    9:26p
 ..              <DIR>        11-23-92    9:26p
 DBLSPACE BIN     50284 02-12-93    6:00a
 FORMAT   COM     22717 02-12-93    6:00a
 NLSFUNC  EXE      7036 02-12-93    6:00a
 COUNTRY  SYS     17066 02-12-93    6:00a
 KEYB     COM     14983 02-12-93    6:00a
 KEYBOARD SYS     34694 02-12-93    6:00a
 ANSI     SYS      9065 02-12-93    6:00a
 ATTRIB   EXE     11165 02-12-93    6:00a

    :        :        :        :         :
 DEFAULT  SET      4482 02-08-93    7:51p
 DEFAULT  SLT        21 02-08-93    1:58p
 MWAVSOS  DLL      7888 02-12-93    6:00a
 MWAVMGR  DLL     21712 02-12-93    6:00a
```

```
MWAVTSR   EXE     17328 02-12-93    6:00a
COMMAND   COM     52925 02-12-93    6:00a
QBASIC    INI       132 02-20-93   12:10p
MOUSE     INI        28 02-03-93   11:54a
DEFAULT   CAT        66 02-08-93    7:51p
         129 file(s)     5826340 bytes
                        16607232 bytes free
```

To execute one of these commands, you can precede the command name with the DOS subdirectory name. For example, the following command invokes FORMAT to prepare a floppy disk in drive A for use:

```
C:\> \DOS\FORMAT   A:  <ENTER>
```

As you can see, the command line not only contained the FORMAT command, but also the directory containing FORMAT.COM. You can execute all external DOS commands in this manner, by preceding the command name with the directory name DOS.

You can also invoke commands such as FORMAT and DISKCOPY without specifying the DOS directory. As you will learn momentarily, DOS lets you specify one or more directories within which you want it to look automatically for your external commands. In most cases, the DOS directory is one of the directories included. Therefore, you can issue the previous command as simply

```
C:\> FORMAT   A:  <ENTER>
```

and DOS finds FORMAT.COM in the directory DOS.

Displaying Your Directory Structure

As the number of files and directories on your disk increases, the difficulty in locating a specific file on your disk also increases. If you are using DOS 5 or later, you can use the DIR /S switch to display every file on your disk:

```
C:\> DIR   /S <ENTER>
```

In this case, DIR not only displays every file and directory that resides within the root, but also those in directories beneath the root.

If you instead issued the command

```
C:\> DIR   \DOS   /S <ENTER>
```

DIR would display all the files in the DOS directory, as well as files and directories beneath the DOS directory.

Beginning with version 2, DOS provides the TREE command, which not only allows you to list the files on your disk, but also provides you with a visual presentation of your directories.

Using the previous directory structure of the floppy disk in drive A, the TREE command will display the following:

```
C:\> TREE A:  <ENTER>
Directory PATH listing
Volume Serial Number is 1837-14F3
A:
   ├─ DOS
   ├─ LOTUS
   └─ DBASE
```

Note that the directories appear to grow out of the root directory like branches of a tree (hence, the command's name). TREE also allows you to display all of the files in each directory. To do so, you must include the /F (files) qualifier, as shown here:

```
C:\> TREE   A:   /F <ENTER>
```

If you are having trouble locating a file, you can use either DIR /S or the TREE command to locate the file.

Path Names

As you know, DOS assigns a unique file name to each of the files that reside on your disk. When you are using DOS directories, however, you often must precede your file name with a subdirectory name. When you do so, you create a DOS path name. Simply stated, a *path name* is a list of directories that DOS must traverse to find your external commands or files. For example, in the command

```
A:\> TYPE   \LOTUS\DATA\NOTES.DAT <ENTER>
```

the path name and file name are as follows:

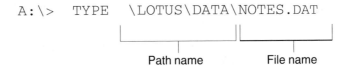

Given the directory structure shown here:

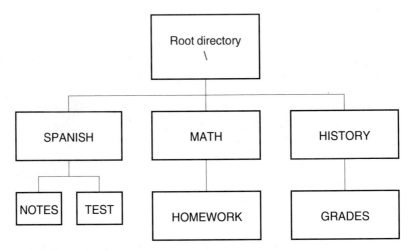

the following are valid DOS path names:

```
\
\SPANISH
\MATH
\HISTORY
\SPANISH\NOTES
\SPANISH\TEST
\MATH\HOMEWORK
\HISTORY\GRADES
```

As you work with directories, you will encounter the term "path name" on a regular basis.

Telling DOS Where to Look for External Commands

You learned in this chapter that to execute an external DOS command, you need to precede the command name with a subdirectory path:

```
C:\> \DOS\FORMAT  A:  <ENTER>
```

You can issue all external DOS commands in this fashion. DOS, however, provides you with an easier way to invoke your commonly used external commands. Each time you type in a command at the prompt, DOS first checks to see if the command is one of the internal commands that it always keeps in memory. If it is, DOS executes the command. If it isn't, DOS searches the current directory. If DOS finds the command as an external command, DOS executes it. Otherwise, DOS displays the message

```
Bad command or file name
```

The PATH command allows you to alter this processing a little. PATH allows you to specify additional directories that DOS should search for the external commands when it fails to locate the command in the current or specified directory. For example, since fixed disk users keep external DOS commands in the DOS subdirectory on drive C, they would want to issue the command

```
C:\> PATH C:\DOS <ENTER>
```

If DOS fails to locate the external command as specified, it will use the path entry and search the DOS subdirectory for the command entered. If DOS locates the command, it executes it. If not, DOS displays the message

```
Bad command or file name
```

The PATH command allows you to specify several directories that DOS will traverse in search of your external commands. If you have other directories, you can include the directories in the path. Given the PATH command

```
C:\> PATH  C:\DOS;C:\LOTUS;C:\DBASE <ENTER>
```

if DOS fails to locate the external command that you enter, it will first search the DOS subdirectory for the command, followed by LOTUS and DBASE, in that order. As you can see, the PATH command includes each directory DOS is to search, separated by a semicolon.

If DOS locates the command in one of the specified directories, it executes the command and the command terminates. If it does not locate the command, DOS continues searching the next subdirectory in the command path. If DOS exhausts its list of directories, it displays the following message:

```
Bad command or file name
```

If you simply type **PATH** at the DOS prompt, DOS will display the current command path:

```
C:\> PATH <ENTER>
PATH=C:\DOS

C:\>
```

In this case, DOS automatically searches the DOS directory for your external commands. Your command path may differ from the one shown here.

To delete the command path, place a semicolon in the PATH command line, as shown here:

```
C:\> PATH ;  <ENTER>
```

If you again invoke PATH, you will see that DOS has deleted the list of additional directories that it should search for external commands:

```
C:\> PATH <ENTER>
No Path

C:\>
```

Working Within the Shell

In Chapter 11, "Getting Started with File Organization," you learned how to perform basic subdirectory manipulation with the DOS shell. In this lesson you will learn to copy, rename, and even move files from one DOS directory to another.

Use the same floppy disk that you have worked with throughout this chapter. Invoke the shell and select drive A as the current drive. Select the DBASE directory, and then select the DBASE.DAT file. Using the File menu, select the Copy option to copy the file to the LOTUS directory as NOTES.NEW.

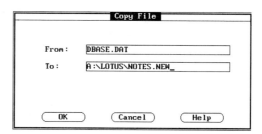

As you know, if the target file name does not change in a file copy operation, DOS does not require you to specify it. In this case, to copy the DBASE.DAT file to the LOTUS directory, keeping the same name, you only have to specify the target directory name, as shown here:

```
┌──────────────────────────────────────────────────┐
│                   ▀▀Copy File▀▀                   │
│                                                    │
│                                                    │
│   From :     ┌────────────────────────────────┐   │
│              │DBASE.DAT                       │   │
│   To :       └────────────────────────────────┘   │
│              ┌────────────────────────────────┐   │
│              │A:\LOTUS_                       │   │
│              └────────────────────────────────┘   │
│                                                    │
│                                                    │
│       (   OK   )      ( Cancel )      ( Help )     │
└──────────────────────────────────────────────────┘
```

Select the LOTUS directory as the current directory. Next, select the files DBASE.DAT and NOTES.NEW. By specifying the directory name DBASE as the target directory, you direct DOS to copy all of the selected files to the DBASE directory. Thus, the shell allows you to copy multiple files at one time.

As you learned earlier, the RENAME command does not allow you to rename a file from one disk to another or from one directory to another. However, when you are using the shell, the Move option on the File menu allows you to move (rather than rename) a file from one disk or directory to another. Select the NOTES.NEW file from the LOTUS directory. Using the Move option, move the file to the root directory on drive A, as shown here:

```
┌──────────────────────────────────────────────────┐
│                   ▀▀Move File▀▀                   │
│                                                    │
│                                                    │
│   From :     ┌────────────────────────────────┐   │
│              │NOTES.NEW                       │   │
│   To :       └────────────────────────────────┘   │
│              ┌────────────────────────────────┐   │
│              │A:\_                            │   │
│              └────────────────────────────────┘   │
│                                                    │
│                                                    │
│       (   OK   )      ( Cancel )      ( Help )     │
└──────────────────────────────────────────────────┘
```

When the command completes, the file will no longer reside in the LOTUS directory, but rather in the root directory. Note that you can move multiple files at one time. To do so, simply select all of the files you want to move. When you specify the target location for the files, the shell will move each file.

From the DOS command line, DOS does not allow you to rename a directory. However, if you select a directory and invoke the File menu, the Rename option allows you to rename a directory, as shown here:

As you can see, the shell not only supports all of the directory capabilities that you have at the command line, but it adds several more.

Cleaning Up the Root Directory

Select drive C as your current drive. Perform a directory listing of the disk's root directory:

```
C:\> DIR <ENTER>
```

As you know, all external DOS commands should reside in a directory called DOS. Later in this book you will learn about the CONFIG.SYS and AUTOEXEC.BAT files. For now, simply note that the following files are the only files that should reside in your root directory:

❏   CONFIG.SYS contains DOS configuration values.

❏   AUTOEXEC.BAT contains a list of commands that DOS executes at system startup.

❏   COMMAND.COM contains DOS internal commands and the command processor that displays the DOS prompt.

The remainder of your root directory entries should be directory names. If your root directory contains files other than these three, you need to "clean up" the directory by moving the additional files to DOS directories or by deleting them if they are no longer required. As you add new software packages to your fixed disk, always create a unique directory for each new program.

Practice

Place a formatted disk in drive A, and create the US, CANADA, and MEXICO directories:

```
A:\> MKDIR   \US <ENTER>
A:\> MKDIR   \CANADA <ENTER>
A:\> MKDIR   \MEXICO <ENTER>
```

Next, issue the following COPY command to create the file SIZE.NTS:

```
A:\> COPY   CON   \CANADA\SIZE.NTS <ENTER>
CANADA contains more square miles than the U.S. <ENTER>
^Z <ENTER>
     1 File(s) copied

A:\>
```

Once this file exists, copy it from the CANADA directory to the US directory, as shown here:

```
A> COPY   \CANADA\SIZE.NTS   \US\SIZE.NTS <ENTER>
```

Remember, since the target file name does not change, you could have also used either of these commands:

```
A:\> COPY   \CANADA\SIZE.NTS   \US\*.* <ENTER>
A:\> COPY   \CANADA\SIZE.NTS   \US <ENTER>
```

Next, create the file CAPITAL.CTY in the MEXICO directory, as shown here:

```
A:\> COPY  CON  \MEXICO\CAPITAL.CTY <ENTER>
Mexico City is the capital of Mexico <ENTER>
^Z <ENTER>
     1 File(s) copied

A:\>
```

Using the TYPE command, display the contents of this file:

```
A:\> TYPE  \MEXICO\CAPITAL.CTY <ENTER>
```

Delete the SIZE.NTS file from the CANADA directory, as shown here:

```
A:\> DEL  \CANADA\SIZE.NTS <ENTER>
```

Using the RENAME command, rename the CAPITAL.CTY file to CAPITAL.MEX in the MEXICO directory:

```
A:\> REN  \MEXICO\CAPITAL.CTY  CAPITAL.MEX <ENTER>
```

Remember, RENAME does not allow you to specify a path name before the target file. The following command will fail:

```
A:\> REN  \MEXICO\CAPITAL.MEX  \MEXICO\CAPITAL.CTY <ENTER>
```

Select drive C as your current drive and issue the TREE command to display the directory structure of your disk:

```
A:\> C: <ENTER>
C:\> TREE  C:\ <ENTER>
```

If you include the /F switch, you can display the name of every file on your disk.

```
C:\> TREE  C:\  /F <ENTER>
```

If you are using DOS 5 or later, issue the following DIR command to display the name of every file on your disk:

```
C:\> DIR  /S  /P <ENTER>
```

The /S switch directs DIR to display the files in the directory specified, as well as files in directories beneath the specified directory. The /P switch directs DIR to pause with each screenful of files.

Issue the PATH command to display the directories DOS automatically searches for external commands:

```
C:\> PATH <ENTER>
```

Invoke the DOS shell and select drive A as the current drive. Next, select MEXICO as the current directory. Highlight the file CAPITAL.MEX and invoke the File menu Copy option. Copy the file to the US directory, as shown here:

```
┌─────────────────────────────────────────────┐
│                  ▐ Copy File ▌                │
├─────────────────────────────────────────────┤
│                                               │
│     From:   ┌─────────────────────────┐       │
│             │ CAPITAL.MEX             │       │
│     To:     └─────────────────────────┘       │
│             ┌─────────────────────────┐       │
│             │ A:\US_                  │       │
│             └─────────────────────────┘       │
│                                               │
│                                               │
│      ( OK )      ( Cancel )      ( Help )      │
└─────────────────────────────────────────────┘
```

If you examine the US directory, you can see that the file now resides in the directory.

displays the files in the current directory:

```
Volume in drive A has no label
Volume Serial Number is 4428-16F4
Directory of A:\HISTORY\NOTES

.               <DIR>      04-09-93    7:04a
..              <DIR>      04-09-93    7:04a
        2 file(s)              0 bytes
                         317440 bytes free
```

The command

```
C:\> DIR A:.. <ENTER>
```

displays the files in the HISTORY directory, as shown here:

```
Volume in drive A has no label
Volume Serial Number is 4428-16F4
Directory of A:\HISTORY

.               <DIR>      04-09-93    7:01a
..              <DIR>      04-09-93    7:01a
CIVILWAR LS1        42     04-09-93    7:02a
NOTES           <DIR>      04-09-93    7:04a
        4 file(s)             42 bytes
                         317440 bytes free
```

How Many Current Directories Are There?

So far, you have worked with DOS subdirectories that only reside on drive A. Since most systems should have at least two disks, it makes sense that DOS should keep track of a current directory for each.

If you use the CHDIR command to select the HISTORY subdirectory as the default directory for drive A, DOS will change the subdirectory for drive A as desired, while leaving the root directory as the current directory for drive C:

Select both of the files in the US directory. Next, invoke the Move option from the File menu. Type **\CANADA** to move the files out of the US directory and into the CANADA directory. When this command completes, the files no longer exist in the US directory; instead, they have been placed in CANADA.

Finally, with US as the current directory, select the Rename option and rename the directory as AMERICA:

 Remember Only the shell allows you to rename a DOS directory or to move files from one directory to another.

Review

1. What DIR command would list files with the COM extension that reside in the directory UTIL?

2. What is a path name?

3. What command would display the contents of the file STATES.CAP that resides in the directory HISTORY?

4. Why does the following command fail?

```
C:\> REN  \HISTORY\STATES.CAP  \HISTORY\STATES.NTS <ENTER>
```

5. What is the function of the TREE command?

6. What is the function of the following command:

```
C:\> PATH   C:\DOS;C:\UTIL  <ENTER>
```

7. How can you rename a subdirectory?

8. What files should reside in your hard disk's root directory?

Key Points

Displaying the Files in a Specific Directory

To perform a directory listing of the files that reside in a DOS directory other than the current directory, simply place the directory name in the DIR command line, as shown here:

```
C:\> DIR   \SUBDIR  <ENTER>
```

Displaying the Contents of a File in a DOS Directory

Just as the TYPE command allows you to display the contents of a file in the current directory by using the command

```
C:\> TYPE FILENAME.EXT  <ENTER>
```

TYPE also allows you to display the contents of a file that resides in a different directory. To do so, simply precede the file name with the name of its directory, as shown here:

continues . . .

```
C:\> TYPE   \SUBDIR\FILENAME.EXT <ENTER>
```

Deleting a File in a Directory

To delete a file that resides in a directory other than the current directory, simply precede the file name with its directory name, as shown here:

```
C:\> DEL   \SUBDIR\FILENAME.EXT <ENTER>
```

Renaming a File in a Directory

To rename a file that resides in a directory other than the current directory, precede the source file name with the directory name:

```
C:\> REN   \SUBDIR\FILENAME.EXT   NEWNAME.EXT <ENTER>
```

Note that you do not precede the target file name with a directory name. RENAME knows the target file will reside in its original directory. If you precede the target file name with a directory name, the RENAME command will fail.

PATH Command

The PATH command allows you to define a list of directories that DOS will search for external commands each time it fails to locate the command in the current directory. For example, the command

continues . . .

Key Points (continued)

```
C:\> PATH   C:\DOS  <ENTER>
```

directs DOS to search the DOS directory on drive C for external commands. Likewise, the following PATH command tells DOS to first look in the DOS directory and, if necessary, in a directory called BATCH:

```
C:\> PATH   C:\DOS;C:\BATCH   <ENTER>
```

Root Directory Files

As you organize your hard disk, keep in mind that your files and commands should reside in specific directories. The only files your root directory should contain are CONFIG.SYS, COMMAND.COM, and AUTOEXEC.BAT.

CHAPTER

Understanding DOS Device Names

As you have learned, you must assign unique names to each of your files on disk. In a similar manner, DOS assigns each of your computer's devices a unique name. Throughout this book, you have been using the device name CON to create files from the keyboard.

In addition to the CON device name, DOS also uses the names shown here:

Name	Function
COM1	First serial device connected to your system
LPT1	First parallel device connected to your system
PRN	First parallel device connected to your system
AUX	First serial device connected to your system
LPT*n*	Additional (optional) parallel devices connected to your system; DOS supports LPT1, LPT2, LPT3
COM*n*	Additional (optional) serial devices connected to your system; DOS supports COM1, COM2, COM3, and COM4

As you will learn in this chapter, a few of these names reference the same device. You will also learn how to set several characteristics for your screen display and keyboard. In Chapter 14, "Using Your Printer," you will learn how you use your system printer under DOS. You must be familiar with DOS device names before you can work with your printer.

Using CON for Input and Output

Throughout this book, you have used the device name CON to create files from your keyboard, as shown here:

```
C:\> COPY  CON  CONSOLE.NTS <ENTER>
The CON device can be <ENTER>
used for input or output. <ENTER>
^Z <ENTER>
      1 File(s) copied

C:\>
```

When you use CON as the source of your file-copying operations, CON refers to your keyboard:

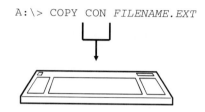

A:\> COPY CON *FILENAME.EXT*

DOS also allows you to use the CON device name as the target of a file-copying command, as shown here:

```
C:\> COPY  CONSOLE.NTS   CON <ENTER>
The CON device can be  <ENTER>
used for input or output.  <ENTER>
     1 File(s) copied

C:\>
```

When you use CON as the target of a file-copying command, CON points to your screen display:

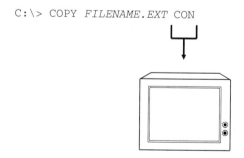

C:\> COPY *FILENAME.EXT* CON

To determine if CON is referencing the screen or the keyboard, simply ask yourself if CON is the source or the target. If CON is the source device, it references the keyboard; if CON is the target, it references the screen display.

Serial Versus Parallel Devices

When your computer communicates with (sends data to or from) the devices attached to your system, it normally does so in one of two ways: parallel or serial communication. Your computer stores information (numbers, characters, and so on) as a series of ones and zeros, called *binary digits,* or *bits.* Each letter of the alphabet, for example, has a unique series of binary digits, as shown here:

Letter	Binary Representation
A	01000001
B	01000010
C	01000011
D	01000100
.	.
.	.
.	.
Z	01011010

To simplify the manipulation of these binary digits, computers group the digits into groups of eight bits, called *bytes*:

You learned earlier that a byte can be viewed as a character's worth of information; now you know why.

When your computer sends data to a parallel device, your computer uses eight wires to transmit data, which allows it to send a byte of information at a time (see Figure 13-1). Thus, a parallel device actually transmits data one character at a time. As you will see, this mode of transmission is much faster than serial data communication.

Parallel data communications

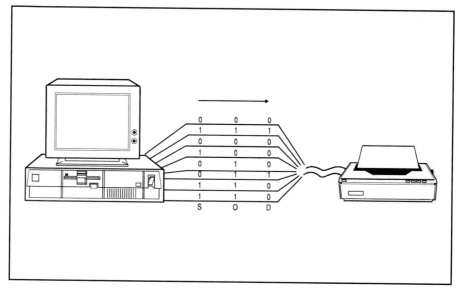

When your computer transmits data to a serial device, it sends data over one wire, one bit at a time, as shown in Figure 13-2. Since serial devices can use only one wire to transmit data, instead of eight, serial communication is much slower than parallel communication.

You need to distinguish between parallel and serial devices because your printer is either a serial or parallel device. Depending upon its type, the steps you must perform to use your printer are different.

Most computers come with at least one parallel and one serial connection, as shown in Figure 13-3. These connections are called *ports*. DOS assigns a unique name to each port. The parallel port, for example, is called LPT1, while the serial port is COM1. In the past, most line printers were parallel devices, so the letters "LPT" stood for "line printer." Similarly, older data communications modems connected to the serial port, so the letters "COM" stood for "communications." The number 1 in both LPT1 and COM1 tells you that these are the first of several possible ports. Remember, DOS supports three parallel ports (LPT1 through LPT3), as well as four serial ports (COM1 through COM4). As you will see, copying files to these devices is quite straightforward.

FIGURE
13-2

Serial data communications

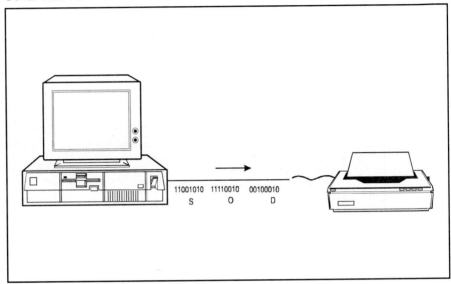

FIGURE
13-3

Serial and parallel ports

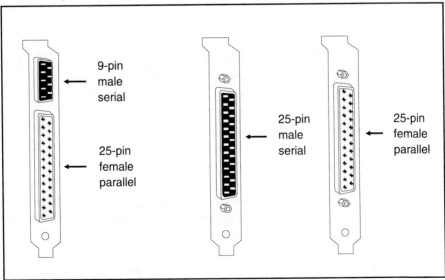

Accessing LPT1 and COM1

If you are not sure whether your printer is a parallel device connected to LPT1 or a serial device connected to COM1, you can either refer to your printer documentation or examine the cables that connect your printer to your computer, as shown in Figure 13-4.

Next, create the following file:

```
C:\> COPY  CON  DEVICES.DAT <ENTER>
LPT1 is  a  parallel  device. <ENTER>
COM1 is a serial device. <ENTER>
^Z <ENTER>
     1 File(s) copied

C:\>
```

Turn on your printer and make sure that its online light is lit. Next, issue either the command

```
C:\> COPY  DEVICES.DAT  LPT1 <ENTER>
```

Serial and parallel cables

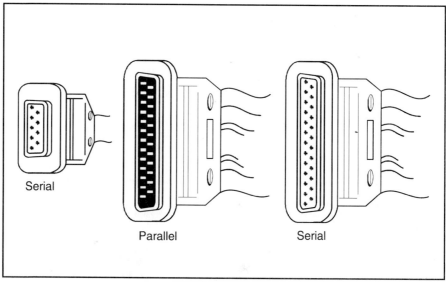

Serial

Parallel

Serial

or the command

```
C:\> COPY  DEVICES.DAT  COM1  <ENTER>
```

depending on your printer type. In either case, your printer should print the contents of the file.

If you are using a serial printer and the text is printed as unrecognizable characters, your printer and your computer are not transmitting and receiving at the same speed. You will need to refer to your printer documentation to see what your printer's data communications parameters are. Keep these parameter values available so you have them when you examine the MODE command later in this chapter.

PRN and AUX

Since most line printers attach to the LPT1 device, DOS also defines the device name PRN as referencing that port. Because PRN is easier to remember, DOS allows you to use it to reference your printer, as shown here:

```
C:\> COPY  DEVICE.DAT  PRN  <ENTER>
```

Many people classify a device such as a mouse or modem as an auxiliary device. Because many of these devices connect to your computer's serial port COM1, DOS also allows you to refer to COM1 as AUX (for "auxiliary"). Assuming you have a serial printer (rather than a mouse or modem) attached to COM1, issue the following command:

```
C:\> COPY  DEVICES.DAT  AUX  <ENTER>
```

Using the MODE Command

As you will see throughout the remainder of this book, many of your devices allow you to customize them for your specific needs. The MODE command provides you with many such capabilities. MODE is an external DOS command.

To begin, let's use MODE to change your screen display. By default, your screen is set up to display 25 rows of 80-character lines (see Figure 13-5). However, if you have a CGA, EGA, or VGA video adapter, DOS allows you to increase your text size by using MODE as shown here:

```
C:\> MODE  40 <ENTER>
```

When you press ENTER, DOS will change your display to 40 characters a line, which makes characters larger. The screen will still display 25 lines of text. To reset your screen to 80 columns, use the following command:

```
C:\> MODE  80 <ENTER>
```

Default screen display

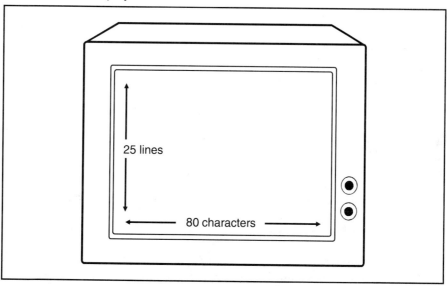

25 lines

80 characters

DOS will restore your screen to its default settings.

MODE supports several values in the command line. The format of the MODE command for changing screen settings is

```
MODE n
```

where *n* specifies one of the following values:

Value	Meaning
MONO	Specifies a monochrome display adapter whose column width is always 80 characters
40	Selects 40-column mode for a color display
80	Selects 80-column mode for a color display
BW40	Selects 40-column mode for a color display with color disabled
BW80	Selects 80-column mode for a color display with color disabled
CO40	Selects 40-column mode for a color display with color enabled
CO80	Selects 80-column mode for a color display with color enabled

If you are using DOS 4 or later and an EGA or VGA monitor, you can use the MODE command to change the number of lines of text displayed to 43 (EGA and VGA) or 50 (VGA only). Before you can use the MODE command to set the number of lines to 43 or 50, you must first install the ANSI.SYS device driver as discussed in Chapter 27, "Customizing Your System Using CONFIG.SYS." The format of the MODE command in this case is as follows:

```
MODE  CON[:]   [COLS=NumberOfColumns] [LINES=NumberOfLines]
```

The number of columns can be either 40 or 80. The following command sets the number of lines to 43.

```
C:\> MODE  CON  LINES=43 <ENTER>
```

Using MODE to Improve Your Keyboard's Responsiveness

If you are using DOS 4 or later, you can use the MODE command to improve your keyboard's responsiveness. Your keyboard has a *typematic rate*, which determines how quickly your computer repeats a character if a key remains depressed. The higher the value you assign to the typematic rate, the faster your keyboard responds. The format of the MODE command to set your keyboard's typematic rate is a follows:

```
MODE CON[:]  [RATE=RepeatRate  DELAY=DelayPeriod]
```

The *RepeatRate* value can range from 1 to 32. Table 13-1 lists the number of characters per second your keyboard will repeat based on different values.

The *DelayPeriod* is a value from 1 to 4 that specifies the amount of time DOS will wait after you first press a key before it begins to repeat characters. Table 13-2 lists the delay periods for each value.

You must set both the rate and delay values at the same time. You cannot invoke MODE with just one value. The following MODE command selects the fastest keyboard setting.

```
C:\> MODE  CON  RATE=32  DELAY=1  <ENTER>
```

Experiment with different settings until you find the keyboard response that is most comfortable.

Using MODE to Set Printer Characteristics

Depending on your printer type (if you have an Epson- or IBM-compatible printer), you may be able to use the MODE command to set the character size and number of characters per line that appear on your printed output. Under DOS 4 or later, the format of the MODE command to customize your printer output is as follows:

```
MODE LPTn[:] [COLS=CharactersPerLine] [Lines=LinesPerInch]
[RETRY=RetrySetting]
```

The *CharactersPerLine* value must be 80 or 132. By default, if you try to print more than 80 characters on a line, your printer will either wrap the characters to the next line or simply ignore them. If you select 132 characters per line, your printer will compress the size of each character, allowing it to fit more characters in the same printout space. The *LinesPerInch* value specifies the number of lines of text per vertical inch on your printout. The value must be 6 or 8. By default, your printer prints

| TABLE 13-1 | Keyboard Repeat Rate Values and Their Corresponding Characters per Second |

Repeat Rate	Characters per Second	Repeat Rate	Characters per Second
1	2.0	17	8.0
2	2.1	18	8.6
3	2.3	19	9.2
4	2.5	20	10.0
5	2.7	21	10.9
6	3.0	22	12.0
7	3.3	23	13.3
8	3.7	24	15.0
9	4.0	25	16.0
10	4.3	26	17.1
11	4.6	27	18.5
12	5.0	28	20.0
13	5.5	29	21.8
14	6.0	30	24.0
15	6.7	31	26.7
16	7.5	32	30.0

TABLE 13-2 Delay Period Values

Delay Period	Delay in Seconds
1	0.25 seconds
2	0.50 seconds
3	0.75 seconds
4	1.0 second

6 lines per inch. If you select 8, your printer will compress each character's height. The *RetrySetting* specifies how DOS should behave when it tries to send characters to the printer and the printer is not ready. Table 13-3 specifies several retry values. By default, DOS uses N, or No action.

Provided your printer is an Epson or IBM compatible, the following MODE command selects the smallest (most condensed) print.

```
C:\> MODE  LPT1:  COLS=132  LINES=8 <ENTER>
```

TABLE 13-3 DOS Printer Retry Options

Retry Option	DOS Action
E	Return an Error status to the command printing the information
B	Return a Busy status to the command printing the information
P	Retry the operation until successful
R	Return a Ready status to the command printing the information
N	Perform no action

Specifying Data Communications Parameters

Because serial devices have only one wire over which they can transmit data, you must ensure that your computer and the devices at the other end of the wire are in agreement as to how they will communicate. The values that the two devices must agree upon are called *data communications parameters*. The MODE command allows you to specify these parameters. Depending on your DOS version, the format of the MODE command to set port characteristics will differ. If you are using DOS 3.3 or earlier, turn to the MODE command in the Command Reference section of this book. If you are using DOS 4 or later, the format of the MODE command is as follows:

```
MODE COMn[:] BAUD=BaudRate [PARITY=Parity] [DATA=DataBits]
[STOP=StopBits] [RETRY=RetryOption]
```

All of the items within brackets are optional. If you do not specify values for these optional parameters, DOS will use the default values defined here:

Parameter	Effect
BaudRate	Specifies the *baud rate*, or speed at which your port will communicate. Valid speeds include 110, 150, 300, 600, 1200, 2400, 4800, 9600, and 19200. MODE requires you to enter only the first two digits of your desired baud rate. The default baud rate is 2400.
Parity	Specifies the type of parity the devices will use. E is even parity, O is odd, M is mark, S is space, and N is no parity. The default parity is E.
DataBits	Specifies the number of data bits in each transmission, either 5, 6, 7, or 8. The default value is 7.
StopBits	Specifies the number of stop bits in each character transmission, either 1, 1.5, or 2. The default for 110 baud is 2. For all other baud rates, the default is 1.
RetryOption	Specifies one of the retry options listed in Table 13-3.

As already stated, the items that appear within the brackets are optional. As such, all of the following are valid MODE commands:

```
C:\> MODE   COM1   BAUD=4800 <ENTER>
C:\> MODE   COM1   BAUD=4800 PARITY=E <ENTER>
C:\> MODE   COM1   BAUD=9600 PARITY=E DATA=8 <ENTER>
C:\> MODE   COM1   BAUD=9600 PARITY=E DATA=8 STOP=2 <ENTER>
C:\> MODE   COM1   BAUD=2400 PARITY=O DATA=8 STOP=2 RETRY=P
<ENTER>
```

Let's take a look at several MODE commands in detail. First, the command

```
C:\> MODE   COM1: /STATUS <ENTER>
```

causes DOS to display the current settings for your device:

```
Status for device COM1:
─────────────────────────
Retry=NONE

C:\>
```

In a similar manner, the command

```
C:\> MODE   COM1   BAUD=4800 <ENTER>
```

sets the baud rate (speed) for COM1 to 4800. Remember, because MODE requires only the first two digits of the baud rate, the following command is functionally identical:

```
C:\> MODE   COM1   BAUD=48 <ENTER>
```

This command sets the speed and parity for COM1:

```
C:\> MODE   COM1   BAUD=4800 PARITY=E <ENTER>
```

The only time that you should have to worry about setting your serial device's characteristics with MODE is when you attach a device to your serial port. In such cases, the documentation that accompanies your device should specify the correct MODE command line.

Directing DOS to Use Your Serial Printer

For most of the printer capabilities examined in the next chapter, it is assumed that your printer is connected to your parallel port. If, instead, you are using a serial printer, you must tell DOS to send its output not to LPT1 but rather to COM1. To do so, use the MODE

command shown here:

```
C:\> MODE  LPT1:=COM1 <ENTER>
```

DOS will then use your serial printer for the default printer operations.

Practice

Use the following COPY CON command in order to create the file CONSOLE.NTS:

```
C:\> COPY  CON  CONSOLE.NTS <ENTER>
The CON device name <ENTER>
can be used for input <ENTER>
and output operations. <ENTER>
^Z <ENTER>
     1 File(s) copied

C:\>
```

Next, issue the command

```
C:\> COPY  CONSOLE.NTS  CON <ENTER>
```

DOS will display the contents of the file on your screen display as shown here:

```
The CON device name
can be used for input
and output operations.
     1 File(s) copied

C:\>
```

As you can see, for input CON points to your keyboard, and for output CON points to your screen display.

Next, turn your printer on and make sure that the online light illuminates. Depending on your system configuration, issue either of these commands:

```
C:\> COPY  CONSOLE.NTS  LPT1 <ENTER>
C:\> COPY  CONSOLE.NTS  COM1 <ENTER>
```

Keep in mind that DOS also assigns the device names PRN and AUX to reference LPT1 and COM1, respectively:

```
C:\> COPY  CONSOLE.NTS  PRN <ENTER>
C:\> COPY  CONSOLE.NTS  AUX <ENTER>
```

If you have a color system, issue the command

```
C:\> MODE  40 <ENTER>
```

DOS will clear your screen display and set the screen to 40 characters per row. To restore the screen to 80-column mode, enter

```
C:\> MODE  80 <ENTER>
```

If you are using DOS 4 or later, hold down a key on your keyboard such as the A key and watch how fast the character repeats. Next, issue the following MODE command to improve your keyboard's responsiveness.

```
C:\> MODE   CON   RATE=32   DELAY=1 <ENTER>
```

Hold down the A key again, and note the speed difference in which the character repeats.

Review

1. The CON device name can reference your screen or keyboard. How can you tell which device CON is referencing?
2. How does serial data communication differ from parallel?
3. What are the COM1 and LPT1 devices?
4. List four capabilities of the MODE command.
5. What is the purpose of the following command?

```
C:\> MODE LPT1:=COM1 <ENTER>
```

6. What are the PRN and AUX devices?

Key Points

Using CON

The CON device name can be used for input and output operations. When you use CON as the source of your file-copying operations, as in the command

```
C:\> COPY CON FILENAME.EXT <ENTER>
```

continues . . .

CON points to your keyboard. When you instead use it as the target of your file-copying operations, as in

```
C:\> COPY FILENAME.EXT CON <ENTER>
```

CON points to your screen display.

Using DOS Device Names with COPY

Just as the COPY command allows you to copy the contents of one file to another, COPY also allows you to copy information to or from a device name as the source or the target of the information, as shown here:

```
C:\> COPY CON FILENAME.EXT
```
Source name

```
C:\> COPY FILENAME.EXT PRN
```
Target name

CHAPTER

Using Your Printer

*I*n Chapter 13, "Understanding DOS Device Names," you learned that you can copy files to your printer by specifying the printer's device name as the target of your file-copying command, as shown here:

```
C:\> COPY FILENAME.EXT  PRN <ENTER>
```

In this chapter you will learn that DOS provides several other printer capabilities, such as printing the current contents of your screen display and echoing to your printer each character that DOS sends to your screen. You will also examine the PRINT command, which allows you to place several files in a waiting line to be printed. PRINT in turn prints these files one after another, while letting you continue to execute other commands as the files print.

Getting Started with Your Printer

If you are using a serial printer, you must give DOS a little more information before you examine DOS printer capabilities in this chapter. If you are not sure whether your system has a parallel printer or a serial printer, check the plug that connects your printer to your computer, as shown here:

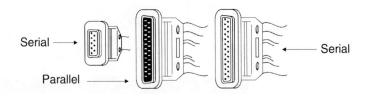

If you are using a parallel printer, as most of you probably are, you can continue reading at the section titled "Printing the Contents of Your Screen Display."

DOS uses the LPT1 device name and its associated port as the default for many operations. Thus, if you have a serial printer, you must first issue the MODE command to route data to the serial port, as shown here:

```
C:\> MODE  LPT1:=COM1 <ENTER>
```

When you do so, DOS will display the following message:

```
Resident portion of MODE loaded

LPT1: rerouted to COM1:

C:\>
```

You are now ready to continue with the lessons in this chapter.

Printing the Contents of Your Screen Display

Issue the following DIR command:

```
C:\> DIR \DOS <ENTER>
```

When DIR completes its directory listing, press the SHIFT-PRTSC key combination (see Figure 14-1). DOS will copy the current contents of your screen display to your printer, as shown in Figure 14-2. This printout of your screen contents is called a *hardcopy listing.*

If nothing happens when you issue the SHIFT-PRTSC key combination, check the following:

❏   Is your printer turned on, and is the online light illuminated?

❏   If you have a serial printer, did you issue the MODE command as previously discussed?

❏   Are you holding the SHIFT key down while you press PRTSC?

❏   If you are using a serial printer, did you use the MODE command to define the printer port's speed, as discussed in Chapter 13, "Understanding DOS Device Names"?

FIGURE
14-1
Location of SHIFT and PRTSC keys

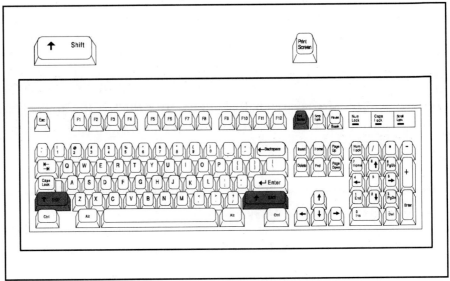

FIGURE
14-2
Printing the screen's contents

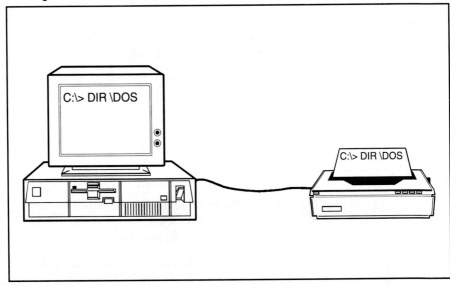

Printing Graphics Images with SHIFT-PRTSC

As long as your screen display contains only text, the SHIFT-PRTSC key combination can print the contents of your screen with no additional preparation. However, if your screen display contains graphics images, such as the spreadsheet graph in Figure 14-3 or even the DOS shell, you must first invoke the GRAPHICS command before DOS can copy the screen contents to your printer. GRAPHICS is an external DOS command.

The Command Reference section of this book provides a complete discussion of the GRAPHICS command-line options. In most cases, you can simply invoke GRAPHICS as follows:

```
C:\> GRAPHICS <ENTER>
```

You need to invoke GRAPHICS only once per user session. Once you have done so, DOS will be able to print text or graphics screen displays when you press SHIFT-PRTSC.

Graphics images

SALES BY MARKET

Echoing Screen Characters to Your Printer

Just as the SHIFT-PRTSC key combination directs DOS to print the current contents of your screen display, the CTRL-PRTSC key combination (see Figure 14-4) directs DOS to echo each character it writes to your screen to your printer as well.

At the DOS prompt, press the CTRL-PRTSC key combination. Nothing should happen. Next, issue the DIR command:

```
C:\> DIR \DOS <ENTER>
```

As DOS writes the characters to your screen display, it also writes them to your printer. If you press the CTRL-PRTSC key combination a second time, DOS will quit sending characters to your printer.

Location of CTRL and PRTSC keys

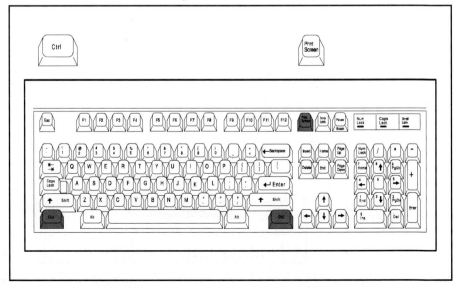

Using the PRINT Command

So far, you have seen three ways to copy information to your printer:

❏ By using LPT1 or COM1 as the target of a file-copying command:

```
C:\> COPY FILENAME.EXT  LPT1 <ENTER>
```

❏ By using the SHIFT-PRTSC key combination to print your screen contents
❏ By using the CTRL-PRTSC key combination to enable character echoing to your printer

As you will see in this section, however, the PRINT command gives you tremendous flexibility as you print your files. PRINT is an external DOS command that resides in the DOS directory.

So that you will have several different files to print, create the following three files:

```
C:\> COPY  CON  VOWELS.DAT <ENTER>
A <ENTER>
E <ENTER>
I <ENTER>
O <ENTER>
U <ENTER>
^Z <ENTER>
     1 File(s) copied

C:\> COPY  CON  NUMBERS.DAT <ENTER>
11111 <ENTER>
22222 <ENTER>
33333 <ENTER>
44444 <ENTER>
55555 <ENTER>
^Z <ENTER>
     1 File(s) copied

C:\> COPY  CON  PRINT.NTS <ENTER>
```

```
The DOS PRINT command <ENTER>
is an external DOS command. <ENTER>
^Z <ENTER>
     1 File(s) copied

C:\>
```

Next, issue the following PRINT command:

```
C:\> PRINT   VOWELS.DAT <ENTER>
```

PRINT may display the following prompt on your screen the first time per session that you invoke it to determine to which device your printer is attached:

```
Name of list device [PRN]:
```

If you are using a serial printer, you will need to type **COM1**. If you are using a parallel printer, you can simply press ENTER, choosing the device PRN by default.

One of the major ways that PRINT differs from COPY is that when you issue a COPY command such as

```
C:\> COPY FILENAME.EXT   LPT1 <ENTER>
```

you must wait for the command to complete before you can continue. When you use the PRINT command, however, DOS immediately redisplays your system prompt, allowing you to continue working as the document prints. If you have a large document that contains several pages of text, waiting for DOS to finish printing the document before you can continue could waste considerable time.

In addition, PRINT allows you to send several files to the system printer at one time. For example, the following command directs PRINT to print the files VOWELS.DAT and NUMBERS.DAT:

```
C:\> PRINT   VOWELS.DAT   NUMBERS.DAT <ENTER>
```

In this case, PRINT will display the following message on your screen:

```
C:\VOWELS.DAT is currently being printed
C:\NUMBERS.DAT is in queue
```

Each time you tell PRINT to print a file while another file is printing, PRINT places the file into a waiting list called a *print queue.* While PRINT is printing the VOWELS.DAT file, the message

```
C:\NUMBERS.DAT is in queue
```

tells you that the NUMBERS.DAT file is waiting to be printed. If you issue the command

```
C:\> PRINT  PRINT.NTS <ENTER>
```

PRINT will add the PRINT.NTS file to the queue, displaying

```
C:\VOWELS.DAT is currently being printed
C:\NUMBERS.DAT is in queue
C:\PRINT.NTS is in queue
```

PRINT prints each file in the order the file enters the queue. Thus, if your print queue contains

```
C:\FIRST.DAT is currently being printed
C:\SECOND.DAT is in queue
C:\THIRD.DAT is in queue
C:\FOURTH.DAT is in queue
```

PRINT will print the files in the same order the files appear in the queue, from top to bottom.

PRINT also supports DOS wildcard characters. For example, the command

```
C:\> PRINT  C:*.DAT <ENTER>
```

results in

```
C:\VOWELS.DAT is in queue
C:\NUMBERS.DAT is in queue
```

Just as the TYPE command cannot display all file types, not all files can be printed with PRINT. If you try to print a program file like COMMAND.COM, your printer will display unrecognizable characters, and your printer's bell will probably sound.

Chapter 15, "Getting the Most from Print," will examine several advanced applications of the PRINT command. For now, however, let's learn how to print files from within the shell.

Printing Files from Within the Shell

Printing files from within the shell is quite straightforward. To begin, select the file you want to print. In this example we will select VOWELS.DAT. Next, using the File menu, select the Print option, as shown in Figure 14-5.

DOS will begin printing your file. Now, select the VOWELS.DAT, PRINT.NTS, and NUMBERS.DAT files. To select multiple files, press the SHIFT-F8 key combination. Next, highlight each file and press the SPACEBAR. After you highlight the last file, press SHIFT-F8 again.

When you invoke the Print option, DOS will print all three files in the order in which they appear in the directory listing.

When you select the system File menu, if the Print option is not available (if it appears in light gray on color systems or does not appear in the menu on monochrome systems), you must first issue the PRINT command from the DOS prompt. If you select the Print option when it is not available, the shell will display the dialog box shown here, which directs you to invoke PRINT.COM:

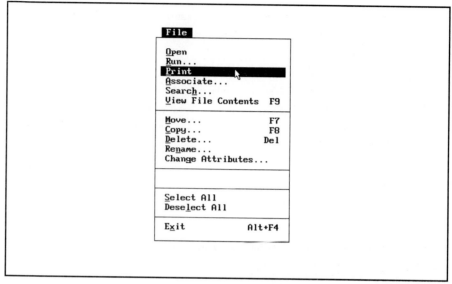

FIGURE
14-5

Selecting the Print option from the File menu

Practice

With a newly formatted disk in drive A, create the FOOTBALL.DAT, BASEBALL.DAT, and HOOPS.DAT files, as shown here:

```
C:\> COPY  CON A:FOOTBALL.DAT <ENTER>
BILLS <ENTER>
BROWNS <ENTER>
BEARS <ENTER>
LIONS <ENTER>
^Z <ENTER>
     1 File(s) copied

C:\> COPY  CON A:BASEBALL.DAT <ENTER>
GIANTS <ENTER>
METS <ENTER>
ANGELS <ENTER>
DODGERS <ENTER>
^Z <ENTER>
     1 File(s) copied
```

```
C:\> COPY  CON A:HOOPS.DAT <ENTER>
LAKERS <ENTER>
SUNS <ENTER>
CELTICS <ENTER>
SONICS <ENTER>
^Z <ENTER>
      1 File(s) copied

C:\>
```

Next, if your system has a serial printer, issue the following MODE command:

```
C:\> MODE  LPT1:=COM1 <ENTER>
```

If your system has a parallel printer, do not issue this command.

When the MODE command completes, issue the following DIR command:

```
C:\> DIR A: <ENTER>
```

When the command completes, press the SHIFT-PRTSC key combination. DOS should begin printing the current contents of your screen display.

Next, issue the command

```
C:\> TYPE  A:HOOPS.DAT <ENTER>
```

When DOS displays the contents of the file, press SHIFT-PRTSC again. DOS will again print the contents of your screen display. Remember, before printing the contents of a screen containing graphics, you must issue the GRAPHICS command.

At the DOS prompt, press the CTRL-PRTSC key combination. Next, issue the following command:

```
C:\> TYPE A:BASEBALL.DAT <ENTER>
```

As DOS writes characters to your screen display, it will also echo them to your printer. Again press CTRL-PRTSC. Because it works as a toggle, the first time you press CTRL-PRTSC enables character echoing, and the second time disables it. When you now issue the command

```
C:\> TYPE A:FOOTBALL.DAT <ENTER>
```

DOS will no longer echo characters to your printer.

Issue the following PRINT command:

```
C:\> PRINT  A:FOOTBALL.DAT <ENTER>
```

DOS should begin printing your file and immediately redisplay its prompt.

This time, direct PRINT to print multiple files:

```
C:\> PRINT  A:FOOTBALL.DAT  A:BASEBALL.DAT  A:HOOPS.DAT <ENTER>
```

PRINT will display a message telling you that it is printing the file FOOTBALL.DAT and has placed BASEBALL.DAT and HOOPS.DAT in the queue.

Remember, the PRINT command fully supports wildcard characters. Issue the following command to see how PRINT works with wildcards:

```
C:\> PRINT  A:*.DAT <ENTER>
```

If you are using DOS, invoke the DOS shell. Select drive A as the current drive. The shell will display your sports files, as illustrated in Figure 14-6.

Select the FOOTBALL.DAT file, and then invoke the Print option from the File menu. DOS will send your file to the printer and redisplay the File System menu. Select all three of the files, and again invoke the Print option. DOS will print each of the files as desired. Last, if you created the files VOWELS.DAT, NUMBERS.DAT, and PRINT.NTS, as discussed earlier in this chapter, use DEL to erase them now.

FIGURE
14-6

The sports files on drive A

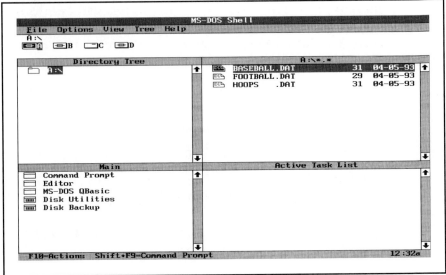

Chapter 15, "Getting the Most from Print," examines the PRINT command in detail. At that time, you will learn how you can customize PRINT for better performance.

Review

1. When do you need to issue the following command?

```
C:\> MODE LPT1:=COM1 <ENTER>
```

2. How do you print the current contents of your screen display? What if the screen contains graphics?

3. What is the function of the CTRL-PRTSC key combination?

4. How does the PRINT command differ from the following command?

```
C:\> COPY FILENAME.EXT  PRN <ENTER>
```

5. What is a queue?

6. What print command would print the contents of the TEST.NTS, CLASS.NTS, and HW.NTS files?

Key Points

The SHIFT-PRTSC key combination directs DOS to print the current contents of your screen display. When the printout completes, press your printer's online button to take the printer off line, press the formfeed button to eject the page, and press the online button to place the printer back on line.

The GRAPHICS Command

By default, the SHIFT-PRTSC key combination prints only text. To print the contents of your screen when it contains graphics, you must first issue the GRAPHICS command. Invoke GRAPHICS only once per user session. The general format of the GRAPHICS command is as follows:

```
C:\> GRAPHICS <ENTER>
```

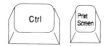

The CTRL-PRTSC key combination works as a toggle. The first time you press it, each character DOS writes to the screen is also echoed by the printer. The second time you press CTRL-PRTSC, character echoing is disabled.

CHAPTER

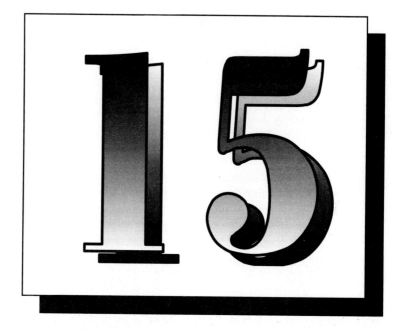

Getting the Most from PRINT

*I*n Chapter 14, "Using Your Printer," you learned several ways to obtain a hardcopy listing, including screen-printing operations, echoing characters to the printer, and the PRINT command. In this lesson you will learn how to optimize PRINT for maximum performance, as well as how to remove one or more files from the print queue. PRINT is a very powerful command; in this lesson you will learn how to increase its capabilities through command-line switches.

Installing PRINT for the First Time

In Chapter 14, you learned that when you invoke the File menu with a file selected and the Print option is either shown in gray or does not appear, the Print option is not available.

If the Print option is not available, you must install the software that creates the DOS print queue and manages the files that it contains. You do so by invoking PRINT from the DOS prompt before using the shell. After you invoke PRINT, you can then print files from within the shell.

The first time you invoke the PRINT command, DOS performs a considerable amount of processing. As shown in Figure 15-1, DOS sets aside storage areas to hold each of the file names that reside in the queue. PRINT also installs the software responsible for managing the files to be printed. To help PRINT perform this special processing, PRINT allows you to set several command-line switches the first time you invoke it. The following sections discuss these switches and what they do.

Specifying the Printer Device

As you have learned, you attach parallel printers to the ports LPT1 through LPT3 and serial printers to the ports COM1 through COM4. As you may recall from Chapter 14, the first time you invoke PRINT, it prompts you to specify the device that your printer is attached to, as shown here:

```
C:\> PRINT <ENTER>
Name of list device [PRN]:
```

Loading PRINT into memory

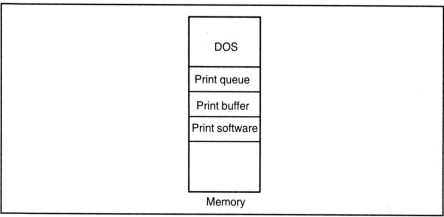

If your printer is attached to the parallel port LPT1, you can simply press ENTER, selecting the default device PRN. If your printer is attached to a serial port, you can type **COM1** and then press ENTER. In either case, DOS will install the print queue and the required software, displaying the following message:

```
C:\> PRINT <ENTER>
Name of list device [PRN]: <ENTER>
Resident part of PRINT installed
PRINT queue is empty

C:\>
```

The PRINT /D switch allows you to specify the printer device in your PRINT command line, as shown here:

```
C:\> PRINT  /D:LPT1 <ENTER>
```

Since you have specified the device name in your PRINT command line, PRINT will not prompt you for one. In Chapter 18, "Using Batch Files," you will learn about a special file named AUTOEXEC.BAT, into which you place commands you want DOS to execute each time it starts. By placing the PRINT command within this file, you can direct DOS to automatically install PRINT's memory-resident software each time your system starts. By including the /D switch, you eliminate PRINT's prompt for a list device.

Increasing the Print Buffer Size

When you direct PRINT to print a file, PRINT performs its processing by reading a portion of the file from disk, printing the information, reading additional information from disk, and then repeating this process. Thus, before PRINT can send information to your printer, the information to be printed must reside in memory. PRINT uses a memory storage region called a *print buffer*, as illustrated in Figure 15-2.

Compared to the electronic speed of your computer, mechanical disk drives, whether floppy or hard, are slow. Anything you can do to reduce disk read or write operations will improve your system performance. By default, PRINT sets aside 512 bytes of storage for its print buffer. This buffer size is equivalent to about one-eighth of a single-spaced typed page. If you often print larger documents than this, PRINT will spend a considerable amount of time just reading information from your disk.

FIGURE 15-2

Use of the memory buffer by the PRINT command

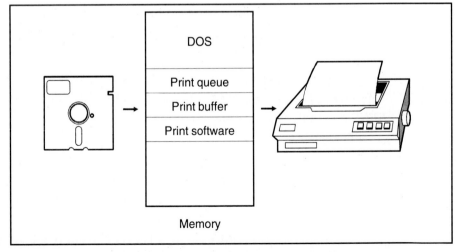

To increase the buffer size and reduce the number of disk read operations, PRINT provides the /B switch, which allows you to increase the size of the print buffer the first time you invoke PRINT. For example, the command

```
C:\> PRINT  /B:4096 <ENTER>
```

defines a print buffer of 4096 bytes, which provides space for about one single-spaced typed page. DOS allows you to specify a value up to 16,384 bytes. As you increase your print-buffer size, do so in increments of 512 bytes (512, 1024, 1536, 2048, and so on). Most users will find a value of 4096 sufficient. Remember, you can specify the /B switch only the first time you invoke the PRINT command.

Making a Larger Print Queue

Your printer can print only one file at a time. As you direct the PRINT command to print additional files, PRINT places the files into a print queue, as shown here:

```
A:\FOOTBALL.DAT is currently being printed
A:\BASEBALL.DAT is in queue
A:\HOOPS.DAT is in queue
```

By default, the print queue can store only ten file names. If you attempt to place an eleventh file in the queue, DOS will display the message

```
PRINT queue is full
```

if you are invoking PRINT from the DOS prompt. If you are invoking the Print option from within the shell, DOS will display the dialog box that is shown here:

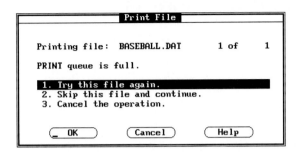

When the print queue becomes full, you must wait for additional files to be printed before you can add files to the print queue. By using the /Q switch the first time you invoke the PRINT command, however, you can direct PRINT to install a queue that is large enough to contain up to 32 file names:

```
C:\> PRINT  /Q:32  <ENTER>
```

Depending on your requirements, you can also create a print queue smaller than ten files by using /Q.

How Does PRINT Work?

PRINT works as a background command, allowing you to continue executing commands at the DOS prompt while your files print. As such, your computer appears to be performing two tasks at once. In actuality, however, your computer is capable of performing only a single task at one time. PRINT gives your computer the appearance of performing two tasks at the same time by quickly switching control of the CPU between DOS and the PRINT command. For example, if you issue the DIR command while you have files printing, DOS scrolls the file names in your directory on the screen while PRINT continues to print your files. Although both tasks appear to be happening at the same time, DIR and PRINT are quickly exchanging control of your computer, as shown here:

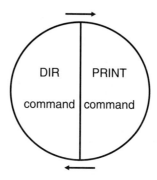

Because this switching occurs very quickly, you usually won't even realize that it is occurring.

DOS provides three PRINT command switches that allow you to further fine-tune PRINT'S performance for your specific system. Let's take a look at each.

Once you invoke the PRINT command, PRINT determines its time to execute by counting clock ticks. Within the IBM PC and PC compatibles, a clock tick occurs about 18.2 times per second (every 0.0549 seconds). By default, each time PRINT obtains control of the processor, it can keep control for 2 clock ticks. The /M switch allows you to set the number of clock ticks for which PRINT can maintain control of the computer. For example, the command

```
C:\> PRINT   /M:64  <ENTER>
```

allows PRINT to maintain control of the system for up to 64 clock ticks (3.5 seconds).

If you make the value much larger than 64, PRINT controls so much of the computer that your overall system response time will suffer, making your keyboard response time sluggish.

PRINT also supports the /S switch, which specifies how long DOS or your current program can run before it must give PRINT a chance. By default, PRINT uses a value of 8 clock ticks for /S. Most users will find this value sufficient.

Because your printer is a mechanical device, it is slower than the electronic speed of your computer. In some cases, when PRINT gains control of the CPU, it can't print additional characters because the printer is still busy. As a result, PRINT gives up its turn. The /U switch allows you to specify the number of clock ticks for which PRINT can wait each time it finds the printer busy. By default, DOS allows PRINT to wait one clock tick. For older printers, increasing this value to 8 or 16 may improve PRINT's performance. The following command lets PRINT wait up to 16 clock ticks if the printer is currently busy:

```
C:\> PRINT  /U:16  <ENTER>
```

When PRINT Has Already Been Invoked

You can specify the switches discussed so far only the first time you invoke the PRINT command. If, when you issue a command such as

```
C:\> PRINT  /Q:32  <ENTER>
```

PRINT displays the message

```
Invalid switch - /Q:32
```

the PRINT command has already been installed. In such a case, issue the command

```
C:\> TYPE \AUTOEXEC.BAT  <ENTER>
```

As you will learn in Chapter 18, the AUTOEXEC.BAT file contains a list of commands that DOS executes each time it starts. By placing a PRINT command within this file, you can install the print queue and print software automatically each time your system starts.

To change the PRINT command defaults, you must edit the system AUTOEXEC.BAT file and add the switches that you desire. Once you do so, reboot DOS to put your change into effect.

Later in this book you will learn how to use EDIT to make changes to files such as AUTOEXEC.BAT. At that time, you might consider adding a command similar to

```
PRINT /D:LPT1 /Q:32 /B:4096
```

or

```
PRINT /D:COM1 /Q:32 /B:4096
```

to your AUTOEXEC.BAT file, depending on your printer type.

Adding and Deleting Files from the Print Queue

Just as the PRINT command allows you to place files into the print queue, as in

```
C:\> PRINT  A:FOOTBALL.DAT  A:BASEBALL.DAT  A:HOOPS.DAT <ENTER>

A:\FOOTBALL.DAT is currently being printed
A:\BASEBALL.DAT is in queue
A:\HOOPS.DAT is in queue

C:\>
```

PRINT also allows you to remove files from the print queue. To do so, you must use the /C switch. Assume that your print queue contains the following files:

```
A:\FOOTBALL.DAT is currently being printed
A:\BASEBALL.DAT is in queue
A:\FILENAME.EXT is in queue
A:\HOOPS.DAT is in queue

C:\>
```

The command

```
C:\> PRINT  A:FILENAME.EXT  /C <ENTER>
```

directs PRINT to remove the file from the print queue, as shown here:

```
C:\> PRINT  A:FILENAME.EXT  /C <ENTER>

A:\FOOTBALL.DAT is currently being printed
A:\BASEBALL.DAT is in queue
A:\HOOPS.DAT is in queue

C:\>
```

DOS will then print a line that contains the message

```
File FILENAME.EXT canceled by operator
```

instead of printing the file.

The /C switch directs PRINT to remove the file that precedes the /C switch, as well as all files that follow the switch. Given the queue

```
C:\> PRINT <ENTER>

A:\FOOTBALL.DAT is currently being printed
A:\BASEBALL.DAT is in queue
A:\HOOPS.DAT is in queue

C:\>
```

the command

```
C:\> PRINT  A:HOOPS.DAT  /C <ENTER>
```

results in the following:

```
C:\> PRINT  A:HOOPS.DAT  /C <ENTER>

A:\FOOTBALL.DAT is currently being printed
A:\BASEBALL.DAT is in queue

C:\>
```

If a file name appears more than once in the print queue, the /C switch directs PRINT to remove every occurrence of the file. The following command, for example, directs PRINT to remove the CLASS.NTS, TEST.NTS, and HW.NTS files from the print queue:

```
C:\> PRINT  CLASS.NTS /C  TEST.NTS  HW.NTS <ENTER>
```

PRINT also supports the DOS wildcard characters when you are using the /C switch. Given the queue

```
C:\> PRINT <ENTER>

A:\FILENAME.EXT is currently being printed
A:\BASEBALL.DAT is in queue
A:\FOOTBALL.DAT is in queue
A:\HOOPS.DAT is in queue
A:\TEST.NTS is in queue

C:\>
```

the command

```
C:\> PRINT A:*.DAT  /C <ENTER>
```

directs PRINT to remove all of the files with the DAT extension from the print queue.

Just as there are times when you need to remove a specific file from the print queue by using /C, there may also be times when you need to cancel the printing of all files in the queue. The /T switch allows you to do just that. The command

```
C:\> PRINT   /T <ENTER>
```

directs PRINT to remove all files from the queue, canceling the file that is currently printing. Once PRINT completes, it will print a line containing the following message:

```
All files canceled by operator
```

PRINT also allows you to add files to the queue by using /P. The /P switch exists primarily to allow you to add and delete files from the print queue in one command line. Given the command

```
C:\> PRINT   FILE.OLD   /C   FILE.NEW   /P <ENTER>
```

DOS will delete the FILE.OLD file from the print queue, while adding the FILE.NEW file at the end of the print queue. Similarly, the command

```
C:\> PRINT   A.DAT   /C   B.DAT   C.DAT   /P   D.DAT <ENTER>
```

will remove the A.DAT and B.DAT files from the print queue, while adding C.DAT and D.DAT.

Practice

Before you get started, find out whether or not DOS is automatically installing your PRINT software and queue for you each time it starts by issuing the following command:

```
C:\> TYPE \AUTOEXEC.BAT <ENTER>
```

Examine the file's contents for the PRINT command, which installs your print queue.

In order to have several files to print, create the files

```
C:\> COPY  CON  A.LTR <ENTER>
A <ENTER>
AA <ENTER>
AAA <ENTER>
AAAA <ENTER>
AAAAA <ENTER>
AAAAAA <ENTER>
^Z <ENTER>
     1 File(s) copied

C:\> COPY  CON  B.LTR <ENTER>
B <ENTER>
BB <ENTER>
BBB <ENTER>
BBBB <ENTER>
BBBBB <ENTER>
BBBBBB <ENTER>
^Z <ENTER>
     1 File(s) copied

C:\> COPY  CON  PRINT.TXT <ENTER>
The DOS PRINT command <ENTER>
supports these switches: <ENTER>
/T, /C, /B, /Q, /M, /U, /S /D /P <ENTER>
^Z <ENTER>
     1 File(s) copied

C:\>
```

Next, issue the command

```
C:\> PRINT  A.LTR  B.LTR  PRINT.TXT <ENTER>
```

DOS will respond with

```
C:\A.LTR is currently being printed
C:\B.LTR is in queue
C:\PRINT.TXT is in queue
```

Immediately type

```
C:\> PRINT   /T <ENTER>
```

at the DOS prompt. DOS will remove all of the files from the print queue, printing the message

```
All files canceled by operator
```

on your printer output.

Using the DOS wildcard characters, issue the command

```
C:\> PRINT   *.LTR <ENTER>
```

DOS will place the following files in the queue:

```
C:\A.LTR is currently being printed
C:\B.LTR is in queue
```

Use the /C switch to remove the B.LTR file from the print queue, as shown here:

```
C:\> PRINT   B.LTR   /C <ENTER>
```

PRINT will later print the message

```
File B.LTR canceled by operator
```

on the printer output, which tells you that the file was indeed removed from the print queue.

Had the print queue contained multiple copies of the B.LTR file, as in

```
C:\A.LTR is currently being printed
C:\B.LTR is in queue
C:\A.LTR is in queue
C:\B.LTR is in queue
```

the command

```
C:\> PRINT  B.LTR  /C <ENTER>
```

would have deleted each occurrence of the file, leaving

```
C:\A.LTR is currently being printed
C:\A.LTR is in queue
```

Review

1. PRINT supports several command-line switches the first time you invoke it. Why are these switches valid only the first time you invoke the PRINT command?

2. What is a print buffer? What switch modifies the size of the print buffer?

3. By default, PRINT supports a queue of ten files. How can you increase the size of the print queue?

4. What is the function of the following command?

```
C:\> PRINT /D:LPT1 <ENTER>
```

5. What are the functions of the PRINT /C and /P switches? How does /C differ from /T?

Key Points

PRINT /D

The PRINT /D switch allows you to specify the printer device the first time you invoke PRINT. If you are using a parallel printer, use LPT1, as shown here:

```
C:\> PRINT /D:LPT1 <ENTER>
```

If you are using a serial printer, use

```
C:\> PRINT /D:COM1 <ENTER>
```

PRINT /B

To print a file, PRINT reads a portion of the file from disk into a memory buffer. The PRINT /B switch allows you to specify the size of the print buffer (in bytes) the first time you invoke PRINT. By default, PRINT uses a 512-byte buffer. The following command selects a buffer size of 4096 bytes:

```
C:\> PRINT /B:4096 <ENTER>
```

PRINT /Q

By default, PRINT creates a print queue that is large enough to store ten files. The /Q switch directs PRINT to create a larger queue, capable of storing up to 32 files. You can specify /Q only the first time you invoke PRINT:

continues . . .

Key Points
(continued)

```
C:\> PRINT /Q:32 <ENTER>
```

PRINT /C

The PRINT /C switch directs PRINT to remove the file that precedes /C from the print queue, as well as any files that follow /C. PRINT will print a line informing the user that the file's printing has been canceled.

PRINT /T

The PRINT /T switch directs PRINT to quit printing the current file and to remove all remaining files from the queue. PRINT will print a line informing the user that all files have been removed from the print queue.

PRINT /P

The PRINT /P switch directs PRINT to place files in the print queue. This switch exists primarily so you can add and delete files to or from the queue in one command. The following command, for example, removes the file OLDFILE.DAT from the queue while adding NEWFILE.DAT.

```
C:\> PRINT OLDFILE.DAT /C NEWFILE.DAT /P <ENTER>
```

CHAPTER

Using EDIT

Since DOS was introduced in 1981, it has included a limited-feature line editor called EDLIN. With the release of DOS 5, this old standby has been rendered obsolete. DOS now includes a second text editor named EDIT, which lets you use the entire screen to edit files, much like a word processor. This type of text editor is called a *full-screen editor.*

As you will learn in this chapter, creating and later changing files by using EDIT is very easy. If you have a mouse, you can use it within EDIT to select specific text or to choose different menu options quickly.

Getting Started with EDIT

To get started with EDIT, you will create the following text file named EDIT.NTS:

```
EDIT is a full screen editor
provided with DOS 5 (or later) to replace
the line editor EDLIN.
```

Invoke EDIT with the file name EDIT.NTS, as shown here:

```
C:\> EDIT  EDIT.NTS <ENTER>
```

EDIT will display an empty editing window within which you can type the file, as shown in Figure 16-1.

Type in the file's first line and press ENTER:

```
EDIT is a full screen editor <ENTER>
```

EDIT will advance the cursor to the start of the second line. As you type, note the numbers that appear at the lower-right corner of your screen. These numbers tell you the cursor's current line number and column position.

FIGURE
16-1

EDIT's initial editing window

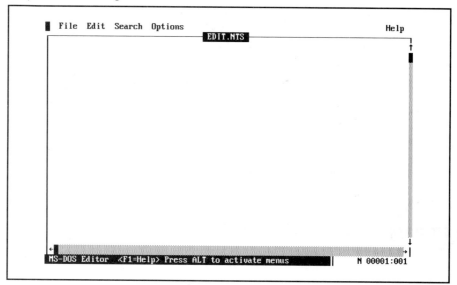

Type in the file's next two lines:

```
provided with DOS 5 (or later) to replace <ENTER>
the line editor EDLIN. <ENTER>
```

Your screen should appear similar to that shown here:

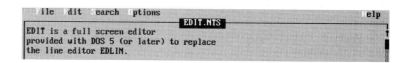

Because your file is now complete, you need a way to print the file or save its contents to disk. If you look at the line appearing immediately above the editing window, you will find the menu options File, Edit, Search, Options, and Help. These menu options let you select EDIT's pull-down menus. To select a specific menu, hold down the ALT key on your keyboard and type the first letter of the desired menu name. For example, if you press ALT-F, EDIT will display its File menu, shown here:

If your system has a mouse and you have successfully installed the mouse driver, EDIT will display a small rectangular mouse pointer on your screen. If you aim the mouse pointer at a menu option and click the left mouse button, EDIT will display the corresponding menu.

Printing the File's Contents

The File menu Print option lets you print the current file's contents. To select the Print option, type **P**, or highlight the option using your keyboard's arrow keys and press ENTER. EDIT will display the following dialog box to determine how much of the document you want to print:

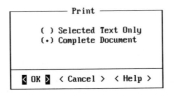

By pressing the TAB key, you can move the dialog box highlight. In this case, highlight OK to print the entire document and press ENTER. EDIT will print your file.

Later in this chapter you will learn how to select a specific section of your file. Once you have selected the text—a key paragraph or page, for example—you could print only that text using the Print dialog box Selected Text Only option.

Should you decide not to print the file, press the TAB key to highlight the Cancel option and press ENTER.

Saving Your File Changes to Disk

After you create or change a file, you must save your changes to disk. To do so, invoke the File menu (ALT-F). In this case, because you are already using the name EDIT.NTS, you can select the Save option.

If you had not yet assigned a name to your file, you would select the Save As option. When you select the Save As option, EDIT will display a dialog box that prompts you for the file name you desire.

Ending Your Editing Session

To exit EDIT to DOS, invoke the EDIT File menu and choose the Exit option. If you have saved your latest file changes to disk, EDIT will end. If you have unsaved changes, however, EDIT will display the following dialog box:

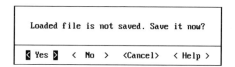

In this case, EDIT is asking you if you want to save your changes, prompting you for a file name if you have not yet specified one. If you select the No option, EDIT will discard your changes. In either case, EDIT will exit to DOS.

If you make changes to a file that you later decide you really didn't want to make, you can discard the changes by exiting EDIT to DOS and not saving the changes to disk.

You should note that, unlike EDLIN, which makes a backup copy of your original file (assigning it the BAK extension), EDIT does not. If you make changes to a file and save the changes, the file's previous contents are lost.

Editing an Existing File

As you have learned, one way to specify a file for editing is to include the file name in EDIT's command line:

```
C:\> EDIT FILENAME.EXT <ENTER>
```

If EDIT is already running, you can use its File menu Open option to select a file. When you select the Open option, EDIT will display the dialog box shown in Figure 16-2.

By default, EDIT displays the files in the current directory that have the TXT extension (TXT indicates a text file). To change the type of files listed, you can change the *.TXT to *.* or *.DAT. If the file extension is correct, you can select a specific file by typing in its name, or by pressing the TAB key to highlight the list of file names and scrolling through the names by using your arrow keys. Once you highlight the desired file, you can press ENTER to select it.

If EDIT can successfully open your file, EDIT will display the file's contents within its editing screen. If EDIT cannot open the file, EDIT will display a dialog box describing the error it encountered.

EDIT's File Open dialog box

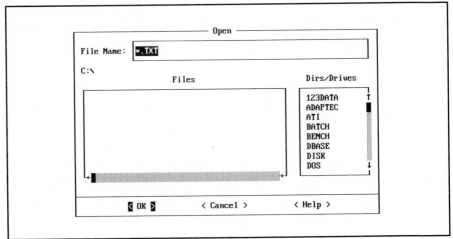

If you have previously been editing a file and you have not saved that file's changes to disk, EDIT will display a dialog box asking if you want to save or discard the changes.

As you can see, the dialog box displays the name of the current drive and directory. If you want to change the current drive or directory, press the TAB key to highlight the dialog box's Dirs/Drives option. Next, using your arrow keys, scroll through the list of names and highlight the drive or directory desired, pressing ENTER to select it.

Creating a New File

Just as there are times when EDIT is running and you want to edit an existing file, there will be times when you want to start a new file. To start a new file, select EDIT's File menu and choose the New option. If you have not yet saved your changes to your previous file, EDIT will display a dialog box asking you if you want to save or discard the changes.

Next, EDIT will display an empty editing window. Unlike the editing window shown in Figure 16-1, which contains a file name, the new editing menu will contain the title "Untitled" until you use the Save As option to assign a file name.

Using the Save As Option

The File menu Save As option lets you assign a name to your file. When you select the Save As option, EDIT displays the dialog box shown in Figure 16-3.

Type in the file name you desire, optionally including a disk drive letter and directory path. As before, you can change the current drive or directory by using the dialog box's Dirs/Drives option.

If you type in the name of a file that already exists on disk, EDIT will display the following dialog box:

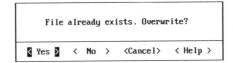

If you want to overwrite the existing file, select the Yes option. If you select the No option, EDIT will redisplay the previous Save As dialog box, letting you type in a new file name.

Searching a Large File for Specific Text

As the size of your files increases, finding a specific location within the file at which you need to edit can become a time-consuming task. If you are looking for a specific word or phrase, you can use EDIT's Search menu (ALT-S) Find option to quickly locate the text. When you invoke the Search menu, EDIT will display the following pull-down menu:

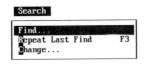

The Save As dialog box

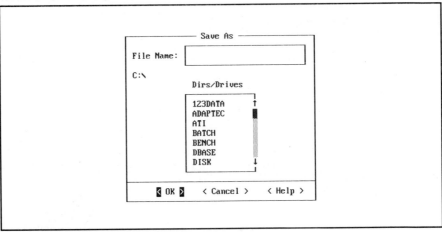

If you select the Find option, EDIT displays the following dialog box:

```
┌──────────────────────── Find ────────────────────────┐
│                                                       │
│  Find What: ┌─────────────────────────────────────┐  │
│             │                                     │  │
│             └─────────────────────────────────────┘  │
│                                                       │
│     [ ] Match Upper/Lowercase       [ ] Whole Word    │
│                                                       │
├───────────────────────────────────────────────────────┤
│        ◄ OK ►          < Cancel >          < Help >   │
└───────────────────────────────────────────────────────┘
```

To locate the word "EDLIN", for example, you would type **EDLIN** at the dialog box's Find What prompt. By pressing the TAB key, you can highlight the Match Upper/Lowercase or Whole Word option. To select one of these options, you must highlight it and press the SPACEBAR.

When you select an option, EDIT will place an "X" next to the option in its dialog box. Pressing the SPACEBAR works as a toggle. The first time you press the SPACEBAR, you select the option. The second time you press it, you deselect the option, removing the "X."

Selecting the Match Upper/Lowercase option directs EDIT to consider upper- and lowercase letters as different. In the case of the word "EDLIN", for example, if you select the Match Upper/Lowercase option, EDIT will consider the words "EDLIN", "Edlin", and "edlin" as different.

Selecting the Whole Word option directs EDIT to match only occurrences of the word that contain the exact number of characters. If you are searching for the word "Opera" and you do not select the Whole Word option, EDIT would consider the word "Operating" a match, since both words begin with "Opera".

When you perform a search operation, EDIT advances the cursor to the next occurrence of the word. In many cases, you may have to perform several searches before you find the occurrence you desire.

The Search menu Repeat Last Find option directs EDIT to search for the next occurrence of the previously specified text. If you look at the Search menu, you'll see the F3 function key next to the Repeat Last Find option. F3 is called a *hot key*, meaning you can press F3 at any time within the editor to repeat the search without having to select the option from the Search menu.

If EDIT cannot find the word or phrase, it will display the following dialog box:

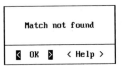

Replacing One Word or Phrase with Another

Just as the Search menu's Find option lets you quickly locate a word or phrase in your file, the Change option lets you quickly replace a word or phrase throughout your document. When you select the Change option, EDIT will display the dialog box shown in Figure 16-4.

Type in the word or phrase you want to replace at the dialog box's Find What prompt, and press the TAB key. EDIT will advance the cursor to the Change To prompt. Type in the new word or phrase. The Match Upper/Lowercase and Whole Word options behave as previously discussed. Press the TAB key to highlight either the Find and Verify or the Change All option.

The Change dialog box

The Find and Verify option directs EDIT to locate the next occurrence of the word and then to display the following dialog box, asking you if you want to replace this occurrence of the word:

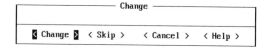

EDIT will repeat this dialog box for each occurrence of the word. If you want to cancel the operation, select the Cancel option.

The Change All option directs EDIT to automatically change every matching occurrence of the word.

Moving and Deleting Text

When you edit your files, there will be times when you need to move text from one location to another or to delete text. EDIT lets you quickly perform these operations by using its Edit menu (ALT-E), shown here:

```
Edit
┌─────────────────────────┐
│ Cut          Shift+Del  │
│ Copy          Ctrl+Ins  │
│ Paste        Shift+Ins  │
│ Clear             Del   │
└─────────────────────────┘
```

The process of moving text from one location to another is called *cutting and pasting.* To perform cut-and-paste operations, EDIT lets you select specific text within your file and move (cut) or copy it to a special storage location in RAM called a *clipboard.* After you move the cursor to the file location at which you want to place the text, the Paste operation copies the clipboard's contents to your file.

To select text for a Cut or Copy operation, using your keyboard, hold down a SHIFT key and press your UP ARROW or DOWN ARROW key. EDIT will highlight text as you select it. If you are using a mouse, you can select text by aiming the mouse pointer at the desired text, holding down the left mouse button, and moving the mouse.

After you select text, choosing the Edit menu's Cut option erases the text from your file, placing it in the clipboard. The Copy option copies the selected text to the clipboard, leaving it in place within your file. Finally, the Clear option deletes the text from your file without copying it to the clipboard.

Changing EDIT's Screen Appearance

EDIT's Options menu (ALT-O) Display option lets you customize EDIT's screen appearance. When you select this menu option, EDIT displays the dialog box shown in Figure 16-5.

To begin, the Colors option lets you select EDIT's foreground and background colors. Use your arrow keys to highlight different colors. By pressing TAB, you can toggle between the foreground and background color lists.

By default, EDIT displays a vertical scroll bar along the right side of its editing window and a horizontal scroll bar along the bottom. If you

FIGURE 16-5

The Display Colors dialog box

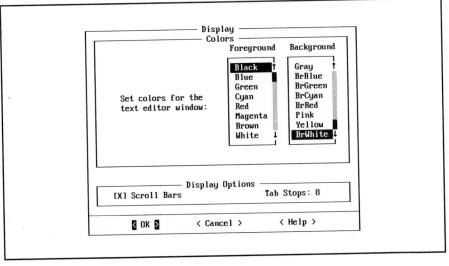

are editing a large file, you can use the small black guide that appears in the bar to help you determine your relative position within the file. If the slide is near the top of the scroll bar, for example, you are editing near the top of the file. Likewise, if the slide is near the bottom of the bar, you are editing near the end of the file. As you traverse the file, the slide will move up and down along the bar with your current document position. If you are using a mouse, you can aim the mouse pointer at one of the scroll bar slides. By holding down the mouse select button, you can drag the slide in either direction, changing your current position within the document as you do so.

If you don't use the scroll bars, you can disable their display by removing the "X" that appears next to the Scroll Bars option by highlighting the option and pressing the SPACEBAR.

By default, EDIT places tab stops every eight characters. To change this setting, highlight the Tab Stops option and type the new value.

If you are satisfied with your selections, highlight the OK option and press ENTER. If you want to discard your changes, select the Cancel option.

Using EDIT's Online Help

Although most of EDIT's features are straightforward and easily accessible through menu options, there may still be times when you have a question about a specific EDIT feature. As a solution, EDIT provides built-in online help. If you press ALT-H, EDIT will display the following menu:

The Getting Started option directs EDIT to display information on basic operations, as shown in Figure 16-6. To display information on one of the listed topics, press the TAB key to highlight the topic and press ENTER. If you are using a mouse, you can aim the mouse pointer at a topic and click the left mouse button.

FIGURE
16-6

EDIT displays its help text by splitting your screen in two sections

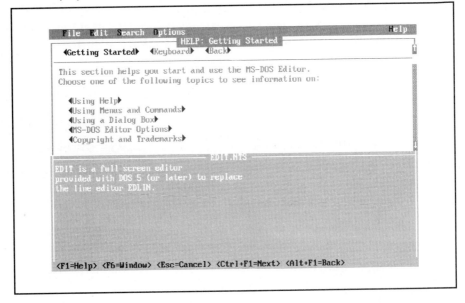

The Help menu Keyboard option directs EDIT to display a menu of options, such as the key combinations listed in Table 16-1, that let you use the keyboard to move the cursor and scroll through the text.

To end a help session, press the ESC key. EDIT will remove the help text from your screen. Table 16-2 lists the keystrokes you can press while EDIT's help is active.

In addition to invoking help through the Help menu, you can press the F1 function key at any time to get help on a topic or dialog box. When help is active, you can press the F6 function key to move between your document window and the window containing the help text.

Practice

If EDIT is not already running, invoke it as follows:

```
C:\>  EDIT <ENTER>
```

TABLE 16-1 EDIT's Cursor-Movement and Text-Scrolling Key Combinations

Key Combination	Function
Arrow keys	Move cursor to position
PGUP	Moves cursor up one text screen
PGDN	Moves cursor down one text screen
HOME	Moves cursor to beginning of line
END	Moves cursor to end of line
CTRL-LEFT ARROW	Moves cursor one word to the left
CTRL-RIGHT ARROW	Moves cursor one word to the right
CTRL-ENTER	Moves cursor to beginning of next line
CTRL-Q-E	Moves cursor to top line of window
CTRL-Q-X	Moves cursor to bottom line of window
CTRL-W or CTRL-UP ARROW	Scrolls text up one line
CTRL-Z or CTRL-DOWN ARROW	Scrolls text down one line
CTRL-HOME or CTRL-Q-R	Moves cursor to beginning of file
CTRL-END or CTRL Q-C	Moves cursor to end of file
CTRL-PGUP	Scrolls text left one screen
CTRL-PGDN	Scrolls text right one screen

When EDIT displays its editing window, type in the following six lines of text:

```
This is line 1.
This is line 4.
This is line 5.
This is line 2.
This is line 3.
This line is in the way.
```

TABLE 16-2

EDIT's Online Help Key Combinations

Key Combination	Function
TAB	Advances to next help topic
SHIFT-TAB	Moves back to previous help topic
Character	Moves to next topic beginning with *Character*
SHIFT-*Character*	Moves to previous topic beginning with *Character*
ALT-F1	Displays help window for previously displayed topic
CTRL-F1	Displays help window for next topic
SHIFT-CTRL-F1	Displays help window for previous topic
F6	Toggles between help window and file window
ESC	Ends the online help session

Your screen should contain the following:

```
█ File  Edit  Search  Options                                    Help
                            ▐Untitled▌                             ↑
This is line 1.
This is line 4.
This is line 5.
This is line 2.
This is line 3.
This line is in the way.
```

Use the ALT-F key combination to invoke the File menu. Select the Print option and print your entire file's contents. Next, select the File menu Save As option and save your file as EDIT TEST.TXT.

As you have read, cut-and-paste operations let you move text from one location in the file to another. Using your arrow keys, move the cursor to the start of the line containing "This is line 4." Hold down the SHIFT key and press the DOWN ARROW twice to select the following lines:

```
This is line 4.
This is line 5.
```

Press the ALT-E key combination to invoke the Edit menu; choose the Cut option. EDIT will remove the text from your file. Next, using the arrow keys, move the cursor to the end of the file.

Press ALT-E to invoke the Edit menu and choose the Paste option. EDIT will restore the text from the clipboard back into your file.

Next, select the line containing "This line is in the way." Using the Edit menu Clear option, remove the line from your file.

Finally, use the File menu Save option to save your file's current contents and the Exit option to return to DOS.

Review

1. What is a full-screen editor?
2. How do you use EDIT to print your file?
3. How do you select text for a cut-and-paste operation?
4. What is the clipboard?
5. What is a hot key?

Key Points

EDIT

Since DOS was introduced in 1981, it has included a limited-feature line editor called EDLIN. With the release of DOS 5, the line editor was replaced by EDIT, a full-screen editor with many features of a modern word processor. To invoke EDIT, type **EDIT** at the command line (optionally followed by the name of a text file whose contents you want to edit, such as AUTOEXEC.BAT).

EDIT has a menu system that allows you to choose operations quickly with either the keyboard or the mouse.

continues . . .

❑ From the File menu, you can start a new file, open an existing file, save a file, save a file with a new name or location, print a file, or exit your editing session.

❑ From the Edit menu, you can cut or copy a bit of text to an electronic memory storage location called a clipboard, paste what is in the clipboard in the current location in text, and delete text.

❑ From the Search menu, you can find a given occurrence of text in your file, repeat the last find, and replace one bit of text with another.

❑ From the Options menu, you can customize many aspects of EDIT, such as the colors of the screen display.

Several of the most frequently used EDIT commands have hot keys associated with them for quick use.

CHAPTER

Controlling DOS Input and Output

*T*he commands you have issued so far in this book have written their output to your screen display and received their input from the keyboard. In this chapter you will learn how to use DOS to control your command's input and output. You will learn how to route the output of a DOS command from the screen display to a file or even to your printer.

The process of routing a command's input away from the keyboard or routing its output away from the screen display is called *I/O* (input/output) *redirection*. To perform I/O redirection, you will use the **>**, **<** , and **>>** symbols in your command line. These symbols are called DOS *redirection operators*. This chapter teaches you how to use each of these operators. You will also learn to use the MORE, SORT, and FIND commands, which help you manipulate your data.

Output Redirection

At the DOS prompt, issue the DIR command. As you would expect, DOS writes DIR's output (the directory listing) to your screen display. Next, make sure that your system printer is turned on and that the online light is lit. Depending upon whether you are using a parallel or serial printer, issue one of the following commands:

```
C:\> DIR  >  PRN <ENTER>
C:\> DIR  >  COM1 <ENTER>
```

The greater-than symbol (**>**) is the *output redirection operator.* When you place this symbol in your command line, DOS redirects the output of your command from the screen display to the destination you specify. In this example, DOS redirects the output of the DIR command from your screen display to your printer, as shown in Figure 17-1.

DOS also allows you to redirect the output of a command to a file. You can redirect the output of the DIR command to a file named FILES.LST with the following command:

```
C:\> DIR > FILES.LST <ENTER>
```

FIGURE
17-1

Redirecting output to a printer

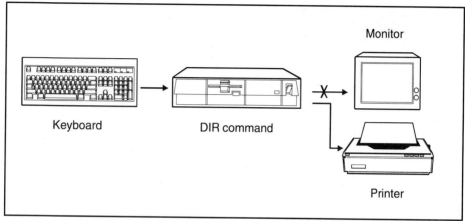

A directory listing reveals the file, as shown here:

```
C:\> DIR   FILES.LST  <ENTER>

 Volume in drive C is DOS 6 DISK
 Volume Serial Number is 16F6-3B73
 Directory of C:\

FILES       LST      1237 03-31-93    9:28a
        1 file(s)        1237 bytes
                  152182784 bytes free

C:\>
```

Using the TYPE command, you can display the file's contents:

```
C:\> TYPE FILES.LST  <ENTER>
```

As you can see, I/O redirection does not change a command's output; it just sends the output to another location.

You can use the output redirection operator with other DOS commands, as shown here:

```
C:\> TREE  >  TREE.LST <ENTER>
C:\> TREE  /F  >  PRN <ENTER>
C:\> CHKDSK  >  DISK.INF <ENTER>
```

You should remember that not all DOS commands and programs support I/O redirection. If you try redirecting the output of your word processor, for example, the word processor will very likely ignore the redirection, displaying its output on the screen.

Appending Output to a File

As you just saw, the output redirection operator lets you route the output of a DOS command to a file or device. DOS provides a second redirection operator, called the *append redirection operator*, that directs DOS to append a command's output to an existing file. This operator is represented by two greater-than symbols (**>>**). For example, given the command

```
C:\> DIR  >> FILENAME.EXT <ENTER>
```

DOS will first examine the current directory to see if it contains the specified file (*FILENAME.EXT*, in this case). If it does, DOS will append the output of the DIR command to this file. If it does not, DOS will create the file and write DIR's output to it.

In order to understand how the append redirection operator works, create the following files:

```
C:\> COPY  CON  ONE.DAT <ENTER>
11 <ENTER>
11 <ENTER>
^Z <ENTER>
     1 File(s) copied

C:\> COPY  CON  TWO.DAT <ENTER>
```

```
22 <ENTER>
22 <ENTER>
^Z <ENTER>
     1 File(s) copied

C:\> COPY  CON   THREE.DAT <ENTER>
33 <ENTER>
33 <ENTER>
^Z <ENTER>
     1 File(s) copied

C:\>
```

Next, issue the following TYPE command:

```
C:\> TYPE   ONE.DAT <ENTER>
11
11

C:\>
```

As you would expect, DOS sends TYPE's output to the screen display.

However, if you include the append redirection operator in the command, as in

```
C:\> TYPE   ONE.DAT  >>   NUMBERS.DAT <ENTER>
```

DOS will redirect the output of the TYPE command, as illustrated in Figure 17-2. Because the file NUMBERS.DAT did not previously exist on disk, DOS will create it. A directory listing of the disk reveals the file, as shown here:

```
C:\> DIR  NUMBERS.DAT <ENTER>

 Volume in drive C is DOS 6 DISK
 Volume Serial Number is 16F6-3B73
 Directory of C:\
```

```
NUMBERS   DAT           8 03-31-93    9:27a
          1 file(s)             8 bytes
                       152162304 bytes free
```

Next, issue the following command.

```
C:\> TYPE  TWO.DAT  >>  NUMBERS.DAT <ENTER>
```

DOS will again redirect the output of the TYPE command from the screen, appending it to the NUMBERS.DAT file. If you examine the file NUMBERS.DAT, you'll find it contains the following:

```
C:\> TYPE  NUMBERS.DAT <ENTER>
11
11
22
22

C:\>
```

Appending output to a file

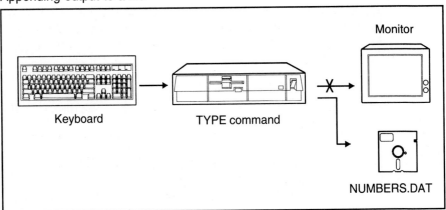

Keyboard   TYPE command

Monitor

NUMBERS.DAT

Repeat this process, appending the output of the THREE.DAT file to NUMBERS.DAT, as shown here:

```
C:\> TYPE  THREE.DAT  >>  NUMBERS.DAT <ENTER>
```

The NUMBERS.DAT file will now contain the following:

```
C:\> TYPE  NUMBERS.DAT <ENTER>
11
11
22
22
33
33

C:\>
```

The output and append redirection operators are very similar in how they function. Both redirect a command's output from the screen to another destination. The operators differ in the way they treat files to which the output is redirected. For example, the command

```
C:\> DIR  > FILENAME.EXT <ENTER>
```

will overwrite the contents of an existing file with *FILENAME.EXT*. The following command, however, appends the output of the DIR command to the specified file, and does not overwrite that file's contents:

```
C:\> DIR  >> FILENAME.EXT <ENTER>
```

Redirecting a Command's Input

As you have learned, unless told to do otherwise, DOS sends the output of a command to your screen display. In a similar way, by default, DOS receives input from the keyboard. Just as the output and append redirection operators allow you to override a command's output destination, the *input redirection operator* (<) allows you to override a command's source of input (the keyboard) and tells DOS to get the input from an existing file instead.

As was the case with output redirection, not all DOS commands support input redirection. This chapter looks at three commands that do support input redirection: MORE, SORT, and FIND.

Displaying a File's Contents with MORE

MORE is an external DOS command that lets you display the contents of a file a screenful at a time. Each time MORE displays a screenful of information, it pauses and displays the following message.

```
-- More --
```

If you want to view the next screenful of information, just press any key. MORE will fill the screen, displaying its prompt and pausing for you to press another key to continue. If you don't want to view any more information, you can press CTRL-C to end the command.

Issue the following command to create the file DOSFILES.DAT:

```
C:\> DIR \DOS  >  DOSFILES.DAT <ENTER>
```

Next, issue this MORE command to display the file's contents a screenful at a time:

```
C:\> MORE  <  DOSFILES.DAT <ENTER>
```

In this case, the input redirection operator directs DOS to route the input of the MORE command away from the keyboard to the file DOSFILES.DAT. To continue displaying the directory listing, press any key. To cancel the MORE command, use the CTRL-C key combination.

Figure 17-3 shows the processing involved with the MORE command. As you can see, the input redirection operator has routed the input of a DOS command from your keyboard to an existing file.

Sorting a File's Contents with I/O Redirection

DOS provides, in addition to MORE, the SORT command, which you can use with redirected input to sort the contents of your files. Like MORE, SORT is an external DOS command. To understand how it works, create a file named VOWELS.DAT, which contains the following:

```
C:\> COPY   CON   VOWELS.DAT <ENTER>
A <ENTER>
E <ENTER>
I <ENTER>
O <ENTER>
U <ENTER>
a <ENTER>
e <ENTER>
i <ENTER>
o <ENTER>
u <ENTER>
^Z <ENTER>
        1 File(s) copied
```

Next, issue the following SORT command to sort the file's contents, displaying the sorted output on the screen:

```
C:\> SORT   <   VOWELS.DAT <ENTER>
```

Processing with MORE

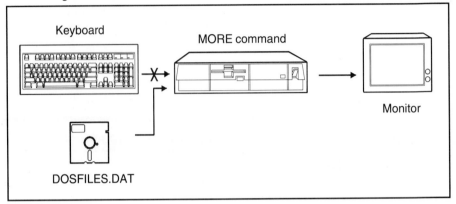

SORT will display the following:

```
C:\> SORT   <   VOWELS.DAT
A
a
E
e
I
i
O
o
U
u

C:\>
```

Notice that SORT treats upper- and lowercase letters as identical.

The SORT command provides the /R switch, which directs it to sort its input in reverse order (highest to lowest). Using the file VOWELS.DAT, the /R switch directs SORT to sort the data in reverse order, as shown here:

```
C:\>   SORT   /R   <   VOWELS.DAT <ENTER>
u
U
```

```
o
O
i
I
e
E
a
A

C:\>
```

Finally, assume your file contains data in a tabular form, as does the file BBALL.TMS, shown here:

```
L.A.       Clippers
L.A.       Lakers
Phoenix    Suns
Seattle    Sonics
N.Y.       Knicks
Boston     Celtics
```

The SORT command allows you to sort your data by a specific column with the /+n switch. Assuming that the team names begin in column 12 of the file, you can sort the file by team names, as shown here:

```
C:\> SORT  /+12  <  BBALL.TMS <ENTER>
Boston     Celtics
L.A.       Clippers
N.Y.       Knicks
L.A.       Lakers
Seattle    Sonics
Phoenix    Suns

C:\>
```

You can use the /R and /+n switches together, as shown here:

```
C:\> SORT  /R  /+12  <  BBALL.TMS <ENTER>
Phoenix    Suns
Seattle    Sonics
```

```
L.A.        Lakers
N.Y.        Knicks
L.A.        Clippers
Boston      Celtics

C:\>
```

Locating a Word or Phrase in a File

In Chapter 16, "Using EDIT," you learned how to use the EDIT Search command to locate a specific word or phrase within a file. The FIND command provides a similar capability from the DOS prompt. FIND is an external DOS command. Given the file BBALL.DAT just shown, you can search the file for the characters "L.A." by using FIND, as shown here:

```
C:\> FIND  "L.A."  <  BBALL.TMS  <ENTER>
```

This command displays each of the teams from L.A., as shown here:

```
C:\> FIND  "L.A."  <  BBALL.TMS  <ENTER>
L.A.      Clippers
L.A.      Lakers

C:\>
```

Notice that the word or phrase you are looking for must appear in quotes. If the word or phrase does not exist in the file, FIND returns you to the DOS prompt, and no file contents are displayed, as shown here:

```
C:\> FIND "Portland"  <  BBALL.TMS  <ENTER>
C:\>
```

FIND also supports three command-line qualifiers that you can use before the word or phrase of interest:

The /C qualifier displays only a count of the number of lines the word or phrase appears in.

The /N qualifier displays the line number of each line containing the word or phrase, as well as the word or phrase itself.

The /V qualifier displays only the lines that do not contain the word or phrase.

With the BBALL.TMS file, the command

```
C:\> FIND  /V  "L.A."  <  BBALL.TMS <ENTER>
```

displays the name of each team not from L.A., as shown here:

```
C:\> FIND  /V  "L.A."  <  BBALL.TMS
Phoenix    Suns
Seattle    Sonics
N.Y.       Knicks
Boston     Celtics

C:\>
```

Likewise, the command

```
C:\> FIND  /N  "L.A."  <  BBALL.TMS <ENTER>
```

directs FIND to display each line containing the characters "L.A." and the line number associated with the line:

```
C:\> FIND  /N  "L.A."  <  BBALL.TMS
[1]L.A.  Clippers
[2]L.A.  Lakers

C:\>
```

The command

```
C:\> FIND  /C  "L.A."  <  BBALL.TMS <ENTER>
```

displays the number of lines in which the characters "L.A." appear in the redirected input:

```
C:\> FIND  /C  "L.A."  <  BBALL.TMS <ENTER>
2

C:\>
```

As you can see, the ability to redirect input to a DOS command provides you with considerable flexibility.

I/O Redirection from Within the Shell

As you have just seen, the I/O redirection operators allow you to redirect the input or output of a DOS command when you invoke the command from the DOS prompt. If you are using the DOS 5 shell, it may not be obvious, but the capability to redirect I/O is still readily available. For example, from the File menu (ALT-F), select the Run option. When DOS displays its dialog box, type **CHKDSK > DISK.STS** to redirect the output of the command to the DISK.STS file, as shown here:

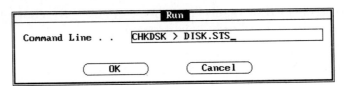

When you press ENTER, the CHKDSK command will execute, sending its output to the DISK.STS file instead of to the screen display.

Repeat this process to invoke the SORT command. When DOS displays its prompt for command-line options, use the input redirection operator to obtain the input of the SORT command from the VOWELS.DAT file, as shown here:

As you can see, the ability to use the I/O redirection operators is fully supported from within the shell.

Practice

Make sure that your printer is on line, and issue either of these commands, depending on your printer type:

```
C:\> DIR  >  PRN <ENTER>
C:\> DIR  >  COM1 <ENTER>
```

DOS suppresses the directory listing display from your screen and routes it instead to the printer.

Repeat the DIR command, this time redirecting the output of the command to a file:

```
C:\> DIR \DOS  >  DIR.LST <ENTER>
```

If you display the contents of the DIR.LST file with the TYPE command:

```
C:\> TYPE  DIR.LST <ENTER>
```

you will see that the file contains the same information that DOS would normally display on the screen with the DIR command.

Using the MORE command, you can view the directory listing a screenful at a time:

```
C:\> MORE  <  DIR.LST <ENTER>
```

So that you have files to use with the append redirection operator, create these files:

```
C:\> COPY  CON  START.DAT <ENTER>
START OF TEXT <ENTER>
^Z <ENTER>
      1 File(s) copied

C:\> COPY  CON  MIDDLE.DAT <ENTER>
MIDDLE OF TEXT <ENTER>
^Z <ENTER>
      1 File(s) copied

C:\> COPY  CON  END.DAT <ENTER>
END OF TEXT <ENTER>
^Z <ENTER>
      1 File(s) copied

C:\>
```

Create the COMPLETE.DAT file, as shown here:

```
C:\> TYPE  START.DAT  >>  COMPLETE.DAT <ENTER>
C:\>
```

If the file specified after the append redirection operator does not exist, DOS creates it.

Use the TYPE command to display the contents of this file:

```
C:\> TYPE  COMPLETE.DAT <ENTER>
```

Using the append operator, append the contents of the MIDDLE.DAT file to the COMPLETE.DAT file:

```
C:\> TYPE  MIDDLE.DAT  >>  COMPLETE.DAT <ENTER>
```

Examine the contents of the file again with the TYPE command:

```
C:\> TYPE  COMPLETE.DAT <ENTER>
```

Finally, append the contents of the END.DAT file to COMPLETE.DAT:

```
C:\> TYPE  END.DAT  >>  COMPLETE.DAT <ENTER>
```

To see that your file is now complete, use the command

```
C:\> TYPE  COMPLETE.DAT <ENTER>
```

Next, create this file:

```
C:\> COPY  CON  NUMBERS.DAT <ENTER>
0 <ENTER>
5 <ENTER>
2 <ENTER>
6 <ENTER>
1 <ENTER>
9 <ENTER>
3 <ENTER>
1 <ENTER>
7 <ENTER>
4 <ENTER>
^Z <ENTER>
     1 File(s) copied
```

Use the SORT command to display the sorted contents of the file NUMBERS.DAT:

```
C:\> SORT  <  NUMBERS.DAT <ENTER>
```

Repeat the command, using the /R qualifier to display the sorted file contents from highest to lowest:

```
C:\> SORT  /R  <  NUMBERS.DAT <ENTER>
```

Next, create this file:

```
C:\> COPY  CON  DOS.NTS <ENTER>
DOS versions 4 and later provide <ENTER>
a menu-driven interface <ENTER>
not present in DOS 3.3. <ENTER>
^Z <ENTER>
     1 File(s) copied

C:\>
```

Now use the FIND command to display each line that contains the word "DOS":

```
C:\> FIND  "DOS"  <  DOS.NTS <ENTER>
```

Repeat the process, using the /N qualifier to display the line numbers for lines containing "DOS":

```
C:\> FIND  /N  "DOS"  <  DOS.NTS <ENTER>
```

Display the number of lines in the file that contain "DOS":

```
C:\>FIND  /C  "DOS"  <  DOS.NTS <ENTER>
```

Finally, using the /V qualifier, display the lines that do not contain the word "DOS":

```
C:\> FIND  /V  "DOS"  <  DOS.NTS <ENTER>
```

As you can see, the FIND command provides considerable flexibility.

Before you continue, delete the temporary files you created in this chapter:

```
C:\>  DEL  DIR.LST <ENTER>
C:\>  DEL  START.DAT <ENTER>
C:\>  DEL  MIDDLE.DAT <ENTER>
C:\>  DEL  END.DAT <ENTER>
C:\>  DEL  COMPLETE.DAT <ENTER>
C:\>  DEL  DOS.NTS <ENTER>
C:\>  DEL  NUMBERS.DAT <ENTER>
```

Review

1. What is the function of the **>**, **>>**, and **<** command-line operators?
2. How do the following two commands differ?

   ```
   C:\> DIR > FILENAME.EXT <ENTER>
   C:\> DIR >> FILENAME.EXT <ENTER>
   ```

3. What is the DOS command that displays the contents of the TAXES.DAT file in sorted order?
4. What is the meaning of the /V, /C, and /N qualifiers for the FIND command?
5. How do you sort the TAXES.DAT file based on data starting in column 15?

Key Points

The Output Redirection Operator (>)

The output redirection operator (>) instructs DOS to redirect the output of a command from the screen display to a file or device. The following command, for example, prints the current directory listing:

```
C:\> DIR > PRN <ENTER>
```

This command redirects the output of the CHKDSK command to a file named DISKINFO.DAT:

```
C:\> CHKDSK > DISKINFO.DAT <ENTER>
```

If the directory already contains a file named DISKINFO.DAT, the output redirection operator directs DOS to overwrite the contents of the file.

The Input Redirection Operator (<)

The input redirection operator (<) lets you tell DOS to redirect a command's source of input from the keyboard to a file or device. The following command directs MORE's source of input from the keyboard to the file FILENAME.EXT.

```
C:\> MORE < FILENAME.EXT <ENTER>
```

continues . . .

The Append Redirection Operator (>>)

The append redirection operator (**>>**) lets you direct the output of a command away from your screen display, appending it to a previously existing file. If the specified file does not exist, DOS will create it. The following command appends the output of the TREE command to a file named TREEINFO.DAT:

```
C:\> TREE >> TREEINFO.DAT <ENTER>
```

The MORE Command

The MORE command allows you to display a file's contents a screenful at a time. With each screenful of information, MORE suspends output and displays the message

```
-- More --
```

To continue the output, press any key. To cancel the file display, press CTRL-C.

The following MORE command displays the contents of the file PHONE.DAT, one screen at a time:

```
C:\> MORE < PHONE.DAT <ENTER>
```

continues . . .

The SORT Command

The SORT command lets you sort redirected input. The /R qualifier directs SORT to sort data in descending order, from highest to lowest. The /+*n* switch allows you to specify a column on which to sort the data.

The FIND Command

The FIND command lets you search redirected input for a specific word or phrase. The /N qualifier directs FIND to precede each line containing the word or phrase with its line number. The /V qualifier directs FIND to display lines that do not contain the word or phrase. The /C qualifier directs FIND to display a count of the number of lines containing the word or phrase.

The following FIND command searches the file PHONE.DAT for numbers with the (212) area code:

```
C:\> FIND "(212)" < PHONE.DAT <ENTER>
```

Using Batch Files

So far in this book, with one exception (PRINT), you have had to wait for the current command to complete before you could issue your next DOS command. In the examples that you have examined, the commands have completed so quickly that you have not had to wait very long before you could issue subsequent commands. When you start running other application programs in the future, however, this may not always be the case. For example, assume you must run several billing programs, each of which takes anywhere from 15 to 30 minutes to complete. If you have to sit and wait at the keyboard while this program executes just so you can execute your next command, you are wasting a considerable amount of time.

DOS provides you with *batch files*, which offer you an alternative way to execute commands that will save you time and keystrokes. A DOS batch file is a text file containing a list of commands that DOS will execute in succession.

Grouping Commands into a Batch File

Assume you are an instructor at a large university. Each week you must compute, sort, and print the grades for each of your classes. To do this, you have three programs that you must execute:

Program Name	Function
CMPGRADE	Computes student grades
SRTGRADE	Sorts student grades
PRTGRADE	Prints student grades

Each Friday, you sit at the computer and invoke the CMPGRADE program to compute your class grades:

```
C:\> CMPGRADE <ENTER>
```

When that program completes, you invoke the SRTGRADE program, which sorts the grades:

```
C:\> SRTGRADE <ENTER>
```

Finally, when the SRTGRADE program completes, you invoke the PRT-GRADE program, which prints all of the grades in sorted order:

```
C:\> PRTGRADE <ENTER>
```

When you invoke one of these three programs, the program runs to completion without further user intervention (meaning that it doesn't require additional input). You do not have to remain at your computer to respond to questions about the processing, but you have to wait at the computer to issue subsequent commands. Such processing is *interactive processing*, which means you are in constant interaction with your computer.

In cases like this, in which a command immediately follows the previous one, DOS allows you to group the commands into a batch file. DOS batch files have the three-letter extension BAT (short for "batch"). For the example just shown, you could create a batch file called GRADES.BAT, as shown here:

```
C:\> COPY CON GRADES.BAT <ENTER>
CMPGRADE <ENTER>
SRTGRADE <ENTER>
PRTGRADE <ENTER>
^Z <ENTER>
     1 File(s) copied

C:\>
```

Rather than type in each command individually, you could then invoke the GRADES.BAT batch file in this manner:

```
C:\> GRADES <ENTER>
```

DOS recognizes GRADES as a batch file by its BAT extension and begins executing the commands the file contains. In this case, DOS would first execute the CMPGRADE program, followed by SRTGRADE and PRTGRADE. The processing that would appear on your screen would be

```
C:\> GRADES <ENTER>

C:\> CMPGRADE

C:\> SRTGRADE

C:\> PRTGRADE

C:\>
```

Once DOS begins executing a batch file, it executes all of the commands in the file in succession, so there is no need for you to sit idly at your computer, waiting to type in the next command. This type of DOS processing is called *batch processing*. When DOS completes the last command in the batch file, it returns control to the DOS prompt.

Creating Your Own Batch Files

Creating DOS batch files is as easy as placing a list of DOS commands into a text file with the BAT extension. Let's create a batch file that performs the following:

❏ Clears the screen display with CLS

❏ Displays the current version number with VER

❏ Prompts the user for the current date with DATE

Create the following batch file and name it GETDATE.BAT:

```
C:\> COPY CON GETDATE.BAT <ENTER>
CLS <ENTER>
VER <ENTER>
```

```
DATE <ENTER>
^Z <ENTER>
     1 File(s) copied

C:\>
```

To invoke this batch file, type **GETDATE** at the DOS prompt:

```
C:\> GETDATE <ENTER>
```

When DOS recognizes that your command is a batch file, it will execute the commands it contains, first clearing the screen and then displaying the following:

```
C:\> GETDATE <ENTER>

C:\> VER

MS-DOS Version 6.00

C:\> DATE
Current date is Tue 04-06-1993
Enter new date (mm-dd-yy):
```

As you can see, DOS executed each of the commands in the batch file, one after another.

In a similar manner, you can create a batch file called DATETIME.BAT that performs the following:

❏   Clears the screen display

❏   Prompts the user to enter the current date

❏   Prompts the user to enter the current time

To create the DATETIME.BAT file, use

```
C:\> COPY  CON  DATETIME.BAT <ENTER>
CLS <ENTER>
```

```
DATE  <ENTER>
TIME  <ENTER>
^Z   <ENTER>
      1 File(s) copied


C:\>
```

As before, you can execute this batch file by typing its name at the DOS prompt:

```
C:\> DATETIME  <ENTER>
```

As you create DOS batch files, keep the following guidelines in mind:

❏ Always give your files meaningful names. The name of the batch file should remind you of the processing the batch file performs.

❏ Batch files must have the BAT extension.

❏ Never give your batch file the same name as a DOS command, such as DATE.BAT. Each time you execute a command, DOS first checks to see if the command is an internal command in memory. If it is not, DOS checks to see if the command is an EXE, COM, or BAT file on disk. Thus, if you name your batch file CLS.BAT, DOS will never find the batch file and will instead execute the CLS command. If you assign a batch file the same name as an external DOS command, the order in which DOS encounters the command or your batch file within a directory search will dictate whether DOS executes your batch file or the DOS command.

Suppressing On-Screen Command Names During Execution

By default, each time DOS executes the commands in a batch file, it does so in sequential order, displaying the name of each command as it executes it:

```
C:\> GRADES <ENTER>

C:\> CMPGRADE

C:\> SRTGRADE

C:\> PRTGRADE
```

In some cases, however, you might not want DOS to display the name of each command it executes within a batch file. The DOS ECHO OFF command allows you to suppress the display of command names.

Given the batch file

```
ECHO OFF
CMPGRADE
SRTGRADE
PRTGRADE
```

DOS will suppress the command-name display, as shown here:

```
C:\> GRADES <ENTER>

C:\> ECHO OFF

C:\>
```

Note that the ECHO OFF command appears only once in the batch file. In a similar manner, if you are using DOS version 3.3 or later, you can precede command names with an @ character, as shown here:

```
@CMPGRADE
@SRTGRADE
@PRTGRADE
```

To suppress the message

```
C:\> ECHO  OFF
```

you can precede the ECHO OFF command in your batch file with an @, as shown here:

```
@ECHO OFF
CMPGRADE
SRTGRADE
PRTGRADE
```

Upon invocation, this batch file will display

```
C:\> GRADES <ENTER>

C:\>
```

Placing Reminders in Your Batch Files

Since we have been discussing the batch procedure GRADES.BAT, which contains the commands

```
CMPGRADE
SRTGRADE
PRTGRADE
```

the processing each program performs is still fresh in your mind. However, a few weeks or months from now, this may not be the case. The REM command allows you to place remarks in your batch file that you can later use to understand or recall the batch file's purpose. DOS also lets you include blank lines in your batch files to improve readability. When DOS encounters a blank line, it ignores the line, continuing the batch file's execution at the command that follows. For example, consider how the remarks and blank lines in this batch file make it more readable:

```
@ECHO OFF
REM Calculate student grades.
CMPGRADE

REM Sort the grades by score.
SRTGRADE
```

```
REM Print the sorted grades by class.
PRTGRADE
```

If you are working in an office with other workers, you will probably want to include remarks that tell other users who wrote the procedure, why, and when:

```
@ECHO OFF
REM ****************************
REM
REM            GRADES
REM
REM  By Kris Jamsa  03/30/93
REM
REM  Compute, sort, and print
REM  class grades.
REM
REM ****************************
```

Suspending a Batch File for User Input

In some cases you may need to ensure that users perform a specific task—such as turning on a printer or inserting a specific disk in a floppy drive—during the execution of a batch file. The PAUSE command allows you to display a message to the screen and suspend processing until a user presses any key to continue.

As an example, if you place the command

```
C:\> PAUSE Make sure the printer is online
```

within a batch file, DOS will later display

```
C:\> PAUSE Make sure the printer is online
Press any key to continue . . .
```

When the user presses any key, DOS will continue the batch file's execution with its next command.

Given the batch file

```
PAUSE Place a new diskette in drive A
FORMAT A:
```

DOS will display

```
C:\> PAUSE Place a new diskette in drive A
Press any key to continue . . .
```

Be aware that if you place an ECHO OFF command within your batch file, as in

```
@ECHO OFF
PAUSE Place a new diskette in drive A
FORMAT A:
```

DOS will suppress the display of the message that PAUSE contains. As a result, DOS will display only

```
Press any key to continue . . .
```

As a solution, for batch files that use ECHO OFF and PAUSE, many users use ECHO for the message PAUSE would normally display, as shown here:

```
@ECHO OFF
REM --Other commands here
ECHO  Turn your printer online
PAUSE
```

Terminating a Batch File

Just as there are many times you need to terminate a DOS command with the CTRL-C key combination, so, too, are there times when you have to cancel the processing of a batch file. Let's use the DATETIME.BAT file as an example:

```
CLS
DATE
TIME
```

When DOS displays the prompt for the system date, press CTRL-C to cancel the DATE command:

```
C:\> DATE
Current date is Tue 04-06-1993
Enter new date (mm-dd-yy):^C
```

When you do so, DOS will display

```
Terminate batch job (Y/N)?
```

Notice the new prompt asking you if you not only want to cancel the DATE command, but also if you want to cancel the processing of the batch file. If you type **Y** and press ENTER, DOS will cancel the processing of the commands that remain in the batch file. If you instead type **N** and press ENTER, DOS will cancel only the DATE command and will continue on to the next command in the batch file, which in this case is the TIME command.

Type **Y** and press ENTER to cancel the batch file. As you can see, DOS will return control to the DOS prompt.

Repeat this same process again, pressing CTRL-C to cancel the DATE command:

```
C:\> DATE

Current date is Tue 04-06-1993
Enter new date (mm-dd-yy): ^C

Terminate batch job (Y/N)?
```

This time, respond to the prompt with **N** to cancel only the DATE command, resuming control at the TIME command:

```
C:\> DATE
Current date is Tue 04-06-1993
Enter new date (mm-dd-yy):^C

Terminate batch job (Y/N)?N

C:\> TIME
Current time is 8:22:07.55a
Enter new time:
```

Invoking a Batch File from Within the Shell

Executing a batch file from within the shell is no different than executing a DOS command. Given the file DATETIME.BAT

```
CLS
DATE
TIME
```

simply highlight the batch file and then invoke it by pressing ENTER. DOS will invoke the batch file, as shown here:

```
C:\> DATE
Current date is Tue 04-06-1993
Enter new date (mm-dd-yy): <ENTER>

C:\> TIME
Current time is 8:30:02.56a
Enter new time:
```

When the batch file completes, DOS will prompt you to press any key to return to the shell.

AUTOEXEC.BAT—A Special Batch File

As you will learn, DOS batch files can be very convenient. In particular, a special batch file named AUTOEXEC.BAT lets you specify a list of commands you want DOS to execute each time it starts. Chapter 1, "Understanding Your System," stated that depending on your system configuration, the steps DOS performs when your computer starts may differ. Actually, however, the steps DOS performs at system startup are dependent on the commands in your AUTOEXEC.BAT file.

Like all DOS batch files, AUTOEXEC.BAT contains a list of DOS commands that DOS executes in succession. What makes AUTOEXEC.BAT special is that each time DOS starts, it searches the root directory for this file. If DOS finds AUTOEXEC.BAT, DOS executes the commands that the file contains. If DOS does not find AUTOEXEC.BAT, DOS executes the DATE and TIME commands.

Because DOS executes the commands in the AUTOEXEC.BAT file each time your system starts, you should place the commands that meet your own requirements (such as PROMPT and PATH) into AUTOEXEC.BAT. Issue this command to see what is in your file:

```
C:\> TYPE  \AUTOEXEC.BAT <ENTER>
```

You should already be familiar with many of the commands that AUTOEXEC.BAT contains. You will examine the remaining commands throughout this book.

Practice

Using the COPY CON command, create a file called DT.BAT, which prompts you to enter the current system date and time:

```
C:\> COPY  CON  DT.BAT <ENTER>
DATE <ENTER>
TIME <ENTER>
^Z <ENTER>
      1 File(s) copied
```

Next, invoke the batch file from the DOS prompt as

```
C:\> DT <ENTER>
```

Invoke the batch file again. When DOS prompts you to enter the system date, press CTRL-C to cancel the command:

```
C:\> DT <ENTER>

C:\> DATE
Current date is Tue 04-06-1993
Enter new date (mm-dd-yy): ^C

Terminate batch job (Y/N)?
```

DOS is asking you if you want to terminate the batch job or just the DATE command.

In this case, type **Y** and press ENTER. As you can see, DOS returns control to the DOS prompt:

```
C:\> DT

C:\> DATE
Current date is Tue 04-06-1993
Enter new date (mm-dd-yy): ^C

Terminate batch job (Y/N)?Y

C:\>
```

Repeat this process, but respond to the prompt

```
Terminate batch job (Y/N)?
```

with **N**. As you can see, DOS continues processing at the TIME command:

```
C:\> DT <ENTER>

C:\> DATE
Current date is Tue 04-06-1993
Enter new date (mm-dd-yy): ^C

Terminate batch job (Y/N)?N

C:\> TIME
Current time is  8:34:52.95a
Enter new time:
```

If you examine the output of the DT.BAT batch file, you can see that DOS displays each command name in the batch file as it executes.

Change the batch file to the following:

```
C:\> COPY  CON  DT.BAT <ENTER>
@DATE <ENTER>
@TIME <ENTER>
^Z <ENTER>
     1 File(s) copied
C:\>
```

When you invoke the batch file now, the @ in front of each command directs DOS to suppress the command-name display:

```
C:\> DT <ENTER>
Current date is Tue 04-06-1993
Enter new date (mm-dd-yy): <ENTER>
Current time is  8:35:52.71a
Enter new time: <ENTER>
```

Using the REM command, place some simple remarks at the beginning of the batch file:

```
C:\> COPY  CON  DT.BAT <ENTER>
@ECHO OFF <ENTER>
REM DT.BAT   04/06/93   K. Jamsa <ENTER>
REM Prompt user for DATE and TIME <ENTER>
DATE <ENTER>
TIME <ENTER>
^Z <ENTER>
     1 File(s) copied

C:\>
```

The ECHO OFF command directs DOS to suppress the display of command names as the batch file executes.

Next, create a batch file called WAIT.BAT, which directs the user to turn on the printer and then sends a list of all of the files on the disk to the printer:

```
C:\> COPY  CON  WAIT.BAT <ENTER>
PAUSE Turn on your printer <ENTER>
DIR  >  PRN <ENTER>
^Z <ENTER>
     1 File(s) copied
```

When you invoke this batch file, DOS will display

```
C:\> PAUSE Turn on your printer
Press any key to continue . . .
```

Next, use the TYPE command to examine the AUTOEXEC.BAT file to see what it contains:

```
C:\> TYPE \AUTOEXEC.BAT <ENTER>
```

Review

1. What is a batch file?

2. Create a batch file called SHOWVER.BAT that clears the screen and displays the current DOS version number.

3. Why won't the following batch file, DIR.BAT, execute?

```
C:\> TYPE DIR.BAT <ENTER>
DIR /W

C:\>
```

4. What does the ECHO OFF command do?

5. What is the function of the @ in the following batch file?

```
@DATE
@TIME
```

6. When do you use the REM command?

7. Create a batch file that will suspend processing until the user presses a key, acknowledging that the correct data disk is in drive B.

8. What is the function of the AUTOEXEC.BAT batch file?

Key Points

DOS Batch Files

A DOS batch file is a text file with the BAT extension that contains a list of DOS commands. To execute the commands, you simply type in the batch file's name at the DOS prompt. DOS will execute the specified commands, starting at the top and working toward the bottom of the file.

continues . . .

Creating Batch Files

For short batch files, many users simply copy the batch file from the keyboard by using COPY CON, as shown here:

```
C:\> COPY CON BATFILE.BAT <ENTER>
DATE <ENTER>
TIME <ENTER>
^Z <ENTER>
  1 File(s) copied
C:\>
```

For larger batch files or if you need to change an entry, use the EDIT text editor (see Chapter 16, "Using EDIT") or another text editor to create the file.

The ECHO OFF Command

The ECHO OFF command directs DOS to suppress the names of commands as they execute in a batch file. Most users precede the ECHO OFF command with the @ character, which also directs DOS to suppress command-name display. The following batch file uses ECHO OFF.

```
@ECHO OFF
CLS
DATE
TIME
```

Suppressing Command-Name Display with @

In addition to the ECHO OFF command, which directs DOS to suppress command names as they execute in a batch file, DOS

continues . . .

allows you to precede commands with the @ character. When DOS encounters the @ character before a command name, it suppresses the command name's display. The following batch file uses the @ character.

```
@DATE
@TIME
```

The REM Command

The REM command allows you to leave remarks in your batch file that will explain the file's processing. DOS does not execute REM; the command is used purely for batch-file documentation. At a minimum, your batch files should contain remarks that state who wrote the batch file, why, and when.

The PAUSE Command

PAUSE allows you to suspend a batch file's processing temporarily, allowing a user to read a message and perform any additional required steps, such as turning the printer on or inserting a specific disk in a drive. Once the user is ready to continue, he or she simply presses a key, and DOS will continue with the next command in the batch file.

The AUTOEXEC.BAT File

Each time your system starts, DOS searches the root directory of the boot device for the AUTOEXEC.BAT file. If DOS locates the file, it executes the commands the file contains. AUTOEXEC.BAT allows you to specify a set of commands you want DOS to execute each time your system starts. If DOS does not find AUTOEXEC.BAT, it executes the familiar DATE and TIME commands.

CHAPTER

Decision Making in Batch Files

As you have already learned, a program is a list of instructions for the computer to perform. In Chapter 18, "Using Batch Files," you actually began to program DOS when you created your first batch files. In general, a batch file is nothing more than a list of commands you want the computer to perform. As you have seen, DOS executes the commands in a batch file sequentially, from top to bottom:

```
CMPGRADE
SRTGRADE
PRTGRAD
```

In this chapter you will examine three new batch-file commands: IF, FOR, and GOTO. These commands allow you to change the order of command execution in a batch file, in some cases repeating commands and in others conditionally executing a command based on the result of a specific test. By using these commands, you can fully exploit DOS batch files by creating batch files with decision-making capabilities.

Making Decisions Within a Batch File

Unless told to do otherwise, DOS will execute the commands in your batch file sequentially from the first batch-file command to the last. The IF command allows you to tell DOS to execute a command only when a specific condition is met. As your batch files increase in complexity, the ability to conditionally execute commands by using IF will be essential. When a batch file executes a command based on the result of a condition tested by an IF command, the batch file is said to perform *conditional batch processing*.

The IF command allows your batch file to test one of three conditions. The first condition is whether or not a file exists as specified on disk. The format of the IF command in this case is

```
IF EXIST FILENAME.EXT DOS_command
```

where *FILENAME.EXT* specifies the file that you are searching for and *DOS_command* is the command that DOS is to execute if the specified file exists. Given the command

```
IF EXIST NOTES.TXT PRINT NOTES.TXT
```

the file DOS is searching for is NOTES.TXT, and the command DOS executes if the file is found is PRINT NOTES.TXT, as shown here:

```
IF EXIST NOTES.TXT                    PRINT NOTES.TXT
```
　　　　　Does this file exist?　　　　　　　　If so, print it.

The following batch file tests to see if the NOTES.TXT file exists on the disk in drive A. If the file exists, DOS copies the contents of the file from drive A to the current drive.

```
CLS
IF EXIST A:NOTES.TXT COPY A:NOTES.TXT *.*
```

In this case, the file name contained a disk drive letter (A:). DOS lets you include disk drive letters and directory names as you require.

The second condition you can test with IF is the success of the previous batch-file command. Many DOS commands specify a value that, upon completion of the command, DOS can evaluate. The DISKCOPY command, for example, supports the following exit-status values:

Exit Value	Meaning
0	Successful copy
1	Unsuccessful copy due to nonfatal disk error
2	User terminated via CTRL-C
3	Unsuccessful copy due to fatal disk error
4	Invalid disk drive

Create the following batch file:

```
C:\> COPY  CON  EXITTST.BAT <ENTER>
@ECHO OFF <ENTER>
DISKCOPY A: A: <ENTER>
IF ERRORLEVEL 2 ECHO User Ctrl-C <ENTER>
^Z <ENTER>
     1 File(s) copied

C:\>
```

Next, invoke the batch procedure as shown here:

```
C:\> EXITTST <ENTER>
```

When DOS invokes the DISKCOPY command, you will see

```
Insert SOURCE diskette in drive A:

Press any key to continue . . .
```

Press the CTRL-C keyboard combination to terminate the command:

```
C:\> EXITTST
Insert SOURCE diskette in drive A:

Press any key to continue . . .
^C
```

Since you have terminated the DISKCOPY command with CTRL-C, DISK-COPY will return an exit status of 2 to DOS. Thus, the condition

```
IF ERRORLEVEL 2 ECHO User Ctrl-C
```

will evaluate as true, and DOS will execute the corresponding ECHO command, displaying the message

```
User Ctrl-C
```

When DOS evaluates the IF ERRORLEVEL condition, DOS tests the exit-status value of the previous program against the specified value. If the program's exit-status value is greater than or equal to the specified value, DOS considers the condition to have been met and executes the specified command. Because of this, you need to take care when you write your batch files. Consider, for example, the following batch file, BADTESTS.BAT, which checks for several conditions:

```
@ECHO OFF
DISKCOPY A: A:
IF ERRORLEVEL  0  ECHO  Successful copy
IF ERRORLEVEL  1  ECHO  Nonfatal disk error
IF ERRORLEVEL  2  ECHO  User Ctrl-C
IF ERRORLEVEL  3  ECHO  Fatal disk error
IF ERRORLEVEL  4  ECHO  Invalid disk drive
```

Invoke the batch as BADTESTS, as shown here:

```
C:\> BADTESTS  <ENTER>
```

When DISKCOPY prompts you to place a source disk in drive A, press CTRL-C to end DISKCOPY. In this case, the batch file will display the following:

```
Successful copy
Non-fatal disk error
User Ctrl-C
```

As you can see, the batch file displayed the messages that correspond to three different conditions. Because the exit-status value was 2, the batch file's first three IF ERRORLEVEL conditions evaluate as true. Remember, IF considers an ERRORLEVEL condition as true if the exit-status value is greater than or equal to the value specified. For more information on creating an IF command that tests for an exact value, refer to the IF command in the Command Reference section of this book.

The last condition that DOS allows your batch files to test is whether two words or phrases are the same:

```
IF phrase_1==phrase_2 DOS_command
```

In Chapter 23, "Batch Files: A Last Look," you will learn that DOS allows you to pass information called batch parameters to your batch files. At that time, you will examine this final IF condition in detail.

Using the DOS 6 CHOICE Command

The DOS IF command lets your batch files make decisions based on different conditions. As you examine the commands listed in the Command Reference section of this book, you will find that several commands provide different exit-status values, which let your batch files determine their degree of success or possible errors. If you are using DOS 6, however, your batch files can invoke the CHOICE command to ask the user a question and then use IF ERRORLEVEL to determine the user's response. For example, your batch file might ask if the user wants to print a specific file, as shown here:

```
Do you want to print FILENAME.EXT [Y/N]?
```

If the user types **Y**, the batch file will print the file. If the user types **N**, the batch file will not.

The DOS 6 CHOICE command displays a message to the user and then waits for the user to press any one in a set of specific keys. For example, the following CHOICE command would display the previous question about printing *FILENAME.EXT*:

```
CHOICE /C:YN Do you want to print FILENAME.EXT
```

In this case, once CHOICE prompts the user for a response, CHOICE will wait until the user types **Y** or **N**. CHOICE will beep the computer's built-in bell if the user types anything else. If the user types **Y**, CHOICE will return the exit status 1. If the user types **N**, CHOICE will return the exit status 2. The following batch file uses CHOICE to determine whether or not you want to print the file CONFIG.SYS:

```
@ECHO OFF
CHOICE /C:YN Do you want to print CONFIG.SYS
IF ERRORLEVEL 1 IF NOT ERRORLEVEL 2 PRINT \CONFIG.SYS
```

The previous CHOICE command used the switch /C:YN to prompt the user for a Yes or No response. As it turns out, if you don't specify a /C switch, the default is /C:YN. Therefore, the following commands are identical in function:

```
CHOICE /C:YN Do you want to print CONFIG.SYS

CHOICE Do you want to print CONFIG.SYS
```

As your batch files become more complex, they might display a menu of options, as shown here:

```
A      Start Excel
B      Invoke Access
C      Start Windows
Q      Quit (to DOS)
Enter choice:[A,B,C,Q]?
```

When the user types **A**, **B**, **C**, or **Q**, the batch file will perform the desired operation. If you are using DOS 6, the CHOICE command lets your batch files wait for and determine a user response. The following CHOICE command waits for the user to type **A**, **B**, **C**, or **Q**:

```
CHOICE /C:ABCQ Enter choice:
```

The letters that follow the CHOICE /C switch specify the keys CHOICE will wait for. If the user types any other key, CHOICE will ignore the keystroke. When the user types one of the specified keys, CHOICE returns an exit-status value that corresponds to the key pressed. Given the previous command, CHOICE will return the exit status 1 if the user presses **A**, 2 for **B**, 3 for **C**, and 4 for **Q**.

Should the user cancel the CHOICE command by pressing CTRL-C, CHOICE returns the exit-status value 0. Within your batch file, you can use the IF ERRORLEVEL command to determine the key pressed. The following batch file, for example, displays a menu of options and then waits to determine the key pressed:

```
@ECHO OFF
:LOOP
CLS
ECHO              Main Menu
ECHO.
ECHO      A       Show the current memory use
ECHO      B       List files in the current directory
ECHO      C       Set the system date
```

```
ECHO    Q       Quit to DOS
ECHO.
CHOICE /C:ABCQ Enter choice:
IF NOT ERRORLEVEL 1 GOTO DONE
IF ERRORLEVEL 1 IF NOT ERRORLEVEL 2 MEM /DEBUG /PAGE
IF ERRORLEVEL 2 IF NOT ERRORLEVEL 3 DIR /P
IF ERRORLEVEL 3 IF NOT ERRORLEVEL 4 DATE
IF ERRORLEVEL 4 GOTO QUIT
PAUSE
GOTO LOOP
:QUIT
```

Case-Sensitive Processing

By default, CHOICE considers upper- and lowercase letters the same. For example, the following CHOICE command waits for the user to type **A**, **B**, **C**, or **Q**:

CHOICE /C:ABCQ Enter choice:

As it turns out, CHOICE will return the same exit-status value if the user types **A** or **a**, or **B** or **b**. Depending on your batch file's processing, there may be times when you want CHOICE to distinguish between upper- and lowercase letters. To do so, include CHOICE's /S switch.

Specifying a Default Choice

In many cases, your menu-driven batch files will have one option that users will select most often. Therefore, CHOICE lets you specify a default option, which, if the user does not respond in a given number of seconds, CHOICE selects for them. Consider, for example, a batch file that asks the user a Yes or No question, such as whether or not they want to print the file FILENAME.EXT. The batch file could invoke the CHOICE command as follows:

```
CHOICE /C:YN Do you want to print FILENAME.EXT
IF ERRORLEVEL 1 IF NOT ERRORLEVEL 2 PRINT FILENAME.EXT
```

Assume that in most cases, the user selects the No option. Using CHOICE's /T switch, you can select N as the default. To do so, you must determine the number of seconds (from 0 to 99) which, if the user fails to respond by, CHOICE selects the default option. The following CHOICE command, for example, directs CHOICE to select the N option after 15 seconds should the user fail to make a response:

```
CHOICE /C:YN /T:N,15 Do you want to print FILENAME.EXT
```

In other words, after 15 seconds, CHOICE behaves as if the user pressed the **N** key, in this case returning the exit-status value 2.

Suppressing CHOICE's Display of Valid Keys

By default, CHOICE displays the keys the user can press in its prompt. For example, the command

```
CHOICE /C:YN Do you want to print FILENAME.EXT
```

will display the letters "Y" and "N" as shown here:

```
Do you want to print FILENAME.EXT [Y/N]?
```

If your batch file displays a menu with several different options, displaying the keys in the prompt is distracting. If you include the /N switch in the command line, CHOICE will not display the keys. For example, the command

```
CHOICE /C:YN /N Do you want to print FILENAME.EXT
```

will not display the keys (nor the question mark), as shown here:

```
Do you want to print FILENAME.EXT
```

Repeating a Command for a Set of Files

The FOR command lets your batch files repeat a specific command for a given set of files. The format of the FOR command is

```
FOR %%variable IN (set_of_files) DO DOS_command
```

where *variable* is a letter to which DOS assigns a file name from a *set_of_files* with each repetition of the loop, *set_of_files* is one or more DOS file names or wildcard characters, and *DOS_command* is the command that FOR will execute for each of the specified files.

To understand how FOR actually works, consider this example:

```
FOR %%I IN (A.DAT B.DAT C.DAT) DO TYPE %%I
```

When the FOR command begins, it assigns the name of the first file in the set to the variable %%I. Thus, when FOR executes the command

```
TYPE %%I
```

DOS actually issues the command

```
TYPE A.DAT
```

because of the substitution.

When the TYPE command completes, FOR examines the set of files and assigns the B.DAT file to %%I, resulting in the command

```
TYPE B.DAT
```

When the TYPE command completes, FOR repeats this process, resulting in the command

```
TYPE C.DAT
```

When this command completes, FOR again examines the set of files. In this case, FOR does not find any additional files, so its processing ends.

The FOR command also supports wildcard characters. For example,

```
FOR %%I IN (*.DAT) DO TYPE %%I
```

displays all the files in the current directory that have the DAT extension. The command

```
FOR %%I IN (*.DAT *.TXT *.NTS) DO TYPE %%I
```

first displays all of the files with the DAT extension, followed by files with the TXT extension, and finally, all files with the NTS extension.

Using GOTO to Skip or Repeat Commands

As you have seen, the IF command allows your batch files to execute commands conditionally, and the FOR command allows you to repeat a specific DOS command for a set of one or more files. However, as your batch-processing needs become more complex, there will be many times when you need to skip one or more commands or repeat a group of commands. The GOTO command allows you to do just that.

The GOTO command allows you to specify a batch-file location at which DOS will continue its processing. For example, consider the following batch file:

```
GOTO DONE
CLS
VER
:DONE
```

When DOS executes this GOTO command, it will skip all of the commands in the batch file and resume control at the DONE label, as shown here:

```
GOTO DONE ─┐
CLS        │
VER        │
:DONE ◄────┘
```

DOS *labels* are simply names that you precede with a colon in your batch file. When DOS encounters the colon at the start of the label name, DOS recognizes that the line contains a label and not a command. Given the batch file VERONLY.BAT, shown here:

```
@ECHO OFF
CLS
GOTO SKIP
DATE
TIME
:SKIP
VER
```

DOS will execute the CLS command, skip the DATE and TIME commands, and continue processing at the VER command:

```
C:\> VER ONLY <ENTER>
MS-DOS Version 6.00

C:\>
```

DOS labels don't have to appear at the end of your batch files. In the following example, DOS will skip the LOOP label, issue the DIR command, and then branch back to the label:

```
:LOOP
DIR
GOTO LOOP
```

DOS will continue processing at the label, again invoking the DIR command. When this command completes, DOS will again branch back to the loop. The net result is that DOS will repeat the DIR command indefinitely until the user presses CTRL-C to terminate the batch file.

You can use the GOTO command in conjunction with the IF command. In the following example, the batch file executes the DISKCOPY command. If DISKCOPY exits with an error-status value greater than 0, an error has occurred and DOS will display the message "Incomplete Copy." If the command is successful, no message is displayed.

```
@ECHO OFF
DISKCOPY A: A:
IF ERRORLEVEL 1 GOTO ERROR
GOTO DONE
```

```
:ERROR
ECHO Incomplete Copy
:DONE
```

When an error occurs (any exit-status value of 1 or greater), the batch file branches to the ERROR label and displays this error message:

```
Incomplete Copy
```

When the command is successful, DOS branches to the DONE label without displaying the error message.

Using the NOT Operator

In some cases, as you create tests with the IF command, you can simplify your processing by using the NOT operator. Consider this command:

```
IF NOT EXIST FILENAME.EXT COPY A:FILENAME.EXT *.*
```

The NOT EXIST expression tells DOS that if the specified file does not exist on disk, it should perform the specified command. In this case, if the FILENAME.EXT file does not exist in the current directory, DOS will copy the file from drive A.

As you will see, the NOT operator allows you to simplify difficult IF conditions. Each of the IF conditions supports the NOT operator.

Practice

Using COPY CON, create the following file:

```
C:\> COPY  CON  BATCH.NTS <ENTER>
The IF command allows you to perform <ENTER>
decision making within a batch file. <ENTER>
```

```
^Z <ENTER>
     1 File(s) copied
C:\>
```

Next, create the IFTST.BAT batch file, as shown here:

```
C:\> COPY  CON  IFTST.BAT <ENTER>
IF EXIST BATCH.NTS TYPE BATCH.NTS <ENTER>
IF EXIST FILENAME.EXT TYPE FILENAME.EXT <ENTER>
^Z <ENTER>
     1 File(s) copied

C:\>
```

When you invoke the command, DOS will display

```
C:\> IFTST <ENTER>

C:\> IF  EXIST  BATCH.NTS  TYPE  BATCH.NTS
The IF command allows you to perform
decision making within a batch file.

C:\> IF  EXIST  FILENAME.EXT  TYPE  FILENAME.EXT

C:\>
```

As you can see, the batch file's first IF command successfully located the file BATCH.NTS. As a result, the batch file used the TYPE command to display the file's contents. The batch file's second IF command, however, did not find a matching file. As a result, it did not issue a TYPE command.

Next, create the FORTST.BAT batch file, as shown here:

```
C:\> COPY  CON  FORTST.BAT <ENTER>
FOR %%I IN (BATCH.NTS *.BAT) DO TYPE %%I <ENTER>
^Z <ENTER>
     1 File(s) copied

C:\>
```

Invoke the command with

```
C:\> FORTST <ENTER>
```

FOR will first assign the file BATCH.NTS to the variable I, displaying the file's contents with the TYPE command. When the TYPE command completes, FOR examines the next file in the set of files. In this case, FOR encounters the file specification *.BAT, so DOS displays the contents of the IFTST.BAT and FORTST.BAT, as well as any other batch files in your directory. When FOR does not find another file in the set, the command terminates.

Create the GOTOTST.BAT batch file, as shown here:

```
C:\> COPY  CON  GOTOTST.BAT <ENTER>
VER <ENTER>
GOTO END <ENTER>
DATE <ENTER>
TIME <ENTER>
:END <ENTER>
^Z <ENTER>
     1 File(s) copied

C:\>
```

When you invoke the batch file, note that DOS displays the current version number and then skips the DATE and TIME commands.

Finally, create the batch file NOTTST.BAT, as shown here:

```
C:\> COPY  CON  NOTTST.BAT <ENTER>
DIR NEWFILE.NTS <ENTER>
IF NOT EXIST NEWFILE.NTS COPY BATCH.NTS NEWFILE.NTS <ENTER>
DIR NEWFILE.NTS <ENTER>
^Z <ENTER>
     1 File(s) copied

C:\>
```

When you invoke this batch file, DOS will display

```
C:\> NOTTST  <ENTER>

C:\> DIR  NEWFILE.NTS
File not found

C:\> IF NOT EXIST NEWFILE.NTS COPY BATCH.NTS NEWFILE.NTS
, 1 File(s) copied

C:\> DIR  NEWFILE.NTS

 Volume in drive C is DOS 6 DISK
 Volume Serial Number is 16F6-3B73
 Directory of C:\

NEWFILE  NTS           80 03-31-93  10:03a
        1 file(s)              80 bytes
                       152174592 bytes free
```

Since the NEWFILE.NTS file does not exist, the command

```
IF NOT EXIST NEWFILE.NTS COPY BATCH.NTS NEWFILE.NTS
```

creates it, and the second DIR command successfully locates the file.
Because the file NEWFILE.NTS now exists on disk, repeat the batch file
and note the processing it performs.

If you are using DOS 6, create the following batch file, ASKDIR.BAT,
that uses CHOICE to determine whether or not you want to display the
current directory listing:

```
@ECHO OFF
CHOICE Do you want to see a directory listing
IF ERRORLEVEL 1 IF NOT ERRORLEVEL 2 DIR
```

Next, create the batch file MYCHOICE.BAT that prompts the user for the letters A, B, C, or D and then echoes the key pressed:

```
@ECHO OFF
CHOICE /C:ABCD Which letter do you like
IF ERRORLEVEL 1 IF NOT ERRORLEVEL 2 ECHO You chose A
IF ERRORLEVEL 2 IF NOT ERRORLEVEL 3 ECHO You chose B
IF ERRORLEVEL 3 IF NOT ERRORLEVEL 4 ECHO You chose C
IF ERRORLEVEL 4 IF NOT ERRORLEVEL 5 ECHO You chose D
```

Review

1. What is conditional batch processing?

2. The IF command allows you to test three conditions. What are they?

3. Write a command that checks to see if the file TEST.DAT exists on disk and prints the file if it exists.

4. What is the function of the following command?

   ```
   FOR %%C IN (*.DAT) DO TYPE %%C
   ```

5. How does DOS distinguish a label from a command?

6. Write a batch file that repeatedly displays the DOS version number until the user presses CTRL-C to terminate the command.

7. Write a batch file that displays the contents of the TEST.DAT, TEST.NTS, and TEST.TXT files.

8. If you are using DOS 6, write a batch file that asks the user if they want to print the file TEST.DAT and, if so, prints the file.

The IF EXIST Condition

The IF EXIST condition directs DOS to test whether a file exists as specified. If the file exists, DOS executes the specified command; otherwise, DOS continues with the next command in the batch file. The following command, for example, tests whether a file named FILENAME.EXT exists and, if so, uses TYPE to display the file's contents:

```
IF EXIST FILENAME.EXT TYPE FILENAME.EXT
```

The IF ERRORLEVEL Condition

The IF ERRORLEVEL condition directs DOS to examine the exit-status value of the previous program. If the exit value is greater than or equal to the value specified, DOS executes the command specified. The following IF command displays the message "Successful SORT" if the previous program exits with an error level of 1 or greater.

```
IF ERRORLEVEL 1 ECHO Successful SORT
```

The FOR Command

The FOR command directs DOS to execute a specific command for each of the files in a given set. DOS uses the files in the set one at a time, issuing the corresponding command. The following FOR command displays the contents of the files A.DAT, B.DAT, and C.DAT, in that order:

```
FOR %%I IN (A.DAT B.DAT C.DAT) DO TYPE %%I
```

continues . . .

Key Points
(continued)

The GOTO Command

The GOTO command allows your batch files to skip or repeat commands as necessary. When DOS encounters the GOTO command, it resumes batch-file processing at the location in the batch file containing the specified label. The following GOTO command branches to a batch-file label named DONE:

```
GOTO DONE
```

In the batch file, the label DONE is preceded by a colon.

The NOT Operator

The NOT operator changes the results of an IF EXIST, IF ERRORLEVEL, or IF *string1==string2* condition. NOT directs DOS to take the opposite of the condition's result. If a condition returns true, NOT results in false, and vice versa. For example, the following command copies the CONFIG.SYS file to drive A only if the file does not currently exist there:

```
IF  NOT  EXIST  A:\CONFIG.SYS  COPY  \CONFIG.SYS  A:\
```

The CHOICE Command

If you are using DOS 6, your batch files can use the CHOICE command to prompt the user to press any one of a specific set of keys. For example, the following CHOICE command directs the user to press **A**, **B**, or **C**:

```
CHOICE /C:ABC Select your option
```

continues . . .

If the user types **A**, CHOICE returns the exit status 1. Likewise, if the user types **B** or **C**, CHOICE returns the exit status 2 or 3. If the user types anything else, CHOICE beeps the computer's built-in speaker.

CHAPTER

I/O Redirection with the DOS Pipe

*I*n Chapter 17, "Controlling DOS Input and Output," you learned that the output redirection operator (>) allows you to redirect the output of a DOS command from your screen display to a file or device. For example, the command

```
C:\> DIR  >  DIR.LST <ENTER>
```

directs DOS to send the output of the DIR command to a file called DIR.LST. You also learned in Chapter 17 that the DOS input redirection operator (<) lets you redirect the input of a DOS command from your keyboard to an existing file. For example, the following command directs DOS to send the sorted contents of the DIR.LST file to your screen display:

```
C:\> SORT  <  DIR.LST <ENTER>
```

You can also combine the DOS input and output redirection operators on the source line in this manner:

```
C:\> SORT  <  DIR.LST > PRN <ENTER>
```

In this case, DOS will sort the contents of the DIR.LST file and write the sorted contents to your printer.

In this chapter you will learn about the last redirection operator, which is called the *DOS pipe*. The pipe operator allows you to make the output of one DOS command the input to another.

Using the DOS Pipe

The pipe operator uses a unique character that looks like a vertical bar (I or ¦). First, locate the key associated with the pipe on your keyboard, shown in Figure 20-1.

Next, issue the following command:

```
C:\> DIR  \DOS  |  MORE <ENTER>
```

FIGURE 20-1

Location of pipe key

The pipe operator directs DOS to send the output of the DIR command to the input of the MORE command. As a result, DOS displays the directory listing one screenful at a time:

```
C:\> DIR  \DOS  |  MORE <ENTER>

 Volume in drive C is DOS
 Volume Serial Number is 1A54-45E0
 Directory of C:\DOS

 .                <DIR>      11-23-92    9:26p
 ..               <DIR>      11-23-92    9:26p
 DBLSPACE BIN     50284 02-12-93    6:00a
 FORMAT   COM     22717 02-12-93    6:00a
 NLSFUNC  EXE      7036 02-12-93    6:00a
 COUNTRY  SYS     17066 02-12-93    6:00a
 KEYB     COM     14983 02-12-93    6:00a
 KEYBOARD SYS     34694 02-12-93    6:00a
 ANSI     SYS      9065 02-12-93    6:00a
```

```
ATTRIB    EXE      11165 02-12-93    6:00a
CHKDSK    EXE      12908 02-12-93    6:00a
EDIT      COM        413 02-12-93    6:00a
EXPAND    EXE      16129 02-12-93    6:00a
MORE      COM       2546 02-12-93    6:00a
MSD       EXE     158470 02-12-93    6:00a
QBASIC    EXE     194309 02-12-93    6:00a
RESTORE   EXE      38294 02-12-93    6:00a
SYS       COM       9379 02-12-93    6:00a
-- More --
```

When you are ready to continue the directory listing, press any key to continue. Figure 20-2 shows how the pipe operator has routed the data. The pipe operator directs the output of the DIR command to become the input of the MORE command.

Repeat this process with the SORT command:

```
C:\> DIR  \DOS |  SORT <ENTER>
```

FIGURE
20-2

Processing of DIR | MORE

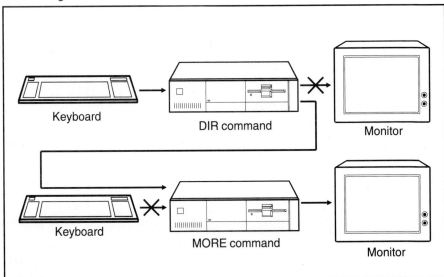

In this case, DOS will display your directory listing with the files sorted by name. The processing for this command is shown in Figure 20-3.

Finally, assume that the directory of the floppy disk in drive A contains three subdirectories, as shown here:

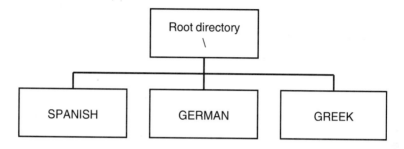

You can display each of the subdirectory names, excluding file names, by using this command:

```
C:\> DIR  A: |  FIND  "<DIR>"  <ENTER>
```

FIGURE 20-3

Processing of DIR | SORT

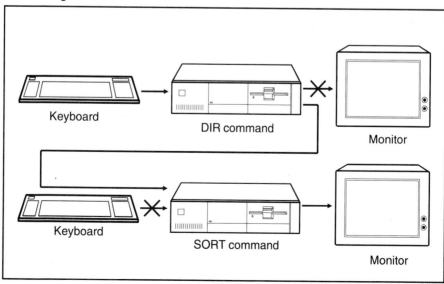

In this case, your output might be

```
C:\> DIR A:  |  FIND  "<DIR>" <ENTER>

SPANISH       <DIR>      03-25-93    2:21p
GERMAN        <DIR>      03-25-93    2:21p
GREEK         <DIR>      03-25-93    2:21p
```

Combining Redirection Operators in the Same Command Line

DOS allows you to place several I/O redirection operators in the same command line. For example, the command

```
C:\> SORT  < FILENAME.EXT > FILENAME.NEW <ENTER>
```

produces the I/O redirection shown in Figure 20-4.

FIGURE 20-4

Processing of SORT < *FILENAME.EXT* > *FILENAME.NEW*

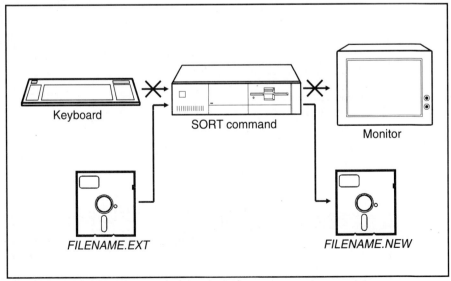

Keyboard   SORT command   Monitor

FILENAME.EXT   FILENAME.NEW

In a similar manner, DOS lets you use multiple occurrences of the DOS pipe. For example, the command

```
C:\> DIR  |  SORT  |  MORE <ENTER>
```

causes DOS to display a sorted directory listing a screenful at a time. The redirection for this command is shown in Figure 20-5.

DOS also allows you to use the pipe in conjunction with the other I/O redirection operators, as shown here:

```
C:\> DIR  |  SORT  > FILENAME.EXT <ENTER>
```

In this case, DOS will write a sorted directory listing to the file *FILENAME.EXT.*

Processing of DIR | SORT | MORE

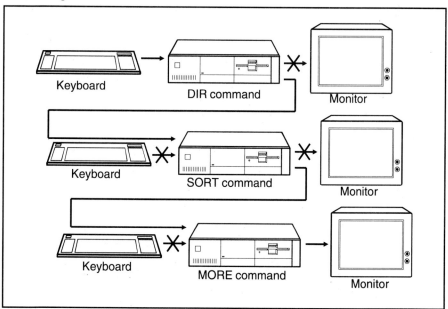

Piping in DOS 5 and Later

To pipe the output of one command into the input of another, DOS actually creates two hidden temporary files that hold the piped data. A *hidden file* is a file that exists on your disk but does not appear in the directory listing. When DOS has finished piping the information, DOS deletes these temporary files. Because DOS must create these files, several possible error conditions may arise. First, if you try to use the pipe with a write-protected floppy disk as the default drive, DOS cannot create the files, and the pipe operation will fail. If this occurs, DOS will display an error message similar to the following:

```
Write protect error writing drive A
Abort, Retry, Fail?
```

Second, should your disk run out of disk space because of the temporary files, the pipe operation will fail, and DOS will display the following:

```
Intermediate file error during pipe
```

If you are using DOS 5 or later, you can use the TEMP environment entry discussed in Chapter 21 to tell DOS where you want it to create its temporary files. In Chapter 27 you will learn how you can use part of your computer's electronic random-access memory to create a fast RAM disk drive. If you direct DOS 5 or later to create its temporary files on the fast RAM drive, DOS can execute your pipe commands much more quickly because it takes it much less time to create the temporary files.

Understanding stdin and stdout

Two terms are often used in discussions of the DOS I/O redirection operators: *stdin* and *stdout*. These are actually the names DOS assigns to the source of the input and the destination of the output for a DOS command. By default, the standard input source (stdin) points to your keyboard and the standard output source (stdout) points to your screen display, as shown here:

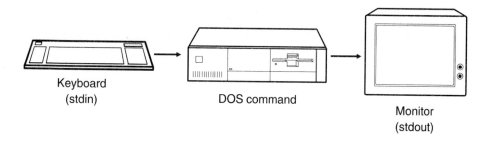

Keyboard
(stdin)

DOS command

Monitor
(stdout)

When you perform input redirection, as in the command

```
C:\> SORT < FILENAME.EXT <ENTER>
```

DOS redefines stdin to point to the new source, as shown here:

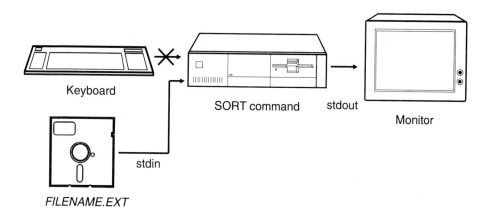

Keyboard

SORT command   stdout

Monitor

stdin

FILENAME.EXT

Likewise, when you perform output redirection, as in

```
C:\> DIR > PRN <ENTER>
```

DOS redefines stdout, as shown here:

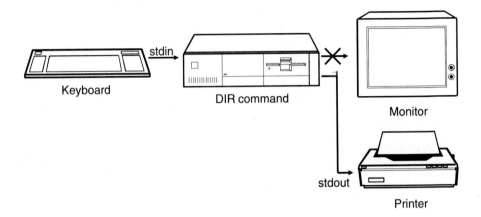

When you use the DOS pipe, as in

```
C:\> DIR  |  MORE <ENTER>
```

DOS redefines stdout for the DIR command and also redefines stdin for MORE, as shown in Figure 20-6.

FIGURE 20-6   Redefinition of stdout and stdin for DIR | MORE

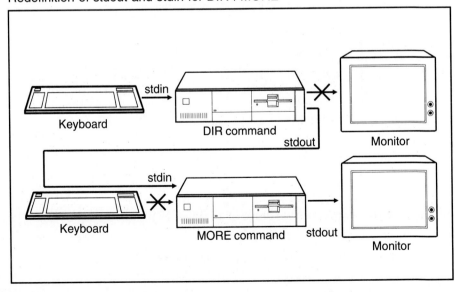

Although you don't need to understand how DOS actually modifies stdin and stdout, you should understand how these two terms relate to I/O redirection.

Practice

Using the DOS pipe operator, issue the following command:

```
C:\> DIR | SORT <ENTER>
```

DOS will display a sorted directory listing.

Change the command slightly and use MORE:

```
C:\> DIR \DOS | MORE <ENTER>
```

Next, use multiple redirection operators in the same command line to print a sorted directory listing of your files:

```
C:\> DIR | SORT > PRN <ENTER>
```

Next, issue the command

```
C:\> DIR \DOS | SORT | MORE <ENTER>
```

to display a sorted directory listing of all your DOS files one screenful at a time.

Finally, use the FIND command to display all the DOS command files with the extension COM, as shown here:

```
C:\> DIR \DOS | FIND "COM" <ENTER>
```

Review

1. How does the DOS pipe operator differ from the DOS input or output redirection operator?

2. What command displays a sorted directory listing using the DOS pipe operator?

3. Modify the command from question 2 to redirect the sorted output to the printer.

4. What is the function of the following command?

```
C:\DOS> DIR \DOS | FIND "EXE" | SORT | MORE <ENTER>
```

Key Points

The Pipe Operator (|)

The pipe redirection operator (|) allows you to make the output of one DOS command become the input of another. The following command, for example, uses the pipe to display a directory listing one screenful at a time:

```
C:\> DIR | MORE <ENTER>
```

CHAPTER

Using the DOS Environment

*M*any of the commands that you will examine in the remainder of this book must get information from DOS in order to complete their processing. These commands communicate with DOS through a location in memory called the DOS environment. Each time DOS starts, it sets aside this region in memory to provide storage for 256 characters of information, as shown in Figure 21-1.

By default, the DOS environment stores such items as the command path defined by the PATH command, the system prompt, and the location on disk of the command processor, COMMAND.COM. To display the current environment's settings, issue the SET command:

```
C:\> SET <ENTER>
COMSPEC=C:\DOS\COMMAND.COM
PATH=C:\DOS
PROMPT=$P$G
```

In this case the DOS environment contains not only the location for COMMAND.COM and the command path, but also the system prompt:

FIGURE 21-1

The environment region in memory

```
┌──────────────────────────────────┐
│        ┌──────────────┐          │
│        │              │          │
│        │     DOS      │          │
│        │              │          │
│        ├──────────────┤          │
│        │ Environment  │          │
│        ├──────────────┤          │
│        │              │          │
│        │              │          │
│        │ Free memory  │          │
│        │              │          │
│        └──────────────┘          │
└──────────────────────────────────┘
```

COMSPEC=C:\DOS\COMMAND.COM	Location of COMMAND.COM
PATH=C:\DOS	Command-file search path
PROMPT=PG	DOS prompt

The number of entries in your environment, as well as their settings, may differ from those shown here.

Adding and Removing Entries in the DOS Environment

The SET command allows you to add, remove, and display entries in the DOS environment. Before you use the entries in the DOS environment in conjunction with DOS commands, you should see how the SET command works.

SET is an internal DOS command. As you have seen, if you invoke SET without specifying additional values in the command line, SET displays the current environment entries. To add an entry to the environment, use SET in the form

```
SET entry_name=desired_value
```

You are working in Chapter 21 of this book. The following SET command creates an entry called CHAPTER and assigns it the value 21:

```
C:\> SET  CHAPTER=21 <ENTER>
```

If you display the contents of the DOS environment again with SET, you will see that DOS has added your entry as desired:

```
C:\> SET <ENTER>
COMSPEC=C:\DOS\COMMAND.COM
PATH=C:\DOS
PROMPT=$P$G
```

```
CHAPTER=21

C:\>
```

SET automatically converts each entry name to uppercase letters. Therefore, the following SET command also creates an environment entry named CHAPTER:

```
C:\> SET chapter=21 <ENTER>
```

Using the same technique, the following SET command creates an entry called BOOK and assigns it the value "DOS Inside & Out," as shown in the following:

```
C:\> SET  BOOK=DOS Inside & Out <ENTER>
```

SET does not change the value you assign to an environment entry to uppercase.

Displaying the contents of the environment yields

```
C:\> SET <ENTER>
COMSPEC=C:\DOS\COMMAND.COM
PATH=C:\DOS
PROMPT=$P$G
CHAPTER=21
BOOK=DOS Inside & Out

C:\>
```

As you can see, the environment entry BOOK appears in upper case, but its value appears in upper and lower case.

To remove an entry from the DOS environment, you use the SET command in the form

```
SET entry_name= <ENTER>
```

For example, to remove the CHAPTER entry, use the command

```
C:\> SET  CHAPTER= <ENTER>
```

If you display the environment entries again, you will see that DOS has removed the CHAPTER entry from the environment:

```
C:\> SET <ENTER>
COMSPEC=C:\DOS\COMMAND.COM
PATH=C:\DOS
PROMPT=$P$G
BOOK=DOS Inside & Out

C:\>
```

Using Environment Entries in Batch Files

In Chapter 19, "Decision Making in Batch Files," you learned that the FOR command uses variables within your batch files, as in

```
FOR %%F IN (A.DAT B.DAT C.DAT) DO TYPE %%F
```

If you are using DOS 3.3 or later, DOS lets your batch files reference *named parameters*, which correspond to DOS environment entries. A named parameter is a variable that appears in a batch file enclosed by percent signs. To begin, create a file named ENV.NTS, as shown in the following:

```
C:\> COPY  CON  ENV.NTS <ENTER>
The DOS SET command <ENTER>
adds, removes and displays <ENTER>
environment entries. <ENTER>
^Z <ENTER>
     1 File(s) copied

C:\>
```

Next, use SET to create an environment entry called NOTES that contains the value ENV.NTS:

```
C:\> SET  NOTES=ENV.NTS <ENTER>
```

Finally, create a batch file called ENVTEST.BAT:

```
C:\> COPY  CON  ENVTEST.BAT <ENTER>
CLS <ENTER>
TYPE  %NOTES% <ENTER>
^Z <ENTER>
     1 File(s) copied

C:\>
```

The line "TYPE %NOTES%" within the batch file references a named parameter, NOTES. When DOS encounters an entry in a batch file that is enclosed in percent signs, as in %NOTES%, DOS searches the environment for an entry with the same name. In the case of the batch file ENVTEST.BAT, DOS locates the environment entry NOTES, which contains the value ENV.NTS. As a result, DOS substitutes the file name for the named parameter, which results in the command

```
TYPE ENV.NTS
```

The FOR command also supports named parameters. Create the environment entry COLORS, as shown here:

```
C:\> SET  COLORS=BLUE,RED,GREEN <ENTER>
```

Next, create this batch file:

```
C:\> COPY  CON  COLORS.BAT <ENTER>
@ECHO  OFF <ENTER>
FOR %%I IN (%COLORS%) DO ECHO %%I <ENTER>
^Z <ENTER>
```

```
    1 File(s) copied

C:\>
```

When you invoke the batch procedure, DOS will display the following:

```
C:\> COLORS <ENTER>
BLUE
RED
GREEN

C:\>
```

As you can see, DOS successfully located the COLORS entry in the environment and substituted its value, as desired.

Changing the DOS Prompt

In Chapter 22, "DOS System Commands," you will use the PROMPT command to set your system prompt. At that time, you will learn that each time DOS completes a command, it searches the environment for an entry in the form

```
PROMPT=
```

If DOS locates the entry, it uses the entry's value to set your prompt.

For an example, issue the command

```
C:\> SET  PROMPT=WHAT? <ENTER>
```

DOS will change your prompt to "WHAT?" as shown here:

```
WHAT?
```

To restore your system prompt to the DOS default, use the SET command
to remove the PROMPT entry, as shown here:

```
WHAT? SET PROMPT= <ENTER>
C>
```

Since you have removed the PROMPT environment entry, DOS uses
its default prompt. In Chapter 22 you will learn about the PROMPT
command's many features. For now, simply understand that the
PROMPT command works by placing an entry in the DOS environment.
Use the following PROMPT command to assign a meaningful system
prompt. Use the characters pg to direct DOS to include your current
drive and directory ($p) followed by a greater-than (>) character ($g):

```
C> SET PROMPT=$p$g <ENTER>
C:\>
```

The "Out of Environment Space" Message

If DOS displays the message

```
Out of environment space
```

when you issue the SET, PROMPT, APPEND, or PATH command, you
have filled the fixed amount of memory set aside for the DOS environment. As your environment entries grow, DOS will try to expand your
environment size up to 32K in order to meet your needs, as shown in
Figure 21-2. However, if you install memory-resident software upon
starting your system, such as GRAPHICS, FASTOPEN, or PRINT, your
environment size becomes fixed, as shown in Figure 21-3.

An easy solution to this error is to restart DOS and issue all the SET
commands you require before you install memory-resident software. As
you will learn later in Chapter 27, "Customizing Your System Using

FIGURE
21-2

The DOS environment can grow up to 32,768 bytes

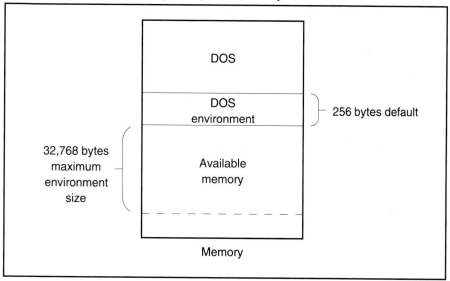

FIGURE
21-3

Memory-resident software restricts the DOS environment's growth

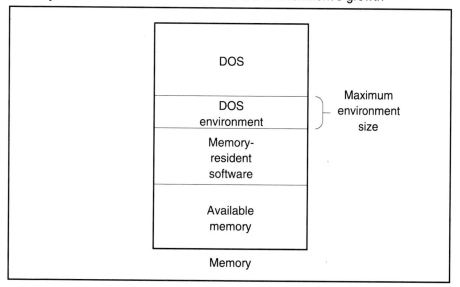

CONFIG.SYS," DOS also allows you to set aside a larger amount of space for the environment by means of the SHELL entry in CONFIG.SYS.

Most users don't have to worry about running out of environment space. However, if you do, you need to know that solutions exist.

Using the TEMP Entry Under DOS 5 or Later

As briefly discussed in Chapter 20, "I/O Redirection with the DOS Pipe," each time you use the pipe operator to pipe one command's output into a second command's input, DOS must create temporary files. By default, DOS creates these files as hidden files (files that do not appear in the directory listing) in the root directory of the current drive.

Using the TEMP environment entry, you can direct DOS to create these files in a different location. Assuming you create a RAM drive whose drive letter is D (see Chapter 27 for information on RAM drives), you can direct DOS to create its temporary files on the RAM drive by assigning TEMP as follows:

```
C:\> SET TEMP=D:  <ENTER>
```

By using the faster RAM drive for the temporary files, you greatly improve the performance of commands that use the DOS pipe.

As you read in Chapter 3, the DOS 5 or later DIR command supports several additional command-line switches, such as /O, which lets you sort files, and /S, which displays files contained in directories beneath the current directory. As you experiment with these switches, you may find several switches that best suit your needs. Rather than having to type these switches every time you invoke DIR, you can assign the switches to an environment entry named DIRCMD. For example, the following SET command assigns switches to DIRCMD that direct DIR to display the directory listing sorted by name, as well as in lowercase letters.

```
C:\> SET DIRCMD=/O:N/L <ENTER>
```

Should you later decide you want to list files in a different way, use
SET to change the DIRCMD entry.

Setting Environment Entries from Within the Shell

If you use the DOS shell, you must end the shell (by pressing F3 or
ALT-F4) if you want to change environment entries. If you exit the shell
only temporarily by pressing SHIFT-F9, your changes to environment
entries will not take effect.

Until you understand the processing that occurs each time you
temporarily exit the DOS shell, using the SET command to define
environment entries can be quite confusing. Each time you temporarily
exit the shell by pressing SHIFT-F9, DOS gives you a working copy of the
current environment entries. Any changes that you make to the environment exist only until you issue the EXIT command to return to the shell.

To verify this, press SHIFT-F9 to temporarily exit the shell. Next, create
the entry shown here:

```
C:\> SET  ENTRY=TEST <ENTER>
```

Use SET to display the entries:

```
C:\> SET <ENTER>
COMSPEC=C:\DOS\COMMAND.COM
PATH=C:\DOS;
PROMPT=$P$G
ENTRY=TEST

C:\>
```

As you can see, your new entry exists.

Next, type **EXIT** to return to the shell. Again press SHIFT-F9 to temporarily exit the shell. Using the SET command, display the environment entries:

```
C:\> SET <ENTER>
COMSPEC=C:\DOS\COMMAND.COM
PATH=C:\DOS
PROMPT=$P$G

C:\>
```

When you used the EXIT command to return to the shell, DOS discarded your temporary environment settings, and thus your setting for ENTRY is lost. If you want the entry to be permanent, you must press F3 to end the shell, use SET to add the entry, and then run the shell again by invoking DOSSHELL.

Practice

At the DOS prompt, issue the SET command to display the current contents of your environment:

```
C:\> SET <ENTER>
```

Create an entry called FILE and assign it the value TEST.DAT:

```
C:\> SET  FILE=TEST.DAT <ENTER>
```

Use SET to display your new entry.

Create the TEST.DAT file as follows:

```
C:\> SET <ENTER>
C:\> COPY  CON  TEST.DAT <ENTER>
```

```
The PROMPT command <ENTER>
creates an environment entry.  <ENTER>
^Z <ENTER>

     1 File(s) copied

C:\>
```

Next, create a DOS batch file called NAMEDVAR.BAT that displays the contents of the file associated with the named variable FILE:

```
C:\> COPY  CON  NAMEDVAR.BAT <ENTER>
TYPE %FILE% <ENTER>
^Z <ENTER>
     1 File(s) copied

C:\>
```

When you invoke this batch file, DOS will display the contents of the TEST.BAT file.

For fun, issue the following command:

```
C:\> SET  PROMPT=COMMAND? <ENTER>
```

Using the SET command, verify that DOS has created a PROMPT= environment entry:

```
COMMAND? SET <ENTER>
```

To restore the prompt to its default, enter

```
COMMAND? SET PROMPT= <ENTER>
C:\>
```

Review

1. What is the DOS environment?

2. How do you display the entries in the DOS environment?

3. Create an environment entry called STATE, and assign it the value "New York".

4. What SET command deletes the STATE entry that you created in question 3?

5. What is a named parameter?

6. Create a batch file that deletes the contents of a file associated with the named parameter DELETE.ME.

Key Points

The SET Command

The SET command lets you add, remove, and display environment entries. To display the environment entries, issue SET as

```
C:\> SET <ENTER>
```

To add an entry to the environment, use the form

```
SET entry=value <ENTER>
```

To remove an environment entry, use

```
SET entry= <ENTER>
```

continues . . .

Key Points
(continued)

Named Parameters

A named parameter is a variable that appears in a batch file surrounded by percent signs, as in

```
TYPE %FILE%
```

When DOS encounters the named parameter (%FILE%), DOS searches the environment for a matching entry. If DOS finds an environment variable with a matching name, it substitutes the variable's value into the command. If DOS does not find a matching entry, DOS assigns the null string to the variable.

CHAPTER

DOS System Commands

*T*his chapter examines several *system commands*, which are commands that affect your overall system rather than a file or directory on your disk. Specifically, this chapter examines the BREAK command, which lets you control extended CTRL-BREAK checking; VERIFY, which lets you enable and disable disk verification; PROMPT, which lets you customize your DOS prompt; MEM, which displays your current memory usage; and the DOS 5 or later DOSKEY command, which lets you recall your previous commands.

Improving CTRL-C Response Time

On several occasions throughout this book, you have used the CTRL-C or CTRL-BREAK key combination to end a DOS command or batch file. In most cases, DOS ended your command immediately and returned control to the DOS prompt. However, if you have a program that performs complex numeric processing, the CTRL-C key combination may at first appear to have no effect. In general, DOS only checks for a CTRL-C each time it writes to your screen display or printer and each time it reads from your keyboard. If you have an application that rarely performs input or output operations, it may take a considerable amount of time before DOS acknowledges that you have pressed CTRL-C.

In such cases, the BREAK command may improve your CTRL-C response time. The BREAK command allows you to increase the number of times that DOS checks to see if you have pressed CTRL-C to terminate the current command. To enable this increased checking, issue the following command:

```
C:\> BREAK ON  <ENTER>
```

The word "ON" directs BREAK to enable extended CTRL-C checking. As such, DOS will not only check for a CTRL-C after basic input and output operations to your screen and printer, but also after disk and file operations. DOS normally does not perform extended CTRL-C checking because the additional checking takes time. The more time DOS spends checking for a CTRL-C, the less time your program gets to run. As a result, your programs run more slowly. If you use the BREAK command to enable extended checking before you execute a specific command, you can later disable it by using the following command:

```
C:\> BREAK OFF <ENTER>
```

If you invoke BREAK without specifying either ON or OFF, DOS will display the current state of extended CTRL-C checking, as shown here:

```
C:\> BREAK <ENTER>
BREAK is on

C:\>
```

Most users keep the default setting of BREAK OFF, trading faster system performance for slower CTRL-C response time.

Verifying the Accuracy of Your Disk Output

Over the last few years, floppy and hard disk technologies have increased tremendously. Even so, it is possible that your disk might not correctly record the information that DOS tells it to write. Although such recording errors are rare, in some cases, depending upon the type of error, DOS might not be aware that such an error has occurred.

If you are running a program on which the accuracy of your data is critical, the VERIFY command might prove useful. VERIFY is similar in format to the BREAK command. Using VERIFY, you can direct DOS to verify that the information written to disk is correctly recorded. The following VERIFY command enables disk verification:

```
C:\> VERIFY ON <ENTER>
```

When disk verification is enabled (on), every piece of information the disk records is compared to the original information DOS directed the disk to write. If the information recorded is different, DOS becomes aware of the error and can correct the information.

Like the BREAK ON command, the VERIFY ON command decreases your system performance. The mechanical nature of your disk drives makes disks much slower than your computer's electronic counterparts, so any time you increase the number of disk operations your system must perform, you slow down the programs you are running. When you enable disk verification, you increase the number of disk operations.

Because of this considerable overhead, and because disk errors of this type are very rare, most users leave disk verification disabled.

If you invoke VERIFY without specifying command-line parameters, VERIFY will display the current state of disk verification, as shown here:

```
C:\> VERIFY <ENTER>
VERIFY is off

C:\>
```

To disable disk verification, issue the following command:

```
C:\> VERIFY OFF <ENTER>
```

Customizing Your DOS Prompt

In Chapter 21, "Using the DOS Environment," you changed your system prompt by using the SET command, something like this:

```
C:\> SET PROMPT=YES?
YES?
```

At that time, you learned that each time DOS completes a command, DOS searches the environment for an entry in the form

```
PROMPT=entry
```

If DOS finds this entry, it uses it to set your system prompt accordingly. If DOS does not find the PROMPT entry, it displays the current disk drive letter and a greater-than symbol as your system prompt:

```
C>
```

In this section you will examine the PROMPT command, which sets your system prompt. PROMPT is an internal DOS command. The following PROMPT command, for example, changes your system prompt to COMMAND?:

```
C:\> PROMPT COMMAND? <ENTER>
COMMAND?
```

If you press the ENTER key several times, you can see that your prompt remains unchanged.

```
COMMAND? <ENTER>
COMMAND? <ENTER>
COMMAND? <ENTER>
```

In addition to using letters and numbers within your prompt, you can also use a special collection of characters, called *metacharacters*, which, preceded by a dollar sign ($), tell DOS what to display as the prompt. The metacharacters are listed in Table 22-1.

To set your prompt to COMMAND>, for example, you would use PROMPT as follows:

```
C:\> PROMPT COMMAND$g <ENTER>
COMMAND>
```

In this case, the $g metacharacter directs PROMPT to display the greater-than symbol. If you instead issued the command as

```
C:\> PROMPT COMMAND> <ENTER>
```

DOS would interpret the character > as the output redirection operator and assume that you were attempting to redirect the output of the PROMPT command. DOS would display the following error message:

```
C:\> PROMPT COMMAND> <ENTER>
File creation error

C:\>
```

TABLE 22-1

Metacharacters for the PROMPT Command

Metacharacter	Effect
$b	Displays the pipe character (I)
$d	Displays the current date
$e	Writes the ASCII escape character
$g	Displays the greater-than symbol (>)
$h	Writes the backspace character, which erases the previous character
$l	Displays the less-than character (<)
$n	Displays the current drive letter
$p	Displays the current drive and directory
$q	Displays the equal sign (=)
$t	Displays the current time
$v	Displays the current DOS version number
$$	Displays the dollar sign ($)
$_	Writes a carriage return and line feed

Most users include the current drive and directory within their prompt. To do so, simply include the $p metacharacter in your PROMPT command. For example, the following prompt command directs DOS to display the current drive and directory followed by a greater-than (>) character:

```
C> PROMPT $p$g <ENTER>
C:\>
```

When you change current directories, your prompt will change as well:

```
C:\> CD DOS <ENTER>
C:\DOS> B: <ENTER>
B:\> C: <ENTER>
C:\DOS>
```

Some people like to place the current directory within left and right brackets for higher visibility. You can do so with the following command:

```
C:\> PROMPT [$P] <ENTER>
[C:\]
```

In this case, the PROMPT command used the uppercase letter "P" within the $P metacharacter. The PROMPT command does not care if you use upper- or lowercase metacharacters.

Displaying the Current Memory Utilization

As programs become more powerful, they also increase in size. Before a program can run, it must reside in your computer's electronic memory. If you run several memory-resident utilities, your computer's memory can become pinched for space. Beginning with DOS 4, the MEM command provides a summary of all your system's current memory utilization.

In its simplest form, you can invoke MEM with no switches. When you do, the DOS 6 MEM command will display the following:

```
C:\> MEM <ENTER>

Memory Type          Total =  Used  +  Free
---------------      ------   ------    ------
Conventional          640K      98K      542K
Upper                 151K      26K      125K
Adapter RAM/ROM       233K     233K       0K
Extended (XMS)       3072K     992K     2080K
Expanded (EMS)         0K       0K        0K
---------------      ------   ------    ------
Total memory         4096K    1349K     2747K


Total under 1 MB      791K     124K      667K


Largest executable program size       542K  (555312 bytes)
Largest free upper memory block       114K  (116528 bytes)
MS-DOS is resident in the high memory area.
```

MEM displays the amount of memory available in the system, as well as the current usage of that memory. MEM also displays the size of the largest program that you can execute. Depending on your system, you may have memory called *expanded memory* (also called *EMS*) If so, MEM will display the amount and its usage. Likewise, you may have memory called *extended memory* (also called *XMS*). Chapter 27, "Customizing Your System Using CONFIG.SYS," briefly discusses the differences between these two memory types.

To determine which programs are using memory, invoke MEM with the /DEBUG switch. MEM will display the name of each program in memory and its size (in bytes), as well as the starting location of the program (its address), as shown here:

```
C:\> MEM  /DEBUG <ENTER>

Conventional Memory Detail:
```

Segment	Size		Name	Type
00000	1039	(1K)		Interrupt Vector
00040	271	(0K)		ROM Communication Area
00050	527	(0K)		DOS Communication Area
00070	2656	(2K)	IO	System Data
			CON	System Device Driver
			AUX	System Device Driver
			PRN	System Device Driver
			CLOCK$	System Device Driver
			A: - C:	System Device Driver
			COM1	System Device Driver
			LPT1	System Device Driver
			LPT2	System Device Driver
			LPT3	System Device Driver
			COM2	System Device Driver
			COM3	System Device Driver
			COM4	System Device Driver
00116	5072	(4K)	MSDOS	System Data
00253	25536	(24K)	IO	System Data
	608	(1K)	SETVERXX	Installed Device=SETVER
	1088	(1K)	XMSXXXX0	Installed Device=HIMEM
	3056	(3K)	EMMQXXX0	Installed Device=EMM386
	4192	(4K)	CON	Installed Device=ANSI
	10000	(10K)	MSCD001	Installed Device=SBPCD
	1488	(1K)		FILES=30
	256	(0K)		FCBS=4
	512	(1K)		BUFFERS=4
	1152	(1K)		LASTDRIVE=M
	3008	(3K)		STACKS=9,256
0088F	80	(0K)	MSDOS	System Program
00894	2640	(2K)	COMMAND	Program
00939	80	(0K)	MSDOS	-- Free --
0093E	528	(0K)	COMMAND	Environment
0095F	80	(0K)	MSDOS	-- Free --
00964	46560	(45K)	MSCDEX	Program
014C2	240	(0K)	MEM	Environment
014D1	14992	(14K)	MOUSE	Program
0187A	87376	(85K)	MEM	Program
02DCF	467712	(456K)	MSDOS	-- Free --

```
Upper Memory Detail:

  Segment  Region       Size        Name         Type
  -------  ------  ----------------  -----------  --------
   0C93B     1          48    (0K)   MSDOS        -- Free --
   0C93E     1       11264   (11K)   MSDOS        -- Free --


   0CD01     2       26816   (26K)   SMARTDRV     Program
   0D38D     2      116528  (113K)   MSDOS        -- Free --

Memory Summary:

  Type of Memory        Size        =      Used      +      Free
  ---------------   ----------------    ----------------   ------------------
  Conventional      655360   (640K)      99872   (98K)     555488   (542K)
  Upper             154656   (151K)      26816   (26K)     127840   (125K)
  Adapter RAM/ROM   238560   (233K)     238560  (233K)          0     (0K)
  Extended (XMS)   3145728  (3072K)    1015808  (992K)    2129920  (2080K)
  Expanded (EMS)         0     (0K)          0    (0K)          0     (0K)
  ---------------   ----------------    ----------------   ------------------
  Total memory     4194304  (4096K)    1381056 (1349K)    2813248  (2747K)


  Total under 1 MB  810016   (791K)     126688  (124K)     683328   (667K)


  Memory accessible using Int 15h           0     (0K)
  Largest executable program size      555312  (542K)
  Largest free upper memory block      116528  (114K)
  MS-DOS is resident in the high memory area.


  XMS version 3.00; driver version  3.09
```

Finally, if you include the /CLASSIFY switch, MEM will display information regarding how DOS is using conventional, extended, and expanded memory, as shown here:

```
C:\> MEM /CLASSIFY <ENTER>


Modules using memory below 1 MB:
```

```
Name          Total      =  Conventional  +  Upper Memory
--------  ---------------     ----------------     ----------------
MSDOS        16189   (16K)     16189   (16K)          0   (0K)
SETVER         624    (1K)       624    (1K)          0   (0K)
HIMEM         1104    (1K)      1104    (1K)          0   (0K)
EMM386        3072    (3K)      3072    (3K)          0   (0K)
ANSI          4208    (4K)      4208    (4K)          0   (0K)
SBPCD        10016   (10K)     10016   (10K)          0   (0K)
COMMAND       3168    (3K)      3168    (3K)          0   (0K)
MSCDEX       46560   (45K)     46560   (45K)          0   (0K)
MOUSE        14992   (15K)     14992   (15K)          0   (0K)
SMARTDRV     26816   (26K)         0    (0K)      26816  (26K)
Free        683328  (667K)    555488  (542K)     127840 (125K)

Memory Summary:

Type of Memory     Size      =     Used      +      Free
----------------  ------------------  --------------------  ------------------
Conventional       655360  (640K)      99872   (98K)     555488  (542K)
Upper              154656  (151K)      26816   (26K)     127840  (125K)
Adapter RAM/ROM    238560  (233K)     238560  (233K)          0    (0K)
Extended (XMS)    3145728 (3072K)    1015808  (992K)    2129920 (2080K)
Expanded (EMS)          0    (0K)          0    (0K)          0    (0K)
------------------  ------------------  --------------------  ------------------
Total memory      4194304 (4096K)    1381056 (1349K)    2813248 (2747K)

Total under 1 MB   810016  (791K)     126688  (124K)     683328  (667K)

Largest executable program size      555312  (542K)
Largest free upper memory block      116528  (114K)
MS-DOS is resident in the high memory area.
```

MEM displays its values in hexadecimal, the base-16 numbering system. As you can see, MEM displays information describing where each program and device driver resides in memory. Chapter 27 examines several DOS 5 or later memory capabilities that let you make the best use of your computer's memory. At that time, you can use the MEM command to view your memory usage in order to determine how much the techniques improve your memory usage.

The DOSKEY Command and DOS Macros

This section examines the DOS 5 or later DOSKEY command, which tracks each command you type at the DOS prompt so you can quickly repeat it. In addition to tracking commands, DOSKEY lets you define single-line *macros* that behave like batch files, letting you abbreviate commonly used commands. Unlike your batch files, which reside in files on disk, DOSKEY macros are stored in your computer's fast electronic RAM. Therefore, macros execute very quickly.

Tracking Commands with DOSKEY

In Chapter 7, "Using Your Keyboard and Mouse," you learned how to edit or quickly repeat the previous command by pressing the F3 function key. You learned that each time you type a command at the DOS prompt, DOS stores the command in a buffer you can access by using the function keys F1 through F4. This type of command buffer is very convenient. Unfortunately, however, it lets DOS keep track of only one command. If you are using DOS 5 or later, the DOSKEY command lets DOS track many commands. The actual number of commands DOSKEY can track depends on the amount of memory you let DOSKEY use and the character length of your commands.

DOSKEY is an external DOS command that resides on disk. The first time you execute the DOSKEY command, DOSKEY loads memory-resident software that remains in memory until you turn off your computer or restart DOS.

Invoke DOSKEY from the DOS prompt, and it will display the following message, informing you it has loaded its memory-resident software:

```
C:\> DOSKEY <ENTER>
DOSKey installed.
```

By default, DOSKEY allocates 512 bytes of memory for a command buffer. If the average character length of your DOS commands is 10, for example, DOSKEY will let you track the previous 50 or so DOS commands. Should your DOSKEY buffer fill, DOSKEY will discard the buffer's oldest command to make room for a new command.

Invoke the DIR, VER, DATE, and CLS commands. Using the UP ARROW and DOWN ARROW keys, you can cycle through your list of previous commands. The UP ARROW key directs DOSKEY to display the command you invoked immediately before the command now displayed. Likewise, the DOWN ARROW key directs DOSKEY to display the command you invoked immediately after the command now displayed. When no more commands precede or follow the command now displayed, DOSKEY ignores subsequent UP ARROW or DOWN ARROW keys.

In addition to letting you cycle through your previous command list by using the UP ARROW and DOWN ARROW keys, DOSKEY lets you use PGUP and PGDN. The PGUP key directs DOSKEY to display the oldest command in the previous command buffer. Likewise, the PGDN key directs DOSKEY to display your most recently used command. Table 22-2 summarizes how DOSKEY uses these keys to traverse the previous command buffer.

By using the keys described in Table 22-2, you can cycle through your list of previous commands. When you need to go back only a few commands, using the arrow keys is very convenient. However, as the number of commands in DOSKEY's previous command buffer becomes large, locating the desired command by using your keyboard's arrow keys

TABLE
22-2

The DOSKEY Previous Command Buffer Traversal Keys

Key	Function
UP ARROW	Displays the command name you invoked immediately before the command now displayed
DOWN ARROW	Displays the command name you invoked immediately after the command now displayed
PGUP	Displays the oldest command name in the previous command buffer
PGDN	Displays the most recently used command name

can become more time consuming. DOSKEY, however, provides several faster ways to locate a command.

DOSKEY refers to the previous command buffer as your *command history*. If you invoke DOSKEY by using the /HISTORY switch, DOSKEY will display all the command names your previous command buffer contains, as shown here:

```
C:\> DOSKEY  /HISTORY <ENTER>
DIR
VER
DATE
CLS
DOSKEY /HISTORY
```

To reduce your typing, DOSKEY lets you abbreviate the /HISTORY switch as simply /H:

```
C:\> DOSKEY  /H <ENTER>
DIR
VER
DATE
CLS
DOSKEY /HISTORY
DOSKEY /H
```

If your previous command buffer is large, DOSKEY lets you refer to commands by number. To begin, press the F7 function key, which directs DOSKEY to display your command history, preceding each command with its corresponding number, as shown here:

```
1: DIR
2: VER
3: DATE
4: CLS
5: DOSKEY /HISTORY
6: DOSKEY /H
```

To select a command by number, press the F9 function key. DOSKEY will prompt you to type in the desired number, as shown here:

```
C:\> Line number:
```

Type in the desired line number and press ENTER. In this case, if you type **3** and press ENTER, DOSKEY will display the DATE command:

```
C:\> DATE
```

DOS won't execute the command until you press ENTER. If you don't want to execute the command, press the ESC key. DOSKEY will erase the current command name from your screen. As the number of characters in your commands becomes large, recalling commands in this way can be very convenient.

DOSKEY gives you one last way to recall a command. Simply type one or more letters of the command name and press the F8 function key. DOSKEY will search the previous command buffer for commands beginning with the letter or letters specified. For example, if you type **V** and press F8, DOSKEY will recall the VER command:

```
C:\> VER
```

As the number of commands in the previous command buffer grows, two or more commands may begin with the letters specified. If you repeatedly press F8, DOSKEY will cycle through each of the matching commands.

Once you recall the desired command, you can execute the command by pressing ENTER, or you can edit the command as you did in Chapter 7, "Using Your Keyboard and Mouse." To help you edit the command, DOSKEY lets you use several editing keys. The RIGHT ARROW and LEFT ARROW keys let you move the cursor one character position to the right or the left. The BACKSPACE key rubs out characters. To delete characters, you can also move the cursor to the position of the character you wish to delete and press the DEL key. To insert characters into the command, place the cursor in the position at which you want to insert the text. Press the INS key until DOSKEY displays a larger cursor, indicating insert mode. Type in the characters as desired.

In addition to the RIGHT ARROW and LEFT ARROW keys, DOSKEY lets you move through the command a word at a time by holding down the CTRL key and pressing either the RIGHT ARROW or LEFT ARROW key. The CTRL-RIGHT ARROW keyboard combination moves the cursor one word to the right, whereas CTRL-LEFT ARROW moves the cursor one word to the left. In addition, the HOME key moves the cursor to the command's first letter and the END key moves the cursor to the end of the command. Table 22-3 summarizes DOSKEY's editing keys.

If the number of commands in your previous command buffer becomes unmanageably large, you can press ALT-F7 to discard the buffer's current contents. Once you empty the buffer in this way, the next command you invoke will become command number 1. Table 22-4 describes the DOSKEY function keys.

TABLE 22-3

The DOSKEY Editing Keys

Key	Function
RIGHT ARROW	Moves the cursor one character position to the right
LEFT ARROW	Moves the cursor one character position to the left
CTRL-RIGHT ARROW	Moves the cursor one word to the right
CTRL-LEFT ARROW	Moves the cursor one word to the left
INS	Toggles insert mode on and off
DEL	Deletes the character at the current cursor position
HOME	Moves the cursor to the start of the command
END	Moves the cursor to the end of the command

| TABLE 22-4 | The DOSKEY Function Keys |

Function Key	Function
F7	Displays all the command names in the buffer, preceding each name with its corresponding number
F8	Displays the first command name that matches the letters you typed immediately before pressing F8. If several command names match, repeatedly pressing F8 will cycle through the matching names
F9	Prompts you to type in a command's corresponding number as displayed by the F7 function key. If the number does not exist, DOSKEY displays the most recently used command
ESC	Directs DOSKEY to remove the current command name, leaving only the DOS prompt
ALT-F7	Directs DOSKEY to discard the current buffer contents

Other DOSKEY Switches

You have just learned that DOSKEY's /HISTORY switch lets you display the current contents of the previous command buffer. In addition to /HISTORY, DOSKEY supports four other switches.

DOSKEY's /BUFSIZE switch lets you specify, in bytes, the amount of memory you want DOSKEY to allocate to store the previous command buffer. By default, DOSKEY allocates 512 bytes.

Because DOSKEY loads memory-resident software and allocates the buffer the first time you invoke it, you must include the /BUFSIZE switch the first time you invoke DOSKEY, or you must use the /REINSTALL switch.

The /REINSTALL switch directs DOSKEY to unload its current memory-resident software and to reload itself using the new switch values. When you reinstall DOSKEY in this way, you discard the current contents of the previous command buffer.

By default, when you edit a previous command, you must first press the INS key to select insert mode. If you don't press INS, you will overwrite letters to the right of the cursor as you type. Depending on your preference, you can direct DOSKEY to automatically begin in insert mode so you don't have to press INS. To do so, invoke DOSKEY using the /INSERT switch:

```
C:\> DOSKEY  /INSERT <ENTER>
```

Table 22-5 briefly describes the DOSKEY switches. If you want more information on these switches, refer to the Command Reference at the end of this book.

TABLE 22-5

The DOSKEY Command Switches

DOSKEY Switch	Function
/BUFSIZE	Specifies the size of DOSKEY's command buffer in bytes
/HISTORY	Displays the names of each command in DOSKEY's buffer
/INSERT	Selects insert mode as the default
/MACROS	Displays the current DOSKEY macro definitions
/OVERSTRIKE	Disables insert mode
/REINSTALL	Installs a new copy of the DOSKEY software in memory

DOSKEY Macros

DOSKEY lets you define *macros*, which are similar to single-line batch files. Like a batch file, each DOSKEY macro has a name. To execute a macro, you type the macro's name at the DOS prompt and press ENTER. Unlike batch files, which reside on disk, DOSKEY stores macros in your computer's fast electronic RAM. Because macros reside in memory, DOS can execute them very quickly; DOS does not have to read the macro from the slow mechanical disk, as it would a batch file. However, because DOSKEY stores macros in RAM, the macros are lost each time you turn off your computer or restart DOS. Unlike batch files, which can contain many lines of commands, DOSKEY macros can hold only a single line.

The following DOSKEY command creates a macro named CMDLIST (an abbreviation for command list) that executes the DOSKEY /HISTORY command to give you a list of your commands:

```
C:\> DOSKEY  CMDLIST=DOSKEY  /HISTORY <ENTER>
```

After you define CMDLIST, you can invoke the macro as follows:

```
C:\> CMDLIST <ENTER>
```

DOS will, in turn, execute the DOSKEY /HISTORY command as desired.

DOSKEY macros take priority over DOS internal commands, external commands, and batch files with the same name. For example, the following DOSKEY command creates a macro named VER that invokes the ECHO command to display this message: "Customized DOS Version!"

```
C:\> DOSKEY  VER=ECHO Customized DOS Version! <ENTER>
```

If you invoke VER from the DOS prompt, your screen will display the following:

```
C:\> VER <ENTER>
C:\> ECHO Customized DOS Version!
Customized DOS Version!
```

Because DOSKEY macros execute first, you may want to define macros for commands you don't want a new user to access, such as FORMAT or even internal commands such as DEL.

DOSKEY macros are not restricted to a single command, but rather to a single line. For example, the following batch file clears your screen, displays the DOS version number, and then invokes DATE:

```
CLS
VER
DATE
```

Because you can easily fit these three commands on one line, you can create a macro named VERDATE that issues all three commands, as shown here:

```
C:\> DOSKEY  VERDATE=CLS  $T  VER  $T  DATE <ENTER>
```

DOSKEY uses the $T character to separate multiple commands that appear on one line.

To invoke the macro, type **VERDATE** at the DOS prompt, as shown here:

```
C:\> VERDATE <ENTER>
```

DOS will execute each of the macro's commands in succession.

Using Macro Command-Line Parameters

As you learned, with DOS batch files you can use the parameters %0 through %9 to access command-line information. In a similar way,

DOSKEY macros use the symbols $1 through $9. The following macro, SHOWPARM, uses the symbols $1 through $9 to display its command parameters:

```
C:\> DOSKEY  SHOWPARM=ECHO  $1 $2 $3 $4 $5 $6 $7 $8 $9 <ENTER>
```

If you invoke SHOWPARM with the letters "X," "Y," and "Z," your screen will display the following:

```
C:\> SHOWPARM  X  Y  Z <ENTER>
C:\> ECHO X Y Z
X Y Z
```

If you invoke the macro with more than nine parameters, DOSKEY ignores the extras.

DOSKEY macros do not provide a command like SHIFT, which rotates parameters. Instead, if you want to access the entire command line, you must use the $*, as shown here, with the macro SHOWALL:

```
C:\> DOSKEY  SHOWALL=ECHO  $* <ENTER>
```

Using the $* symbol, the following macro, TYPE, combines the TYPE command with FOR to support multiple file names and DOS wildcards.

```
C:\> DOSKEY  TYPE=FOR  %I  IN  ($*)  DO  TYPE  %I <ENTER>
```

Using the TYPE macro, you can display the contents of several files in succession, as shown here:

```
C:\> TYPE  CONFIG.SYS  AUTOEXEC.BAT <ENTER>
```

One DOSKEY macro cannot execute another. Therefore, when DOS encounters TYPE within the FOR command, DOS executes the internal TYPE command and not the macro, displaying the file's contents. Because the macro uses the FOR command, the macro fully supports DOS wildcard characters, as shown here:

```
C:\> TYPE  *.BAT <ENTER>
```

Table 22-6 defines symbols you can use within your DOSKEY macros.

I/O Redirection Within a Macro

The commands your macros execute can be very complex, as long as they fit on one line. You may eventually want to include I/O redirection operators within the macro command. Using the I/O redirection operators, however, is more difficult than you might think. The goal of the following macro, PRTFILES, is to redirect the output of the DIR command to the printer:

```
C:\> DOSKEY  PRTFILES=DIR  >  PRN <ENTER>
```

Unfortunately, when you execute this DOSKEY command, DOS assumes you want to redirect DOSKEY's output, not the output of the DIR command, to the printer. If you want to use the I/O redirection operators within your DOSKEY macros, you must use the symbols $G for output redirection, $L for input redirection, GG for append redirection, and $B for the DOS pipe.

TABLE 22-6

Symbols Supported by DOSKEY Macros

Symbol	Meaning
$T	Separates multiple commands
$1 through $9	Represent the macro's command-line parameters
$*	Represents the entire command line

Using the $G symbol, the following DOSKEY command correctly implements the PRTFILES macro:

```
C:\> DOSKEY  PRTFILES=DIR  $G  PRN <ENTER>
```

In a similar way, the macro DIRONLY uses the DOS pipe to display only the directories that reside in the current directory:

```
C:\> DOSKEY  DIRONLY=DIR  $B  FIND  "<DIR>" <ENTER>
```

Table 22-7 summarizes DOSKEY's redirection symbols.

Using DOSKEY's /MACROS switch, you can display the defined macros, as shown here:

```
C:\> DOSKEY  /MACROS <ENTER>
CMDLIST=DOSKEY /HISTORY
VER=ECHO Customized DOS Version!
VERDATE=CLS  $T  VER  $T  DATE
SHOWPARM=ECHO $1 $2 $3 $4 $5 $6 $7 $8 $9
SHOWALL=ECHO $*
TYPE=FOR %I IN ($*) DO TYPE %I
PRTFILES=DIR $g PRN
DIRONLY=DIR $b FIND "$1DIR$g"
```

TABLE 22-7

DOSKEY Macro I/O Redirection Symbols

Symbol	Represents
$G	DOS output redirection operator >
$L	DOS input redirection operator <
GG	DOS append redirection operator >>
$B	DOS pipe operator |

Macro Restrictions

Although DOSKEY macros are very powerful, they do have a few restrictions. First, DOSKEY stores macros in the same memory buffer it allocates for tracking your previous commands. If you create many macros, you may need to use DOSKEY's /BUFSIZE switch to increase the buffer size.

Second, one DOSKEY macro cannot invoke a second macro. For example, the following macro, NESTED, tries to invoke the macro SHOWPARM.

```
C:\> DOSKEY  NESTED=SHOWPARM <ENTER>
```

When you invoke NESTED, DOS will display the "Bad command" error message, as shown here:

```
C:\> NESTED <ENTER>
C:\> SHOWPARM
Bad command or file name
```

Third, you can invoke DOSKEY macros only from the keyboard. If you reference a macro name within a batch file, for example, DOS will not locate the command.

If you create several macros you frequently use, place DOSKEY commands in your AUTOEXEC.BAT to define the macros each time your system starts.

Practice

At the DOS prompt, issue the following BREAK command:

```
C:\> BREAK <ENTER>
```

Invoking BREAK without specifying ON or OFF causes BREAK to display the current state of extended CTRL-BREAK (or CTRL-C) processing. The BREAK ON command enables extended CTRL-BREAK checking, but keep in mind that many of your applications will run more slowly because DOS is spending time testing for a CTRL-BREAK. The BREAK OFF command disables extended CTRL-BREAK checking.

In a similar manner, issue the VERIFY command:

```
C:\> VERIFY <ENTER>
```

DOS will display the current state of disk verification, ON or OFF. As before, when disk verification is enabled, your applications will run more slowly because DOS is repeatedly performing disk I/O operations.

At the DOS prompt, issue the command

```
C:\> PROMPT $t <ENTER>
```

DOS will set your prompt to the current time. Each time you press ENTER, your prompt will change slightly as the current time changes. Experiment with the carriage-return and linefeed characters, displaying the date on one line followed by the current time on the next:

```
C:\> PROMPT $d$_$t <ENTER>
```

Your prompt can become even more complex—it can display the DOS version number, the date, the time, and the current disk drive:

```
C:\> PROMPT $v$_$d$_$t$_$n$g <ENTER>
```

Once you have finished experimenting, you will probably want to place the following PROMPT command in your AUTOEXEC.BAT file:

```
PROMPT $p$g
```

Doing this causes your system prompt always to contain your current drive and directory name.

Issue the following MEM command when you want to display your current memory use:

```
C:\> MEM <ENTER>
```

Next, use MEM's /DEBUG switch to display the current programs that reside in memory, as well as the system's memory utilization:

```
C:\> MEM  /DEBUG <ENTER>
```

If you have not already done so, invoke DOSKEY, as shown here:

```
C:\> DOSKEY <ENTER>
```

Next, invoke the VER, DIR, TIME, CLS, and DATE commands. Using the UP ARROW and DOWN ARROW keys, cycle through your list of previous commands. Press the PGUP key to display the oldest command in the buffer. Use PGDN to display the most recently used command.

Next, use DOSKEY's /HISTORY switch to display your command history:

```
C:\> DOSKEY  /HISTORY <ENTER>
```

Repeat the command using the /H abbreviation:

```
C:\> DOSKEY  /H <ENTER>
```

Press the F7 function key to display the previous command buffer with each command name preceded by its corresponding number. Select a command and use the F9 function key to recall the command by number. Press the ESC key to remove the command name from the screen without executing it.

Type **V** and press F8 to recall the VER command. Type **C** and press F8. DOSKEY will recall the CLS command.

Finally, use the following macro, ALLFILES, to display the name of every file on your disk:

```
C:\> DOSKEY ALLFILES=DIR C:\*.* /S <ENTER>
```

Invoke the macro as shown:

```
C:\> ALLFILES <ENTER>
```

Review

1. What is extended CTRL-BREAK checking?
2. Why does disk verification reduce your overall system performance?
3. How do you display the current state of disk verification (on or off)?
4. What is the function of the following command:

```
C:\> PROMPT $v$_[$p] <ENTER>
```

5. What is the function of the MEM command?
6. How many commands can the DOSKEY buffer store?
7. List three ways to recall a command by using DOSKEY.
8. What happens when DOSKEY runs out of buffer space?

Key Points

BREAK Command

The BREAK command lets you enable and disable extended CTRL-BREAK checking. In general, DOS checks for a CTRL-BREAK or CTRL-C only when it writes to your screen or printer or reads from your keyboard. By issuing the command

```
C:\> BREAK ON <ENTER>
```

you enable extended CTRL-BREAK checking, which increases the number of times DOS checks for a user-entered CTRL-BREAK. However, because DOS will now spend more time checking for CTRL-BREAK, your programs get less time to run and your system performance may decrease. For this reason, most users leave extended CTRL-BREAK checking disabled.

VERIFY Command

The VERIFY command lets you enable and disable disk verification. If you issue the command

```
C:\> VERIFY  ON <ENTER>
```

DOS will enable disk verification, meaning every piece of information DOS directs the disk to store is compared to actual information the disk records. If a disk recording error occurs, DOS is notified of the error and can correct it. Because disk recording errors are rare, and because disk verification increases the number of disk operations (which decreases your system performance), most users leave disk verification disabled.

continues . . .

PROMPT Command

The PROMPT command lets you customize your system prompt. Although PROMPT lets you become very creative with your prompt, most users should use a prompt that contains the current disk drive letter and directory, as shown here:

```
C> PROMPT  $p$g
C:\>
```

Once you determine the prompt you desire, place the corresponding PROMPT command in your AUTOEXEC.BAT file so DOS will use your prompt each time your system starts.

MEM Command

The MEM command displays your current memory use. MEM requires DOS 4 or later. In its simplest form, MEM tells you the amount of memory in your computer, as well as how much is in use.

```
C:\> MEM <ENTER>
```

If you want to know the programs that are using each section of memory, invoke MEM with the /PROGRAM or /DEBUG switch.

continues . . .

DOSKEY Command

The DOSKEY command lets you quickly recall your previous commands. DOSKEY provides a buffer in your computer's fast electronic memory that stores your previously entered commands. Depending on the amount of memory you let DOSKEY allocate and the number of characters in each command, the actual number of commands DOSKEY can track will differ. Using your keyboard's UP ARROW and DOWN ARROW keys, you can quickly cycle through the list of commands.

DOSKEY Macros

A DOSKEY macro is similar to a single-line batch file. Like batch files, each DOSKEY macro has a name. You execute a DOSKEY macro by typing its name at the DOS prompt. Unlike batch files, which reside on disk, DOSKEY macros reside in RAM, which lets DOS execute them very quickly. The format to create a DOSKEY macro is as follows:

```
DOSKEY Name=Command  Parameters <ENTER>
```

CHAPTER

Batch Files:
A Last Look

*B*y now you should be confidently creating DOS batch files to perform or simplify many of your daily tasks. This chapter will round out your knowledge of DOS batch processing. You will learn how to invoke one batch file from within another, as well as how to use parameters to make your batch files suitable for a greater number of applications. By the end of this chapter, you will be able to take advantage of DOS batch processing to its fullest extent.

Invoking a Batch File from Within Another

The batch file examples presented so far have contained only DOS commands. In many cases, however, you can simplify your processing by invoking one batch file from within another. When the name of a second batch file appears within the list of batch-file instructions that DOS is to perform, the second batch file is said to be *nested* within the first batch file.

The CALL command allows one batch file to invoke a second (nested) batch file. CALL is an internal DOS command whose format is

```
CALL bat_file
```

For example, the second line of the following batch file uses CALL to invoke a nested batch file named BATFILE:

```
DATE
CALL BATFILE
TIME
```

When you run this batch file, DOS will first invoke the DATE command. When DATE completes, DOS will use the CALL command to invoke the nested batch file. Finally, after the nested batch file's commands complete, DOS will execute the TIME command. If the batch file specified in the CALL command does not exist, DOS will simply display the message

```
Bad command or file name
```

and continue its processing with the next command in the batch file.

You may be wondering what happens if you simply specify the nested batch file's name without using the CALL command. Let's find out. Create the following batch file, TEST.BAT, which invokes a nested batch file named NESTED:

```
C:\> COPY  CON  TEST.BAT <ENTER>
DATE  <ENTER>
NESTED <ENTER>
TIME  <ENTER>
^Z    <ENTER>
      1 File(s) copied

C:\>
```

Next, create the batch file NESTED.BAT, whose only command is VER:

```
C:\> COPY  CON  NESTED.BAT <ENTER>
VER <ENTER>
^Z <ENTER>
      1 File(s) copied

C:\>
```

When you invoke the batch file TEST, DOS will execute the DATE command, displaying

```
C:\> TEST <ENTER>

C:\> DATE
Current date is Tue 04-06-1993
Enter new date (mm-dd-yy):
```

It will then invoke the nested batch file, NESTED, which in turn will display the DOS version number:

```
C:\> TEST

C:\> DATE
Current date is Tue 04-06-1993
Enter new date (mm-dd-yy): <ENTER>

C:\> NESTED

C:\> VER

MS-DOS Version 6.00

C:\>
```

Because the batch file did not use the CALL command to invoke the nested batch file, when NESTED completes, DOS will never return to the first batch procedure to execute the TIME command, returning to the DOS prompt instead. Thus, if your batch file invokes a nested batch file, you must use the CALL command. If you change the batch file TEST.BAT to use the CALL command, as shown here:

```
DATE
CALL NESTED
TIME
```

the batch file will successfully invoke the nested batch file followed by the TIME command.

Note   The CALL command was introduced in DOS 3.3. If you are using an earlier version of DOS, you must use COMMAND /C BATFILE instead of CALL BATFILE.

Supporting Multiple Applications with One Batch File

As you know, DOS batch files save you time and typing. As an example, create the T.BAT file, which uses the TYPE command to display the contents of the PAYROLL.DAT file:

```
C:\> COPY CON T.BAT <ENTER>
TYPE PAYROLL.DAT <ENTER>
^Z <ENTER>
      1 File(s) copied

C:\>
```

Once you create this file, DOS allows you to abbreviate the command

```
C:\> TYPE PAYROLL.DAT <ENTER>
```

simply as

```
C:\> T <ENTER>
```

which significantly reduces your typing.

This batch file is useful only for displaying the contents of a specific file, PAYROLL.DAT. As you create batch files, keep the idea of supporting multiple applications in mind. A batch file that you can use for several applications is much more useful than a file-specific application like the T.BAT file.

In Chapter 21, "Using the DOS Environment," you learned that DOS batch files support named parameters. The first step in increasing the number of files T.BAT can support might be to use a named parameter, as shown here:

```
C:\> COPY  CON  T.BAT <ENTER>
TYPE %FILE% <ENTER>
^Z <ENTER>
     1 File(s) copied

C:\>
```

In this case, when you invoke T.BAT, DOS will search the environment for an entry in the form FILE=. If DOS finds this entry, it will display the contents of the corresponding file, which means that T.BAT could work for more than one file. Each time you wanted to display a different file, you would simply change the environment entry's value.

As a better solution, however, DOS allows you to include additional information in the batch-file command line. In addition to named parameters, DOS allows you to use up to ten different batch parameters. For example, consider the following command:

```
C:\> BATFILE  ONE  TWO  THREE <ENTER>
```

The command not only includes the batch-file name (BATFILE), but also three parameters. You access the command-line parameters within a batch file by using the variables %0 through %9, in this manner:

%0	Contains the batch-file name
%1	Contains the first batch parameter
%2	Contains the second batch parameter
.	.
.	.
.	.
%9	Contains the ninth batch parameter

Given the command line

```
C:\> BATFILE  ONE  TWO  THREE <ENTER>
```

DOS will associate the parameters %0 to %3 as shown here:

%0   Contains BATFILE
%1   Contains ONE
%2   Contains TWO
%3   Contains THREE

Likewise, given the command line

```
C:\> BATFILE  A  B  C  D  E  F  G  H  I  <ENTER>
```

DOS assigns the parameters this way:

%0	Contains BATFILE	%5	Contains E
%1	Contains A	%6	Contains F
%2	Contains B	%7	Contains G
%3	Contains C	%8	Contains H
%4	Contains D	%9	Contains I

Now that you know how the parameters work, let's use them. Change the T.BAT file to

```
C:\> COPY  CON  T.BAT  <ENTER>
TYPE %1  <ENTER>
^Z  <ENTER>
     1 File(s) copied

C:\>
```

You can now use the T abbreviation to display any file. For example, the command

```
C:\> T  PAYROLL.DAT  <ENTER>
```

displays the contents of the PAYROLL.DAT file, while the command

```
C:\> T  T.BAT <ENTER>
```

displays the contents of the T.BAT file. By using DOS batch parameters, you have changed T.BAT from a file-specific batch file to a batch file that supports multiple applications.

Displaying Batch-File Parameters

To better understand how DOS assigns the command-line values to batch parameters, create the VIEW.BAT file:

```
C:\> COPY  CON  VIEW.BAT <ENTER>
@ECHO %0 %1 %2 %3 %4 %5 %6 %7 %8 %9 <ENTER>
^Z <ENTER>
      1 File(s) copied

C:\>
```

The batch file VIEW.BAT uses the ECHO command to display the value of each parameter. If you invoke VIEW without a command line, the only parameter defined is %0 (which contains the batch file's name). Invoking VIEW without parameters will display the following:

```
C:\> VIEW <ENTER>
VIEW

C:\>
```

If you include the command-line values 1, 2, and 3, the batch file will display the following:

```
C:\> VIEW  1  2  3 <ENTER>
VIEW 1 2 3

C:\>
```

In a similar manner, the command

```
C:\> VIEW  Read the book DOS Inside & Out <ENTER>
```

results in the following:

```
VIEW Read the book DOS Inside & Out

C:\>
```

If your command line contains more than nine entries, as in

```
C:\> VIEW  1  2  3  4  5  6  7  8  9  10  11  12  13 <ENTER>
```

VIEW will still display only the first nine, as shown here:

```
VIEW 1 2 3 4 5 6 7 8 9

C:\>
```

As you will learn later in this chapter, you can use the SHIFT command to allow a batch file to manipulate more than nine parameters.

Using the IF String1==String2 Condition

When you were introduced to conditional batch processing and the IF command in Chapter 19, "Decision Making in Batch Files," you learned that the condition

```
IF string1==string2 DOS_command
```

would make more sense once you had examined DOS parameters. Here's why. Assume that you track several stocks based on these files:

File	Contents
HIGHTECH.DAT	High-tech computer stocks
AUTO.DAT	Automotive stocks
PENNY.DAT	Miscellaneous penny stocks

To display the stock values for a specific day, you could use a command such as

```
C:\> TYPE  HIGHTECH.DAT <ENTER>
```

In a similar manner, you can create a batch file called STOCK.BAT that contains the following:

```
C:\> COPY  CON  STOCKS.DAT <ENTER>
IF %1==HIGHTECH TYPE HIGHTECH.DAT <ENTER>
IF %1==AUTO TYPE AUTO.DAT <ENTER>
IF %1==PENNY TYPE PENNY.DAT <ENTER>
^Z <ENTER>
     1 File(s) copied

C:\>
```

Later, to display the values of your high-tech stocks, you would invoke the batch file as follows:

```
C:\> STOCKS  HIGHTECH <ENTER>
```

DOS will compare the value of %1 to the letters "HIGHTECH" within your batch file. As a result, the command

```
IF %1==HIGHTECH TYPE HIGHTECH.DAT
```

will become true, and DOS will display the contents of the HIGH-TECH.DAT file. Likewise, if you issue the command

```
C:\> STOCKS  AUTO <ENTER>
```

the batch file will match the following IF command, displaying the contents of the AUTO.DAT file:

```
IF %1==AUTO TYPE AUTO.DAT
```

Keep in mind that the tests within a batch file are case sensitive. For example, the command

```
C:\> STOCKS  penny <ENTER>
```

will not match any of the conditions within the batch file.

Checking for a Missing Parameter

As the complexity of your batch files increases, there may be times when you need to ensure that the user has specified a specific batch parameter. With the sample STOCKS.BAT file, for example, the user needs to include HIGHTECH, AUTO, or PENNY. If a user omits the parameter, the value of %1 will be empty. When comparing strings, the IF command needs two strings to compare. If one of the strings does not exist, IF will display the syntax error message, as shown here:

```
IF ==HIGHTECH TYPE HIGHTECH.DAT
Syntax error
```

To prevent such inadvertent errors, group both %1 and the values you want to compare within single quotes, as shown here:

```
IF '%1'=='HIGHTECH' TYPE HIGHTECH.DAT
```

Should the user invoke the batch file with the parameter HIGHTECH, DOS will substitute the value for %1, resulting in the following:

```
IF 'HIGHTECH'=='HIGHTECH' TYPE HIGHTECH.DAT
```

To test whether or not a parameter has a value, use the condition

```
IF '%1'='' DOS_command
```

If the user omits the first parameter, as in

```
C:\> STOCKS <ENTER>
```

the value of %1 is empty, so the previous condition becomes

```
IF ''='' DOS_command
```

Since both strings are equal, DOS will execute the command.

This batch file tells the user to specify a value in the command line:

```
C:\> COPY CON STOCKS.DAT <ENTER>
@ECHO OFF <ENTER>
IF '%1'='' ECHO SPECIFY HIGHTECH AUTO OR PENNY <ENTER>
IF '%1'='HIGHTECH' TYPE HIGHTECH.DAT <ENTER>
IF '%1'='AUTO' TYPE AUTO.DAT <ENTER>
IF '%1'='PENNY' TYPE PENNY.DAT <ENTER>
^Z <ENTER>
     1 File(s) copied

C:\>
```

In this case, if the user invokes the batch file as

```
C:\> STOCKS <ENTER>
```

the batch file will display the message

```
SPECIFY HIGHTECH AUTO OR PENNY
```

You will use the test for empty parameters in the next section as you work with the SHIFT command.

Supporting More Than Nine Batch Parameters

DOS provides support for the parameters %1 through %9. If you specify more than nine entries on your command line, DOS will acknowledge and work with only the first nine. If you must process more than nine parameters, the SHIFT command provides you with a solution. SHIFT is an internal DOS command that directs DOS to move each of the parameters one position to the left. For example, given the batch file

```
C:\> COPY  CON  SHIFTTST.BAT <ENTER>
@ECHO OFF <ENTER>
ECHO %0 %1 %2 %3 %4 %5 %6 %7 %8 %9 <ENTER>
SHIFT <ENTER>
ECHO %0 %1 %2 %3 %4 %5 %6 %7 %8 %9 <ENTER>
^Z <ENTER>
     1 File(s) copied

C:\>
```

the command

```
C:\> SHIFTTST  1  2  3  4  5 <ENTER>
```

results in the following output:

```
C:\> SHIFTTST  1  2  3  4  5 <ENTER>
SHIFTTST 1 2 3 4 5
1 2 3 4 5

C:\>
```

Each time DOS encounters the SHIFT command within a batch file, it rotates each parameter one location to the left. As a result, %1 moves to %0, %2 moves to %1, and so on:

%0 %1 %3 %4 %5 %6 %7 %8 %9   Empty
value

%0 %1 %3 %4 %5 %6 %7 %8 %9

If your command line contains more than nine parameters, as in

```
C:\> SHIFTTST  1  2  3  4  5  6  7  8  9  10  11  12  13
<ENTER>
```

DOS will rotate the additional parameters into %9 with each
SHIFT command:

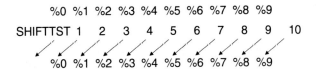

%0 %1 %2 %3 %4 %5 %6 %7 %8 %9

SHIFTTST 1 2 3 4 5 6 7 8 9 10

%0 %1 %2 %3 %4 %5 %6 %7 %8 %9

The following batch procedure uses the GOTO command to display all
of the parameters on the command line:

```
@ECHO OFF
:LOOP
IF '%1'=='' GOTO DONE
ECHO %1
SHIFT
GOTO LOOP
:DONE
```

The procedure begins by examining the value of %1. If %1 is empty, the
procedure terminates. If it is not, DOS displays the value of %1, shifts
all of the parameters one position to the left, and loops to the beginning
to test the new value of %1. When SHIFT does not have a value to assign
to %1, the variable becomes empty, and the procedure terminates.

Practice

The CALL command allows you to invoke one batch procedure from within another. To verify this, create the following batch files:

```
C:\> COPY  CON  CALLTEST.BAT <ENTER>
CALL DATETIME <ENTER>
VER <ENTER>
^Z <ENTER>
     1 File(s) copied

C:\> COPY  CON  DATETIME.BAT <ENTER>
DATE <ENTER>
TIME <ENTER>
^Z <ENTER>
     1 File(s) copied

C:\>
```

Invoke the CALLTEST.BAT batch file and note the processing. Then remove the CALL command from the batch file named DATETEST, as shown here:

```
C:\> COPY  CON  CALLTEST.BAT <ENTER>
DATETIME <ENTER>
VER <ENTER>
^Z <ENTER>
     1 File(s) copied

C:\>
```

When you invoke CALLTEST, DOS will never execute the VER command because the file does not include CALL.

Next, create the ECHOTEST.BAT file, which displays the batch file name using %0 and the first five batch parameters:

```
C:\> COPY  CON  ECHOTEST.BAT <ENTER>
@ECHO %0 %1 %2 %3 %4 %5 <ENTER>
^Z <ENTER>
     1 File(s) copied

C:\>
```

Invoke the batch file with

```
C:\> ECHOTEST  A  B  C <ENTER>
```

The batch file will display the batch file name and the three parameters.

Next, invoke the batch file with

```
C:\> ECHOTEST  1  2  3  4  5  6  7  8 <ENTER>
```

In this case, the batch file displays only the first five parameters. Remember, the ECHO command uses only %0 through %5.

Change ECHOTEST.BAT slightly to include the SHIFT command:

```
@ECHO OFF
ECHO %0 %1 %2 %3 %4 %5
SHIFT
ECHO %0 %1 %2 %3 %4 %5
```

Experiment with the previous command lines to see how the SHIFT command works.

Finally, create the T.BAT file:

```
C:\> COPY  CON  T.BAT <ENTER>
@ECHO OFF <ENTER>
:LOOP <ENTER>
IF '%1'=='' GOTO DONE <ENTER>
FOR %%I IN (%1) DO TYPE %%I <ENTER>
SHIFT <ENTER>
```

```
GOTO LOOP <ENTER>
:DONE <ENTER>
^Z <ENTER>
     1 File(s) copied

C:\>
```

T.BAT displays the contents of each file name you specify. Because it uses the FOR command, T.BAT supports wildcard characters. By using SHIFT to traverse the batch parameters, T.BAT lets you include several file names in its command line. T.BAT allows you to issue such commands as

```
C:\> T  PAYROLL.DAT <ENTER>
C:\> T  PAYROLL.DAT  T.BAT  ECHOTEST.BAT <ENTER>
C:\> T  *.BAT  *.DAT <ENTER>
```

Thus, T.BAT greatly increases the flexibility of the TYPE command.

Review

1. What is a nested batch file?
2. When do you need the CALL command?
3. Given the following command line, what values will DOS assign to parameters %0 to %3?

   ```
   C:\> BATFILE MAY JUNE JULY <ENTER>
   ```

4. Create a batch file that displays the contents of a file specified by the first batch parameter.
5. What is the function of the SHIFT command?

The CALL Command

The CALL command allows one batch file to invoke another. The CALL command can be as simple as

```
CALL BATFILE
```

or it can contain batch parameters (information passed to the batch file) as shown here:

```
CALL BATFILE PARAM1 PARAM2 ...
```

When DOS completes the nested batch file, DOS returns to the first batch file. If you invoke a nested batch file without using CALL, DOS will never return to the first batch file, returning instead to the DOS prompt.

COMMAND /C BATFILE

DOS 3.3 is the earliest version of DOS to provide the CALL command for invoking nested batch files. DOS users who have used DOS 3.2 or earlier may have invoked nested batch files by using

```
COMMAND /C BATFILE
```

If you are using DOS 3.3 or later, your batch files should use the CALL command.

continues . . .

Key Points
(continued)

The SHIFT Command

The SHIFT command directs DOS to rotate each of the batch parameters one position to the left; %1 stores the value previously stored in %2, %2 stores %3's value, and so on. If more than nine batch parameters are in the command line, SHIFT places the next additional parameter in %9.

Using DOS Pretender Commands

*T*hroughout this book, all of the commands that you have examined have used drives A, B, and C. Because these floppy and hard disk drives are physically connected to your computer, they are called *physical disk drives*. DOS also allows you to reference *logical disk drives*, which do not exist physically on your system. You can use logical drives to abbreviate long DOS subdirectory names.

This chapter first examines the APPEND command, which allows you to define the list of subdirectories DOS will examine in search of your data files. Just as the PATH command defines the command-file search path, the APPEND command defines the data-file search path.

Next, this chapter introduces the SUBST command, which lets you abbreviate long directory names with a logical disk drive letter.

Finally, you will briefly examine the JOIN command, which allows you to make two disk drives appear as one. Because JOIN and SUBST work with disk drives that do not physically exist on your system, they are called *pretender commands*.

Defining a Data-File Search Path

Earlier, you learned that the command

```
C:\> PATH  C:\DOS;C:\UTIL;C:\BATCH <ENTER>
```

directs DOS to search the DOS, UTIL, and BATCH subdirectories on drive C each time it fails to locate an external DOS command in the current subdirectory. You can use the APPEND command in a similar manner to specify the subdirectories in which DOS will search for a data file each time it fails to locate the file in the specified subdirectory.

Let's look at one example. Assume your directory structure contains the directories shown here:

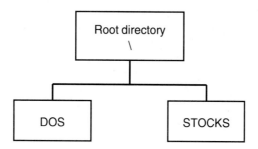

Next, assume your current directory is not the STOCKS subdirectory. To access files that reside in the STOCKS directory, you must specify the subdirectory name before your file names, as in

```
C:\> TYPE  \STOCKS\HIGHTECH.DAT <ENTER>
```

or

```
C:\> PRINT  \STOCKS\AUTO.DAT <ENTER>
```

Using the APPEND command, you can eliminate the need to specify a complete directory name for your commonly used directories. For example, if you instead issue the command

```
C:\> APPEND  C:\STOCKS <ENTER>
```

DOS will automatically search the STOCKS subdirectory each time it fails to locate the data file in the current directory. Thus, regardless of the default disk drive or directory, DOS allows you to execute the previous commands as

```
C:\> TYPE  HIGHTECH.DAT <ENTER>
```

or

```
C:\> PRINT  AUTO.DAT <ENTER>
```

When DOS fails to locate the file in the current directory or in the directory you specify, DOS will search the list of directories specified in the APPEND command.

If you simply invoke APPEND without specifying command-line parameters, APPEND will display the current data-file search path, as shown here:

```
C:\> APPEND <ENTER>
APPEND=C:\STOCKS

C:\>
```

To remove the data-file search path, place a semicolon in the APPEND command line, as shown here:

```
C:\> APPEND; <ENTER>
```

If you invoke APPEND again without command-line parameters, it will display

```
C:\> APPEND <ENTER>
No Append

C:\>
```

If you examine the APPEND command in the Command Reference section of this book, you will find that APPEND supports several command-line switches. Unlike the PATH command, which automatically places an entry in the DOS environment, you must include the /E switch the first time you invoke the APPEND command in order for APPEND to create an environment entry. More important, not all DOS commands support the data-file search path. To increase the number of applications that support APPEND, you must include the /X switch when you invoke APPEND:

```
C:\> APPEND  /X <ENTER>
```

This greatly increases the number of applications that support data-file search paths. If you are using DOS 5 or later, use the switch as /X:ON. Finally, the /PATH switch lets you control whether or not DOS searches the data-file search path when it fails to locate a file whose name is preceded by a directory path. The /PATH:ON switch directs DOS to search the data-file search path for such files. The /PATH:OFF switch directs DOS to search only the data-file search path when the file name is not preceded by a directory name.

You may be wondering if you can inadvertently delete a file in another directory once you define a data-file search path. Fortunately, the developers of DOS have protected you from such a possibility. If you attempt to delete a file by using

```
C:\> DEL FILENAME.EXT <ENTER>
```

and DOS does not locate the file in the current directory, it will not search the data-file search path for the entry. Therefore, if the file resides in a different directory, it will not be deleted. The same is true for the RENAME command.

Placing too many subdirectory paths in a PATH command can decrease your overall system performance, and the same holds true for APPEND. If a subdirectory is not likely to contain a commonly used data file, don't place the subdirectory in the APPEND data-file search path; doing so will result in wasted time because of the searching overhead. Also, place the subdirectories most likely to contain your data files first in the data-file search path to reduce the amount of searching that DOS must perform.

Abbreviating Long Directory Names

As you increase the number of subdirectories on your disk, your subdirectory structure will become quite complex, as illustrated in

Figure 24-1. Your DOS commands will become equally complex since you must specify complete path names, as shown here:

```
C:\> DIR   \INCOME\1993\QTR1 <ENTER>

C:\> TYPE  \INCOME\1993\QTR2\PAYCHECK.$$$ <ENTER>

C:\> DEL   \EXPENSES\1993\MAY1993\*.OLD <ENTER>

C:\> COPY \EXPENSES\1993\MAY1993\*.OLD \EXPENSES
          \1993\MAY1993\SAVE.EXP
```

If you find yourself repeatedly accessing files that reside in a specific subdirectory, the SUBST command may let you reduce your typing. SUBST allows you to abbreviate a long DOS subdirectory name as a disk drive specifier. For example, given the command

```
C:\> SUBST  E: C:\EXPENSES\1992\JULY1992\BUSINESS <ENTER>
```

DOS will allow you to refer to the subdirectory simply as E:. This means that the command

```
C:\> TYPE  E:PAPER.EXP <ENTER>
```

is equivalent to

```
C:\> TYPE  C:\EXPENSES\1992\JULY1992\BUSINESS\PAPER.EXP <ENTER>
```

As you can see, referring to the subdirectory as drive E saves you considerable typing. Since drive E does not physically exist as a disk drive on your system, it is called a *logical* disk drive.

If the subdirectory you are abbreviating contains additional DOS subdirectories, you can still access them by specifying drive E, as shown here:

```
C:\> TYPE  E:SUBDIR\FILENAME.EXT <ENTER>
```

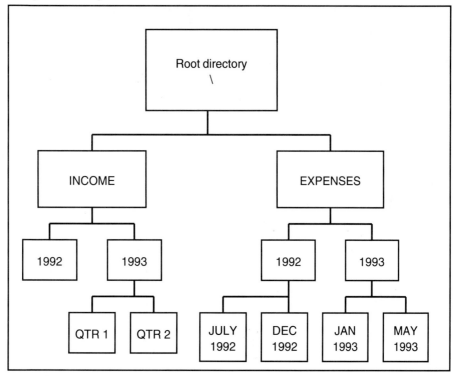

FIGURE 24-1

Sample directory structure

Once you have created a logical disk drive with the SUBST command, that disk drive is available from within the DOS shell, as shown in Figure 24-2.

If you select the logical disk drive as the current disk drive, DOS will display the files that the abbreviated subdirectory contains.

If you invoke SUBST without specifying any command-line parameters, it will display the current directory substitutions:

```
C:\> SUBST <ENTER>
E: => C:\EXPENSES\1992\JULY1992\BUSINESS

C:\>
```

To remove the logical disk drive, invoke the SUBST command with the /D switch, as shown here:

```
C:\> SUBST   E:  /D  <ENTER>
```

If you invoke the SUBST command again, you will see that the directory substitutions have been eliminated.

```
C:\> SUBST  <ENTER>

C:\>
```

If SUBST displays the message

```
Invalid parameter
```

you may have to update the LASTDRIVE entry in CONFIG.SYS (discussed in Chapter 27, "Customizing Your System Using CONFIG.SYS") to accommodate more drive letters.

FIGURE 24-2

Logical disk drive E shown in the DOS shell

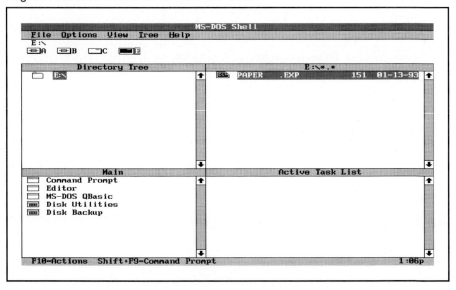

Many older software programs do not support DOS subdirectories. In some cases, the SUBST command can provide you with an alternative. By substituting a disk drive letter for the directory name, you can probably trick the program into running. Also, if the number of characters in your DOS PATH command becomes too large, you might consider abbreviating several of the directory names with disk drive letters.

Making Two Disk Drives Appear to Be One

If you have a floppy disk system, there may be times when a program you are running requires more disk space than one floppy disk can provide. In such cases, the JOIN command allows you to make two disks seem to be one.

 Note DOS 6 does not support the JOIN command.

To begin, you must use an empty directory on your primary disk:

```
A:\> MKDIR  \JOINDIR  <ENTER>
```

Next, use the JOIN command to join the secondary disk to the new subdirectory:

```
A:\> JOIN  B:  \JOINDIR  <ENTER>
```

JOIN will join drive B to the directory JOINDIR on drive A. In this case, the previous MKDIR command created the directory. If the directory you specify in a JOIN command does not exist, JOIN will create it.

When you issue the command

```
A:\> DIR  \JOINDIR  <ENTER>
```

DIR will not only display all of the files in the real /JOINDIR directory, but also the ones on the disk in drive B. DOS pretends they are a single directory.

DOS will not allow you to access a disk drive directly once you have joined it to a directory. In this case, if you issue the command

```
A:\> DIR   B: <ENTER>
```

DOS will display the message

```
Invalid drive specification
```

If you invoke JOIN without specifying any command-line parameters, JOIN will display its currently joined disks, as shown here:

```
A:\> JOIN <ENTER>
B: => A:\JOINDIR

A:\>
```

To remove a disk join, use the /D switch, as shown here:

```
A:\> JOIN   B: /D <ENTER>
```

If you invoke JOIN again without specifying a command-line argument, it will show you that it has removed the joined disk:

```
A:\> JOIN <ENTER>

A:\>
```

If you use the DOS shell on a regular basis, you know that each time you change the default drive within the shell, the shell performs a time-consuming directory read of the new disk. When you change directories on the same drive, however, the shell does not perform the directory read. If you change between two drives on a regular basis, you might consider joining one of the drives to the other. In so doing, you can simply change directories to the joined directory whenever you want to access the other drive's files, thereby avoiding the time-consuming directory read of the disk.

Practice

As you have read, the APPEND command allows you to define a data-file search path that DOS examines each time it fails to locate a data file in the specified subdirectory. To begin, create the directory TEMPDIR, as shown here:

```
C:\> MKDIR   \TEMPDIR <ENTER>
```

Using the CHDIR command, select TEMPDIR as the current directory:

```
C:\> CHDIR   \TEMPDIR <ENTER>
```

Next, create the file TESTAPPD.DAT, as shown here:

```
C:\TEMPDIR> COPY CON TESTAPPD.DAT <ENTER>
This is a test file for the APPEND command. <ENTER>
^Z <ENTER>
  1 File(s) copied

C:\TEMPDIR>
```

Use the TYPE command to display the file's contents.

```
C:\TEMPDIR> TYPE  TESTAPPD.DAT <ENTER>
This is a test file for the APPEND command.

C:\TEMPDIR>
```

Next, select the DOS directory as the current directory:

```
C:\TEMPDIR> CHDIR  \DOS <ENTER>
```

Issue the following TYPE command to display TESTAPPD.DAT's contents.

```
C:\DOS> TYPE  TESTAPPD.DAT <ENTER>
File not found

C:\DOS>
```

Because the file TESTAPPD.DAT does not reside in the DOS directory, TYPE could not find it.

Issue the following APPEND command, which directs DOS to search the TEMPDIR directory for data files:

```
C:\DOS> APPEND  \TEMPDIR <ENTER>
```

Next, repeat the previous TYPE command:

```
C:\DOS> TYPE  TESTAPPD.DAT <ENTER>
This is a test file for the APPEND commmand.

C:\DOS>
```

In this case, because DOS searched the directory TEMPDIR, TYPE was able to locate and display the file TESTAPPD.DAT.

Issue the following APPEND command to view the current data-file search path:

```
C:\DOS> APPEND <ENTER>
```

Next, remove the data-file search path by including a semicolon in the APPEND command line, as shown here:

```
C:\DOS> APPEND ; <ENTER>
```

Issue the following SUBST command to substitute the DOS directory on drive C as the logical disk drive E:

```
C:\> SUBST   E:   C:\DOS <ENTER>
```

Next, issue a directory listing of drive E:

```
C:\> DIR   E: <ENTER>
```

As you will see, DIR displays the files that reside in your DOS directory.

Issue the following SUBST command to display the current directory substitutions:

```
C:\> SUBST <ENTER>
E: => C:\DOS
```

If you invoke the shell, you will see that DOS has created the logical disk drive E.

To remove the disk drive substitution, invoke SUBST with the /D switch:

```
C:\> SUBST   E:  /D <ENTER>
```

Issue the following directory command:

```
C:\> DIR   E: <ENTER>
```

Because drive E is no longer defined, DOS will display the message

```
Invalid drive specification
```

In addition, drive E will no longer appear on the shell menu of available drives.

If you are not using DOS 6, the JOIN command allows you to make two disk drives appear as one. Place a floppy disk that contains files in drive A. Invoke DOSSHELL and select drive A as the current drive. As you will find, the shell performs a directory read of the files on the disk. Exit the shell by pressing F3. Next, create the directory JOINDIR on drive C. Issue the following command to JOIN drive A to the directory:

```
C:\> JOIN  A:  C:\JOINDIR <ENTER>
```

Next, invoke DOSSHELL. Select JOINDIR as the current directory. As you will see, the shell displays the names of the files that reside on the disk in drive A without performing the slow disk read. Exit the shell by pressing F3. Remove the directory JOIN by issuing the following command:

```
C:\> JOIN  A: /D <ENTER>
```

Review

1. What is a data-file search path?
2. What APPEND command places the NOTES and MISC subdirectories into the data-file search path?
3. What is the function of the SUBST command?
4. What DOS command would you use to abbreviate the subdirectory \PAYROLL\EXPENSES\BUDGET as drive E?
5. How do you remove a directory substitution?
6. When do you need to use the JOIN command?

Key Points

The APPEND Command

The APPEND command allows you to define or display a data-file search path. For example, the command

```
C:\> APPEND C:\NOTES;C:\LTRS <ENTER>
```

directs DOS to search the NOTES directory, followed by the LTRS directory on drive C, each time it fails to locate a file in the directory specified.

To display the current data-file search path, invoke APPEND as

```
C:\> APPEND <ENTER>
```

APPEND /E /X:ON /PATH:ON

By default, APPEND does not place an entry in the DOS environment, as does the PATH command. The /E switch directs APPEND to place an entry into the environment in the form

```
APPEND=C:\SUBDIR
```

In addition, by default, not all DOS commands support APPEND. The /X:ON switch increases the number of commands that support APPEND. Finally, the /PATH switch lets you control whether or not

continues . . .

DOS will search the data-file search path for a file name preceded by a directory path. The /E, /X, and /PATH switches are valid only the first time you invoke APPEND. For more information on these switches, refer to APPEND in the Command Reference section later in this book.

The SUBST Command

The SUBST command allows you to abbreviate a long directory name as a disk drive specifier. Once the substitution exists, DOS allows you to access the directory by using the substituted disk drive name. The following command abbreviates the DOS directory on drive C as drive E:

```
C:\> SUBST   E:   C:\DOS  <ENTER>
```

To display current disk drive substitutions, invoke SUBST without command-line parameters:

```
C:\> SUBST  <ENTER>
E:  => C:\DOS
```

To later remove a substitution, use the /D switch.

```
C:\> SUBST   E:  /D  <ENTER>
```

continues . . .

*Key Points
(continued)*

The JOIN Command

If you are not using DOS 6, the JOIN command allows you to make two disk drives appear as one. To use JOIN you must use an empty directory on one drive and then join the second drive to it. If the directory you specify in a JOIN command does not exist, JOIN will create it. Once you join a disk to a directory, a directory listing of the "joined" directory displays any files stored on the second drive. To remove the join, use the /D switch.

```
C:\> JOIN B: /D <ENTER>
```

CHAPTER

Advanced File
Manipulation

*T*his chapter examines several key DOS file-manipulation commands: ATTRIB, COMP, FC, REPLACE, XCOPY, and EXPAND. By the end of this chapter, you will be familiar with the DOS file-manipulation capabilities you will need in order to get the most from DOS.

Several commands you will examine in this chapter have complex command-line switches. You will learn here only about the switches you will need to get started with these commands. For more specifics, refer to the Command Reference at the end of this book.

Setting or Displaying File Attributes

As you know, each time you create or change a file, DOS assigns a date and time stamp to the file. When you use DIR, DOS displays each file's date and time:

```
C:\> DIR <ENTER>
 Volume in drive C is DOS 6 DISK
 Volume Serial Number is 16F6-3B73
 Directory of C:\

CONFIG    SYS       128 08-09-93   10:31a
AUTOEXEC  BAT       119 08-09-93   11:42a
DOS              <DIR>    07-22-93    7:19a
WP51             <DIR>    08-12-93    4:05a
BACKUP           <DIR>    08-13-93    1:29p
        5 file(s)         247 bytes
                    151519232 bytes  free
```

One item that doesn't appear in the directory listing is the file attribute that DOS also assigns to every file. A *file attribute* tells DOS whether or not it can delete or modify the file, as well as whether or not the file needs to be backed up to a floppy disk with the BACKUP command (discussed in Chapter 26). Specifically, the attributes you assign to a file can include the following:

❏ **Read-only** Prevents a DOS command from changing the file in any way. Commands that do not change the file in any manner (such as TYPE or PRINT) have complete access to the file. Commands that attempt to change a read-only file will fail.

❑ **Archive** Indicates to DOS that the file has been modified or created since the last system backup; when you later execute the BACKUP command to back up the file, DOS changes the attribute to the archived attribute.

❑ **Hidden** Directs DOS not to display the file's name in a directory listing, hiding the file's existence from the user.

❑ **System** Indicates the file is a special DOS system file. You should reserve the system attribute for use by DOS.

The ATTRIB command lets you display or set the attribute for one or more files. For example, to display the attribute of each file in the current directory, issue the command

```
C:\> ATTRIB  *.*  <ENTER>
```

ATTRIB will display each file name that appears in the directory listing preceded by letters that indicate the file's current attribute settings, as shown here:

```
     SH        C:\IO.SYS
     SH        C:\MSDOS.SYS
  A            C:\COMMAND.COM
               C:\CONFIG.SYS
               C:\AUTOEXEC.BAT
```

If a file name is not preceded by attribute letters, the file does not have any attributes set. Table 25-1 summarizes the attribute letters you may see. As shown in the previous output, a file may have one or more of the attribute values.

You have already learned that write-protecting your floppy disks can prevent an errant DOS command such as DEL *.* from inadvertently deleting your files. However, you cannot use a write-protect tab to protect the files on a hard disk. The ATTRIB command gives you a means of protecting important files that don't change often by setting the files to read-only access.

TABLE 25-1	Attribute Letters Displayed by ATTRIB

Attribute Letter	Meaning
A	Archiving (backing up) of the file is required.
R	The file is a read-only file.
S	The file is a DOS system file.
H	The file is a hidden file that will not appear in the directory listing.

To better understand how file attributes work, create the ATTRIB.NTS file, as shown here:

```
C:\> COPY  CON  ATTRIB.NTS  <ENTER>
The ATTRIB command sets or displays  <ENTER>
a file's attributes.  <ENTER>
^Z  <ENTER>
     1 File(s) copied

C:\>
```

Using the ATTRIB command, display this file's attributes:

```
C:\> ATTRIB  ATTRIB.NTS  <ENTER>
  A           C:\ATTRIB.NTS
```

In this case, the uppercase "A" indicates the file has the archive-required attribute set. Each time you create or change a file, DOS sets the archive-required attribute. When you later back up the file to floppy disk, DOS removes the attribute.

To set or remove a file attribute yourself, you invoke ATTRIB, using one or more of the letters that appear in Table 25-1 with a plus sign to assign the attribute and a minus sign to remove it. Table 25-2 contains several different combinations you could use to change file attributes.

TABLE 25-2 Sample Attribute Combinations for the ATTRIB Command

Attribute Letters	Attribute Setting
+R	Sets the file to read-only
+A	Sets the file's archive-required attribute
+R +A	Sets the file to read-only and archive-required
–R +A	Removes a file's read-only attribute while setting archive-required
+R –A +H	Sets the file's read-only attribute, removes the file's archive-required attribute, and sets the file to hidden

Next, set the file to read-only access by using the ATTRIB command:

```
C:\> ATTRIB  +R  ATTRIB.NTS <ENTER>
```

If you again display the file's attributes, you will see

```
C:\> ATTRIB  ATTRIB.NTS <ENTER>
  A    R     C:\ATTRIB.NTS
```

As you can see, the file's archive-required attribute has not changed. The uppercase "R" indicates that the read-only attribute has been set, so DOS cannot change or delete the file. If you try to delete the file from the DOS prompt, DEL will fail, displaying the following:

```
C:\> DEL  ATTRIB.NTS <ENTER>
Access denied

C:\>
```

If you try to delete it from within the shell, DOS will display the dialog box shown here:

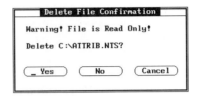

Before you can delete or change a read-only file, you must first remove the read-only attribute by using –R in the ATTRIB command line, as shown here:

```
C:\> ATTRIB  -R  ATTRIB.NTS <ENTER>
```

If you again attempt to delete the ATTRIB.NTS file, you will be successful:

```
C:\> DEL  ATTRIB.NTS <ENTER>
C:\>
```

In a similar manner, you can set or remove a file's archive-required attribute by using +A or –A in the ATTRIB command line, as shown here:

```
C:\> ATTRIB  +A FILENAME.EXT <ENTER>
```

Later in this chapter, you will use the archive attribute with the XCOPY command. At that time you will gain a greater appreciation for its use.

In the examples presented so far, you have used only one file, which resided in the current directory. ATTRIB fully supports wildcard characters. For example, the following command directs ATTRIB to display the attributes for files with the COM extension in the DOS directory:

```
C:\> ATTRIB  \DOS\*.COM <ENTER>
```

In addition, you can use the /S switch to direct ATTRIB to process all of the files in directories beneath the specified directory. To display the attributes of all of the files on your hard disk, for example, you can use the following command:

```
C:\> ATTRIB  C:\*.*  /S <ENTER>
```

If you are using the shell, select the file or files whose attributes you want to set. Next, invoke the File menu Change Attributes option. The shell will display the following dialog box:

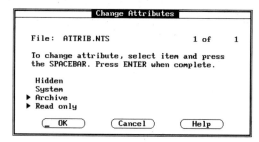

Using your arrow keys and SPACEBAR, highlight the attributes you want to assign to the file. When you select the OK option, the shell will assign the new attributes.

Many people fail to use ATTRIB simply because they don't know which files they should set the attributes for. As a general guideline, protect files such as EXE and COM files by setting them to read-only. The ATTRIB command provides you with a tool to protect your files; for ATTRIB to be effective, you must use it.

Although the ATTRIB command lets you set the –S switch, you should reserve the use of the system attribute for DOS. For more information on hidden files, refer to ATTRIB in the Command Reference at the end of this book.

Comparing the Contents of Two Files

The COMP command is an external DOS command that allows you to compare the contents of two files. COMP displays the first ten differences on your screen.

DOS 6 does not provide the COMP command. Instead, use the FC command discussed later in this chapter. The following COMP command compares the contents of the file FIRST.DAT to the file SECOND.DAT:

```
C:\> COMP  FIRST.DAT  SECOND.DAT <ENTER>
```

If the files are identical, COMP will display the following:

```
Comparing FIRST.DAT and SECOND.DAT
Files compare OK

Compare more files (Y/N)?
```

However, if the files are different, COMP will display a message similar to the following:

```
Comparing FIRST.DAT and SECOND.DAT
Compare error at OFFSET n
File 1 = nn
File 2 = nn
```

The value n specifies the byte position of the character within the files that differ. If, for example, the fifth character in the files differs, COMP would display the value 5. The values nn are the actual values that appear in both files. Unfortunately, by default, COMP displays the byte offset and file values in hexadecimal, the base-16 numbering system. Hexadecimal values are typically used and understood by programmers.

To better understand how COMP works, create the following files:

```
C:\> COPY  CON  TWO_ES.DAT <ENTER>
A <ENTER>
B <ENTER>
C <ENTER>
D <ENTER>
E <ENTER>
E <ENTER>
F <ENTER>
G <ENTER>
H <ENTER>
^Z <ENTER>
```

```
      1 File(s) copied

C:\> COPY  CON  A_TO_I.DAT <ENTER>
A <ENTER>
B <ENTER>
C <ENTER>
D <ENTER>
E <ENTER>
F <ENTER>
G <ENTER>
H <ENTER>
I <ENTER>
^Z <ENTER>
      1 File(s) copied

C:\>
```

Next, invoke COMP, as shown here:

```
C:\> COMP  TWO_ES.DAT  A_TO_I.DAT <ENTER>
```

In this case, COMP will display the following:

```
C:\> COMP  TWO_ES.DAT  A_TO_I.DAT <ENTER>
Comparing TWO_ES.DAT and A_TO_I.DAT...
Compare error at OFFSET F
file1 = 45
file2 = 46
Compare error at OFFSET 12
file1 = 46
file2 = 47
Compare error at OFFSET 15
file1 = 47
file2 = 48
Compare error at OFFSET 18
file1 = 48
file2 = 49
```

As you can see, COMP displays the values in each file that differ. However, as discussed, it displays the values using hexadecimal. If you are using DOS 5, you can use the /A switch to direct COMP to display the differences in their ASCII, or character, form. The following command uses /A:

```
C:\> COMP  TWO_ES.DAT  A_TO_I.DAT  /A <ENTER>
Comparing TWO_ES.DAT and A_TO_I.DAT...
Compare error at OFFSET F
file1 = E
file2 = F
Compare error at OFFSET 12
file1 = F
file2 = G
Compare error at OFFSET 15
file1 = G
file2 = H
Compare error at OFFSET 18
file1 = H
file2 = I
```

Each time COMP ends a comparison, it displays the following prompt:

```
Compare more files (Y/N)?
```

If you respond with **Y** to compare more files, COMP will display the following prompt asking you to type in the file name you want to compare:

```
Name of first file to compare:
```

When you type in a file name, COMP will repeat this process, prompting you to enter the second file name to compare.

In addition to the /A switch, COMP supports the switches listed in Table 25-3. For more information on each of these switches, refer to the Command Reference at the end of this book.

TABLE 25-3 Other COMP Command-Line Switches

Switch	Function
/D	COMP displays differences in decimal.
/L	COMP displays line numbers of differences.
/N = *number*	COMP compares only the number of lines specified.
/C	COMP considers upper- and lowercase letters as the same.

Once again, you can easily invoke COMP from within the DOS shell by using the File menu Run option. When the shell displays the command-line dialog box, type in the names of the files you want to compare:

Comparing Files Using FC

If you are using MS-DOS version 2.0 or later, you can use the FC (file compare) command to compare files. Unlike COMP, which displays the differences between files as byte offsets and single values, FC performs line-by-line comparisons. To begin, create the following files:

```
C:\> COPY  CON  WEEK.DAY <ENTER>
Sunday <ENTER>
Monday <ENTER>
Tuesday <ENTER>
Wednesday <ENTER>
Thursday <ENTER>
```

```
Friday <ENTER>
Saturday <ENTER>
^Z <ENTER>
      1 File(s) copied

C:\> COPY  CON  WORK.DAY <ENTER>
Monday <ENTER>
Tuesday <ENTER>
Wednesday <ENTER>
Thursday <ENTER>
Friday <ENTER>
^Z <ENTER>
       1 File(s) copied

C:\>
```

Next, invoke the FC command to compare the two files, as shown here:

```
C:\> FC  WEEK.DAY  WORK.DAY <ENTER>
```

In this case, FC will display the following:

```
C:\> FC  WEEK.DAY  WORK.DAY <ENTER>
Comparing files WEEK.DAY and WORK.DAY
***** WEEK.DAY
Sunday
Monday
Tuesday
***** WORK.DAY
Monday
Tuesday
*****

***** WEEK.DAY
Saturday
***** WORK.DAY
*****
```

FC first tells you the file WEEK.DAY begins with the lines Sunday, Monday, Tuesday, while WORK.DAY begins Monday, Tuesday. Next, FC tells you the file WEEK.DAY contains the line Saturday and WORK.DAY does not.

As you can see, FC's output is more meaningful than COMP's output. Table 25-4 lists the switches you can include in FC's command line. For more information on these switches, refer to the Command Reference at the end of this book.

TABLE 25-4

FC Command-Line Switches

FC Switch	Function
/A	Directs FC to display only the first and last lines of a set of lines that differ, instead of displaying the entire set
/B	Directs FC to perform a byte-by-byte file comparison similar to COMP
/C	Directs FC to consider upper- and lowercase letters as the same
/L	Directs FC to perform a line-by-line comparison. FC normally works in this mode with the exception of comparing files with the EXE, COM, LIB, OBJ, BIN, or SYS extension
/LB*nn*	Directs FC to allow *nn* consecutive lines to differ before FC cancels the command. By default, FC uses 100
/N	Directs FC to display the line numbers that correspond to lines that differ
/*nnn*	Requires FC to match *nnn* consecutive lines before it can consider the files to be resynched
/T	Directs FC not to expand tab characters into spaces
/W	Directs FC to compress white space by considering several successive blanks or tabs as one space or tab character

Updating Specific Files with REPLACE

Over the past few years, it has seemed as if new versions of software products are shipping almost as fast as you can install them. For some applications, the REPLACE command may provide a useful method of selectively upgrading your files. Assume, for example, that you receive a collection of floppy disks containing upgraded programs or files. By using the REPLACE command, you can quickly replace your existing files on your hard disk with the new files.

By default, REPLACE works very much like the COPY command, copying all of the files from a source disk to the target disks. For example, the command

```
C:\> REPLACE  A:*.*  \SUBDIR  /A <ENTER>
```

directs REPLACE to add all of the files that exist on drive A to the directory SUBDIR on drive C. Because the /A switch is used, if there are files in the SUBDIR directory whose names match those on the replacement disk, REPLACE will ignore them, adding only nonexistent files.

To better understand how REPLACE works, consider the following example. Assume that the disk in drive A contains these files:

```
C:\> DIR  A:
 Volume in drive A has no label
 Volume Serial Number is 1A49-12ED
 Directory of A:\

FIRST    DAT       128 03-09-93  10:31a
SECOND   DAT       119 03-09-93  11:42a
THIRD    DAT     47845 03-09-93   5:00a
FOURTH   DAT     12637 03-13-93  11:39a
FIFTH    DAT      8125 03-13-93  11:39a
        5 file(s)      68854 bytes
                      290816 bytes free
```

Assume that the directory SUBDIR contains these files:

```
C:\> DIR  \SUBDIR <ENTER>
 Volume in drive C is DOS 6 DISK
 Volume Serial Number is 16F6-3B73
 Directory of C:\SUBDIR

 .           <DIR>          03-13-93  11:40a
 ..          <DIR>          03-13-93  11:40a
 FIRST    DAT     32911 03-09-93   5:00a
 SECOND   DAT     10652 03-09-93   5:00a
 THIRD    DAT     47845 03-09-93   5:00a
          5 file(s)       91408 bytes
                      151396352 bytes free
```

The following REPLACE command will replace each file in the directory SUBDIR with its matching counterpart from the disk in drive A:

```
C:\> REPLACE  A:*.*  \SUBDIR <ENTER>

Replacing C:\SUBDIR\FIRST.DAT

Replacing C:\SUBDIR\SECOND.DAT

Replacing C:\SUBDIR\THIRD.DAT

3 file(s) replaced
```

In this case, REPLACE replaces only existing files; it will not add files to the directory that do not already exist. If you want to add files, you can use the /A switch, as previously discussed and shown here:

```
C:\> REPLACE  A:*.*  \SUBDIR  /A <ENTER>

Adding C:\SUBDIR\FOURTH.DAT

Adding C:\SUBDIR\FIFTH.DAT

2 file(s) added
```

In some cases, your hard disk may have one or more copies of a file in different directories that need to be replaced. The /S switch tells REPLACE to search all of the subdirectories that reside below the current directory of the target disk.

REPLACE is a powerful DOS command that supports multiple command-line switches. Table 25-5 briefly describes each of these switches. For more information on REPLACE, refer to the Command Reference at the end of this book.

Once again, you can use the shell's File menu Run option to invoke FC from within the shell.

Using XCOPY for Extended File Copying

You have used the COPY command extensively since early in this book to perform your file-copying operations. DOS also provides extended

TABLE 25-5

REPLACE Command-Line Switches

REPLACE Switch	Function
/A	Directs REPLACE to add only those files not found on the target disk
/P	Directs REPLACE to individually prompt you to confirm each replacement or addition
/R	Directs REPLACE to replace files marked read-only. By default, REPLACE stops at the first read-only file it encounters
/S	Directs REPLACE to search directories below the target directory for matching files
/U	Directs REPLACE to replace only those files on the target disk that are older than the replacement copies
/W	Directs REPLACE to pause, waiting for you to press a key before beginning the replacement

file-copying capabilities with the XCOPY command. By using the XCOPY command, you can

❑ Perform selective file-copying operations based on a file's creation and modification date

❑ Perform selective file-copying operations based on a file's archive attribute

❑ Copy files that reside in subdirectories below the current directory, creating an identical directory structure on the target disk

❑ In its most basic form, you can use the XCOPY command just like the COPY command:

```
C:\> XCOPY FILENAME.EXT  A:  <ENTER>
```

In this case, XCOPY will copy the file *FILENAME.EXT* from the current directory to the floppy disk in drive A. In a similar way, the following command directs XCOPY to copy all the files in the current directory to the disk in drive A:

```
C:\> XCOPY  *.*  A:  <ENTER>
```

Like ATTRIB and REPLACE, XCOPY supports the /S switch, which directs it to process files that reside below the current or specified directory. For example, assume that the disk in drive A contains the following files:

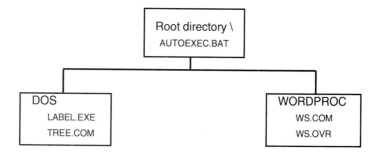

The following XCOPY command will copy all the files drive A contains to the current directory, including files in the subdirectories. If necessary, XCOPY will create the directories on the current disk.

```
C:\> XCOPY  A:*.*  *.*  /S <ENTER>
Reading source file(s)...
A:AUTOEXEC.BAT
A:DOS\LABEL.EXE
A:DOS\TREE.COM
A:WORDPROC\WS.COM
A:WORDPROC\WS.OVR
        5 File(s) copied
```

There may be times when you want to copy files selectively with XCOPY. When you include the /P switch in your command line, XCOPY will prompt you to determine whether or not you want to copy each file:

```
FILENAME.EXT (Y/N)?
```

To copy the file, type **Y** and press ENTER. To exclude the file from being copied, type **N** and press ENTER.

You can also use XCOPY with the /D switch to copy files selectively based on their date stamp. The command

```
C:\> XCOPY  A:*.*  *.* /D:12-25-93 <ENTER>
```

directs XCOPY to copy all files that were created or changed since December 25, 1993.

Many users wonder when they should use XCOPY instead of COPY. Here are a few suggestions. COPY is an internal DOS command, whereas XCOPY is an external command that resides on disk. As a result, for simple copy operations, COPY will execute much faster. When you need to perform selective file-copy operations or copy files that reside in DOS subdirectories, use XCOPY.

There are often times when you need to copy files in a directory on your hard disk to a floppy disk. If you are copying a large number of files, the floppy disk will fill, and DOS will display the message

```
Insufficient disk space
```

If you use the COPY command, there is no easy way to continue the copying operation from the point at which the disk filled. If you use the XCOPY command, however, you can easily continue the copying operation where you left off with a new floppy disk. To do so, you must use the ATTRIB command in conjunction with XCOPY.

To start, use ATTRIB to set all of the files in the directory to archive-required:

```
C:\> ATTRIB  +A  \SUBDIR\*.*  <ENTER>
```

Next, invoke XCOPY with the /M switch, as shown here:

```
C:\> XCOPY  \SUBDIR\*.*  A:  /M <ENTER>
```

The /M switch directs XCOPY to copy matching files whose archive-required attribute is set. When XCOPY successfully copies the file to the floppy disk, XCOPY clears the archive-required attribute. When the floppy disk fills and DOS displays the message

```
Insufficient disk space
```

you can place a new floppy disk in drive A and reissue the command:

```
C:\> XCOPY  \SUBDIR\*.*  A:  /M <ENTER>
```

Because XCOPY cleared the archive-required attribute of each file as it copied it, XCOPY knows exactly where it left off. Copying files from your fixed disk to floppy disks becomes much easier. Table 25-6 summarizes each of XCOPY's command-line switches.

To invoke XCOPY from within the shell, use the File menu Run option.

TABLE
25-6

XCOPY Command-Line Switches

XCOPY Switch	Function
/A	Directs XCOPY to copy only matching files whose archive-required attribute is set
/D:*mm-dd-yy*	Directs XCOPY to copy only matching files created or changed on or after the date specified
/E	Directs XCOPY to create subdirectories on the target even if the directory is empty
/M	Directs XCOPY to copy only matching files whose archive-required attribute is set. When XCOPY successfully copies the file, XCOPY clears the attribute
/P	Directs XCOPY to prompt "*FILENAME.EXT* (Y/N)?" before copying each file. If you type **Y**, XCOPY will copy the file. If you instead type **N**, XCOPY will not copy the file
/V	Directs XCOPY to compare the contents of the file copied to the original file to verify that the copy operation was successful
/S	Directs XCOPY to also copy files that reside in directories beneath the target directory
/W	Directs XCOPY to wait until you press a key before beginning the file-copy operation

Expanding Files from the DOS 5 and 6 Distribution Disks

To reduce the number of floppy disks used to hold the DOS 5 and 6 program, many of the files are stored on the DOS distribution disks in a compressed format. If you perform a directory listing of one of the distribution disks, you will see files with underscore characters in the last position of the file extension, as shown here:

```
C:\> DIR A:
 Volume in drive A is DISK      2
 Volume Serial Number is 1964-0711
 Directory of A:\

COUNTRY   SY_       5086 04-09-91    5:00a
DISPLAY   SY_      11186 04-09-91    5:00a
EGA       CP_      19714 04-09-91    5:00a
   :       :          :      :         :
UNDELETE  EX_       9391 04-09-91    5:00a
UNFORMAT  COM      18576 04-09-91    5:00a
XCOPY     EX_      11868 04-09-91    5:00a
CGA       VI_       6920 04-09-91    5:00a
        26 file(s)      346049 bytes
                         1024 bytes free
```

When you install DOS on your disk, the SETUP command automatically expands the files into their decompressed format. However, if you accidentally delete a DOS file and want to copy the file from the distribution disks, you may need to expand the file yourself.

The DOS 5 EXPAND command exists to decompress files you need to copy from a DOS 5 or later distribution disk. Assuming you delete the file UNDELETE.EXE, you can copy the compressed file from the distribution disk back into your DOS directory by using the following EXPAND command:

```
C:\> EXPAND  A:UNDELETE.EX_  \DOS\UNDELETE.EXE <ENTER>
```

The only time you need the EXPAND command is to copy files from the DOS 5 or later distribution floppies.

DIR Revisited

As you have learned, the ATTRIB command lets you set and display a file's attributes. If you are using DOS 5 or later, the DIR command lets you selectively display directory listings based on selected file attributes. The DIR /A switch lets you specify one or more of the attribute settings listed in Table 25-7.

For example, the following DIR command displays all hidden files in the root directory:

```
C:\> DIR  /A:H  \*.*  <ENTER>
```

TABLE 25-7

DIR /A Attribute Settings

Attribute Setting	Function
A	Displays only files whose archive-required attribute is set
–A	Displays only files whose archive-required attribute is not set
D	Displays only directory names
–D	Does not display directory names
H	Displays only hidden files
–H	Displays only non-hidden files
R	Displays only read-only files
–R	Displays only files that are not read-only
S	Displays only DOS system files
–S	Displays only non-system files

Likewise, this command displays all of the read-only files in the current directory:

```
C:\> DIR   /A:R  <ENTER>
```

Using the /A switch with /S, the following DIR command displays the name of every read-only file on your disk:

```
C:\> DIR   /A:R   /S   \*.*  <ENTER>
```

Practice

Use the following ATTRIB command to display the attributes of the files in the current directory:

```
C:\> ATTRIB   *.*  <ENTER>
```

Using ATTRIB's /S switch, display the attributes of every file on your disk, as shown here:

```
C:\> ATTRIB   \*.*   /S  <ENTER>
```

Create the ATTRIB.NTS file, as shown here:

```
C:\> COPY   CON   ATTRIB.NTS  <ENTER>
The ATTRIB command sets or displays  <ENTER>
file attributes.  <ENTER>
^Z  <ENTER>
     1 File(s) copied

C:\>
```

Next, use the following ATTRIB command to set the ATTRIB.NTS file to read-only access:

```
C:\> ATTRIB  +R  ATTRIB.NTS <ENTER>
```

Using the TYPE command, verify that you can still display the contents of the file:

```
C:\> TYPE  ATTRIB.NTS <ENTER>
The ATTRIB command sets or displays
file attributes.

C:\>
```

If you try to delete the file with DEL, DOS will display the following:

```
C:\> DEL  ATTRIB.NTS <ENTER>
Access denied

C:\>
```

Before you can delete the file, you must remove the read-only attribute:

```
C:\> ATTRIB  -R  ATTRIB.NTS <ENTER>
```

If you again attempt to delete the file, as shown here:

```
C:\> DEL  ATTRIB.NTS <ENTER>
C:\>
```

you will be successful.

If you are not using DOS 6, create two files called A.DAT and B.DAT, as shown here:

```
C:\> COPY  CON  A.DAT <ENTER>
A <ENTER>
AA <ENTER>
```

```
AAA <ENTER>
^Z <ENTER>
      1 File(s) copied

C:\> COPY  CON  B.DAT <ENTER>
B <ENTER>
BB <ENTER>
BBB <ENTER>
^Z <ENTER>
      1 File(s) copied

C:\>
```

Next, using COMP, compare the contents of the two files:

```
C:\> COMP  A.DAT  B.DAT <ENTER>
```

Remember, COMP displays its values in hexadecimal. The value 41 represents the letter "A," while the value 42 represents the letter "B." If you want to display the values in ASCII, use COMP's /A switch, as shown:

```
C:\> COMP  A.DAT  B.DAT  /A <ENTER>
```

Copy the contents of the file A.DAT to A.NEW:

```
C:\> COPY  A.DAT  A.NEW <ENTER>
      1 File(s) copied

C:\>
```

Next, issue the following COMP command:

```
C:\> COMP  A.DAT  A.NEW <ENTER>
```

COMP will tell you that the files are identical.

To see how XCOPY works, copy all files from the DOS directory to floppy disks in drive A. If you issue the following COPY command:

```
C:\> COPY  \DOS\*.*  A: <ENTER>
```

COPY will begin copying the files to drive A. When the disk fills, DOS will display the message

```
Insufficient disk space
```

Unfortunately, COPY does not provide you with an easy way to continue copying files at the last file copied. If you use XCOPY, however, copying an entire directory of files is very easy.

To start, set the attributes of all the files that you want to copy to archive-required by using ATTRIB, as shown here:

```
C:\> ATTRIB +A  C:\DOS\*.* <ENTER>
```

Next, issue the following XCOPY command:

```
C:\> XCOPY  C:\DOS\*.*  A:  /M <ENTER>
```

The /M switch directs XCOPY to copy only those files whose archive-required attribute is set. When you use /M, XCOPY will clear the archive-required attribute each time it successfully copies a file.

When your floppy disk fills, DOS will display a message indicating there is not enough disk space. Insert a new floppy disk in drive A and reissue the XCOPY command:

```
C:\> XCOPY  C:\DOS\*.*  A:  /M <ENTER>
```

Repeat this process until XCOPY copies the last file in the directory.

If you are using DOS 5 or later, issue the following DIR command to list every file on your disk:

```
C:\> DIR  \*.*  /S <ENTER>
```

Using the output redirection operator, you can print the name of every file, as shown here:

```
C:\> DIR  \*.*  /S  >  PRN <ENTER>
```

For more information on redirecting input and output, refer to Chapter 17, "Controlling DOS Input and Output."

Review

1. What file attributes does the ATTRIB command let you set?
2. What ATTRIB command sets the AUTOEXEC.BAT file to read-only?
3. How can you set all the files in the DOS directory to read-only?
4. What ATTRIB command displays the file attributes of every file on your disk?
5. When should you use XCOPY instead of COPY?
6. When do you need the DOS 5 EXPAND command?

Key Points

ATTRIB Command

The ATTRIB command lets you set and display a file's attributes. The following ATTRIB command displays the attributes for files in the DOS directory:

```
C:\> ATTRIB  \DOS\*.* <ENTER>
```

ATTRIB may precede each file's name with one or more of the following letters:

continues . . .

A   Archive required

R   Read-only file

H   Hidden file

S   DOS system file

To set a file's attribute, invoke ATTRIB, using +*attribute* to assign an attribute or –*attribute* to remove it. For example, the following ATTRIB command sets the AUTOEXEC.BAT file to read-only:

```
C:\> ATTRIB  +R  AUTOEXEC.BAT  <ENTER>
```

COMP Command

The COMP command compares the contents of two files, displaying the byte offsets of the characters that differ between the two files, as well as the characters themselves. If the files COMP compares are the same, COMP will display the following message:

```
Files compare OK
```

The following COMP command compares the two files FILENAME.EXT and FILENAME.NEW:

```
C:\> COMP  FILENAME.EXT  FILENAME.NEW  <ENTER>
```

DOS 6 does not support the COMP command.

*Key Points
(continued)*

REPLACE Command

The REPLACE command lets you selectively update files on your disk. By using REPLACE, you can copy all of the replacement files, only those files that don't exist on your target disk, only those files that do exist, or only those files newer than their counterparts. The following REPLACE command replaces all the files in the directory SOMEAPP with their counterparts from the floppy disk in drive A:

```
C:\> REPLACE  A:*.*   \SOMEAPP <ENTER>
```

XCOPY Command

The XCOPY command lets you selectively copy files based on the file's date stamp or file attributes. XCOPY also lets you copy files that reside in directories beneath your source directory. If you must copy a directory of files to multiple floppy disks, XCOPY provides your best solution.

EXPAND Command

The DOS 5 EXPAND command lets you copy compressed files from the DOS 5 distribution disk to your hard disk in a decompressed format. The following EXPAND command copies the file UNDELETE.EXE from the distribution disk in drive A:

```
C:\> EXPAND  A:UNDELETE.EX_   \DOS\UNDELETE.EXE <ENTER>
```

Likewise, if you are using DOS 6, the DECOMP command decompresses the distribution files.

Protecting Your Files with the DOS 6 MSBACKUP Command

*B*eginning with DOS 6, the MSBACKUP command provides a menu-driven, fast, backup utility. This chapter describes how to install and configure MSBACKUP and then how to perform complete disk, as well as incremental and differential backup, operations. MSBACKUP provides many performance and functional improvements over the previous DOS BACKUP command. If you haven't been performing regular backups in the past, MSBACKUP's capabilities just might motivate you to do so.

Installing and Configuring MSBACKUP

When you invoke MSBACKUP for the first time, MSBACKUP will display a dialog box that tells you that you must configure it for your system.

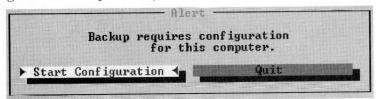

Choose the Start Configuration option to configure the system. MSBACKUP will display its Video and Mouse Configuration dialog box. Choose the OK option. MSBACKUP will then determine your system's floppy disk type. Perform the operations as MSBACKUP prompts you. Generally, you will choose the OK option for each dialog box displayed. Eventually, MSBACKUP will display its Floppy Disk Compatibility Test dialog box.

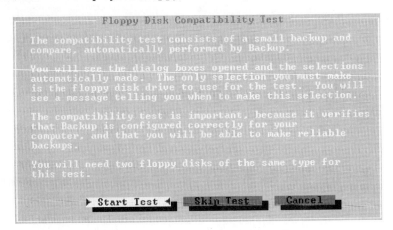

The compatibility test requires two unused floppy disks. If you have two disks available, perform the test by choosing the Start Test option. Otherwise, choose the Skip Test option. After the test completes (or if you skip the test) MSBACKUP will display its Configure dialog box.

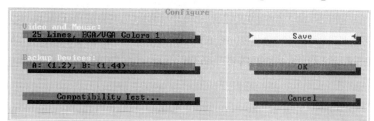

Choose the Save option. MSBACKUP will end the configuration, displaying its main menu. You are now ready to begin your backup operations.

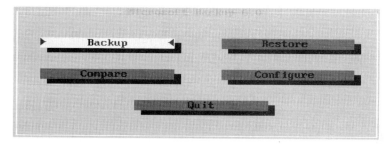

Performing Backup Operations

MSBACKUP lets you perform three different types of backups: full, incremental, or differential. Each backup operation backs up different files on your disk. To begin, a full backup backs up every file on your disk. A full backup is often called a complete disk backup. Next, an incremental backup backs up every file you have created or changed since the last backup operation. Incremental backups are sometimes called daily backups. Third, a differential backup backs up the files you have created or changed since the last full backup operation. Although MSBACKUP supports several different command-line switches (see this book's Command Reference), most users will perform their backup and restore operations directly from MSBACKUP's main menu, invoking MSBACKUP from the DOS prompt as follows:

```
C:\> MSBACKUP <ENTER>
```

Setup Files Make MSBACKUP Easy to Use

If you have worked with the DOS BACKUP command, you have issued commands using specific wildcard combinations to back up the files you desire. If you included the /A switch, BACKUP performed an incremental backup; otherwise, it backed up every file on your disk. MSBACKUP, on the other hand, lets you specify the files (and directories) you want to back up, as well as the backup type within a *setup file*. MSBACKUP lets you define up to 49 different setup files. In most cases, however, you will use only two or three. Typically, users will create one file that oversees their incremental backups and one for a full disk backup. As a rule, assign meaningful names to your setup files that define the operation they perform. For example, you might want to use the setup file names FULLDISK.SET and INCREMEN.SET. When you invoke MSBACKUP to perform a backup operation, you simply select the setup file for the type of backup you desire.

Creating Your Setup Files

Setup files define the files you want to back up, as well as the backup operation that you want to perform (full, incremental, or differential). In this section you will create the setup files FULLDISK.SET and INCRE-MEN.SET, which will let you quickly perform a full or incremental backup of your files on drive C.

Invoke MSBACKUP and select the BACKUP option. MSBACKUP will display its Backup screen. Press the TAB key until MSBACKUP highlights the Backup From option. Using your arrow keys, highlight the disk you want to back up and press the SPACEBAR. As you press the SPACEBAR, MSBACKUP will display the message All files next to the drive letter, telling you it will back up every file on that disk. If you want to back up more than one disk, repeat this process, selecting the desired disk drives.

Press the TAB key to highlight the Backup Type option and press ENTER. MSBACKUP will display its Backup Type dialog box.

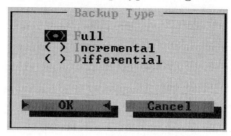

Use your keyboard arrow keys to highlight the desired backup type, in this case Full, and press the SPACEBAR followed by ENTER. Press the TAB key to highlight the Backup To option. If it does not currently say MS-DOS Drive and Path, press ENTER. MSBACKUP will display the Backup To dialog box.

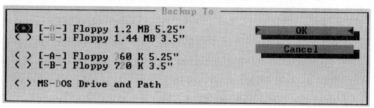

Select the MS-DOS Drive and Path and then select OK. Next, press the TAB key and type in the path **A:** as shown here:

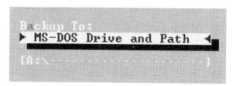

The setup you have just defined will back up every file on disk. Press the ALT-F keyboard combination to select the File menu.

Select the Save Setup As option. MSBACKUP will display the Save Setup File dialog box, shown here:

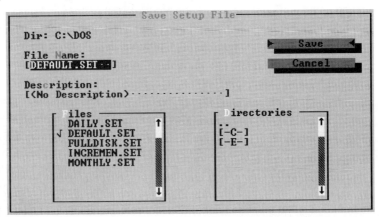

Type in the setup file name **FULLDISK.SET** and press ENTER. MSBACKUP will save the configuration to the file. Next, to create the setup file INCREMEN.SET, press the TAB key and highlight the Backup Type option, again pressing ENTER. When MSBACKUP displays the Backup Type dialog box, select the Incremental option, followed by OK. Next press the ALT-F keyboard combination to select the File menu. As before, choose the Save Setup As option and type in the file name **INCREMEN.SET**. Your two backup setup files are now ready for use.

Performing a Full Backup

After you define your backup setup files, performing backups is very easy. From the Backup screen, use your keyboard arrow keys to highlight the Setup File option and press ENTER. MSBACKUP will display its list of available setup files from within Setup File dialog box, shown here:

Because a full disk backup copies every file on your disk, they can be quite time consuming. Therefore, most users will only perform a full disk backup once a month. In fact, many users refer to a full disk backup as a monthly backup. To perform a full disk backup, highlight the file name FULLDISK.SET and press the SPACEBAR followed by ENTER. Next, place an unused, formatted floppy disk in drive A. Press the TAB key to highlight the Start Backup option. As the backup begins, MSBACKUP will display a screen summarizing the operation, as shown here:

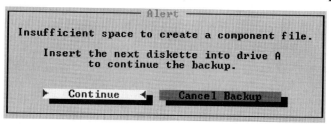

MSBACKUP will begin copying files to the floppy disk. As MSBACKUP successfully backs up a file, it will place a check mark next to the file name. Eventually, the floppy disk in drive A will fill, and MSBACKUP will display the Alert dialog box, prompting you to insert a new floppy disk.

```
───────────── Alert ─────────────
 Insufficient space to create a component file.

     Insert the next diskette into drive A
            to continue the backup.

  ▶  Continue  ◀        Cancel Backup
```

Remove the floppy disk from the drive, placing on the disk a label that contains the backup type (Monthly Backup), the date, and the disk number. Place the disk into a disk storage container. Next, place a second unused floppy in the drive and select the Continue option. Repeat this process of inserting and labeling floppy disks until the backup completes. When the backup ends, MSBACKUP will display the Backup Complete dialog box.

Select the OK option to continue. Place your monthly backup floppy disks in a safe location. A month from now, after you successfully perform your next full disk backup, you can replace these backup floppies with the newer backups.

Performing a Daily Backup

Because the monthly backup backs up every file on your disk, it can be a quite time-consuming process and use up a considerable number of floppies. Luckily, you only have to perform the operation once a month. For the other days in the month, you can perform a daily or incremental backup. The incremental backup backs up only those files you have created or changed since the last (full or incremental) backup operation.

Because you previously created the setup file INCREMEN.SET, performing a daily backup is very easy. From the Backup menu, select the Setup File option. MSBACKUP will display a dialog box containing its list of available setup files. Highlight the file name INCREMEN.SET and press the SPACEBAR, followed by ENTER. Next, place an unused floppy disk in drive A and select the Start Backup option. MSBACKUP will begin backing up files to the disk. Depending on the number and size of the files you have created or changed since the last backup operation, the backup may require two or more disks. Should a disk fill, MSBACKUP will display a dialog box prompting you to insert a new disk. Label the old disk with a label containing the backup type (Daily Backup), the date, and the disk number. Place the daily backup disks in a safe location.

Selecting and Excluding Specific Files

Each of the previous backup operations has assumed that you wanted to back up every file on your disk. Most users, however, have many different application programs on their disk, such as Windows, 1-2-3, or dBASE. Because they can easily install these programs from the original floppies, backing up the files from their hard disk simply consumes time and floppies. MSBACKUP lets you select or exclude specific files for backing up. To exclude or select specific directories, choose the Select Files option from the Backup menu. MSBACKUP will display the Select Backup Files dialog box shown below, which contains a copy of your directory tree.

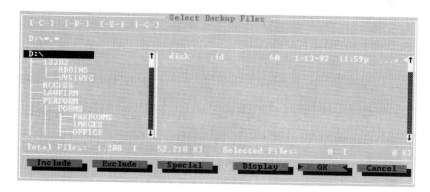

Using your keyboard arrow keys, individually highlight each directory you want to back up and press the SPACEBAR. MSBACKUP will display a triangle next to the directory name, indicating it will back up the directory's files. To exclude a directory, don't press the SPACEBAR to select it; or, if the directory is already selected, press the SPACEBAR a second time, deselecting it (MSBACKUP will change the triangle's appearance indicating the exclusion). After you select the last files you desire, select the OK option. Use the File menu Save option to save the selected directories within the desired setup file.

Note   Just as MSBACKUP lets you select specific directories for backing up, you can also press the TAB key and select individual files for backing up. As before, MSBACKUP will display a triangle next to the file name.

Understanding Backup Sets

To simplify the process of restoring files, the MSBACKUP command supports backup sets and catalogs. Each backup set has a catalog that describes the following:

❑ The number of files backed up

❑ Specifics about each file backed up

❑ The MSBACKUP setup file used to perform the backup

❑ The date of the backup

MSBACKUP stores the catalog files in the DOS directory. Depending on the backup type, the files will have one of the extensions specified in Table 26-1.

The catalog file's eight-character name tells you specifics about the catalog. Each character in the file name has a specific meaning and use, as briefly described in Table 26-2.

When you need to restore files from a specific date, you can use the catalog's name to determine the correct catalog file. If you need to restore your entire disk, MSBACKUP examines all the catalog files to determine the latest versions of all your files. Each time you success-fully perform a full disk backup, MSBACKUP removes all the old catalog files from your disk.

TABLE 26-1

MSBACKUP Catalog Extensions

File Extension	Backup Type
DIF	Differential backup
FUL	Full backup
INC	Incremental backup

TABLE 26-2	The Meaning of Letters in an MSBACKUP Catalog's File Name	

Character Position(s)	Meaning
1	The first drive backed up. For example, drive C would be C*XXXXXXX*.
2	The last drive backed up. For example, drive E would be *X*E*XXXXXX*.
3	The last digit of the backup year. For example, 1993 would be *XX*3*XXXXX*.
45	The month of the backup. For example, September would be *XXX*09*XXX*.
67	The day of the backup. For example, the third would be *XXXXX*03*X*.
8	A letter describing which catalog this is if you performed several backups on the same day. The first catalog gets the letter A, the second B, and so on.

Restoring Files

Unlike previous versions of DOS that used the BACKUP and RESTORE commands, the MSBACKUP command performs both of these operations. Should you ever need to restore one or more files from a backup floppy, invoke MSBACKUP from the DOS prompt, as shown here:

```
C:\> MSBACKUP <ENTER>
```

When MSBACKUP displays its main menu, select the Restore option. MSBACKUP will display the Restore screen, shown here:

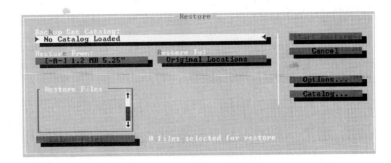

From the Restore screen, you can restore your entire disk or selectively restore files or directories.

Restoring Your Entire Disk

To restore all of the files on your disk, press the TAB key to highlight the Backup Set Catalog option and press ENTER. MSBACKUP will display the Backup Set Catalog dialog box, which contains its list of available catalog files.

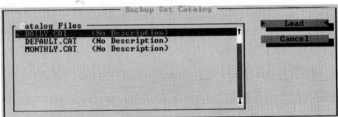

Highlight the desired catalog file and press the SPACEBAR. You will want to begin with your monthly backup (the catalog file with the FUL extension). Select the Load option. Make sure the restore to option is set to original locations. Highlight the Select Files option and choose All Files. Select the Start Restore option. MSBACKUP will display an Alert dialog box that prompts you to insert the first floppy disk.

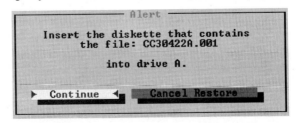

Insert the floppy disk and select Continue. Repeat this process for each floppy in the backup set.

After MSBACKUP completes, you must select the next catalog file, repeating this process.

Restoring Specific Files or Directories

The steps you need to restore a specific directory or file is very similar to those you performed for a disk backup. To begin, select the desired catalog file. When MSBACKUP displays the Restore screen, choose the Select Files option. MSBACKUP will display the Select Restore Files dialog box, which contains a directory tree of files available for restoration.

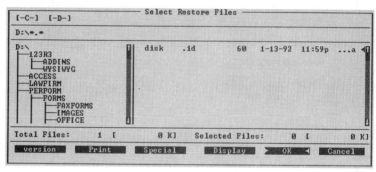

Using your keyboard arrow keys, highlight the directory containing the files you want to restore and press the SPACEBAR. MSBACKUP will display a triangle next to the directory name indicating its selection. Repeat this process for each directory you want to restore. Select the OK option. Next, select Start Restore. As before, MSBACKUP will display the Alert dialog box, asking you to insert the first backup floppy. Insert the disk and select Continue. Repeat this process for each floppy disk in the backup set.

After the restore operation completes, select additional catalog files performing this same processing.

Practice

Unlike other chapters, much of this chapter's discussion has been done in a "hands-on" fashion. If you have not yet created the setup files

INCREMENT.SET and FULLDISK.SET, do so now. Next, invoke the MSBACKUP command and perform a full disk backup operation. After the backup operation completes, place the backup floppy disks in a safe location. Tomorrow, after you finish your day's work, invoke MSBACKUP and use the setup file INCREMENT.SET to perform an incremental backup operation.

Review

1. Why would you use a MSBACKUP setup file?

2. What is the meaning of the MSBACKUP catalog name CC30315A.INC?

3. Why would you want to exclude some files or directories from being backed up?

4. How can you exclude or include specific files to be backed up?

Key Points

MSBACKUP

The DOS 6 MSBACKUP command is a menu-driven utility that lets you easily perform full, incremental, or differential backup operations. A full backup operation backs up every file on your disk. An incremental backup backs up only those files you have created or changed since the last (full or incremental) backup operation. Likewise, a differential backup backs up those files you created or changed since the last full backup. MSBACKUP also gives you the ability to select and exclude specific directories. In this way, you don't have to spend time backing up program files you could install using the original program disks. MSBACKUP also performs file restore operations.

CHAPTER

Customizing Your System Using CONFIG.SYS

515

*D*OS allows you to customize various characteristics of the operating system. In this chapter you will learn several ways to improve your system performance. Each time DOS starts, it searches the root directory of your boot disk for a file named CONFIG.SYS. If DOS locates this file, it reads the file's contents and uses the information the file contains to configure itself in memory. If DOS does not locate CONFIG.SYS, it uses its own default values to load the operating system. CONFIG.SYS is simply a text file that you can create or edit with a word processor or an editor such as EDIT. CONFIG.SYS contains several one-line entries that define specific characteristics of DOS. In this chapter you will examine each of the CONFIG.SYS entries in detail, including the guidelines that you should follow for each in order to get the best performance from DOS. Each CONFIG.SYS entry directly influences a different aspect of the operating system; if you place an errant or careless entry in CONFIG.SYS, you can actually decrease system performance.

Keep in mind that the only time that DOS examines CONFIG.SYS is during system startup. If you change a CONFIG.SYS entry, you must restart DOS for the change to take effect.

Using BREAK at System Startup

Earlier in this book you learned that the BREAK command allows you to enable extended CTRL-BREAK processing. In general, DOS checks to see if you have pressed CTRL-BREAK or CTRL-C to end the current program each time it writes to your screen or printer, or reads from your keyboard. You read in Chapter 22, "DOS System Commands," that if you invoke the following BREAK command, DOS will increase the number of times that it tests for a user-entered CTRL-BREAK, which means it will respond to a CTRL-BREAK much faster in most cases.

```
C:\> BREAK  ON  <ENTER>
```

This improved response is not without cost. Because DOS must now spend additional time testing for CTRL-BREAK, your programs will in turn run slower. Because of this performancc cost, most users leave extended CTRL-BREAK checking disabled. If you are a programmer developing and testing a new application, however, you might want to enable extended checking. If you place the entry BREAK=ON in CONFIG.SYS, DOS will start with extended CTRL-BREAK checking enabled. If DOS fails to find a BREAK entry in CONFIG.SYS, it will leave extended checking disabled.

Using BUFFERS to Reduce Disk I/O Operations

Whenever possible throughout this book, you have taken steps to reduce the number of disk I/O operations that DOS must perform because disk drives are mechanical and therefore much slower than your computer's electronic components. To assist you in this process, DOS allows you to set aside areas in memory called *disk buffers.* As shown in Figure 27-1, each disk buffer can store 512 bytes of data, which is typically the size of a sector on your disk.

When DOS reads or writes information to your disk, the smallest amount of data that DOS can transfer is a sector. Assume, for example,

Storage space of a disk buffer

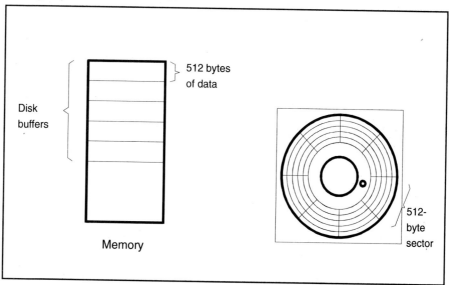

that you have a program that reads employee information like that shown in Table 27-1. Each employee record is 128 bytes in length. When your program reads information for the first employee, it only needs the first 128 bytes of information in the file. However, because the smallest amount of disk space DOS can transfer is 512 bytes, DOS reads the entire 512 bytes of information from the disk into a disk buffer that resides in memory, as shown in Figure 27-2. Thus, the disk buffer contains not only the information for the first record, but also for records 2 through 4, as shown in Figure 27-3.

However, because DOS has read a sector of information into the disk buffer, you can decrease the number of disk I/O operations required. When your program needs to read the second record from the employee file, for example, DOS first checks to see if the information is already present in memory within a disk buffer. If it is, DOS uses that information without having to perform a slow disk read operation. If the program needs to access records 1 through 4 in succession, DOS has eliminated three slow disk movements.

When DOS needs to read information from disk, it follows these steps:

1. DOS first checks to see if the data is already present in memory in a disk buffer.

2. If the data resides in the disk buffer, DOS uses the data.

3. If the data does not reside in memory, DOS reads the disk sector containing the data from disk into a disk buffer in memory.

TABLE 27-1

Payroll Employee Records

Name	Address	Pay Grade	Dependents
Jones	1327 First St.	5	2
Kent	926 Downing	4	5
Lowry	1822 Fourth Ave.	4	1
Smith	173 Fifth St.	5	5
Wilson	19 Jones Dr.	7	3

FIGURE
27-2

DOS reading a sector from a disk

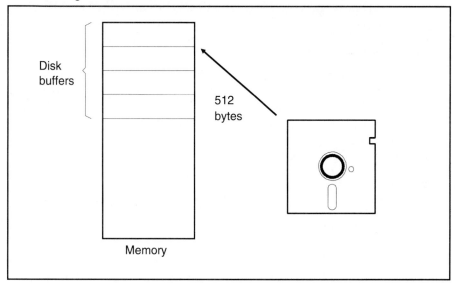

FIGURE
27-3

DOS storing record information in memory

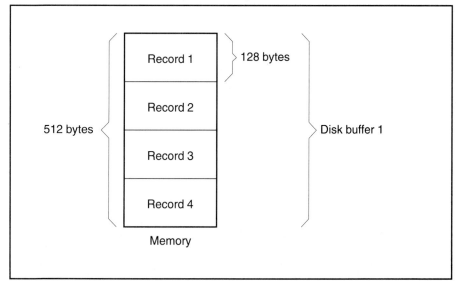

As you increase the number of disk buffers, you increase the probability of DOS finding the information, so you reduce the number of disk I/O operations required. The BUFFERS entry in CONFIG.SYS allows you to increase the number of disk buffers for which DOS sets aside space each time your system starts. The most basic form of a BUFFERS entry is as follows:

```
BUFFERS=number_of_buffers
```

where *number_of_buffers* is a number from 1 to 99. For example, the following entry sets aside space in memory for 25 disk buffers:

```
BUFFERS=25
```

Many users often ask why they shouldn't use the maximum number of disk buffers. Since DOS checks the contents of each disk buffer before reading data from disk, too many disk buffers can degrade your system performance, because DOS will spend a considerable amount of time simply traversing disk buffers in search of the data, as Figure 27-4 shows. In addition, each disk buffer consumes 528 bytes of memory. If you specify too many disk buffers, you will allocate memory that your programs or DOS could use more effectively.

For most users, a value of 25 disk buffers will prove most efficient. If DOS does not find an entry for BUFFERS in CONFIG.SYS, it uses one of the default values shown in Table 27-2.

TABLE 27-2

Determination of DOS Default Disk Buffers

Criterion	Number of Buffers
Disk drive > 360Kb	3
Memory > 128Kb	5
Memory > 256Kb	10
Memory > 512Kb	15

Record read from disk into buffer

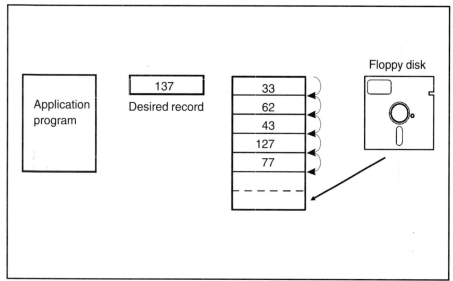

Using COUNTRY to Specify Date, Time, and Currency Formats

Chapter 28, "International DOS Support," examines the steps that international users must take to work with DOS. That chapter discusses in detail the CONFIG.SYS COUNTRY entry.

Using DEVICE to Provide Additional Software Support

Each device on your system—whether it is a keyboard, printer, screen, disk drive, or mouse—requires specific software that enables DOS to interact with the hardware device. This software is called a *device driver*. For most of your common hardware devices (such as disk drives, the printer, the screen, and the keyboard), DOS provides all of the software you need. However, if you purchase a mouse or some other hardware device, you may have to install additional software to support it. The process of making this software available to DOS is called installing a device driver.

The CONFIG.SYS DEVICE entry allows you to install a device driver at system startup. The format of this entry is

```
DEVICE=FILENAME.EXT [driver_parameters]
```

where *FILENAME.EXT* is the name of the file containing the device driver that you want to install and *driver_parameters* specifies optional parameters for use by the device driver. Device driver files typically use the extension SYS. List the files DOS provides with the SYS extension as shown here to see the device drivers DOS contains:

```
C:\> DIR  \DOS\*.SYS   <ENTER>

 Volume in drive C is DOS
 Volume Serial Number is 1A54-45E0
 Directory of C:\DOS

COUNTRY  SYS    17066 02-12-93    6:00a
KEYBOARD SYS    34694 02-12-93    6:00a
ANSI     SYS     9065 02-12-93    6:00a
EGA      SYS     4885 02-12-93    6:00a
HIMEM    SYS    14224 02-12-93    6:00a
RAMDRIVE SYS     5873 02-12-93    6:00a
DISPLAY  SYS    15789 02-12-93    6:00a
DRIVER   SYS     5406 02-12-93    6:00a
CHKSTATE SYS    41600 02-12-93    6:00a
DBLSPACE SYS      339 02-12-93    6:00a
        10 file(s)     148941 bytes
                    16607232 bytes free
```

As you can see, DOS provides several device driver files. The following list describes the standard ones:

❑   ANSI.SYS provides enhanced cursor, screen, and keyboard capabilities for specific software programs.

❏ COUNTRY.SYS contains country-specific date, time, and currency formats for international DOS users (see Chapter 28).

❏ DISPLAY.SYS provides code-page switching support for international DOS users (see Chapter 28).

❏ DBLSPACE.SYS lets you move the DBLSPACE device driver from the top of conventional memory to the bottom.

❏ DRIVER.SYS provides support for a system with an external floppy disk drive.

❏ EGA.SYS provides support for systems that are using an EGA and the DOS 5 or later Task Swapper.

❏ HIMEM.SYS provides support for extended memory.

❏ KEYBOARD.SYS contains country-specific keyboard templates (see Chapter 28).

❏ PRINTER.SYS provides printer code-page switching support for international DOS users (see Chapter 28).

❏ RAMDRIVE.SYS provides RAM disk support, allowing you to create a fast disk drive in your computer's memory.

❏ SMARTDRV.SYS provides support for a disk cache, which reduces disk input and output operations, in turn improving your overall system performance.

DOS 5 also provides two device driver files with the EXE extension: SETVER.EXE and EMM386.EXE. If you are using DOS 6, DOS includes the device drivers POWER.EXE and INTERLNK.EXE.

To install a device driver, use the DEVICE entry to tell DOS the name of the driver as well as the directory where it resides. For example, to install the ANSI.SYS device driver, your DEVICE entry becomes:

```
DEVICE=C:\DOS\ANSI.SYS
```

Several third-party software packages make extensive use of the ANSI.SYS driver. The documentation that accompanies such software will direct you to ensure that the ANSI.SYS driver is installed. *DOS: The Complete Reference, Fourth Edition,* by Kris Jamsa, Osborne/McGraw-Hill: Berkeley, 1993, shows you several ways to use the ANSI.SYS device driver for setting your screen colors, defining function keys, and so on. The following section examines the device driver DRIVER.SYS, which lets you use an external floppy drive. The other device drivers previously listed will be discussed throughout the remainder of this book.

Using an External Floppy via DRIVER.SYS

All of the computers examined throughout this book have built-in floppy disk drives. Some systems, however, have an external floppy disk drive, as shown here:

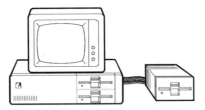

If your system has external floppy disk drives, you must use the DRIVER.SYS device driver. The format of this device entry is

```
DEVICE=DRIVER.SYS [/D:drive_number] [/C] [/F:form_factor]
  [/H:max_head_number] [/N] [/S:sectors_per_track]
  [/T:tracks_per_side] [/I]
```

where the following definitions apply:

The *drive_number* is the disk-drive number from 0 to 255 where drive A is 0, drive B is 1, and so on.

The /C switch directs DOS to provide *change-line support*: some floppy disk drives provide an electronic signal called a change line that is turned on each time a floppy disk latch is opened, and closed, to inform DOS that a new floppy disk may have been inserted.

The *form_factor* specifies the device type as follows:

0	160Kb, 180Kb, 320Kb, or 360Kb drive
1	1.2Mb drive
2	720Kb 3.5-inch drive
3	8-inch single-density floppy disk drive
4	8-inch double-density floppy disk drive
5	Hard drive
6	Tape drive
7	1.44Mb floppy or an optical drive (requires DOS 5 or later)
8	2.88Mb floppy (requires DOS 5 or later)

The *max_head_number* specifies the maximum number of heads on the disk from 1 to 99. The default is 2.

The /N switch informs DOS that the device is not removable.

The *sectors_per_track* specifies the number of sectors on each track from 1 to 99. The default value is 9.

The *tracks_per_side* specifies the number of tracks per side from 1 to 999. The default value is 80.

If your computer's BIOS does not support 3 1/2-inch disks, use the /I switch.

To install software support for a third floppy disk capable of storing 720Kb, you enter

```
DEVICE=C:\DOS\DRIVER.SYS /D:2
```

If you purchase an external floppy disk drive, the documentation that accompanies the device should include the correct DRIVER.SYS entry.

Directing DOS to Report a Specific Version with SETVER

There are several different DOS versions currently in use. Many new programs rely on capabilities of the newer versions of DOS. When you run such a program, the program asks DOS for its version number. If the DOS version supports the program, the program will run. Otherwise, the program will display an error message telling you that your DOS version does not support it, and it will end. In some cases, a program may test for a specific DOS version such as 3.3 or 4.0. If you try to run these programs under DOS 5, the programs will display the version number error message and will end.

To help you run such programs, DOS 5 or later provides a device driver named SETVER.EXE. Using the CONFIG.SYS DEVICE entry, you can install this driver as shown here:

```
DEVICE=C:\DOS\SETVER.EXE
```

After you install SETVER, you can use it to trick the programs that test for a specific version number into running. For example, assume you have a program named V4_ONLY that tests for DOS 4. The following SETVER command directs DOS to report its version number as 4.0 whenever the program asks.

```
C:\> SETVER  V4_ONLY  4.0  <ENTER>
```

When you issue the command, SETVER will store the program name and DOS version, displaying the following:

```
C:\> SETVER  V4_ONLY  4.0  <ENTER>
WARNING - Contact your software vendor for information about
whether a specific program works with MS-DOS version 6.0. It
is possible that Microsoft has not verified whether the
program will successfully run if you use the SETVER command
to change the program version number and version table. If
you run the program after changing the version table in
MS-DOS version 6.0, you may lose or corrupt data or intro-
duce system instabilities. Microsoft is not responsible for
any loss or damage, or for lost or corrupted data.

Version table successfully updated
The version change will take effect the next time you restart
your system
```

In order for SETVER to return the correct value for V4_ONLY, you must reboot your system. If you invoke SETVER without a command line, SETVER will display its current version number assignments, as shown in the following:

```
C:\> SETVER <ENTER>
WIN200.BIN      3.40
WIN100.BIN      3.40
WINWORD.EXE     4.10
EXCEL.EXE       4.10
HITACHI.SYS     4.00
REDIR4.EXE      4.00
NET.EXE         4.00
NET.COM         3.30
    :            :
REDIR50.EXE     5.00
MSCDEX.EXE      5.00
V4_ONLY         4.00
```

When the developers of V4_ONLY later send you the DOS 5 version, you can remove the V4_ONLY entry from SETVER, as shown here:

```
C:\> SETVER  V4_ONLY  /DELETE <ENTER>
```

As before, SETVER will display a message informing you that you must reboot your system for the change to take effect.

```
C:\> SETVER  V4_ONLY  /DELETE <ENTER>
Version table successfully updated
The version change will take effect the next time you restart
your system
```

Changing a Block Device's Characteristics

Hardware devices are categorized as either a *block device* or *character device*, depending on how they exchange information with the computer. Printers or keyboards exchange information a character at a time, and are hence character devices. Your disks, on the other hand, exchange information with the computer in blocks of characters (typically a sector). The CONFIG.SYS DRIVPARM entry lets you change one or more attributes of your block devices. The format of the DRIVPARM entry is as follows:

```
DRIVPARM=[/D:drive_number] [/C] [/form_factor] [/H:max_head_num-
    ber] [/N] [/S:sectors_per_track] [/T:tracks_per_side] [/I]
```

where the entry's switches correspond to those discussed in the previous section on the DRIVER.SYS device driver.

Using FCBS to Specify File Control Block Support

DOS applications written early in the 1980s used a facility called a file control block, or FCB, to open, read, and write to files. Beginning with version 2.0, DOS started using a facility called a file handle instead.

If you are running an older program and begin to encounter errors, you may need to specify an FCBS entry in CONFIG.SYS. The format for this entry is as follows:

```
FCBS=max_open,leave_open
```

where the following is true:

max_open specifies the number of file control blocks, from 1 to 255, that DOS can have open at one time; the default is 4.

leave_open specifies the maximum number of files, from 1 to 255, that DOS cannot automatically close if it needs to open additional files. The default value is 0.

The only time you need to include this entry in CONFIG.SYS is when you are experiencing errors in older software applications. In such cases, try this setting:

```
FCBS=20,4
```

If you are not experiencing such errors with older programs, you will not need to use the FCBS entry.

Using FILES to Open More Than Eight Files at Once

By default, DOS allows you to open eight files at one time. However, as you learned when you examined I/O redirection, DOS predefines several input and output destinations, as shown here:

stdin	Source of input
stdout	Destination for output
stderr	Destination of error messages
stdprn	Standard printer device
stdaux	Standard auxiliary device

These predefined destinations use up five of the eight files that DOS allows you to open at one time, leaving you with only three files your own program can open at a time.

Many applications require support for more than three open files at one time. In such a case, you must use the CONFIG.SYS FILES entry. The format for this entry is

```
FILES=number_of_files
```

where *number_of_files* specifies the number of files that DOS will support from 8 up to 255. For most users, 20 files should be sufficient:

```
FILES=20
```

If DOS does not find a FILES entry in CONFIG.SYS, it uses the default value of 8.

Using INSTALL to Load Memory-Resident DOS Commands

Many DOS programs remain present in memory to enhance your DOS processing capabilities. Such programs are called memory-resident programs. To provide a more efficient use of memory, DOS 4 provides the CONFIG.SYS INSTALL entry, which allows you to direct DOS to place one or more of the following programs into memory during system startup:

❑ FASTOPEN.EXE

❑ SHARE.EXE

❑ KEYB.COM

❑ NLSFUNC.EXE

These programs will be discussed in the next two chapters. The format of the INSTALL entry is as follows:

```
INSTALL=FILENAME.EXT [command_line]
```

where *FILENAME.EXT* is the name of the program to install, and *command_line* is the program's optional command line.

For example, the following INSTALL entry invokes FASTOPEN during system startup to track 50 recently used directory entries on drive C:

```
INSTALL=C:\DOS\FASTOPEN.EXE C:=50
```

The advantage of using INSTALL over invoking the program from your AUTOEXEC.BAT file is that DOS tries to make better use of memory when you use INSTALL. If you are using DOS 5 or later, you may want to use the LOADHIGH command in your AUTOEXEC.BAT file in place of the INSTALL entries. (See the Command Reference for more information on the LOADHIGH command.)

Using LASTDRIVE to Specify the Last Valid Disk Drive Letter

As you learned in Chapter 24, "Using DOS Pretender Commands," the SUBST command allows you to abbreviate long subdirectory names with a logical disk drive letter. By default, DOS only supports drives A through E. If you plan to create several logical disk drives, you must place a LASTDRIVE entry in CONFIG.SYS to tell DOS to recognize the drives. The format of this entry is

```
LASTDRIVE=drive_letter
```

where *drive_letter* is a letter from A to Z. For example, the following LASTDRIVE entry directs DOS to support drives A through J:

```
LASTDRIVE=J
```

Placing Remarks in CONFIG.SYS

When you examined batch files earlier in this book, you learned the REM command lets you place comments or remarks within your batch files that explain their processing. Beginning with version 4, DOS lets you place comments in your CONFIG.SYS file. Assume, for example, you purchase a third-party mouse that requires a device driver named CHEESE.SYS. Using the CONFIG.SYS DEVICE entry, you can install the driver as shown here:

```
DEVICE=CHEESE.SYS
```

If another user examines your CONFIG.SYS file, they may have a difficult time understanding the device driver's purpose. Using the REM entry, however, you can include an explanation, as shown here:

```
REM Install a device driver for my mouse
DEVICE=CHEESE.SYS
```

In addition to using REM to comment within your CONFIG.SYS file, you can also use REM to disable entries. For example, assume you want to temporarily remove the ANSI.SYS device driver. Rather than removing the DEVICE entry from your file, you can simply place "REM" in front of it, as shown here:

```
REM DEVICE=C:\DOS\ANSI.SYS
```

When DOS encounters the REM entry, DOS assumes it corresponds to a remark, and ignores it. When you later want to use ANSI.SYS, you can remove the word "REM" and restart your system.

Using SHELL to Define the Location of Your Command Processor

As you have learned, COMMAND.COM contains internal commands such as CLS, DATE, and TIME, as well as the software responsible for displaying the DOS prompt and processing your commands. COMMAND.COM is one of the three files you should keep in the root directory of a hard disk:

- ❏ COMMAND.COM
- ❏ CONFIG.SYS
- ❏ AUTOEXEC.BAT

If you examine the files in your DOS directory, you will find the file COMMAND.COM. If you have a copy of COMMAND.COM in your root directory and in the DOS directory, you are unnecessarily using up disk space. Using the CONFIG.SYS SHELL entry, you can direct DOS to look for COMMAND.COM in the DOS directory, as opposed to the root. The following SHELL entry does just that:

```
SHELL=C:\DOS\COMMAND.COM  C:\DOS /P
```

When DOS locates the SHELL entry in CONFIG.SYS, DOS will search the specified subdirectory for the COMMAND.COM file. If DOS locates

COMMAND.COM, your system will start; otherwise, DOS will display the following error message:

```
Bad or missing Command Interpreter
```

In DOS versions 5 and earlier, you must locate a bootable floppy disk to start your system. If you are using DOS 6, however, DOS will display the following message.

```
Bad or missing Command Interpreter
Enter name of correct Command Interpreter (eg, C:\COM-
MAND.COM)
```

DOS 6 will then display the DOS prompt, allowing you to invoke the command processor yourself. If COMMAND.COM resides in a directory other than the root, such as (C:\DOS), type in the complete path name to the file (C:\DOS\COMMAND.COM).

Within the CONFIG.SYS SHELL entry, the path name C:\DOS\COM-MAND.COM tells DOS the name and location of the command interpreter. The path name C:\DOS tells DOS the value to assign to the COMSPEC environment entry discussed in Chapter 21, "Using the DOS Environment."

You must include the /P switch in the entry. Without it, DOS will not execute the AUTOEXEC.BAT file if it exists.

In Chapter 21, you learned that the DOS environment cannot continue to grow once you install memory-resident software. As a result, it is quite possible for a SET command to fail because there is no more room in the environment. When that occurs, SET will display the message

```
Out of environment space
```

The SHELL entry provides a solution. The /E switch in the entry

```
SHELL=C:\DOS\COMMAND.COM C:\DOS /P /E:4096
```

allows you to specify the desired size for the DOS environment in bytes from 160 to 32,768. By creating a large environment at system startup, you can avoid running out of environment space.

Using STACKS to Control Hardware Interrupts

To maximize your computer's performance, many of the hardware devices on your system perform a specific task and then interrupt DOS to tell DOS that the task is complete. For example, when DOS directs your disk drive to write a sector of information to disk, DOS continues its processing while the disk drive records information. When the drive later completes the request, it interrupts DOS to tell it that the data has been successfully recorded.

Each time DOS is interrupted, it temporarily stops the task it was performing to handle the interruption. To remember the task it was performing prior to the interruption, DOS places information in a facility called a *stack*. When DOS later resumes its processing, it removes the information from the stack.

In rare instances, DOS may receive more interruptions at one time than it can handle. When this occurs, your system may quit running and DOS will display the message

```
Fatal:  Internal Stack Failure, System Halted
```

If this occurs, you should place a STACKS entry in CONFIG.SYS, which increases the size and number of stacks available to DOS. The format of the STACKS entry is

```
STACKS=number_of_stacks,size_of_stack
```

where *number_of_stacks* specifies a value from 0 to 64. The *size_of_stack* value specifies the size of each stack in bytes, from 0 to 512. In most cases, the following setting is more than sufficient:

```
STACKS=8,512
```

Using SWITCHES to Specify Keyboard Operations

As you read in Chapter 7, "Using Your Keyboard and Mouse," several styles of keyboards have emerged over the past few years that provide extended capabilities. Unfortunately, not all software programs support these keyboards. Beginning with DOS 4, the CONFIG.SYS SWITCHES entry directs DOS to use only an enhanced keyboard's conventional capabilities. The format of the SWITCHES entry is as follows:

```
SWITCHES=/K
```

This is useful when operating older software packages.

DOS 5 or Later Memory Management

One of the most important enhancements DOS 5 or later provides over previous DOS versions is improved memory management. As application programs get larger, most users find themselves looking for ways to get the most from their available memory. DOS 5 or later provides CONFIG.SYS entries and DOS commands that let you use your computer's conventional memory, as well as expanded or extended memory if it is present. Before you can understand DOS memory management, you need to have an understanding of your computer's memory and its characteristics.

Understanding Memory Types

There are three memory types your PC can use. Typically, most computers have 640Kb of conventional memory, which is the computer's primary memory. DOS and the programs you execute reside in conventional memory. Using the CHKDSK command (or MEM with DOS 4 or later), you can display the amount of conventional memory in your computer, as well as the amount currently in use.

```
C:\> CHKDSK  <ENTER>

Volume DOS 6 DISK  created 03-26-1993 6:40a
Volume Serial Number is 16F6-3B73

 200065024 bytes total disk space
     77824 bytes in 2 hidden files
    299008 bytes in 66 directories
  57765888 bytes in 2732 user files
 141922304 bytes available on disk

      4096 bytes in each allocation unit
     48844 total allocation units on disk
     34649 available allocation units on disk

    655360 total bytes memory
    543968 bytes free
```

Each time your start DOS, DOS loads itself into the lower part of conventional memory. If you install memory-resident programs, DOS places the programs in the next available lower memory areas. The amount of memory that remains unused determines the largest program your computer can run. The following illustration shows the conventional memory layout.

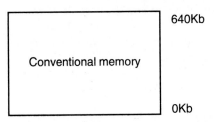

640Kb

Conventional memory

0Kb

Although conventional memory cannot exceed 640Kb, the original IBM PC can address up to 1 megabyte of memory. If you subtract 640Kb from 1Mb, you'll find the PC has a 384Kb gap between the end of conventional memory and the highest memory location the IBM PC can access. As Figure 27-5 shows, your computer uses a portion of this memory to interface to your video display and a portion for the ROM BIOS routines

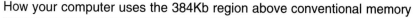

FIGURE 27-5 How your computer uses the 384Kb region above conventional memory

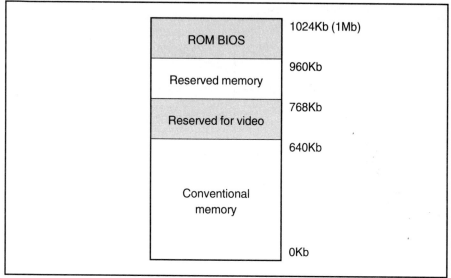

(your computer's built-in input/output routines), leaving a portion of the 384Kb region unused.

Although a portion of the 384Kb region above conventional memory is unused, the region isn't big enough to be of much use on its own. However, by using a memory board called expanded memory and powerful software called an EMM driver you can expand the amount of memory the PC can use from 640Kb to up to 32Mb!

In general, the EMS software uses a 64Kb region of the memory in the reserved memory above 640Kb and below 1Mb. As Figure 27-6 shows, the expanded memory software divides this region into four 16Kb regions, called page buffers.

Next, when you run a program that supports expanded memory, the program is loaded into conventional memory, and its data is loaded into the expanded memory board. Such data might include a very large database. The program must divide its data into 16Kb sections called pages, as shown in Figure 27-7.

When the PC needs to access data contained in an expanded memory page, the expanded memory software maps the address of the 16Kb page containing data to an address of one of the page buffers that the PC can

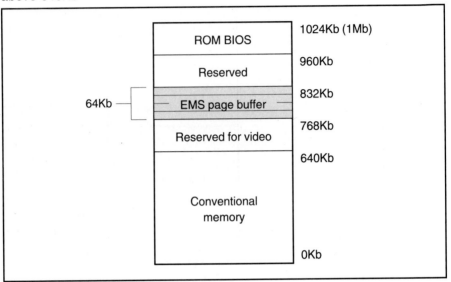

FIGURE 27-6 The expanded memory software uses a 64Kb region in the memory above 640Kb

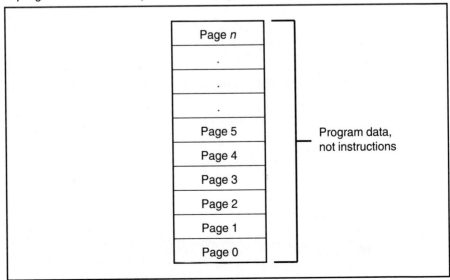

FIGURE 27-7 A program divides its expanded memory data into 16Kb regions called pages

access. To understand how expanded memory works, you need to remember the original IBM PC could not access memory above 1Mb. To the PC, expanded memory is not addressed like standard memory. Instead, the PC knows there are 64Kb bytes of memory (four 16Kb pages) it can access. The memory itself resides on an expanded memory board. The job of the expanded memory software is to map information contained in the expanded memory into the page frame.

The advantage of expanded memory is that it lets the original IBM PC break the 640Kb boundary. The disadvantages of expanded memory are that not all programs support it and those that do may execute slowly because of the continual time-consuming address mappings required to map different pages in and out of the page buffers.

To use expanded memory, you will need an expanded memory board (or a board that simulates expanded memory) and a device driver for the board, which you must install using the CONFIG.SYS DEVICE entry. The device driver should come on a floppy disk that accompanies your memory board from the manufacturer.

Although expanded memory broke the IBM PC's 640Kb memory restriction, the overhead of swapping pages in and out of the page buffers left hardware developers looking for a more efficient way of accessing memory above 1Mb. When IBM introduced the PC AT (80286) in 1984, they also introduced the notion of extended memory. Like expanded memory, extended memory combines hardware and software to access program data stored in memory above 1Mb. The 80286 can use up to 16Mb of extended memory. The 80386 and 80486 can each access up to 4 gigabytes (4 billion bytes) of extended memory! Note that the original IBM PC (8088) cannot use extended memory.

Because extended memory does not swap pages in and out of page buffers that reside below 1Mb, extended memory is much faster than expanded memory. The best way to view extended memory is as one large storage location, as shown in Figure 27-8.

When you run a program written to use extended memory, DOS loads the program into conventional memory. The program, in turn, loads its data into extended memory, as shown in Figure 27-9.

When the program needs to access data stored in extended memory, the extended memory software lets the program access the data directly, without the page mapping done by expanded memory.

FIGURE
27-8
Extended memory is one large memory region that resides above 1Mb

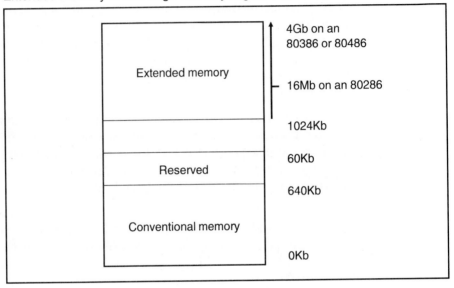

FIGURE
27-9
DOS loads programs that support extended memory into conventional memory; the program, in turn, loads its data into extended memory

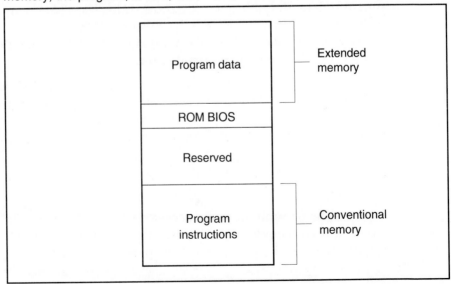

Extended memory requires a software device driver that lets DOS use the memory. In many cases, a device driver on floppy disk will accompany your extended memory board. If you are using DOS 5 or later or Microsoft Windows 3.1, the device driver file HIMEM.SYS provides DOS access to extended memory. Using the CONFIG.SYS DEVICE entry, you can install the driver as follows:

```
DEVICE=C:\DOS\HIMEM.SYS
```

If you are not using DOS 5 or later, change the directory path to WINDOWS as shown here:

```
DEVICE=C:\WINDOWS\HIMEM.SYS
```

How You Can Use Extended and Expanded Memory

Although extended and expanded memory let DOS break the 640Kb boundary, both techniques have a big limitation. In most cases, you can only store a program's data above 1Mb. The program's instructions must still reside below 1Mb. The 80286, 386, and 486 have two modes of operation. Under DOS, these computers run in *real mode*, which means program instructions must reside below 1Mb.

Under other operating systems such as OS/2, UNIX, or even Microsoft Windows (running in 386 Enhanced mode) your computer runs in *protected mode*, which lets a program's data and instructions reside in extended memory.

Unfortunately (because DOS runs in real mode and program instructions must reside below 1Mb), even if your computer has a large amount of extended memory, many application programs still don't take advantage of it. Thus, users most commonly use extended and expanded memory for large disk buffers, called disk caches, or for fast electronic RAM drives, discussed next.

Creating a RAM Drive

If you have unused memory available, either conventional, expanded, or extended, DOS lets you use the memory to create an electronic (or RAM) disk drive. Because RAM drives reside in your computer's fast electronic memory, they are many times faster than a mechanical hard disk. When you create a RAM drive, DOS assigns to the drive the first unused drive letter such as D or E. Because of these drives' tremendous speed, many users use RAM drives to store temporary files. Because they store files in your computer's electronic memory, the information RAM drives contain is lost when you turn off your computer's power or restart DOS. RAM drives, therefore, are well suited for temporary files.

The RAMDRIVE.SYS device driver lets you install a RAM drive. To install the driver, you must use the CONFIG.SYS DEVICE entry. The format of RAMDRIVE.SYS is as follows:

```
DEVICE=C:\DOS\RAMDRIVE.SYS [[DiskSize SectorSize]
 [DirectoryEntries]] [/A|/E]
```

The *DiskSize* specifies the size of the disk in kilobytes. If you don't specify a value, the default size is 64Kb. RAMDRIVE.SYS lets you specify a size from 16 through 4096Kb (4 megabytes).

The *SectorSize* specifies the RAM drive's sector size. The default sector size is 512 bytes. RAMDRIVE.SYS lets you specify sector sizes of 128, 256, or 512 bytes.

The *DirectoryEntries* specifies the number of files and directories the RAM drive can store in its root directory. Like all disk drives, RAM drives restrict the number of files you can store in the root directory. By default, the RAM drive's root directory can hold 64 entries. RAMDRIVE.SYS lets you specify from 2 to 1,024 entries.

By default, RAMDRIVE.SYS creates the RAM drive in conventional memory. The /E switch directs RAMDRIVE.SYS to create the RAM drive in extended memory. Likewise, the /A switch directs RAMDRIVE.SYS to use expanded memory. You will learn later in this chapter the various advantages of these two options.

The following CONFIG.SYS entry creates a 64Kb RAM drive in conventional memory:

```
DEVICE=C:\DOS\RAMDRIVE.SYS
```

When you start your computer, your screen will display a message similar to the following, possibly using a different disk drive letter or disk size.

```
Microsoft RAMDrive version n.nn virtual disk D:
    Disk size: 64k
    Sector size: 512 bytes
    Allocation unit: 1 sectors
    Directory entries: 64
```

To access the drive in this example, use the drive letter D, as shown in the following:

```
C:\> DIR  D: <ENTER>
```

Likewise, the following entry creates a 512Kb RAM drive in extended memory:

```
DEVICE=C:\DOS\RAMDRIVE.SYS  512  /E
```

If you are using DOS 5 or later, DOS uses the TEMP environment entry discussed in Chapter 21, "Using the DOS Environment," to determine where it should create its temporary files during I/O redirection operations. By assigning TEMP to your fast RAM drive, you can improve your system performance.

Remember that the information stored in a RAM drive is lost when you turn off your computer or restart DOS. If you need the files the RAM drive contains, make sure you copy the files back to your hard disk or floppy before you turn your computer off.

Before you can install a RAM drive into extended or expanded memory, the corresponding memory management software must already be active. Place the RAMDRIVE.SYS DEVICE entry in CONFIG.SYS after the DEVICE entry for your extended memory or expanded memory device driver.

 Note If the letter of the new RAM drive, when added with any other logical drives, is higher than the default letter E, you must include a LASTDRIVE statement in CONFIG.SYS to tell DOS to recognize it, for example, LASTDRIVE=F.

Creating a Disk Cache

As you have learned, disk buffers improve your system performance by reducing the number of disk I/O operations DOS must perform. Each disk buffer consumes 528 bytes of conventional memory. Depending on your DOS version, or if you are using Windows 3.1, the SMARTDRV.SYS or SMARTDRV.EXE device driver lets you install disk-caching software into extended or expanded memory.

A disk cache is a very large disk buffer. Each time DOS needs to perform a disk read, DOS just searches the disk cache for the data. Disk caches have several advantages over the DOS disk buffers. First, because disk caches reside in extended or expanded memory, they don't use up conventional memory DOS can make use of to hold program instructions. Second, disk caches can be very large, up to 8Mb. Finally, most disk-caching software is very specialized and executes very quickly.

Using SMARTDRV in DOS 5

If you are using DOS 5, you must use the CONFIG.SYS DEVICE entry to load SMARTDRV.SYS. The format of SMARTDRV.SYS is as follows:

```
DEVICE=C:\DOS\SMARTDRV.SYS [InitialCacheSize] [MinimumCacheSize]
   [/A]
```

The *InitialCacheSize* specifies the starting cache size in kilobytes from 128Kb to 8192Kb (8 megabytes). The default cache size is 256Kb. Depending on your memory and cache usage, it is possible for some programs to reduce the cache size.

The *MinimumCacheSize* specifies the smallest size in kilobytes to which a program can reduce the cache. For example, using Microsoft Windows, you can create a very large disk cache using SMARTDRV.SYS. Should Windows later need to use other portions of the cache, Windows will reduce the cache size. The default value is 0. By default, SMARTDRV.SYS installs the cache in extended memory. The /A switch directs SMARTDRV.SYS to use expanded memory instead.

The following CONFIG.SYS entry installs a 256Kb disk cache in extended memory:

```
DEVICE=C:\DOS\SMARTDRV.SYS
```

When you start your computer, your screen will display a message similar to the following:

```
Microsoft SMARTDrive Disk Cache version 3.13
   Cache size: 256K in Extended Memory
   Room for 16 tracks of 32 sectors each
   Minimum cache size will be 0K
```

Likewise, the following entry creates a 128Kb disk cache in expanded memory:

```
DEVICE=C:\DOS\SMARTDRV.SYS 128  /A
```

Because expanded memory must swap pages to access the cache, an extended memory disk cache will have better performance.

Before you can install disk-caching software into extended or expanded memory, the corresponding memory management software must be active. Place the DEVICE entry for SMARTDRV.SYS in CONFIG.SYS after the entry for the memory management device driver.

Using SMARTDRV in DOS 6

If you are using DOS 6, you install disk caching by installing the SMARTDRV.EXE device driver. Most users will place a SMARTDRV command in their AUTOEXEC.BAT file. The format of the SMARTDRV command is as follows:

```
SMARTDRV [[Drive[+|-] ...] [/E:ElementSize]
    [InitialCacheSize] [MinimumCacheSize]
    [/B:BufferSize] [/C] [/R] [/L] [/Q] [/S]
```

Drive[+ | –] specifies the disk drive to cache. If you don't specify a plus or minus sign, SMARTDRV performs read caching but not write caching. If you specify a plus sign, SMARTDRV performs both. If you specify a minus sign, SMARTDRV disables caching.

/E:ElementSize specifies the amount of data (in bytes) that SMARTDRV moves at one time. You must specify 1024, 2048, 4096, or 8192 bytes. The default size is 8192.

InitialCacheSize specifies, in Kb, the cache size when SMARTDRV starts.

MinimumCacheSize specifies, in Kb, the size to which applications (such as Windows) wanting extended memory can reduce the cache. When the application ends, the previous cache size will resume.

/B:*BufferSize* specifies, in Kb, the size of SMARTDRV's read-ahead buffer. The default size is 16Kb.

/C directs SMARTDRV to write all cached (output) data from memory to disk. /R clears the current cache and restarts SMARTDRV. /L directs SMARTDRV to load itself into conventional memory as opposed to upper memory. /Q directs SMARTDRV not to display error messages as it starts. Finally, /S directs SMARTDRV to display its status information.

Before you can invoke SMARTDRV, you must first install the HIMEM.SYS device driver, which gives DOS access to extended memory. The following SMARTDRV command allocates a 2Mb cache, enabling read and write caching for drive C:

```
C:\> SMARTDRV C+ 2048 <ENTER>
```

The SMARTDRV command provides several command-line switches, which are discussed in detail in the Command Reference later in this book.

Reducing the Number of DOS Disk Buffers

As you learned in Chapter 24, the CONFIG.SYS BUFFERS entry lets you specify the number of DOS disk buffers. If you install a disk cache, using SMARTDRV.SYS or SMARTDRV.EXE, you need to reduce the number of DOS disk buffers within CONFIG.SYS. For example, the following entry reduces the number of buffers to 3:

```
BUFFERS=3
```

Viewing Your Memory Usage

You have learned that the CHKDSK command displays statistics about your conventional memory usage. If you are using DOS 4 or later, the MEM command displays detailed information about conventional expanded and extended memory usage. When you invoke the MEM command under DOS 6, your screen will display output similar to the following:

```
C:\> MEM <ENTER>

Memory Type         Total =  Used  +  Free
----------------    ------   ------   ------
Conventional         640K      98K     542K
Upper                151K      26K     125K
Adapter RAM/ROM      233K     233K      0K
Extended (XMS)      3072K     992K    2080K
Expanded (EMS)        0K       0K       0K
----------------    ------   ------   ------
Total memory        4096K    1349K    2747K

Total under 1 MB     791K     124K     667K

Largest executable program size        542K   (555312 bytes)
Largest free upper memory block        114K   (116528 bytes)
MS-DOS is resident in the high memory area.
```

As you can see, MEM provides you with considerable insight into your system's current memory use.

DOS 5 or Later Memory Management

Each time your system starts, DOS loads itself into conventional memory. If you are using DOS 5 or later, you can direct DOS to load part of itself into the *high memory area*, which is the first 64Kb of extended memory, as shown in Figure 27-10.

By loading DOS into the high memory area, you free up additional conventional memory for your programs. To load DOS into the high

Under DOS 5, you can load DOS into the high memory area (the first 64Kb of extended memory)

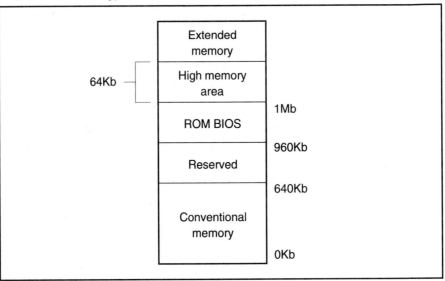

memory area, you must include the CONFIG.SYS DOS entry as shown in the following:

```
DOS=HIGH
```

The 384Kb memory area above conventional memory and below 1Mb is often called *reserved memory.* As you saw earlier, expanded memory makes use of 64Kb of this area. In DOS 5 or later, you can use portions of reserved memory for software device drivers and memory-resident DOS commands. To use reserved memory, you must have a 386 or 486 computer and then include the letters UMB in the CONFIG.SYS DOS entry as shown here:

```
DOS=UMB
```

The UMB entry does not actually use reserved memory, it simply tells DOS you will later access it using the CONFIG.SYS DEVICEHIGH entry or the LOADHIGH command.

UMB is an abbreviation for *upper memory block* (a 64Kb region in reserved memory unused by a hardware device). By using reserved memory for software drivers or memory-resident commands, you free up conventional memory. The following CONFIG.SYS entry tells DOS you will later use reserved memory and you want DOS to load itself in high memory:

```
DOS=UMB,HIGH
```

If you aren't using extended memory, you can direct DOS to load itself in conventional memory, while telling DOS you will later use reserved memory as shown here:

```
DOS=UMB,LOW
```

Finally, if you use the NOUMB entry, DOS will not let you use reserved memory later.

As you have read, the CONFIG.SYS DEVICE entry installs a software device driver. DOS places the corresponding software into conventional memory. In DOS 5 or later, the CONFIG.SYS DEVICEHIGH entry lets you install a device driver into reserved memory. Before you can use DEVICEHIGH, your CONFIG.SYS must contain entries similar to those shown here:

```
DEVICE=C:\DOS\HIMEM.SYS
DEVICE=C:\DOS\EMM386.EXE NOEMS
DOS=UMB
DEVICEHIGH=C:\DOS\ANSI.SYS
```

In this case, DOS will try to load the ANSI.SYS device driver into reserved memory. Also, the HIMEM.SYS driver provides extended memory support. The EMM386.EXE device driver provides access to the reserved memory. The NOEMS parameter tells DOS you don't want the driver to simulate expanded memory. Do not try to install the HIMEM.SYS or EMM386 device drivers in reserved memory; these drivers must reside in conventional memory.

If you also want DOS to load itself into high memory, change the DOS entry to include HIGH as shown here:

```
DOS=UMB,HIGH
```

If DOS does not have enough reserved memory to hold the driver software, it will load the driver in conventional memory as if you had used a DEVICE entry instead of DEVICEHIGH.

As you have read, the CONFIG.SYS INSTALL entry lets you load four specific memory-resident DOS commands efficiently into memory. In DOS 5 or later, the LOADHIGH command lets you load memory-resident programs into reserved memory. LOADHIGH is not a CONFIG.SYS entry—it is an internal DOS command.

Before you can use LOADHIGH, your CONFIG.SYS file must contain a DOS=UMB entry just as if you were using DEVICEHIGH. The following LOADHIGH command, for example, installs the FASTOPEN memory-resident software into reserved memory. If insufficient reserved memory is available, LOADHIGH will load the command into conventional memory.

```
C:\> LOADHIGH  FASTOPEN  C:=50 <ENTER>
```

DOS lets you abbreviate LOADHIGH as LH. If your AUTOEXEC.BAT loads memory-resident software, you may be able to load the software into reserved memory using LOADHIGH.

As you have learned, use of DEVICEHIGH and LOADHIGH to load device drivers and memory-resident programs into reserved memory frees memory for your programs. In some cases, a program's initial starting address may reside below 64Kb.

Some programs cannot execute below 64Kb and will display the error message "Packed file corrupt" when you execute them in this low memory region. If this error message occurs, use the DOS 5 or later LOADFIX command to direct DOS to load the program above 64Kb.

The format of the LOADFIX command is as follows:

```
LOADFIX ProgramName [parameters]
```

where *ProgramName* specifies the program you are trying to run, and *parameters* specifies the program's optional command-line parameters. You will not need to use LOADFIX unless you experience the "Packed file corrupt" error message.

DOS 6 System Configuration Options

Depending on their system configurations, users can have different CONFIG.SYS files for different types of processing. For example, when they plan to use a network, they use the CONFIG.SYS file that contains the network device drivers. Likewise, if they need to free up conventional memory for a large program, they use a second CONFIG.SYS file. Rather than forcing you to constantly change CONFIG.SYS files, DOS 6 provides CONFIG.SYS entries that let you customize your system startup. Using these entries, you can create a menu of options from which you can select the desired configuration.

To create a DOS 6 customized startup, you divide up your CONFIG.SYS file into groups of related entries. For example, you would group the entries you use for a network configuration in one section, and those you use without the network in another. Each group of entries has a unique name containing up to 70 characters. You place the block name within left and right brackets such as [*GroupName*]. Regardless of the different configurations you use, you will normally have several entries that are common to each group, such as your FILES, BUFFERS, or STACKS entries. As such, DOS provides a special block named [COMMON] within which you can place such entries. The following CONFIG.SYS file contains three blocks, one for a network configuration, one for no network, and one for common entries:

```
[COMMON]
FILES=50
BUFFERS=30
DEVICE=C:\DOS\HIMEM.SYS
DEVICE=C:\DOS\EMM386.EXE NOEMS
DOS=HIGH,UMB

[NETWORK]
DEVICEHIGH=C:\NETDRIVE.EXE
DEVICEHIGH=C:\NETPRINT.EXE

[NoNETWORK]
DEVICEHIGH=RAMDRIVE.SYS 512
DEVICEHIGH=ANSI.SYS
```

To select the configuration you desire, you create a menu of options using the CONFIG.SYS MENUITEM entry. To use MENUITEM you specify the block name and optional menu text, as shown here:

```
MENUITEM=BlockName[,MenuText]
```

For example, the following entries create options for the network and no network configurations:

```
[MENU]
MENUITEM=NETWORK,Network configuration
MENUITEM=NoNETWORK,No network support
```

When you combine the entries with the previous configuration blocks, CONFIG.SYS becomes the following:

```
[MENU]
MENUITEM=NETWORK,Network configuration
MENUITEM=NoNETWORK,No network support

[COMMON]
FILES=50
BUFFERS=30
DEVICE=C:\DOS\HIMEM.SYS
DEVICE=C:\DOS\EMM386.EXE NOEMS
DOS=HIGH,UMB

[NETWORK]
DEVICEHIGH=C:\NETDRIVE.EXE
DEVICEHIGH=C:\NETPRINT.EXE

[NoNETWORK]
DEVICEHIGH=RAMDRIVE.SYS 512
DEVICEHIGH=ANSI.SYS
```

Note that the [COMMON] block is special. DOS performs the entries listed in the [COMMON] block regardless of the configuration option you select.

If you restart the system containing this CONFIG.SYS file, DOS will display the following menu on your screen:

```
MS-DOS 6 Startup Menu

    1. Network configuration
    2. No network support

Enter a choice: 1
```

To select an option, you can type the option's number or highlight the option using your arrow keys and press ENTER.

If you look closely at the format of the MENUITEM entry, you will find the menu text is optional. If you don't specify options text, DOS will display the block name in the startup menu. For example, the following menu does not specify menu option text.

```
[MENU]
MENUITEM=NETWORK
MENUITEM=NoNETWORK
```

When your system starts, DOS will display the following:

```
MS-DOS 6 Startup Menu
    1. NETWORK
    2. NoNETWORK
Enter a choice: 1
```

Specifying a Menu Color

The CONFIG.SYS MENUCOLOR entry lets you specify the color of the startup menu. The format of the entry is as follows.

```
MENUCOLOR=Foreground[,Background]
```

The foreground and background colors are specified using a color value from 0 through 15, as listed in Table 27-3.

TABLE 27-3 DOS 6 CONFIG.SYS MENUCOLOR Color Values

Color Value	Color	Color Value	Color
0	Black	8	Gray
1	Blue	9	Bright Blue
2	Green	10	Bright green
3	Cyan	11	Bright cyan
4	Red	12	Bright red
5	Magenta	13	Bright magenta
6	Brown	14	Yellow
7	White	15	Bright white

The following entry directs DOS to display bright white menu text on blue background:

```
[MENU]
MENUCOLOR=15,1
MENUITEM=NETWORK,Network configuration
MENUITEM=NoNETWORK,No network configuration
```

Selecting a Default Menu Option

If you examine the startup screens displayed for the previous menu configurations, you will find that DOS lists option 1 as the default. Depending on your configuration, you might want to specify a different option as the default. The CONFIG.SYS MENUDEFAULT option lets you specify the default menu option. In addition, MENUDEFAULT lets you specify a time-out period from 0 to 90 seconds after which DOS automatically selects the option. By specifying a time-out option, you can ensure that your system starts, even if you are away from the keyboard. The format of the MENUDEFAULT entry is as follows:

```
MENUDEFAULT=BlockName[,Timeout]
```

The following MENUDEFAULT entry directs DOS to select the NET-WORK configuration after 30 seconds:

```
[MENU]
MENUITEM=NETWORK,Network configuration
MENUITEM=NoNETWORK,No network support
MENUDEFAULT=NETWORK,30
```

When you specify a default option and time out, DOS will display a count down of the number of seconds remaining until it selects the option, as shown here:

```
MS-DOS 6 Startup Menu

    1. Network configuration
    2. No network support


Enter a choice: 1                        Time remaining: 15
```

Including One Block's Options Within Another Block

As you have learned, to configure CONFIG.SYS, you divide the file into multiple blocks. Depending on how you divide your entries, there may be times when one of your blocks contains entries defined in another. Rather than duplicating the entries, you can use the INCLUDE entry to include the second block's entries, as shown here:

```
INCLUDE=BlockName
```

For example, assume your CONFIG.SYS file contains a block called [HIGH_MEMORY], as shown here:

```
[HIGH_MEMORY]
DEVICE=C:\DOS\HIMEM.SYS
DEVICE=C:\DOS\EMM386.EXE NOEMS
DOS=HIGH,UMB
```

Within a block such as [NETWORK], you can include the [HIGH_MEM-ORY] entries as shown here:

```
[MENU]
MENUCOLOR=15,1
MENUITEM=NETWORK,Network configuration
MENUITEM=NoNETWORK,No network configuration

[COMMON]
FILES=50
BUFFERS=30

[HIGH_MEMORY]
DEVICE=C:\DOS\HIMEM.SYS
DEVICE=C:\DOS\EMM386.EXE NOEMS
DOS=HIGH,UMB

[NETWORK]
INCLUDE=HIGH_MEMORY
DEVICEHIGH=C:\NETDRIVE.EXE
DEVICEHIGH=C:\NETPRINT.EXE

[NoNETWORK]
INCLUDE=HIGH_MEMORY
DEVICEHIGH=C:\DOS\RAMDRIVE.SYS 512 /E
DEVICEHIGH=C:\DOS\ANSI.SYS
```

Creating Several Menu Levels

Depending on your system configuration, there may be times when you can't easily express the different configuration options using just one menu. To solve this, the SUBMENU entry lets you specify additional menus. The format of the SUBMENU entry is as follows:

```
SUBMENU=BlockName[,MenuText]
```

The block name specifies a CONFIG.SYS block that contains additional MENUITEM entries. When your system starts, DOS will find the [MENU] block and process the entries it contains. If you select an entry that corresponds to a submenu, DOS will display a second menu, followed possibly by a third or fourth. Assume, for example, that if the user selects the "No network support" option, you want to further prompt the user

for how they want to load DOS into memory. The following CONFIG.SYS
file uses the SUBMENU entry to do just that:

```
[MENU]
MENUCOLOR=15,1
MENUITEM=NETWORK,Network configuration
SUBMENU=NoNETWORK,No network configuration

[COMMON]
FILES=50
BUFFERS=30

[HIGH_MEMORY]
DEVICE=C:\DOS\HIMEM.SYS
DEVICE=C:\DOS\EMM386.EXE NOEMS
DOS=HIGH,UMB

[NETWORK]
INCLUDE=HIGH_MEMORY
DEVICEHIGH=C:\NETDRIVE.EXE
DEVICEHIGH=C:\NETPRINT.EXE

[NoNETWORK]
MENUITEM=DOS_HIGH,Load DOS High and use UMB
MENUITEM=DOS_LOW,Load DOS Low without UMB
MENUITEM=DOS_UMB,Load DOS Low with UMB

[DOS_HIGH]
INCLUDE=HIGH_MEMORY
DEVICEHIGH=C:\DOS\RAMDRIVE.SYS 512 /E
DEVICEHIGH=C:\DOS\ANSI.SYS

[DOS_LOW]
DEVICE=C:\DOS\HIMEM.SYS
DEVICE=C:\RAMDRIVE.SYS 512 /E
DEVICE=C:\DOS\ANSI.SYS

[DOS_UMB]
DEVICE=C:\DOS\HIMEM.SYS
DEVICE=C:\EMM386.EXE NOEMS
DOS=LOW,UMB
```

```
DEVICEHIGH=C:\RAMDRIVE.SYS 512 /E
DEVICEHIGH=C:\ANSI.SYS
```

Further Controlling Your System Startup

In addition to letting you create menu-driven, customized startups, DOS 6 lets you bypass the CONFIG.SYS and AUTOEXEC.BAT processing altogether, or selectively perform or ignore each CONFIG.SYS entry. Each time your system starts, DOS 6 displays the following message:

```
Starting MS-DOS...
```

If you press the F5 key, DOS will bypass your CONFIG.SYS and AUTOEXEC.BAT processing, displaying its prompt. Bypassing the startup in this way is useful when one or more entries is preventing DOS from successfully starting your system.

If you instead press the F8 function key, DOS will individually prompt you for each CONFIG.SYS entry as to whether or not you want to perform the entry. For example, the following entry prompts whether or not you want to install the ANSI.SYS device driver:

```
DEVICE=C:\DOS\ANSI.SYS [Y,N]?
```

If you type **Y**, DOS will install the driver. If you instead type **N**, DOS will not install the driver. In either case, DOS will continue the same processing with the next entry.

Using SET in CONFIG.SYS

As you read in Chapter 19, the DOS SET command lets you assign environment entries. If you are using DOS 6, you can use SET from within your CONFIG.SYS file. For example, assume that you have commands in your AUTOEXEC.BAT file that are dependent on a network or no-network configurations. Using SET within CONFIG.SYS, you can assign a value to the NETWORK entry, as shown here:

```
[NETWORK]
INCLUDE=HIGH_MEMORY
DEVICEHIGH=C:\NETDRIVE.EXE
DEVICEHIGH=C:\NETPRINT.EXE
SET NETWORK=YES

[NoNETWORK]
INCLUDE=HIGH_MEMORY
DEVICEHIGH=C:\DOS\RAMDRIVE.SYS 512 /E
DEVICEHIGH=C:\DOS\ANSI.SYS
SET NETWORK=NO
```

Within your AUTOEXEC.BAT file, you can use the named parameter %NETWORK% to test for the network configuration, as shown here:

```
IF %NETWORK%==YES NET_COMMAND
```

Practice

Remember, DOS uses the entries in CONFIG.SYS during system startup. If you place an errant entry in this file, DOS might not be able to start. Thus you should always make a copy of CONFIG.SYS before you modify its contents:

```
C:\> COPY  CONFIG.SYS  CONFIG.SAV <ENTER>
```

In addition, you should use the following FORMAT command to create a bootable floppy disk that you can place in a safe location:

```
C:\> FORMAT  A:  /S <ENTER>
```

If you make a change to your CONFIG.SYS file that prevents your system from starting, you can boot your system using the floppy disk and then edit the CONFIG.SYS file to correct it.

Because each user has different hardware requirements, it is difficult to develop a practice section for the DOS system configuration parameters. Rather than modifying CONFIG.SYS as an exercise, let's review its current contents in your system. Issue the following TYPE command to view the current contents of your CONFIG.SYS file:

```
C:\> TYPE  \CONFIG.SYS <ENTER>
```

Look up each entry in your CONFIG.SYS and make sure you understand the entry's function and setting.

At a minimum, your CONFIG.SYS file should contain a FILES entry set to at least 20 and a BUFFERS entry set to at least 25, as shown here:

```
FILES=20
BUFFERS=25
```

If you are using DOS 5 or later and your computer has available extended memory, invoke the MEM command and note the current memory use. Next, place the following entries in your CONFIG.SYS file:

```
DEVICE=C:\DOS\HIMEM.SYS
DEVICE=C:\DOS\EMM386.SYS  NOEMS
DOS=UMB,HIGH
```

Next, place your current DEVICE entries after the entries just shown, and change each DEVICE entry to DEVICEHIGH. Also, if your CONFIG.SYS contains an INSTALL entry, remove the entry and place a corresponding LOADHIGH entry in your AUTOEXEC.BAT file. Reboot your system and invoke the MEM command. Note the increase in available conventional memory. Depending on the amount of extended memory in your system, you might want to install the SMARTDRV.SYS device driver to load a high-performance disk cache. If you do so, reduce the number of buffers in your BUFFERS entry to 3. Finally, if you are using DOS 6, take a few moments and experiment with the CONFIG.SYS customize startup entries.

Review

1. When does DOS use the CONFIG.SYS file?

2. How does the CONFIG.SYS BREAK=ON entry differ from the BREAK ON command?

3. What is the function of a DOS disk buffer?

4. What CONFIG.SYS entry allocates 25 disk buffers?

5. What is a device driver?

6. What CONFIG.SYS entry installs the ANSI.SYS device driver?

7. When do you need to include a CONFIG.SYS FCBS entry?

8. By default, DOS supports eight open files at one time. Your programs, however, are restricted to only three. Why?

9. What CONFIG.SYS entry directs DOS to support 20 files?

10. When do you need to use the CONFIG.SYS STACKS entry?

11. What is a RAM disk?

12. What CONFIG.SYS entry creates a 256Kb RAM disk?

13. What CONFIG.SYS entry creates a 256Kb RAM disk in extended memory?

Key Points

The BREAK Entry

The CONFIG.SYS BREAK entry allows you to enable extended CTRL-BREAK checking at system startup. By default, DOS leaves extended CTRL-BREAK checking disabled. Using the following entry, you can enable checking:

```
BREAK=ON
```

Remember, extended CTRL-BREAK checking adds system overhead, which decreases your overall performance.

continues . . .

The BUFFERS Entry

The CONFIG.SYS BUFFERS entry allows you to improve your system performance by reducing the number of slow disk drive operations DOS must perform. Most users should use, at a minimum, the following BUFFERS entry:

```
BUFFERS=25
```

If you use the SMARTDRV.SYS device driver to install a disk cache, reduce the number of buffers to 3.

The DEVICE Entry

The CONFIG.SYS DEVICE entry directs DOS to install a software device driver into conventional memory. The following CONFIG.SYS entry, for example, directs DOS to install the ANSI.SYS device driver.

```
DEVICE=C:\DOS\ANSI.SYS
```

The DRIVPARM Entry

The CONFIG.SYS DRIVPARM entry directs DOS to change the characteristics of a block device such as your disk or a tape drive. The following DRIVPARM entry, for example, directs DOS to provide change-line support for drive A:

```
DRIVPARM=/D:0 /C
```

continues . . .

Key Points
(continued)

The FCBS Entry

The CONFIG.SYS FCBS entry allows you to increase the number of file control blocks DOS can use to support older application programs. If your older programs don't experience errors when trying to open files, you don't need to use the FCBS entry. If your older programs do experience strange errors, use the following entry:

```
FCBS=20,4
```

The FILES Entry

The CONFIG.SYS FILES entry specifies the number of files DOS can open at one time. By default, DOS can open eight files. However, five of those files are used to support redirection. Most users should provide support for at least 20 file handles, as shown here:

```
FILES=20
```

The INSTALL Entry

The CONFIG.SYS INSTALL entry directs DOS to install one of the following memory-resident programs: FASTOPEN, SHARE, KEYB, or NLSFUNC. By using INSTALL, DOS can better use your available memory. If you are using DOS 5 or later, use the LOADHIGH command (in your AUTOEXEC.BAT file) instead of the CONFIG.SYS INSTALL entry.

continues . . .

The LASTDRIVE Entry

The CONFIG.SYS LASTDRIVE entry lets you specify the letter of the last disk drive DOS can access. By default, drive E is the last drive DOS can access. If you plan to create several logical disk drives using the SUBST command, you will need the LASTDRIVE entry. The following entry allows DOS to access drives A through K:

```
LASTDRIVE=K
```

The REM Entry

The CONFIG.SYS REM entry lets you place explanatory remarks within your CONFIG.SYS file to explain different entries. For example, the following entry justifies the BUFFERS entry that follows:

```
REM Install 50 buffers to support the DATABASE
BUFFERS=50
```

The SHELL Entry

The CONFIG.SYS SHELL entry lets you specify the name of, and the directory containing, the command processor. In the case of COMMAND.COM, you can use the SHELL entry to increase the environment size as well. The following SHELL entry directs DOS to locate COMMAND.COM in the DOS directory and to support an environment of 4098 bytes:

```
SHELL=C:\DOS\COMMAND.COM  C:\DOS  /E:4098 /P
```

continues . . .

Key Points
(continued)

The STACKS Entry

The CONFIG.SYS STACKS entry directs DOS to set aside more memory for stack space to handle hardware interrupts. The only time you need to use the STACKS entry is when your system halts and displays the following error message:

```
Fatal: Internal Stack Failure, System Halted
```

The SWITCHES Entry

To assist older programs that only support the conventional keyboard, the CONFIG.SYS SWITCHES entry directs DOS to treat an enhanced keyboard as a conventional keyboard.

Conventional Memory

Conventional memory is your computer's memory from 0 to 640Kb. When your computer starts, DOS loads itself into the lower portion of conventional memory. If you invoke memory-resident programs, DOS loads them into the next available conventional memory location.

Expanded Memory

Expanded memory lets the original IBM PC (8088) break the 640Kb boundary. Expanded memory combines hardware memory boards and powerful software.

continues . . .

Expanded memory uses a 64Kb region immediately above conventional memory as a buffer for four 16Kb pages. When you run a program written to use expanded memory, DOS loads the program into the 640Kb conventional memory. The program then loads its data into the expanded memory area. The program divides its data into 16Kb pages. When the program needs to access data stored in a specific page, the expanded memory software brings the page from expanded memory into one of the 16Kb page frames. If the page frames are currently full, the expanded memory software maps one page out so it can map another page in.

Extended Memory

Extended memory is the memory above 1Mb in an 80286, 80386, or 80486. Extended memory combines hardware memory boards with a software device driver you must load using the CONFIG.SYS DEVICE entry. When you execute a program that uses extended memory, DOS loads the program into conventional memory. The program in turn loads its data into extended memory. When the program needs to use data stored in extended memory, the extended memory software lets the program access the data directly without the time-consuming mapping to a page buffer that occurs with expanded memory. As a result, extended memory is much faster than expanded.

The RAMDRIVE.SYS Device Driver

The RAMDRIVE.SYS device driver lets you install a RAM drive in your computer's fast electronic memory. After you create a RAM drive, you access the drive using the drive letter RAMDRIVE.SYS displays on your screen, which is typically D or E. Because of their tremendous speed, RAM drives are very convenient for storing temporary files. Because RAM drives reside in your computer's electronic memory, the files the drive contains are lost when you turn off your computer's power or restart DOS.

continues . . .

The SMARTDRV.SYS Device Driver

The SMARTDRV.SYS device driver installs a disk cache into extended or expanded memory. A disk cache works as a high-performance, large disk buffer. Because the disk cache resides in either extended or expanded memory, the cache does not consume conventional memory that DOS can use to run larger programs.

The DOS Entry

The CONFIG.SYS DOS entry lets you direct DOS 5 or later to install itself in high memory. In addition, the DOS entry lets you request a link to reserved memory DOS can later use to install a device driver or command in reserved memory (using DEVICEHIGH or LOADHIGH).

The DEVICEHIGH Entry

The CONFIG.SYS DEVICEHIGH entry directs DOS 5 or later to install a device driver into reserved memory, making more conventional memory available to DOS for other programs. To use the DEVICEHIGH entry, your CONFIG.SYS file must contain a DOS=UMB entry, and the EMM386.EXE driver must be installed. The following DEVICEHIGH entry installs the RAMDRIVE.SYS driver in reserved memory:

```
DEVICEHIGH=C:\DOS\RAMDRIVE.SYS
```

If DOS does not have enough reserved memory to hold the driver, it will load the driver into conventional memory as if you had used the DEVICE entry.

continues . . .

*Key Points
(continued)*

The LOADHIGH Command

The LOADHIGH command lets you load memory-resident software into the reserved area of memory above conventional memory and below 1Mb. Loading memory-resident software into reserved memory frees conventional memory for other programs. To use LOADHIGH, you must be using a 386 or 486, with the DOS=UMB entry in CONFIG.SYS and the EMM386.EXE device driver installed. If your computer does not have enough reserved memory available for the program, LOADHIGH will load the program into conventional memory. The format of LOADHIGH is as follows:

```
LOADHIGH CommandName [parameters]
```

The LOADFIX Command

If you load DOS into high memory and load your device drivers and memory-resident programs into reserved memory, you may actually free up so much conventional memory that a program's starting address is actually below 64Kb. Unfortunately, some programs cannot execute in this address range and will display the message "Packed file corrupt" when you attempt to execute them. Using the DOS 5 or later LOADFIX command, you can instruct DOS to load the program into memory above the 64Kb address, thus resolving the problem.

DOS 6 Custom Startup

If you are using DOS 6, you can use CONFIG.SYS entries to create a menu of customized startup options. In addition, by pressing the F5 function key when DOS 6 first starts, you can direct DOS to bypass the processing of CONFIG.SYS. In a similar way, by pressing F8, you can direct DOS to prompt you before performing each CONFIG.SYS entry.

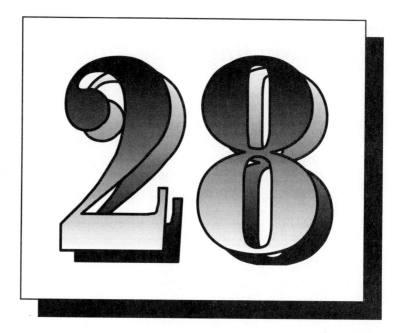

CHAPTER

28

International DOS
Support

O ver the past few years, the number of international DOS users has increased dramatically. Many U.S. companies find that as much as one-third of their business goes to Canada and abroad. To support the growing number of international users, DOS offers several commands and CONFIG.SYS entries that provide country-specific keyboard layouts and character sets, simplifying the international user's interface to DOS.

This chapter examines the NLSFUNC, CHCP, and KEYB commands, which you will need if you want international DOS support. If you do not need to use the international capabilities that are built into DOS, you may want to proceed to Chapter 29, "A Closer Look at Disks."

Understanding Code Pages

This chapter uses the term *code page* extensively. A code page defines a set of characters used in a specific language. You have probably seen typewriters that allow you to change the letter associated with each key simply by changing the typewriter ball. Code pages work in a similar fashion: when you change code pages, you change the set of characters that DOS will display on your screen.

DOS provides support for the following code pages:

Code Page	Country
437	United States
850	Multilingual
852	Slavic (requires DOS 5 or later)
860	Portuguese
863	French-Canadian
865	Nordic

Each of the concepts discussed in this chapter is closely related to DOS code pages.

Using COUNTRY to Specify Country-Specific Formats

Just as most countries have unique languages, they also have unique date, time, and currency symbols. The CONFIG.SYS COUNTRY entry directs DOS to support a specific country's date, time, and currency format. The general form of this entry is

```
COUNTRY=country_code[,[code_page][,country_info_file]]
```

where the following is true:

The *country_code* entry is a three-digit number that identifies the desired country, as shown in Table 28-1.

TABLE 28-1

Country Codes

Country Code	Country
001	United States
002	French-Canadian
003	Latin American
031	Netherlands
032	Belgium
033	France
034	Spain
036	Hungary
038	Yugoslavia

**TABLE
28-1
Cont.**

Country Codes

Country Code	Country
039	Italy
041	Switzerland
042	Czechoslovakia
044	United Kingdom
045	Denmark
046	Sweden
047	Norway
048	Poland
049	Germany
055	Brazil
061	English (International)
081	Japan
082	Korea
086	Chinese (simplified)
088	Chinese (traditional)
351	Portugal
358	Finland
785	Arabic countries
972	Israel

The *code_page* entry is the three-digit value associated with the desired code page.

The *country_info_file* entry is the name and location of the file containing the country-specific formats. In most cases, this file is C:\DOS\COUNTRY.SYS.

For example, to direct DOS to use the symbol set for Finland, your entry is the following:

```
COUNTRY=358,,C:\DOS\COUNTRY.SYS
```

To select a specific code page, you can use the COUNTRY entry as shown here:

```
COUNTRY=061,850,C:\DOS\COUNTRY.SYS
```

In this case, DOS will select the country code symbols for Australia.

The COUNTRY entry can be used only to define date, time, and currency symbols. To select a unique keyboard layout, you must use the KEYB command.

Selecting a Keyboard Template

Just as different countries have different character sets, they also have unique keyboard layouts. The KEYB command is an external DOS command that allows you to select a specific keyboard template.

The format of the KEYB command is as follows:

```
KEYB [keyboard[,[code_page][,keyboard_file]][/ID:nnn][/E]
```

where the following is true:

The *keyboard* entry specifies the two-letter keyboard code for the desired keyboard, as shown in Table 28-2.

The *code_page* entry specifies the three-digit code page to use in conjunction with the keyboard.

The *keyboard_file* entry specifies the name and location of the file containing the keyboard templates. In most cases, this file will be called KEYBOARD.SYS.

TABLE 28-2

Keyboard and Template Codes

Keyboard	Country
US	United States
CF	French-Canadian
LA	Latin American
NL	Netherlands
BE	Belgium
FR	France
SP	Spain
IT	Italy
SF	Switzerland (French)
SG	Switzerland (German)
UK	United Kingdom
DK	Denmark
SV	Sweden
NO	Norway
GR	Germany
PO	Portugal
SU	Finland
BR	Brazil
CZ	Czech
SL	Slavic
HU	Hungary
PL	Poland
YU	Yugoslavia

The /ID:*nnn* entry specifies a three-digit keyboard layout template (see Table 28-2). When a country has two or more templates, this switch allows you to specify the desired keyboard.

The /E switch informs KEYB you are using an enhanced keyboard.

To select the keyboard template for Norway, you use the KEYB command as follows:

```
C:\> KEYB NO,850,C:\DOS\KEYBOARD.SYS <ENTER>
```

Remember from Chapter 27 that if you are using DOS 4, you can use the CONFIG.SYS INSTALL entry to select a keyboard template at system startup:

```
INSTALL=C:\DOS\KEYB.COM FR,850,C:\DOS\KEYBOARD.SYS
```

Likewise, if you are using DOS 5 or later, you can use the LOADHIGH command from within your AUTOEXEC.BAT file as shown here:

```
LOADHIGH C:\DOS\KEYB.COM FR,850,C:\DOS\KEYBOARD.SYS
```

Once you install a keyboard template, you can toggle between the international keyboard and the United States keyboard by using the CTRL-ALT-F1 and CTRL-ALT-F2 key combinations. CTRL-ALT-F1 selects the U.S. keyboard, and CTRL-ALT-F2 selects the international keyboard.

If you will be using an international keyboard on a regular basis, install the corresponding KEYB command in CONFIG.SYS. Your keyboard template will then be readily available each time DOS starts.

Code-Page Switching

Most international users select only one keyboard template and code page. However, if you must work with several international languages, you may have to perform code-page switching. To do so, you must use the NLSFUNC and CHCP commands and the DISPLAY.SYS and

PRINTER.SYS device drivers. Not all devices support code-page switching; for those that do, you must install device driver support.

Screen Support for Code-Page Switching

The DISPLAY.SYS device driver provides code-page switching support for your screen display. The format of the DISPLAY.SYS entry is

```
DEVICE=C:\DOS\DISPLAY.SYS CON:=[(display_type[,hardware_code-
page] [,(additional_codepages, subfonts)])]
```

where the following is true:

The *display_type* entry specifies your display type. Valid entries are EGA and LCD (VGA systems can use EGA).

The *hardware_codepage* entry specifies the code page supported by your screen display. Valid entries include 437, 850, 852, 860, 863, and 865.

The *additional_codepages* entry specifies the number of code pages that DOS can prepare for use. EGA can be set from 0 or 6, and LCD can be set from 0 or 1.

The *subfonts* entry specifies the number of subfonts supported by your display.

A DISPLAY.SYS entry for an EGA monitor might be

```
DEVICE=C:\DOS\DISPLAY.SYS CON:=(EGA,437,(2,1))
```

Remember, the only time you need to include this entry in CONFIG.SYS is when you are going to perform code-page switching.

Printer Support for Code-Page Switching

Like monitors, not all printers support code-page switching. If your printer does support it, the documentation that accompanied your printer should contain the correct PRINTER.SYS entry. The format of this entry is

```
DEVICE=C:\DOS\PRINTER.SYS LPTn:=(printer_type[,[hardware_code-
page] [,additional_codepages]])
```

where the following is true:

LPT*n* specifies the desired printer port number (LPT1, LPT2, and so on).

The *printer_type* entry specifies your printer type. Valid entries include

Entry	Printer
4201	IBM Proprinter 4201, 4202
4208	IBM Proprinter 4207, 4208; Proprinter X24, XL24
5202	IBM Proprinter 5202 Quietwriter

The *hardware_codepage* entry specifies the code page supported by your printer. Valid entries include 437, 850, 852, 860, 863, and 865.

The *additional_codepages* entry specifies the number of code pages that DOS can prepare for use. This number is printer specific.

As an example, to use a Proprinter connected to LPT1 with the French code page, the following PRINTER.SYS entry will be correct:

```
DEVICE=C:\DOS\PRINTER.SYS LPT1:=(4201,867,1)
```

Using NLSFUNC to Provide National Language Support

Before you can perform code-page switching, you must issue the NLSFUNC command. (NLSFUNC stands for National Language Support Function.) The format of this command is

```
NLSFUNC [country_file]
```

where *country_file* specifies the name of the file containing the country-specific information. In most cases, this file is C:\DOS\COUNTRY.SYS. The following command loads the national language support software:

```
C:\> NLSFUNC C:\DOS\COUNTRY.SYS
```

Also keep in mind that the DOS 4 CONFIG.SYS INSTALL entry and the DOS 5 or later AUTOEXEC.BAT LOADHIGH command allow you to install national language support during system startup in this manner:

```
INSTALL=C:\DOS\NLSFUNC.EXE C:\DOS\COUNTRY.SYS
```

```
LOADHIGH C:\DOS\NLSFUNC.EXE C:\DOS\COUNTRY.SYS
```

Using CHCP to Select a Code Page

Once you have invoked NLSFUNC to prepare your system for code-page switching, you can use the CHCP command to select a new code page. The format of this command is

```
CHCP [codepage]
```

where *codepage* is the three-digit value that specifies the desired code page.

If you simply invoke CHCP with no command-line parameter, DOS will display the current code page, as shown here:

```
C:\> CHCP <ENTER>
Active codepage: 437

C:\>
```

To select the Nordic code page, use the command

```
C:\> CHCP  865 <ENTER>
```

Displaying the active code page again produces

```
C:\> CHCP <ENTER>
Active codepage: 865

C:\>
```

The CHCP command allows you to select a code page for your screen and printer at the same time. If you want to select code pages for these devices independently, you must use the MODE command.

Using MODE for Code-Page Support

The MODE command is a key component in code-page switching, and it has several new forms. The following sections describe the MODE command's uses for international support.

Preparing a Code Page

Before you can use a code page, you must prepare your screen display or printer for use with the code page. To prepare your screen display, the format of the MODE command is as follows:

```
MODE CON CODEPAGE PREPARE=((code_page,code_page) display_type.CPI)
```

where *display_type*.CPI is a file containing code-page information (CPI) for your specific display type, such as EGA.CPI. For example, the following command prepares an EGA or VGA monitor to use code pages 863 and 865:

```
C:\> MODE CON CP PREPARE=((863,865) C:\DOS\EGA.CPI) <ENTER>
```

Likewise, the following command prepares only code page 850 for use:

```
C:\> MODE CON CODEPAGE PREPARE=((850) C:\DOS\EGA.CPI) <ENTER>
```

Once you have prepared a code page for use, the CHCP command allows you to select it:

```
C:\> CHCP 850 <ENTER>
```

Preparing a code page for use by your printer is a similar process. In this case, use the MODE command

```
MODE LPTn CODEPAGE PREPARE=((code_page) device.CPI)
```

where LPT*n* is the desired printer port and *device*.CPI is the file containing the code-page information for your printer (4201.CPI, 4208.CPI, or 5202.CPI). For example, the command

```
C:\> MODE LPT1 CODEPAGE PREPARE=((865) C:\DOS\4201.CPI) <ENTER>
```

prepares code page 865 for use by an IBM Proprinter.

Selecting a Code Page

The MODE command also allows you to select code pages on a device-by-device basis. Once you have prepared a code page, you can select it for use with either of the following MODE commands:

```
MODE CON CODEPAGE SELECT=codepage
MODE LPT1 CODEPAGE SELECT=codepage
```

For example, the following command selects code page 865 for your screen display:

```
C:\> MODE CON CODEPAGE SELECT=865 <ENTER>
```

Refreshing a Code Page

Each time you select a code page for a device, DOS downloads code-page information to the device. If DOS downloads code-page information to your printer and you later turn your printer off, the code-page information is lost. To restore the current code page for the device, you need to use the MODE command, as shown here:

```
C:\> MODE LPT1 CODEPAGE REFRESH <ENTER>
```

Displaying the Current Code-Page Status

If you forget which code pages are active, you can issue the command

```
C:\> MODE CON CODEPAGE /STATUS <ENTER>
```

or the command

```
C:\> MODE LPT1 CODEPAGE /STATUS <ENTER>
```

In the case of the CON code-page status, MODE will display something like this:

```
C:\> MODE  CON  /STATUS <ENTER>

Status for device CON:
----------
Columns=80
Lines=25

Active code page for device CON is 437
Hardware code pages:
  code page 437
Prepared code pages:
```

```
code page 437
code page 850

MODE status code page function completed
```

Abbreviating MODE Commands

Because many MODE commands can become quite long, DOS allows you to abbreviate several of the command's key words, as shown here:

Keyword	Abbreviation
CODEPAGE	CP
PREPARE	PREP
SELECT	SEL
REFRESH	REF
/STATUS	/STA

You will find the abbreviations useful if you frequently issue MODE commands.

Practice

There is a tremendous number of international configurations possible with DOS, so no single set of hands-on practice commands would suit everyone's setup. Be sure to modify the commands that are presented here to include the correct country code or code-page values for your requirements.

To inform DOS that you want to use country-specific date, time, and currency symbols, place the COUNTRY entry in CONFIG.SYS. For the German symbol set, your entry would be

```
COUNTRY=049,437,C:\DOS\COUNTRY.SYS
```

If you need to install a keyboard template, use the KEYB command. With DOS version 4, you can use the INSTALL entry in CONFIG.SYS to invoke KEYB at system startup, as shown here:

```
INSTALL=C:\DOS\KEYB.COM GR,860,C:\DOS\KEYBOARD.SYS
```

Likewise, if you are using DOS 5 or later, you can use the LOADHIGH command, as shown here:

```
LOADHIGH C:\DOS\KEYB.COM GR,860,C:\DOS\KEYBOARD.SYS
```

Your system is now ready to support the German keyboard template and symbol set.

If you plan to use code-page switching, you must install either the DISPLAY.SYS or PRINTER.SYS device driver in CONFIG.SYS, as discussed earlier in this chapter. If you are using DOS 5 or later, use the DEVICEHIGH entry to load the device drivers. Also use the INSTALL CONFIG.SYS entry or LOADHHIGH command to invoke NLSFUNC during system startup. Refer back to Chapter 27 if you need a review of how to work with CONFIG.SYS.

Review

1. What is a code page?
2. What is the function of COUNTRY.SYS?
3. How do you select the French-Canadian keyboard template?
4. How do you toggle between a foreign keyboard template and the U.S. keyboard template?
5. When do you need code-page switching?
6. What is the function of DISPLAY.SYS?
7. What is the function of PRINTER.SYS?
8. What is the NLSFUNC command?
9. What steps are required for code-page switching?

10. How do you change the code page for your screen display without affecting your printer?

Key Points

The CONFIG.SYS COUNTRY Entry

The CONFIG.SYS COUNTRY entry allows international DOS users to select the date, time, and currency symbol set for their country. For example, the following COUNTRY entry selects the German symbol set:

```
COUNTRY=049,437,C:\DOS\COUNTRY.SYS
```

The KEYB Command

The KEYB command allows international DOS users to install a keyboard template specific to their country. Once an international keyboard is active, the user can toggle from the international keyboard to the U.S. keyboard by pressing CTRL-ALT-F1, or from the U.S. to the international keyboard by pressing CTRL-ALT-F2. If you need an international keyboard template, you should execute KEYB in the DOS 4 CONFIG.SYS INSTALL entry or the DOS 5 or later LOADHIGH command.

The NLSFUNC Command

The NLSFUNC command prepares a system for code-page switching. Before you can change code pages with CHCP or the MODE command, you must execute NLSFUNC. If you need code-page switching support, you should execute NLSFUNC by using the DOS 4 CONFIG.SYS INSTALL entry or DOS 5 or later LOADHIGH command.

CHAPTER

A Closer Look at Disks

By now you should feel comfortable working with hard and floppy disks. In this chapter you will take a closer look at how DOS stores information on your disk and examine several DOS commands that can improve your disk performance.

Taking Apart a Floppy Disk

In previous chapters you have issued commands that prepare a disk for use by DOS, copy the contents of one disk to another, and perform complex file manipulation. To better understand the steps each command actually performs, you should take a look at the actual components of a disk.

Take out an unused floppy disk. Its components are labeled in the following illustration:

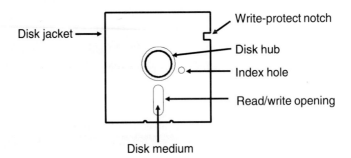

You have already used write-protect tabs to cover the write-protect notch, which prevents DOS from modifying the contents of the disk. Now take a look at the *disk storage medium.* This is nothing more than a thin piece of specially coated plastic, like the tape of an audio cassette. Your disk drive records information on disk by magnetizing it to the coated plastic. Always keep your disks away from large electronic or magnetic devices. The energy these devices may generate can change the information recorded on your disk.

The *disk jacket* is the cover that surrounds your disk storage medium. When you are not using a disk, this jacket protects the disk from dust, smoke, and fingerprints. When the disk is in use, the disk jacket keeps the disk from being crushed as you insert and remove it from the drive.

The *disk hub* is a reinforced portion of the disk that rotates the disk within the drive. Whenever you insert a disk in a drive and close the latch, the disk begins to spin quite rapidly within the drive. In order to spin the disk, the disk drive "grabs" the disk at the hub. The hub should have a reinforced metal ring for additional strength. If it does not, you should consider a different brand of disk.

If you grab the disk hub and rotate the disk carefully, you will eventually find a small hole in the disk that you can see through. This is called the *index hole.* Your disk drive uses it to mark a starting point for storing information. The index hole serves as a timing mechanism that your computer uses when it first formats the disk for use.

Again, without touching your disk storage medium, locate the disk's read/write opening. Your disk drive reads and writes information to the disk medium through this opening. If you touch the disk storage medium through this opening, you risk damaging the disk and losing the information that it contains.

Open up your unused disk in order to view its inner construction, as shown in Figure 29-1. As you can see, the disk is really quite simple.

3 1/2-Inch Floppy Disks

With the success of laptop computers as well as the IBM PS/2 line of computers, the use of 3 1/2-inch microfloppy disks, such as the one illustrated here, has grown tremendously:

FIGURE
29-1 Inner construction of a floppy disk

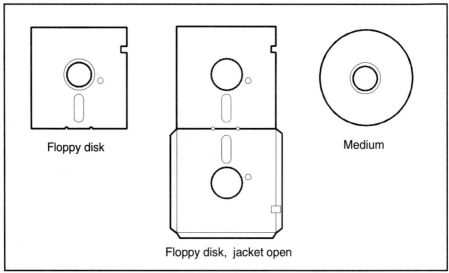

Floppy disk

Medium

Floppy disk, jacket open

Microfloppy disks, like the standard 5 1/4-inch floppy disks, are used to store programs and data. However, microfloppy disk jackets are not flexible; they are made out of a hard plastic that provides them with better protection. Also unlike standard floppy disks, microfloppy disks do not expose the disk storage medium, which means they are protected better from dust, smoke, and fingerprints. If you do want to examine the medium, you move the small metal portion of the disk called a *shutter*.

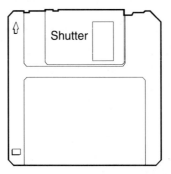

Shutter

Sliding the shutter to the left exposes the disk storage medium, as shown here:

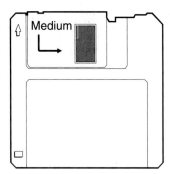

Turn the microfloppy disk over. Locate the disk spindle and sector notch:

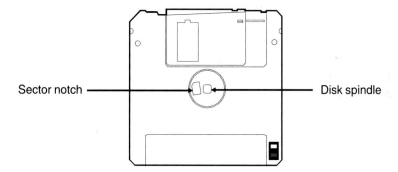

When you insert a microfloppy disk into the disk drive, the disk begins spinning just as a standard floppy disk does. The drive uses the *disk spindle* to rotate the microfloppy disk. With a standard 5 1/4-inch floppy disk, the drive uses an index hole for timing; for a microfloppy disk, it uses the *sector notch*. The microfloppy drive locates this notch and immediately knows the orientation of the disk.

A microfloppy disk does not have a write-protect notch; it has a *write-protect hole* instead:

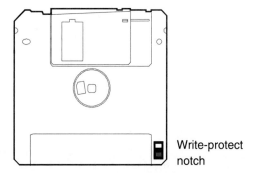

Write-protect
notch

When the hole is exposed, the disk is write protected. When the hole is covered, DOS is free to access the disk as it requires. You can tell the difference between a 1.44Mb and 720Kb 3 1/2-inch floppy disk by the presence of a second hole—the *high-density hole*—on the 1.44Mb disk, directly across from the write-protect hole, as shown here:

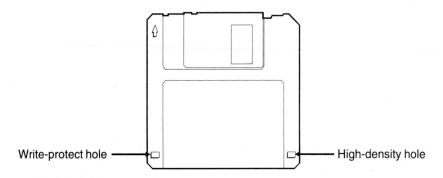

Write-protect hole ⎯⎯⎯⎯⎯⎯   ⎯⎯⎯⎯⎯ High-density hole

If you take care of your floppy and microfloppy disks, they should last a long time. Figure 29-2 demonstrates some guidelines for the proper care and handling of your disks.

Hard Disks

Hard disks are also used to store programs and data. Working with a hard disk is identical to working with a floppy disk, except that you typically reference a hard disk as drive C, and the hard disk can store considerably more files.

FIGURE
29-2
Rules for handling floppy disks

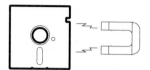

Never place the disk near
magnetic devices.

Always place disks back
into disk envelopes when
you are not using them.

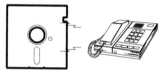

Keep your disk away from
your telephone.

Store your floppy disks in
a safe location.

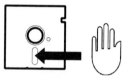

Never touch your floppy
disk medium.

Always make a backup
copy of your floppy disk.

Never smoke near floppy
disks.

Keep room temperature in
the range of 50F to 110F.

Never bend floppy disks.

Hard disks are also faster than floppy disks. Unlike the plastic storage medium used by floppy and microfloppy disks, a hard disk has a solid metal medium, which allows the recording mechanism to be more precise. The metal platters can spin about ten times as fast as a floppy disk can, giving you much better performance.

Unlike a floppy disk, which uses a single platter for storing data, a hard disk can contain several platters, as shown in Figure 29-3. The multiple platters provide increased storage space, so the hard disk can store much more information than a floppy disk.

Disk Storage Capacities

Each time DOS displays a directory listing of your disk, the last item it displays is the amount of disk space available. The amount of storage space on a disk depends on the disk type. Standard 5 1/4-inch disks, for example, provide space for 368,640 bytes. Microfloppy disks can store 737,280, 1,474,560, or 2,949,120 bytes, depending again on the disk type. Finally, 5 1/4-inch quad-density disks can store 1,228,800 bytes. Table 29-1 summarizes disk storage capacities.

Hard disk

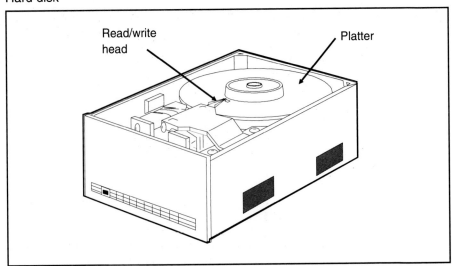

TABLE 29-1	Storage Capacities of Floppy Disks		
Disk Size	**Disk Description**	**Capacity**	**DOS Versions**
5 1/4	360Kb	368,640 bytes	DOS 2.0 or later
5 1/4	1.2Mb	1,228,800 bytes	DOS 3.0 or later
3 1/2	720Kb	737,280 bytes	DOS 3.2
3 1/2	1.44Mb	1,474,560 bytes	DOS 3.3
3 1/2	2.88Mb	2,949,120 bytes	DOS 5.0 or later

It's not critical that you remember the exact number of bytes that your disks can store. It is important to remember, however, that several different types of disks exist and that each is capable of storing different amounts of information.

Tracks, Sectors, and Sides

To fully understand how some disks can store more information than others, you need to know how DOS stores information on your disk. Visualize your disk as containing many circular rings, similar to the grooves on a record album. These are called *tracks:*

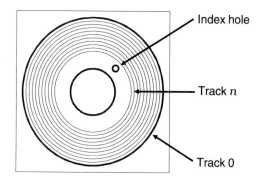

DOS uses tracks to locate and store information on your disk. Each track contains several different storage locations, called *sectors*, as shown here:

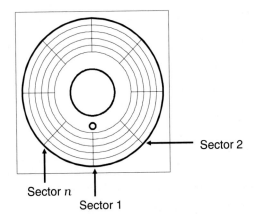

Sector 2

Sector *n*

Sector 1

When DOS reads or writes information to your disk, it does so a sector at a time. In most cases, DOS uses both sides of a disk for storage. With this in mind, you can determine the amount of data your disk can store by using the equation

Storage = tracks per disk * sectors per track * bytes per sector * sides

Using a standard 5 1/4-inch disk as an example, the storage capacity is the following:

Storage = 40 * 9 * 512 * 2
Storage = 368,640 bytes

Understanding how DOS stores files on your disk can often help you use your disk more efficiently.

Examining Your Disk with CHKDSK

The CHKDSK command allows you to find out if your disk contains damaged locations or lost files. When DOS writes information to your disk, an error can occur (although it is uncommon). Depending on the kind of error, DOS might not even be aware it occurred. The CHKDSK command allows you to examine your disk for such errors.

CHKDSK is an external DOS command; to invoke it, issue the command

```
C:\> CHKDSK <ENTER>
```

CHKDSK will examine your disk and display information on the following:

❑ Disk volume name and serial number (if one exists)

❑ Total disk space in bytes

❑ Disk space consumed by DOS hidden files

❑ Disk space consumed by DOS subdirectories

❑ Disk space consumed by user files

❑ Disk space consumed by damaged sectors

❑ Available disk space in bytes

❑ Size of each file allocation unit

❑ Number of allocation units on disk

❑ Available allocation units on disk

❑ Total memory present in the system

❑ Available memory unused by DOS

For example, CHKDSK might display

```
C:\> CHKDSK <ENTER>


Volume DOS 6 DISK  created 03-26-1993 6:40a
Volume Serial Number is 16F6-3B73

 200065024 bytes total disk space
     77824 bytes in 2 hidden files
    286720 bytes in 63 directories
  48140288 bytes in 2515 user files
 151560192 bytes available on disk

      4096 bytes in each allocation unit
     48844 total allocation units on disk
     37002 available allocation units on disk

    655360 total bytes memory
    574176 bytes free

C:\>
```

In order for a disk to be bootable by DOS, the disk must contain not only COMMAND.COM, but also two other hidden files. Remember, a hidden file is a file that resides on your disk but does not appear in the directory listing. DOS hides these files to prevent their accidental deletion. The CHKDSK command displays the number of hidden files on your disk. If you have used the LABEL command to assign a name to your disk, DOS creates a hidden file to store the volume name.

Much of the information CHKDSK displays is self-explanatory. However, certain information deserves additional explanation.

To improve your disk organization, each time DOS creates a file on your disk, it allocates file space by *allocation units*, or *clusters*. The allocation unit shown in the following illustration is four sectors in length:

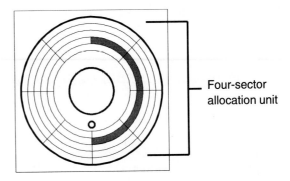

Four-sector allocation unit

Rather than being spread out across multiple sectors of a disk, as shown in the following illustration, the file is confined to four adjacent sectors.

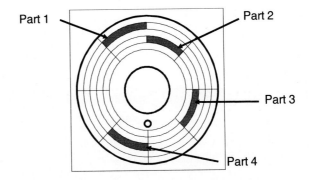

Part 1 Part 2 Part 3 Part 4

The advantage of allocating file space in this manner is speed. When DOS reads your file, it can do so quickly because it does not have to locate sectors all over the disk. When DOS later increases the size of the file, it allocates a cluster of disk space. In most cases, the fact that DOS uses disk clusters to store files is of little interest to the user. However, if you create many small files on your disk, you need to remember that DOS must allocate at least one cluster per file. Assume, for example, that you create the file ONE.DAT, which contains one character (1 byte) of information, as shown here:

```
C:\> COPY  CON  ONE.DAT <ENTER>
1^Z <ENTER>
    1 File(s) copied

C:\>
```

Although the file contains only 1 byte, DOS must still allocate a complete disk cluster to hold the file. If the disk cluster size is 2048 bytes, 2047 bytes of the cluster are unused. As you create files on your disk, keep in mind that your smaller files may be using up a lot more disk space than you think.

If CHKDSK displays the message

```
nnn lost allocation units found in n chains.
Convert lost chains to files (Y/N)?
```

it has located damaged files on your disk. If this occurs, reinvoke CHKDSK with the /F qualifier, as shown here:

```
C:\> CHKDSK  /F <ENTER>
```

When CHKDSK asks you whether or not you want to convert the lost chains to files, type **Y** and press ENTER. CHKDSK will create several files in your root directory named FILE*nnnn*.CHK, where *nnnn* are numbers such as 0001. (CHKDSK creates the files FILE0000.CHK and so on.) Use the TYPE command to display the contents of these files. In some cases, the files may contain important data.

Using FORMAT to Prepare Your Disks

Earlier in this book you used the FORMAT command to prepare floppy disks for use. The FORMAT command provides considerable functionality. The Command Reference section of this book examines each of FORMAT 's switches. The most frequently used qualifiers are discussed here.

As you know, not all disks are bootable. To be bootable, a disk must contain several key files. If you attempt to boot DOS with a disk that does not contain these files, your system will not start and DOS will display the following message:

```
Non-System disk or disk error
Replace and press any key when ready
```

A bootable DOS disk must contain the COMMAND.COM file along with the two hidden DOS files. To create a bootable disk, use the /S switch of the FORMAT command, as shown here:

```
C:\> FORMAT A: /S <ENTER>
```

In this case, FORMAT will work in this manner:

```
Insert new diskette for drive A:
and press ENTER when ready... <ENTER>

Checking existing disk format.

Verifying 360K

100 percent completed.

Format complete.
System transferred

Volume label (11 characters, ENTER for none)? <ENTER>
```

```
    362496 bytes total disk space
    119808 bytes used by system
     29696 bytes in bad sectors
    212992 bytes available on disk

      1024 bytes in each allocation unit.
       208 allocation units available on disk.

Volume Serial Number is 1837-14F3

Format another (Y/N)?
```

When FORMAT completes, the disk in drive A will contain not only the hidden system files, but also COMMAND.COM. If you restart DOS, the disk can boot DOS as desired.

If your computer is an IBM PC AT or compatible, it probably has a 1.2-megabyte floppy disk drive. This disk drive uses a different floppy disk (called a *quad-density disk*) that is capable of storing almost four times as much information as a standard 5 1/4-inch floppy disk (360Kb disk). If you are using quad-density disks, the output of the FORMAT command looks like this:

```
C:\> FORMAT A: <ENTER>
Insert new diskette for drive A:
and press ENTER when ready...

Checking existing disk format.

100 percent completed.

Format complete.
System transferred

Volume label (11 characters, ENTER for none)?

   1213952 bytes total disk space
    119808 bytes used by system
   1094144 bytes available on disk
```

```
     512 bytes in each allocation unit.
     2137 allocation units available on disk.

Volume Serial Number is 225D-14F8

Format another (Y/N)?
```

In some cases, you may need to exchange files with someone who has a 360Kb disk drive. To exchange files with this user, you must format a 360Kb disk in your 1.2-megabyte drive with the /4 switch, as shown here:

```
C:\> FORMAT  A:  /4  <ENTER>
```

If you have a 1.2Mb drive and you don't tell FORMAT to do otherwise, FORMAT will try to format the disk as a 1.2Mb disk. If the drive contains a 360Kb disk, such a format operation will fail, or at the least, leave you with tens (or hundreds) of thousands of bytes in bad sectors and an unreliable disk.

The only time you need to use the /4 switch is to format a 360Kb disk in a 1.2Mb drive.

If you are using 3 1/2-inch drives, your drive may be a 720Kb, 1.44Mb, or 2.88Mb drive. As such, a similar problem of having to format a disk smaller than the drive's normal capacity can arise. If you need to format a smaller 3 1/2-inch disk, refer to FORMAT's /F switch in the Command Reference section of this book.

Finally, the /V switch prevents FORMAT from prompting you for a volume name. For example, the following command directs FORMAT to assign a volume label named DOSDISK to the newly formatted disk:

```
C:\> FORMAT A: /V:DOSDISK  <ENTER>
```

Because the command line includes a volume label, FORMAT will not prompt you for one.

Comparing Your Disks with DISKCOMP

Just as the DISKCOPY command copies the contents of one floppy disk to another, the DISKCOMP command compares two disks' contents, sector by sector. If DISKCOMP locates differences, it will display the following message:

```
Compare error on
side n, track nn
```

If your computer has two floppy disks of the same capacity, the simplest way to invoke DISKCOMP is as follows:

```
C:\> DISKCOMP A: B: <ENTER>
```

DISKCOMP will prompt you to insert the disks, as shown here:

```
Insert FIRST diskette in drive A:
Insert SECOND diskette in drive B:
Press any key to continue . . .
```

Most users use DISKCOMP to ensure that a DISKCOPY command was successful. If DISKCOMP locates differences, DISKCOPY should be repeated. If the disks are identical, DISKCOMP will display

```
Compare OK
Compare another diskette (Y/N) ?
```

If you use the DOS 5 or later DISKCOPY command to duplicate your disks, DISKCOPY automatically assigns a different disk serial number to the target disk. If you invoke DISKCOMP from a version of DOS earlier than version 5, the different serial numbers cause DISKCOMP to detect a difference.

If your computer has only a single floppy disk drive, you can invoke DISKCOMP as follows:

```
C:\> DISKCOMP   A:   A:  <ENTER>
```

DISKCOMP will prompt you to insert each floppy disk as it needs it.

You may wonder why DISKCOMP encounters differences when two disks contain the same files. Remember, DISKCOMP compares disks on a sector-by-sector basis. If you use the COPY command to copy files from one disk to another, you have no way to ensure that the files were placed in the same sectors in both disks, even if they were copied successfully. If the files reside in different sectors, DISKCOMP considers the disks different.

Improving File-Open Response Time with FASTOPEN

Each time you issue a command such as

```
C:\> TYPE FILENAME.EXT <ENTER>
```

DOS must locate the specified file on disk, open it, and then display the file's contents. To locate a file, DOS must first search the directory for the file's directory entry. The directory entry contains the file's starting location on disk. Depending on the number of files in the directory or your disk speed, the search for the file's directory entry may be time consuming.

If you use the same files repeatedly (in a database application, for example), the FASTOPEN command can help. FASTOPEN works only with hard disks.

When you invoke FASTOPEN, DOS begins keeping track of files as you open them. If you have to reopen a file later, DOS has the starting location of the file in memory already, which means it does not have to locate the file by searching your disk. Thus, DOS can open your file much more quickly.

The format of the FASTOPEN command is

```
FASTOPEN drive:=[file_count] [/X] [...]
```

where the following is true:

drive specifies the disk drive on which DOS is to track entries. The drive must be a hard disk drive.

file_count specifies the number of file entries to track. This value must be between 10 and 999; the default value is 48.

/X directs DOS to place the buffers in expanded memory.

Most users don't open very many files on a regular basis, so the value 50 should give you optimal performance.

If you are using DOS 4, invoke FASTOPEN using the INSTALL entry in CONFIG.SYS. This entry, for example, directs FASTOPEN to track 50 files on drive C:

```
INSTALL=C:\DOS\FASTOPEN.EXE  C:=50
```

If you are using DOS 5 or later, you can use the LOADHIGH command within your AUTOEXEC.BAT file, as shown in this entry:

```
LOADHIGH  C:\FASTOPEN.EXE  C:=50
```

If your computer has more than one hard disk, you can direct FASTOPEN to track files on both disks. For example, the following FASTOPEN command provides support for drives C and D:

```
C:\> FASTOPEN C:=50 D:=50 <ENTER>
```

Providing File-Sharing Support in a Local Area Network

Many offices today are recognizing the benefits of sharing files between users by means of a local area network (see Figure 29-4). If your computer is part of a local area network, you will need the SHARE command, which helps DOS perform the coordination necessary for computers to share files. In most cases, the person who installed your network should place the correct INSTALL= entry in CONFIG.SYS for you.

The format of the SHARE command is

```
SHARE /F:filespace /L:locks
```

FIGURE 29-4

File sharing and local area networks

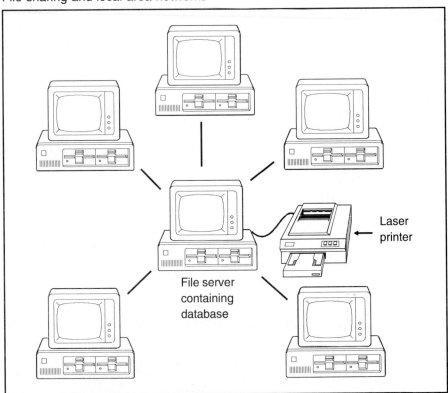

Laser printer

File server containing database

where the following is true:

/F:*filespace* specifies the amount of memory to set aside for file sharing. Each shared file requires space for the file name (up to 63 characters) plus 11 bytes for file-sharing overhead. The default value is 2048.

/L:*locks* specifies the number of locks you want SHARE to support. The default value is 20.

As an example, the CONFIG.SYS entry

```
INSTALL=C:\DOS\SHARE.EXE /F:4096 /L:25
```

sets aside 4096 bytes of memory for shared file names and overhead bytes, along with support for 25 file locks.

If you are connected to a local area network, ask the individual who installed your network if you need to invoke SHARE.

If you are using DOS 4 and you have hard disk partitions larger than 32Mb, you need to invoke the SHARE command to avoid damage to your disk. DOS 4 was the first DOS version to support hard disk partitions larger than 32Mb (DOS 4 supports 512Mb partitions, and DOS 5 or later supports 2Gb partitions). Unfortunately, under DOS 4, older programs that used file control blocks (see Chapter 27, "Customizing Your System Using CONFIG.SYS") to write to files can't support partitions larger than 32Mb. If you run one of these programs, the program may write its data to disk at any location on your disk, possibly overwriting your existing files or making your disk unbootable. By invoking the SHARE command, you eliminate the possibility of a program damaging your disk and files in this way. You need to invoke SHARE only if you are using DOS 4 and disk partitions larger than 32Mb.

Using SYS to Create a Bootable Disk

Earlier in this chapter you learned how to use the /S switch of the FORMAT command to create a bootable disk. In some cases, however, you will want to transfer the DOS operating system files to a disk that is already formatted and contains files. This is most common for application programs that are designed to boot under DOS but were not shipped with the hidden files and COMMAND.COM. In such cases, the SYS command may allow you to transfer the system files.

The format of the SYS command is

```
SYS [source_path] target_drive
```

where *source_path* specifies the location of the COMMAND.COM file that SYS must copy to the target disk and *target_drive* specifies the disk drive to which the operating system files should be transferred. If you don't specify a source path, SYS uses the current directory.

As an example, the command

```
C:\> SYS  C:\  A:  <ENTER>
```

transfers the system files to the disk in drive A. If successful, SYS will display the following message:

```
System transferrcd
```

In some cases, however, SYS cannot transfer the files to the target disk. In such cases, SYS will display the following:

```
No room for system on destination disk
```

If this occurs, format an unused disk with FORMAT /S, and then copy the files from the original disk to the newly formatted disk.

Using the DOS 6 DEFRAG Command

Beginning with DOS 6, you can use the DEFRAG command to quickly defragment the files on your disk. Invoke DEFRAG from the DOS prompt as shown here:

```
C:\> DEFRAG <ENTER>
```

DEFRAG will display a dialog box asking you to select the desired disk drive, as shown in Figure 29-5.

With your keyboard arrow keys, highlight the desired drive and press ENTER. DEFRAG will analyze the files on your disk, eventually displaying its recommendation, as shown in Figure 29-6.

Select the Optimize option. DEFRAG will begin analyzing your files, removing fragmentation. When DEFRAG displays its message box telling you it has finished the optimization, select OK. DEFRAG will display the dialog box shown in Figure 29-7, asking you if you want to defragment another disk, change DEFRAG's configuration information, or exit. Select the Exit option to return to DOS.

DEFRAG and FASTOPEN

As previously discussed in this chapter, the DOS FASTOPEN command improves your system performance by keeping information about a file's starting location in RAM. When you use DEFRAG to defragment files, DEFRAG moves files around on the disk. As a result, FASTOPEN's table of file locations is invalid. Unfortunately, the only way to discard

DEFRAG's prompt for a disk drive

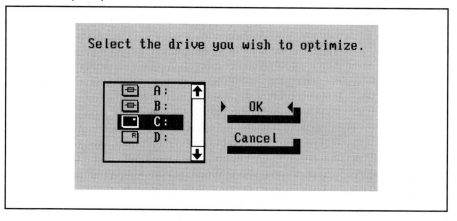

DEFRAG's Recommendation dialog box

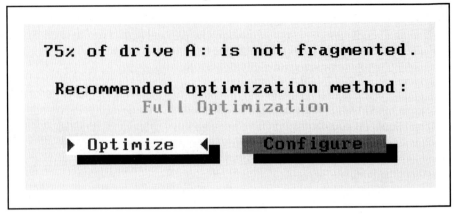

FASTOPEN's entries is to reboot your system. As such, if you are using
FASTOPEN, DEFRAG will display the dialog box shown in Figure 29-8
when it completes, telling you it will restart your system. Press ENTER
to reboot.

DEFRAG's completion options

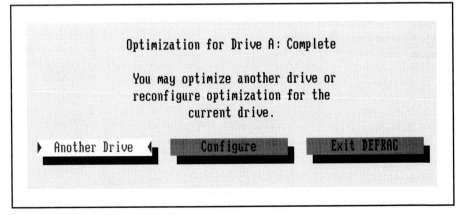

FIGURE 29-8

DEFRAG's reboot dialog box

DOS's FASTOPEN program has been detected!

DEFRAG will now Reboot your system to prevent FASTOPEN from writing incorrect information to your hard disk.

Please remove any diskette from drive A:

▶ Reboot ◀

Disk Operations Within the Shell

If you are using the DOS shell, you can easily execute each of the commands discussed in this chapter. For example, to invoke the CHKDSK command, press ALT-F to invoke the File menu, shown here:

Next, select the Run option. When the shell displays the Run dialog box, type **CHKDSK**, as shown here:

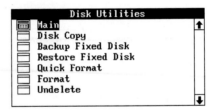

When you press ENTER, the shell will execute the CHKDSK command.

You can use this same technique to run the DISKCOMP command. To invoke the FORMAT command, press the TAB key until the shell highlights the Main program group. Next, using your keyboard's arrow keys, highlight the Disk Utilties option and press ENTER. The shell will display the following menu of options:

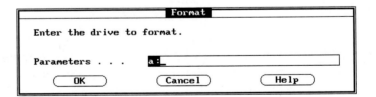

Highlight the Format option and press ENTER. The shell will display the following dialog box:

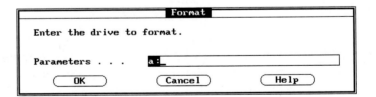

If you need to include the /S or /4 switch, for example, you can simply type in the switch. When you press ENTER, the shell will execute the FORMAT command.

Practice

Issue the following CHKDSK command:

```
C:\> CHKDSK <ENTER>
```

CHKDSK will display the current status of your disk. Remember, if CHKDSK displays the message

```
nnn lost allocation units found in n chains.
Convert lost chains to files (Y/N)?
```

CHKDSK has found damaged files on your disk. If this message appears (there is no need to respond Y or N at this point), you must invoke CHKDSK again with the /F switch to correct the errors:

```
C:\> CHKDSK /F <ENTER>
```

Place an unused floppy disk in drive A and issue the following FORMAT command:

```
C:\> FORMAT  A:  /S <ENTER>
```

With the newly formatted floppy disk in drive A, press the CTRL-ALT-DEL keyboard combination to restart DOS. Because you have created a bootable floppy disk, the disk can start DOS. Remove the floppy disk from drive A and boot your system from your hard disk by again pressing CTRL-ALT-DEL.

If you are using DOS 4, examine the contents of CONFIG.SYS by using the TYPE command:

```
C:\> TYPE  \CONFIG.SYS <ENTER>
```

Check to see if the file contains an INSTALL= entry that invokes the FASTOPEN command. If, not, you should consider adding one. Likewise, if you are using DOS 5 or later, type the contents of your AUTOEXEC.BAT file and search for a LOADHIGH command that installs FASTOPEN:

```
C:\> TYPE  \AUTOEXEC.BAT <ENTER>
```

If the file does not contain such a command, you should probably add one.

Finally, format an unused floppy disk by using the command

```
C:\> FORMAT A: <ENTER>
```

Because you did not include the /S switch in the FORMAT command line, the newly formatted disk will not be bootable. However, using the SYS command shown next, you can place the system files DOS needs to boot on the disk:

```
C:\> SYS A: <ENTER>
```

Review

1. What is the function of each of the following?

   ❏ Disk envelope
   ❏ Disk hub
   ❏ Index hole
   ❏ Write-protect notch
   ❏ Read/write opening

2. Determine the disk storage capacity of a hard disk that has 512-byte sectors, 306 tracks per side, 2 disk platters, and 17 sectors per track.

3. What is the function of the CHKDSK command?

4. When do you use the command CHKDSK /F?

5. What is an allocation unit?

6. What FORMAT command creates a bootable floppy disk from the disk in drive A?

7. When do you issue the following command?

```
C:\> FORMAT  A: /4 <ENTER>
```

8. What is the function of the DISKCOMP command?

9. If two disks contain the same files, why can DISKCOMP still discover differences?

10. What is the function of the FASTOPEN command?

11. Under DOS 4, what CONFIG.SYS INSTALL entry installs support for 50 files for the disk in drive C?

12. If you are using DOS 5 or later, what is the LOADHIGH command to invoke FASTOPEN, providing support for 50 files on drive C?

13. What is the function of the SYS command?

Key Points

Allocation Units

Each time DOS allocates space on disk for a file, it does so by using an allocation unit's worth of disk space. An allocation unit contains two or more sectors. By grouping sectors within allocation units, DOS makes sure your file is contained in adjoining sectors, which improves disk performance.

FORMAT /S

The FORMAT /S switch directs FORMAT to create a bootable DOS disk by copying the DOS hidden files and COMMAND.COM to the target disk. The following FORMAT command, for example, formats the floppy disk in drive A as a bootable disk:

continues . . .

```
C:\> FORMAT A: /S <ENTER>
```

FORMAT /4

The FORMAT /4 switch directs DOS to format a 360Kb floppy disk in a 1.2-megabyte floppy disk drive. Without the /4 switch, FORMAT will attempt to format the disk as a 1.2-megabyte floppy disk and fail. The following command formats a 360Kb disk in a 1.2Mb drive:

```
C:\> FORMAT  A:  /4 <ENTER>
```

FORMAT /V:label

The FORMAT /V switch directs DOS to use the disk label specified for the target disk instead of prompting you to enter a volume label. The following FORMAT command uses /V to assign a disk volume label named BUDGET:

```
C:\> FORMAT  A:  /V:BUDGET <ENTER>
```

The DISKCOMP Command

The DISKCOMP command compares two floppy disks on a sector-by-sector basis. If differences exist between the two disks, DISKCOMP will display the sides and track numbers that differ. DISKCOMP is useful for verifying that a DISKCOPY command was

continues . . .

successful. The following command directs DISKCOMP to compare
the floppy disk in drive A to the disk in drive B:

```
C:\> DISKCOMP  A:  B: <ENTER>
```

The FASTOPEN Command

The FASTOPEN command directs DOS to track frequently used
files on disk, allowing them to be opened much more quickly during
subsequent DOS commands. FASTOPEN supports only hard disks.
The following FASTOPEN command directs FASTOPEN to track 50
files on drive C:

```
C:\> FASTOPEN  C:=50 <ENTER>
```

If you are using DOS 4, you can invoke FASTOPEN at system
startup by using the CONFIG.SYS INSTALL entry. If you are using
DOS 5 or later, you can instead use the LOADHIGH command.

The SHARE Command

The SHARE command installs memory-resident software for file
sharing on systems connected to a local area network. If your system
is not part of a local area network, do not execute the SHARE
command. If you are using DOS 4 and you need to use the SHARE
command, place an INSTALL entry in your CONFIG.SYS file to do
so. If you are using DOS 5 or later and require SHARE, use the
LOADHIGH command to invoke SHARE.

continues . . .

Key Points
(continued)

The SYS Command

The SYS command transfers the hidden files required by DOS to boot to a target disk. The following SYS command copies the DOS system files to the disk in drive A:

```
C:\> SYS  A:  <ENTER>
```

The DEFRAG Command

If you are using DOS 6, you can use the DEFRAG command to defragment the files on your disk quickly. In general, you invoke DEFRAG from the DOS prompt as follows:

```
C:\> DEFRAG <ENTER>
```

CHAPTER

DOS File and Disk Recovery

As you have learned, an errant DEL command can quickly erase all of the files in a directory. Likewise, an errant FORMAT command can quickly destroy a disk. To help minimize the amount of information such operations can destroy, DOS 5 introduced the MIRROR, UN-DELETE, and UNFORMAT commands. If you are using DOS 6, the MIRROR command no longer exists, but as you will learn, much of its functionality has moved to UNDELETE. This chapter examines the steps you must perform to recover your files and disks using these commands. In addition, the chapter discusses the DOS 6 MSAV anti-virus utility.

Using the DOS 5 MIRROR Command

If you are using DOS 5, the MIRROR command loads memory-resident software and stores key information on your disk that can be used by both the UNFORMAT and UNDELETE commands. To better understand how MIRROR works, let's first look at how MIRROR assists UNFORMAT. Remember, DOS 6 does not support the MIRROR command.

Mirroring Key Disk Information

To keep track of which files are stored in which sectors on your disk, DOS uses a table of values called the *file allocation table*. In general, each entry in the table tells DOS if a section of the disk is in use, available for use, or marked by FORMAT as unusable because of a damaged location. The file allocation table essentially serves as the road map DOS follows to locate your files. DOS stores the file allocation table on your disk.

One of the steps FORMAT performs when it prepares a disk for use is to create a new file allocation table for the disk, overwriting an existing table if one was present. FORMAT does not, however, overwrite the information the disk contains. The following illustration shows a disk containing a file allocation table and data:

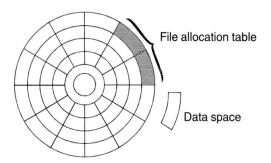

File allocation table

Data space

If you format the disk, FORMAT will overwrite the existing file allocation table. However, as shown here, FORMAT will leave the disk's data unchanged:

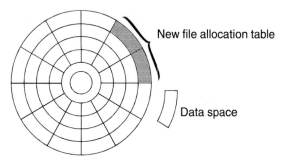

New file allocation table

Data space

Unfortunately, because the file allocation table that describes which pieces of data on the disk belong to which file is gone, DOS has no way of using the data.

The MIRROR command makes a copy of the file allocation table and the disk's root directory and stores the copy in the disk's data section, as shown here:

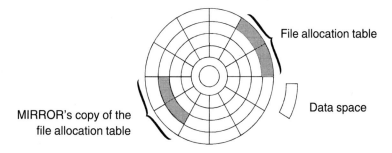

File allocation table

Data space

MIRROR's copy of the
file allocation table

If you accidentally format the disk, MIRROR's copy remains on the disk, as shown here:

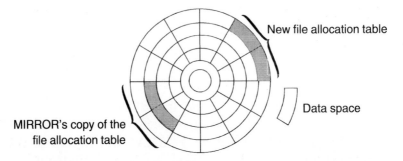

If you invoke the UNFORMAT command, UNFORMAT will use MIRROR's file to rebuild the disk's file allocation table and root directory. If the disk does not contain MIRROR's file, UNFORMAT may be able to recover some or all of your files, but there is no guarantee.

Keep in mind that each time you create a new file or increase or decrease the size of an existing file, DOS updates the file allocation table to note the change. When DOS changes the file allocation table, its values will no longer match those stored in MIRROR's copy on disk. If you later need to unformat the disk, UNFORMAT will use MIRROR's outdated copy of the disk information. Although UNFORMAT can probably recover most of your disk, you may lose some information.

The more often you invoke the MIRROR command, the more current your copy of the disk information will be. Most people place the MIRROR command in their AUTOEXEC.BAT file to ensure that it runs each time their system starts. MIRROR stores the disk information in the file MIRROR.FIL.

Saving File Deletion Information

In addition to storing the file allocation table information, MIR-ROR can also track information about each file you delete. If you later need to undelete one or more files, the UNDELETE command can use this information.

To better understand how you can undelete files, you need to understand how DOS stores files on your disk. To begin, every file has one or more entries in the file allocation table that tell DOS where the file actually resides on the disk. Also, each file has a directory entry that contains the file's name, size, attributes, and date and time stamp, as well as the file's starting entry in the file allocation table.

When you delete a file by using DEL, DOS doesn't actually erase the file's information from the disk. Instead, DOS marks each of the file's file allocation table entries as available for use by other files. Likewise, DOS marks the file's directory entry as available for reuse by assigning the following special character to the first letter of the file's name: σ. If you delete a file named FILENAME.EXT, for example, DOS would assign the special character to the first letter of the name, resulting in σILENAME.EXT. When DIR encounters this special character in a directory entry, DIR knows the file has been deleted, and therefore DOS does not display the entry.

When you invoke MIRROR's file delete tracking, MIRROR will record information about each file you erase, including the file's file allocation table entries and its directory entry. If you accidentally delete a needed file, the UNDELETE command can use MIRROR's file delete tracking information to undelete the file.

 Note If you accidentally delete one or more files, do not store any information on your disk until you successfully undelete the file. As you just read, when you delete a file, DOS marks the file's file allocation table entries available for reuse. If you store another file on your disk, DOS may use the entries, overwriting the information stored for the file you wanted to undelete. Once the file's information is overwritten, UN-DELETE cannot recover the file.

Putting MIRROR to Use

If you invoke MIRROR as follows, MIRROR will copy the current contents of your disk's file allocation table and root directory:

```
C:\> MIRROR <ENTER>
```

MIRROR will not, however, install its file delete tracking software.

To track file deletions, you must invoke MIRROR with the /T switch. The following MIRROR command uses /T to direct MIRROR to track up to 500 deleted files on drive C:

```
C:\> MIRROR /TC-500 <ENTER>
```

When you invoke this command, MIRROR will display the following:

```
Creates an image of the system area.
Drive C being processed.
The MIRROR process was successful.
Deletion-tracking software being installed.
The following drives are supported:
Drive C - 500 files saved.

Installation complete.
```

The first three lines of output tell you MIRROR successfully copied the system information (the file allocation table and root directory) for use by UNFORMAT. The last four lines tell you MIRROR has successfully installed its file delete tracking software.

If you are using DOS 5, place the preceding MIRROR command in your AUTOEXEC.BAT file to enable file delete tracking.

Recovering a Disk with UNFORMAT

The best way to fully understand the unformat process is to try using it. Place an unused floppy disk in drive A and format the disk, as shown here:

```
C:\> FORMAT A: <ENTER>
```

After the FORMAT command is completed, create the following directories:

```
C:\> MKDIR   A:PROGRAMS <ENTER>
C:\> MKDIR   A:KEYDATA <ENTER>
```

Next, copy the following file to the disk:

```
C:\> COPY   CON   A:FILENAME.EXT <ENTER>
This is a very important <ENTER>
report or letter. <ENTER>
^Z <ENTER>
     1 File(s) copied

C:\>
```

Next, format the disk.

```
C:\> FORMAT A: <ENTER>
```

When the format operation completes, a directory listing of the disk reveals the following:

```
C:\> DIR A: <ENTER>
 Volume in drive A has no label
 Volume Serial Number is 3452-15E6
 Directory of A:\

File not found
```

Next, use the following UNFORMAT command to recover the disk:

```
C:\> UNFORMAT A: <ENTER>
```

UNFORMAT will prompt you to place the disk you want to recover into drive A, as shown here:

```
Insert disk to rebuild in drive A:
and press ENTER when ready.
```

When you press ENTER, UNFORMAT will display output similar to the following:

```
Insert disk to rebuild in drive A:
and press ENTER when ready.


Restores the system area of your disk by using the image file created by the MIRROR command.


    WARNING !!        WARNING !!


This command should be used only to recover from the inadvertent use of
the FORMAT command or the RECOVER command. Any other use of the UNFORMAT
command may cause you to lose data!  Files modified since the MIRROR image
file was created may be lost.


Searching disk for MIRROR image.


The last time the MIRROR or FORMAT command was used was at 14:31 on 04-15-93.


The MIRROR image file has been validated.


Are you sure you want to update the system area of your drive A (Y/N)?
```

As you can see, UNFORMAT prompts you to determine if you want to restore the disk's previous contents. Type **Y** and UNFORMAT will rebuild the disk, displaying the following:

```
The system area of drive A has been rebuilt.

You may need to restart the system.
```

A directory listing of the disk reveals that UNFORMAT was successful, as shown here:

```
C:\> DIR  A: <ENTER>

Volume in drive A has no label
 Volume Serial Number is 2244-0EE8
 Directory of A:\

PROGRAMS       <DIR>      09-15-91   2:30p
KEYDATA        <DIR>      09-15-91   2:30p
FILENAME EXT          45 09-15-91   2:30p
  3 file(s)              45 bytes
                     339968 bytes free
```

Understanding a Safe Format

Unless you tell it not to, the DOS 5 or later FORMAT command performs a *safe format* operation, meaning that it does not destroy the data stored on a disk and that it makes a copy of the root directory and file allocation tables.

When you use FORMAT to format a disk that already contains information, FORMAT will display the following message on your screen as it copies the unformat information:

```
Saving UNFORMAT information.
```

If the disk does not have enough available space to store the information, UNFORMAT will display the following message, telling you it is unable to store the unformat information and asking you if you want to continue the format operation:

```
Drive A Error Insufficient space for the MIRROR image file.
There was an error creating the format recovery file.
This disk cannot be unformatted.
Proceed with the Format (Y/N)?
```

When you create a MIRROR file in this way, FORMAT ensures you always have a current file from which UNFORMAT can rebuild your disk.

There may be times when you want FORMAT to completely overwrite a disk's data so another user cannot unformat the disk and access the information the disk contained. To perform such a format operation, include the /U switch in your FORMAT command. For more information on /U, refer to the Command Reference at the end of this book.

Undeleting Files with UNDELETE

The DOS UNDELETE command lets you undelete one or more previously erased files. If you are using DOS 5, UNDELETE provides you with two ways to undelete files. First, UNDELETE can use the file delete tracking information recorded by the MIRROR command. Because MIRROR records the name and disk location of each file you delete, using the file tracking information provides a very good way to successfully recover files. If file delete tracking software has not been active, however, UNDELETE can use a second technique, recovering files using only the information available from DOS.

If you are using DOS 6, UNDELETE can use a third technique called data sentry protection. When you use data sentry protection, UNDELETE makes a copy of every file you delete, placing the copy in a directory named SENTRY. Using data sentry protection, you are almost assured of a successful file recovery. Unfortunately, data sentry protection can consume considerable disk space depending on the size and number of files you delete.

Undeleting Files Using Only Information Available from DOS

As discussed, using only the information available from DOS to undelete files is the least reliable method. However, if you did not have file delete tracking active, it is your only choice. Assume, for example, that the current directory contains the files FILENAME.ONE and FILENAME.TWO, as shown here:

```
C:\SUBDIR> DIR <ENTER>

 Volume in drive C is DOS 6 DISK
 Volume Serial Number is 1967-6547
 Directory of C:\SUBDIR


 .               <DIR>      11-23-92   12:46p
 ..              <DIR>      11-23-92   12:46p
FILENAME ONE         51 11-23-92   12:46p
FILENAME TWO         22 11-23-92   12:46p
        4 file(s)             73 bytes
                       34934784 bytes free
```

The following DEL command will delete the two files:

```
C:\SUBDIR> DEL *.* /DOS <ENTER>
```

Using the following UNDELETE command you can attempt to undelete the deleted files in the current directory:

```
C:\SUBDIR> UNDELETE *.* /DOS <ENTER>
```

UNDELETE, in turn, will individually display informaton about each deleted file, asking you if you want to undelete the file, and if so, the first letter of the original file name. Given the two files FILENAME.ONE and FILENAME.TWO, the process becomes the following:

```
C:\SUBDIR> UNDELETE *.* /DOS <ENTER>

UNDELETE - A delete protection facility
Copyright (C) 1987-1993 Central Point Software, Inc.
All rights reserved.

Directory: C:\SUBDIR
File Specifications: *.*

   Delete Sentry control file not found.
```

```
        Deletion-tracking file not found.

        MS-DOS directory contains     2 deleted files.
        Of those,    2 files may be recovered.

    Using the MS-DOS directory method.

            ?ILENAME ONE    51 4-23-93 12:46p  ...A  Undelete (Y/N)?Y
             Please type the first character for ?ILENAME.ONE: F

    File successfully undeleted.

            ?ILENAME TWO    22 4-23-93 12:46p  ...A  Undelete (Y/N)?Y
             Please type the first character for ?ILENAME.TWO: F

    File successfully undeleted.
```

When you have to rely on only the information available from DOS, you have to specify the first letter of each file you undelete.

Undeleting Files Using File Delete Tracking

As you have read, file delete tracking is memory-resident software that records information about each file you delete. Specifically, the file delete tracking records the file's directory entry and locations where the file resided on disk. If you are using DOS 5, you can start file tracking using the MIRROR command's /T switch. For example, the following command enables file tracking on drive C.

```
C:\> MIRROR /TC-500  <ENTER>
```

In this case, MIRROR will record information for up to 500 deleted files.

If you are using DOS 6, you can enable file delete tracking using UNDELETE's /T switch. For example, the following command directs UNDELETE to track up to 500 deleted files on drive C.

```
C:\> UNDELETE /TC-500 <ENTER>
```

As before, assume the current directory contains the files FILENAME.ONE and FILENAME.TWO and that you delete the files. With file delete tracking active, UNDELETE knows the complete file name for each deleted file. Therefore, the UNDELETE process becomes the following:

```
C:\> UNDELETE *.* <ENTER>

UNDELETE - A delete protection facility
Copyright (C) 1987-1993 Central Point Software, Inc.
All rights reserved.

Directory: C:\SUBDIR
File Specifications: *.*

    Delete Sentry control file not found.
   Searching deletion-tracking file....
    Deletion-tracking file contains    2 deleted files.
   Of those,    2 files have all clusters available,
                0 files have some clusters available,
                0 files have no clusters available.

    MS-DOS directory contains    2 deleted files.
   Of those,    2 files may be recovered.

Using the Deletion-tracking method.

    Searching deletion-tracking file....
FILENAME TWO    22 4-23-93 12:46p  ...A  Deleted: 4-23-93 12:48p
All of the clusters for this file are available. Undelete (Y/N)?Y

File successfully undeleted.

    Searching deletion-tracking file....
FILENAME ONE    51 4-23-93 12:46p  ...A  Deleted: 4-23-93 12:48p
All of the clusters for this file are available. Undelete (Y/N)?Y

File successfully undeleted.
```

Most users will place either the previous MIRROR (DOS 5 users) or UNDELETE (DOS 6 users) commands in their AUTOEXEC.BAT files to ensure that file delete tracking is active each time their system starts.

Undeleting Files Using Data Sentry Protection

If you are using DOS 6, you can direct DOS to perform data sentry protection by invoking UNDELETE using the /S switch. For example, the following command enables data sentry protection for drive C:

```
C:\> UNDELETE /SC <ENTER>
```

Once again, using the files FILENAME.ONE and FILENAME.TWO, the undelete processing using data sentry protection becomes the following:

```
C:\> UNDELETE *.* <ENTER>

UNDELETE - A delete protection facility
Copyright (C) 1987-1993 Central Point Software, Inc.
All rights reserved.

Directory: C:\SUBDIR
File Specifications: *.*
   Searching Delete Sentry control file....
   Delete Sentry control file contains    2 deleted files.
   Searching deletion-tracking file....
   Deletion-tracking file contains    0 deleted files.
   Of those,    0 files have all clusters available,
                0 files have some clusters available,
                0 files have no clusters available.

   MS-DOS directory contains    2 deleted files.
   Of those,    0 files may be recovered.
Using the Delete Sentry method.
```

```
    Searching Delete Sentry control file....
FILENAME TWO  22 4-23-93 12:46p ...A  Deleted: 4-23-93 12:50p
This file can be 100% undeleted. Undelete (Y/N)?Y

File successfully undeleted.

    Searching Delete Sentry control file....
FILENAME ONE   51 4-23-93 12:46p ...A  Deleted: 4-23-93 12:50p
This file can be 100% undeleted. Undelete (Y/N)?Y

File successfully undeleted.
```

Using data sentry protection provides the most reliable data recovery, but at the cost of disk space. When you delete a file with data sentry protection active, DOS places a copy of the file in the SENTRY directory. Over time, the number of files in the SENTRY directory can become quite large and can consume considerable disk space. If you are sure you don't need to undelete any files, you can remove the files in the SENTRY directory by invoking UNDELETE with the /PURGE switch, as shown here:

```
C:\> UNDELETE  /PURGE <ENTER>
```

Deleted Files Can Be Overwritten

If you accidentally delete one or more files, do not store any more information on the disk until you undelete the files. If you store information, DOS may overwrite the data contained in the file you want to undelete. If you try to undelete a file whose contents have been overwritten, UNDELETE will display the following:

```
None of the clusters for this file are available.
The file cannot be recovered. Press any key to continue.
```

Virus Protection Using the DOS 6 MSAV Command

If you are using DOS 6, you should regularly invoke the MSAV command to examine your disk for computer viruses. The simplest way to use MSAV is to invoke it from the DOS prompt as shown here:

```
C:\> MSAV <ENTER>
```

MSAV will display its menu of options, as shown in Figure 30-1.

Using your keyboard arrow keys, highlight the Detect & Clean option and presss ENTER. MSAV will begin examining the files on the disk, as shown in Figure 30-2.

If MSAV encounters a virus, it will remove the infection and continue searching your files. When the operation is complete, MSAV will display summary information, as shown in Figure 30-3, that lists the number of files searched and the number of infections removed.

FIGURE 30-1   MSAV's main menu

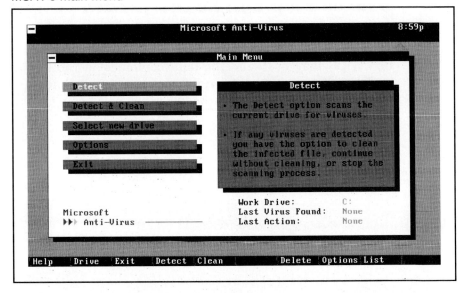

FIGURE
30-2
MSAV's Detect & Clean operation

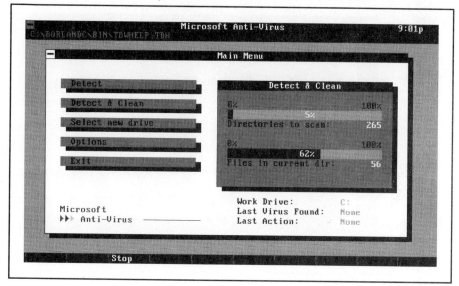

When you press ENTER, MSAV will redisplay its menu, from which you can select a second drive for examination or exit to DOS.

Working Within the Shell

If you need to undelete one or more files while you're working within the shell, press the TAB key until the shell highlights the program list. Next, select the Disk Utilities option. The shell will display the following options:

FIGURE
30-3 MSAV's summary information

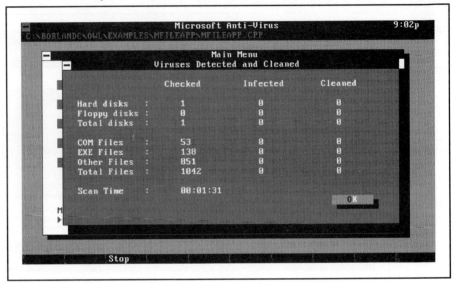

Highlight the UNDELETE option and press ENTER. The shell will display the following dialog box:

Type in the name of the file you want to undelete and press ENTER. The shell will invoke the UNDELETE command, which will function as shown throughout this chapter.

If you need to unformat a disk, use the File menu option to invoke the UNFORMAT command with the correct disk drive letter.

Practice

Use the following FORMAT command to prepare an unused floppy disk for use:

```
C:\> FORMAT A: <ENTER>
```

When FORMAT completes, create the following files on the disk:

```
C:\> COPY CON A:BUDGET.NTS <ENTER>
This is a budget file. <ENTER>
^Z <ENTER>
     1 File(s) copied

C:\> COPY CON A:HOMEWORK.TXT <ENTER>
This is a homework assignment. <ENTER>
^Z <ENTER>
     1 File(s) copied

C:\>
```

Repeat the FORMAT command:

```
C:\> FORMAT A: <ENTER>
```

When FORMAT completes, perform the following DIR command:

```
C:\> DIR A: <ENTER>
```

Invoke the UNFORMAT command to recover the disk's contents:

```
C:\> UNFORMAT A:  <ENTER>
```

When UNFORMAT completes, use the DIR command to verify the files have been recovered.

Delete the file BUDGET.NTS, as shown here:

```
C:\> DEL A:BUDGET.NTS  <ENTER>
```

Next, invoke UNDELETE to undelete the file. Because you have not selected file delete tracking for drive A, you must type in the first letter of the file's name to successfully undelete the file.

If you are using DOS 5, issue the following MIRROR command to enable file delete tracking for drive A:

```
C:\> MIRROR A:  /TA-25  <ENTER>
```

If you are using DOS 6, invoke UNDELETE with the /T switch to enable file delete tracking.

```
C:\> UNDELETE /TA-25  <ENTER>
```

Next, delete the file HOMEWORK.TXT:

```
C:\> DEL A:HOMEWORK.TXT  <ENTER>
```

Use the following UNDELETE command to recover the file:

```
C:\> UNDELETE A:*.*  <ENTER>
```

In this case, because file delete tracking was active, you didn't have to type the first letter of the file name. If you have not already done so, you should place a MIRROR or UNDELETE command in your AU-TOEXEC.BAT file to enable file delete tracking.

If you are using DOS 6, invoke the MSAV command to examine your disk for computer viruses.

```
C:\> MSAV <ENTER>
```

Each time you get a floppy disk from another user, you should use MSAV to immediately examine the disk.

Review

1. How is it possible for DOS to unformat a disk?
2. What happens when DEL deletes a file?
3. List two functions MIRROR provides.
4. Why should you not copy information to a disk containing files you want to undelete?
5. What is a safe format?
6. What is data sentry protection?
7. How do you invoke file delete tracking using DOS 6?

Key Points

The MIRROR Command

MIRROR is a DOS 5 command that copies a disk's file allocation table and root directory to a file named MIRROR.FIL that UNFORMAT can use to rebuild the disk following an accidental disk format operation. The more often you invoke MIRROR, the more current MIRROR's copy of your disk's key data will be. As a result, UNFORMAT will have a better chance of successfully recovering your disk.

In addition, MIRROR can install file delete tracking software that records information UNDELETE can use to recover an accidentally deleted file.

The UNFORMAT Command

The UNFORMAT command lets you rebuild a disk that has been accidentally formatted. If you are using DOS 5, UNFORMAT makes use of the file MIRROR.FIL (which contains a copy of the disk's file allocation table and root directory) created by the MIRROR command. The more current the contents of MIRROR's file, the more successful UNFORMAT will be in rebuilding the disk.

The UNDELETE Command

The UNDELETE command lets you undelete an accidentally deleted file. If you delete one or more files by mistake, do not store any information on your disk until you undelete the files. If you do, you may overwrite the deleted file's information, making it impossible for UNDELETE to recover the file.

The MSAV Command

If you are using DOS 6, the MSAV command lets you examine your disks for computer viruses. If MSAV encounters a virus, it will remove it from your disk. You should always use MSAV to immediately examine a floppy disk given to you by another user.

Advanced Shell
Concepts

639

hapter 6, "Getting Started with the DOS Shell," introduced you to the DOS 5 and 6 shell. Since that time, you have used the shell to perform a wide variety of tasks. This chapter examines the remaining shell topics and teaches you how to use the shell's Task Swapper to load several programs into memory at one time.

Customizing the Shell's Appearance

All of the shell-related screens presented in this book have shown the shell in graphics mode. The shell, however, lets you run it in text mode. If you are using a CGA monitor, the shell lets you select 25-line mode. If you have an EGA monitor, the shell lets you use 25- or 43-line mode. If you have a VGA monitor, you can use 25-, 43-, or 50-line mode. To change the current video mode, press ALT-O to select the Options menu, which is shown here:

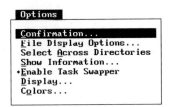

Next, select the Display option. The shell will display the following dialog box of video options:

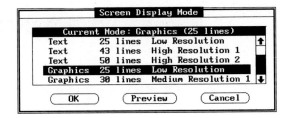

Highlight the option you desire and press ENTER; press ESC to cancel the dialog box.

In addition to letting you select text or graphics mode, the shell also lets you change the shell's current colors. From the Options menu, select the Colors option. The shell will display the following dialog box of available color options:

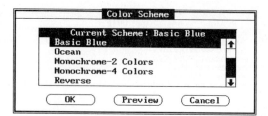

Using your keyboard arrow keys, you can highlight a color entry and press ENTER. If you want to know how a color will look, highlight the color name and press the TAB key until the shell highlights the Preview option. When you press ENTER, the shell will temporarily display the screen using the selected color.

If you like the current color, press the TAB key to select the OK option. The shell will use the new color. If you decide not to change the color, press the ESC key.

Searching Your Disk for a Specific File

As the number of files and directories on your disk increases, there may be times when you misplace a file. By using the File menu Search option, however, you can quickly locate the file. When you select the Search option, the shell will display the following dialog box:

Type in the name of the file you desire. If you are interested in a group of files, you can type in a wildcard combination. When you press ENTER, the shell will search your disk for the file, displaying the directory name of each matching file, as shown here:

From the list of files, you can select one or more files for a file operation. If you instead press the ESC key, the shell will remove the list. If the shell does not find a matching file, it will display a message stating so.

Customizing the File List

By default, the shell displays the name of every nonhidden and nonsystem file. In some cases you may want to restrict the type of file name displayed, possibly to only files with the TXT extension. To do so, select the Options menu File Display Options entry. The shell will display the dialog box shown in Figure 31-1.

The File Display Options dialog box

The *.* characters direct the shell to display every file. If you want to display only files with the TXT extension, for example, you would change the name entry to *.TXT. Note the other dialog box options. By pressing the TAB key, you can select the "Display hidden/system files" option. If you press the SPACEBAR, the shell will place an "X" next to the option, selecting it. When the option is selected, the shell displays files with the hidden or system attribute set, as well as all other files.

In a similar way, selecting the "Descending order" option directs the shell to display files sorted from highest to lowest. If you select the "Sort by" option, you can change the field in which the shell sorts your file list. By using your keyboard's UP ARROW and DOWN ARROW keys, you can select the field you desire. If you press ENTER, the shell will put your changes into effect. If you press ESC or select the Cancel option, the shell will leave your current settings unchanged.

Controlling the Directory Tree and File List

By default, the shell displays a single directory tree and file list, as well as the program list. As you have learned, the View menu Dual File List option lets you split the screen into two directory trees and file lists, as shown in Figure 31-2. When you display dual lists, the shell lets you select a different drive or directory for each list.

If you don't need to use options from the program list, you can increase the size of your directory tree and file list by selecting the View menu Single File List option. When you select this option, the shell will expand the size of the directory tree and file list, as shown in Figure 31-3.

Depending on your needs, you may want to list specifics about every file on your disk. To do so, select the View menu All Files option. The shell will display an alphabetical listing of your disk's files in the right half of your screen and specifics about the current file in the left half, as shown in Figure 31-4. To restore the shell to its original setting, select the View menu Program/File Lists option.

FIGURE 31-2

Displaying dual directory trees and file lists

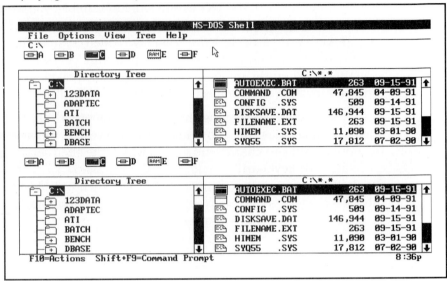

FIGURE 31-3

Displaying a single directory tree and file list

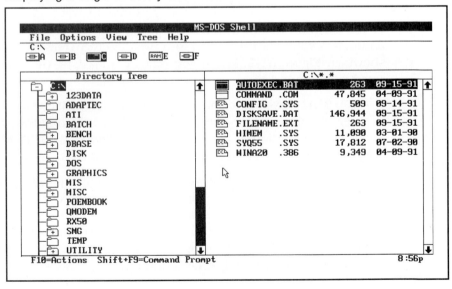

FIGURE
31-4

Using the All Files option

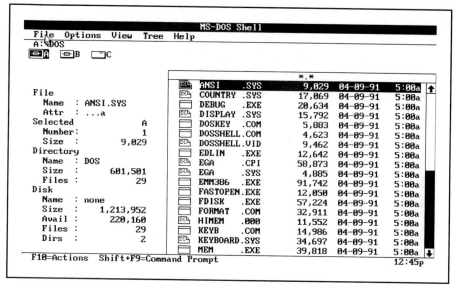

Associating a File Type to a Specific Program

As you have learned, by highlighting a file with the EXE, COM, or BAT extension and pressing ENTER, you direct the shell to run that command. In a similar way, the shell lets you associate files with a specific extension to a specific command. When you later highlight a file with a matching extension and press ENTER, the shell will automatically run the associated command, using the file selected. For example, you might associate files with the TXT extension to EDIT, the DOS editor. When you later highlight a file with the TXT extension and press ENTER, the shell will run EDIT, letting you edit the file.

To associate a file type with a program, highlight a file with the desired extension and select the File menu Associate option. The shell will display the following dialog box:

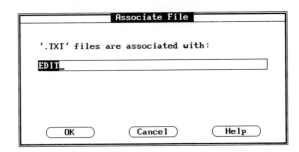

Type in the program name to which you want to associate the file type and press ENTER.

Creating and Working with Program Groups

A *program group* is two or more related programs, such as your word processor, spell checker, and thesaurus. If you examine the shell's program list, you will find the Disk Utilties program group within the shell's Main group. In the case of Disk Utilities, the group contains several disk-related utility commands. In this section, you will learn how to create your own program group entries.

If you have a program you use on a regular basis, you may find it most convenient to add the program entry to the Main group itself. If you have several related programs, however, you'll want to create a separate program group to organize your programs, much as you would store related files in a directory.

To add a program group, first select the shell's program list. Next, invoke the File menu. When the program list is selected, the shell changes the list of File menu options, as shown here:

Table 31-1 briefly describes each menu option.

To add a program group, select the File menu and choose the New option. The shell will display the following dialog box, asking you if you want to add a program item or program group:

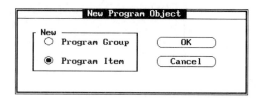

To add a program group, select the Program Group option and press ENTER or click the OK option using your mouse. The shell will display the dialog box shown in Figure 31-5, prompting you to type in the group specifics.

TABLE 31-1 Shell File Menu Options When the Program List Is Selected

Option	Function
New	Adds a new program or group entry to the current program group
Open	Displays the contents of the selected program group or starts a program
Copy	Copies a program entry into a specific program group
Delete	Removes an empty program group from within the current group or removes a program entry from a group
Properties	Specifies the characteristics of a program or program group
Reorder	Moves a program or group entry within the program group menu
Run	Lets you run a command by typing in the command name and its optional parameters
Exit	Exits the DOS shell to the DOS prompt

FIGURE
31-5

The Add Group dialog box

```
                          ┌───────────────┐
                          │   Add Group   │
                          ┌───────────────────────────┐
                          │                           │
                          │ Required                  │
                          │                           │
                          │  Title . . . .  ┌────────┐ │
                          │                 └────────┘ │
                          │ Optional                  │
                          │                           │
                          │  Help Text . .  ┌────────┐ │
                          │                 └────────┘ │
                          │  Password   . .  ┌───────┐ │
                          │                  └───────┘ │
                          │                           │
                          │   (  OK  )  ( Cancel )  ( Help ) │
                          └───────────────────────────┘
```

The dialog box Title option lets you specify a title containing up to 23 characters that will appear within the group menu and as the group title bar when the group is open.

The Help Text option lets you specify up to 255 characters of online help the shell will display about the group should a user highlight the group and press F1. If you type in the text as sentences, the shell will later format the text to fit within the dialog box. If you want to control line breaks within the text, insert the caret character (^) immediately followed by the letter "m" each time you want the shell to perform a carriage return and linefeed operation.

The Password option lets you specify a password up to 20 characters long that the user must type to access the group. Do not rely on the password as a security measure. Instead, you should use the password only to prevent another user from adding or deleting program entries within the group.

After you complete the group fields, press ENTER or use your mouse to click the OK option.

Editing an Existing Program Group

Should you later need to change a group's title, help text, or password, highlight the group and select the Properties option from the File menu.

If the group has a password, the shell will display a dialog box asking you to enter the password. If you type the correct password, the shell will display a dialog box similar to the following, which allows you to edit the group fields:

```
┌──────────────────── Program Item Properties ────────────────────┐
│                                                                  │
│  Program Title . . . . [Command Prompt_                       ]  │
│                                                                  │
│  Commands  . . . . . . [COMMAND                               ]  │
│                                                                  │
│  Startup Directory . . [                                      ]  │
│                                                                  │
│  Application Shortcut Key      [                              ]  │
│                                                                  │
│  [ ] Pause after exit          Password . .  [             ]     │
│    ( OK )      ( Cancel )     ( Help )      ( Advanced... )       │
└──────────────────────────────────────────────────────────────────┘
```

To change a field, click the field using your mouse or press the TAB key to highlight the field. Next, edit the text as desired. Select OK to save your changes.

Removing a Program Group

If you delete the programs associated with a group from your disk, you will also want to remove the group entry from the program list. Before you can remove a program group, you must first remove each program entry within the group. To do so, select the group and highlight an entry. Next, invoke the File menu and choose the Delete option. The shell will display a dialog box similar to the following, asking you to confirm the deletion:

```
┌──────────────────── Delete Item ────────────────────┐
│                                                      │
│                                                      │
│     1. Delete this item.                             │
│     2. Do not delete this item.                      │
│       ( _ OK )        ( Cancel )        ( Help )     │
└──────────────────────────────────────────────────────┘
```

Select the dialog box option 1 to delete the entry. Repeat this process for each program entry in the group. Next, press ESC to exit the program group to the next higher level. Select the File menu Delete option. The shell will display a dialog box asking you to confirm the deletion. Select option 1 to delete the group. If the group has a password, the shell will prompt you to enter the password before it removes the group.

Changing the Order of Group Items

For convenience, you probably want to place your most commonly used program and group entries at the top of the group list. To move an entry, highlight the entry and select the File menu Reorder option. Next, highlight the entry in the list before which you want to move the program or group and press ENTER. You must repeat this process for each entry you wish to move.

Creating and Working with Program Entries

Just as there will be times when you want to create program groups, there may also be times when you want to add an entry to a group. For example, you might want to add an Unformat option to the Disk Utilities group.

To add a program item to a group, select the desired group, invoke the File menu, and choose the New option. The shell will display a dialog box asking you if you want to add a program or group item. Select the Program Item option. The shell will display the following dialog box, prompting you to enter the program item information:

```
┌────────────────────── Add Program ──────────────────────┐
│                                                          │
│  Program Title . . . . [                              ]  │
│                                                          │
│  Commands  . . . . . . [                              ]  │
│                                                          │
│  Startup Directory . . [                              ]  │
│                                                          │
│  Application Shortcut Key    [                       ]   │
│                                                          │
│  [X] Pause after exit     Password . . [            ]    │
│     ( OK )      ( Cancel )     ( Help )    ( Advanced... )│
└──────────────────────────────────────────────────────────┘
```

The Program Title option lets you specify up to 23 characters that will appear in the group menu as the entry's title. In the case of the Unformat example, your title might simply be Unformat.

The Commands option lets you specify commands the shell needs to issue for this entry. If the shell needs to perform two or more commands, such as first selecting a specific directory and then running the program, separate the commands with a semicolon. The number of characters in the commands can total 255. If one of the commands is a DOS batch file, use the CALL command to invoke it. In the case of the Unformat command, you might enter the command UNFORMAT %1. The %1 is called a *replaceable parameter.* When it encounters the %1, the shell will display a dialog box asking the user to enter the desired value. In this way, the user can type in the disk drive desired.

The Startup Directory option lets you specify a directory name you want the shell to select as the current directory before the program runs. If you don't specify a directory, the shell uses the current directory.

The Application Shortcut Key option lets you specify a hot-key combination that directs the Task Swapper (discussed in "Using the Task Swapper" later in this chapter) to automatically select the program if the program is present in the Active Task List. To select a hot key, hold down the SHIFT, ALT, or CTRL key and press a key. If you press the SHIFT key and F10 for example, the dialog box will display the hot key as "Shift+F10." The following key combinations are reserved by the shell:

CTRL-C	CTRL-[	SHIFT-CTRL-M	SHIFT-CTRL-[
CTRL-M	CTRL-5*	SHIFT-CTRL-I	SHIFT-CTRL-5*
CTRL-I	CTRL-H	SHIFT-CTRL-H	

*Indicates the numeric keypad number 5.

The "Pause after exit" option directs the shell to display a message asking the user to press any key to continue when the program ends, before returning to the shell. With this option disabled, you may not be able to view the program's last screenful of output before your screen redisplays the shell.

The Password option lets you specify a password of up to 20 characters that a user must enter before running the program. As discussed, with program group passwords, do not rely on the password for security. Instead, use a password only to prevent a user from changing one of the program entry's properties.

For most programs, the information you specify in this dialog box will be enough to successfully run the program. As such, you can press ENTER or click the OK option to place the entry in the program list. If you want to specify online help text or the program's memory requirements, select the Advanced option. The shell will display the following dialog box:

```
┌──────────────────────────┤ Advanced ├──────────────────────────┐
│                                                                │
│  Help Text      └                                          ┐  │
│                                                                │
│  Conventional Memory   KB Required   [              ]          │
│                                                                │
│  XMS Memory  KB Required  [          ]    KB Limit  [       ]  │
│                                                                │
│  Video Mode   ◉ Text      Reserve Shortcut Keys [ ] ALT+TAB    │
│               ○ Graphics                        [ ] ALT+ESC    │
│  [ ] Prevent Program Switch                     [ ] CTRL+ESC   │
│         (    OK    )        ( Cancel )         (  Help  )      │
└────────────────────────────────────────────────────────────────┘
```

The Help Text option lets you specify up to 255 characters of online help. The shell will display the help text when the user highlights the program entry and presses F1. If you type in the help text as sentences, the shell will later format the text to best fit within the help dialog box. If you want to control line breaks within the text, insert a caret character (^) immediately followed by the letter "m" each time you want the shell to perform a carriage return and linefeed operation.

The Conventional Memory KB Required option lets you specify the minimum amount of conventional memory, in kilobytes, the program requires before the Task Swapper can run the program. The default value is 128Kb. The XMS Memory KB Required option lets you specify the minimum amount of extended memory the program must have before the Task Swapper can run it. The default value is 0. The XMS Memory KB Limit option specifies the maximum amount of extended memory, in kilobytes, the program can use. The default value is 384Kb or, if the system has less than 384Kb, the amount of the extended memory.

When the Task Swapper changes from one active task to another, the Swapper must save the current task's screen display. The Video Mode option controls how much memory the Swapper must reserve to store the screen display. Unless you are using a CGA monitor, select text mode for all programs. If you are using a CGA monitor and the Task Swapper does not correctly restore your screen, select graphics mode.

By default, pressing ALT-ESC or CTRL-ESC directs the Task Swapper to either cycle through active tasks or display the Active Task List. If you have a program whose execution you don't want interrupted, select the Prevent Program Switch option. When you select this option, the only way to return to the shell when the program runs is to end the program.

The Task Swapper uses the ALT-TAB, ALT-ESC, and CTRL-ESC key combinations to cycle through active tasks or to select the Active Task List. If your program also uses one of these key combinations, you must reserve the key for the program's use. When you reserve a key combination, the Task Swapper will not respond to that key combination when the program is running.

Editing a Program Group Entry

If you need to change a program entry's commands, online help, or an advanced option used by the Task Swapper, highlight the program entry and choose the File menu Properties option. The shell will display a dialog box allowing you make your changes. After you do so, select OK to save your changes.

Copying a Program Entry to a New Group

If you accidentally place a program entry in the wrong group or later want to move an entry to a different group, highlight the entry and select the File menu Copy option. Next, display the group within which the item you want appears and press F2. The item will appear in the group's program list. Next, select the entry's original group and remove the entry by using the File menu's Delete option. The shell will display a dialog box asking you to confirm the deletion. Select option 1 to delete the entry.

Using the Task Swapper

DOS is a *single-task operating system,* which means it can run only one program at a time. Assume, for example, that you are creating a report with your word processor and you need to look up several values contained in a spreadsheet. If you are working from the DOS prompt, you must exit the word processor, run the spreadsheet program, and restart your word processor.

Using the DOS shell, however, you can load several programs into memory, quickly switching between the programs as your needs require. In the previous scenario, you could start both the word processor and the spreadsheet. When you switch from one program to another, DOS suspends the first program's execution until you select it again.

To load two or more programs into memory in this way, you must first enable *task swapping*. DOS refers to each program you run as a *task* and the process of changing from one program to another as task swapping. To enable task swapping, invoke the Options menu and select the Enable Task Swapper option. The shell will display a small diamond next to the menu option when task swapping is enabled.

Next, run the first program you want to load into memory. Press the CTRL-ESC key combination. DOS will suspend your program's execution, redisplaying the shell. As shown earlier in Figure 31-4, the shell divides your program list area in half. One half contains the program list and the second half contains the list of tasks currently loaded in memory. To select a task from the list, press the TAB key until the shell highlights the Active Task List. Next, using your keyboard's arrow keys, highlight the desired task and press ENTER.

To select an active task without using the task list, press the ALT-TAB key combination. The shell will cycle through each available task.

To remove a task from the Active Task List, select the program and end it as you normally would. If, for some reason, a program hangs and you cannot end it, highlight the task's name in the Active Task List and press the DEL key to remove it.

DOS will not let you exit the shell if you have active tasks. If you try to do so, the shell will display the following dialog box:

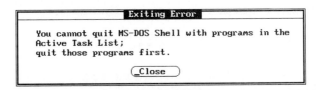

The Task Swapper exists to let you quickly switch from one commonly used program to another. If you try to load too many programs, you will eventually run out of memory and the shell will display the following dialog box:

If this message appears, remove one or more tasks and then try to load the new task.

Practice

If you are using an EGA or VGA, experiment with the shell's 43- or 50-line display mode, using the Options menu Display option. Next, using the Options menu Colors option, preview the available colors. If you find a color combination you like, press ENTER to select it.

Press ALT-F to invoke the File menu and choose the Search option. When the shell displays the dialog box prompting you to enter a file name, type ***.BAT** and press ENTER. The shell will display a list of every batch file on your disk.

Next, enable task swapping, using the Options menu Enable Task Swapper option. Select the DOS directory as the current directory. Highlight the file name EDIT.COM and press ENTER. After EDIT displays its editing screen, press CTRL-ESC to return to the shell. Highlight the file HELP.EXE and press ENTER. When HELP displays its first screen, press CTRL-ESC.

Press the ALT-TAB key combination to cycle through the available tasks. Exit EDIT by using the File menu Exit option. Next, select the HELP task. Let the program complete, returning control to the shell.

Review

1. What does it mean to associate files?
2. What is a program group?
3. What is the Task Swapper?
4. Why won't DOS let you exit the shell while active tasks exist?
5. List the ways to switch from one active task to another.

Key Points

Advanced Shell Topics

The DOS 5 and 6 shell can be modified in several important ways to make it more powerful and easy to use. You can change the colors of the screen display and, depending on your type of monitor, you can choose from among several different screen resolutions in text mode. You can choose among several different combinations of the display of file and program lists.

Just as you can choose the icon of an executable file (COM, EXE, or BAT), you can also associate a data file type (such as DOC or TXT) with an executable program, so that choosing the file opens both the program and the file.

Program groups are groups of related programs. You can add or remove programs to and from an existing group, move programs from one group to another, create new program groups, and delete program groups. You can also specify online help text for the entries in your groups.

The DOS 5 and 6 shell allows task swapping, enabling you to switch between several applications without having to close and reopen each. There are several ways of switching between the applications on the Active Task List, and you can add and remove tasks to and from the Active Task List.

DOS 6 System Commands

DOS 6 provides several new utility commands that let you double your hard disk's storage capacity, easily exchange files between a notebook computer and desktop computer, control the PC's power consumption, and use the network facilities provided with Windows for Workgroups. This chapter examines the DOS 6 DBLSPACE, INTERLNK, INTERSVR, POWER, and NET commands. If you are not using DOS 6, read through the discussion of these utilities. You will probably find that these utilities are reason enough to upgrade to DOS 6.

Using DBLSPACE to Increase Your Disk's Storage Capacity

The DOS 6 DBLSPACE command compresses the files stored on your hard disk into compact form that saves disk space. In short, DBLSPACE lets you double your disk capacity. If you are using a 200Mb hard disk, for example, running DBLSPACE might increase the disk's storage capacity to 400Mb! Unlike other compression techniques, which require you to constantly compress and decompress files as you use them, DBLSPACE's compression is transparent to your work with DOS. As you create, edit, rename, and delete files (using the same commands you've always worked with) the files remain in their compressed format. As a result, DBLSPACE doubles the storage capacity of your hard disk without impacting your work.

Putting DBLSPACE to Work

After you install DOS 6, you need to invoke DBLSPACE from the DOS prompt to compress your disk. Before you invoke DBLSPACE, however, you should first back up all of the files on your disk using MSBACKUP, just in case. After the backup operation completes, invoke DBLSPACE from the DOS prompt as shown here:

```
C:\> DBLSPACE <ENTER>
```

DBLSPACE will display the introductory screen shown here:

```
Microsoft DoubleSpace Setup


Welcome to DoubleSpace Setup.
The Setup program for DoubleSpace frees space on  your hard
disk by compressing the existing files on the disk.

Setup also installs the DoubleSpace device driver to manage
the compressed data.

  o To set up DoubleSpace now, press Enter.
  o To learn more about DoubleSpace Setup, press F1.
  o To quit Setup without installing DoubleSpace, press F3.

ENTER=Continue  F1=Help  F3=Exit
```

Press ENTER to continue the DBLSPACE operation. DBLSPACE will display the menu of options as shown here:

```
Microsoft DoubleSpace Setup


There are two ways to run Setup:
Use Express Setup if you want DoubleSpace Setup to compress
drive C and determine the compression settings for you.

This is the easiest way to install DoubleSpace.
Use Custom Setup if you are an experienced user who wants to
specify the compression settings and drive configuration
yourself.

   ┌─────────────────────────────────────────┐
   │   Express Setup (recommended)           │
   │          Custom Setup                   │
   └─────────────────────────────────────────┘

To accept the selection, press ENTER.
To change the selection, press the UP or DOWN ARROW key
until the item you want is selected, and then press ENTER.

ENTER=Continue  F1=Help  F3=Exit
```

Choose the Express installation. DBLSPACE will display specifics about your disk and information describing the amount of time the compression will require, as shown here:

```
Microsoft DoubleSpace Setup

DoubleSpace is ready to compress drive C. This will take 16
minutes.
Note : During this process, DoubleSpace will restart your
         computer to enable the DoubleSpace device driver.

To compress this drive, press C.
To return to the previous screen, press ESC.

 C=Continue  F1=Help  F3=Exit  Esc=Previous screen
```

Press C to continue the compression. DBLSPACE will first run the CHKDSK command to ensure your disk's file allocation tables contain valid entries. DBLSPACE will then make temporary changes to your AUTOEXEC.BAT file and will restart your system. After your system restarts, DBLSPACE continues the disk compression. The amount of time the compression operation requires will depend on the number and size of files on your disk. For larger disks, the amount of time the compression consumes may reach two hours or more. After the compression completes, DBLSPACE will run the DOS 6 DEFRAG command to optimize the newly compressed disk. When DEFRAG completes, DBLSPACE will display a summary screen, as shown here:

```
Microsoft DoubleSpace Setup

DoubleSpace has finished compressing drive C.
     Free space before compression:  32.4 MB
     Free space after compression:  178.7 MB
     Compression ratio:              2.0 to 1
     1 time to compress:             2 hours
DoubleSpace has created a new drive H that contains 5.9 MB
of uncompressed space. This space has been set aside for
files that must remain uncompressed.
```

```
To exit from DoubleSpace and restart your computer, press
ENTER.

ENTER=Continue    F1=Help
```

Note the capacity of the compressed disk. Press ENTER to restart your system. You can now use your compressed disk just as you previously used drive C.

Understanding the Compressed and Uncompressed Disks

When you use DBLSPACE to compress your disk, DBLSPACE conceptually divides your disk into two parts. DBLSPACE creates a compressed volume that consumes most of your disk space, as well as an uncompressed volume. The uncompressed volume serves two functions. First, some applications must store information in an uncompressed format. One of the best examples of such an application is the Windows permanent swap file. Second, and most important, DOS uses the uncompressed volume to boot. Here's how. When your system first starts, the uncompressed disk is actually your computer's drive C. Your compressed drive does not yet exist. During the startup process, DOS creates a drive letter and assigns your uncompressed drive to it. DOS then

TABLE 32-1   Files DOS Stores on the Uncompressed Disk

Filename	Contents
IO.SYS	The initial DOS boot code and input/output drivers
MSDOS.SYS	The MS-DOS operating system kernel
DBLSPACE.BIN	The compression software used to manage your compressed disk
DBLSPACE.000	The compressed disk's data
DBLSPACE.INI	DBLSPACE configuration and initialization specifics

assigns your compressed disk to drive C, and processes the CONFIG.SYS and AUTOEXEC.BAT files that reside on the compressed disk. DOS places the five files listed in Table 32-1 on your uncompressed disk.

The file named DBLSPACE.000 actually contains the data stored on your compressed disk. In other words, there really isn't a compressed disk. Instead DOS compresses all of the information, storing the compressed data in a file. DOS then makes the file appear as a disk volume.

The DBLSPACE.SYS Device Driver

If you examine your CONFIG.SYS file, you might find a DEVICEHIGH entry for the DBLSPACE.SYS device driver. If DOS encounters the DBLSPACE.SYS entry with a /MOVE switch, DOS will move the driver DBLSPACE.BIN (loaded into conventional memory at startup) to an upper memory block. If your CONFIG.SYS file does not contain a DBLSPACE.SYS entry, you will still have full access to your compressed data. DOS, however, will leave the driver DBLSPACE.BIN in conventional memory.

Using INTERLNK and INTERSVR

If you are using a laptop or notebook computer, there are probably times when you need to exchange files between your smaller system and your desktop PC. To make it easier to exchange information between two systems, DOS 6 provides the INTERLNK and INTERSVR commands. Using these two commands and connecting the computers over serial or parallel ports, two computers can quickly exchange files or share a disk or printer.

Working with Clients and Servers

When you use the DOS 6 INTERLNK and INTERSVR commands, one system is a *server* and the second is a *client*. The server is typically the desktop computer and is the system whose disk and printers can be shared by the second computer, or the client. The server computer runs the DOS 6 INTERSVR command, while the client runs INTERLNK.

When you connect two computers using INTERSVR and INTERLNK, the server computer's disks and printers become available to the client. The client accesses the devices using a drive letter or printer name. For example, assume, as shown in Figure 32-1, the server has a printer attached to LPT1, and the drives A, B, and C. Likewise, assume the client has drives A, B, and C.

After you connect the computers, as shown in Figure 32-2, the client would access the server's disk drives using the drive letters D, E, and F. In addition, the client could access the server's printer using the device name LPT2.

 Note If the client's logical drive letters (in this example, D, E, and F) go beyond the DOS default of E, make sure the client has a LASTDRIVE statement (in this case, LASTDRIVE=F) in its CONFIG.SYS that allows it to recognize those letters.

Installing the INTERLNK Device Driver

The client computer connects to the server by running the INTERLNK command. Before a client can invoke INTERLNK, however, the client

 FIGURE 32-1 Server and client disk drive and printer names

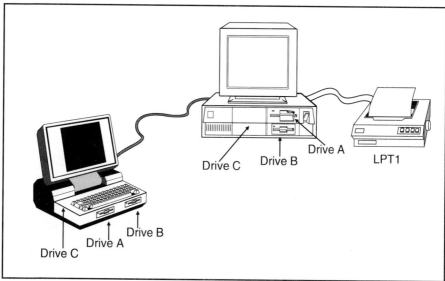

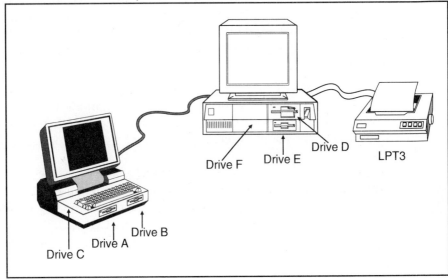

FIGURE
32-2

Client remote disk and printer names

must first install the INTERLNK device driver using the CONFIG.SYS DEVICE= entry. The format of the INTERLNK entry is as follows:

```
DEVICE=C:\DOS\INTERLNK.EXE [/DRIVES:n] [/NOPRINTER]
[/COM[:] [n|Port] [/LPT[:][n|Port] [/AUTO]
[/NOSCAN] [/LOW] [/BAUD:Rate] [/V]
```

The /DRIVES:n switch specifies the number of server disk drives the client can access. The default is 3. If you specify 0, the client only accesses server printers. The /NOPRINTER switch prevents the client from using the server's printers. The /COM switch specifies the client serial port through which the connection is made. You can specify a port number, such as /COM:1, or a port address, such as /COM:3F8. The /LPT switch specifies the client parallel port through which the connection is made. You can specify a port number such as /LPT:1, or you can specify a port address, such as /LPT:378. The /AUTO switch directs DOS to leave the driver installed in memory only if the driver establishes a connection when the system starts. In contrast, the /NOSCAN switch loads the driver, directing the driver not to establish a connection during startup. The /LOW switch loads the driver into conventional memory. By default, the driver uses the upper memory area. The /BAUD switch specifies the communication speed for serial port connections. Valid rates include 9600, 19200, 38400, 57600, and 115200 bps. The default baud rate is 115200. Finally, the /V switch reduces possible PC timer conflicts during serial port connections. Use /V if one of the systems hangs during file or printer operations.

The following DEVICEHIGH entry loads the INTERLNK driver for serial communication through COM1:

```
DEVICEHIGH=C:\DOS\INTERLNK.EXE   /COM:1
```

After you place the entry in CONFIG.SYS and restart your system, INTERLNK is ready for use. Assuming your computer is connected to a server that is running INTERSVR, you can establish a connection by invoking INTERLNK as follows:

```
C:\> INTERLNK
```

If INTERLNK establishes a connection, it will display the following:

```
C:\> INTERLNK <ENTER>
    This Computer            Other Computer
      (Client)                  (Server)
    ------------        -------------------------
      D:     equals     A:
      E:     equals     C: (61Mb)   DOS 6
      LPT2: equals      LPT1:
      LPT3: equals      LPT2:
```

Using INTERSVR to Create a Server

Just as the client computer must invoke INTERLNK to perform a connection, the server computer must invoke INTERSVR. Unlike INTER-LNK, which requires a device driver, INTERSVR does not. The format of the INTERSVR command is as follows:

```
INTERSVR [Drive:]  [/X:Drive]  [/COM[:][n|Port]
[/LPT[:][n|Port]  [/Baud:Rate]  [/B]  [/V]  [/RCOPY]
```

If you specify a drive, INTERSVR will only allow the client to access that specific drive. By default, INTERSVR allows the client to access all drives. The /X switch lets you exclude access to a specific drive. For example, if you want the client to access all drives but drive C, you would use /X:C. The /COM switch specifies the server serial port through which the connection will be made. You can specify a port number, such as /COM:1, or a port address, such as /COM:3F8. The /LPT switch specifies the server parallel port through which the connection will be made. You can specify a port number as /LPT:1 or you can specify a port address, such as /LPT:378. The /BAUD switch specifies the communication speed for serial port connections. Valid rates include 9600, 19200, 38400, 57600, and 115200 bps. The /B switch directs the server to display its screen output in black and white. The /V switch reduces possible PC timer conflicts during serial port connections. Use /V if one of the systems hangs during file or printer operations. Finally, the /RCOPY switch directs INTERSVR to copy the files INTERLNK.EXE and INTERSVR.EXE to a remote computer using serial ports.

Unlike INTERLNK, which requires a device driver, you simply invoke INTERSVR from the DOS prompt. The following command invokes INTERSVR for a serial connection using COM1:

```
C:\> INTERSVR /COM:1 <ENTER>
```

INTERSVR will display the screen shown in Figure 32-3.

When INTERSVR is running, you cannot run other commands on the server. After the client has finished its file or printer operations, you can end INTERSVR by pressing the ALT-F4 keyboard combination.

DOS 6 Advanced Power Management

With the tremendous popularity of notebook and laptop computers, manufacturers have been trying to find ways to increase the computer's battery life. Intel and Microsoft have recently created the Advanced Power Management (APM) specification, which combines hardware and software to reduce the PC's power consumption during the computer's idle times. Because the APM specification is new, very few computers support

FIGURE 32-3   The INTERSVR connection screen

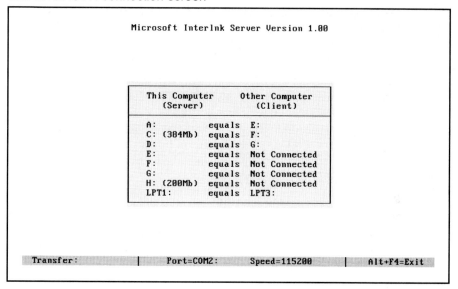

it yet. If you have a newer computer that does, you can use the DOS 6 POWER command to control its power consumption. Before you can invoke the POWER command, you must first install POWER.EXE within your CONFIG.SYS file. The format of the DEVICE entry to do so is as follows:

```
DEVICE=C:\DOS\POWER.EXE [ADV[:MAX | REG | MIN] | STD |
OFF][/LOW]
```

ADV[:MAX | REG | MIN] specifies the amount of power management desired. MAX directs POWER to make power management the primary consideration, possibly at the cost of application performance. REG is the default setting and directs POWER to balance application performance with power management. MIN directs POWER to only reduce power consumption when applications and devices are idle.

STD directs POWER to only use those APM features your hardware supports. If your hardware does not support APM, power management is turned off.

OFF directs POWER to turn off power management.

/LOW directs POWER to load its memory-resident software in lower (conventional) memory. By default, the POWER command loads itself into upper memory.

The following CONFIG.SYS entry loads maximum support for power conservation:

```
DEVICE=C:\DOS\POWER.EXE ADV:MAX
```

After you have installed the POWER.EXE device driver, you can use the POWER command to control the power management settings. The format of the POWER command is as follows:

```
POWER [ADV: [MAX | REG | MIN] | STD | OFF]
```

The following command selects minimum power conservation:

```
C:\> POWER ADV:MIN
```

To display the current power management setting, invoke POWER with no arguments, as shown here:

```
C:\> POWER <ENTER>
```

Connecting to Windows for Workgroups

Each day, approximately 30,000 new computers are connected to local area networks. As a result, Microsoft, late in 1992, released Windows for Workgroups, a powerful network-based version of Microsoft Windows that lets users connected to local area networks share files, printers, exchange electronic mail, and more. Windows for Workgroups makes it very easy for a team of workers to share the data and information they need to get their jobs done. Unfortunately, not all PCs are capable of running Windows for Workgroups (it requires at least a 286 and 3Mb of memory). Likewise, not all users are sold on the Windows environment. To help users who aren't running Windows for Workgroups still share printers, disks, and electronic mail, Microsoft provides Workgroup Connection software. This section examines this software and the benefits it provides to DOS users.

Installing the Workgroup Connection Software

To use the DOS 6 Workgroup Connection software, your computer must be connected to a local area network, within which at least one computer is running Windows for Workgroups or Microsoft's LAN Manager. After you install DOS 6, you must install the software on your disk. To do so, place the Workgroup Connection disk into drive A or B and then invoke the WCSETUP program.

```
A:\> WCSETUP <ENTER>
```

The installation program will first ask you for your network username and password. The username is the name members of your workgroup will use to identify you. Choose a username consistent with the members of your group. At Microsoft, for example, usernames often use an individual's first name immediately followed by the first letter of their last name. My username, for example, would be KRISJ. Your password prevents others from logging into the workgroup and, thus, should be known only to you. Choose a meaningful password you won't forget. The password should contain at least six characters. Passwords can contain up to 14 characters.

The installation software will also ask you to type in your computer's name. Use a name that clearly defines the PC and its location, such as JAMSA_10A. Finally, the installation will ask you for your workgroup name. Make sure you use a meaningful group name such as MANAGE-MENT or TEACHERS. The work group name must be used by all members of your workgroup.

The installation may modify your CONFIG.SYS and AUTOEXEC.BAT files. As your system starts carefully watch your screen for possible error messages. If an error message appears, contact your network administrator. If no error messages appear, you should be able to connect to the workgroup.

Connecting to the Workgroup

Before you can access the workgroup, you must first log on. To do so, issue the NET LOGON command from the DOS prompt as shown here:

```
C:\> NET LOGON <ENTER>
```

Your screen will prompt you to determine whether or not you want to start a workgroup service, as shown here:

```
The WORKSTATION service is not started.
Is it OK to start it? (Y/N) [Y]:
```

Press ENTER to select the default answer Y. Your screen will then prompt you for your username, as shown here:

```
Type your user name, or press ENTER if it is <USER>:
```

If the prompt contains your username, press ENTER. Otherwise, type your correct username. Your screen will then prompt you for your password.

```
Type your password:
```

Type in your password and press ENTER. After you successfully log on to the workgroup, the Workgroup Connection software will attempt to reestablish previous connections you had with other computers. The connections may be for a shared directory or printer. Eventually, the DOS prompt will reappear, and you can begin to use network resources.

Using Shared Resources

The Workgroup Connection software lets you share directories and printers with other users. The shared resources reside on the computer running Windows for Workgroups or the LAN Manager. If you are running only the Workgroup Connection software, another user cannot access your directories or printers. Also, the computer owning the shared resources must grant users explicit access to use them. If, for example, the computer lets you access a directory named BUDGET, you cannot access other directories on the computer.

To use a shared resource, you need to know the resource's name. Workgroup names are very consistent, taking the form *COM-PUTER\RESOURCE*. For example, if the computer named WORK_STA-TION_1 allows sharing of the directory BUDGET, you would specify the name as \\WORK_STATION_1\BUDGET.

To access a shared directory, you assign a logical drive letter to the directory name. For example, you might reference \\WORK_STA-TION_1\BUDGET using drive H. To use a shared printer, you redirect a local printer port such as LPT1 or LPT2 to a shared printer queue. After you have done so, you can print to the shared queue from DOS or from within an application program such as WordPerfect!

 Note If your logical drive letter (in this example, H) exceeds the DOS default of E, make sure you have a LASTDRIVE statement (in this case, LASTDRIVE=H) in your CONFIG.SYS file to enable DOS to recognize the drive.

Viewing Network Information

The NET VIEW command lets you display information about available shared resources. To display information about computers in your workgroup that share resources, invoke NET VIEW as follows:

```
C:\> NET VIEW <ENTER>
```

If you only want to view resources for a specific computer, you can include the computer's name, as shown here:

```
C:\> NET VIEW \\WORK_STATION_1 <ENTER>
Shared resources at \\WORK_STATION_1
Sharename     Type          Comment
```

```
------------------------------------------------------------
-
LASER          Print
BUDGET         Disk
The command completed successfully.
```

The NET USE command enables you to view your current network connections.

```
C:\> NET USE <ENTER>
Status          Local name       Remote name
------------------------------------------------------------
-
OK              H:               \\WORK_STATION_1\BUDGET
OK              LPT1             \\WORK_STATION_1\LASER
The command completed successfully.
```

Connecting to a Shared Directory

Before you can use a shared directory, the computer at which the directory resides must first give you access to the directory. You can then assign the directory to an unused disk drive letter using the NET USE command.

Before you invoke the NET USE command to connect to a shared directory, make sure your CONFIG.SYS file contains a LASTDRIVE entry that lets you use drive letters A through K as a minimum.

```
LASTDRIVE=K
```

If your CONFIG.SYS file did not previously contain a LASTDRIVE entry, restart your system for the change to take effect. Next, assuming you want to use the shared directory REPORTS, which resides on the computer WORK_STATION_1, you can connect to the directory using a NET USE command similar to the following:

```
C:\> NET USE H:   \\WORK_STATION_1\REPORTS <ENTER>
```

In this case, you would refer to the shared directory as drive H. The following DIR command, for example, would display the files the directory contains:

```
C:\> DIR H: <ENTER>
```

Within an application program such as WordPerfect or Excel, you can open files that reside in the shared directory by preceding the filename with the drive specifier H:.

When you no longer need to use the files in the shared directory, you can end the connection by invoking NET USE with the /DELETE switch, as shown here:

```
C:\> NET USE H: /DELETE <ENTER>
```

Connecting to a Shared Print Queue

If your network has a laser printer containing many fonts, each of the computers can share the printer by connecting to a shared printer port. For example, if the computer WORK_STATION_1 has a shared print queue named LASER, you can redirect output for LPT1 to the queue as shown here:

```
C:\> NET USE LPT1  \\WORK_STATION_1\LASER <ENTER>
```

After you redirect LPT1, any output sent to LPT1 will print on the shared printer.

To view the files that currently reside in shared print queues, you can invoke the NET PRINT command with a workstation name, as shown here:

```
C:\> NET PRINT \\WORK_STATION_1 <ENTER>
```

Likewise, to view the jobs in a specific print queue, you can include the queue's name in the NET PRINT command, as shown here:

```
C:\> NET PRINT \\WORK_STATION_1\LASER <ENTER>
```

Each job in a print queue is assigned a unique number. Using the NET PRINT command's /PAUSE, /RESUME, and /DELETE switches you can control the printing of one of your jobs. The following NET PRINT command, for example, removes job 23 from the LASER print queue:

```
C:\> NET PRINT  \\WORK_STATION_1 23 /DELETE <ENTER>
```

When you no longer want to use the shared printer, you can end the printer redirection using the NET USE /DELETE switch, as shown here:

```
C:\> NET USE LPT1 /DELETE <ENTER>
```

Making Connections Persistent

If you use directories and printers on a regular basis, continually connecting to the drives and printers each time you start your system could become quite time consuming. Rather than forcing you to issue NET USE commands for each resource every time you log on, the Workgroup Connection software lets you create *persistent connections* that it will automatically try to establish for you each time you log on. To direct the Workgroup Connection software to make each of your future connections persistent, invoke NET USE with the /PERSISTENT switch as shown here:

```
C:\> NET USE /PERSISTENT:YES <ENTER>
```

The Workgroup Connection software will record any connections you later make as persistent. When you later log on to the workgroup, the software will reestablish the connections, as shown here:

```
H: connected to \\WORK_STATION_1\BUDGET
```

If a computer owning a shared resource is not on (or running Windows for Workgroups or the LAN Manager) and the connection cannot be established, the Workgroup Connection software will display a prompt similar to the following:

```
Cannot reconnect H: to \\WORK_STATION_1\BUDGET (Error 53).
 Do you wish to continue restoring connections? (Y/N) [Y]:
```

If you want the software to try to establish connections to other computers, type **Y**; otherwise, type **N**.

Should you later want to create "nonpersistent" connections, invoke NET USE with the /PERSISTENT switch as shown here:

```
C:\> NET USE /PERSISTENT:NO <ENTER>
```

Logging Off the Workgroup

As a rule, when you have finished using workgroup resources, you should log off the network using the NET LOGOFF command as shown here:

```
C:\> NET LOGOFF <ENTER>
```

If you don't log off the workgroup, another user gaining access to your computer can access not only the files on your disks, but also files residing in shared directories.

Changing Your Network Password

To reduce the possibility of other users gaining access to your workgroup files, you should change your password on a regular basis. To do so, invoke the NET PASSWORD command as shown here:

```
C:\> NET PASSWORD <ENTER>
```

The Connection software will prompt you to type your current password, as shown here:

```
Type the old password:
```

After you type your current password and press ENTER, the software will prompt you for a new password.

```
Type your new password:
```

Type in the password you desire and press ENTER. The software will ask you to type the password a second time to confirm that you typed it correctly.

```
Confirm the password by typing it again:
```

Type in the new password and press ENTER. Use the new password the next time you log on to the workgroup.

Turning Off Network Support

If you examine your AUTOEXEC.BAT file, you will find that the Workgroup Connection setup program placed a NET START command in the file that loads memory-resident workgroup support. If, after installing the Workgroup Connection software, you experience problems with an existing program, you can remove the software from memory using the NET STOP command.

```
C:\> NET STOP <ENTER>
```

Should you later need to use the Workgroup Connection, you can issue the NET START command from the DOS prompt.

```
C:\> NET START <ENTER>
```

Using the Network Pop-up Interface

Earlier you learned how to connect to shared directories and print queues using the NET USE command. The Workgroup Connection software also provides a memory-resident "pop-up" dialog box interface you can use to perform such connections. To load the pop-up software, use the NET START command as shown here:

```
C:\> NET START POPUP <ENTER>
Pop-up for Workgroup Connection loaded into memory.
Use Alt+N to activate.
The command completed successfully.
```

Next, by pressing the ALT-N keyboard combination, you can invoke the Disk Connections dialog box, as shown in Figure 32-4.

The dialog box lets you specify the drive letter and shared directory with which you want to work. By pressing the TAB key, you can move from one field in the box to another. If you know the name of the shared directory, you can type it. Otherwise, you can select the name by selecting the Browse option. If you select the Browse option, a second dialog box will appear containing the names of computers and their shared directories. Using the TAB and arrow keys, highlight the desired directory and press ENTER.

The pop-up interface also lets you end a connection. To do so, highlight the shared directory from within the list of current connections. Next, select the Disconnect option.

Just as you can use the pop-up interface to connect to shared directories, you can also use it to connect or disconnect shared print queues. When the Connection software displays the dialog box shown in Figure 32-4, press the ALT-S keyboard combination. The software will then display the Print Connections dialog box, shown in Figure 32-5.

By following the previously discussed steps, you can use this dialog box to connect or disconnect shared print queues.

FIGURE
32-4

The pop-up Disk Connections dialog box

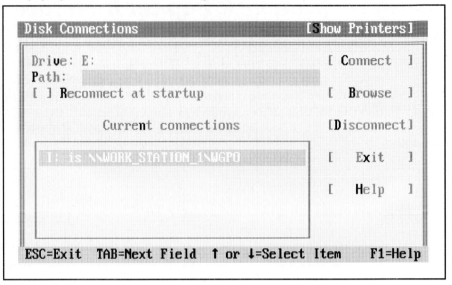

FIGURE
32-5

The Print Connections dialog box

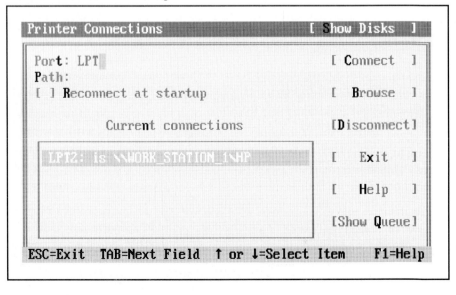

Using Microsoft Mail

One of the most powerful capabilities the DOS 6 Workgroup Connection provides is the ability to exchange electronic mail (e-mail) with other users. Before you can send and receive e-mail, you must set up your e-mail account. The MAIL command will perform the setup operations with you the first time you invoke it. Before you perform the e-mail setup, talk to your network administrator to determine your e-mail name (probably the same as your logon name) and the name of the shared directory that contains the post office.

After MAIL is installed, you can invoke MAIL from the DOS prompt as shown here:

```
C:\> MAIL <ENTER>
```

MAIL, in turn, will display its menu-driven interface, as shown in Figure 32-6.

FIGURE 32-6

MAIL's menu-driven interface

```
Microsoft (R) Mail V3.0b                    New mail:  0  Unread mail:  0

Address  Read  Compose  Delete  Storage  Print  Options  Update
Select items of mail to read, or read all unread mail if none selected

  FROM        SUBJECT                              DATE      TIME    PRI
```

From within MAIL, you can send, receive, and print e-mail messages using various menu options. Unfortunately, a complete discussion of MAIL's capabilities would require a chapter of its own. In most cases, you will find the operations you need to regularly perform within MAIL to be very straightforward.

Receiving Notification of New Mail

If you use MAIL on a regular basis, you might want your computer to notify you of the receipt of new mail. If so, invoke the memory-resident MICRO command from the DOS prompt as shown here:

```
C:\> MICRO <ENTER>
```

If you later receive mail, MICRO will display a brief message on your screen notifying you of the mail. You can then invoke MAIL to read the new message.

Practice

If you have not yet invoked DBLSPACE to increase your disk's storage capacity, turn to Chapter 26 and use the MSBACKUP command to perform a complete backup of your disk. When the backup completes, invoke DBLSPACE as shown here:

```
C:\> DBLSPACE <ENTER>
```

Most users will want DBLSPACE to perform an Express compression operation. Follow the remaining prompts as discussed in this chapter.

The most common way to connect two computers is using a NULL-modem cable between the computer's serial ports. If you have a NULL-modem cable, connect it to COM1 on each system. You may have to temporarily disconnect a mouse or other device. Next, on the client computer, place the following entry in CONFIG.SYS and reboot:

```
DEVICE=C:\DOS\INTERLNK.EXE   /COM:1
```

At the server system, invoke INTERSVR as follows:

```
C:\> INTERSVR /COM:1 <ENTER>
```

From the client, invoke INTERLNK to establish or view the connection.

```
C:\> INTERLNK <ENTER>
```

When the connection is established, use DIR to view files on the server disk. Use PRINT to print a file to the remote printer. To end the connection, press ALT-F4 on the server to end INTERSVR.

Review

1. What is the CONFIG.SYS entry to load the INTERLNK driver for a connection over COM1?

2. What is the INTERSVR command to establish a connection over COM1?

3. What steps must you perform to access the workgroup?

4. What is the command to access the shared directory BUDGET that resides on the computer named FINANCE, assuming you want to access the directory as drive I?

5. What is the command required to access the print queue LASER that resides on the workstation PRODUCTION, assuming you want to access the print queue using LPT1?

6. What happens when you copy a compressed file to a floppy disk?

7. What is the purpose of the DBLSPACE.SYS device driver?

8. What is APM?

Key Points

Doubling Your Disk's Storage Capacity

DBLSPACE is a DOS 6 command that transparently compresses the files stored on your disk. As a result of the compression, most users can nearly double the storage capacity of their disks. To compress your disk you simply invoke DBLSPACE from the DOS prompt as shown here:

```
C:\> DBLSPACE <ENTER>
```

DBLSPACE will compress each of your existing files, which may require several minutes to a few hours.

Compressed and Uncompressed Drives

DBLSPACE creates two logical drives on your disk. One drive is compressed and one is not. The compressed drive contains your existing files and will be the drive you regularly use as drive C. Each time you create a file on the compressed drive, the file is automatically compressed. Should you later copy the file to an uncompressed drive, the file is stored in its uncompressed format. The uncompressed drive serves two purposes. First, DOS uses the drive to boot. During the system startup, DOS changes drive letters making your compressed drive appear as drive C. Second, some programs have files whose contents cannot be compressed. In such cases, you can store the file on the compressed drive.

The DBLSPACE.SYS Device Driver

DOS provides the DBLSPACE.SYS device driver, which lets you move the DBLSPACE.BIN software from conventional memory to an upper memory block. The format of the CONFIG.SYS entry is as follows.

continues . . .

```
DEVICEHIGH=C:\DOS\DBLSPACE.SYS   /MOVE
```

If the entry is not in your CONFIG.SYS file, the DOS 6 disk compression will still work. The only difference is that DOS will leave DBLSPACE.BIN in conventional memory.

DBLSPACE and SMARTDRV

If you are using DBLSPACE, you should still use the SMARTDRV disk-caching software discussed in Chapter 31, "Improving Your System Performance." SMARTDRV is fully compatible with DBLSPACE, and its use will significantly improve your system performance.

Clients and Servers

When you connect two computers, one computer is called the client and the second, the server. The server computer contains disks and printers that it allows the client computer to use. The server computer runs the DOS 6 INTERSVR command while the client runs INTERLNK.

INTERLNK Device Driver

Before a client computer can access the server, the client must first install the INTERLNK device driver using the CONFIG.SYS DEVICE entry. After the driver is installed, the client can use the INTERLNK command to enable or disable drive redirection.

continues . . .

INTERSVR Command

To establish a connection, the server computer must be running the INTERSVR command. When INTERSVR is active, you cannot issue other commands at the server.

Workgroup Connection

The DOS 6 Workgroup Connection software provides commands that DOS users connected to a local area network can use to share directories and printers, or to exchange electronic mail. To use the Connection software, one or more computers must be running Windows for Workgroups or Microsoft's LAN Manager.

Connection Steps

To access the workgroup, users will normally perform these steps:

❏ Invoke NET START (typically from within AUTOEXEC.BAT)

❏ Log onto the workgroup using NET LOGON

❏ Connect to shared directories or printers using NET USE or the pop-up interface

❏ Log off the network using NET LOGOFF

Command Reference

APPEND

Defines a data-file search path

When DOS cannot find a data file as specified (or in the current directory), it searches to see whether the user has defined a data-file search path (a sequence of directories DOS can follow to carry out a command). The APPEND command allows you to define disk drives and subdirectories to be included in this path. Hence, this command defines a data-file search path that DOS uses whenever it fails to locate a file in either the current directory or a specified directory.

Format

```
APPEND[d:][p][;[d:][p]...]
APPEND[/X][/E]
APPEND[;]
```

or, in DOS 5 or later:

```
APPEND[/X:on|off][/PATH:on|off]
```

d: A disk drive to include in the data-file search path.

p A subdirectory to include in the data-file search path.

/X Aids in SEARCH-FIRST, FIND-FIRST, and EXEC options.

/E Places an APPEND entry in the DOS environment in a manner similar to a PATH entry (see PATH).

/X:on|off A DOS 5 or later switch that works like the /X parameter in earlier DOS versions. When /X:on is specified, the application can look for data files in the appended directories. When you specify /X:off, the application can look only in the current directory. You can abbreviate /X:on as simply /X.

/PATH:on|off A DOS 5 or later switch that specifies how applications use the data-file search path when looking for files with disk drive or directory information specified. The default setting is /PATH:on. This allows searching the appended directories, even if a drive or directory is specified in the request. If you specify /PATH:off, the appended directories are searched only if the request does not include a drive or directory.

Notes

To reduce overhead with each file reference, place the directories most likely to contain data files at the beginning of the APPEND path. When DOS cannot locate a file in the current directory, it searches the first entry in the APPEND path; if it can't locate the file in that directory, it searches the second, third, and so on. If commonly used data files reside in the directories specified at the end of the APPEND path, DOS has to perform needless directory searches.

Not all commands use the data-file search path by default. To increase the number of commands that use it, use the /X parameter.

If you invoke APPEND with no command-line parameters, APPEND displays the current data-file search path.

To remove the current data-file search path, invoke APPEND followed by a semicolon (see the preceding Format section).

APPEND supports network drives and path names. Do not use the APPEND command with Microsoft Windows.

Examples

In the following example, if DOS cannot find the data file in the current directory, it searches the root directories on drives C, B, and A, in that order:

```
C:\> APPEND C:\;B:\;A:\ <ENTER>
```

The following APPEND command tells DOS to search the directories \DOS, \UTIL, and \MISC, all of which reside on drive C:

```
C:\> APPEND C:\DOS;C:\UTIL;C:\MISC <ENTER>
```

ASSIGN

Routes disk drive references from one disk drive to another

Many older software packages expect to find data or overlay files on drive A. If you want to install such software on a fixed disk, you must trick the software into looking for the files on the fixed disk. ASSIGN lets you do this by routing disk drive references from one disk drive to another.

Format

```
ASSIGN[source_drive=target_drive[...]]
```

or, in DOS 5:

```
ASSIGN [/STATUS]
```

source_drive   The disk drive identifier of the disk from which I/O references are routed.

target_drive   The disk drive identifier of the disk to which I/O operations are routed.

/STATUS   A DOS 5 parameter that displays the currently active drive assignments. This parameter may be abbreviated /S or /STA.

Notes

Invoking ASSIGN without command-line parameters restores the default disk drive assignments.

Do not place a colon after each disk drive identifier in the ASSIGN command line.

Do not use an ASSIGNed disk with the BACKUP, DISKCOMP, DISK COPY, FORMAT, JOIN, LABEL, PRINT, RESTORE, or SUBST commands.

Most users should consider using the SUBST command instead of ASSIGN. Microsoft recommends this to ensure compatibility with future versions of DOS. The following ASSIGN and SUBST commands are functionally equivalent:

```
C:\> ASSIGN A=C <ENTER>
C:\> SUBST A: C:\ <ENTER>
```

The ASSIGN command is not supported by DOS 6.

Examples

In the following example, DOS disk I/O operations, which reference drive A, are routed to the disk in drive C:

```
C:\> ASSIGN A=C <ENTER>
```

If you then issue a command such as DIR A:, DOS will list the files on drive C.

You can perform multiple disk drive assignments on one command line, as follows:

```
C:\> ASSIGN A=C B=C <ENTER>
```

ATTRIB

Displays or modifies a file's attribute byte

This command displays or modifies a file's attribute byte, which contains information about the file. Several DOS commands, such as BACKUP, RESTORE, and XCOPY, use a file's attribute to enable selective file processing. By using these commands in conjunction with ATTRIB, you can gain considerable file-processing control.

Format

```
ATTRIB[+A|-A][+R|-R] file_spec[/S]
```

or, in DOS 5 or later:

```
ATTRIB[+A|-A][+R|-R][+S|-S][+H|-H]
    file_spec[/S]
```

+A   Sets a file's archive bit.

–A   Clears a file's archive bit.

+R   Sets a file's read-only bit.

–R   Clears a file's read-only bit.

+S   Sets the file's system bit (DOS 5 or later).

–S   Clears the file's system bit (DOS 5 or later).

+H   Sets the file's hidden bit (DOS 5 or later).

–H   Clears the file's hidden bit (DOS 5 or later).

file_spec   The complete DOS file specification, including the disk drive and path name, of the file(s) to be modified. ATTRIB supports DOS wildcard characters.

/S   Tells DOS to process all files in the subdirectories below the specified directory (DOS 3.3 and later).

Notes

Every file on the disk has specific characteristics or attributes. The ATTRIB command lets you change a file's attributes. Users most commonly change the read-only and archive attributes. A file with the read-only attribute set cannot be overwritten or deleted.

The archive attribute helps DOS determine which files on the disk need to be backed up. Whenever you create a file or change an existing file's contents, DOS sets the file's archive attribute. The BACKUP command searches the disk for files whose archive attribute is set and then, having copied the files to a backup disk, clears the file's archive bits.

In DOS 5 or later, you can change a file's system and hidden bits. The system attribute is normally reserved for the files DOS uses whenever your system is started. A file whose hidden bit is set will not appear in a directory listing.

Examples

In the example that follows, ATTRIB sets the CONFIG.SYS file to read-only:

```
C:\> ATTRIB +R CONFIG.SYS <ENTER>
```

To show the current attributes of all files in the current directory, use the following:

```
C:\> ATTRIB *.* <ENTER>
```

In DOS 5 or later, the command that follows hides the file MY_NOTES.TXT:

```
C:\> ATTRIB +H MY_NOTES.TXT <ENTER>
```

BACKUP

Backs up one or more files to a new disk

The BACKUP command works closely with the operating system's directory entries to select specific files for backup. Note that DOS directory fields (information about each file in the directory) relate closely to parameters included in the BACKUP command line (see the Format section for a complete list of these parameters). In DOS 6, BACKUP has been replaced by the MSBACKUP command.

Format

```
BACKUP source:[file_spec]target:[/A]
    [/D:mm-dd-yy][/L:log_file][/M][/S]
    [T:hh:mm:ss][/F[:Size]]
```

source: Specifies the source disk that contains the file(s) that are to be backed up.

file_spec   The path name(s) for the file(s) to back up.

target: Specifies the target disk.

/A   Appends source files to files on the target disk.

/D:mm-dd-yy   Backs up files modified since this date.

/L:*log_file* Places an entry for all files in the file specified by *log_file*. BACKUP.LOG is the default.

/M Backs up files modified since the last backup.

/S Backs up all subdirectory files.

/T:*hh:mm:ss* Backs up files modified since the specified time (DOS 3.3 or later).

/F Tells DOS to format an unformatted disk (DOS 3.3 or later). If you are using DOS 5, you can specify the size of the floppy disk BACKUP is to format; use /F:*size*, where *size* is one of the following:

160	160K	160KB			
180	180K	180KB			
320	320K	320KB			
360	360K	360KB			
720	720K	720KB			
1200	1200K	1200KB	1.2	1.2M	1.2Mb
1440	1440K	1440KB	1.44	1.44M	1.44Mb
2880	2880K	2880KB	2.88	2.88M	2.88Mb

Notes

Whenever you use your computer, back up your files. If you are using a fixed disk, backups are easy. Depending on the size of the disk and the number of files it contains, backups may take considerable time. Make sure that you have enough formatted floppy disks. The following formulas show how many floppy disks you need:

Bytes in use = Total disk space – Bytes available
Disks needed = Bytes in use / Floppy disk capacity

The BACKUP command completes with one of the following exit status values:

0   Successful backup

1   No files found to back up

2   Sharing conflicts prevented some files from being backed up

3   User termination via CTRL-C

4   An error prevented system backup

Examples

The following example backs up all files on drive C to the disk in drive A:

```
C:\> BACKUP C:\*.* A: /S <ENTER>
```

The following example uses the /A parameter to add C:TEST.DAT to the files contained on the backup disk in drive A:

```
C:\> BACKUP C:TEST.DAT A: /A <ENTER>
```

The following example backs up only those files that were created since April 30, 1993:

```
C:\> BACKUP C:\*.* A: /S /D:4-30-93 <ENTER>
```

The following command performs an incremental backup operation:

```
C:\> BACKUP C:\*.* A: /S /A /M <ENTER>
```

BREAK

Enables or disables DOS extended CTRL-BREAK checking

By default, after completing keyboard, screen, and printer I/O operations, DOS checks for a user-entered CTRL-BREAK. If you enable extended

CTRL-BREAK checking by entering **BREAK=ON**, DOS also checks for a CTRL-BREAK after completing services performed by the operating system, such as disk read or write operations.

Format

```
BREAK[=][on|off]
```

on   Enables extended CTRL-BREAK checking.

off   Disables extended CTRL-BREAK checking.

Notes

Because DOS must check for a CTRL-BREAK upon completing each system service, you increase the amount of time the system uses to complete operations by using the BREAK command. Programmers might want to set BREAK to ON during program development, but most users will leave the setting at the default BREAK=OFF.

Invoked without a command-line parameter, BREAK will display the current state of checking (either ON or OFF).

By default, DOS boots with extended CTRL-BREAK checking turned off. To enable extended checking at system startup, place the entry

```
BREAK=ON
```

in the file CONFIG.SYS and reboot.

Example

The following command enables DOS extended CTRL-BREAK checking:

```
C:\> BREAK ON  <ENTER>
```

CALL

Invokes a batch file from within another batch file

DOS has difficulty invoking one batch file from within another. This is especially true when the invocation of a procedure appears in the middle of the batch file. If you must invoke a batch procedure from within a batch file, the CALL command enables you to do so.

Format

```
CALL BatchFile[argument[...]]
```

BatchFile   The name of the second batch file to invoke.

argument   A command-line parameter for the second batch file.

Notes

The CALL command requires DOS 3.3 or later.

This command is similar to the function provided by using COMMAND /C within a batch file (see COMMAND).

Example

You can include CALL in one batch file in order to invoke another, as in the following example:

```
CLS
CALL MYPROC
DATE
```

CHCP

Displays or changes the current code page

Whenever DOS displays a character on screen, it must first map the character's ASCII value to a specific letter in a chosen character set. DOS uses code pages to map characters to letters.

Format

CHCP [code_page]

code_page Specifies the desired code page. This parameter must have been previously prepared by the system as either the primary or secondary code page in CONFIG.SYS. Valid code-page entries include the following:

437	United States	852	Slavic (DOS 5 or later)
850	Multilingual	863	French Canadian
860	Portuguese	865	Nordic

Notes

CHCP, which requires DOS 3.3 or later, allows you to set temporarily the desired code page for a device. If you intend to use the specified code page regularly, use the COUNTRY= entry in CONFIG.SYS rather than the CHCP command.

DOS allows you to use different character sets, thus offering international character support. To select an alternative code page (that is, a special character set), you previously must have issued the NLSFUNC command (see NLSFUNC). By entering a code-page value with the CHCP command, you reassign an alternative character set to be used by DOS.

Invoked without a command-line parameter, CHCP displays the current code page.

Example

The following command tells CHCP to select the Nordic code page:

```
C:\> CHCP 865 <ENTER>
```

CHDIR

Changes or displays the default directory

To organize your files, DOS lets you group related files into directories. The CHDIR command changes or displays the current directory name for a specified disk drive.

Format

```
CHDIR[drive:][path]
CD[drive:][path]
```

drive: Specifies as the default the disk drive that contains the directory you want. If you omit this parameter, CHDIR uses the default drive.

path   Specifies the path name for the current directory you want. If you omit the path, CHDIR will display the name of the current directory.

Notes

The abbreviated form of CHDIR is CD.

Whenever you specify a path name for CHDIR, the command does the following: If a slash precedes the path name (as in \SUBDIR), the search for the directory begins at the root directory. If the path name does not begin with a slash (as in SUBDIR), the search begins at the current directory. If you don't include a directory path, CHDIR displays the current directory.

Examples

Using CD without a path name displays the name of the current directory:

```
C:\> CD <ENTER>
C:\SUBDIR
```

This command is valid with a disk drive specifier, as shown here:

```
C:\> CHDIR A: <ENTER>
A:\UTIL
```

Likewise, the following command selects the subdirectory BATCH as the default directory:

```
C:\> CHDIR \BATCH <ENTER>
```

CHKDSK

Checks a disk's current status

CHKDSK examines the disk's file allocation tables and directory structures and reports errors and inconsistencies, providing you with the opportunity to correct the errors.

Format

```
CHKDSK [drive:][path][file_name][/F][/V]
```

drive: The disk drive CHKDSK is to examine.

path   Specifies a subdirectory that contains the files CHKDSK is to examine for disk fragmentation.

file_name   The file name and extension of the file(s) CHKDSK is to examine for disk fragmentation.

/F   Fixes errors found in a directory or file allocation table.

/V   Displays the names of all files on the disk.

Notes

CHKDSK reports on the status of the following disk conditions:

❑   The amount of free, used, and corrupted disk space

❑   The number of hidden files

❑   The amount of free and used memory

Occasionally, as normal day-to-day operations of a disk cause wear and tear on the storage media, files become corrupted and lose sectors. CHKDSK allows you to view and even repair such problems.

A file can also become fragmented, with its contents dispersed to different locations on the disk. CHKDSK also displays information on fragmented files.

CHKDSK does not work with joined or substituted disks (see JOIN and SUBST).

If you are operating on a local area network, do not try to repair the disk. When DOS has files open (as may be the case with a network), it cannot correctly update the file allocation table.

By default, CHKDSK only reports disk errors—it does not attempt to fix them. To write actual corrections to disk, use the /F parameter.

At least once a month, you should issue the CHKDSK command:

```
C:\> CHKDSK /F <ENTER>
```

to examine the fixed disk. DOS sometimes finds errors when it writes information to disk. Depending on the error, you may not realize that one has occurred. The CHKDSK command is your only tool for testing the "health" of the disk.

If CHKDSK finds lost information caused by an error, it displays the following:

```
nnn lost clusters found in n chains.
Convert lost chains to files  (Y/N)?
```

If you respond with **Y**, CHKDSK creates a file(s) containing the information referenced by the lost pointers. This occurs only if you have used the /F parameter. These files are placed in the root directory and named FILE0000.CHK, FILE0001.CHK, and so on. Use the TYPE command to examine the contents of these files. If they don't contain useful information, simply delete them.

Do not use the command CHKDSK /F from within Microsoft Windows or from within the MS-DOS shell when task swapping is enabled. Doing so might damage files stored on your disk.

Examples

The following command displays the state of the current disk:

```
C:\> CHKDSK  <ENTER>
```

If you include a file specification or wildcard character, as follows:

```
C:\> CHKDSK *.*  <ENTER>
```

CHKDSK reports on file fragmentation for the current directory.

To direct CHKDSK to repair any errors it may find, use the /F parameter, as shown here:

```
C:\> CHKDSK /F <ENTER>
```

If you invoke CHKDSK with the /V parameter:

```
C:\> CHKDSK /V <ENTER>
```

CHKDSK displays the name of every file on the disk.

CHOICE

Displays a user prompt and returns an error level that corresponds to a specific key pressed

If you are using DOS 6, you can use the CHOICE command in your batch files to allow the user a chance to choose between alternative courses of action easily.

Format

```
CHOICE   [/C[:]Keys [/N] [/S] [/T[:]Seconds,Default]
         [UserPrompt]
```

/C[:]Keys   Specifies the letters the user can press. If you don't specify /C, CHOICE uses the letters YN as the default.

/N   Directs CHOICE not to display the valid letters in the user prompt.

/S   Directs CHOICE to be case sensitive. If you don't specify /S, CHOICE considers upper- and lowercase letters the same.

/T[:]*Seconds,Default* Specifies the number of seconds, from 0 through 99, that CHOICE will wait for a user response and the default selection should the time limit expire.

UserPrompt A character string containing the prompt CHOICE displays to the user.

Notes

When the user presses one of the valid keys, CHOICE returns an exit status value that corresponds to the key. If the valid keys are ABC, A corresponds to the exit status 1, B to 2, and C to 3.

If the user presses a key that is not one of the specified options, CHOICE will beep the computer's built-in speaker. If the user presses CTRL-C to cancel the command, the error level 0 is returned.

CHOICE requires DOS 6.

Examples

The following batch file commands use CHOICE to decide whether or not the user wants to run CHKDSK:

```
@ECHO OFF
CHOICE  Run CHKDSK
IF ERRORLEVEL 1 IF NOT ERRORLEVEL 2 CHKDSK
```

When you invoke this batch file, CHOICE will display the following:

```
Run CHKDSK[Y,N]?
```

The following commands illustrate how you can use CHOICE within a menu-based batch file:

```
@ECHO OFF
ECHO  A  Run WordPerfect
```

```
ECHO   B   Run Lotus 1-2-3
ECHO   C   Run Windows
ECHO   D   Quit
CHOICE /C:ABCD /N Selection:
IF ERRORLEVEL 1 IF NOT ERRORLEVEL 2 WP
IF ERRORLEVEL 2 IF NOT ERRORLEVEL 3 123
REM Other commands here
```

Finally, this command gives the user ten seconds to respond to a yes or no prompt about defragmenting the disk. If the user fails to respond, the default is N:

```
CHOICE  /T:10,N  Run  DEFRAG
```

CLS

Clears the screen display

The CLS command clears the screen display and places the cursor (and DOS prompt) in the home (upper-left) position.

Format

```
CLS
```

Notes

This command does not affect the way DOS displays information on screen; it merely clears the screen of all information.

COMMAND

Loads a secondary command processor

COMMAND is used most often to invoke nested batch files in DOS versions earlier than 3.3.

Format

```
COMMAND [drive:][path][Ctty_Device]
  [/C string][/E:num_bytes][/K:Filename.Ext][/P][/MSG]
```

drive: Specifies the disk drive that contains the secondary command processor. If you do not specify a drive, DOS uses the default drive.

path   The path name of the subdirectory that contains the command processor. If you do not specify a path name, DOS uses the default directory.

Ctty_Device   A DOS 5 parameter that lets you specify an alternative device for I/O operations. For more information on changing this device, refer to the **CTTY** command.

/C string   Tells DOS to execute the command specified by *string*. Ordinarily, this parameter is used for nested batch-file invocations. If this parameter is used with /P, DOS ignores /P.

/E:num_bytes   Specifies the size of the area DOS is to allocate for the secondary command processor's environment space. This parameter must be between 160 and 32,767 bytes; the default is 160 bytes.

/K:Filename.Ext   A DOS 6 switch that specifies a program or batch file to run before displaying the DOS prompt.

/P   Tells DOS to leave the secondary command processor permanently in memory.

/MSG   Directs DOS to store error messages in memory, for floppy disk-based systems.

Notes

COMMAND is commonly used to invoke nested batch procedures, as shown here:

```
CLS
COMMAND /C BATFILE
DATE
```

For information about terminating a secondary command processor, see EXIT.

If you are using DOS 3.3 or later, use the CALL command to invoke your nested batch files.

The /K switch provides a convenient way for you to run a specific batch file each time you create a DOS window from within Microsoft Windows. For example, if you have a batch file named SET_ENV.BAT that defines your system prompt and other environment settings, you can use the Windows PIF Editor to edit the file DOSPRMPT.PIF adding the /K switch /K:SET_ENV.BAT to the optional parameters field.

Example

Using COMMAND, the batch file NESTED.BAT invokes the batch file TIMEDATE.BAT.

```
ECHO OFF
CLS
VER
COMMAND /C TIMEDATE
VOL
```

COMP

Compares the contents of two files

COMP compares the contents of two files and displays the first ten differences between the files as hexadecimal offsets into the file. DOS 6 does not support the COMP command.

Format

```
COMP file_spec1 file_spec2
```

or, using DOS 5:

```
COMP file_spec1 file_spec2 [/D]
  [/A][/L][/N=number][/C]
```

file_spec1* and *file_spec2   Completes DOS path names of the files to be compared. COMP supports DOS wildcard characters.

/D   Displays any differences in decimal (DOS 5 only).

/A   Displays any differences in ASCII (DOS 5 only).

/L   Displays the line numbers in which differences occur, instead of displaying offsets (DOS 5 only).

/N=*number*   Compares only the number of lines specified (DOS 5 only).

/C   Treats upper- and lowercase letters identically (DOS 5 only).

Notes

COMP compares two files and displays the differences as hexadecimal values. If the files are identical, COMP displays the message:

```
Files compare OK
```

After files have been compared, COMP asks the following:

```
Compare more files (Y/N)?
```

To compare additional files, press **Y**; otherwise, press **N**. If COMP locates more than ten differences, it displays

```
10 Mismatches - ending compare
```

COMP will not compare files of different sizes.

If you are copying a critical file from one disk or directory to another, you can verify that the copy was successful by using the COMP command after the copy procedure is complete. If differences exist between the two files, you know that an error occurred. If no differences exist, the copy was successful.

Examples

In the following example, COMP compares the contents of the file A.DAT to those of B.DAT:

```
C:\> COMP A.DAT B.DAT <ENTER>
```

Assuming that each file contains the following:

```
C:\> TYPE A.DAT <ENTER>
A
AA

C:\> TYPE B.DAT <ENTER>
B
BB
```

the command displays this:

```
Compare file C:A.DAT and file C:B.DAT
Compare error at OFFSET 0
File 1 = 41
File 2 = 42
```

```
Compare error at OFFSET 3
File 1 = 41
File 2 = 42

Compare error at OFFSET 4
File 1 = 41
File 2 = 42

Compare more files (Y/N)?
```

If you are using DOS 5, you can the display the differences between the two files in ASCII, as follows:

```
C:\> COMP A B /A <ENTER>
```

If you omit the file name from the secondary file, DOS matches the file name on the specified drive to the primary file, as follows:

```
C:\> COMP A.DAT B: <ENTER>
```

If you do not specify a file in the COMP command line, COMP prompts you for it, as shown here:

```
C:\> COMP <ENTER>
Enter the primary file name.
A.DAT <ENTER>

Enter the 2nd file name or drive id.
B.DAT <ENTER>
```

COPY

Copies one or more files to a new destination

The COPY command copies one or more files to a new disk drive, directory, or file name.

Format

```
COPY source_file [/V][/A][/B]
target_file [/V][/A][/B]

COPY source1+source2[/V][/A][/B][...]
target_file [/V][/A][/B]
```

source_file   Specifies the file to be copied.

target_file   The name of the destination file.

/V   Uses disk verification to check whether a successful copy occurred.

/A   Informs COPY that the preceding file was an ASCII file.

/B   Informs COPY that the preceding file was a binary file.

source1+source2   Indicates that you can use any number of source files.

Notes

The COPY command fully supports DOS wildcard characters. To combine multiple files into one file, use the plus sign (+) between the desired source files.

COPY will not allow you to copy a file over itself. The names of source and target files must differ in some way. If the target file already exists, COPY will overwrite the file.

The COPY command only copies files contained in the current directory or a specified DOS directory. To copy files that reside in several subdirectories, use XCOPY.

The /V parameter adds processing overhead but prevents a hardware error from rendering inconsistent the contents of source and target files.

Examples

The following command copies a spreadsheet file (BUDGET.DAT) from the Lotus 1-2-3 directory to a floppy disk in drive A:

```
C:\> COPY \123\BUDGET.DAT A: <ENTER>
```

The following command copies the contents of the CONFIG.SYS file to a file with the same name in drive B:

```
C:\> COPY A:CONFIG.SYS B:CONFIG.SYS <ENTER>
```

This command is identical in function to the following:

```
C:\> COPY A:CONFIG.SYS B: <ENTER>
```

or to the commands

```
C:\> B: <ENTER>
B:\> COPY A:CONFIG.SYS <ENTER>
```

The following command copies all the files on drive A to drive B:

```
C:\> COPY A:*.* B:*.* <ENTER>
```

The following command uses the plus sign to append files TWO.DAT and THREE.DAT to file ONE.DAT, thereby creating a file called FOUR.DAT:

```
C:\> COPY ONE.DAT+TWO.DAT+THREE.DAT FOUR.DAT <ENTER>
```

CTTY

Modifies standard input (stdin) to point to alternative device

The CTTY command changes standard I/O from a default device to an alternative device. Valid device names include AUX:, COM1:, and COM2:. To return standard input to the console device, the command CTTY CON must be issued through the auxiliary device.

Format

CTTY *device_name*

device_name   The name of the device you want for standard input.

Notes

Most end users have no need to issue this command. If you invoke CTTY without your computer attached to the serial port, you will have to reboot DOS in order to continue.

Example

This command sets the standard input/output to COM1:

```
A> CTTY COM1: <ENTER>
```

DATE

Sets the system date

The DATE command sets the system date DOS uses to assign date stamps to each file you create or modify.

Format

```
DATE  [mm-dd-yy]
DATE  [dd-mm-yy]
DATE  [yy-mm-dd]
```

mm   The desired month (1 to 12).

dd   The desired day (1 to 31).

yy   The desired year (80 to 99). DATE also allows you to include the century, in the form 19*yy* or 20*yy*.

Notes

The *mm-dd-yy* date format depends on the COUNTRY specifier in CONFIG.SYS (see CONFIG). You can also use slashes (/) instead of dashes (-). If you do not specify a date, DATE displays the current date.

Prior to DOS 3.3, the DATE command did not modify the AT computer's system clock. Users of DOS versions earlier than 3.3 must use the Setup disk provided with the *Guide to Operations* in order to change the AT system clock.

The actual date is an optional command-line parameter. If you omit the date, DATE prompts you for it. Although you do not have to type in a date, doing so is good practice. DOS uses the system's current date and time to time-stamp files whenever a file is created or modified.

Examples

Since the command line in the following example does not include the date, DATE prompts the user for it:

```
C:\> DATE <ENTER>
The current date is: Mon 04-05-1993
Enter the new date: (mm-dd-yy)
```

If you simply want to display the system date without modifying it, press the ENTER key at the date prompt. DATE leaves the system date unchanged.

In the following example, the DATE command sets the system date to December 8, 1993:

```
C:\> DATE 12/08/93 <ENTER>
```

This command has the same effect as

```
C:\> DATE 12/08/1993 <ENTER>
```

DBLSPACE

Compresses the information stored on a disk, increasing the disk's storage capacity

DBLSPACE compresses the information stored on a disk, essentially doubling the disk's storage capacity. DBLSPACE works with hard or floppy disks. After you compress a disk, you work with the disk's files, just as you always have. In other words, DOS transparently compresses and decompresses as you use them, so your operations are unaffected.

Format

```
DBLSPACE [/CHKDSK [/F] [Drive:]]
   [/COMPRESS Drive: [/NEWDRIVE=Drive:] [/RESERVE=Megabytes]]
   [/CONVSTAC=StackerVolume: [/NEWDRIVE=Drive:] [/CVF=xxx]]
```

```
[/CREATE Drive: [/NEWDRIVE=Drive:] /SIZE=Megabytes]
        [RESERVE=Megabytes]]
[/DEFRAGMENT [Drive:]]
[/DELETE Drive:]
[/FORMAT Drive:]
[/INFO Drive:]
[/LIST]
[/MOUNT[=xxx] Drive: /NEWDRIVE=Drive:]
[/UNMOUNT Drive:]
[/RATIO[=x.x] [Drive: | /ALL]]
[/SIZE[=Megabytes | /RESERVE=Megabytes] Drive:]
```

/CHKDSK   Directs DBLSPACE to examine the internal structure of the compressed volume file.

/COMPRESS   Directs DBLSPACE to compress the files on the drive specified. DBLSPACE uses the drive letter specified after the /NEWDRIVE switch as the uncompressed drive volume. The /RESERVE switch specifies the amount of disk space in megabytes that DBLSPACE must leave on the uncompressed volume.

/CONVSTAC   Directs DBLSPACE to convert a Stacker disk volume into DBLSPACE format. The /NEWDRIVE switch specifies the drive letter of the newly compressed drive. The /CVF switch specifies the three-digit (000 through 254) file extension of the compressed volume file.

/CREATE   Directs DBLSPACE to create a compressed drive using free space on the specified drive.

/DEFRAGMENT   Directs DBLSPACE to defragment the files stored on the compressed volume specified.

/DELETE   Directs DBLSPACE to delete a compressed drive.

/FORMAT   Directs DBLSPACE to format a compressed drive.

/INFO   Directs DBLSPACE to display specific information about a compressed drive.

/LIST   Directs DBLSPACE to display information about a system's compressed and uncompressed drives.

/MOUNT   Directs DBLSPACE to mount a compressed drive, preparing the drive for use. The *xxx* values correspond to the three-digit file extension of the drive to mount. The *Drive*: parameter specifies the disk containing the compressed volume file. The /NEWDRIVE switch lets you specify the desired drive letter for the newly mounted drive.

/UNMOUNT   Directs DBLSPACE to dismount a compressed drive.

/RATIO   Directs DBLSPACE to change a drive's compression ratio. The *x.x* parameter specifies the desired compression ratio from 1.0 to 16.0. The *Drive*: parameter specifies the disk drive for which you want to change the compression ratio.

/SIZE   Directs DBLSPACE to change the size of a compressed drive.

Notes

The first time that you invoke the DBLSPACE command, DBLSPACE executes the DBLSPACE setup and installation, typically compressing your hard disk. After that, most users will not invoke DBLSPACE again. However, as you can see, DBLSPACE contains several command-line switches that power users may include to further customize their disk compression.

DBLSPACE requires DOS 6.

Examples

If you have not yet invoked DBLSPACE to compress your disk, the following DBLSPACE command will begin the software installation and disk compression:

```
C:\> DBLSPACE <ENTER>
```

Simply perform the operations as prompted. Depending on your disk's capacity and current files, the compression operation might require an hour or more.

The following DBLSPACE command uses the /INFO to direct DBLSPACE to provide more specifics about a compressed drive:

```
C:\> DBLSPACE /INFO <ENTER>
DoubleSpace is examining drive C.


Compressed drive C (DOS 6 DISK) was created on 4-24-1993 at 12:08am. Drive C
is stored on uncompressed drive H in the file DBLSPACE.000.


                         Compressed    Uncompressed
                          Drive C        Drive H


      Total space:       337.11 MB      190.79 MB
      Space used:        221.69 MB      187.66 MB
      Space free:        115.42 MB**      3.13 MB


      The actual compression ratio is 1.7 to 1.


**  based on estimated compression ratio of 2.0 to 1.
```

Likewise, this command directs DBLSPACE to display information about a system's available drives:

```
C:\> DBLSPACE /LIST <ENTER>
Drive  Type                        Total Free  Total Size  CVF Filename
-----  -------------------------   ----------  ----------  ---------------
  A    Floppy drive                  0.00 MB     0.69 MB
  C    Compressed hard drive       115.42 MB   337.11 MB   H:\DBLSPACE.000
  E    Available for DoubleSpace
  F    Available for DoubleSpace
  G    Available for DoubleSpace
  H    Local hard drive              3.14 MB   190.79 MB
```

The following command directs DBLSPACE to check the internal consistency of the compressed drive C: using the /CHKDSK switch:

```
C:\> DBLSPACE /CHKDSK C: <ENTER>
```

If DBLSPACE encounters errors during the CHKDSK operation, repeat the command including the /F switch.

The following DBLSPACE command uses the /DEFRAGMENT switch to defragment the compressed drive D:

```
C:\> DBLSPACE /DEFRAGMENT D: <ENTER>
```

DEFRAG

Eliminates file fragmentation to improve performance

As you create, delete, and change files, a file's contents may get stored in locations spread out across your disk. Files whose contents are not stored in consecutive locations are fragmented files. Such files decrease system performance by increasing the number of disk operations required to read the file. The DEFRAG command moves files on your disk to place them in consecutive storage locations.

Format

```
DEFRAG [Drive:][/B][/F][/S[:]SortOrder]
[/SKIPHIGH][/V]
```

or

```
DEFRAG [Drive:][/B][/SKIPHIGH][/U][/V]
```

Drive: Specifies the drive letter corresponding to the disk you want to defragment. If you don't specify a drive letter, DEFRAG will prompt you for one.

/B Directs DEFRAG to boot your system after it completes. If you use FASTOPEN, include the /B switch when you invoke DEFRAG.

/F Directs DEFRAG not only to defragment files but also to remove any holes (unused clusters) between files.

/S[:]*SortOrder* Specifies the order in which DEFRAG sorts files in each directory:

N	Name A to Z	–N	Name Z to A
E	Extension A to Z	–E	Extension Z to A
D	Date oldest first	–D	Date newest first
S	Size smallest first	–S	Size largest first

If you don't specify a sort order, DEFRAG leaves the directory order unchanged.

/SKIPHIGH Directs DEFRAG to load into conventional memory. By default, DEFRAG loads itself into upper memory if the memory space is available.

/U Directs DEFRAG to defragment files and leave existing holes (unused clusters) that exist between files.

/V Directs DEFRAG to verify that the data it writes to disk during a cluster move operation is recorded correctly. Using /V slows down the defragmentation operation.

Notes

If your programs or files seem to take longer to load, or your disk's activation light seems to remain on for longer periods of time, your files may be fragmented. As a general rule, if you regularly create, delete, and change files, you should defragment your disk once a month.

To support batch processing, DEFRAG uses the following exit status values:

Exit Status	Meaning
0	Successful defragmentation
1	Internal error
2	Disk has 0 free clusters; DEFRAG requires at least one
3	User CTRL-C
4	General error
5	Disk read error
6	Disk write error
7	Cluster error; use CHKDSK /F
8	Memory error
9	Insufficient memory

DEFRAG requires DOS 6

Examples

DEFRAG is a menu-driven utility program. As such, most users simply invoke DEFRAG as follows, using its menus to select desired options:

```
C:\> DEFRAG <ENTER>
```

If you are using DOS FASTOPEN invoke DEFRAG using the /B switch:

```
C:\> DEFRAG /B <ENTER>
```

DEL

Deletes one or more files from disk

Use the DEL command to delete from the disk a file that no longer is needed.

Format

```
DEL [drive:][path]file_name[.ext][/P]
```

drive: Specifies the disk drive that contains the file to be deleted. If you omit this parameter, DEL uses the default drive.

path   Specifies the name of the subdirectory that contains the file to be deleted. If you omit the path, DEL uses the current directory.

file_name[.ext]   The name of the file to be deleted. DEL fully supports DOS wildcard characters.

/P   A DOS 4 or later switch that directs DEL to prompt you before deleting the file specified.

Notes

For compatibility with earlier versions of DOS, you can invoke the DEL command as ERASE.

Unless you explicitly use a drive or path specifier, DEL deletes files in the current directory only. You can delete several files simultaneously by including each file name on the same command line.

You cannot use DEL to remove subdirectories: use RMDIR.

If you attempt to delete all the files in a directory, DOS asks

```
Are you sure (Y/N)?
```

to ensure that you truly want the command performed. To proceed, type **Y** and press ENTER; otherwise, type **N** and press ENTER.

Using DOS 4 or later, if you invoke DEL with wildcard characters and the /P parameter, DOS prompts you for each individual file to determine whether you want to delete it:

```
FILENAME.EXT, Delete (Y/N)?
```

Type **Y** and press ENTER to delete the file. If you type **N** and press ENTER, DEL will leave the file on disk.

If you are using DOS 5 or later, you may be able to use the UNDELETE command to restore one or more recently deleted files.

Examples

In the following example, DEL erases the contents of the CONFIG.OLD file from drive B:

```
C:\> DEL B:CONFIG.OLD <ENTER>
```

Similarly, the following command:

```
C:\> DEL AUTOEXEC.OLD <ENTER>
```

deletes a file from within the current subdirectory.

If you are using DOS 4 or later, you can use the /P parameter to tell DEL to prompt you before deleting a file:

```
C:\> DEL *.BAK /P <ENTER>
```

DELTREE

Deletes all of the files and subdirectories in a directory

The DELTREE command lets you remove a directory, its files, and its lower-level subdirectories in one step.

Format

```
DELTREE [/Y] Pathname
```

Pathname

Specifies the directory DELTREE is to delete.

/Y   Directs DELTREE not to prompt you before deleting the directory.

Notes

DELTREE will delete all of the files in a directory and its subdirectories, regardless of the file's current attribute settings. If DELTREE successfully removes a directory, DELTREE returns the exit status value 0.

Note   DELTREE supports the DOS wildcard characters. However, use wildcards with caution. The wrong wildcard combination could quickly erase many directories from your disk.

Examples

The following DELTREE command deletes the directory OLDNEWS, as well as the subdirectories OLDNEWS contains:

```
C:\> DELTREE OLDNEWS <ENTER>
```

If you do not include the /Y switch, DELTREE will prompt you to type **Y** to delete a directory or **N** to leave the directory alone, as shown here:

```
C:\> DELTREE OLDNEWS <ENTER>
Delete directory "OLDNEWS" and all its subdirectories? [yn]
```

If you type **Y**, DELTREE will delete the directory. If you type **N**, DELTREE will leave the directory unchanged. To eliminate this prompt, invoke DELTREE with the /Y switch.

DIR

Displays a directory listing of files

A directory is a list of file names. DIR displays the names of all files in the directory specified.

Format

```
DIR [file_spec][/P][/W]
```

or, using DOS 5 or later:

```
DIR [file_spec][/P][/W][A:attributes]
   [/O:sort_order][/S][/B][/L]
```

file_spec   The file(s) for which DIR is to display a directory listing. The file specification can include a disk drive identifier and path name. If you do not place a file specification in the command line, DIR displays a listing of all files in the current directory. DIR fully supports DOS wildcard characters.

/P Pauses after each screenful of information.

/W Displays the files in short form (file name only), with five file names across the screen.

/A:*attributes* A DOS 5 or later switch that tells DIR to display only files that meet specific attribute criteria.

/O:*sort_order* A DOS 5 or later switch that tells DIR to display the directory listing in an order other than by name.

/S A DOS 5 or later switch that displays the files that reside in lower-level subdirectories.

/B A DOS 5 or later switch that displays file names and extensions only.

/L A DOS 5 or later switch that displays file names in lowercase letters.

Notes

By default, the DIR command displays each file's complete name, file size in bytes, and date and time of creation (or last modification). The DIR command also displays the amount of free disk space in bytes, and in DOS 5 also displays the total number of bytes in files in the directory. By default, DIR does not display hidden files.

DIR always displays the drive letter and directory name in which the files are stored.

When you use the /B parameter available in DOS 5 or later, the drive letter and directory name are not displayed.

If you simply invoke DIR with a file name, like this:

```
C:\> DIR FILENAME <ENTER>
```

the extension defaults to *.

When using DOS 5 or later, you can use the /O:*sort_order* parameter to modify the order in which files are displayed. Valid sort orders include the following:

N	A to Z by name
–N	Z to A by name
C	By compression ratio smallest to largest (DOS 6)
–C	By compression ratio largest to smallest (DOS 6)
E	A to Z by extension
–E	Z to A by extension
D	By date oldest to newest
–D	By date newest to oldest
S	By size smallest to largest
–S	By size largest to smallest
G	Directories grouped before files
–G	Directories grouped after files

If you are using DOS 5 or later, you can also use the environment entry DIRCMD to define the default format DIR uses to display files. For example, the following SET command assigns DIRCMD the parameters /L and /S (lowercase and subdirectories):

```
C:\> SET DIRCMD=/L/S <ENTER>
```

With DOS 5 or later, you can use the /A:*attributes* parameter to control which files the DIR command displays. Only the names of those files whose file attributes match those in the *attributes* string are listed. Valid attribute values include the following:

H	Hidden files
–H	Files that are not hidden files
S	System files
–S	Files that are not system files
D	Directories
–D	Files that are not directories
A	Files needing archiving

–A	Files already archived
R	Read-only files
–R	Files that are not read-only

You can combine attributes, as well. For example, /A:A–R tells DIR to display all files requiring archiving that are not read-only files.

Examples

The following example causes DIR to display a directory listing of all files on drive A. The two lines are functionally equivalent and produce the same results:

```
C:\> DIR A: <ENTER>

C:\> DIR A:*.* <ENTER>
```

If many files exist on drive A, they may scroll off the screen during the directory listing. If this happens, invoke DIR as follows:

```
C:\> DIR A:*.* /P <ENTER>
```

Whenever DIR completes a screenful of files, it will pause, displaying a prompt similar to the following:

```
Strike a key when ready . . .
```

When this occurs, press any key for DIR to continue.

The file specification of the DIR command can be as specific as you like. The following command displays the directory listing of the CONFIG.OLD file, which resides in the subdirectory on the current disk:

```
C:\> DIR \DOS\CONFIG.OLD <ENTER>
```

If you are using DOS 5 or later, use the following command to tell DIR to display a directory listing sorted by size:

```
C:\> DIR /O:S <ENTER>
```

The following DOS 5 or later command tells DIR to display all files that reside on your disk, showing their names in lowercase letters.

```
C:\> DIR  \*.*  /S  /L <ENTER>
```

Finally, this DOS 5 or later command tells DIR to display only the names of subdirectories that reside in the current directory:

```
C:\> DIR /A:D <ENTER>
```

DISKCOMP

Compares two floppy disks

The DISKCOMP command compares the contents of two floppy disks and displays differences if the disks are not identical.

Format

```
DISKCOMP[primary_drive:[secondary_drive]][/1][/8]
```

primary_drive   Specifies the first drive to be used for the disk comparison. If you do not specify a primary drive, DISKCOMP uses the default.

secondary_drive   Specifies the second drive to be used for the disk comparison. If you do not specify a secondary drive, DISKCOMP uses the default.

/1   Instructs DISKCOMP to perform a single-sided disk comparison.

/8   Instructs DISKCOMP to perform an eight-sector-per-track disk comparison.

Notes

If you have a single-floppy system, the DISKCOMP command will perform a single-drive comparison, prompting you to enter the source and target disks at the correct time.

If the contents of the disks are identical, DISKCOMP displays the following message:

```
Compare OK
```

Otherwise, DISKCOMP displays in hexadecimal values the location (disk's side and track) of the differences.

Many users issue the DISKCOMP command immediately after using DISKCOPY to copy the contents of one disk to another. DISKCOMP detects any errors that occurred during the disk copy.

DISKCOMP returns the following exit status values:

0   Disks compare OK
1   Disks are not the same
2   User termination via CTRL-C
3   Unrecoverable disk error
4   Invalid syntax, insufficient memory, or invalid drive

Examples

In the following example, DISKCOMP compares the contents of the disk in drive A to those of drive B:

```
C:\> DISKCOMP A: B:  <ENTER>
```

If there are errors, DISKCOMP displays the locations of the differences:

```
Compare error on side n track n
```

If you need to compare single-sided disks, use the following command:

```
C:\> DISKCOMP A: B: /1 <ENTER>
```

DISKCOPY

Copies a source floppy disk to a target disk

The DISKCOPY command copies the contents of one floppy disk to another, creating an identical copy.

Format

```
DISKCOPY[source_drive:[target_drive]][/1][/V]
```

source_drive   Specifies the disk drive that contains the floppy disk to be copied. If you do not specify a source drive, DOS uses the default drive.

target_drive   Specifies the disk drive that contains the disk to be copied to. If you do not specify a target drive, DOS uses the default drive.

/1   Tells DISKCOPY to copy only the first side of the source disk to the target disk.

/V   Enables disk verification (DOS 5 or later). Disk verification double-checks that all information written to the disk is recorded correctly.

Notes

If you have a single-floppy system, DISKCOPY performs a single-drive copy, prompting you to enter the source disk and target disk at the correct time.

DISKCOPY supports the following exit status values:

0   Successful disk copy

1   Non-fatal disk read/write error

2   Disk copy ended by user CTRL-C

3   Disk copy ended due to fatal error

4   Initialization error prevented copy

DISKCOPY destroys the previous contents of the target disk. If the source and target disks are different types of disks (a 360Kb and a 1.2Mb disk, for example), DISKCOPY displays an error message and terminates.

If the target disk has not been formatted, DISKCOPY formats it during the copy operation.

Do not use DISKCOPY with joined or substituted disks (see JOIN and SUBST).

Examples

The following command assumes that you have two compatible floppy disk drives on your system:

```
C:\> DISKCOPY A: B: <ENTER>
```

After DISKCOPY begins copying a disk, it reads several tracks of data from the source and then writes them to the target disk. In a single-floppy drive system, DISKCOPY repeats this process, prompting you for the source and target disks, as shown here:

```
A: DISKCOPY <ENTER>
Insert SOURCE diskette in drive A:
```

```
Press any key when ready

Copying 40 tracks
9 Sectors/Track, 2 Side(s)

Insert TARGET diskette in drive A:
Press any key when ready

Insert SOURCE diskette in drive A:

Press any key when ready
Insert TARGET diskette in drive A:

Press any key when ready
Copy another diskette (Y/N)?
```

DOSKEY

Recalls previously entered commands

DOSKEY is a DOS 5 or later command that lets you recall and edit previously entered commands and create macros (similar to batch files) that DOS stores in memory.

Format

```
DOSKEY[/REINSTALL][/BUFSIZE=size][/MACROS]
  [/HISTORY][/INSERT | /OVERSTRIKE]
  [macro_name=macro]
```

/REINSTALL   Installs a new copy of the DOSKEY program in memory.

/BUFSIZE=size   Specifies the size of the command and macro buffer in memory. If you are creating many macros, use a buffer size of 4096. The default size is 512.

/MACROS   Displays the current list of macros.

/HISTORY   Displays a list of all commands stored in the buffer (the command history).

/INSERT   Lets you remain in insert mode after you press ENTER.

/OVERSTRIKE   Disables insert mode.

macro_name=macro   Lets you create a macro.

Notes

With DOSKEY enabled, you can use the keyboard arrow keys to toggle through previously entered commands. When the command you want is displayed, execute it by pressing ENTER. To edit the command, use the following:

Key	Action
UP ARROW	Recalls the command preceding the one displayed
DOWN ARROW	Recalls the command after the one displayed
PGUP	Recalls the oldest command in buffer
PGDN	Recalls last command placed in buffer
LEFT ARROW	Moves cursor left one character
RIGHT ARROW	Moves cursor right one character
CTRL-LEFT ARROW	Moves cursor back one word
CTRL-RIGHT ARROW	Moves cursor forward one word
HOME	Moves cursor to start of line
END	Moves cursor to end of line
ESC	Clears command from display
F7	Displays all commands in memory, preceded by a line number
ALT-F7	Erases all commands stored in memory
F8	Searches memory for command matching partial command line displayed

Key	Action
F9	Specifies a command line by number
F10	Displays all macros stored in memory
ALT-F10	Clears all macros

Macros are similar in concept to DOS batch files. A macro can contain one or more commands. When you create a macro, it must fit on one page. DOS stores the macro in RAM. To execute a macro, enter its name.

Like DOS batch files, macros support command-line parameters. Instead of using the symbols %0 to %9, macros use $1 through $9. Macros also support the following metacharacters:

Character	Meaning
$G or $g	DOS output redirection operator
$L or $l	DOS input redirection operator
$B or $b	DOS pipe operator
$T or $t	Command separator
$*	Entire command line, minus the macro name

Examples

The following command loads DOSKEY with a 4096-byte buffer for commands and macros:

```
C:\> DOSKEY /BUFSIZE=4096 <ENTER>
```

This command:

```
C:\> DOSKEY /HISTORY <ENTER>
```

tells DOSKEY to display all of the commands in the command buffer.

Likewise, the following command tells DOSKEY to display all of its macros:

```
C:\> DOSKEY /MACROS <ENTER>
```

To create a macro named CP that abbreviates the COPY command, use the following:

```
C:\> DOSKEY CP=COPY $1 $2 <ENTER>
```

As you can see, the CP macro uses the symbols $1 and $2 to access its command-line parameters. Once you create the macro, you access it by using the name CP.

Finally, the following command:

```
C:\> DOSKEY HIST=DOSKEY /HISTORY $T DOSKEY
    /MACROS <ENTER>
```

creates a macro (HIST) that displays not only the commands currently stored in the DOSKEY buffer but also the current macros.

HIST uses the $T metacharacter to separate the two commands.

DOSSHELL

Starts the DOS shell user interface

Starting with version 4, DOS provides a menu-driven, graphically oriented, user-friendly shell interface that allows you an easy-to-use alternative to the DOS command line for giving commands.

Format

```
DOSSHELL [/T[:L|M|H {Resolution]]] [/B]
        [/G[:L|M|H [Resolution]]]
```

/T   Starts the DOS shell in low-, medium-, or high-resolution text mode.

/G   Starts the DOS shell in low-, medium-, or high-resolution graphics mode.

/B   Starts the DOS shell in black and white.

Notes

The file DOSSHELL.INI contains the shell's program group, screen color, resolution, and other settings. If you move the file from the DOS directory, place a SET command in your AUTOEXEC.BAT file that defines the file's new directory, as shown here:

```
SET  DOSSHELL=C:\NEWDIR
```

Example

Most users invoke the DOSSHELL from the command prompt as follows and then use the shell's Options menu to specify graphics or text mode settings:

```
C:\> DOSSHELL  <ENTER>
```

ECHO

Displays or suppresses batch command messages

By default, whenever you execute DOS batch files, DOS displays the name of each command as it executes. You can stop this command-name display by using the ECHO OFF command. In addition, many batch files use ECHO to display messages to the user.

Format

```
ECHO[ON | OFF | message]
```

ON   Enables the display of batch commands as they execute.

OFF   Disables the display of batch commands as they execute.

message   Contains the text ECHO is to display.

Notes

If you are using DOS 3.3 or later, you can suppress command-name display by preceding command names in a batch file with an @ sign, as shown here:

```
@ECHO OFF
DATE
```

Many batch files use ECHO to display messages for users. For example, the following batch file displays the message "Hello there!"

```
@ECHO OFF
ECHO Hello there!
```

If you aren't using DOS 5 and you want ECHO to display a blank line, you must place the ALT-255 keyboard combination after the ECHO command, as follows:

```
@ECHO OFF
ECHO Skipping one 1
ECHO ALT-255
ECHO Done
```

To enter the ALT-255 keyboard combination, hold down the ALT key. At the same time, *using the numeric keypad,* type in the value **255**. When you release the ALT key, you will see the cursor move one position to the

right. The ALT-255 keyboard combination creates a special blank character. When this character appears in an ECHO command line, ECHO
displays a blank line.

Beginning with DOS 3.3, you can direct ECHO to display a blank line
by simply placing one of several special characters immediately after the
ECHO command. You can use a period, or the characters +, /,[,], or a
colon. The following example uses a period:

```
@ECHO OFF
ECHO Skipping one line
ECHO.
ECHO Done
```

Examples

The following batch file uses ECHO to display several messages on the
screen:

```
@ECHO OFF
ECHO *********************
ECHO * Batch File Example *
ECHO *                    *
ECHO * Messages displayed *
ECHO *      by  ECHO      *
ECHO *********************
```

When you invoke this batch file, it displays the following:

```
*********************
* Batch File Example *
*                    *
* Messages displayed *
*      by  ECHO      *
*********************
```

EDIT

Invokes the DOS full-screen editor

Beginning with DOS 5, DOS provides a full-screen editor that lets you quickly create or change ASCII files, while viewing the file's contents on your screen.

Format

```
EDIT [Filename] [/B] [/G] [/H] [/NOHI]
```

Filename   Specifies the name of the file you want to edit.

/B   Directs EDIT to display its output in black and white.

/G   Directs EDIT to perform fast CGA screen updates.

/H   Directs EDIT to display its output using the maximum number of screen lines that your video card supports.

/NOHI   Directs EDIT not to use high-intensity display attributes.

Notes

To use EDIT, the file QBASIC.EXE must reside in the current directory or within a directory specified in the command path.

Within EDIT, you can use menu options to save and print the current file's contents.

Example

The following command invokes EDIT with the file CONFIG.SYS:

```
C:\> EDIT \CONFIG.SYS <ENTER>
```

EXIT

Terminates a secondary command processor

Many application programs provide an option that lets you temporarily exit the application to the DOS prompt. After you finish issuing DOS commands, you can return to the application by typing **EXIT**.

Format

```
EXIT
```

Notes

The DOS shell lets you temporarily exit the shell to the DOS prompt. When you are ready to resume work in the shell, type **EXIT** at the prompt and press ENTER.

EXPAND

Expands a DOS compressed file

To reduce the number of distribution disks, many DOS 5 or later files are shipped on disk in a compressed format. If you examine your distribution disks, you will see files whose last letter of their extension is an underscore (_) character, such as UNDELETE.EX_. During the DOS 5 installation, SETUP expands these files onto your hard disk as necessary. Should you ever need to copy one of these files to your disk after installation, you will need to expand it.

Format

```
EXPAND source_file target_file
```

source_file   The complete path name of the file whose contents you want to expand.

target_file   The name of the expanded file.

Notes

You cannot use a compressed file until you expand it.

Example

The following expands the file UNDELETE.EX_ on the floppy disk in drive A to your DOS directory as UNDELETE.EXE:

```
C:\> EXPAND A:UNDELETE.EX_ \DOS\UNDELETE.EXE <ENTER>
```

FASTHELP

Provides online help for DOS commands

Format

```
FASTHELP [CommandName]  (DOS 6)
```

or

```
HELP [CommandName]  (DOS 5)
```

CommandName Specifies a specific DOS command for which you want to display help text.

Notes

In DOS 6, the command is FASTHELP. In DOS 5, it is called HELP. Both DOS 5 and DOS 6 let you obtain help on a specific command by invoking the command followed by the /? switch, as shown here:

```
C:\> CLS /? <ENTER>
Clears the screen.

CLS
```

If you do not include a command name, FASTHELP displays a single-line description of each command. In DOS 5, see also the HELP command.

Examples

The following command displays help text on CHKDSK:

```
C:\> FASTHELP CHKDSK <ENTER>
Checks a disk and displays a status report.

CHKDSK [drive:][[path]filename] [/F] [/V]


  [drive:][path]  Specifies the drive and directory to check.
  filename        Specifies the file(s) to check for fragmentation.
  /F              Fixes errors on the disk.
  /V              Displays the full path and name of every file on the disk.


Type CHKDSK without parameters to check the current disk.
```

In DOS 5, the following command displays help text on CHKDSK:

```
C:\> HELP CHKDSK <ENTER>
```

Finally, the following command displays a one-line summary of each DOS command:

```
C:\> FASTHELP <ENTER>
```

FASTOPEN

Increases directory search performance

Whenever you invoke a program or open a file, DOS must search the disk to determine where the file resides. Because the disk is a mechanical device, this search is time consuming. By increasing the number of directory entries DOS keeps in memory, FASTOPEN increases the speed with which DOS locates files on disk.

Format

FASTOPEN *d*:[=*entries*][...][/X]

d: Specifies the disk drive for which DOS is setting aside storage space for directory entries.

entries Specifies the number of directory entries for which DOS is reserving space. This value must be in the range of 10 to 999. The default value is 48.

/X A DOS 5 or later parameter that tells FASTOPEN to create the table of directory entries in expanded memory. Using this parameter limits the number of entries to 305.

Notes

Whenever DOS opens a file for reading or writing, it must locate that file on disk. DOS does this by first searching the directory specified (or the current directory) for the file's starting location.

Beginning with DOS 3.3, you can use FASTOPEN to set aside memory for a table of commonly used files and their starting locations. When you later open a file, DOS examines this table for the file's starting address. If DOS locates the file in the table, it doesn't have to read this information from disk. This saves considerable time.

The FASTOPEN command allows you to specify the size of the table of file names DOS stores in memory. If several disks are specified, the sum of the number of directory entries cannot exceed 999 (305 if using the /X parameter).

 Note If you are using a third-party disk defragmenter and the command FASTOPEN, always immediately reboot your system after the defragmenter completes.

Example

In the example that follows, DOS remembers 50 directory entries for drive C:

```
C:\> FASTOPEN C:=50 <ENTER>
```

FC

Displays the actual differences between two files

FC stands for *file compare*. FC compares two files and displays those lines that differ.

Format

```
FC[/A][/B][/C][/LB n][/N][/T][W][/nnnn]
  file1 file2
```

/A Tells FC to display only the first and last lines in a group of lines that differ, rather than all the lines that differ between two ASCII files.

/B Performs a binary comparison of the files.

/C Ignores the case of letters.

/L Performs an ASCII-file comparison.

/LB n Uses an internal buffer of *n* lines.

/N Displays the line numbers of lines that differ in two ASCII files.

/T Treats tabs as tabs, rather than expanding tabs into spaces.

/W Compresses white space (spaces or tabs).

/nnnn Specifies the number of lines that must again match after a difference before FC assumes the files are synchronized. The default is 2.

file1 The complete file specification of the first file to compare.

file2 The complete file specification for the second file to compare.

Notes

FC displays differences between files by displaying the first file name, the line preceding the lines that don't match, the lines that differ, and finally the line following the lines that don't match. Then the same information is displayed for the second file.

FC compares and displays binary files in the form:

aaaaaaaa bb cc

where *aaaaaaaa* is the offset address of the values that differ, and *bb* and *cc* are the values that differ.

If FC encounters too many errors, it terminates, displaying the following message:

```
Resynch failed. Files are too different.
```

Using FC to compare two files is often more helpful than using COMP because FC provides more information.

Examples

The following command compares two binary files, using the /B parameter:

```
C:\> FC /B TEST.EXE OLDTEST.EXE <ENTER>
```

In this case, the output might be

```
00000002: 9A 66
00000004: 06 20
00000006: 01 03
0000000A: 00 CE
0000000E: 20 14
0000000F: 00 04
00000011: 02 08
00000012: 32 97
```

Similarly, assuming that the files A.DAT and B.DAT contain the following:

A.DAT	B.DAT
4	4
5	5
A	B
A	B
A	B
6	6
7	7
8	8

the command

```
C:\> FC A.DAT B.DAT <ENTER>
```

will display

```
***** A.DAT
5
A
A
A
6
```

```
***** B.DAT
5
B
B
B
6
*****
```

FC, if you include the /N parameter, will display

```
C:\> FC /N A.DAT B.DAT <ENTER>

***** A.DAT
    2:   5
    3:   A
    4:   A
    5:   A
    6:   6

***** B.DAT
    2:   5
    3:   B
    4:   B
    5:   B
    6:   6
*****
```

If you want FC to ignore differences between upper- and lowercase letters, add the /C parameter, as follows:

```
C:\> FC /C FILE.1 FILE.2 <ENTER>
```

FDISK

Defines disk partitions on a DOS fixed disk

DOS allows you to divide the fixed disk into logical collections of cylinders, called *partitions*. By so doing, you can place several operating systems into different partitions on one fixed disk. The FDISK command allows you to add, change, display, and delete disk partitions.

Format

```
FDISK
```

Notes

If your computer is new and DOS cannot locate the fixed disk, you must issue the FDISK command to define the disk to DOS. FDISK is a menu-driven program that allows you to divide your disks into multiple sections called *partitions*. In most cases, however, your computer dealer will have done this for you.

For a complete guide to FDISK, refer to *DOS: The Complete Reference, 4th Edition* (Osborne/McGraw-Hill, 1993).

The first sector on any fixed disk contains a master boot record that contains information that defines the partition the computer uses for booting. FDISK is your means of interfacing with the master boot record.

Example

To use FDISK, place your DOS disk in the drive and type

```
A> FDISK <ENTER>
```

FDISK, a menu-driven program, responds with its first menu:

```
          MS-DOS Version 6.00
       Fixed Disk Setup Program
    (C)Copyright Microsoft Corp. 1983-1993
            FDISK Options

Current fixed disk drive: 1
Choose one of the following:
1: Create DOS Partition or Logical DOS Drive
2: Set active partition
3: Delete DOS Partition or Logical DOS Drive
4: Display partition information

Enter choice:[1]

Press Esc to exit FDISK
```

FIND

Searches file(s) or piped input for a character string

The FIND command lets you locate a sequence of characters or words within a file or within redirected output. FIND can also be used as a filter with piped input.

Format

FIND[/C][/I][/N][/V] "*string*"[*file_spec*][...]

/C   Tells FIND to display a count of occurrences of the string. If /C is used with /N, the /N parameter is ignored.

/I   A DOS 5 or later switch that directs FIND to consider upper- and lowercase letters as the same.

/N   Tells FIND to precede each line containing the string with that line's number.

/V   Tells FIND to display each line that does not contain the string.

string   Specifies the string FIND is to search for. This string must be enclosed in quotation marks.

file_spec   The name of the file in which to search for the string. This can be a series of file names, separated by spaces. FIND does not support DOS wildcard characters.

Notes

The string FIND is searching for must be enclosed in quotation marks. If the string includes quotation marks as characters, you must use two sets of quotation marks—one set for the string and one for the command, as follows:

```
C:\> FIND """Look"" he said" FILENAME.EXT <ENTER>
```

Prior to DOS 5, command-line parameters had to come between FIND and the string to be found. In DOS 5, they can occur in any order.

Examples

In the following example, FIND is used as a filter to list each subdirectory in the current directory. If the current directory contains the following information:

```
C:\> DIR <ENTER>

 Volume in drive C is MSDOS 5
 Volume Serial Number is 1931-9E01
 Directory of C:\SUBDIR
```

```
.                  <DIR>        01-20-93      6:44p
..                 <DIR>        01-20-93      6:44p
ONE                <DIR>        01-20-93      6:44p
FILENAME EXT           6 01-20-93            6:45p
TWO                <DIR>        01-20-93      6:45p
READ      ME           4 01-20-93            6:45p
NOTES     DOC          3 01-20-93            6:45p
THREE              <DIR>        01-20-93      6:45p
         8 file(s)             13 bytes
                      85256192 bytes free
```

you can use the FIND command as follows to display directory names only:

```
C:\> DIR | FIND "<DIR>"  <ENTER>
.                  <DIR>        01-20-93      6:44p
..                 <DIR>        01-20-93      6:44p
ONE                <DIR>        01-20-93      6:44p
TWO                <DIR>        01-20-93      6:45p
THREE              <DIR>        01-20-93      6:45p
```

To list all files that are not directories, use the FIND /V parameter, as follows:

```
C:\> DIR A: | FIND /V "<DIR>"  <ENTER>
```

The following command displays each occurrence of the string "begin" in the TEST.PAS file:

```
C:\> FIND "begin" TEST.PAS  <ENTER>
```

The following command also displays each occurrence of "begin". In this example, however, each line is preceded by its line number:

```
C:\> FIND /N "begin" TEST.PAS  <ENTER>
```

The following command displays the number of occurrences of "begin" in the file:

```
C:\> FIND /C "begin" TEST.PAS <ENTER>
```

FOR

Provides repetitive execution of DOS commands

The FOR command is used most commonly within DOS batch files to repeat a specific command for a given set of files.

Format

```
FOR %%variable IN (set) DO DOS_command
```

%%variable   The FOR-loop control variable that DOS manipulates with each iteration. The variable name can be any single printable character except %, =, |, /, <, >, or a comma.

set   A list of valid DOS file names. This list can contain DOS file names separated by commas, wildcard characters, or both. The list must be enclosed in parenthesis.

DOS_command   The command to be executed with each iteration.

Notes

The FOR command can be used from the DOS prompt. Use the %% symbols before the variable name when working within batch files. Use the single % from the DOS prompt.

Examples

The following shows how FOR works in a batch file:

```
FOR %%V IN (ONE.BAT, TWO.DAT, THREE.INI) DO TYPE %%V
```

In this case, FOR assigns the variable file name ONE.BAT during the first iteration of the command, and displays the contents of the file:

```
TYPE ONE.BAT
```

On the second iteration, FOR assigns the variable file name TWO.DAT and displays the contents of the file:

```
TYPE TWO.DAT
```

On the third iteration, FOR assigns the variable file name THREE.INI, and again displays the contents of the file:

```
TYPE THREE.INI
```

When FOR prepares for the fourth iteration, it fails to find any additional file names. Processing is complete.

FORMAT

Formats a disk for use by DOS

The manufacturers of floppy disks have no way of knowing on what computer—or operating system—the disks will be used. Therefore, before you can use a new disk, you must format it for DOS. The FORMAT command lets you format a disk that is to be used with DOS.

Format

```
FORMAT d:[/V:label][/S][/B][/Q]
FORMAT d:[/F:size][/U][/S][/B][/Q]
FORMAT d:[/1][/4][/U][/V:label][/S][/B][/Q]
FORMAT d:[/8][/U][/S][/B][/Q]
FORMAT d:[/T:tracks][/N:sectors][/S][/B][/Q]
```

/1   Tells FORMAT to format the disk as a single-sided disk.

/4   Tells FORMAT to format the disk as double-sided in a quadruple-density disk drive.

/8   Tells FORMAT to format the disk with 8 sectors per track; most disks use 9 or 15 sectors.

/N:*sectors*   Defines the number of sectors to a track. This parameter requires DOS 3.3 or later.

/T:*tracks*   Defines the number of tracks to a side. This parameter requires DOS 3.3 or later.

/F:*size*   Beginning with DOS 4, specifies the size of the floppy disk to format, where size is one of the following:

160	160K	160Kb			
180	180K	180Kb			
320	320K	320Kb			
360	360K	360Kb			
720	720K	720Kb			
1200	1200K	1200Kb	1.2	1.2M	1.2Mb
1440	1440K	1440Kb	1.44	1.44M	1.44Mb
2880	2880K	2880Kb	2.88	2.88M	2.88Mb

/S   Tells FORMAT to place the system files on the disk, thereby making the disk bootable.

/B   Tells FORMAT to reserve space for the system files on the target disk. Unlike the /S parameter, /B does not actually place the files on disk. The /S and /V parameters cannot be used in conjunction with the /B parameter.

/V:*label*   Tells FORMAT to include the volume label specified.

/U   Unconditional format (DOS 5); destroys all information previously recorded on a disk. You cannot unformat a disk that has been unconditionally formatted.

/Q   Performs a *quick format* of a previously formatted disk (DOS 5 or later), overwriting the root directory and file allocation table. A quick format does not search the disk for bad sectors.

Notes

Inadvertently formatting a fixed disk can be disastrous. FORMAT first prompts you as follows:

```
WARNING, ALL DATA ON NON-REMOVABLE DISK
DRIVE N: WILL BE LOST!
Proceed with Format (Y/N)?
```

To proceed with the formatting process, type **Y**; otherwise, type **N**. Depending on which version of DOS you are using, FORMAT may also prompt you to enter the volume label of the hard disk before formatting. If the label you enter does not match the hard disk label, FORMAT will not continue. When the formatting process is complete, FORMAT displays the following:

❏   Total disk space

❏   Corrupted disk space marked as defective

❏   Total disk space consumed by the operating system

❏   Total disk space available for file utilization

FORMAT reports on defective space it finds during formatting. FORMAT also places entries for each defective sector into the file allocation table (an area that DOS uses to keep track of the locations of files). This prevents DOS from using the corrupted sectors for data storage.

The FORMAT /S command copies the hidden files that are needed in order to boot DOS to the target disk.

Do not use FORMAT in conjunction with ASSIGN, JOIN, or SUBST.

FORMAT will not work with drives that are being used in a network configuration.

If you are using DOS 5 or later, you may be able to recover an inadvertently formatted hard disk by using the UNFORMAT command.

FORMAT supports the following exit status codes:

0	Successful format
3	Format terminated by user with CTRL-C
4	Fatal error
5	User typed **N** at the prompt to continue

Examples

This command formats the disk in drive A as bootable:

```
C:\> FORMAT A:/S <ENTER>
```

When invoked, the command will display the following:

```
Insert a new diskette for drive A:
and press ENTER when ready.
```

Many users frequently have to format double-density disks in their 1.2Mb drives. Use the /4 parameter in the FORMAT command to tell FORMAT to create a 360Kb disk:

```
C:\> FORMAT A: /4 <ENTER>
```

The /B and /S parameters are similar. The following command tells FORMAT to reserve space for the operating system's boot files (files that are necessary for the operating system to boot), instead of placing those files on disk:

```
C:\> FORMAT A: /B <ENTER>
```

If you include the /B parameter, the SYS command can later update the disk as required.

If you are using DOS 5 or later, the following command tells FORMAT to perform a quick format of a previously formatted floppy disk that currently resides in drive A:

```
C:\> FORMAT A: /Q <ENTER>
```

GOTO

Branches to the label specified in a batch file

The GOTO command tells DOS to branch to a label specified in a batch file. Label names contain any of the characters valid for DOS file names. If the label does not exist, DOS terminates execution of the batch file.

Format

```
GOTO label_name
```

label_name   Specifies the name of a label within a DOS batch procedure.

Notes

DOS label names can be virtually any length. However, DOS distinguishes only the first eight characters of a label name. It will consider the label names DOS_LABEL1 and DOS_LABEL2 to be equivalent, because their first eight characters are equivalent.

In the batch file, a colon must precede the label.

If the label specified in a GOTO command does not exist or is not preceded by a colon, DOS will terminate the batch file and display an error message.

Example

The following batch procedure repeatedly displays a directory listing of the current drive. It runs until the user presses CTRL-C or CTRL-BREAK:

```
:LOOP
DIR
GOTO LOOP
```

GRAFTABL

Improves extended character display in graphics mode

The GRAFTABL command allows you to display extended ASCII characters when the display is in medium-resolution graphics mode. DOS 6 does not support GRAFTABL.

Format

```
GRAFTABL [code_page | /STATUS | /?]
```

code_page Specifies the code page to be used for the display. Possible values are as follows:

437	United States
850	Multilingual
852	Slavic (DOS 5 or later)
860	Portuguese
863	French Canadian
865	Nordic

/STATUS Tells GRAFTABL to display the code page currently in use.

/? Tells GRAFTABL to display the code page plus a list of available options.

Notes

Most users will not have to use the GRAFTABL command. If you do, you probably should place the GRAFTABL command in your AUTO-EXEC.BAT file.

GRAFTABL is a memory-resident program that supports the following exit status values:

0	Table successfully loaded
1	Table replaced an existing table
2	File error preventing loading of a new table
3	Invalid command-line parameter
4	Incorrect DOS version

Examples

If you specify the /STA parameter in the GRAFTABL command line, as follows:

```
C:\> GRAFTABL /STATUS <ENTER>
```

GRAFTABL displays the current code page, as shown here:

```
USA version of Graphic Character Set Table is already loaded.
```

The following command:

```
C:\> GRAFTABL 437 <ENTER>
```

tells GRAFTABL to use the code page for the United States when displaying extended characters.

GRAPHICS

Provides print-screen support for graphics mode

The GRAPHICS command lets you use print-screen operations to print contents of screens that contain graphics.

Format

```
GRAPHICS
[pro_file][printer_type][/B][/LCD][/R][/PRINTBOX:id]
```

pro_file The path name of a file that contains the profiles of supported printers. By default, DOS looks for GRAPHICS.PRO. This parameter requires at least DOS 4.

printer_type Specifies the target printer type. Possible values are as follows:

COLOR1	Color printer with black ribbon
COLOR4	Color printer with RGB ribbon
COLOR8	Color printer with cyan, magenta, yellow, and black ribbon
GRAPHICS	Graphics printer
GRAPHICSWIDE	Graphics printer with 11-inch carriage (DOS 4 or later)
LASERJETII	Hewlett-Packard Laserjet II (DOS 5 or later)
PAINTJET	Hewlett-Packard Paintjet (DOS 5 or later)
QUIETJET	Hewlett-Packard Quietjet (DOS 5 or later)
QUIETJETPLUS	Hewlett-Packard Quietjet Plus (DOS 5 or later)
RUGGEDWRITER	Hewlett-Packard Rugged Writer (DOS 5 or later)
RUGGEDWRITERWIDE	Hewlett-Packard Rugged Writer Wide (DOS 5 or later)
THERMAL	Thermal printer
THINKJET	Hewlett-Packard Thinkjet (DOS 5 or later)

/B Tells GRAPHICS to print the background color. The default is not to print the background color.

/LCD Directs GRAPHICS to use the LCD aspect ratio. The /LCD switch is identical to /PRINTBOX:LCD.

/R Tells GRAPHICS to reverse the color of the screen image—black images on the screen are printed as white, white images as black.

/PRINTBOX:*id* Selects the printbox size. The following values are valid: std for standard and lcd for liquid crystal display.

Notes

The GRAPHICS command invokes a program that remains in memory until the computer is rebooted. Therefore, this command needs to be invoked only once during a user session.

If you use the GRAPHICS command to print graphics images to the printer, and the printouts are too dark, use the /R parameter.

Examples

The following command loads the memory-resident software required to support print-screen operations that contain graphics images:

```
C:\> GRAPHICS <ENTER>
```

This command tells DOS to print white screen images as black, and black screen images as white:

```
C:\> GRAPHICS /R <ENTER>
```

HELP

Starts the DOS 5 online help facility

DOS 5 provides an online help facility that you can use to get information about a command, its format, and switches. The command in DOS 5 is HELP, optionally followed by the name of the commmand you want help for. In DOS 6, the command is FASTHELP. You can also summon help by typing the name of the DOS command followed by the /? switch.

Format

```
HELP [CommandName]
```

Notes

DOS 5 provides an interactive online help facility that provides descriptions, examples, and explanations of different DOS commands. After you invoke HELP, you can use the arrow keys or mouse to select and display information on different commands.

Example

When you invoke HELP without specifying a command, HELP displays a list of the DOS commands as shown here:

```
 File  Search                                                   Help
┌──────────────────── MS-DOS Help: Command Reference ─────────────────┐
│                                                                     ▲│
│ Use the scroll bars to see more commands. Or, press the PAGE DOWN key. For│
│ more information about using MS-DOS Help, choose How to Use MS-DOS Help │
│ from the Help menu, or press F1.                                    │
│                                                                     │
│  <ANSI.SYS>           <Fc>                   <Net Time>             │
│  <Append>             <Fcbs>                 <Net Use>              │
│  <Attrib>             <Fdisk>                <Net Ver>              │
│  <Break>              <Files>                <Net View>             │
│  <Buffers>            <Find>                 <Nlsfunc>              │
│  <Call>               <For>                  <Path>                 │
│  <Chcp>               <Format>               <Pause>                │
│  <Chdir (cd)>         <Goto>                 <Power>                │
│  <Chkdsk>             <Graphics>             <POWER.EXE>            │
│  <Choice>             <Help>                 <Print>                │
│  <Cls>                <HIMEM.SYS>            <Prompt>               │
│  <Command>            <If>                   <Qbasic>               │
│  <Copy>               <Include>              <RAMDRIVE.SYS>         │
│  <Country>            <Install>              <Rem>                  │
│  <Ctty>               <Interlnk>             <Rename (ren)>         │
│  <Date>               <INTERLNK.EXE>         <Replace>             │
│  <Dblspace>           <Intersvr>             <Restore>            ▼│
 <Alt+C=Contents> <Alt+N=Next> <Alt+B=Back>              N 00006:002
```

The following HELP command displays a screenful of information on the XCOPY command:

```
C:\> HELP XCOPY <ENTER>
```

IF

Provides conditional processing within DOS batch files

The IF command lets your batch files test whether a specific file exists, whether two character strings are equal, or whether the preceding command was successful.

Format

```
IF [NOT] condition DOS_command
```

NOT   Performs a Boolean NOT on the result of the condition.

condition   Must be one of the following:

ERRORLEVEL *value*	True if the preceding program's exit status is greater than or equal to the value
EXIST *file_spec*	True if the file specified exists
string1==string2	True if the two strings are identical

DOS_command   The name of the DOS command to perform if the condition is true.

Notes

Be careful when you use IF to test a program's exit status value. IF evaluates to true if the exit status is greater than or equal to the value specified. If you combine two IF commands, you can determine the exact exit status value:

```
IF ERRORLEVEL 1 IF NOT ERRORLEVEL 2 ECHO One
IF ERRORLEVEL 2 IF NOT ERRORLEVEL 3 ECHO Two
IF ERRORLEVEL 3 IF NOT ERRORLEVEL 4 ECHO Three
```

If you use IF to compare two strings, you should group the strings within single quotation marks. The IF command requires two strings to compare. If only one string is present, IF displays a "Syntax error" message.

If the user does not specify a value for %1 in the following example, IF will compare the null string ' ' to the string 'CONFIG.SYS':

```
IF '%1'=='CONFIG.SYS' TYPE %1
```

If the single quotation marks are not present, IF has only one string to compare and generates an error.

Although most users use the IF statement only from within batch files, IF is fully supported from the command line.

If you are using DOS 6, see the CHOICES command.

Examples

The following batch file uses IF to determine whether CONFIG.SYS exists in the current directory and, if so, copies it to drive A. Note the use of NOT to determine whether the file does not exist:

```
@ECHO OFF
IF EXIST CONFIG.SYS COPY CONFIG.SYS A:
IF NOT EXIST CONFIG.SYS ECHO File not found
```

Here, if the DOSPGM program exits with a status greater than or equal to 3, a message to that effect is displayed:

```
@ECHO OFF
DOSPGM
IF ERRORLEVEL 3 ECHO T H R E E
```

The following example uses the IF command to determine whether the value of a batch parameter is defined:

```
@ECHO OFF
IF '%1'=='' ECHO Not defined
IF NOT '%1'=='' ECHO The value is %1
```

INTERLNK

Redirects requests for a client drive or printer to a server

The DOS 6 INTERLNK and INTERSVR commands allow two computers to easily exchange files or share disks or printers over a serial or parallel cable. These two commands provide an ideal way for a user with a laptop computer to upload files to or retrieve files from a desktop PC.

Format

```
INTERLNK [Client[:]=[Server[:]]
```

Client   Specifies the local drive letter with which you want to refer to a specific disk drive on the server.

Server   Specifies the server disk you want to access.

Notes

Before you can use the INTERLNK command, you must first install the INTERLNK.EXE device driver in your CONFIG.SYS file. The format of DEVICE entry is as follows:

```
DEVICE=C:\DOS\INTERLNK.EXE [/DRIVES:NumberOfDrives]
      [/NOPRINTER][/AUTO][/BAUD:Rate][/LOW]
```

```
[/NOSCAN][/V][/COM[:][Number|Address]]
[/LPT[:][Number|Address]]
```

For specifics on each driver switch, refer to the book *DOS: The Complete Reference*, Fourth Edition.

To connect the computer, use a null-modem cable if you are using serial ports, or a bidirectional parallel cable if you are using parallel ports.

INTERLNK requires DOS 6.

Examples

The following CONFIG.SYS entry loads the INTERLNK device driver to support data exchange over a parallel cable connected to LPT1:

```
DEVICE=C:\DOS\INTERLNK.EXE /LPT1 /DRIVES:5
```

The following command directs INTERLNK to route references to the local (client) disk drive F to the server drive C:

```
C:\> INTERLNK F:=C:  <ENTER>
```

When you later refer to drive F, INTERLNK will route the request to drive C. To view the current mappings, invoke INTERLNK as follows:

```
C:\> INTERLNK <ENTER>

Port=COM1

This Computer          Other Computer
  (Client)                (Server)
-------------    ---------------------
  D:     equals    A:
  E:     equals    B:
  F:     equals    C: (499Kb)
  LPT2: equals     LPT1:
  LPT3: equals     LPT2:
```

As you can see, INTERLNK also displays available server printers. In this case, you can access the server's LPT1 printer using the client port name LPT2.

If you want to disable disk reference, invoke INTERLNK with the drive letter followed by an equal sign, as shown here:

```
C:\> INTERLNK F= <ENTER>
```

INTERSVR

Loads server that allows remote disk and printer access

The DOS 6 INTERSVR command works with the INTERLNK command to allow two computers to quickly exchange files over a serial or parallel cable connection.

Format

```
INTERSVR [Drive:]  [/X=Drive:]  [/LPT:[Number |
        Address]]  [/COM:[Number | Address]
          [/BAUD:Rate]  [/B]  [/V]  [/RCOPY]
```

Drive   Specifies a specific server drive you want available for client users. If you don't specify a drive, INTERSVR makes all drives available.

/X=Drive   Specifies a server drive you want to exclude client users from accessing.

/LPT:[Number | Address]   Specifies the LPT port number or address through which the connection will be make.

/COM:[Number | Address]   Specifies the COM port number or address through which the connection will be made.

/BAUD:*Rate* Specifies the data communication rate for a serial connection. Valid rates include 9600, 19200, 38400, 57600, and 115200. The default is 115200.

/B Directs INTERSVR to display a black-and-white screen.

/V Prevents INTERSVR conflicts with the computer's built-in timer. Use this switch if a computer quits running during a serial connection.

/RCOPY Directs INTERSVR to copy the INTERLNK and INTERSVR files to a remote client over serial lines.

Notes

The INTERSVR command does not require a device driver; to create a server, you simply invoke INTERSVR.

See INTERLNK. INTERSVR requires DOS 6.

Example

The following command makes all the server's drives available for redirection and specifies the connection between computers will occur using LPT1:

```
C:\> INTERSVR /LPT1 <ENTER>
```

In a similar way, this command specifies the connection will occur over COM1, but it excludes the redirection of drive D:

```
C:\> INTERSVR /COM1 /X=D <ENTER>
```

If the client computer to which you want to connect does not contain the INTERLNK and INTERSVR commands, you can copy the files to the client using a null-modem cable and serial ports. The following command directs INTERSVR to copy the files to the client:

```
C:\> INTERSVR /RCOPY <ENTER>
```

After you issue this command, follow the prompts INTERSVR displays.

JOIN

Joins a disk drive to an empty subdirectory

JOIN makes two disks seem like one by joining a disk to a DOS path that represents an empty subdirectory. DOS 6 does not support the JOIN command.

Format

```
JOIN[d1:[d2:path]][/D]
```

d1:   Specifies the disk drive to be joined to the path provided.

d2:path   Specifies the directory to be joined.

/D   Disconnects a previously joined disk.

Notes

Users with two floppy-drive systems often have applications that must open more files than can fit on a single disk. By using the JOIN command, they can "join" the disk in drive B to a subdirectory in drive A, making the two disk drives seem to be one large disk.

If you issue a JOIN command without any parameters, JOIN displays the current joins. DOS will join a disk only to an empty DOS directory.

Do not use JOIN in conjunction with the BACKUP, CHKDSK, DISK-COMP, DISKCOPY, FDISK, FORMAT, LABEL, RECOVER, RESTORE, or SYS commands.

Examples

The following command joins drive A to the empty subdirectory JOINDIR, which resides on drive C:

```
C:\> JOIN A: \JOINDIR <ENTER>
```

In this case, references to C:JOINDIR are identical to references to drive A. If drive A contains subdirectories, simply refer to them as follows:

```
C:\> DIR \JOINDIR\SUBDIR <ENTER>
```

To remove a join, use the /D parameter:

```
C:\> JOIN A: /D <ENTER>
```

KEYB

Loads a foreign keyboard set

To support fully international configurations, DOS provides support for various keyboard templates. The KEYB command loads memory-resident software to replace the standard keyboard layout provided by DOS.

Format

```
KEYB[keyboard_code[,code_page],[filespec]]]
   [/E][/ID:keyboard]
```

keyboard_code   Specifies the two-letter code associated with the desired keyboard.

code_page   The desired code page (see CHCP).

filespec   The name of the file containing the keyboard definitions (normally, KEYBOARD.SYS).

/E   Setup for an enhanced keyboard (DOS 5 or later).

/ID:keyboard   Specifies the keyboard type (DOS 5 or later); only needed for countries with two or more layouts.

Notes

Once a new keyboard is installed, you can toggle between it and the default keyboard by pressing CTRL-ALT-F1 for the default keyboard and CTRL-ALT-F2 for the foreign keyboard. Common keyboard layouts (and the matching keyboard codes) include

BE	Belgium	PL	Poland
BR	Brazil	PO	Portugal
CF	Canadian French	SF	Swiss French
CZ	Czech	SL	Slavic
DK	Denmark	SG	Swiss German
FR	France	SP	Spain
GR	Germany	SU	Finland
HU	Hungary	SV	Sweden
IT	Italy	UK	United Kingdom
LA	Latin America	US	United States

NL   Netherlands   YU   Yugoslavia
NO   Norway

If you are using a secondary keyboard template, place the corresponding KEYB command in the AUTOEXEC.BAT file to ensure that the keyboard you want is in effect whenever your system starts.

DOS versions prior to 3.3 provide individual country keyboard commands in the form KEYB*xx*.COM, where *xx* is the two-letter code that represents a specific country.

KEYB supports the following exit status values:

0   Keyboard successfully loaded
1   Invalid keyboard, code page, or syntax
2   Invalid keyboard definition file
4   CON device error
5   Error preparing code page

Examples

Use this command if you want DOS to use the United Kingdom keyboard template:

```
C:\> KEYB UK <ENTER>
```

This command selects the French keyboard template and informs DOS that the file KEYBOARD.SYS resides in the subdirectory C:\DOS:

```
C:\> KEYB FR,850,C:\DOS\KEYBOARD.SYS <ENTER>
```

LABEL

Specifies a disk volume label

DOS allows you to define a name (called a *volume label*) for each disk. Disk labels help you organize your floppy disks and can prevent an inadvertent format of your hard disk. The LABEL command allows you to display and set the volume label of a given disk.

Format

LABEL[*target_drive*:][*volume_label*]

target_drive: The disk drive that contains the disk to be labeled.

volume_label   An 11-character volume label. All characters valid in DOS file names are valid in volume labels.

Notes

Whenever you issue the DIR command, DOS displays the volume label of the disk for which it is displaying the directory, as shown here:

```
Volume in drive A is DOSLABEL
Directory of  A:\
```

It is also possible to use software to obtain the disk volume label from within your DOS programs. By so doing, you can ensure that the user has the correct disk in the drive.

If you do not specify a volume label in the command line, LABEL prompts you for one, as follows:

```
Volume in drive C is DOSDISK
Volume label (11 characters, ENTER for none)?
```

If you do not want to change the disk label, press ENTER; otherwise, type in the volume name you want.

Using DOS 4 or later, the FORMAT command prompts you to enter the disk volume label before it formats your hard disk. By assigning a unique label to the disk, you reduce the possibility of inadvertently formatting your hard disk.

The VOL command also displays volume label (see VOL).

Examples

The following command gives the name DOSDISK to the floppy disk in drive A:

```
C:\> LABEL A:DOSDISK <ENTER>
```

Since the command line contains a label name, LABEL does not prompt the user for information.

In the following command, the label name is not specified in the command line:

```
C:\> LABEL <ENTER>
```

In such a case, LABEL prompts:

```
Volume in drive C is DOSDISK
Volume label (11 characters, ENTER for none)?
```

If you are using DOS 5 or later, the LABEL command also displays the disk's serial number, as shown here:

```
Volume in drive C is DOSDISK
Volume Serial Number is 1234-5678
Volume label (11 characters, ENTER for none)?
```

Either enter the label name you want, or press the ENTER key to leave the current label name unchanged. If you are using DOS 5 or later, after you press ENTER you will see another prompt, which allows you to indicate whether you wish to delete the current volume label.

LOADFIX

Loads a program into the conventional memory above 64Kb

In DOS 5 or later, you can use the DOS=HIGH,UMB CONFIG.SYS entry to load DOS into the high-memory area and to maintain a link to reserved memory for use by DEVICEHIGH and LOADHIGH to load device drivers and memory-resident programs into reserved memory. Each of these techniques frees conventional memory for DOS, possibly letting commands execute in the conventional address space below 64Kb.

Some programs cannot execute below 64Kb and will display the error message "Packed file corrupt" when you execute them. Using LOADFIX, you can direct DOS to load these programs above 64Kb, thus solving the problem.

Format

```
LOADFIX pathname [parameters]
```

pathname   The path name of the program to execute.

parameters   The program's optional command-line parameters.

Notes

LOADFIX requires DOS 5 or later. You will not need to use LOADFIX unless you experience the "Packed file corrupt" error message.

Example

The following command loads the program SOMEPROG.EXE above 64Kb in conventional memory:

```
C:\> LOADFIX  SOMEPROG.EXE parameters <ENTER>
```

LOADHIGH

Loads a program into reserved memory

Conventional memory is your computer's memory from 0 to 640Kb. *Reserved memory* is the memory from 640Kb to 1Mb and normally is used for device I/O. *Extended memory* is the memory beyond 1Mb. Most programs run in conventional memory. Beginning with DOS 5, the LOADHIGH command lets DOS load memory-resident programs into the unused portions of reserved memory. By loading programs into reserved memory, you leave more conventional memory available to your application programs.

Format

```
LOADHIGH pathname [parameters]
```

or

```
LH pathname [pathname]
```

pathname The complete path name, including the disk drive letter, of the program DOS is to load into reserved memory.

parameters The optional command-line parameters.

Notes

To use LOADHIGH, you must load EMM386.EXE and direct DOS to save the link between reserved and conventional memory by using CONFIG.SYS's DOS=UMB entry as shown here:

```
DEVICE=C:\DOS\EMM386.EXE NOEMS
DOS=UMB
```

If the reserved memory available is insufficient to load the program, DOS will load the program into conventional memory. DOS does not indicate when this has occurred.

DOS lets you abbreviate LOADHIGH as LH.

Example

The following command loads a memory-resident program named SOMEPROG.EXE into reserved memory:

```
C:\> LOADHIGH SOMEPROG.EXE <ENTER>
```

MEM

Provides information on current memory usage

MEM is a DOS 4 or later command that displays your system's current memory usage. MEM is used most often by programmers.

Format

```
MEM[/DEBUG][/PROGRAM][/CLASSIFY][/FREE][/PAGE][/MODULE Name]
```

/DEBUG   Tells MEM to display the location of each device driver in memory as well as each program's memory usage. This parameter can also be abbreviated as /D.

/PROGRAM   Tells MEM to display all programs that currently reside in memory and a summary of their usage. This parameter can also be abbreviated as /P.

/CLASSIFY   Classifies programs by memory use (DOS 5).

/FREE   A DOS 6 switch that directs MEM to display the free areas in conventional and upper memory. You can abbreviate this switch as /F.

/PAGE   A DOS 6 switch that directs MEM to pause after each screenful of information. You can abbreviate this switch as /P.

/MODULE *Name*   Directs MEM to display information about how a specific program is currently using memory.

Notes

With the introduction of the DOS 5 memory-management tools, the MEM command has become a very convenient way to determine your system's memory utilization. MEM will display information about

```
Conventional, extended, and expanded memory use.

Available conventional and upper memory.

Program and device driver memory use.
```

Examples

If you invoke MEM with no switches, MEM will display a summary of your memory use:

```
C:\> MEM <ENTER>

Memory Type         Total  =  Used   +  Free
----------------    ------    ------    ------
Conventional          640K       57K      583K
Upper                  59K       43K       16K
Adapter RAM/ROM       325K      325K        0K
Extended (XMS)       7168K     2624K     4544K
Expanded (EMS)       7488K     2704K     4784K
----------------    ------    ------    ------
Total memory        15680K     5753K     9927K

Total under 1 MB      699K      100K      599K

Largest executable program size        583K  (596528 bytes)
Largest free upper memory block         11K   (10784 bytes)
MS-DOS is resident in the high memory area.
```

The following command displays specifics about how programs and drivers are using memory:

```
C:\> MEM /DEBUG <ENTER>
```

If you are using DOS 6, you can display the previous output a screenful at a time using the /PAGE switch:

```
C:\> MEM /DEBUG /PAGE <ENTER>
```

Finally, the following MEM command tells you the memory use for a specific program, which in this case is COMMAND.COM:

```
C:\> MEM /MODULE COMMAND <ENTER>

COMMAND is using the following memory:

  Segment  Region        Size         Type
  -------  ------   ----------------   --------
   00667                2640    (3K)   Program
   00711                1040    (1K)   Environment
                   ----------------
  Total Size:          3680    (4K)
```

MEMMAKER

Optimizes memory use on a 386 or higher

MEMMAKER optimizes your system's memory use by moving device drivers and memory-resident programs from conventional to upper memory. MEMMAKER may change your CONFIG.SYS, AUTOEXEC.BAT, and Windows SYSTEM.INI files.

Format

```
MEMMAKER [/BATCH] [/SWAP:Drive] [/UNDO]
        [/W:WindowsBuffer1,WindowsBuffer2]
```

/BATCH   Directs MEMMAKER to select its default options for all prompts, running without user intervention.

/SWAP:*Drive*   Specifies the drive letter of your original startup disk. The switch is only necessary if you are using a third-party software program that changes the startup drive to possibly a compressed drive.

/UNDO   Directs MEMMAKER to undo its most recent changes to CONFIG.SYS, AUTOEXEC.BAT, and SYSTEM.INI.

/W:*WindowsBuffer1*,*WindowsBuffer2* Specifies the amount of memory in Kb (1024 bytes) DOS reserves for Windows translation buffers. The default is 12Kb. If you don't use Windows, use the value 0,0.

Notes

If you run MEMMAKER in batch mode, MEMMAKER records information about each of its changes to the file MEMMAKER.STS. Using EDIT or TYPE, you can display the file's contents.

If MEMMAKER changes your CONFIG.SYS, AUTOEXEC.BAT, or SYSTEM.INI files MEMMAKER stores each file's original contents in files with the OLD extension (such as CONFIG.OLD).

When Windows runs in protected mode, Windows allocates two buffers in the upper-memory area that it uses for input and output operations to devices that must operate beneath 1Mb. If you don't use Windows, use the value 0 for each buffer to prevent the buffer allocation.

MEMMAKER requires DOS 6.

Examples

The following command invokes MEMMAKER, allowing you to respond to MEMMAKER's prompts so you can control the changes made:

```
C:\> MEMMAKER <ENTER>
```

The following command directs MEMMAKER to prevent the allocation of the two 12Kb Windows translation buffers:

```
C:\> MEMMAKER /W:0,0 <ENTER>
```

MIRROR

Stores critical disk information

A DOS 5 command, MIRROR saves critical disk information to a file named MIRROR.FIL, from which the UNFORMAT command can later rebuild an inadvertently formatted or recovered disk. (If you recover a disk that is not damaged, you may scramble it beyond recognition.)

Format

```
MIRROR [d:][/Tdrive[-entries]]
  [[/Tdrive[entries]]...][/1]
MIRROR [d:][/PARTN]
MIRROR [d:][/U]
```

d: Specifies the drive letter for which you want MIRROR to record the critical disk information. If you don't specify a drive letter, MIRROR uses the default.

/1   Keeps only the latest information about the disk. By default, MIRROR makes a backup copy of the previous information, storing the information in the file MIRROR.BAK.

/Tdrive[-entries]   Installs a memory-resident program that records information about every file deleted from the disk specified. The *entries* option specifies the number of deleted files that MIRROR should track, from 1 to 999. If this information is available, the UNDELETE program uses it.

/U   Tells MIRROR to remove the memory-resident delete tracking program from memory, disabling file-delete tracking.

/PARTN   Saves the hard disk partition information to a floppy disk.

Notes

The MIRROR command saves a copy of the root directory and file allocation table. The more often you invoke MIRROR, the less likely you are to inadvertently lose files.

MIRROR stores information in a file named MIRROR.FIL, which resides in the root directory. The UNFORMAT command uses this information to rebuild a damaged disk. The size of MIRROR.FIL depends on your disk type.

If you invoke MIRROR with /T*drive*, MIRROR will create a file to store information about each file you delete. The UNDELETE command uses (but does not require) this file. If you want to track multiple drives, they must all be entered at the same time. To change an existing configuration, use the /U parameter to first disable tracking.

Use /PARTN to save a copy of the disk's partition table information to a floppy disk. Store the floppy disk safely.

Examples

The following command tells MIRROR to record the file allocation table and the root directory for drive C and to install file-delete tracking for that drive:

```
C:\> MIRROR C: /TC <ENTER>
```

The following command tells MIRROR to save drive C's partition table information:

```
C:\> MIRROR C: /PARTN <ENTER>
```

MIRROR will prompt you for the letter of the disk drive containing the disk on which you want the partition table information written.

MKDIR

Creates the subdirectory specified

DOS subdirectories let you organize your files by grouping related files into a list called a *directory.* The MKDIR command creates directories on your disk.

Format

```
MKDIR [drive:]path
MD [drive:]path
```

drive: Specifies the drive on which to create the subdirectory. If a drive is not specified, MKDIR uses the default drive.

path   Specifies the name of the directory that MKDIR is to create.

Notes

The abbreviated form of the MKDIR command is MD.

Every DOS disk has a root directory (\) from which all other sub-directories grow. If you do not use DOS subdirectories, your disks are restricted to a limited number of files in the root directory.

You use MKDIR to create subdirectories. Whenever you create a subdirectory, one of two things happens. If the directory name starts with a backslash (as in \SUBDIR), DOS starts with the root directory to create the subdirectory. If the name does not start with a backslash (as in SUBDIR), DOS creates the directory within the current directory.

Follow these "rules of thumb" when you create DOS directories:

❑   DOS directory names have the same format as DOS file names.

❑   DOS can process a *path name* (the representation of all directories and subdirectories) of up to 63 characters.

❑ If you do not specify a complete path name when you create a subdirectory, DOS assumes that you are creating the directory in the current directory.

❑ To manipulate directories on other disks, precede the directory name with a disk drive identifier (as in B:\CARS).

❑ Do not create directory names identical to the names of files contained in the same directory.

❑ Root directories on each disk are restricted to a specific number of files because of the disk layout. Subdirectories, however, can contain an unlimited number of files.

Examples

In the following example, MKDIR creates a directory called IBM in the root directory:

```
C:\> MKDIR \IBM <ENTER>
```

Similarly, the following command creates a subdirectory called NOTES in the IBM directory:

```
C:\> MKDIR \IBM\NOTES <ENTER>
```

Assuming that the current directory is still the root, this command:

```
C:\> MKDIR MISC <ENTER>
```

also creates a subdirectory in the root. In this case, the subdirectory name does not contain a slash, so MKDIR creates the directory in the current directory (which, in this case, is still the root).

MODE

Specifies device characteristics

The MODE command allows you to set parameters or characteristics for many types of devices. MODE specifies how DOS should interact with the device.

Format

```
VIDEO DISPLAY:
MODE n
MODE [n],m,[t]
```

or, using DOS 5 or later:

```
MODE CON[:][COLS=columns][LINES=lines]
COM PORTS:
MODE COM#[:] baud[,parity[,data[,stop[,P]]]]
```

or, using DOS 5 or later:

```
MODE COM#[:] BAUD=baud [PARITY=parity]
  [DATA=data][STOP=stop]
  [RETRY=r]
```

To configure for a parallel printer:

```
MODE LPT#[:][cpl][,vli][,P]
```

or, using DOS 5 or later:

```
MODE LPT#:[COLS=cpl][LINES=vli][RETRY=r]
```

To accomplish printer redirection:

```
MODE LPT#[:]=COM#[:]
```

To configure international code pages:

```
·MODE device CODEPAGE operation
```

To fine-tune your keyboard response (using DOS 5 or later):

```
MODE CON[:][RATE=rate][DELAY=delay]
```

n   Specifies the screen-display attribute, which must be one of the following:

40	40-column display
80	80-column display
BW40	Black-and-white 40-column display
BW80	Black-and-white 80-column display
CO40	Color 40-column display
CO80	Color 80-column display
MONO	Monochrome display

m   Specifies the direction to shift the screen display one character, either to the left or to the right.

t   Asks MODE to display a test pattern to aid in character alignment.

columns   The number of characters per line on the screen: can be either 40 or 80.

lines   The number of lines on the screen: 25, 43, or 50.

COM#   Specifies the serial port number, such as COM1.

baud   Specifies the device baud rate: 110, 150, 300, 600, 1200, 2400, 4800, 9600, or 19200. MODE requires only that you specify the first two digits of the baud rate.

parity   Specifies the device parity: E for even parity, N for no parity, and O for odd parity. The default is even parity.

data   Specifies the number of data bits: 7 or 8. The default number is 7 data bits.

stop   Specifies the number of stop bits: 1 or 2. For 110 baud, the default is 2; otherwise, it is 1.

P   Specifies continuous retries on time-out errors. (This parameter makes a part of MODE memory resident.)

r   Specifies the retry action on time-out errors. (This parameter makes a part of MODE memory resident.) Options are as follows:

E	Returns a busy status error (the default)
B	Returns a busy status (same as using P parameter)
R	Returns a ready status
None	Performs no action

cpl   Characters per line on the printer (80, 132).

vli   Vertical lines per inch (6, 8).

LPT#   Specifies the parallel printer number, such as LPT1.

device   Specifies the device for which to manipulate a code page (CON, LPT*n*).

operation   The code-page operation has several options. Use one of the following:

prepare=[[*code_page*][*filename*]]
select=*code_page*
refresh
/STATUS

rate   Specifies the keyboard typematic rate in clock ticks. Values range from 1 to 32.

delay Specifies the length of time you must hold down a key before DOS begins to repeat the character. The values are 1, 2, 3, and 4; they correspond to 0.25, 0.50, 0.75, and 1.0 seconds.

Notes

MODE is one of the most difficult DOS commands, mainly because it is used for complex concepts (such as serial data communication or printer redirection). Unless you are using a serial laser printer or modem, chances are you will never have to issue the MODE command. If you are using the MODE command, your printer or modem documentation probably specifies the MODE command you need to issue. Place this command into the AUTOEXEC.BAT file so that you can forget about it.

By default, DOS uses the parallel printer port for printed data. If your printer is connected to a serial device, you can redirect the parallel output to the serial device by using MODE.

If you are using DOS 3.3 or later, the MODE command allows preparation and selection of code pages for the screen display and printer. The PREPARE operation tells DOS to prepare a code page for use on the device specified. The SELECT operation chooses a specific code page to be used by the device. If you download a code page to your printer device while the printer is turned off, you can restore the code page by using the REFRESH operation. Finally, the /STATUS operation lists the code pages currently in use or prepared for the device specified.

MODE supports the following abbreviations:

CP   CODEPAGE
/STA   /STATUS
PREP   PREPARE
SEL   SELECT
REF   REFRESH

Examples

This command sets the screen display to 40 columns per line:

```
C:\> MODE 40 <ENTER>
```

If you are using DOS 5 or later, an equivalent command is

```
C:\> MODE CON: COLS=40 <ENTER>
```

The following command routes data from the parallel port (LPT1) to the serial port (COM1):

```
C:\> MODE LPT1:=COM1: <ENTER>
```

The next command specifies the data-communication parameters for COM1:

```
C:\> MODE COM1 96,N,8,1 <ENTER>
```

If you are using DOS 3.3 or later and an EGA monitor, the following command prepares the display for the Multilingual and Portuguese code pages:

```
C:\> MODE CON CODEPAGE PREPARE=(850,860)
    C:\DOS\EGA.CPI <ENTER>
```

Note that you must specify the code-page information file (CPI) in the command line. In DOS 4 or later, this command line would be entered with an extra set of parentheses:

```
C:\> MODE CON CODEPAGE PREPARE=((850,860) C:\DOS\4201.CPI) <ENTER>
```

After you prepare a code page for a device, you select the code page by means of the SELECT option, as shown here:

```
C:\> MODE CON CODEPAGE SELECT=860 <ENTER>
```

If your printer supports code pages, the following command prepares the printer for the Multilingual and Portuguese code pages:

```
C:\> MODE LPT1 CODEPAGE PREPARE=(850,860) C:\DOS\4201.CPI <ENTER>
```

If you are using DOS 4 or later, this command line would be entered with an extra set of parentheses:

```
C:\> MODE LPT1 CODEPAGE PREPARE=((850,860) C:\DOS\4201.CPI) <ENTER>
```

MORE

Displays a command's output a screenful at a time

MORE enables you to view a file or a program's output one screenful at a time. Press any key when you are ready to view the next screenful of information.

Format

```
DOS_command | MORE < DOS_file
MORE < DOS_file
```

Notes

The MORE command reads data from the standard input device, displaying the information on the standard output device, a page at a time, until an end-of-file marker is encountered. Each time a page of data is displayed on the screen, MORE displays the message:

```
-- MORE --
```

Press any key to continue the output or press CTRL-C to terminate the command.

Examples

The following command displays the files in the directory a screenful at a time:

```
C:\> DIR | MORE <ENTER>
```

By including the SORT command, you can enhance the previous command to display a sorted directory listing one screenful at a time:

```
C:\> DIR | SORT | MORE <ENTER>
```

To display the contents of a file named DATA.DAT one screenful at a time, use MORE as shown here:

```
C:\> MORE < DATA.DAT <ENTER>
```

MOVE

Moves a file from one directory to another

The MOVE command lets you move a file from one directory to another or rename an existing directory. MOVE does not let you move directories.

Format

```
MOVE Source Target
```

Source   Specifies the file or files that you want to move or the directory you want to rename. MOVE fully supports wildcard characters.

Target Specifies the directory into which you want to move the files or the desired name of a directory that you are renaming.

Notes

The MOVE command lets you move one or more files from one directory to another or rename a directory. If a file exists in the target directory with the same name as you are using in the MOVE operation, the original file (if not read-only) is overwritten. MOVE lets you move files from one disk to another. If MOVE succeeds, MOVE returns an exit status of 0.

The MOVE command lets you rename a directory. You cannot MOVE a directory, however. MOVE requires DOS 6.

Examples

The following MOVE command renames the directory OLDNAME to NEWNAME:

```
C:\> MOVE OLDNAME NEWNAME <ENTER>
```

The next MOVE command moves the file BUDGET.DAT from the REPORTS directory into the directory FINANCE:

```
C:\> MOVE \REPORTS\BUDGET.DAT  \FINANCE <ENTER>
```

MOVE fully supports wildcard characters. The following command moves the files with the TAX extension from the BUDGET directory to the directory PAYMENTS:

```
C:\> MOVE \BUDGET\*.TAX  \PAYMENTS <ENTER>
```

You can use MOVE to move a directory. If you try to do so, the command will fail, as shown here:

```
C:\> MOVE \BUDGET \COMPANY\BUDGET <ENTER>
c:\budget => c:\company\budget [Permission denied]
```

MSAV

Examines your computer's memory and disks for viruses

The MSAV command scans your computer's memory and disk files for known viruses. If a virus is detected, MSAV may be able to remove the infection.

Format

```
MSAV  [[Drive:][...] | Path]
      [/A][/C | /S][/F][/L][/N][/P][/R]
      [/VideoSetting][/IM][/LE][/NGM][/PS2]
```

Drive: Specifies a disk drive whose files MSAV will scan for viruses. The ellipses (...) indicate you can specify several disk drives.

Path   Specifies a directory whose files MSAV will scan for viruses.

/A   Directs MSAV to scan all drives except A and B.

/C   Directs MSAV to scan the specified files and remove any viruses it encounters.

/F   Directs MSAV to turn off the display of file names it has scanned when you use /N or /P.

/L   Directs MSAV to scan all drives except network drives.

/N   Directs MSAV not to display information as it scans, but rather to write the information to the file MSAV.TXT, whose contents you can later view using the DOS TYPE command.

/P   Directs MSAV to display a command-line interface as opposed to its graphical menu display.

/R   Directs MSAV to create the file MSAV.RPT, which lists the files scanned, number of viruses found, and the viruses removed. By default, MSAV does not create this file.

/S   Directs MSAV to scan the specified disk for viruses, identifying them, but not correcting them.

/VideoSetting   Directs MSAV to use a specific video mode. The value specified must be one of the following:

25	25-line text mode
28	28-line VGA text mode
43	43-line EGA and VGA text mode
50	50-line VGA mode
60	60-line mode for video 7 adapters
IN	Directs MSAV to use color
BW	Directs MSAV to use black and white
MONO	Directs MSAV to use monochrome
LCD	Directs MSAV to support an LCD monitor
FF	Directs MSAV to perform fast CGA screen updates
BF	Directs MSAV to use the BIOS for video output
NF	Directs MSAV to disable the use of alternative fonts
BT	Directs MSAV to support a graphics mouse cursor in Windows

/IM   Directs MSAV not to support a mouse.

/LE   Directs MSAV to exchange the left and right mouse buttons.

/NGM   Directs MSAV to use a text or block mouse cursor.

/PS2   Directs MSAV to support a PS/2 system mouse.

Notes

MSAV will scan your computer's memory and files on disk for known viruses. In most cases, MSAV can eliminate the virus. The more often you invoke MSAV, the less likely a VIRUS can damage your disk or files. Because MSAV executes very quickly, you might consider placing the MSAV command in your AUTOEXEC.BAT file, especially if you frequently exchange disks or files with other users.

MSAV requires DOS 6. See also VSAFE.

Examples

MSAV provides a set of menus that let you quickly select the options you desire. As such, most users simply invoke MSAV as follows:

```
C:\> MSAV <ENTER>
```

The following MSAV command directs MSAV to scan drive C for viruses, reporting the existence of a virus without correcting it:

```
C:\> MSAV  C: /S <ENTER>
```

MSBACKUP

Invokes the DOS 6 menu-driven backup utility.

Format

```
MSBACKUP  [SetupFile]  [/T[D|I|F]]  [/BW|/LCD|/MDA]
```

SetupFile   Specifies the name of a setup file that contains the desired backup options. If you don't specify a file name, MSBACKUP uses the name DEFAULT.SET.

/T   Specifies the desired backup type: Differential, Incremental, or Full.

/BW   Runs MSBACKUP in black and white.

/LCD   Runs MSBACKUP using an LCD video display mode.

/MDA   Runs MSBACKUP using a monochrome display adapter video mode.

Notes

MSBACKUP setup files specify which files you want to back up, backup options (such as verification), and the backup type. You create setup files within MSBACKUP. A differential backup operation backs up all files specified in the setup file that have changed since the last full disk backup. An incremental backup backs up all specified files that have been changed since the last incremental or full backup operation. A full backup operation backs up every file on your disk.

MSBACKUP requires DOS 6.

Example

MSBACKUP provides a menu-driven user interface. Therefore, most users will invoke MSBACKUP as follows:

```
C:\> MSBACKUP <ENTER>
```

MSBACKUP, in turn, will display its menu-driven interface as shown in the following:

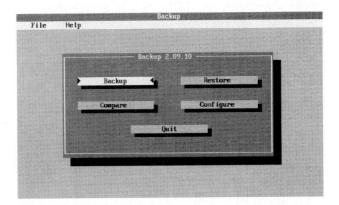

MSD

Provides detailed technical specifics about your computer's hardware configuration.

Format

```
MSD [/B] [/I] [/F Filename.Ext]
    [/P Filename.Ext] [/S Filename.Ext]
```

/B   Directs MSD to run in black and white.

/I   Directs MSD not to perform its initial hardware detection. Use this switch if MSD fails to start.

/F Filename.Ext   Directs MSD to prompt you for your name, company, address, and phone number, and then writes them plus a complete hardware report to the file specified.

/P Filename.Ext   Directs MSD to write a complete hardware report to the file specified.

/S *Filename.Ext*   Directs MSD to write a summary report to the file specified.

Notes

MSD is a Microsoft diagnostic utility that provides detailed information about your computer's memory, port, and IRQ settings, as well as device drivers and TSRs.

Example

When you invoke MSD, your screen displays a menu of settings options, as shown here:

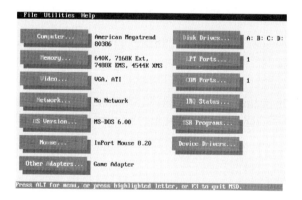

NLSFUNC

Provides device support for international code pages

NLSFUNC (National Language Support Function) is used by international DOS users to change character sets.

Format

```
NLSFUNC[file_spec]
```

file_spec   The complete DOS file specification for the file that contains the country information. This file is usually COUNTRY.SYS.

Notes

The only users who will have to issue the NLSFUNC command are those concerned with code-page support for international character sets. If you are modifying code pages, you must issue the NLSFUNC command before you can invoke CHCP.

If you are using DOS 4 or later, you can use the CONFIG.SYS INSTALL= entry to load NLSFUNC during system startup.

Example

The following command informs DOS that the country information file (COUNTRY.SYS) resides in the directory on drive C:\DOS:

```
C:\> NLSFUNC C:\DOS\COUNTRY.SYS <ENTER>
```

PATH

Defines a command-file search path

The PATH command defines the search path (the list of directories that DOS will follow) to locate an external command. By defining a command-file search path, you can easily execute your commonly used commands regardless of your current directory.

Format

PATH[*drive:*][*path*][;[*drive:*][*path*]...]

drive: The disk drive that DOS is to include in the command-file search path.

path   A DOS subdirectory to include in the command-file search path.

Notes

Each time you type in a command name from the DOS prompt, DOS first checks whether the command is an internal command that resides in RAM. If so, DOS executes the command. Each time DOS fails to locate a command internally, it searches the current directory or the directory specified in the command line. If DOS cannot find a matching EXE, COM, or BAT file, DOS checks whether you have defined a command-file search path. If so, DOS searches each of the directories specified in the command path for the command.

The PATH command enables you to define disk drives and subdirectories to be included in this search path.

To reduce overhead with each file reference, place the directories that are most likely to contain command files first in your PATH command. Each time DOS fails to locate a command in the current directory, it searches the first entry in your PATH path. If DOS still doesn't locate your file in that directory, it searches the second, third, and so on. If your commonly used commands reside in the directories specified at the end of the PATH command, DOS has to perform needless directory searches.

Examples

In the following example, if DOS cannot find the command, it will search the root directories on drives C, B, and A, in that order:

```
C:\> PATH C:\;B:\;A:\ <ENTER>
```

In a similar manner, the following PATH command tells DOS to search
C:\DOS, C:\BATCH, and then C:\MISC:

```
C:\> PATH C:\DOS;C:\BATCH;C:\MISC <ENTER>
```

PAUSE

Suspends execution of a batch file and displays an optional message

The PAUSE command temporarily suspends a batch file's processing
until the user presses a key to continue.

Format

```
PAUSE [message]
```

message   An optional message of up to 121 characters that PAUSE is
to display when it suspends batch processing.

Notes

When it encounters a PAUSE command within a batch file, DOS will
display a message similar to the following:

```
[optional message text]
Strike a key when ready . . .
```

The optional message is normally an instructional message the batch file displays to the user, such as to turn on the printer.

To continue batch processing, press any key; otherwise, press CTRL-BREAK. If you press CTRL-BREAK, DOS will display the following:

```
Terminate batch job (Y/N)?
```

To terminate the batch file, type **Y**; otherwise, type **N**.

The ECHO OFF command (see ECHO) suppresses the display of messages from PAUSE.

Examples

When DOS 5 or later encounters the PAUSE command with a batch procedure, as shown here:

```
PAUSE Insert a blank disk in drive B
```

it will pause and display

```
C:\> PAUSE Enter a blank disk in drive B
Press any key to continue . . .
```

In a similar manner, the command

```
PAUSE
```

will not display an instructional message but will still suspend processing. The following shows what happens if PAUSE is invoked with a DOS version prior to DOS 5:

```
C:\> PAUSE <ENTER>
Strike a key when ready . . .
```

POWER

Uses the Advanced Power Management (APM) specification supported by some computers to reduce the computer's power consumption when programs are idle.

Format

```
POWER [ADV[:MAX\REG\MIN]|STD|OFF
```

ADV Specifies the type of power conservation desired: maximum, regular, or minimum.

STD Directs POWER to use only those power consumption capabilities supported by your computer or to turn off APM if the hardware does not support it.

OFF Turns off advanced power management.

Notes

Not all hardware supports advanced power management. Before you can use the POWER command, you must first install the device driver POWER.EXE within your CONFIG.SYS file. The format of the entry is the same as the POWER command with the exception that the driver supports the optional /LOW switch, which directs DOS to install the driver in low memory. By default, the driver uses upper memory if it is available.

Example

The following CONFIG.SYS entry installs the POWER.EXE device driver:

```
DEVICE=C:\DOS\POWER.EXE
```

After the driver is installed, you can use the POWER command to change its settings.

PRINT

Prints a DOS file via the print queue

The PRINT command prints one or more ASCII files from the DOS prompt.

Format

```
PRINT [/D:device_name][/C][/T][/P]
   [/B:buffer_size][/M:max_ticks]
   [/Q:queue_size][/S:time_slice]
   [/U:busy_ticks]file_spec[...]
```

/D:*device_name*   The name of the device that DOS is to use for the printer. The default device is PRN or LPT1.

/C   Cancellation of printing the file that precedes the /C and all those that follow.

/T   Cancellation of all the print jobs in the printer queue.

/P   Addition of the preceding file name and all those that follow to the print queue.

/B:*buffer_size*   The amount of memory (in bytes) that is set aside for PRINT. The default size is 512. By increasing this size in multiples of 512 (1024, 2048, 4096), you will improve PRINT's performance by decreasing the number of required disk I/O operations. However, increasing this value consumes memory.

/M:*max_ticks* The maximum number of CPU clock ticks that PRINT can consume before it must return control to DOS. This value can range from 1 to 255; the default value is 2. This parameter is only valid the first time that you invoke PRINT. Increasing this value will improve PRINT's performance, because it has more control of the CPU. However, if you make this value too large, the rest of your applications will become sluggish when PRINT is working.

/Q:*queue_size* The number of entries that the PRINT queue can store. This value can range from 4 to 32; the default value is 10. This parameter is only valid the first time you invoke PRINT.

/S:*time_slice* The number of CPU clock ticks that PRINT must wait before it can run again. (CPU clock ticks occur 18.2 times per second on the IBM PC.) This value must be in the range from 1 to 255; the default value is 8. This parameter is only valid the first time you invoke PRINT.

/U:*busy_ticks* The number of CPU clock ticks that PRINT will wait before the printer becomes available for the next series of characters. This value can range from 1 to 255; the default value is 1. This parameter is only valid the first time you invoke PRINT.

_file_spec_ The complete path name of the file to be added to, or removed from, the print queue. PRINT supports DOS wildcard characters.

Notes

The PRINT command sends files to the printer in a background mode, which means that you can continue processing in the foreground while printing takes place in the background.

The PRINT command lines the files in a print queue that are then printed in order of their entry in the queue.

Experiment with the PRINT parameters /B, /M, and /U. For starters, try this PRINT command:

```
C:\> PRINT /D:LPT1: /B:4096 /M:24 /U:8 <ENTER>
```

Once you are satisfied with PRINT's performance and your overall system performance, place the associated PRINT command in the AUTO-EXEC.BAT file, so you have a consistent PRINT installation for each user session.

Examples

The following command installs a print queue with storage for 32 files:

```
C:\> PRINT /Q:32 <ENTER>
```

Remember that many parameters are only valid the first time you issue a PRINT command.

The next command prints all the files in the current directory that have an extension of DAT:

```
C:\> PRINT *.DAT <ENTER>
```

In a similar manner, this command prints the CONFIG.SYS file:

```
C:\> PRINT CONFIG.SYS <ENTER>
```

The following command terminates all current print jobs:

```
C:\> PRINT /T <ENTER>
```

This command removes the AUTOEXEC.BAT file from the print queue:

```
C:\> PRINT AUTOEXEC.BAT /C <ENTER>
```

PROMPT

Defines the system prompt that appears on the display

The PROMPT command defines how the DOS prompt appears on the screen display.

Format

PROMPT[*prompt_string*]

prompt_string   The character string that defines the DOS prompt. The prompt can contain characters or the following metastrings:

$$	$ character	$n	Current drive
$_	Carriage return/line feed	$p	Current drive and directory
$b	| character	$q	= character
$d	Date	$t	Current time
$e	ESC character	$v	DOS version
$g	> character	$l	< character
$h	Backspace		

Notes

If no string is specified, PROMPT resets the system prompt to the default drive. The DOS prompt can be a help facility for users. Perhaps the most helpful is setting the prompt to display your current directory name, as follows:

```
C> PROMPT $p$g <ENTER>
C:\>
```

The PROMPT command creates an entry in the DOS environment. If you are using DOS 3.3 or higher, your batch files can use the named parameter %PROMPT% to determine and save the current system prompt.

Examples

The following command simply sets the DOS prompt to YES >:

```
C> PROMPT YES$g <ENTER>
YES>
```

The next command sets the system prompt to the current system time:

```
C> PROMPT $t <ENTER>
```

To display only the hours and minutes, you can change the prompt to

```
C> PROMPT $t$h$h$h$h$h$h <ENTER>
```

The following prompt, however, which is most common, simply displays the current drive and directory:

```
C> PROMPT $p$G <ENTER>

C:\>
```

RECOVER

Recovers a damaged disk or file

If a DOS disk or file becomes damaged and loses sectors (the areas on the disk that contain information), the RECOVER command can retrieve portions of the disk or file stored in good sectors. Data from the bad sectors cannot be recovered. DOS 6 does not support the RECOVER command.

Format

```
RECOVER[d:][path]filename.ext
```

d: The drive identifier of the file or disk to be recovered. If you do not specify this parameter, RECOVER uses the default.

path   The path name of the subdirectory that contains the file to be recovered. If you do not specify this parameter, DOS uses the default.

filename.ext   The name of the damaged file to be recovered.

Notes

The RECOVER command sometimes enables you to recover a portion of a file if the file develops a bad sector. However, RECOVER can only save a portion of the file from the undamaged sectors. Do not rely on this command; perform file and disk backups regularly. For a text file, you can edit the file later to restore the missing contents. For bad sectors in an executable file, do not execute the file—remember, the file is missing sectors.

If you use RECOVER to recover a complete disk, the command will create files in the root directory with names in the form FILE*nnnn*.REC, where *nnnn* is a four-digit number beginning with 0001 (FILE0001.REC).

RECOVER does not work with disk drives connected to a network.

Examples

The following command attempts to recover the contents of the disk in drive A:

```
C:\> RECOVER A: <ENTER>
```

In this case, RECOVER will create several files with names that are in the format FILE*nnnn*.REC, where *nnnn* represents the number of the file created. The command

```
C:\> RECOVER FILENAME.EXT <ENTER>
```

will simply recover the contents of the *FILENAME.EXT* file up to the damaged sector.

REM

Documents a DOS batch file

The REM command enables you to place comments or remarks within a DOS batch file to explain the batch file's processing.

Format

```
REM [message]
```

message A character string up to 123 characters long.

Notes

DOS does not execute lines containing the REM command; instead, DOS simply ignores the line and continues the batch file's execution with the next line. This makes REM useful for disabling lines that you might want to use later—just insert "REM" at the front of the line and remove it later, when you want to use the line again.

Place the ECHO OFF command at the start of a batch file to prevent DOS from displaying each REMark on the screen as the batch file executes.

At a minimum, your batch files should use REM to explain a batch file's purpose, the author, and when the batch file was written.

```
@ECHO OFF
REM Name: DISPLAY.BAT
REM Purpose: Display the contents of each
REM          file specified.
REM Written by: Kris Jamsa
REM Date Written: 4/05/93
:LOOP
   IF '%1'=='' GOTO DONE
   FOR %%I IN (%1) DO TYPE %%I
   SHIFT
   GOTO LOOP
:DONE
```

Example

The following batch file uses REM to add several meaningful comments to the batch file presented in the Notes section that explain the batch file's processing:

```
@ECHO OFF
REM Name: DISPLAY.BAT
REM Purpose: Display the contents of each
REM          file specified.
REM Written by: Kris Jamsa
REM Date Written: 4/05/93
REM The format to invoke DISPLAY.BAT is:
REM
REM DISPLAY FILENAME.EXT[optional file names]
REM
REM Loop through all of the file names specified
:LOOP
   REM When %1 is null, the batch file is done
   IF '%1'=='' GOTO DONE
   REM By using the FOR command, the batch
```

```
REM file supports wildcards
FOR %%I IN (%1) DO TYPE %%I
REM Assign the next file name to %1
SHIFT
GOTO LOOP
:DONE
```

RENAME

Renames the file(s) specified

The RENAME command renames one or more files on your disk.

Format

```
RENAME oldfile_spec newfile_name
REN oldfile_spec newfile_name
```

oldfile_spec   The complete path name of the file to be renamed. It can contain a drive and DOS subdirectory path. RENAME supports DOS wildcard characters for this parameter.

newfile_name   The target file name for the rename operation. It cannot have a drive or DOS subdirectory path. RENAME supports DOS wildcard characters for this parameter.

Notes

Because of its frequency of use, DOS permits you to abbreviate RENAME as REN.

The REN command does not rename DOS subdirectories.

You must specify a target file after indicating the file you want to rename. The target and source files must reside in the same directory on the same disk drive, because RENAME does not copy the contents of a file. RENAME simply renames the file in its directory entry.

To move a file from one drive or directory to another, first copy the file to the desired drive or directory and then delete the file using DEL.

Examples

The following command renames the file CONFIG.BAK as CONFIG.SAV:

```
C:\> REN CONFIG.BAK CONFIG.SAV <ENTER>
```

The next command renames all the files in the current directory that have the extension BAK, giving them the same file name and a new extension of SAV:

```
C:\> REN *.BAK *.SAV <ENTER>
```

REPLACE

Replaces or updates selected files

The REPLACE command allows selective file replacements and updates when new versions of software become available.

Format

```
REPLACE source_file_spec
[target_file_spec][/A][/P][/R][/S][/U][/W]
```

source_file_spec   The complete DOS source file specification for the files that REPLACE is to use. REPLACE supports wildcards.

target_file_spec The complete DOS destination file specification of the files being added or released.

/A Adds, rather than replaces, files to the target directory. With this parameter, REPLACE only places those files onto the target that are not currently present.

/P Displays a prompt to user before replacing or adding each file.

/R Replaces the files on the target location currently marked as read-only. Without this parameter, REPLACE stops replacement operations with the first file marked read-only.

/S Searches the subdirectories on the target location for other occurrences of the file to be replaced. This parameter cannot be used with /A.

/U Replaces only those files in the target directory that are older than the files in the source. This is a DOS 5 parameter.

/W Inserts a pause for a keypress before beginning to replace files, letting you change floppy disks.

Notes

The REPLACE command exists primarily to aid program developers when they have updates to programs that users may have distributed across several directories. Most users will never issue the REPLACE command.

If you use REPLACE to update your fixed disk with a new version of DOS, keep in mind that REPLACE cannot update the hidden system files IO.SYS and MSDOS.SYS, which are required for your system to boot.

REPLACE uses the following exit status values:

0   All files successfully replaced
2   Source files were not found
3   Source path was not found

5	File access violation
8	Insufficient memory
11	Invalid command-line syntax
15	Invalid drive specified

Examples

The following command replaces any files in the current directory that have the DAT extension using files that reside on drive A.

```
C:\> REPLACE A:*.DAT C:  <ENTER>
```

The following command will replace each file on drive C that has the extension DAT with the corresponding file from drive A.

```
C:\> REPLACE A:*.DAT C:\ /S <ENTER>
```

RESTORE

Restores files saved by BACKUP

The BACKUP command places files onto a disk in a manner only accessible by RESTORE. To copy a file from the backup disk, you must use RESTORE. In DOS 6, backup and restore operations are done by the MSBACKUP command.

Format

```
RESTORE source_drive:file_spec
 target_drive:file_spec[/P]
 [/S][/B:mm-dd-yy][/A:mm-dd-yy]
 [/E:hh:mm:ss][/L:hh:mm:ss][/M][/N][/D]
```

source_drive:file_spec   The files to be restored. Each file name must match the name of the file as it was originally backed up; *source_drive* is the drive that contains the backup files.

target_drive:file_spec   The disk drive to which the files will be restored.

/P   Displays a prompt to the user before restoring those files that are read-only or have been modified since the backup.

/S   Restores files contained in subdirectories.

/B:*mm-dd-yy*   Restores only those files modified on or before the date specified.

/A:*mm-dd-yy*   Restores only those files modified after the specified date.

/E:*hh:mm:ss*   Restores only those files modified at or before the time specified. This parameter requires DOS 3.3 or later.

/L:*hh:mm:ss*   Restores only those files modified at or after the time specified. This parameter requires DOS 3.3 or later.

/M   Restores only those files modified since the last backup.

/N   Restores only those files no longer existing on the target disk.

/D   Displays the names of the files on the backup disk that match the file specification without actually performing the restore operation (DOS 5).

Notes

The RESTORE command will not restore the hidden system files that DOS uses to boot your system.

If you do not perform regular system backups using BACKUP, the RESTORE command is essentially worthless to you. Back up your disks regularly and place those backups in a safe location. DOS 3.3 enables you to keep a log of the files contained on your backup disks. Use this log to locate specific files on your disks for restoration. Remember to create meaningful labels for your backup disks.

RESTORE supports the following exit status values:

0   Successful file restore

1   No matching files found to restore

3   User termination with CTRL-C

4   Fatal processing error; restore incomplete

Examples

The following command will restore all files from the backup disk in drive A, including those in subdirectories:

```
C:\> RESTORE A: C:*.* /S <ENTER>
```

If the backup operation requires several floppy disks, RESTORE will prompt you to place each subsequent backup disk in the specified drive as needed.

The next command restores all the files from the backup disk that contain the extension DAT:

```
C:\> RESTORE A: C:*.DAT /P <ENTER>
```

RESTORE will prompt you with

```
Warning! File FILENAME.EXT was changed after backed up.
Replace the file (Y/N)?
```

before it restores files that have been modified since the backup.

RMDIR

Removes the directory specified

The RMDIR command removes an empty directory from your disk.

Format

```
RMDIR[drive:]path
RD[drive:]path
```

drive: The drive from which the subdirectory will be removed. If this parameter is not specified, RMDIR uses the default drive.

path   The name of the subdirectory to remove.

Notes

Because of its frequency of use, DOS permits you to abbreviate RMDIR as RD.

Use the RMDIR command to remove a specified directory. This command only removes empty subdirectories that do not contain files. RMDIR will not remove the current directory.

Examples

The following command attempts to remove the IBM subdirectory from the root directory of the current drive. If the directory contains files, RMDIR cannot remove the directory.

```
C:\> RMDIR \IBM <ENTER>
```

Similarly, the command

```
C:\> RMDIR \MISC\IBM\SALES <ENTER>
```

removes the empty subdirectory SALES from the directory \MISC\IBM on the current drive.

SET

Places or displays DOS environment entries

When DOS boots, it reserves an area of memory called the *environment*, which provides a storage location for system specifics. DOS commands such as PROMPT and PATH place entries in the environment. The SET command sets or displays entries in the DOS environment.

Format

```
SET [name=[value]]
```

name   The name of the DOS environment entry to which you are assigning a value.

value   A character string that defines the assigned value.

Notes

The DOS environment always contains the COMSPEC= and PATH= entries. COMSPEC= tells DOS where to locate the command processor COMMAND.COM. PATH= defines the current command search path.

Other commands that set environment entries include PROMPT, PATH, and APPEND. If you are using DOS 5, the DIRCMD entry defines the format DIR uses to display directory listings (see DIR). The SET command converts all entry names to uppercase.

The SET command entered with no parameters displays the current environment.

You may have used the batch parameters %0 to %9. Beginning with DOS 3.3, you can use the named parameters that are environment entries whose names are surrounded by percent signs, such as %NAME%. Consider the following batch file:

```
CLS
TYPE %FILE%
```

When DOS encounters "%FILE%" in the batch file, DOS will search your environment entries for an entry matching FILE=. Assuming that your environment contains the following:

```
COMSPEC=C:\DOS\COMMAND.COM
PATH=C:\DOS;C:\BATCH
PROMPT=[$p]
FILE=TEST.BAT
```

DOS would display the contents of the file TEST.BAT.

Examples

With no command-line parameters, SET displays the current environment entries:

```
C:\> SET <ENTER>
COMSPEC=C:\DOS\COMMAND.COM
PATH=C:\DOS
```

The following example creates a new environment entry called FILE and assigns it the value TEST.DAT:

```
C:\> SET FILE=TEST.DAT <ENTER>
```

You can verify this by again issuing the SET command:

```
C:\> SET <ENTER>
COMSPEC=C:\DOS\COMMAND.COM
PATH=C:\DOS
FILE=TEST.DAT
```

To remove the value for an entry, use SET as shown here:

```
C:\> SET FILE= <ENTER>
```

Invoking SET now displays

```
C:\> SET <ENTER>
COMSPEC=C:\DOS\COMMAND.COM
PATH=C:\DOS
```

SETVER

Assigns a DOS version number to a program

Many older application programs, and in some cases older DOS commands, do not run in DOS 5 or later. The SETVER command instructs DOS to respond that it is an earlier version when a specific program asks for the version number.

Format

```
SETVER [program_name][version]
SETVER program_name /DELETE [/QUIET]
```

program_name The complete path name of the program to which you want SETVER to assign a different DOS version.

version   The DOS version number you want assigned to the program. The number must be in the range 2.11 to 9.99.

/DELETE   The parameter to remove the version number assignment from the program.

/QUIET   Suppresses SETVER messages for table-entry delete operations.

Notes

Use the following CONFIG.SYS DEVICE= entry to load SETVER as a device driver:

```
DEVICE=C:\DOS\SETVER.EXE
```

SETVER creates a list of programs that you want run under different versions of DOS. Each time you change this list, you must restart your system for the change to take effect.

If you do not type in a program name, SETVER will display the current version number assignments.

SETVER supports the following exit status values:

  0   Successful assignment
  1   Invalid command-line parameter
  2   Invalid file name specified
  3   Insufficient memory
  4   Invalid version number format
  5   Program name not found in list
  6   MS-DOS system files not found
  7   Invalid drive specified
  8   Too many command-line parameters
  9   Command-line parameters missing
 10   Error reading MS-DOS system files
 11   Corrupt version list
 12   MS-DOS system files do not support version list

13 Insufficient space in list for a new entry

14 Error writing MS-DOS system files

Examples

The following command lists the current version number assignments:

```
C:\> SETVER <ENTER>
```

The next command tells SETVER to assign DOS 3.2 to the command EXE2BIN.EXE:

```
C:\> SETVER EXE2BIN.EXE 3.2 <ENTER>
```

To remove a command from the set version list, include the /DELETE parameter, as shown here:

```
C:\> SETVER TEST.EXE /DELETE <ENTER>
```

SHARE

Installs DOS file-sharing support

SHARE lets users in a network access the same file at the same time.

Format

```
SHARE [/F:file_space][/L:locks]
```

/F:file_space Memory allocation (in bytes) for the area in which DOS will store file-sharing information. Each open file requires 11 bytes plus the length of the file name (up to 63 characters). The default file space is 2048 bytes.

/L:*locks*   The number of files that can be locked at the same time. The default is 20.

Notes

You issue the SHARE command only if your computer is part of a local area network. Ask the person responsible for the network for the proper SHARE values.

DOS versions later than 3.0 support file and record locking. Each time a file is opened with file sharing installed, DOS checks whether the file is locked against the open operation. If it is, the file cannot be opened. In addition, DOS checks for locking during each read and write operation.

The SHARE command invokes a memory-resident program that performs the file and record locking. SHARE can only be invoked once. When it has been invoked, the only way to remove file sharing is to reboot. The SHARE command slows down the speed of all your file operations, so only install it when file sharing is in effect.

If you are using DOS 4 or later, you can use the CONFIG.SYS INSTALL= entry to install file sharing each time your system starts. If you are using DOS 4 and disk partitions larger than 32Mb, make sure you invoke SHARE to prevent damage from a program using file control blocks. If you are using DOS 5 or later, you can invoke SHARE by using LOADHIGH.

Examples

The following command invokes file sharing with default values of 2048 and 20 locks:

```
C:\> SHARE <ENTER>
```

The next command installs file-sharing support with 40 locks:

```
C:\> SHARE /L:40 <ENTER>
```

SHIFT

Shifts each batch parameter left one position

Your DOS batch files can easily access the first nine batch file command-line parameters using the symbols %1 through %9. If the user invokes your batch file with more than nine parameters, you can use the SHIFT command to access them.

Format

```
SHIFT
```

Notes

This command shifts each batch parameter one position to the left. If more than ten parameters are passed to a DOS batch procedure, you can use the SHIFT command to access each parameter past %9. If no parameter exists to the right of a parameter, SHIFT will assign the parameter a NULL string.

There is no way to undo the effects of the SHIFT command. A parameter in the leftmost position (%0) is lost once SHIFT has executed.

Example

The following batch file displays all the batch parameters specified on the command line:

```
@ECHO OFF
:LOOP
  SHIFT
  IF '%0'== '' GOTO DONE
  ECHO %0
  GOTO LOOP
:DONE
```

If the previous file was named TEST.BAT, invoking the batch file by entering

```
C:\> TEST 1 2 3 4  <ENTER>
```

would display

```
C:\> TEST 1 2 3 4  <ENTER>
1
2
3
4
```

SMARTDRV

Improves performance by installing a disk cache, which reduces disk operations

SMARTDRV is a memory-resident program that reduces the number of slow disk read and write operations by buffering information in your computer's fast electronic RAM.

Format

```
SMARTDRV [[Drive[+|-]...] [/E:ElementSize]
[InitialSize][WindowsSize]]
[/B:ReadAheadBuffer] [/C][/L][/Q][/R][/S]
```

Drive[+|–]   A drive letter followed by a plus sign enables read and write caching for that drive. A minus sign disables caching. If you don't specify a plus or minus sign, SMARTDRV enables read caching while disabling write caching. The ellipses (...) indicates that you can specify several drives.

/E:ElementSize   Specifies the amount of information (in bytes) SMARTDRV moves to or from disk at one time. Valid element sizes are 1024, 2048, 4096, and 8192. The default is 8192.

InitialSize   Specifies in Kb (1024 bytes), the size of SMARTDRV's initial cache. In general, the larger the cache, the better your system performance.

WindowsSize   Specifies the size in Kb (1024 bytes) to which SMARTDRV will reduce the cache size when Windows runs, to give Windows more memory with which it can operate.

/B:ReadAheadBuffer   Specifies the size in Kb (1024 bytes) of a buffer into which SMARTDRV reads extra disk sectors in attempting to reduce subsequent disk read operations.

/C   Directs SMARTDRV to immediately flush all cached (output) data to disk.

/L   Loads SMARTDRV into conventional memory, as opposed to upper memory.

/Q   Directs SMARTDRV not to display initialization error messages.

/R   Directs SMARTDRV to clear the current cache contents and to restart.

/S   Directs SMARTDRV to display status information.

Notes

Because your disk drive is a mechanical device, it is much slower than your computer's electronic components. SMARTDRV uses your computer's extended memory to create a large buffer into which it can read extra information in an attempt to satisfy future disk read operations. In addition, SMARTDRV buffers information that programs write to disk, and later performs the actual disk write operation at a more suitable time.

The SMARTDRV disk cache eliminates your need to use the DOS CONFIG.SYS BUFFERS entry. Depending on the amount of extended memory your system contains, the size of the SMARTDRV buffer you allocate will differ. Use the following table as a guideline:

Extended Memory	Initial Buffer	Windows Buffer
1 to 2Mb	1Mb	256Kb
3 to 4Mb	1 to 1.5Mb	512Kb
5 to 6Mb	2Mb	1Mb
>6Mb	2Mb	2Mb

Place the SMARTDRV command in your AUTOEXEC.BAT file.

Examples

The following SMARTDRV command allocates an initial 2Mb buffer for drive C, allowing Windows to reduce the buffer size to 1Mb:

```
SMARTDRV C+ 2048 1024
```

SMARTDRV allows you to specify the buffering of several disks. The following command selects a 1Mb buffer and enables caching for drive C and drive D:

```
SMARTDRV C+ D+ 1024
```

Using the /S switch, the following command displays SMARTDRV's status information:

```
C:\> SMARTDRV /S <ENTER>
Microsoft SMARTDrive Disk Cache version 4.0
Copyright 1991,1992 Microsoft Corp.

Room for 128 elements of 8,192 bytes each
There have been 689 cache hits
    and 208 cache misses

Cache size: 1,048,576 bytes
Cache size while running Windows: 262,144 bytes

          Disk Caching Status
drive   read cache   write cache   buffering
-------------------------------------------------
  A:        yes          no            no
  B:        yes          no            no
  C:        yes          yes           no

For help, type "Smartdrv /?".
```

Because SMARTDRV may perform write caching, information you thought was recorded to disk may actually still reside in memory.

Before you restart or turn off your computer, you should use SMARTDRV's /C switch to first flush all the information to disk:

```
C:\> SMARTDRV /C <ENTER>
```

SORT

Sorts and displays the contents of a file or redirected program output

The SORT command lets you view a file's contents or a program's output in sorted order.

Format

```
DOS_COMMAND | SORT[/R][/+n]
SORT[/R][/+n] < file
```

/R   Data sort in reverse order.

/+n   Number of the column on which to sort the data.

Notes

The SORT command reads data from the standard input device, sorting the information and displaying it on the standard output device until an end-of-file marker is encountered. SORT is usually used with the < and | redirection operators.

SORT does not make any distinction between upper- and lowercase letters.

Examples

The following command displays a sorted directory listing:

```
C:\> DIR | SORT <ENTER>
```

The following command tells SORT to sort the information contained in the DATA.DAT file:

```
C:\> SORT < DATA.DAT <ENTER>
```

In a similar manner, the command

```
C:\> SORT /R < DATA.DAT <ENTER>
```

tells SORT to sort the same file; this time, in reverse order.

If your data file contains

```
Bill M
Mary F
Kris M
Kal  M
Jane F
Mike M
Ed   M
```

The command

```
C:\> SORT /+6 < FILENAME.EXT <ENTER>
```

tells SORT to sort the file based on the data starting in column 6. In this case, SORT's order will be

```
Mary F
Jane F
Bill M
Kris M
Kal  M
Mike M
Ed   M
```

SUBST

Substitutes a drive name for a path name

Some older programs do not support DOS subdirectories. If you are using such a program, you can trick the program into using a subdirectory by substituting the desired directory name with a disk drive letter.

Format

```
SUBST [d:][path_name][/D]
```

d: The drive identifier that will be used to reference the path.

path_name   The path name to be abbreviated.

/D   The parameter to remove a previous disk substitution.

Notes

Because path names can become large, you can use the SUBST command to substitute a drive identifier for a path name. If you invoke SUBST without any parameters, current substitutions will be displayed. By default, the last disk drive that DOS will reference is drive E.

```
C:\> SUBST E: \DIRNAME <ENTER>
```

To specify a disk drive greater than E, use the LASTDRIVE= entry in CONFIG.SYS. For instance, the following entry tells DOS to support the drive letters A through K:

```
LASTDRIVE=K
```

Do not use the following commands with a substituted disk:

BACKUP	FDISK	RESTORE
CHKDSK	FORMAT	SYS
DISKCOMP	LABEL	UNDELETE
DISKCOPY	RECOVER	UNFORMAT

Examples

In the following example, DOS enables you to abbreviate the subdirectory \REPORTS\1993 to the drive letter E:

```
C:\> SUBST E: \REPORTS\1993 <ENTER>
```

A command such as

```
C:\> DIR E: <ENTER>
```

will then display the contents of the directory. If that subdirectory contains other subdirectories, you can still use the drive letter, as shown in the following:

```
C:\> DIR E:SUBDIR <ENTER>
```

Invoking SUBST without command-line parameters displays current substitutions:

```
C:\> SUBST
E: => C:\REPORTS\1993 <ENTER>
```

SYS

Creates a bootable disk

To start your system, DOS requires that two hidden files reside in the disk's root directory. Use the SYS command to copy these hidden files from a bootable disk to a newly formatted disk.

Format

```
SYS source_drive: target_drive:
```

source_drive: A parameter available beginning with DOS 4 to specify from where the DOS system files should be copied.

target_drive: The target drive for the hidden operating system files.

Notes

The SYS command enables you to transfer to the target disk the hidden operating system files that perform the initial system startup. The SYS command does not copy the COMMAND.COM file to the target disk. To do so, you must use the COPY command.

DOS will only transfer files to an empty target disk or to a disk that was formatted previously with the /S or /B parameter (see FORMAT).

SYS does not work with a disk that uses the JOIN or SUBST command.

Prior to DOS 4, the hidden system files had to be the first two files in the root directory. If the root directory already contains files, you probably won't be able to transfer the hidden files to the disk. In such cases, SYS will display the following message:

```
No room for system on destination disk
```

Example

In this example, SYS will transfer the hidden operating system files to the disk in drive A.

```
C:\> SYS A: <ENTER>
```

TIME

Displays and sets the system time

DOS uses the current system time to update the directory each time you create or modify a file.

Format

```
TIME[HH:MM[:SS[.hh]]][AM | PM]
```

HH:MM   The desired hours (0 to 23) and minutes (0 to 59).

SS   The desired seconds (0 to 59).

hh   The desired hundredths of a second (0 to 99).

Notes

If you are using DOS 5 or later, you can enter a time based on a 12-hour clock and include either the letters "AM" or "PM" following the time as appropriate, so the following TIME commands are identical:

```
TIME 14:30
TIME 2:30P
TIME 2:30PM
```

Examples

If you do not specify a time on the command line, as in

```
C:\> TIME <ENTER>
```

TIME will prompt you for one:

```
Current time is 16:08:41.15
Enter new time:
```

To leave the time unchanged, simply press ENTER. Otherwise, type in the time desired and press ENTER.

The following command sets the clock to 12:00 noon:

```
C:\> TIME 12:00 <ENTER>
```

The next command sets the clock to midnight:

```
C:\> TIME 00:00:00.000 <ENTER>
```

TREE

Displays directory structure

DOS refers to the directories on your disk as the *directory tree.* The TREE command displays all of the directories on your disk and, optionally, the files each directory contains.

Format

```
TREE[d:][path][/F][/A]
```

d: The drive identifier of the disk for which TREE is to display the directory structure.

path The name of a directory at which you want the directory tree to begin. If you don't specify a directory, DOS uses the root directory.

/F The parameter that also displays the name of each file in a directory.

/A   The parameter that displays the directory tree using standard text characters instead of graphics characters. This parameter requires DOS 4 or higher.

Notes

Beginning with DOS 4, the TREE command uses graphics-like characters to display the directory structure.

If you use the I/O redirection operators, you can print the directory tree, as shown here:

```
C:\> TREE > PRN <ENTER>
```

Example

The following command displays the directory structure of the disk:

```
C:\> TREE <ENTER>
```

To display the files in each directory, use the /F parameter:

```
C:\> TREE A: /F <ENTER>
```

TYPE

Displays a text file's contents

The TYPE command displays the contents of a text file on the screen.

Format

```
TYPE file_spec
```

file_spec   The complete DOS file specification for the file to be displayed. It can contain a drive identifier and path name.

Notes

The TYPE command is restricted to ASCII files. Do not use TYPE with files containing a COM or EXE extension—these files contain characters that will cause the screen to beep and display meaningless characters.

When you use the TYPE command, don't forget that you can control the output by using the MORE command:

```
A> TYPE FILENAME.EXT | MORE <ENTER>
```

and also by pressing the CTRL-S key combination. When it encounters the CTRL-S, DOS suspends scrolling the current output until you press another key.

Examples

The following command tells TYPE to display the contents of the CONFIG.SYS file:

```
C:\> TYPE \CONFIG.SYS <ENTER>
```

In a similar manner, the command

```
C:\> TYPE \AUTOEXEC.BAT <ENTER>
```

tells TYPE to display the contents of the file AUTOEXEC.BAT, which resides in the root directory.

UNDELETE

Recovers a previously deleted file

When you delete a file, the file actually remains on your disk until DOS overwrites the file's contents with another file. The DOS 5 UNDELETE command recovers recently deleted files. If you don't immediately recover a deleted file, however, the file may be overwritten by the next command, making its undeletion impossible.

Format

```
UNDELETE[pathname][/LIST][/DT | /ALL | /DOS]
```

or in DOS 6

```
UNDELETE [/LIST | /ALL | /PURGE[:Drive] | /STATUS
              | /LOAD | /U | /S[:Drive] | /TDrive[-entries]]
```

pathname   The subdirectory path of the file or files you want to undelete. If you don't specify a path name, UNDELETE uses the current directory.

/LIST   The parameter that lists all of the files available for recovery.

/DT   The parameter for recovery of only those files listed in the delete tracking (DT) file.

/ALL

The parameter for recovery of all of the files listed by DOS as deleted without a prompt to enter the first letter of the file. Instead, UNDELETE assigns the character # to the first letter of each file. If a file exists with the same name, UNDELETE will attempt instead to use the characters % & - 0 1 2 3 4 5 6 7 8 9, in that order.

/DOS   The parameter for recovery of only those files listed by DOS as deleted (ignoring the delete tracking file). DOS will prompt you to enter the first letter of each file name.

/LOAD   Loads Undelete's memory-resident software using the files in the file UNDELETE.INI. If the file does not exist, UNDELETE uses default values. This is a DOS 6 switch.

/PURGE[:*Drive*]   Deletes (purges) the contents of the SENTRY directory on the drive specified. If you don't specify a drive, UNDELETE uses the current drive. This is a DOS 6 switch.

/S[:*Drive*]   Directs UNDELETE to initiate data sentry protection on the drive specified. If you don't specify a drive, UNDELETE uses the current drive. This is a DOS 6 switch.

/T*Drive*[–*entries*]   Loads a memory-resident delete tracking program that tracks from 1 to 999 deleted files in the root directory file PCTRACKR.DEL. This is a DOS 6 switch.

Notes

If you are recovering files using /DOS, the recovered files may contain errors due to file fragmentation.

If you inadvertently delete a file, do not copy any files to the disk until you successfully recover the deleted file.

When DOS deletes a file, it replaces the first character in the file's name with a Greek symbol. To recover a file, UNDELETE may ask you to type in the file's original first character.

In DOS 6, UNDELETE incorporates many features of the DOS 5 MIRROR command, which no longer exists. The DOS 6 UNDELETE command provides two types of undelete protection. First, delete-file tracking (also in DOS 5) stores information about each file you delete, such as where the file began, and the clusters it consumed. Using the delete-file tracking information is effective until the file's disk storage locations are overwritten. Second, the DOS 6 UNDELETE command supports sentry protection in which files are not actually deleted from disk, they are moved to the SENTRY directory. If disk space becomes low, UNDELETE will purge the SENTRY directory. You can also purge the files yourself using UNDELETE's /PURGE switch.

The DOS 6 UNDELETE command lets you specify various options using the root directory file UNDELETE.INI. Using UNDELETE's /U switch, you can create the file. For more information on UNDELETE.INI, refer to the book *DOS: The Complete Reference*, Fourth Edition.

Examples

The following UNDELETE command displays the names of all files available for recovery in the current directory:

```
C:\> UNDELETE /LIST /DT <ENTER>
```

If you have enabled file-delete tracking using MIRROR, UNDELETE uses the information MIRROR has saved.

The following command undeletes all of the recoverable files in the current directory based on delete tracking information:

```
C:\> UNDELETE *.* /DT <ENTER>
```

Likewise, the following command undeletes all of the recoverable files in the current directory using only DOS file information:

```
C:\> UNDELETE *.* /DOS <ENTER>
```

The following DOS 6 command loads UNDELETE's data sentry protection:

```
C:\> UNDELETE /S <ENTER>
```

The next DOS 6 command loads UNDELETE's file-delete tracking software, just as you would use the MIRROR command in DOS 5:

```
C:\> UNDELETE /TC <ENTER>
```

UNFORMAT

Restores an erased or formatted disk

UNFORMAT is a DOS 5 or later command that works in conjunction with the MIRROR command (in DOS 5) to rebuild an inadvertently formatted disk or a disk damaged by inadvertently entering the RECOVER command.

Format

```
UNFORMAT D:[/J][/P]
UNFORMAT D:[/L][/TEST][/P]
UNFORMAT D:[/L][/PARTN]
```

D: The disk drive letter of the disk to rebuild.

/J Verifies that the current root directory and file allocation table match the last file created by MIRROR. This parameter does not rebuild the disk. This switch requires DOS 5.

/L Lists each file and subdirectory UNFORMAT finds.

/TEST Displays how UNFORMAT will rebuild the disk, without actually executing the command.

/P Sends screen output to the printer, as well as to the screen.

/PARTN Restores a corrupted partition table using the file MIRROR previously recorded to a floppy disk. This switch requires DOS 5.

Notes

UNFORMAT cannot restore a disk formatted with the /U parameter.

UNFORMAT will always attempt to use the information previously stored by the MIRROR command. If the MIRROR file is not available or is very old, you can direct UNFORMAT to try to recover the disk using only the current file allocation table and root directory. This method, however, is much less reliable.

Using the DOS FORMAT command, create a bootable floppy disk and copy to the disk the UNFORMAT, UNDELETE, RESTORE, and DOSBACK commands. Label the disk "Emergency Disk" and place the disk in a safe location.

Examples

The following DOS 5 command uses UNFORMAT to restore a corrupted partition table for drive C:

```
A> UNFORMAT C: /PARTN <ENTER>
```

In this case, UNFORMAT will prompt you to place the floppy disk containing the correct partition table information saved by MIRROR into a floppy drive.

The following UNFORMAT command uses the /TEST parameter to determine whether UNFORMAT can rebuild a formatted floppy disk in drive A:

```
C:\> UNFORMAT A: /TEST <ENTER>
```

VER

Displays the DOS version number

The VER command displays the current DOS version number.

Format

```
VER
```

Notes

DOS version numbers consist of a major and minor version number. For DOS 3.2, 3 is the major version number, and 2 is the minor version number.

Example

The following command tells VER to display the current version number:

```
C:\> VER <ENTER>
```

For DOS 3.3, the output is

```
IBM Personal Computer DOS Version 3.30
```

Likewise, for DOS 6, the output is

```
MS-DOS Version 6.00
```

VERIFY

Enables or disables disk verification

Periodically, a disk drive may not correctly record the information on disk as DOS intended. Although rare, such occurrences can leave incorrect data on your disk. If you enable disk I/O verification by issuing the VERIFY command, DOS will double-check the data it writes to disk by rereading each sector and comparing it with the original data. If a discrepancy exists, DOS will detect it. However, because DOS must reread each sector that it writes to disk, disk verification slows down the speed of operation.

Format

```
VERIFY[ON | OFF]
```

ON   The parameter that enables DOS disk verification.

OFF   The parameter that disables DOS disk verification.

Notes

If you invoke VERIFY without a command-line parameter, it will display its current state, ON or OFF.

The VERIFY command ensures that DOS is successfully recording all the information it is writing to disk. VERIFY does this by comparing each disk sector immediately after it is written to the sector with the information that should have been recorded. Any difference indicates that DOS has recorded data incorrectly.

Although this seems to be a good idea, such disk errors are rare. VERIFY increases the overhead on your system by writing and rereading multiple sectors. Most users should use the default value of

Format

VOL[*drive:*]

drive: The disk drive that contains the disk for which VOL is to display the disk volume label. If you do not specify this parameter, VOL uses the default drive.

Notes

Disk labels can consist of the same characters as DOS file names. To assign a volume label, use the LABEL command.

If you are using DOS 4 or later, the VOL command also displays the disk's serial number.

Examples

In the following example, VOL displays the disk volume label of the disk contained in the current drive:

```
C:\> VOL <ENTER>
Volume in drive C is DOSDISK
```

If you are using DOS 4 or later, VOL will also display the disk serial number, as shown here:

```
C:\> VOL <ENTER>
Volume in drive C is DOS
Volume Serial Number is 4E13-1342
```

VSAFE

Installs memory-resident virus detection software

The DOS 6 MSAV scans your computer's disk and memory for known viruses. MSAV only performs a one-time virus search. The VSAFE command, however, installs memory-resident software that detects and intercepts operations frequently performed by destructive viruses. The best virus defense is to use both VSAFE and MSAV.

Format

```
VSAFE  [/OptionNumber[+|-] [...]] [/Ax]
       [/Cx] [/D] [/N] [/NE] [/NX] [/U]
```

/OptionNumber[+|–]   Directs VSAFE to turn on or off detection of the following options:

1   Intercepts low-level formatting operations; default: On

2   Intercepts a program's attempt to become memory resident; default: Off

3   Intercepts disk write operations; default: Off

4   Intercepts file operations that open executable files; default: On

5   Checks all disks for boot sector viruses; default: On

6   Intercepts attempts to modify the boot record or partition table; default: On

7   Intercepts attempts to change a floppy disk's boot record; default: Off

8   Intercepts attempts to change an executable file; default: On

/Ax   Directs VSAFE to use the key specified for ALT key activation. For example, /AX selects ALT-X.

/Cx   Directs VSAFE to use the key specified for CTRL key activation. For example /CX selects CTRL-X.

/D Directs VSAFE to turn off checksum operations.

/N Allows network drivers to be loaded after VSAFE is active.

/NE Directs VSAFE not to monitor expanded memory.

/NX Directs VSAFE not to monitor extended memory.

/U Removes VSAFE from memory.

Notes

The VSAFE program consumes approximately 22Kb of memory. If you direct VSAFE to monitor a specific operation, such as a program attempting to become memory resident, and such an event occurs, VSAFE will sound a bell and display a message describing the attempted operation.

To prevent the operation, select Stop, and the offending program will end. To allow the operation, select Continue. If you select Boot, your system will restart.

You can use VSAFE within Windows; however, you must first place the following entry in your WIN.INI file:

```
LOAD=C:\DOS\WNTSRMAN.EXE
```

VSAFE requires DOS 6.

Example

The following command loads VSAFE into memory:

```
C:\> VSAFE <ENTER>
```

If you press VSAFE's activation keyboard combination (ALT-V is the default), VSAFE will display its menu. To enable or disable VSAFE's monitoring of specific events, type the event's number. VSAFE will display a check mark after each event it will monitor. Press ESC to hide the menu.

XCOPY

Copies source files and subdirectories to a target disk

The XCOPY command copies one or more files providing extended capabilities not available with the COPY command.

Format

```
XCOPY source_file_spec[target_file_spec]
   [/A][/D:mm-dd-yy][/E][/M][/P][/S][/V][/W]
```

source_file_spec   The complete DOS file specification for the source files to be copied by XCOPY.

target_file_spec   The destination name for the files copied by XCOPY.

/A   Copies only files that have the archive bit set.

/D:mm-dd-yy   Copies only files created on or after the specified date.

/E   Places subdirectories on the target disk if the subdirectory is currently empty.

/M   Functions like the /A parameter; however, /M tells XCOPY to clear each file's archive bit as it copies the file.

/P   Tells XCOPY to prompt

```
FILENAME.EXT (Y/N)?
```

before copying each file.

/S   Copies the contents of lower-level subdirectories to the target location.

/V   Compares the contents of the target file and the source file to verify that the file copy was successful.

/W   Tells XCOPY to prompt

```
Press any key to begin copying file(s)
```

before beginning.

Notes

The XCOPY command copies source files and subdirectories to a target destination. Unlike COPY and DISKCOPY, the XCOPY command copies files contained in DOS subdirectories on a selective basis. Many users invoke XCOPY to repair disk fragmentation or use it as a system backup mechanism.

Because the XCOPY command provides many more capabilities than the standard COPY command, many users are using XCOPY in place of COPY for their file manipulation. In the future the use of XCOPY should continue to grow, and its functionality should increase.

Examples

The following XCOPY command copies the files in the current directory of drive C to the disk in drive A. Using the /S parameter, the command creates an identical copy of the directory on the floppy drive, including all of the files that reside in subdirectories below the current directory:

```
C:\> XCOPY *.*  A:\ /S <ENTER>
```

The following command copies all of the files in the current directory that have been created or modified since December 31, 1993, to the disk in drive A:

```
C:\> XCOPY *.* /D:12/31/93 A: <ENTER>
```

To use XCOPY to copy the entire contents of a fixed disk to floppy disks, first set the attribute of each file on the fixed disk to indicate that each requires a backup, as shown here:

```
C:\> ATTRIB +A \*.* /S <ENTER>
```

Next, issue the command:

```
C:\> XCOPY \*.* A:\ /M /E /S <ENTER>
```

XCOPY will begin transferring files to the floppy disk, maintaining the existing disk structure. When the target disk becomes full, simply insert a new floppy disk in drive A and again invoke the command:

```
C:\> XCOPY \*.* A:\ /M /E /S <ENTER>
```

XCOPY will continue where it left off, because it has been clearing the archive bit on each file it successfully copies to the target disk.

APPENDIX

Answers to Review Questions

Chapter 1

1. The three steps are input, output, and processing.

2. Input is the process of getting information (data) into the computer.

3. Processing is the execution of a computer program (software) that takes the input information and converts it into the desired output.

4. Output is the display or printing of meaningful information for the end user.

5. Figure A-1 shows the correct device labels.

6. Disks exist to store programs and information.

7. Figure A-2 shows the disk drive names.

8. A computer is PC compatible if it can execute programs written specifically for the IBM PC and can freely exchange disks. In most cases, the systems can even exchange such hardware devices as a screen or keyboard.

9. Unlike floppy disks, which are removable, a hard disk is attached to your computer's chassis and cannot be removed. Although both

FIGURE	Devices labeled as input, output, or both
A-1	

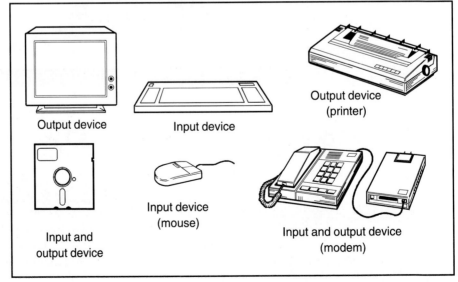

FIGURE A-2

Correctly labeled disk drives

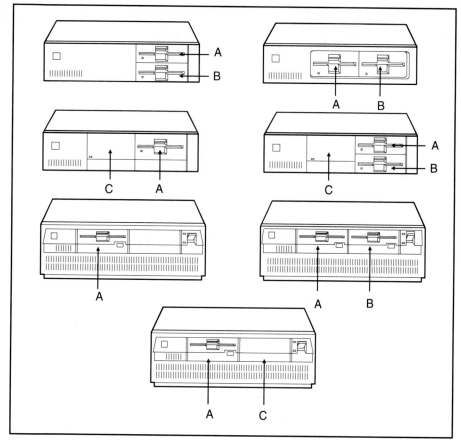

hard and floppy disks exist to store programs and information, hard disks are much faster than floppies and can store much more information.

10. Most systems have a screen display, a keyboard, a chassis, and a printer. In addition, many users add optional hardware devices such as a mouse, modem, or surge suppressor. A mouse is an input device that can simplify your traversal of DOS 5's menu interface. A modem allows two systems to communicate over phone lines. Finally, a surge suppressor protects your system against harmful "spikes" on your power lines while in some cases allowing you to turn specific hardware devices on and off individually.

11. Cycling your computer's power is the process of turning off your computer, waiting about ten seconds, and then turning your system back on. In many cases, cycling your computer's power will clear hardware errors.

12. Each time you turn on your computer's power, the computer performs a series of tests to check the status of its internal components. In most cases, if your system encounters an error during the self-test, it will display a message that you can report to your retailer.

Chapter 2

1. Software is categorized as either system or application software. System software includes such programs as the operating system. Application programs include such programs as a word processor or spreadsheet.

2. "DOS" stands for "disk operating system."

3. An operating system is a special program that serves as the overseer of your computer's resources (such as your disk drives). In addition, the operating system allows you to execute other programs.

4. DOS version numbers are composed of two parts: a major number and a minor number. For DOS 5.0, 5 is the major version number and 0 is the minor number. When software developers release a new version of a software package, they use guidelines to determine which version number to increment. If the upgrade is simply for error fixes or minor enhancements, they increment the minor version number. If the upgrade contains many significant changes, the developers update the major version number.

5. MS-DOS and PC-DOS both refer to DOS, the disk operating system for personal computers. MS-DOS, licensed by Microsoft, is used most commonly in conjunction with PC-compatible clones. PC-DOS, from IBM, is most often found on the IBM PC, the PC AT, and the PS/2 line of computers. For the end user, PC-DOS and MS-DOS appear identical in terms of how they function, and both use the same set of commands.

6. No matter which disk type you are using, all disk drives contain a disk activation light that tells you when the drive is in use. Each time your computer must read information from or write information to your disk, it illuminates this light. Never open your disk drive or turn off your computer while this light is on, or you risk damaging your disk and losing the information that the disk contains.

7. DOS displays its prompt when it is ready for you to enter a command. The most common prompt is C:\>. When this prompt is displayed on your screen, DOS is asking you to type in a command. To execute a command, type in the command name and press ENTER.

8. First, you can power your computer off and on. Second, you can press the CTRL-ALT-DEL keyboard combination.

9. The CLS command stands for "clear screen." When you invoke CLS from the DOS prompt, DOS will erase all of the characters on your screen display and place the DOS prompt in the upper-left corner of the screen.

Chapter 3

1. The VER command displays the DOS version number.

2. The command sets the current system date to December 25, 1991. Since the DATE command line contains the desired date (12-25-91), DATE will not prompt you to enter a date.

3. Prior to DOS 4, use the following command:

```
C:\> TIME 18:30 <ENTER>
```

If you are using DOS 4 or later, use this command:

```
C:\> TIME 6:30p <ENTER>
```

4. This error message occurs when you mistype a command or when the command that you enter does not reside on the current disk or in the directory of files you are currently using.

5. Each time DOS starts, it loads several small, commonly used commands, such as CLS, DATE, TIME, and VER, into memory. Since these commands are always in memory, DOS does not need to load them from disk when you execute them; they are internal commands. However, external commands, such as FORMAT and DISKCOPY, reside on disk. When executing an external command, DOS must load the command from disk into memory.

6. The DATE and TIME commands allow you to display either the date or time, respectively, without changing it. When DATE prompts

```
Current date is Mon 091991
Enter new date (mm-dd-yy):
```

simply press ENTER to leave the date unchanged. When TIME prompts

```
Current time is 6:41:21.64p
Enter new time:
```

press ENTER to leave the time unchanged.

7. The DIR command displays the contents of your disk. To locate a specific external DOS command like FORMAT, use

```
C:\> DIR \DOS\FORMAT  <ENTER>
```

8. If you are using a 5 1/2-inch disk, you can write-protect it simply by placing a write-protect tab over the write-protect notch in the upper-right corner of your disk. If you are instead using a 3 1/2-inch floppy disk, simply slide the write-protect switch down, exposing a hole through the disk. You should always, on a regular basis, write-protect your original DOS disks and other disks whose contents you do not anticipate changing.

9. The DISKCOPY command allows you to make duplicate copies of your disk. If your floppy disks A and B are the same size, you can issue the following DISKCOPY command:

```
C:\> DISKCOPY A: B: <ENTER>
```

If the disk sizes differ, or if you only have one floppy, you can perform a single-drive copy, as shown here:

```
C:\> DISKCOPY A: A: <ENTER>
```

10. You should never use the original disks of any software package on a regular basis. Instead, you should use DISKCOPY to create a set of working copies. Then, you can use the working copies of your disks daily and place the original disks in a safe location.

11. Many DOS commands require you to copy information from one disk to another. The source disk is the disk you are copying from, and the target disk is the disk you are copying to.

12. The FORMAT command prepares a disk for use by DOS. Before DOS can use a disk, it must be formatted.

13. A disk volume label is a name that you can assign to a disk to improve your disk organization. Volume labels can contain up to 11 characters. When the FORMAT command prompts

```
Volume label (11 characters, ENTER for none)?
```

it is asking you to type in an optional label name. Name your disks according to their use.

14. Although floppy disk technology has improved considerably in the past few years, it is still possible for your disk to contain damaged locations that cannot store information. The FORMAT command locates damaged areas on your disk, marking them as unusable for DOS. If FORMAT encounters such errors, it displays the message

```
nnnn bytes in bad sectors
```

Chapter 4

1. DOS organizes the programs and information on your disk by placing them into unique storage facilities called files.

2. A directory is a list of files. Every DOS disk maintains a list of the files contained on the disk.

3. The DIR command displays the directory listing of your disk.

4. File names consist of one to eight characters, with an optional one- to three-character extension. When you use DOS file names, you must separate these two parts with a period.

5. DOS allows you to use all of the letters of the alphabet and the numbers 0 to 9, as well as the following characters:

   ! @ # $ ^ & ( ) – { } ' % ~ _

6. DISKCOMP.COM is a file containing a DOS command. ANSI.SYS is an operating system file used by DOS. DOS AUTOEXEC.BAT is a DOS batch file that contains a list of DOS commands. JONES.LTR is a file containing a letter to a person named Jones.

7. The /P switch directs DIR to suspend its output with each screenful of file names, displaying the message

   ```
   Press any key to continue...
   ```

   This allows you to examine all of the file names on the screen before pressing a key to continue.

8. The /W switch suppresses DIR's display of each file's size, date, and time stamp. The display then shows five files across the screen.

9. The DIR command displays the disk drive letter; the disk volume name; the volume serial number; the file name, extension, and size in bytes, and the creation/modification date and time for each file; the number of files on the disk; and the available disk space.

10. DOS wildcard characters include the asterisk (*) and question mark (?). They allow you to perform DOS file operations on a group of files. The question mark directs DOS to ignore the character in a specific location within a file name or extension. The asterisk directs DOS

to ignore not only the character replaced by the asterisk, but also any characters that follow.

11. The first command directs DIR to list all of the files in the DOS directory that have the extension COM. The second directs DIR to list all of the files in the DOS directory that begin with the letter "A." The third directs DIR to list all of the files in the DOS directory that begin with "DISKCO" and have the extension COM. In the case of your DOS disks, the output might include the files DISKCOPY.COM and DISKCOMP.COM.

Chapter 5

There are no review questions for Chapter 5.

Chapter 6

1. From the DOS prompt, type **DOSSHELL**, as shown here:

```
C:\> DOSSHELL <ENTER>
```

2. Press the TAB key to move from one section of the shell to the next. If you are using a mouse, you can simply click the item in the section that you desire.

3. To invoke a shell menu, hold down the ALT key and type the first letter of the name of the desired menu, such as ALT-F for the File menu. If you are using a mouse, you can click the menu name to select it.

4. A dialog box is a framed window-like prompt the shell displays when it needs additional input before it can complete a command. The dialog box may contain a prompt for a specific file name, or it might contain a list of possible choices.

5. To exit the shell, press ALT-F4 or invoke the File menu and select the Exit option.

6. An icon is a symbolic representation of an object. The shell uses different icons to represent different file types and disk drives.

Chapter 7

1. When you invoke a DOS command, DOS executes the command, assuming the command is a valid internal or external command. Second, DOS buffers the command line that you entered so you can later edit it before entering your next command.

2. The function keys are used as follows:

Key	Function
F1	Copies a character from the corresponding character position in the previous command line
F2	Copies all of the characters up to but not including the character that you type immediately after pressing F2
F3	Copies all of the characters remaining in corresponding character positions in the previous command line
F4	Directs DOS to skip all the characters up to, but not including, the character you type immediately after pressing F4
BACKSPACE	Deletes the character in the current command line that immediately precedes the cursor
INS	Allows you to insert characters into the command line when performing command-line editing
DEL	Allows you to delete characters from the command line when performing command-line editing
ESC	Directs DOS to ignore the current command line

3. Press F1 twice, press the INS key, and type **R**. Then press F3.

4. Before you can use the mouse within the DOS 5 shell, you must install the mouse driver for your mouse as directed in your documentation. If you are using the DOS 4 shell, you must edit the file DOSSHELL.BAT.

Chapter 8

1. The file BUDGET.RPT is the source file (the file to be copied), and the file BUDGET.SAV is the target file (the file within which the copy will be placed).

2. The command copies all of the files on drive A having the EXE extension to files also on drive A with the extension SAV.

3. The COPY command overwrites existing files on disk. In Chapter 25, "Advanced File Manipulation," you will learn how to protect your files from being inadvertently overwritten.

4. The command renames the file BUDGET.RPT as BUDGET.SAV. In this case, RENAME simply substitutes the base name BUDGET for the wildcard.

5. If you are using DOS 5, you may be able to recover the file by using the UNDELETE command. If you are not using DOS 5 but you have a third-party disk utility program, you may be able to undelete the files. Finally, provided you have performed regular backups as discussed in Chapter 26, "Protecting Your Files with BACKUP and RESTORE," you can restore your file from a backup disk.

6. The /P switch directs DEL to prompt you with the following before deleting a file from your disk:

```
FILENAME.EXT, Delete (Y/N)?
```

If you type **Y**, DEL will delete the file. If you type **N**, DEL will leave the file on disk. The /P switch is most convenient when you are using wildcards within DEL, as shown here:

```
C:\> DEL *.* /P <ENTER>
```

```
C:\> VERIFY OFF <ENTER>
```

Remember, if you are concerned about a file copy, add the /V parameter to the individual COPY or XCOPY commands, like this:

```
C:\> COPY FILENAME.EXT A: /V <ENTER>
```

DOS will verify the contents of the file as it is recorded to disk.

Examples

The following command enables disk I/O verification:

```
C:\> VERIFY ON <ENTER>
```

Invoking VERIFY without command-line parameters causes VERIFY to display its current state:

```
C:\> VERIFY <ENTER>
VERIFY is on.
C:\>
```

VOL

Displays a disk volume label

The VOL command displays a disk volume label (or name) for the drive specified. DOS volume labels are 11-character names assigned to a disk.

Chapter 9

1. The default is the disk drive that, unless told to look elsewhere, DOS searches for your external commands and files. The DOS prompt normally contains the drive letter for the default drive.

2. To change the default drive from the DOS prompt, you type the drive letter of the desired drive, followed by a colon, and then press ENTER. When you change the default disk drive, the DOS prompt changes.

3. The following command lists all files on the root directory of drive A:

    ```
    C:\> DIR  A:  <ENTER>
    ```

4. To execute a DOS command that resides on a disk other than the default disk drive, you specify the disk drive letter of the disk containing the file before the command name, as in

    ```
    C:\> A:BUDGET <ENTER>
    ```

5. It copies the contents of the COMMAND.COM file to drive A, naming the new file TEST.COM.

6. All three commands have the same effect: each copies the COMMAND.COM file to drive A.

7. The RENAME command does not allow you to specify a disk drive letter before the target file name. Since RENAME does not allow you to rename a file from one disk drive to another, the target file name must always reside on the same disk as the source.

8. The following command would delete the TEST.COM file from the disk in drive A:

    ```
    C:\> DEL A:TEST.COM <ENTER>
    ```

9. To select a disk from within the shell, press the TAB key until a disk is highlighted. Then use the RIGHT ARROW and LEFT ARROW keys to highlight the desired drive and press ENTER. Also, you can hold down the CTRL key and press the letter of the disk drive desired. With a mouse, click on the icon of the drive you want to select.

Chapter 10

1. A text file is a file that contains letters, numbers, and punctuation marks—characters that are similar to what you would find in a letter, a memo, or other forms of text (text files contain no formatting information).

2. DOS assigns the name CON to your keyboard. When you see CON as your source in a file copy operation, as in

```
C:\> COPY CON FILENAME.EXT <ENTER>
```

DOS will place the text that you enter into the specified file. When you have finished typing text, press the F6 key followed by ENTER. F6 places the end-of-file character in your file.

3. The TYPE command displays the contents of the file specified in the TYPE command line.

4. Simply precede the file name with the disk drive that contains the desired file, as in

```
C:\> TYPE  A:FILENAME.EXT <ENTER>
```

5. From the File System menu, select the desired file. Next, from the File menu, select the View File Contents option, and DOS will display the file. If the file is longer than can be shown on the screen, use the PGUP and PGDN keys to browse through it. When you have finished, press ESC to return to the File System menu.

Chapter 11

1. Just as a directory is a list of files, a subdirectory is a sublist of files. Usually, the files that are in a DOS subdirectory are logically related in some way.

2. The MKDIR command creates DOS subdirectories. It can be abbreviated as MD.

3. Just as DOS defines the default or current directory as the directory it searches by default for your external commands and files, DOS also defines the current directory as the list of files it will search for your external DOS commands and files.

4. The CHDIR command selects the current directory. It can be abbreviated as CD.

5. DOS treats files and subdirectories differently on disk. DEL deletes a file. To remove a subdirectory, you must use RMDIR.

6. These are abbreviations for the current directory (.) and the subdirectory that resides immediately above the current directory (..).

7. Each time you format a disk, DOS sets aside a specific amount of space for the root directory. Once this space fills with file names, DOS cannot create additional files in your directory. However, unlike the root directory, subdirectories can store an unlimited number of files.

8. Press the TAB key until the shell highlights the directory tree label. Next, using the UP ARROW and DOWN ARROW keys, highlight the desired directory and press ENTER (or click on it with the mouse).

9. Select the directory to remove as the current directory. Next, from the File menu, select the Delete option. When DOS displays a dialog box, select the Yes option and press ENTER.

10. The directory structure for these commands is shown in Figure A-3.

Commands with their directory structures

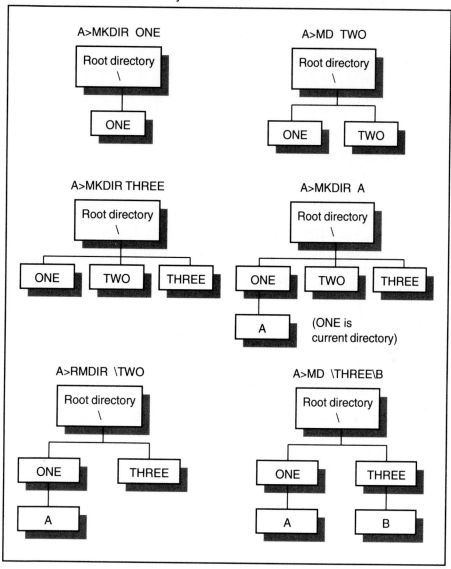

Chapter 12

1. The correct command would be

```
C:\> DIR  \UTIL\*.COM <ENTER>
```

2. A path name is a list of directory names DOS will traverse to find an external command or file.

3. The correct command would be

```
C:\> TYPE  C:\HISTORY\STATES.CAP <ENTER>
```

4. The RENAME command does not allow you to include a disk drive letter or directory name before the target file name. The correct RENAME command in this case is the following:

```
C:\> REN  \HISTORY\STATES.CAP  STATES.NTS <ENTER>
```

5. The TREE command displays your disk's directory structure, often referred to as the directory tree.

6. Each time you issue a DOS command, DOS first searches for the command as an internal command in memory. If DOS finds the command, DOS executes it. If not, DOS searches for the command in the current directory or the directory specified. If DOS finds the command, DOS executes it. Otherwise, DOS checks to see if you have defined a command path, or list of directories DOS should automatically search for your external commands. The PATH command defines the command path. In this case, DOS will automatically search the directories DOS and UTIL on drive C each time it fails to locate an external command.

7. The DOS shell lets you rename a directory. To do so, highlight the directory and select the File menu's Rename option.

8. The only files that should reside in your hard disk's root directory are CONFIG.SYS, COMMAND.COM, and AUTOEXEC.BAT. The remainder of the root directory entries should be directory names.

Chapter 13

1. If CON is the source in a file-copying operation, as in

```
C:\> COPY CON FILENAME.EXT <ENTER>
```

CON references the keyboard. If, instead, CON is the target, as in

```
C:\> COPY FILENAME.EXT CON <ENTER>
```

it references your screen display.

2. Serial data communication carries one bit (binary digit) at a time over a single wire. Parallel data communication uses several wires, which allows your computer to transmit eight bits at a time. Parallel communication, therefore, is faster than serial communication.

3. The device name COM1 is assigned to the first serial port on your system. Likewise, LPT1 is assigned to the first parallel port.

4. You can use MODE to set your screen attributes (such as width, color, and so on), your serial port's data communication parameters, printer characteristics (such as the default printer), and your keyboard's responsiveness. As you will see later in Chapter 28, "International DOS Support," MODE is also instrumental in international character-set support.

5. By default, DOS directs all of its basic printer operations to the parallel port LPT1. If you are instead using a serial printer attached to COM1, you can direct DOS to use that printer with the command just shown. DOS will then write any information originally destined for LPT1 to COM1.

6. Because LPT1 is often used to attach line printers to your computer, DOS also assigns the device name PRN to LPT1. Likewise, because many auxiliary devices are attached to COM1, DOS also assigns the device name AUX to COM1. Thus, the following commands are functionally equivalent:

```
C:\> COPY FILENAME.EXT LPT1 <=> C:\> COPY FILENAME.EXT PRN
C:\> COPY FILENAME.EXT COM1 <=> C:\> COPY FILENAME.EXT AUX
```

Chapter 14

1. If your system has a serial printer and you want to perform the screen-printing and character-echoing operations, you must tell DOS to write the characters to your serial port (COM1), as opposed to the default parallel port (LPT1).

2. The SHIFT-PRTSC key combination directs DOS to print the current contents of your screen display. If your screen contains graphics characters, you must first issue the GRAPHICS command.

3. The CTRL-PRTSC key combination works as a toggle. The first time you press it, DOS enables character echoing to your printer, which means that each of the characters written to your screen display is also sent to your printer. When you press CTRL-PRTSC a second time, DOS disables character echoing.

4. The most significant difference between using PRINT and COPY to send files to your printer is that PRINT returns control to the DOS prompt, immediately allowing you to issue subsequent commands while the document continues to print. With COPY, the document must be completely printed before you are returned to the DOS prompt. If your file is long, COPY could waste a significant amount of time during which you could be using your computer productively. In addition, after PRINT finishes the last page of printed output, PRINT will automatically eject the page from the printer.

5. A queue is a waiting line. In the case of the PRINT command, a queue is the list of files that are waiting to be printed.

6. The following command would print them:

```
C:\> PRINT  TEST.NTS  CLASS.NTS  HW.NTS  <ENTER>
```

Chapter 15

1. The first time you invoke the PRINT command, PRINT must set aside space for the print queue and install the software that manages the files in the queue. Once the command completes, the print queue size and attributes have been defined, so you cannot change them with PRINT switches.

2. Before PRINT can print the contents of a file, PRINT must read the file's information from disk into memory. Once PRINT sends this information to the printer, it reads additional information from the file into memory. This region of memory is called the print buffer. By default, DOS sets aside a buffer size of 512 bytes. By using the /B switch, you can increase this size, which will reduce the number of slow disk reads that DOS must perform and improve PRINT 's performance. Most users will get better performance from a buffer size of 4096 bytes.

3. The /Q switch allows you to increase the size of the print queue to up to 32 file entries. Remember, this switch can be used only the first time you invoke the PRINT command.

4. The /D switch specifies the device that PRINT should send its output to. In this case, PRINT will use the device LPT1.

5. The /C switch directs DOS to remove the file that precedes the switch, as well as the files that follow, from the print queue. The /P switch directs DOS to add the file that precedes the switch to the print queue, as well as all of those that follow. The /T switch directs PRINT to remove all files from the print queue.

Chapter 16

1. A full-screen editor lets you display your document using the entire screen. Using your keyboard's arrow keys or the mouse, you can move the cursor throughout the document to add, change, or delete text at any location. EDIT is a full-screen editor. EDLIN (included in DOS releases prior to DOS 5) is a line editor because it lets you work with only one line of the file at a time.

2. To print your document within EDIT, press the ALT-F key combination to select the File menu and press P, the Print option.

3. To select text by using your keyboard, move the cursor to the start of the desired text. Next, hold down the SHIFT key and press your keyboard's RIGHT ARROW, LEFT ARROW, UP ARROW, and DOWN ARROW keys. To select the text by using your mouse, move the cursor to the start of the desired text. Next, hold down the left mouse button and move the mouse pointer over the desired text. As you select text, EDIT will highlight the selected text.

4. The clipboard is a temporary storage location to which you can copy or move text from your document. Once the text is in the clipboard, you can paste the text into your file at a different location.

5. A hot key is a key or key combination you can press to select a specific menu option without having to select the option from the menu. For example, pressing the F3 function key directs EDIT to perform the Search menu's Repeat Last Find operation.

Chapter 17

1. The > operator redirects the output of a command from the screen display to a file or device. The >> operator redirects the output of a command from the screen display, appending it to the specified file. The < operator redirects the input of a DOS command from the keyboard to the specified file.

2. The first command redirects the output of the DIR command from the screen display to the *FILENAME.EXT* file. If a file with the same name already exists on disk, DOS will overwrite its contents. The second command also redirects its output from the screen display to a file. In this case, however, if a file already resides on disk with the same name, DOS will append the redirected output to it.

3. This command displays TAXES.DAT in sorted order:

```
C:\> SORT < TAXES.DAT <ENTER>
```

4. The /V qualifier directs FIND to display only the lines of the file that do not contain the specified word or phrase. The /C qualifier directs

FIND to display only a count of the number of lines that contain the specified word or phrase. The /N qualifier directs FIND to precede each line displayed with its line number.

5. This command is correct:

```
C:\> SORT /+15 < TAXES.DAT <ENTER>
```

Chapter 18

1. A batch file is a text file that contains a list of DOS commands that DOS executes sequentially.

2. Here is the SHOWVER.BAT file:

```
CLS
VER
```

3. This batch file has the same name as an internal DOS command: DIR. DOS will always execute the DOS command first and will therefore never locate the batch file.

4. The ECHO OFF command directs DOS to suppress the display of command names as your batch file executes.

5. The @ also directs DOS to suppress the display of DOS command names as the batch file executes. If you precede a DOS command name with an @, DOS will suppress that command name.

6. The REM command allows you to place remarks or comments within your batch files to explain the processing involved. The REM command is not an executable command; it simply documents your batch file.

7. Here is the appropriate batch file:

```
PAUSE Insert the data disk in drive B
```

8. AUTOEXEC.BAT contains a list of commands that DOS executes each time your system starts. The AUTOEXEC.BAT file must reside in the root directory of the disk you are starting DOS from in order for DOS to execute the command. If the file does not exist, DOS executes the DATE and TIME commands instead.

Chapter 19

1. Conditional batch processing occurs when a batch file contains the IF command, which allows it to optionally execute commands based upon the result of a tested condition. If the condition specified is true, DOS executes the command; otherwise, DOS continues processing with the next command in the file.

2. The first condition is the existence of a specific file, as in

    ```
    IF EXIST FILENAME.EXT DOS_command
    ```

    The second condition is the exit status value of the previous command, as in

    ```
    IF ERRORLEVEL 2 DOS_command
    ```

    The third condition is whether or not two words or phrases are identical, as in

    ```
    IF %1==Blue DOS_command
    ```

3. The correct command is

    ```
    IF EXIST TEST.DAT PRINT TEST.DAT
    ```

4. It displays the contents of each file on disk that has the DAT extension.

5. The first character of a DOS label name is a colon. When DOS encounters the colon during the processing of your batch files, it recognizes that the line contains a label instead of a command and doesn't attempt to execute it.

6. The batch file is shown here:

    ```
    :LOOP
    VER
    GOTO LOOP
    ```

7. Each of these three batch files will display the files correctly:

    ```
    TYPE TEST.DAT
    TYPE TEST.NTS
    TYPE TEST.TXT
    ```

```
FOR %%1 IN (TEST.DAT TEST.NTS TEST.TXT) DO TYPE %%1

FOR %%1 IN (TEST.*) DO TYPE %%1
```

8. @ECHO OFF choice. Do you want to print TEST.DAT if ERROR-LEVEL 1. If not ERRORLEVEL 2 print TEST.DAT.

Chapter 20

1. The I/O redirection operators allow you to redirect the input or output of a command to a device or file. The pipe operator allows you to redirect the output of one DOS command to become the input to another.

2. This command displays a sorted directory listing:

   ```
   C:\> DIR | SORT <ENTER>
   ```

3. This command sends a sorted directory listing to the printer:

   ```
   A:\> DIR | SORT > PRN <ENTER>
   ```

4. The command displays a sorted directory listing of all the DOS command files with the extension EXE on your screen, one screenful at a time.

Chapter 21

1. The DOS environment is a region in memory that is set aside each time DOS boots. It stores such information as the system prompt, a command search path, the location of the COMMAND.COM command processor, and named variables that you can access from your batch files.

2. The SET command allows you to add, remove, and display entries in your environment. To simply display the environment entries, issue the command

```
C:\> SET <ENTER>
```

3. The correct command is

```
C:\> SET STATE=New York <ENTER>
```

4. This command deletes the STATE entry:

```
C:\> SET STATE= <ENTER>
```

5. A named parameter is a variable that appears in a batch file enclosed by percent signs. When DOS encounters a named parameter in your batch file, it searches the environment for a matching entry. If DOS locates a matching entry in the environment, it substitutes the value associated with the named variable.

6. The batch file should look like this:

```
C:\> COPY CON DELTEST.BAT <ENTER>
DEL %DELETE.ME% <ENTER>
^Z <ENTER>
        1 File(s) copied

C:\>
```

Chapter 22

1. By default, each time DOS writes to your screen or printer or reads from your keyboard, DOS checks to see if you have pressed the CTRL-BREAK or CTRL-C keyboard combination to end the current command. The BREAK ON command allows you to increase the number of times DOS checks for a CTRL-BREAK or CTRL-C. When you

issue the BREAK ON command, DOS enables extended CTRL-BREAK checking, which means it will test for a CTRL-BREAK or CTRL-C each time it performs a system service, such as file operation. By checking for CTRL-BREAK more often, DOS can respond sooner when you want to end a command. However, because DOS spends more time checking for CTRL-BREAK, your programs will run more slowly. Therefore, most users leave extended CTRL-BREAK checking off.

2. Because disks are mechnical devices, disk I/O operations are slow. When you enable disk verification by using the VERIFY command, you increase the number of disk operations your system must perform. Therefore, your system performance decreases. Because disk recording errors are rare, most users leave disk verification disabled.

3. To display the current state of disk verification, invoke VERIFY as follows:

```
C:\> VERIFY <ENTER>
```

VERIFY will display the message that VERIFY is on or off, depending on whether you have disk verification enabled or disabled.

4. The command directs DOS to display a prompt containing the current DOS version number on one line, followed by the current drive and directory within brackets on the next.

5. The MEM command displays the system's current memory usage.

6. The number of commands DOSKEY can store depends on the amount of memory you allocate for DOSKEY's buffer, the number of characters in each command, and the number of DOSKEY macros you create. By default, DOSKEY uses a 512-byte buffer.

7. Three ways to recall a command using DOSKEY are

❏ Use the UP ARROW and DOWN ARROW keys to cycle through the previous command buffer.

❏ Press the F7 key to display the number of each command in the previous command buffer, and then press F9, typing in the number of the desired command at DOSKEY's "Line Number:" prompt.

❏ Type the first few letters of the command name and then press F8.

8. DOSKEY will discard the oldest commands in the previous command buffer to make space for new commands.

Chapter 23

1. A nested batch file is a batch file that is invoked from within another batch file.

2. You use the CALL command to invoke a nested batch file. When you want to invoke one batch file from within another, use the CALL command.

3. %0 will contain BATFILE; %1 will contain MAY; %2 will contain JUNE; and %3 will contain JULY.

4. This batch file displays the contents of a file specified by %1:

```
C:\> COPY CON DISPLAY.BAT <ENTER>
TYPE %1 <ENTER>
^Z <ENTER>
        1 File(s) copied

C:\>
```

5. The SHIFT command lets you access more than nine batch parameters. Each time you invoke the SHIFT command from within a DOS batch file, DOS rotates each batch parameter one position to the left. If no parameters exist to the right of a batch parameter, DOS assigns the empty value to the batch parameter.

Chapter 24

1. A data-file search path is a list of subdirectory names that DOS will examine in search of your data files each time it fails to locate the

file in the current or specified subdirectory. The APPEND command creates a data-file search path. For example, with

```
C:\> APPEND C:\DOS;C:\MISC <ENTER>
```

DOS will examine the DOS and MISC subdirectories (in that order) each time it fails to locate a data file.

2. The command is

```
C:\> APPEND C:\NOTES;C:\MISC <ENTER>
```

3. The SUBST command allows you to abbreviate a long directory name as a disk drive specifier. Some older software programs do not support DOS path names. The SUBST command allows you to abbreviate a path name as simply a disk so these programs can continue to execute.

4. The command is

```
C:\> SUBST E: \PAYROLL\EXPENSES\BUDGET <ENTER>
```

5. Place the \D switch immediately after the logical disk drive specifier in the SUBST command line, as shown here:

```
C:\> SUBST E:/D <ENTER>
```

6. The JOIN command allows you to make two disk drives appear as one. If you have a floppy disk system, you can use JOIN to make your two floppy disks appear as one larger disk drive.

Chapter 25

1. Prior to DOS 5, the ATTRIB command let you set a file's read-only and archive-required attributes. Beginning with DOS 5, ATTRIB also lets you set a file's hidden and system attributes.

2. The proper ATTRIB command is

```
C:\> ATTRIB  +R  \AUTOEXEC.BAT <ENTER>
```

3. You can set all the files in the DOS directory to read-only with this command:

```
C:\> ATTRIB  +R  \DOS\*.* <ENTER>
```

4. The following ATTRIB command displays the file attributes of every file on your disk:

```
C:\> ATTRIB  C:\*.*  /S <ENTER>
```

5. If you need to perform selective file copies based on a file's archive attribute or date stamp, or if you need to copy files that reside in directories beneath the target directory, use XCOPY. For normal file copy operations, use COPY.

6. The only time you need to use the EXPAND command is to copy compressed files from DOS 5 distribution disks.

Chapter 26

1. MSBACKUP setup files specify the files that you want to back up, as well as the backup type you want to perform, such as a full, incremental, or differential backup.

2. The file extension INC indicates that the backup was an incremental backup operation. The file name CC30315A describes specifics about the backup. The letters "CC" indicate that drive C was the first and last drive backed up. The 3 specifies the backup was performed in 1993. The 0315 specify the month and day (March 15). Finally, the A specifies that this catalog file corresponds to the first backup operation performed on that day.

3. Most users have several large application programs on their disk that they could reinstall using the original floppy disks that accom-

panied the program. Therefore, backing up the directories on a regular basis unnecessarily consumes time and backup floppies.

4. To exclude or select specific directories, choose the Select Files option from the Backup menu. MSBACKUP will display the Select Backup Files dialog box. Using your keyboard arrow keys, individually highlight each directory you want to back up and press the SPACEBAR. MSBACKUP will display a triangle next to the directory name, indicating it will back up the directory's files. To exclude a directory, don't press the SPACEBAR to select it; or, if the directory is already selected, press the SPACEBAR a second time to deselect it (MSBACKUP will change the triangle's shape, indicating the exclusion). After you select the last files you desire, select the OK option. Use the File menu Save option to save the selected directories within the desired setup file.

Chapter 27

1. Each time DOS starts, it searches the root directory of the boot disk for the file CONFIG.SYS. If DOS finds the file, it uses the file's contents to configure itself in memory. If the file does not exist, DOS uses its own default values. If you make a change to CONFIG.SYS, you must restart DOS for the change to take effect.

2. By default, DOS disables extended CTRL-BREAK checking because of its system overhead. The BREAK ON command enables extended CTRL-BREAK checking. You can issue the BREAK ON command at any time. If you want DOS to boot with extended CTRL-BREAK checking enabled, you can place the BREAK=ON entry in your CONFIG.SYS file.

3. A disk buffer reduces the number of slow disk read and write operations that DOS must perform.

4. The proper CONFIG.SYS entry is

    BUFFERS=25

5. A device driver is special software that lets DOS communicate with a specific hardware device. If you purchase a mouse, for example, you will have to install a device driver before you can use the mouse.

6. The proper CONFIG.SYS entry is

```
DEVICE=C:\DOS\ANSI.SYS
```

7. Older software programs written for DOS versions prior to DOS 2 used file control blocks to access files. Beginning with version 2, DOS uses file handles instead. If you are running older programs that experience errors when they access files, you may need to use the FCBS entry.

8. To support I/O redirection, DOS predefines five input and output destinations: stdin, stdout, stderr, stdprn, and stdaux. These destinations use up five of the eight file handles.

9. The proper CONFIG.SYS entry is

```
FILES=20
```

10. In rare instances, your computer cannot handle the number of hardware interrupts that occur. If your system halts and displays the message

```
Fatal: Internal Stack Failure, System Halted
```

you will need to use a STACKS entry.

11. A RAM disk is a fast disk that resides in your computer's electronic memory. You can access a RAM disk with a single drive letter, just as you would a floppy or hard disk. Unlike a floppy or hard disk, a RAM drive loses its contents when you turn off your computer or restart DOS.

12. The proper CONFIG.SYS entry is

```
DEVICE=C:\DOS\RAMDRIVE.SYS  256
```

13. The proper CONFIG.SYS entry is

```
DEVICE=C:\DOS\RAMDRIVE.SYS  256  /E
```

Chapter 28

1. A code page is a character set. Most international users choose to work with their own character sets, and DOS code pages allow that.

2. The COUNTRY.SYS device driver contains country-specific date, time, and currency symbols. Just as each country has its own character set, most countries use their own symbols.

3. Either issue the command

```
C:\> KEYB CF,850,\DOS\KEYBOARD.SYS <ENTER>
```

or place the same command in CONFIG.SYS with the INSTALL entry.

4. CTRL-ALT-F1 selects the U.S. template, and CTRL-ALT-F2 selects the international template.

5. Code-page switching is necessary for users, such as international bankers, who have to work with several different character sets during the same DOS session. Most users select a country-specific code page and never change it.

6. DISPLAY.SYS supports code-page switching for screen display.

7. PRINTER.SYS supports code-page switching for IBM printers.

8. "NLSFUNC" stands for "National Language Support Function." The command consists of memory-resident software that must be installed for code-page switching to work.

9. Install DISPLAY.SYS and PRINTER.SYS as needed in CONFIG.SYS and invoke NLSFUNC. Prepare the code pages for the device by using MODE in AUTOEXEC.BAT. Then select the desired code page by using CHCP or MODE.

10. CHCP selects a code page for the printer and screen display at the same time. To prepare individual devices, you must use MODE.

Chapter 29

1. The disk envelope protects the disk from dust, smoke, and fingerprints. The disk hub is used by the disk drive to rotate the disk. The index hole is used by the disk drive timing mechanism. The write-protect notch is used to control whether you can write information to the disk. When the notch is exposed, DOS can modify the contents of the disk; when covered with a write-protect tab, DOS cannot modify the disk's contents. The read/write opening is the opening through which the drive's read/write head records information.

2. Use the equation:

Storage = tracks per disk * sectors per track
* bytes per sector * sides
= 306 * 17 * 512 * 4 = 10,653,696 bytes

3. CHKDSK examines the structure of your disk and displays a status report. If your disk contains inconsistencies, many of them can be corrected with the CHKDSK /F switch.

4. If CHKDSK displays the message

```
nnn lost allocation units found in n chains
Convert lost chains to files (Y/N)?
```

you can direct CHKDSK to convert the lost chains to files by invoking CHKDSK /F. This will create several files in the root directory of your disk. They will contain the previous lost files, renamed in the form FILEnnn.CHK.

5. Each time DOS creates a file on disk, it allocates several sectors of storage space for the file. This is called an allocation unit, or cluster. The CHKDSK command reports on the number of bytes in the allocation unit. By grouping the sectors of a file into clusters, DOS increases your disk performance.

6. The correct command is

```
C:\> FORMAT A: /S <ENTER>
```

7. If your system has a 1.2Mb disk drive and you need to exchange files with someone who uses 360Kb disks, the /4 switch of the FORMAT command directs DOS to format a 360Kb disk in a 1.2Mb disk drive.

8. This command compares two floppy disks on a sector-by-sector basis. Most people use DISKCOMP only to ensure that a DISKCOPY command was successful.

9. DISKCOMP performs a sector-by-sector comparison of two disks. Just because two disks contain the same files doesn't mean that the

files reside in the same sectors. Only the DISKCOPY command copies the contents of two disks on a sector-by-sector basis.

10. The FASTOPEN command allows hard disk users to improve their response time by directing DOS to store the names and starting locations on disk of their commonly used files in memory. Normally, DOS must read the starting location of your file from disk, which is a slow process. Since floppy disks are often readily exchanged, FASTOPEN supports only hard disks.

11. The correct command is

```
INSTALL=C:\DOS\FASTOPEN.EXE   C:=50
```

12. The correct LOADHIGH command is the following:

```
LOADHIGH   C:\DOS\FASTOPEN.EXE   C:=50
```

13. The SYS command directs DOS to copy hidden system files to the specified target drive. DOS requires these files to boot your system.

Chapter 30

1. Unless told specifically to do otherwise (by the use of the /U switch), the FORMAT command does not overwrite the data stored on a disk. Instead, FORMAT creates a new file allocation table and root directory. The MIRROR command places a copy of the root directory and file allocation table in a file named MIRROR.FIL on the disk. If the disk is accidentally formatted, the UNFORMAT command can use the information in MIRROR.FIL to rebuild the disk.

2. When DEL deletes a file, DOS marks the file's file allocation table entries as available for reuse and assigns the character σ to the first letter of the file name within the directory list. DEL does not actually erase the file from your disk. Therefore, should you need to undelete a file, the UNDELETE command can correct the file's name in the directory entry and reallocate the file's file allocation table entries.

3. MIRROR copies the file allocation table and root directory for use by the UNFORMAT command. If delete tracking is enabled, MIRROR stores the directory entry and file allocation table entries of each file

you delete. If necessary, the UNDELETE command can use this information to undelete a file.

4. When you delete a file, DOS marks the file's file allocation table entries as available for use by another file. If you store information on the disk, DOS may assign one of the file allocation entries belonging to a file you want to undelete, in turn overwriting the needed information. Once a deleted file's data has been overwritten, UNDELETE cannot recover the file.

5. The DOS 5 FORMAT command, unless told to do otherwise, performs a safe format, meaning that it does not overwrite the information stored in the data portion of a disk and that it copies the current root directory and file allocation table values to a file the UNFORMAT command can use to rebuild the disk.

6. Beginning with DOS 6, the UNDELETE command supports data sentry protection, which directs DOS to make a copy of every file you delete, placing the file in a directory (named SENTRY). Should you later need to undelete, the UNDELETE command can use the copy. In this way, you greatly improve your chances of successfully undeleting a file. The disadvantage of using data sentry protection is that you consume a large amount of disk space to hold files you previously deleted.

7. In DOS 5 you used the MIRROR command to invoke file-delete tracking. The MIRROR command, however, does not exist in versions prior to DOS 6. To invoke file-delete tracking under DOS 6, invoke UNDELETE using the /T switch. For example, the following command directs UNDELETE to perform file-delete tracking for drive C:

```
C:\> UNDELETE /TC <ENTER>
```

Chapter 31

1. A file association is a relationship within the DOS shell between files with a particular extension and a specific program. When you highlight a file whose type is associated with a program and press

ENTER, the shell will run the corresponding program, specifying the file name in the program's command line.

2. A program group is a collection of two or more related commands for which you create an entry in the DOS shell's program list. When you highlight a program list and press ENTER, the shell will display the list of programs that correspond to the group. From that list, you can highlight and run a specific program.

3. The Task Swapper is an option within the DOS 5 shell that, when enabled, lets you load two or more programs into memory, switching between the programs as your needs require.

4. If one or more of the active tasks had not saved your current information to disk and you were to exit the shell, the information would be lost. By forcing you to exit each program before exiting the shell, DOS reduces the chance of lost information.

5. If you press CTRL-ESC, DOS will redisplay the shell. By using the TAB key, you can highlight the Active Task List, selecting the task you desire by using your arrow keys or mouse. Likewise, if you press the ALT-TAB key combination within the shell, DOS will cycle from one active task to the next.

Chapter 32

1. The following CONFIG.SYS DEVICEHIGH= entry installs the INTER-LNK driver for a connection using COM1:

```
DEVICE=C:\DOS\INTERLNK.EXE   /COM:1
```

2. The following INTERSVR command directs the server to use COM1:

```
C:\> INTERSVR   /COM:1 <ENTER>
```

3. To connect to a workgroup, you must first start the workgroup connection software using NET START. This is typically done from

within AUTOEXEC.BAT. Next, you must log on to the workgroup using NET LOGON.

4. The following NET USE command connects to the shared directory BUDGET that resides on the FINANCE computer using the logical drive I:

```
C:\> NET USE I:  \\FINANCE\BUDGET <ENTER>
```

5. The following NET USE command redirects LPT1 to the print queue LASER that resides on the PRODUCTION computer:

```
C:\> NET USE LPT1  \\PRODUCTION\LASER <ENTER>
```

6. Each time you use a compressed file, DBLSPACE decompresses the file. Therefore, if you copy a compressed file to a floppy, the floppy will contain the decompressed file.

7. The DBLSPACE.SYS device driver lets you move the DBLSPACE.BIN driver from conventional memory to upper memory. The DBLSPACE.SYS driver is not required for accessing the compressed drive.

8. APM is an abbreviation for advanced power management. APM is a specification that defines how the PC uses power during idle time. Several newer laptop computers provide chips that support APM. The DOS 6 POWER command lets you control the APM power chips, and hence your PC's power consumption.

Index